# THE PURSUIT OF LIBERTY
## Volume II: Since 1860

# THE PURSUIT OF LIBERTY

## A History of the American People

### Volume II: Since 1860

**R. JACKSON WILSON**
*Smith College*

**JAMES GILBERT**
*University of Maryland*

**STEPHEN NISSENBAUM**
*University of Massachusetts*

**DONALD SCOTT**
*Brown University*

**CARVILLE EARLE**
*University of Maryland—Baltimore County*

**RONALD HOFFMAN**
*University of Maryland*

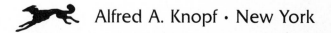 Alfred A. Knopf · New York

First Edition
987654321
Copyright © 1984 by Alfred A. Knopf, Inc.

**Library of Congress Cataloging in Publication Data**
Main entry under title:

The Pursuit of liberty.

   Bibliography: p.
   Includes index.
   1. United States—History.   I. Wilson, Raymond Jackson.
E178.1.P985    1983        973       83–14932
ISBN 0–394–32109–X
ISBN 0–394–33476–0 (pbk. : v. 1)
ISBN 0–394–33477–9 (pbk. : v. 2)

Cover photograph: © Peter Beney/The Image Bank

Cover design and graphic supervision: Lorraine Hohman

Graphic assistance and layouts: Susan Detrich

Maps: David Lindroth

Photo research: Alan Forman

Manufactured in the United States of America

# Authors' Preface

When the oldest of the authors of *The Pursuit of Liberty* was in the eighth grade, he had to take his first course on the history of the United States. His teacher was a legend in the school, a tough, slightly forbidding woman, who was determined that her students were going to learn *something* about the history of their country.

She gave her roomful of fourteen-year-olds a demanding task. They had to memorize any 200 facts about American history, including dates. When the final examination came, they had to write down their list of facts in the correct chronological order. You could choose any facts, as long as there were 200 of them and they were in chronological order. You might start with "1492—Columbus discovers America." Or you could begin with "1607—First English colony in America at Jamestown, Virginia." (In both cases, you would be a bit wrong. But that didn't matter. These facts were in the textbook, and the important thing was that you had learned them.)

Nowadays, of course, everything about learning history has changed. The authors' own children come home from history classes with their heads full of "concepts." They don't think "1607—Jamestown" (or even "1587—Roanoke," which is closer to the truth). Instead, they are taught to talk about large and abstract events, such as "The Confrontation of European and Native-American Cultures." They study grand processes such as "Industrialization," "Immigration," and "Urbanization." They seem to learn history in a more sophisticated and better way than memorizing some list of 200 facts.

But there is a problem. Students who study American history today seem to know something in general, but nothing in particular. They have mastered the art of discussing abstractions and generalizations, but these are not connected with any firm grasp of relevant factual information. Have our best and most innovative teachers simply replaced 200 facts with 20 vague concepts? The old problem was that history was a grab bag of names and dates and places. Students learned something in particular and nothing much in general. But the new problem, knowing the general but not the particular, is just as serious. Either way, studying history runs the risk of being a plain waste of time.

This dilemma is partly the result of the nature of history itself. There *are* large and general tendencies and there *are* particular facts. The difficult thing is to see how the two fit together. We tend to look at history the way we look at a painting. We focus on the foreground—the facts. Or we think about the background, about the general way the picture is structured and the kinds of claims it makes on our imagination. But when we study history, it is difficult to put the foreground and the background, the facts and the general concepts, together. We seem to choose between foreground and background, unable to see how each makes sense in terms of the other.

When most history textbooks try to bring specific facts and general concepts together, they do so by simply *telling* readers that this or that fact is an example of this or that general tendency. First comes a heading, something like "The Contact of European and Native American Cultures" or "Industrialization." Then comes a sentence or two of generalization. A little further on come the facts, such as "1607—Jamestown" or "The first transcontinental railroad was completed in 1869."

Some important things are lost in this way of writing history. We are not asked to see or understand the relationship between fact and general concept at all. Did something called "industrialization" *cause* the first transcontinental railroad or did a host of facts, such as the building of that railroad, cause industrial development? Concrete facts and general concepts merely coexist in such textbooks, each of them inert and incapable of giving any sort of life to the other.

Perhaps worse, when students study history in textbooks of this sort, they get no sense of the human *experience* involved in either the specific events they find listed there or the generalizations they read and underline to study for next week's test. Most history textbooks contain no narrative, no stories, no accounts of the dramatic, sometimes triumphant, often shameful efforts and struggles of human beings. Human action is squeezed out of history and we are left with dead "events" and equally lifeless generalizations.

We have written *The Pursuit of Liberty* with the belief that we have found ways to solve these kinds of problems. We started with two convictions. First, we had to make it possible for students to see and *understand* the ways that specific sequences of human action were related to the general background in which they took place. Second, historians ought not to keep a secret of the remarkably exciting and dramatic ways people actually acted in the past.

Both these convictions shaped our book and explain its unusual structure. The chapters are laid out in pairs. In the first chapter of each pair, we tell the story of a very specific and very concrete event: a witchcraft hysteria in the village of Salem Farms, Massachusetts, in 1692, for example; or the massacre of Sioux Indians by a troop of U.S. cavalry at Wounded Knee in the Dakotas in 1890.

The second chapter in each pair explores the background of the story we tell in the first half of the pair. In these chapters, we suggest general explanations for the specific events previously narrated. The chapter on Salem witchcraft is followed by a chapter on Puritanism in seventeenth-century New England that tries to make sense of the fact that hundreds of otherwise reasonable people suddenly accused their neighbors of being witches and hanged a large number of them. A chapter on the westward expansion of white society in the nineteenth century tries to make the same kind of sense of the massacre at Wounded Knee.

And so we go through *The Pursuit of Liberty,* alternating between the specific and the general, between narrative and explanation. In the end we think our readers will have a much better grasp of the way history works, of the way that all the specific actions of people are shaped by the historical setting in which they take place. And we have faith, too, that some of our readers will learn the most important thing that history has to teach all of us: we all live in history, profoundly shaped by the society around us, by what it has been as well as by what it is now.

If this lesson is learned, then our readers will have learned what we already know, that learning history is a way of discovering our kinship with all those real people who have come before us, who have acted out their struggles, terrors, and occasional exaltations with the same anxiety and effort that go so deeply into all our lives. The past is inescapable, for everyone, whether one knows it or not.

It is better to know it.

R. Jackson Wilson
James Gilbert
Stephen Nissenbaum
Donald Scott
Carville Earle
Ronald Hoffman

*September 1983*

# Acknowledgments

Books like *The Pursuit of Liberty* contain two unavoidable lies. They are on the title page. This page lists the names of the people known as "the authors," as though they alone had produced all the ideas in the book. And the same title page gives the name of the "publisher," as though some kind of anonymous corporate body had given physical life to the book. The truth is more complicated. Authors do not work and write alone, and the publisher is not in reality a corporation but a collection of very specific and very human beings. And so the purpose of these acknowledgments is really to set down the truth, to correct the little implicit lies of the title page by talking about some of the people who made the book possible.

But even here, the whole truth cannot be told. There are too many people. To start with, the writing of history always depends on the work of other historians, and we owe an incalculable debt to the honest labor of whole generations of men and women who have labored to bring into the light the history of the United States as we know it. Almost as many men and women, most of them now mature citizens of the Republic, have been our students and they have helped us more than they knew. We can only thank them abstractly and hope that some of their children will learn something about their past from our book. Closer to home, we cannot name all the mates and friends and children who have encouraged us. Nor can we even name all the women and the men who have for us *been* the abstraction called "Alfred A. Knopf, Inc."; nor the literally dozens of colleagues around the country, most of them strangers to us, who have read and commented on the manuscript over the years we have been at work on it. We can only retreat into the usual formula and say that without all of these people—*all* of them—these pages honestly would never have seen the light of day.

What we can do to set the record a bit straighter, however, is at least to thank a few of the people who have contributed most directly to what is right about *The Pursuit of Liberty* (and who bear none of the blame for whatever may be wrong with it). For years, Paula Franklin, Nancy Woloch, and William Graebner have read our chapters with care, with an ardent concern for the teaching of history, and, when necessary, with righteous anger at our short-comings. Our book is much better than it could have been without their help. For us, "Alfred A. Knopf " has been a lot of people, but two men in particular have given us patient support and effective work when work and support were needed most. John Sturman has dealt with our manuscript tirelessly, carefully, and above all intelligently. And David Follmer has, over the years, been remarkably able to find ways to stop us from failing, even when we tried.

# Contents

# American Images

# Economics and History

# Americans at War

# Boxes

# Illustrations

*Appears in "Americans at War."

# Illustrations *(continued)*

*Appears in "Americans at War."

# Maps and Charts

# 21 ▪ Abraham Lincoln: From Politics to Martyrdom

As the winter of 1860–1861 ended, the new president came quietly, even somewhat secretly, into Washington to take his oath of office. He was about to face a reality no other American president had had to face: a divided Union. And no one, not even men who had agreed to serve in his cabinet, not even the political friends who had helped engineer his nomination and win his election, knew what his strategies and policies would be. Most people who thought about Abraham Lincoln much at all thought of him as a Western lawyer, as a pretty good stump speaker, and—above all—as a shrewd politician. And they were, in the main, right. Abraham Lincoln had shown a remarkable ability to find moderate positions about slavery, positions he knew were not far off the opinions of the kinds of Northern voters who had elected him.

What no one could have predicted was that four years later, a dead Abraham Lincoln would leave the capital as the greatest national hero since George Washington. When his body returned westward, back to Illinois, it was no longer the political figure, or even the political leader, that people mourned. It was a dedicated, heroic martyr to what Lincoln had managed to define as a national crusade. What Abraham Lincoln accomplished was to transform an ugly civil war into a spiritual struggle for principles much higher than the political unity of a nation. His death put the seal on that transformation.

He began his presidency by playing a complicated political "game," as he sometimes called it. The game became war. And war changed Abraham Lincoln. The change was not complete: the shrewd politician remained always a part of him. But he began to see the war as something more than politics, more even than battle and suffering. Part of him began to think of it as a religious experience, in which a nation that seemed to have been chosen by God for special blessings was now being put through a special trial and

ABRAHAM LINCOLN, 1860 AND 1865
The first portrait shows Lincoln in June 1860, at the opening of his presidential campaign. The second, taken just four days before his assassination, reveals the psychological and physical toll the Civil War exacted from Lincoln. *(Chicago Historical Society)*

punishment. He began to insist more and more that the war was a kind of blood sacrifice demanded by God as a payment for the long sin of slavery. And when, at the war's end, he paid with his own blood, a dramatic proof seemed to be given that his redefinition of the war was correct.

As Lincoln prepared to take office, the political situation was so delicate and so dangerous that even his practical skills had a slender chance. Seven states in the lower South had already seceded and had established a new federal government for themselves—the Confederate States of America. Several states in the upper South, particularly Virginia, Maryland, and Kentucky, were poised to join the new Confederacy. All the federal officials in the seceded states had either given allegiance to the Confederacy or had been replaced by secessionists. The Confederacy had taken over almost all the federal property within its borders—the post offices, the customs and land offices, even the forts and arsenals. All that remained of visible federal authority were two forts. One was Fort Pickens—far off in Pensacola, Florida; the other was Fort Sumter in Charleston harbor—in the heart of secession country.

Then, as inauguration day approached, there was a strange lull. Everyone waited to see what Lincoln would do. He made no public statements. The only prediction anyone could hazard was that his actions would be—characteristically—cautious, secretive, and essentially political. In Lincoln's mind, the best direction things could go was clear: secession would somehow be stopped without violence; the Union would be restored. And this would be done without any compromise on the basic Republican position on slavery in the Western territories. The problem was, did he have the means and the power to work out such a political solution?

The answer would surely lie with Virginia. If he could manipulate events carefully enough, Virginia might not secede. If Virginia stayed in the Union, then surely Maryland and Kentucky, probably Tennessee and Missouri, would follow Virginia's lead. Time would take its toll on the weak and isolated Confederacy. Good sense might win out, and one by one the seceding states could come back into the Union.

At this point, Lincoln saw the problem in terms that were legal, political, and constitutional. It was illegal for any state to secede. He had no doubt of that. But it was equally unconstitutional for the federal government to interfere at all with slavery in any of the states. The political bargain he wanted was for the upper South to accept this political settlement, remain in the Union, and keep their slave system as long as they could make it last.

But it was a very tricky situation. If Lincoln did anything that even seemed hostile, he might provoke the border states and the upper South, especially Virginia, into joining the Confederacy, leaving the Union in a much more vulnerable position if and when war came. But he could not simply ignore secession: the people who had elected him expected Lincoln to stand up to the slave power, not give in to it. Should he try to get national institutions going again and send Republican postmasters, judges, and customs officials into the Confederacy? Should he try to reclaim federal property? What about Fort Pickens and Fort Sumter? There had already been one crisis over Fort Sumter. On December 26, Major Robert Anderson had moved his Union garrison out of Fort Moultrie, moved them far out in the harbor, into Sumter. But outraged South Carolinians had demanded the total evacuation of federal troops. After three days of vacillation, President Buchanan had rejected the Confederate demand and the first Sumter crisis had died down. But Fort Sumter had become an important symbol: to the North it was an emblem of the endurance of the Union, to the South it was a galling sign of Yankee "aggression."

Lincoln announced his policy in his first act as president, his inaugural address. He began by reassuring the South. His administration would not "directly or indirectly interfere with the institution of slavery where it exists." Lincoln then flatly declared that the Union remained unbroken. "No state," he insisted, "can lawfully get out of the Union; and acts of violence within any state or states against the authority of the United States are insurrectionary." He warned that he would use "the power confided to me to hold, occupy, and possess the property and places belonging to the government." But then, his resolve to defend the Union unmistakable, he assured the South that there would be "no bloodshed or violence unless it be forced upon the national authority." He would deliver the mails only if the South wanted them delivered, and he would not "force obnoxious strangers into the South to carry out Federal business." Even though he had "the strict legal right" to do so, he would "forgo, for the time, the use of such offices" because any attempt to do otherwise "would be so irritating and so nearly impracticable."

Finally, Lincoln insisted again on his peaceful intentions. "In your hands, my dissatisfied fellow country-men, and not mine, is the momentous issue of Civil War—the government will not assail you. You can have no conflict, without being yourself the aggressors."

Lincoln was carefully walking a political tightrope, trying to avoid as long as possible any action that would set events on an irreversible course to war. His policy was designed to buy some political time to get his administration set up and to let Unionist sentiment in the South regroup. But the policy was also aimed toward making sure that if war *did* come, the responsibility for starting it would lie not with Lincoln but with "his dissatisfied fellow country-men." It would be easier to rally the political support needed to wage war if the Confederacy rather than Lincoln was seen as the aggressor. Also, if Lincoln started the war, all the remaining slave states would probably join the Confederacy, and then Britain and France, leaping at the chance to split the American empire, might formally recognize the Confederacy as a separate nation.

Lincoln's policy of "masterly inactivity" as the *New York Times* dubbed it, rested on the assurance of his military advisers that Fort Sumter could hold out indefinitely and stand as a continuing symbol of the unbroken Union. But the day after Lincoln delivered his inaugural address, Major Anderson sent the surprising word that his provisions would last for only four to six weeks. He would have to surrender Fort Sumter unless 70,000 troops were sent to relieve him.

So Sumter would have to be reinforced or evacuated. Neither alternative was very desirable in political terms. Sending military relief would certainly bring civil war. It would surely drive the upper South and quite possibly the border states as well into the Confederacy. But evacuation also had political risks. It would probably avoid war for a time and might help Southern Unionists. But it might push reunion even further away by confirming the secessionists' claim that the North lacked the will to fight, thus strengthening their political grip on the Confederate states. The impact of evacuation on Northern opinion could be even more disastrous. Most Northerners, and especially the Republican majority that had elected Lincoln, would surely consider evacuation a betrayal of his pledge to "hold and possess" federal property. This might so discredit him as a political leader that his capacity to govern would collapse. And that, Lincoln feared, would lead to the collapse of the Republican party, the political force that had finally succeeded in wresting the federal government away from the slave power. Everything the Republicans had fought for during six long years would be lost forever.

Lincoln, characteristically, proceeded cautiously. He asked each of the members of his cabinet for a written response to the suggestion that provisions only—not fresh troops—be sent to Fort Sumter. Only one man, Attorney General Montgomery Blair, urged that course. The others feared that even this would lead to war. Secretary of State William Seward argued most vehemently against sending provisions, insisting that the evacuation of Sumter was the only possible way, short of war, to end the crisis and restore the Union. Lincoln listened to the debate but did not express a firm position of his own. Those around him certainly thought he had accepted the overwhelming opinion of his cabinet that the fort would have to be surrendered. In fact (unknown to Lincoln), Seward privately assured some Confederate commissioners who had come to Washington to demand recognition of the Confederacy that Sumter *would* be evacuated. The commissioners knew that Lincoln could not possibly accept their demand for recognition, but they hoped to use his formal refusal to prove their contention that his real intent was hostile. Arguing that Sumter was about to be evacuated, Seward persuaded the commissioners to delay asking for an immediate answer to their demand. He himself favored evacuation and was dead certain that the inexperienced Lincoln would follow his seasoned advice.

But Lincoln had not decided to pull out of Fort Sumter. Seward and the others had misread his silence as an endorsement of evacuation. (Lincoln usually listened to advice, but he rarely revealed his own intentions until he was ready to act.) Though it seemed likely that Sumter would have to be abandoned, Lincoln was reluctant to take the step and played for more time. He had ordered the troops waiting aboard ship in Pensacola harbor to move into Fort Pickens. This quiet, relatively unprovocative act might let him turn Pickens into the symbol of an unbroken Union. He sent Stephen Hurlbut, a Charleston-born friend, to South Carolina to find out how strong the Union sentiment there really was.

But the clamor for action was mounting. The rumors of an impending evacuation of Sumter were eroding Lincoln's support, and disillusionment over his "weakness" and "inaction" began to set in. "The country feels no more assurance as to the future than it did on the day Mr. Buchanan left Washington," the *New York Times* editorialized. "The people want something to be decided on—some standard raised—some policy put forward which shall serve as a rallying point for the abundant but discouraged loyalty of the American heart." Lincoln's old friend Senator Lyman Trumbull, of Illinois, introduced a resolution into the Senate declaring that it was "the duty of the President to use all the means in his power to hold and protect the property of the United States."

Hurlbut reported back that Unionism was utterly dead in South Carolina and all but extinct in other seceding states. He was sure that the Confederacy would accept nothing but "unqualified recognition of absolute independence," and he believed that nothing done "by the government will prevent the possibility of armed collision." Major Anderson in the meantime sent back word that he could hold out no longer than April 15. So on March 29, Lincoln ordered that an expedition to provision Sumter be prepared, "to be used, according to circumstance."

Still, the president hesitated. For weeks he had waited for word from Pensacola, but when it finally came, on April 6, it was not what Lincoln had hoped to hear. The order to garrison Fort Pickens, sent by sea rather than land, had taken a long time to get there. When it finally had arrived, it had not been obeyed! The captain of the troopship, acting on orders issued under Buchanan, would not take orders from the army and refused to act until a navy superior told him to. Now lack of supplies would force the surrender of Sumter before Pickens could be established as the symbol of the Union. And so, finally, Lincoln sent a message to Governor Pickens of South Carolina, informing him that "an attempt will be made to supply Fort Sumter with provisions only, and that if such attempt be not resisted, no effort to throw in men, arms, or ammunition will be made without further notice, or in case of an attack upon the fort." On April 9, the expedition, carrying provisions for a year, set forth with an armed escort.

Lincoln's message to Governor Pickens surprised and angered Southern leaders, who thought that Seward had spoken for Lincoln when he had promised the evacuation of Sumter. But secessionists were also becoming impatient with the inactivity of *their* leaders. The United States flag fluttering above the fort, in full view of Charlestonians, was a continuing affront to the idea of Southern independence. The Confederates acted. At 4:30 A.M. on April 12, 1861, before the relief expedition had time to arrive, shore batteries opened fire on Fort Sumter. The next day Major Anderson withdrew his forces, and on the following day, April 14, Lincoln, declaring that the South had fired the first shot, issued a call for 75,000 volunteers to put down the insurrection.

Lincoln's efforts to avoid the war had been political—naturally enough, for the situation *was* political until one side or the other began to shoot. And the political task had suited his personality and his talents. Now, confronted with a war that quickly became more deadly and more enduring than anyone on either side expected, what would Lincoln do? What was there in his character that would emerge under the intense pressure of armed conflict?

Initially, some of his work was still mainly political. He had to organize the government for war. He had to take full control of his party, which was as yet merely a loose electoral coalition. Few Republicans felt much loyalty to the "little Illinois lawyer"—as Seward had once called Lincoln. He had become president through a combination of adroit maneuvering and accident. Now he had to spend enormous amounts of time handing out the favors and the offices that would create political loyalties.

But in the midst of the politics, a new kind of Lincoln began to find his voice. He developed a special way of talking about the war—no longer as a war for the Union, or just as a combat forced on the government by a few hotheads in the South. In his language, the war gradually became a test of the principles of freedom and democracy—for white people, at least. On July 4, in a message calling Congress into special session, Lincoln stated the argument he was to use for the next four years: that the struggle was not between North and South, or between Union and secession, but a struggle for the rights of the people. The real issue, he declared,

> embraces more than the fate of these United States. It presents to the whole family of man the question whether a constitutional republic, or a democracy—a govern-ment of the people, by the same people—can or cannot maintain its territorial integrity against its domestic foes. It presents the question whether discontented individuals, few in number, can arbitrarily break up their government and thus practically put an end to free government upon the face of the earth.

These brief words summarized a brilliant rhetorical strategy. There were three interlocking steps. First, identify the Union cause as the cause of "the people," the cause of democracy. Second, make the outcome a test case of the cause of democracy not just in the United States but for the whole world, the "family of man." Third, make the outcome the *ultimate* test case: if democracy cannot survive here and now, then it can never survive anywhere "upon the earth."

From that July 4 address to the end of the Civil War in 1865, Abraham Lincoln continued to insist on these principles. They were a little illogical: there was no sound reason why democracy might not fail in the United States and still succeed in other places. And they were a little unrealistic: there was in fact little or no democracy for the "family of man" in the world. But neither logic nor realism was at stake for Lincoln. He understood the necessity of enabling his countrymen to believe they were embarked on an ennobling crusade. And he plainly came to believe it himself.

Lincoln's definition of the war got its most famous statement two years later, in November of 1863. He traveled to Gettysburg, Pennsylvania, where the Union armies had turned back a Confederate advance in one of the bloodiest battles of the war just three months earlier. Lincoln's speech came at the end of a long ceremony dedicating a military cemetery. This short address came to represent his greatest performance as a writer, speaker, and ideological leader of his people. His strategy had not changed. He still defined the war as a war for democracy, for all the world, and for all time. But the tactics had become even more skillful.

First, Lincoln sanctified democracy by making it into an *inheritance*. "Four score and seven years ago," he began, "our fathers brought forth on this continent a new nation, conceived in Liberty, and dedicated to the proposition that all men are created equal." No more skillful sentence was ever written by an American president. "Four score and seven years" sounded much more ancient and more holy than "eighty-seven." And "our fathers brought forth . . . conceived . . ." was the language of procreation and birth. It stood in superb dramatic contrast to the place of death he had come to dedicate. Again, the logic and the accuracy were questionable. The United States was already heavily populated by immigrants whose "fathers" had not "brought forth"

**MARY TODD LINCOLN**

Mary Todd Lincoln (1818–1882) encouraged her husband's political ambitions and fully sup-ported his presidential as-pirations. But her White House years were espe-cially difficult. Born in Ken-tucky, she was suspected of disloyalty to the Union. Washington society con-demned her as both a crude Westerner and an excessively extravagant hostess. The death of her son, Willie, in 1862 and the assassination of her husband undermined her physical and mental health. In her last years, she was a desperate and pathetic woman bordering on insanity. *(UPI)*

the nation at all. And it was equally true that the fathers who had "conceived" the nation included a great many slaveholding Virginians and South Carolinians. But once again, logic and realism were not what counted. Lincoln was making the war into an act of faith.

In his next paragraph—and the Gettysburg Address consisted of only two paragraphs—he began to make this religious message clear. The first sentence used the words "dedicate," "consecrate" and "hallow": "But in a larger sense, we cannot dedicate, we cannot consecrate, we cannot hallow, this ground. The brave men, living and dead, who struggled here, have consecrated it." (Those brave men, of course, were all Union soldiers, for nothing in Lincoln's way of defining the struggle could admit Confederate dead to a share in the "unfinished work . . . so nobly advanced.") The issue was, in the end, dedication—not the dedication of a cemetery but the need for dedication of those who lived on to complete the "work." And so Lincoln ended with a ringing plea that "we here highly resolve that these dead shall not have died in vain—that this nation, under God, shall have a new birth of freedom—and that government of the people, by the people, for the people, shall not perish from the earth."

Lincoln had, by the force of his words more than by any other means, made the war into a crusade. But while he worked out the definition of the crusade as a struggle to defend democracy for all time, a nagging, often private dilemma would not go away. Lincoln's fine speech at Gettysburg did not mention the problem of slavery. Was that part of the crusade? Did "our fathers" include black fathers? Did "a new birth of freedom" include freedom and some measure of equality for black men and women? This part of Lincoln's drama was never settled with anything like the clarity and coherence of his mighty assertion of liberty and democracy as the real stakes of war. But his halting, indecisive attempts to confront the issue of slavery are still a central thread in the story of his movement toward heroic martyrdom.

While Lincoln was defining the war as democracy's struggle for survival, other men around him wanted a different, more radical definition. For them, slavery *was* the issue. Charles Sumner, a Massachusetts senator and the leader of the abolitionist wing of the Republican party, insisted that Lincoln strike immediately at slavery—both as an act of justice and as a military measure to weaken the Confederacy. Frederick Douglass, the leading black abolitionist, declared that "the innermost logic of events will force it upon them in the end: that the war is a war for and against slavery." A leading white abolitionist, Wendell Phillips, spoke in even more demanding terms to the North: "Seize the thunderbolt God has forged for you, and annihilate the system that has troubled your peace for seventy years."

But Lincoln hung back. He knew that somehow slavery was the "root of the rebellion." And he knew he did not like it. He could not remember a time when he did not believe that "if slavery is not wrong, nothing is wrong." At the same time, he shared the view of most Northern white voters that black people were racially inferior to whites. Even if he considered fighting the war

**LINCOLN AND HIS CABINET**

Lincoln selected his cabinet carefully, making sure that the many factions of his party were represented. From left to right: Edwin M. Stanton, Secretary of War; Salmon P. Chase, Secretary of the Treasury; Lincoln; Gideon Welles, Secretary of the Navy; Caleb Smith, Secretary of the Interior; William H. Seward, Secretary of State; Montgomery Blair, Postmaster General; Edward Bates, Attorney General. *(UPI)*

*against* slavery, he could not conceive of it as a war *for* black freedom and equality. He was also deeply convinced that the Constitution did not give him any power to interfere with slavery within the states.

Most of all, the idea of emancipating blacks by executive order went against Lincoln's political instincts. He knew that a leader who defied public opinion might lose his capacity to lead at all. He had not been elected on an abolitionist platform (and no Republican could have been elected that way). The support he enjoyed early in the war came to him as the friend of the Union, perhaps as the friend of democracy and liberty for whites, but not as the friend of black slaves. Most of all, Lincoln feared that the political outcome of any attempt to emancipate the slaves would be to drive the border states, especially Kentucky, into the Confederacy. "To lose Kentucky," he said, "is nearly the same as to lose the whole game. Kentucky gone, we could not hold Missouri, nor, as I think, Maryland. These all against us, the job on our hands is too large for us. We would as well consent to the separation at once, including the surrender of this capital."

But Frederick Douglass was right: the "innermost logic of events" did keep forcing the question of slavery to the surface. In the most practical way, military commanders operating in places like Missouri or Maryland had to deal with the status of slaves. Twice, in August of 1861 and then again in May of 1862, Union generals in the field issued orders declaring the slaves of rebels or slaves who had come within Union battle lines, free. Lincoln quickly and unambiguously canceled both orders, to the grief of abolitionist sentiment in the North.

Lincoln was in trouble. And he groped for a solution. He proposed the old idea of "colonization"—sending freed slaves out of the country. He even had agents scouting out suitable land in Central America. He promoted the idea of encouraging slaveholders to give up their slaves voluntarily, in return for federal government compensation.

But he was beginning a private journey toward a new policy. During the spring of 1862, he slipped down into the telegraph room of the White House. It was the only place he could hide from the nagging politicians and office seekers that dogged his tracks all day. There he wrote out a draft proclamation of emancipation—which he put away to use in case he needed it.

It waited for two months, until July of 1862. He continued to try to rally support for his plan for voluntary, gradual, and compensated emancipation followed by colonization. But the support did not come quickly enough nor in great enough strength. On July 13, Lincoln hinted to two members of his cabinet that emancipation might become a "military necessity." A week later, on July 21, he called the rest of the cabinet together to read them his draft of an emancipation proclamation. The cabinet was stunned by the policy change. They argued the question back and forth while the president listened. Finally, he was persuaded to wait again. The Union was still losing battle after battle. At home and in Europe, a proclamation might seem to be only a clumsy attempt to draw public attention away from the military blundering and defeats. Back into Lincoln's desk drawer went the draft, to wait for at least a Union victory.

While he waited, the president suffered, publicly and privately. In public, he was accused of being "an Ass for the Slave Power to ride." Horace Greeley, editor of the influential Republican paper the *New York Tribune,* printed an open letter to the president: "On the whole face of this wide earth, Mr. President, there is not one determined, intelligent champion of the Union cause who does not feel that all attempts to put down the Rebellion and at the same time uphold its inciting cause are preposterous and futile."

The *Tribune* letter gave Lincoln a chance to restate, in the clearest possible way, his continued analysis of the relationship between the war and slavery. He did wish, he wrote in reply, that "all men everywhere be free." But—and the "but" was the same one that had dogged him since his election—"My paramount object is to save the Union and is *not* either to save or to destroy Slavery. If I could save the Union without freeing any slave I would do it, and if I could save it by freeing all the slaves, I would do it, and if I could do it by freeing some and leaving others alone, I would also do that."

That answer might satisfy some—even most—of Northern opinion. But the private suffering was harder to deal with. Lincoln had begun to brood over the meaning of the war—especially of the Union defeats—in a way that went far beyond politics and public opinion. After one particularly disastrous military failure, he sat in his study at night and thought about God. "We are whipped again." That much was clear. If God was all powerful, as Lincoln devoutly believed he was, then why did the slaveholders keep winning? Maybe God had something in mind that neither Union nor Confederacy could know. "God wills this contest, and wills that it should not end yet," he thought. "By his mere quiet power, he could have either saved or destroyed the Union without human contest." Alone, at night, Lincoln began to wonder whether he "might be an instrument in God's hands for accomplishing a great work." He even began to look for some kind of sign from God.

The sign—or something like it—came on the battlefield. The Confederates invaded Maryland at summer's end, in 1862. This time they were stopped cold. The Union commander wired that he had won a great victory—a claim Lincoln soon learned was somewhat exaggerated. But he proclaimed the victory anyway. Lincoln went to his cabinet and told them he had made a covenant with God that when victory came in Maryland, he "would consider it an indication of the Divine Will" that he should "move forward in the cause of emancipation."

The next day, September 22, 1862, Lincoln issued his Emancipation Proclamation. He had come only a little distance. The proclamation did not free a single slave until New Year's Day, 1863. And then it declared only that the slaves in Confederate territory were to be freed. Since most of that territory was still very firmly in the hands of the Southerners, the proclamation could hardly be enforced. In fact, the proclamation suggested a very odd paradox: that slavery was illegal in rebel states but still perfectly all right in Union states like Kentucky or Missouri—in the city of Washington itself, if it came to that.

But Lincoln had done one decisive thing. He had settled one question firmly that no one had considered settled before. If the Union won the war, then slavery in the American South would effectively come to an end. Now, the war was a war for the Union; it was a war for the principles of democracy and liberty; but it was also a war against slavery. It was not yet a war *for* black rights—and it never would become quite that. But it was a very different thing from the intricate political "game" it had been when the president took office.

Abraham Lincoln's sense that the Civil War had some sort of deep, religious meaning deepened over the next year and a half. The casualty lists grew to appalling proportions on both sides. Gettysburg came and went. And so did other titanic battles. The president looked older and more melancholy every week. Enduring, enduring—this had become his form of dedication.

The contest proceeded, still. But the months and the battles were good to the Union, whose armies now advanced in the unanticipated role of liberating armies for black slaves. No one, including Lincoln, had any clear idea what liberation might mean in fact and in practice. But Frederick Douglass's "logic of events" had done its work. When on March 4, 1865, Lincoln again climbed the steps of the Capitol, to deliver his second inaugural address, the end was in sight. He knew everything he said would be studied with care by men and women, blacks and whites, in the North and in the South. And so he tried once more to say what the war signified, to give some explanation of the reasons he thought the nation had to endure what it was going through.

When the war had begun almost four years earlier, he began, no one on either side had guessed that it would last so long, or that it would be transformed into a war against slavery. But that had been God's will. He had given the Americans this long and "terrible war," perhaps as a punishment for the "offense" of slavery. "Fondly do we hope, fervently do we pray," he went on, "that this mighty scourge of war may speedily pass away." "Fervently do we pray." "Mighty scourge." "Pass away." His language had the accents of the Old Testament prophets. And he did not hold back: "Yet if God wills that it continue until all the wealth piled by the bondsman's two hundred and fifty years of unrequited toil shall be sunk, and until every drop of blood drawn with the lash shall be paid by another drawn with the sword, as was said three thousand years ago, so still must be said, 'the judgements of the Lord are true and righteous altogether.' "

But in the religious world of Abraham Lincoln and of most of his countrymen (North and South), the Lord did not only judge. He forgave. So Lincoln ended with a plea that echoed more the New Testament than the Old. "With malice toward none; with charity for all; with firmness in the right as God gives us to see the light, let us strive to finish the work we are in; to bind up the nation's wounds, to care for him who shall have borne the battle, and for his widow, and his orphan—to do all which may achieve a just and lasting peace, among ourselves and with all nations." Here were the words so central to the New Testament: "Charity." "Light." "Care." "Peace." When he lay dead a few weeks later, the vocabularies of both Testaments would echo back over him, and he would be compared to Moses, then to Jesus.

At Appomattox Courthouse in Virginia, April 9, 1865, Robert E. Lee surrendered his Army of Northern Virginia to Ulysses S. Grant. By April 14—which was Good Friday—it had all begun to sink in: armed resistance in the South was practically over. The sadness that had seemed to weigh so heavily on Lincoln lifted a bit. In the afternoon, riding in a carriage, his wife, Mary, said to him that he seemed "so gay, so cheerful." "Well I might," Lincoln answered. "I consider this the day the war has come to a close." That night, they would go to the theater. A new English comedy, *Our American Cousin,* had just opened at Ford's Theater, and the Lincolns were in just the right mood for such a play. During the third act, John Wilkes Booth—a member of the famous Booth family of actors, slipped into the president's box. He pointed a derringer at Lincoln's head and pulled the trigger. Lincoln slumped forward, with the bullet that had passed through his brain now lodged just behind his right eye. He probably never knew what had happened.

He was carried, deeply unconscious, to a house across the street. All through the night, the hopeless vigil of the doctors, of high government officials, and of Lincoln's son, Robert, continued. Then, at 7:22 in the morning, Lincoln died. The secretary of war, Edwin Stanton, was heard to mutter, "Now he belongs to the ages."

Stanton was right. What now began was a drama of grief that seemed almost boundless. War and victory had made Lincoln a hero. Now death transformed him into a near saint. "The heart grows sick and faint," wrote the *Washington National Republican* on this day before Easter. "The pen almost refuses to trace the details of the tragedy." Crowds had gathered in the rain outside the house where Lincoln lay dying. At 7:30, "the tolling of bells announced to the lamenting people that he had ceased to breathe. His great and loving heart was still." Immediately, the streets were crowded with "people, men, women, and children, thronging the thoroughfares. It seemed as if everyone was in tears." As the bells tolled, offices, government buildings, and stores all closed. The black crepe of mourning replaced the red, white, and blue bunting that only a few days earlier had been put up to celebrate Lee's surrender. It was the same everywhere. As the telegraph hurried the news over the land, people gathered in the streets to express and share their horror, bewilderment, and grief.

To many, the loss was personal—something that had happened directly to them, not just to the nation. Some could barely contain their rage and struck out at anyone who uttered anything against the fallen president. Black freedmen were numbed by the word that the president was dead. One young girl remarked that she thought she could "never love God anymore." Walt Whitman expressed his sense of loss in a poem. News of the assassination had come to him just as the lilacs, portent of spring, rebirth, and renewal, had come into blossom:

> When lilacs last in the dooryard bloom'd
> And the great star early droop'd in the western
>   sky in the night,
> I mourn'd, and yet shall mourn with ever-returning spring.
> Ever-returning spring, trinity sure to me you bring,
> Lilac blooming perennial and drooping star in the west,
> And thought of him I love.

The press and public orators struggled to find ways to comprehend and interpret the "awful tragedy of last night." What "dumbfounded" the people, wrote the *New York Herald,* was that such a thing could have happened to the American republic. The real "horror of the deed," the *Boston Transcript* insisted, was "the fact that the victim was the kindliest and most magnanimous of great magistrates and seemed to fall martyr to his own goodness." In Lincoln's hometown, a newspaper that had not always supported the president described the tragedy in this way:

Just in the hour when the crowning triumph of his life awaited him; . . . when he could begin clearly to see the promised land of his longings—the restored Union—the assassin's hand at once put a rude period to his life and to his hopes. As Moses of old, who had led God's people through the gloom and danger of the wilderness, dies when on the eve of realizing all that his hopes had pictured, so Lincoln is cut off just as the white wing of peace begins to reflect its silvery radiance over the red billows of war.

As the first shocked grief poured forth, plans for the funeral and burial were made. Several groups laid claim to the body. The City Council in Springfield, Illinois, insisted that Springfield "should be the final resting place for all of him that remains mortal." New York papers urged construction of a monument that would contain his remains. The Commission of Public Monuments in Washington declared that the body ought to be deposited in the vault that had been prepared for George Washington under the rotunda of the Capitol. But the distraught widow insisted (as had Washington's family) that "his dust shall lie among his own neighbors and kin." Lincoln would be returned to Springfield for burial, but not directly and immediately as Mary Lincoln wanted. Her husband also belonged to the public. Secretary of War Stanton, in charge of the official arrangements, thought it was important that as many people as possible have a chance to take part in the farewell to Lincoln.

At noon on Wednesday, April 19, the official funeral service took place in

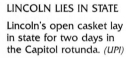

**LINCOLN LIES IN STATE**

Lincoln's open casket lay in state for two days in the Capitol rotunda. *(UPI)*

REWARD POSTER FOR THE CAPTURE OF THE CONSPIRATORS

Lincoln's assassination was part of a broader scheme. Booth's accomplices also intended to kill Vice President Johnson and Secretary of State Seward, who was badly beaten in an attack upon him by the conspirators. *(Culver Pictures)*

the East Room of the White House. At the same hour, people all over the country gathered in their churches for simultaneous services. Lincoln's pastor eulogized the president and pointed to the belief in the "justness and goodness of God" that had been "an anchor to his soul" and had "emboldened him in his path of duty." Then a solemn procession, led by a regiment of black troops, followed by half a dozen other military units, thirty bands, and then another black regiment, carried the body past a vast crowd of blacks and whites, soldiers and wounded veterans, to the rotunda of the Capitol, where the open casket lay in state for two days. "The procession of saddened faces came pressing forward at the rate of three thousand persons per hour. The Rotunda, which was lighted only by a sort of twilight hue, was filled with solemn stillness, unbroken save by the rustling of the dresses of female mourners, and occasionally a deep sigh from some of those passing the coffin."

Then, on April 21, a nine-car funeral train left Washington for the long journey back to Springfield. The train retraced the route that just four years earlier had carried Lincoln to his inauguration. It stopped in ten cities along the way. Everywhere it was the same: a procession through the city, ceremonies in a hall where the body lay in state, throngs of people filing past the coffin to get a last glimpse of the "face of our great friend." In Philadelphia, 100,000 people joined the procession; 300,000 more looked on, as the hearse bearing the casket made its way to Independence Hall, "the Temple of American Liberty," to lie in state. When the body arrived at the hall, three women placed a cross of pure white flowers on the casket. It was, according to the silk streamer attached to it, "A Tribute to our Great and Good President Fallen a Martyr to the Cause of Human Freedom—'In my Hand No Price I Bring, Simply My Cross to Cling.' "

In every city, banners along the route that the procession took proclaimed their messages: "His Memory, like the Union he Preserved, is not for a day, but for all time"; "God's noblest work, an honest man"; "Weep, generous nation, weep; the sad, swift removal of him whom Heaven indulgent sent to man. Too good for earth, to Heaven art thou fled, and left the Nation in tears." At numerous ceremonies, Lincoln's second inaugural address was read again and again. Orators and clergymen tried to capture the meaning of the man and the tragedy. Lincoln's "death, which was meant to sever the Union beyond repair, binds it more firmly than ever," George Bancroft declared. "The country may need this imperishable grief, to touch its inmost feelings.

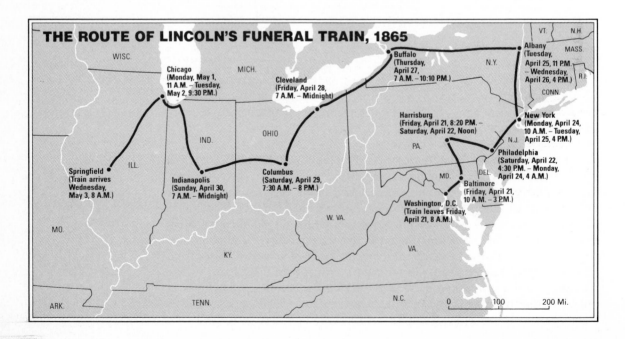

**THE ROUTE OF LINCOLN'S FUNERAL TRAIN, 1865**

Chicago (Monday, May 1, 11 A.M. – Tuesday, May 2, 9:30 P.M.)

Cleveland (Friday, April 28, 7 A.M. – Midnight)

Buffalo (Thursday, April 27, 7 A.M. – 10:10 P.M.)

Albany (Tuesday, April 25, 11 P.M. – Wednesday, April 26, 4 P.M.)

Harrisburg (Friday, April 21, 8:20 P.M. – Saturday, April 22, Noon)

New York (Monday, April 24, 10 A.M. – Tuesday, April 25, 4 P.M.)

Philadelphia (Saturday, April 22, 4:30 P.M. – Monday, April 24, 4 A.M.)

Springfield (Train arrives Wednesday, May 3, 8 A.M.)

Indianapolis (Sunday, April 30, 7 A.M. – Midnight)

Columbus (Saturday, April 29, 7:30 A.M. – 8 P.M.)

Baltimore (Friday, April 21, 10 A.M. – 3 P.M.)

Washington, D.C. (Train leaves Friday, April 21, 8 A.M.)

0    100    200 Mi.

LINCOLN'S FUNERAL TRAIN

This nine-car funeral train carried Lincoln across the land to his grave in Springfield, Illinois.
*(Culver Pictures)*

The grave that receives the remains of President Lincoln, receives a martyr
to the Union, and the monument which rises over his body will bear witness
to the Union."

Not only the cities mourned. As the train passed hamlet, countryside, and
town, it went through arches with banners and emblems, past bands playing
requiems, and regiments of militiamen and Union soldiers. Everywhere, at
every hour and in every kind of weather, people thronged to see the train.
At midnight, in Syracuse, New York, 35,000 people stood in a drenching
rain as the train passed by. During the nights, all along the way, a "pillar of
fire" guided the cortege as "at every crossroads the glare of innumerable
torches illuminated the whole population from age to infancy, kneeling on
the ground, their clergymen leading them in prayers and hymns."

After twelve days and more than 1,600 miles, the funeral train reached
Springfield, Illinois. At ten in the morning on May 3, the casket was closed
for the last time, carried to the waiting hearse, and taken by one last procession
to the "City of the Dead" in Oak Ridge cemetery.

The long journey was over. Stanton had said that Lincoln belonged to the
ages. As the funeral train had made its way across the nation, the people
themselves had poured out on him the accumulated grief of four years of war

**THE EXECUTION OF THE CONSPIRATORS**

John Wilkes Booth, killed trying to resist capture, escaped trial for the assassination of Lincoln. But four others were tried and, on July 7, 1865, publicly executed. One of them, Mary E. Surratt, in whose boarding house some of the plotting had taken place, was clearly innocent of any involvement in the crime. She was merely a victim of the hysteria and desire for revenge that Lincoln's assassination provoked. *(Culver Pictures)*

and taken possession of him. "Give him place, oh, ye prairie," the Reverend Henry Ward Beecher had said as the cortege passed through New York. "Ye winds that move over the mighty prairies of the west, chant his requiem. Ye people, behold the martyr, whose blood pleads for fidelity, for law, for liberty." From Lincoln's words and acts, out of their own needs, from historical myth and their religious traditions, they had transmuted the Lincoln many of them had once ridiculed and condemned into Lincoln the martyr—the good and pure Lincoln, who befriended the lowly slave, and sacrificed himself for liberty and the Union. "Washington the Father, Lincoln the Savior of his Country," countless banners along the way proclaimed.

# War and Reunion

When Lincoln summoned the North to combat, few people were really surprised—war talk had been going on for a long time. But neither side was at all ready for war. The United States scarcely had a military establishment: its army existed mainly to fight Indians and consisted of about 20,000 soldiers scattered in remote frontier forts. Its navy was made up of about ninety ships, most of which were obsolete, out of commission, or in foreign ports. In addition, Americans were largely an agricultural people, living in a huge, sparsely populated, and highly decentralized society.

## BUILDING AND EQUIPPING ARMIES

The first task was to create armies. There was no shortage of men willing to fight. Northerners and Southerners both greeted the call to arms with naive, almost innocent, enthusiasm. All over the nation men, many scarcely more than boys, rushed to volunteer. The big question was "not who shall go to the wars, but who shall stay at home." Local communities themselves organized companies, platoons, and regiments. With a motley assortment of uniforms and weapons, with fiery speeches, and with knapsacks crammed with cakes and mementoes from wives, mothers, and sweethearts, the volunteers went off to war, flushed with idealism, eager to serve the sacred cause of Union or Southern independence. Death did not frighten them. Each side expected its valor in a righteous cause to bring quick victory. If death did come it would be heroic: "And for life," wrote one young man in words many on both sides would have echoed, "if the Nation will take me, I do not see that I can put myself— experience and character—to any more useful use."

The flood of volunteers had to be turned into disciplined armies. There was not much to build

**CONFEDERATE VOLUNTEERS**

This photograph of a group of eager and proud Confederate volunteers captures the enthusiasm and confidence with which both sides greeted the outbreak of war. In both North and South recruits rushed to have their new status recorded by photographers. *(Cook Collection, Valentine Museum)*

on. Their only military experience was the musters of local militias, to which most able-bodied white men had gone each month for a little haphazard drill, a lot of speechmaking, and even more drinking. More serious was the lack of an adequate and experienced officer corps. Of the little over 1,000 officers with any formal military training (about three-quarters of whom joined the Confederacy), none had ever commanded more than a few battalions. At the company, platoon, and regimental levels (and often even at higher levels), command was often conferred because of political connections or local prominence rather than because of military competence. Throughout the war, but especially in the first two years, the war efforts of both sides and particularly the

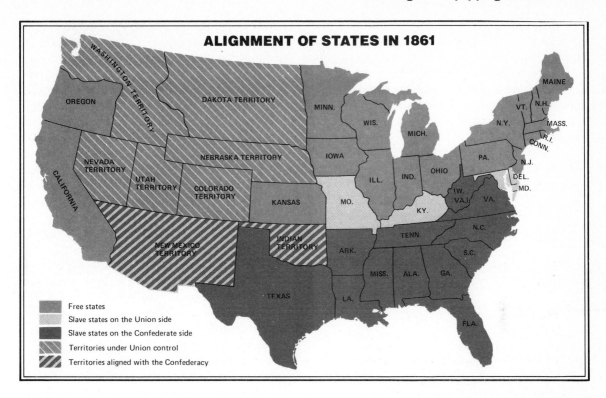

**ALIGNMENT OF STATES IN 1861**

Legend:
- Free states
- Slave states on the Union side
- Slave states on the Confederate side
- Territories under Union control
- Territories aligned with the Confederacy

North were plagued by wildly incompetent officers.

Creating and fielding armies also demanded kinds of economic and governmental organization that neither side had. Both sides and particularly the North possessed considerable resources, but in 1861 neither economy (especially the South's) was designed for feeding, equipping, and transporting large armies. The North's textile mills, for example, produced hundreds of thousands of yards of cloth each year, but this cloth was still turned into finished clothing (like uniforms) in small workshops. And the nearly 10,000 miles of Southern railroad (as much railway, in proportion to population, as the North had) did not constitute a genuine transportation system, since few of the railroads were hooked up to each other.

There was a similar lack of administrative machinery. Except for the postal service, the federal government played little role in people's lives. With a minuscule military establishment, no fed-

eral taxes or national banking system, and no educational or welfare agencies, the experienced officials or bureaucratic mechanisms needed to prepare for and conduct war did not exist. Near chaos reigned for much of the first year. Leroy P. Walker, the Confederacy's first secretary of war (whose filing system consisted of piling papers on a chair), turned away tens of thousands of volunteers because he did not know what to do with them. The Union's secretary of war, Simeon Cameron, like Walker a political appointee with no relevant experience, was equally unable to cope with the flood of recruits and military contracts. As a result, corrupt profiteers had a heyday, getting exhorbitant prices for often worthless equipment. One large lot of Northern uniforms, for example, was made of "shoddy," a cheap cotton fabric that disintegrated in a hard rain. Not until well into the second year of the war did many of these problems begin to get worked out. Lincoln shipped Cameron off to a relatively innocuous ambassadorship in Russia and replaced him with Edwin Stanton, who ran the War Department from then on with incorruptible efficiency. Davis, too, found more competent personnel, and by 1862 the Confederacy had an ordance chief who was able to procure 20 million cartridges for a 400,000 man army. (When the Confederacy declared war it had only 20 cartridges per soldier).

# STRATEGY—THEORY AND PRACTICE

Economic strength and military power go hand in hand, and when war began, the North seemed to have an overwhelming economic advantage. Its population of 22,000,000 was more than dou-

### JEFFERSON DAVIS

Though a reluctant secessionist, Davis (1808–1889) was a firm and unrelenting champion of the Confederacy. Like Lincoln, he was often vilified by opponents who objected to his handling of the war. Imprisoned for two years after the war, he remained a believer in the righteousness of the Southern cause to the end of his life. He refused to request official amnesty and never regained United States citizenship. *(UPI)*

ble that of the South; its industrial output and its overall wealth were more than ten times that of the South. It even outstripped the agricultural South in the production of food. Jefferson Davis (a West Point graduate who would have preferred to lead the Confederate armies rather than head its government) chose a defensive strategy to offset the effects of the North's enormous economic potential. It would cost far less in men and resources to force the Union to fight in the South than it would to invade the North and try to defeat its armies there. Davis's strategy was to have the Confederate army fight close to its economic base and use the military advantages of defense, familiar territory, and short supply lines to win a few major battles. The North, Davis believed, would find the price of victory too high and would grant the Confederate States of America independence, just as a war-weary and frustrated Britain had granted the American colonies their independence.

Northern strategy, not surprisingly, was almost the mirror opposite. By the nature of its paramount goal—to save the Union—the North had to go on the offensive. Only if the South was thoroughly defeated, Lincoln and his military advisers believed, could it be forced to give up its claim to independence. Lincoln knew that even with its economic superiority the North faced a task that would strain its will and resources to the utmost. And he recognized, too, the link between economic and military strength. To strangle the South economically, he declared a naval blockade, hoping to keep the Confederacy from importing the war materials it needed. On the military front, he planned a two-pronged attack. In the West, Northern armies would invade and try to cut the Confederacy in two, while in the East, they would strike at the Southern capital of Richmond.

These were the grand designs. But geography and the conventions of military doctrine shaped how they were put into practice. Until the last year of the war, almost all the fighting in the East took place in the narrow area between the Blue Ridge Mountains and the Atlantic Ocean and be-

**A UNION IRONCLAD**

In an attempt to break the Northern naval blockade, the Confederacy devised the first "ironclad" vessel, a wooden ship plated with armor. In March 1862, the first battle of the ironclads took place, a standoff between the Confederate *Merrimac* and the Union *Monitor.* By the end of 1864, the Union navy had more than seventy ironclads in commission, many resembling the one shown in this photograph. *(UPI)*

tween the James and the Potomac rivers, the narrow corridor between the two capitals. In the thinking of the day, capital cities had great military, political, and symbolic significance. According to strategic doctrine, capturing the enemy's capital could itself bring victory, and loss of one's own might well bring defeat. So for three years, as if locked in an elaborate and bloody chess match, the Army of the Potomac and the Army of Northern Virginia slugged it out in battle after battle, with neither army, until the very end, either annihilating the other or capturing the enemy's capital.

The war in the West was very different. There, the vast and changing border between Union and Confederacy stretched on for over a thousand miles. In this vast theater, warfare took many forms. The long border exposed both sides to quick strikes and raids. Along the Missouri and Kansas border, a marauding guerrilla warfare of the most brutal sort took place. (Indeed, Jesse and Frank James, the most notorious bandits in American history, got their start as members of William C. Quantrill's guerrilla band). In the

West, too, the Mississippi, Tennessee, and Cumberland rivers opened up avenues into the heart of the Confederacy.

## WAR, DIPLOMACY, AND NORTHERN MORALE

The fortunes of war are not sealed only on the battlefield. From the perspective of long-range strategy, the Union successes in the West put the Union in a fairly strong position. But it did not seem that way to the Northern people. The Civil War was the first American war to get vivid daily newspaper coverage, and it was in the Eastern theater that the most dramatic, closely watched, and highly publicized fighting took place. There in the early years of the war the North took a pounding, and this was far more important than what happened at Shiloh and Corinth in shaping the politics and diplomacy that could determine the outcome of the war.

Diplomacy played an important part in the Confederacy's overall strategy. From the outset,

# AMERICANS AT WAR

## The Civil War

The Union and the Confederacy were not old enemies, facing each other across well-defined and fortified frontiers. When the fighting began, the Confederacy had two major armies in Kentucky, which was claiming "neutral" status. And the Union had an important fortress and two large armies inside northern Virginia.

These facts defined the war from the beginning in two important ways. First, the Civil War would not be a war of fixed fronts, with armies digging in along entrenched lines. It would be a war of movement. Second, the struggle would take place in two distinct geographical theaters. The war would have an "east," in Virginia, where federal troops were already inside the Confederacy. And it would have a "west" in the valleys of the Ohio, the Mississippi, and the Tennessee rivers.

If the war could be won (or lost) quickly, as a lot of people on both sides expected it would be, then the decisive action would surely come in the east. If the war had to be fought in the heartland beyond the Appalachian Mountains—in Kentucky, or Tennessee, or Mississippi—then it would be long and bitter.

During the first spring and early summer of war, 1861, not much happened on the battlefields. Both sides were getting ready. Then Lincoln decided to try for the quick victory that would end the war. He ordered General Irvin McDowell, who commanded about 30,000 inexperienced troops, to march south from Washington toward the Virginia town of Manassas, to do battle with a smaller Confederate army commanded by General P. G. T. Beauregard. In mid-July, McDowell moved. Beauregard waited just south of a muddy little creek (or "run" as country people called it) named Bull Run. The two armies met on July 21. Several times the federal soldiers charged Beauregard's lines. Each time, they were driven back. Then Beauregard ordered a counterattack. The heat, the clamor, and the unexpectedly heavy casualties all took their toll on the young and green federal soldiers. The Union forward units panicked and ran back across Bull Run. The panic spread, and before it was over, McDowell had to retreat all the way to Washington.

The retreating soldiers brought only a few of their dead and wounded. But they also brought a blunt, wordless message. The war would not be won and lost in a few weeks in northern Virginia. It would be long and bloody. The first force of Union volunteers had enlisted for three months. Now Lincoln set out to raise a force of hundreds of thousands, recruited not for a few weeks but for three years. The Confederate leaders began the same grim task.

The winter of 1861–1862 was another sea-

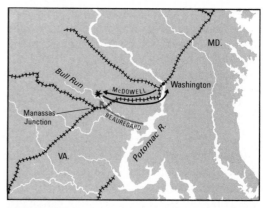

**THE FIRST BATTLE OF BULL RUN, JULY 21, 1861**

son of regrouping, supply, and training on both sides. And when the war heated up again, it was in the West, and it was savage. The Confederate armies in Kentucky were grouped around Bowling Green in the east and Columbus in the west. A Union commander, Ulysses S. Grant, received permission to move south from Illinois to drive a wedge between the armies and try to gain control of the Tennessee River. He succeeded in capturing two Confederate forts just inside Tennessee before the Confederate commanders could get their armies in position to challenge his advance. Then he quickly headed southward up the river. By early April, he had reached Pittsburg Landing, near the Mississippi border and a crucial rail junction at Corinth, Mississippi.

Meanwhile the two Confederate forces in the West, split by Grant's maneuver, had fallen back, abandoning the western half of Tennessee. The two armies, one commanded by Beauregard, the other by Albert Sidney Johnston, came together in northern Mississippi. Sooner or later they and Grant's force would have to meet. The Southern commanders decided to strike at Grant before Union reinforcements, racing down from Louisville, could reach him. They attacked near a Tennessee country church called Shiloh on April 6.

The struggle was ferocious and vast. The Confederate generals had 55,000 troops to throw at Grant, who had about 40,000 men. The first day ended in stalemate, but the corpses piled up. Then Grant's reinforcements arrived, and after the second day, the Southerners had to break off their attack.

Neither army had been broken or destroyed at Shiloh. But two things were now clear. First, the Confederate forces had not been able to drive Grant's threatening army out of the Deep South. Second, the war was going to be more savage than even Bull Run had hinted it would be. On the fields and in the woods at Shiloh, 13,000 Union soldiers and 10,000 of the Confederacy's best troops lay dead. Many thousands of others on both sides were wounded. Victory was now a question of which side could stand the carnage longer, could continue to pour men and guns into one titanic battle after another, and could go on hauling away the wagonloads of the dead and wounded.

Strategically, the Union was very close to accomplishing a major goal—controlling the Mississippi. In April 1862, the same month as Shiloh, Flag Officer—soon to be Admiral—David Farragut had captured Mobile and New Orleans for the Union. A little later, he

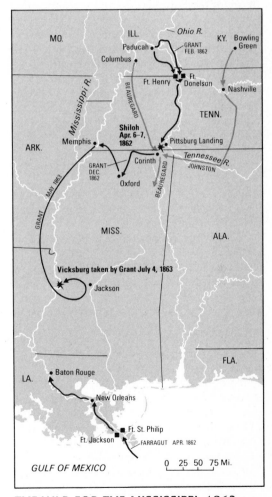

THE WAR FOR THE MISSISSIPPI, 1862–1863

had moved up the Mississippi to Baton Rouge. Grant took Corinth, Union forces occupied Memphis, and now most of the river was theirs, except for the strong Confederate fortress at Vicksburg.

While the Union attack in the West went forward, the war in the East became a bloody standoff. Neither the Union's failures nor the Confederacy's successes were decisive enough to bring either side within sight of final victory or defeat.

The main Union army in Virginia, the Army of the Potomac, was now commanded by young George B. McClellan, who had convinced Lincoln to let him try to take Richmond, not by land this time, but by sea and up the peninsula between the York and James rivers—that same peninsula where Charles, Lord Cornwallis, had surrendered to George Washington in 1781. Confederate armies led by a new commander, Robert E. Lee, and his ablest lieutenant, General Thomas J. "Stonewall" Jackson, met the threat and turned McClellan back. The major battles of the campaign lasted seven days and cost Lee 20,000 dead, McClellan 15,000. But Lee had won. The Army of the Potomac was driven back down the peninsula.

Lincoln ordered McClellan's army home to Washington, determined to attack Richmond overland. But Lee and Jackson now moved north, hoping to defeat other Union forces near Washington before McClellan's army could complete its withdrawal and regroup. And they succeeded. A second battle near Manassas, the Second Battle of Bull Run, August 29–30, 1862, was the most decisive Confederate victory yet.

Now Lee took the offensive. He moved his army into Maryland, knowing that the federal army would have to place itself between him and the capital, leaving Virginia's farmers free to take in the fall harvest without the presence of massive Union armies. McClellan moved out to meet the threat and threw an army of almost 90,000 at Lee's 50,000 near Sharpsburg, Maryland, at a stream called Antietam Creek.

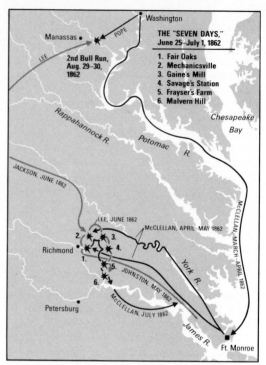

**THE PENINSULAR CAMPAIGN AND THE SECOND BATTLE OF BULL RUN, 1862**

On September 17, Lee's men and McClellan's fought three pitched battles on the same field. The Confederate lines bent under overwhelming pressure. Then, when it was clear that one more Union assault would bring a massive defeat, Jackson rushed to Lee with reinforcements. Still, McClellan might have won with one more charge. But he held back, and even gave Lee another day to withdraw.

Antietam was the bloodiest single day of the war. At its end, 13,000 men in Union blue and almost 11,000 in Confederate gray lay dead. Lincoln called it a victory and used it as the occasion for the Emancipation Proclamation. But he mourned McClellan's failure to follow up on his apparent advantage, and he relieved McClellan as commander. In the East, as in the West, some things had become clear, at least for the time being. Nei-

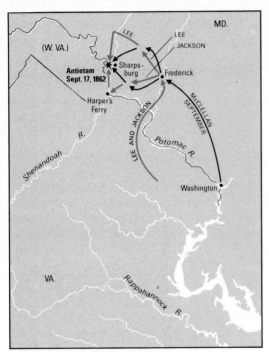

**THE BATTLE OF ANTIETAM, 1862**

ther side had an overwhelming advantage in the field. The Union was not able to manage a successful offensive against Richmond. But neither was Lee able to operate successfully outside Virginia. Any Union commander who wanted to defeat Lee had to be prepared to accept truly appalling casualties and keep attacking, again and again.

Such an officer was the man Lincoln chose to replace McClellan, General Ambrose E. Burnside. Burnside shocked Lee and Jackson by driving his Army of the Potomac across the Rappahannock River, near Fredericksburg, Virginia, and attacking strong Confederate positions on the high ground near the town. The Confederates held. Burnside sent his men again up the heights. Again they failed. The bewildered general commanded another attack. Another failure. And by the end of the battle, Burnside had lost 12,000 men in his disastrous effort. The two exhausted armies dug in for a winter of waiting on the opposite shores of the Rappahannock.

The next spring, another new general, "Fighting Joe" Hooker, took charge of the Army of the Potomac. But his luck against Lee was no better than McClellan's or Burnside's had been. Hooker tried moving upriver, then across the Rappahannock, to outflank Fredericksburg. Lee and Jackson met him at Chancellorsville, in early May 1863, and defeated him decisively. But by now the Confederacy was so weakened that no Southern general could assemble the supplies and fresh troops necessary to take decisive advantage of any victory. Once more, Lee had won; but he had won only time and stalemate. And time and stalemate were now clearly the allies of the Union.

At the end of April 1863, Grant had put the Mississippi River town of Vicksburg under heavy siege. The situation was critical. If Vicksburg fell, as it must if not given massive support from the east, then Confederate communications with the states west of the river would be cut. Lee had to decide whether to send an army west to raise the siege. He decided on another, daring strategy, designed to try for a victory that might force the Union to move part of Grant's forces east. So once more Lee invaded, this time not just into Maryland, but into Pennsylvania.

As Lee moved north, Hooker moved too, keeping his army between the enemy and Washington. But Hooker did not attack. Chancellorsville had been a painful lesson. He finally asked Lincoln to remove him from command, and the hapless Army of the Potomac now received yet another new commander, George G. Meade. With Lee about ten miles inside Pennsylvania, Meade moved in on the rear of the advancing Confederates.

On July 1, 1863, Lee sent a brigade of infantry into the town of Gettysburg, hoping to seize shoes for his army. The infantry stumbled onto some Union cavalry units, and there was a brief skirmish. Messengers on both sides rode away toward their main armies, asking for quick reinforcements.

ULYSSES S. GRANT *(Library of Congress)*

ROBERT E. LEE *(Cook Collection, Valentine Museum)*

Neither commander had chosen Gettysburg as a battlefield. But Lee could not keep moving northward once the Army of the Potomac had found him and was at his rear, able to cut him off from Virginia. The Union commander, Meade, could not give Gettysburg to Lee. The town was just too important. It was a junction for a dozen different roads, one of them leading straight into Baltimore.

All day long on July 1, both armies rushed men toward Gettysburg. Lee was a bit closer, so he managed to get 25,000 soldiers into action on that first day. Meade managed to move up about 20,000. The Union's forward units fought and fell back, then fought again. (One Northern unit, after ferocious fighting, retreated in a panic through the town of Gettysburg, to take up new positions on Cemetery Hill. As they rushed sweating and frightened past the gates of the town's cemetery there, some of them may have noticed a small sign, a memory of more peaceful days. It read, "All persons found using firearms in these grounds will be prosecuted with the utmost rigor of the law." The good citizens of Gettysburg wanted their dead to sleep in peace.)

At the end of the first day's fighting, Meade's soldiers had fallen back into tight and powerful defensive positions on the long hook-shaped ridge south and west of Gettysburg. Time was on his side. Every hour, he could expect fresh men and supplies. Lee was reluctant to attack because he did not know where the rest of the great Army of the Potomac was, or how long it would take it to fall upon him. But he was encouraged by the success of his men on that first day, when they had seemed able to drive the Union troops back toward the ridge top with ease. In fact, Lee was fighting a war of morale, hoping that he could break the spirit of the Union soldiers at Gettysburg and that a victory here would damage the Union's will to continue the war.

So Lee decided to try to turn both Union flanks on July 2. He ordered General Richard

Ewell to take Cemetery Hill, on the Union right, "if practicable." But Ewell, who commanded the corps that Stonewall Jackson had once led, was not willing to risk his men. He was certain that the enemy was securely dug in on the hill and had a lot of artillery ready to fire into his advancing troops. So he held back.

Lee also ordered a larger force, commanded by General James P. Longstreet, to attack the Union left and to try to take the hills, known as Little Round Top and Round Top, at the southern end of Cemetery Ridge. Longstreet's desperate charge fell short and only succeeded in driving some Union cavalry units off the forward slopes of the ridge.

Lee's hope had been that attacks by Ewell and Longstreet would tempt Meade to move forces out of the center of his line, to defend its open flanks. Meantime, he was massing almost the entire Confederate artillery in the center, ready for an assault on the third day. Despite Ewell's decision not to attack Cemetery Hill, and despite Longstreet's bloody and costly failure, Lee decided to go ahead with his plan. In fact, given the state of battle and the state of the war, he probably had no choice but to launch an all-out attack.

By noon on July 3, the Confederates had everything ready. About 143 cannon were massed near the center of the field. At 1:00, Lee ordered them to fire. They were answered by a barrage of equal ferocity from the heights. It was the single most heavy exchange of artillery of the entire war. But as the exchange wore on, two things happened. The Confederate guns dug themselves more deeply into the earth on each recoil, pointing their barrels higher. Their shots began to fly above the Union positions, where the infantry crouched behind defenses they had dug for themselves the day before. Second, Union commanders, understanding that a massive infantry assault would soon be coming, ordered their artillery gradually to fall silent and wait. In fact, Meade had anticipated Lee's strategy, and was ready for the assault on his center. He had placed a lot of

## GETTYSBURG, JULY 1–3, 1863

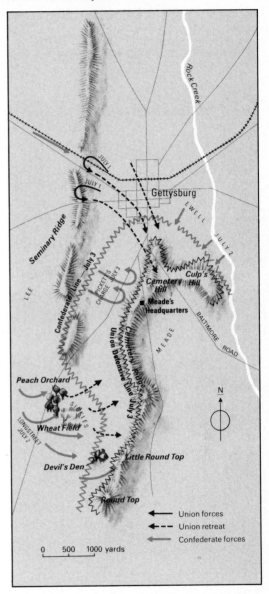

artillery there and had some of his best and toughest troops defending that part of the line.

Lee and his generals may have been convinced that they had a good chance to break

## THE CHATTANOOGA CAMPAIGN, 1863

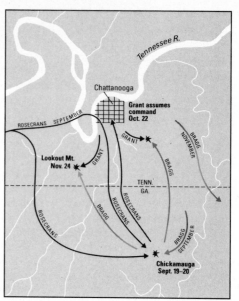

the Union's lines. Or Lee may have felt that he had no choice but to continue his attack, no matter what. He could hardly take up a defensive position this deep into enemy territory. And he could not retreat without dooming Vicksburg to surrendering to Grant. Whatever the reason, Lee ordered 13,000 men, commanded by General George Pickett, to charge Cemetery Ridge. Pickett formed his men in parade-ground order and sent them forward. The Union artillery opened up, followed by a withering fire from a strong center held by some of the most seasoned troops in the Army of the Potomac. And still the Confederates came. A few of them actually reached Union breastworks

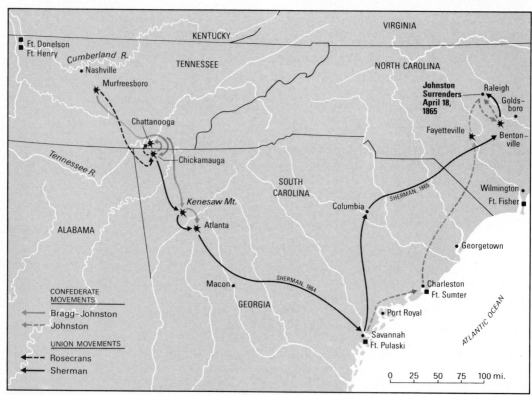

### SHERMAN'S MARCH THROUGH THE CONFEDERACY, 1864–1865

along the ridge line. But only a few. The rest were dead or wounded on the field, and the few who did make it to Union lines had no choice but to die, surrender, or run back down the slope under the same deadly fire.

As the charge began, Pickett had had three brigade commanders. Two were now dead and the third badly wounded. The thirteen colonels in his division were all dead. And three-fourths of his men were dead, wounded, or captured.

All in all, the Confederate armies had lost between 25,000 and 30,000 men at Gettysburg. (Lee had lost seventeen generals in the three days of battle.) Meade had lost about 23,000 men. But he had held. And on the day of Pickett's dreadful charge, the news came to both sides that Vicksburg had fallen to Grant.

The end was all but inevitable, but still the fighting and dying continued. Union troops occupied Chattanooga, Tennessee, in

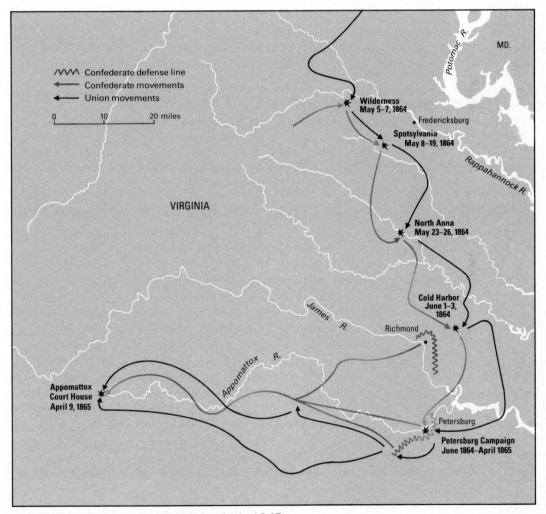

THE FINAL VIRGINIA CAMPAIGN, 1864–1865

August. Then a Union force moved down into Georgia. They were beaten there in the fierce battle of Chickamauga, one of the few fights in which the Confederates outnumbered the Union troops. But the victory counted for little. A month later, in the Battle of Chattanooga, Grant's army drove the South off its positions on the ridges and mountains around the city.

Once the Union armies had taken unchallenged control of Chattanooga, Atlanta lay before them, and then the sea. The South, already divided along the Mississippi, could now be split a second time by a line of soldiers stretching from Kentucky across Tennessee and Georgia to the Atlantic. This mission was not to be Grant's. Lincoln called him East to take command of the Army of the Potomac. The West was left under the command of William Tecumseh Sherman.

In the spring of 1864, the end drew nearer—though still it would not come. Grant embarked on the most vicious offensive of the war, attacking Lee day after day in May in a terrible struggle known as the Wilderness campaign. The Southerners fell back, but they continued to kill with deadly skill. They cost Grant 55,000 casualties in a little less than a month. But they suffered 30,000 of their own, losses they could no longer afford.

Meanwhile, in May, Sherman had begun his move southeastward from Chattanooga. It took him three months to reach Atlanta, but reach it he did. Then he set off on one of the most remarkable military marches in history. He ordered his men to advance along a front fully sixty miles wide, feeding off the countryside and destroying civilian property as they went. By December, he was in Savannah.

For nine months, the armies of Grant and Lee had been entrenched around Richmond, Grant waiting, Lee unable to attack. Defeat for the Confederacy was becoming more and more obvious with every dispatch from Georgia. Then Grant finally moved to surround Lee's force. The Confederate army, now numbering only about 25,000, made a desperate lunge westward, trying to escape encirclement, but it failed. Lee surrendered his army at Appomattox Court House, Virginia, on April 9, 1865. There were a few days more of scattered fighting in the Carolinas. But the war had finally ended. So had the lives of 600,000 soldiers.

Davis hoped to secure recognition and support from the European powers, especially England and France. The South's confidence that Britain would come to its aid lay in the importance of its cotton to the English economy. Nearly 20 percent of Britain's population was dependent on textiles for its livelihood; cotton goods made up over 40 percent of its exports, and it depended on the South for more than 80 percent of its raw cotton (700 million pounds per year). This situation, and the fact that Britain's own imperial designs in the Western Hemisphere would be well served if the American Union fell apart, brought that country very close to recognizing the Confederacy. As it was, in thinly disguised fashion Britain supplied the South with blockade-running ships and, at the risk of provoking war with the North, had even taken orders for two ironclad rams that could easily have broken the Northern blockade. Still, prudence and certain hard economic facts—the fact that Britain, having stockpiled a great deal of cotton before hostilities, had not yet felt much of an economic pinch; the fact that its merchants were profiting handsomely from trade with both sides, the fact that it imported a great deal of Northern wheat—dictated caution. Though leaning heavily toward the Confederacy, the British government chose to look carefully before it leapt; it waited to see how the war was going before it did anything that might provoke the North's open hostility. Lincoln knew that the British had their eyes trained on the battlefield. That was one of the reasons he so hastily proclaimed Antietam a major victory and issued the Emancipation Proclamation. He hoped to swing British public opinion behind the Northern cause.

Those at home also watched the Eastern theater with concern. Northern morale—the willingness of the people of the North to endure the suffering of war—was almost as important for Northern victory as what happened on the battlefield. Lincoln knew that one of his greatest tasks was to keep up support for the war, and he tried at every point to strengthen commitment to the Union as a cause worthy of any sacrifice. Moreover, Confederate strategy was aimed directly at Northern morale. Davis expected Southern independence to come from the Confederacy's ability to hold off defeat until a weary Northern public turned against the war. The strategic importance Lee attached to the destruction of a Northern army lay in the impact he hoped it would have on Northern and foreign opinion. Lincoln was acutely aware of how precarious Northern morale was in the summer and fall of 1862. Enthusiasm for the war had waned with the end of any hope for a quick victory, and many people were beginning to wonder if there would be any victory. Discontent with the administration's conduct of the war was mounting, and the war weariness threatened to slip into opposition to the war itself. Already there were those argued that the North should stop fighting and negotiate with the Confederacy about rejoining the Union. Lincoln issued his Emancipation Proclamation partly to line up antislavery fervor solidly behind the administration. He considered the organized opposition to the war to be a form of treason and jailed some of its leaders. If things in the East kept going as they were, the North's will to fight might well give out.

## LEADERSHIP AND OPPOSITION IN WARTIME

As the war ground on inexorably, opposition to Lincoln and Davis mounted. Northerners and Southerners increasingly blamed the seeming weakness and incompetence of their respective leaders for the hardship, suffering, and frustration they had to endure. Throughout the war, opponents portrayed Lincoln as a well-meaning but hapless bungler. To many Southerners, Davis seemed petty, aloof, bogged down in detail, and incapable of strong leadership. But oddly enough, Lincoln and Davis were also accused of being *too* forceful and were vilified as dictators and tyrants.

In large measure, the charge of tyranny reflected the fact that the war led to an unprecedented centralization of governmental power on both sides. In 1863, the North reinstituted a national banking system. The Confederate and Union governments both instituted new forms of taxation. The North imposed duties on most goods and adopted an income tax, while the South instituted a tax that required each planter and farmer to contribute 10 percent of his produce to the government. By early 1863, both sides had turned to conscription to help fill their armies. The opposition to the draft was intense, especially because the conscription acts contained exemption clauses that let the rich avoid the draft by hiring substitutes. Finally, both presidents deployed executive authority in unprecedented ways. Lincoln used his authority as commander in chief to initiate limited emancipation and Davis used executive authority to impress slaves for work on military projects. Both Lincoln and Davis at times suspended the right of habeas corpus so that those suspected of aiding the enemy could be arrested and detained without trial. (In the North, more than 13,000 persons were detained in this way.) From an administrative point of view, these were all pragmatic measures dictated by military necessity, but to the Northerners and Southerners who experienced them, they were forms of centralization and regimentation—tyranny—that went against longstanding traditions of local autonomy.

Lincoln and Davis also found it increasingly difficult to muster the unified support needed to carry out the policies necessary for victory. The Republican party itself was divided, and Lincoln constantly had to try to balance the conflicting demands of moderates and radicals in his own

DRAFT RIOT IN NEW YORK CITY, 1863

Violent riots broke out in New York and other Northern cities in reaction against Abraham Lincoln's conscription policies. Most of the rioters were workers who were especially angered because men with enough money could buy their way out of being drafted. This newspaper illustration depicts the murder of Colonel H. F. O'Brien near his home on July 14, 1863. The riots were only one manifestation of widespread dissatisfaction with Lincoln's administration. In the South, Jefferson Davis also met with major resistance to his policies. *(Culver Pictures)*

camp. Most Northern Democrats had initially lined up behind the war effort, but partisan politics quickly reasserted itself. The Democrats, even while supporting the war, subjected Lincoln's leadership and policies to unrelenting attack. Finally, the growing war-weariness sapped support for the war effort itself. By the summer of 1864, the North, with its overwhelming economic and military strength, was on the brink of triumph. But war-weariness was so strong that Lincoln thought it likely that Northern voters would repudiate him in the fall elections and elect General George McClellan on a Democratic "peace" ticket instead. But Lincoln was rescued by the fall of Atlanta, his own political skills, and his ability to provide the Northern public with a sense of the higher, sacred meaning of the war. He won a solid victory, gaining the support he needed to see the cause through to victory.

There was far less opposition to the war effort in the Confederacy than in the Union. But Jefferson Davis had even greater problems getting the support he needed than Lincoln did. Many planters, though steadfastly loyal to the Confederacy, opposed Davis's policies and did all they could to evade or subvert them. Davis's efforts also ran afoul of the doctrine of states' rights. His own vice president, Alexander Stephens, led the opposition to Davis's alleged usurpations of state sovereignty, and the governors of Georgia and North Carolina continually obstructed Davis's efforts to develop and carry out a unified policy.

This dissension and disaffection proved insurmountable, even for one as singlemindedly dedicated to Southern independence as Jefferson Davis, and, in the fall of 1864 and the winter of 1865 the Confederacy essentially disintegrated.

## THE TOLL OF TOTAL WAR

On April 9, 1865, the Civil War, the War Between the States, the War for Southern Independence, the War of the Rebellion, as it is variously called, was finally over, taking the lives of 618,000 soldiers—360,000 from the Union and 258,000 from the Confederacy. In the North, there was an outpouring of uncontainable jubilation, then a sense of completion and deliverance that was sealed in the ritual of mourning and transfiguration that carried Lincoln to his martyr's grave. To the ex-slaves, it was also time for jubilation—the day of deliverance longed for and promised in so many spirituals. Among the defeated whites of the South, especially those of the planter class, there was shock and disbelief, fear and uncertainty; their ordeal, it seemed, was far from over. All around them was chaos and destruction—no money, little food, a society and economy in shambles. Many wondered how or if they would survive and what might become of them. Would their lands be seized? Would they be tried and hanged as traitors, especially now that some Southern fanatic had killed the seemingly magnanimous Lincoln? Some also experienced an overpowering sense of loss. Not only had the Confederate armies been defeated, Southern civilization seemed also to have been destroyed. It was more than some could bear. On June 17,

### THE DESTRUCTION OF CHARLESTON, SOUTH CAROLINA

As the armies of Sherman and Grant pressed into the Confederacy, they left much of the South in ruins, visiting a destruction upon the civilian population that few other Americans have ever experienced. *(Library of Congress)*

# Mary Boykin Chesnut

Mary Boykin Chesnut wrote one of the most revealing pieces of Southern literature to come out of the Civil War era, a book first published under the title *A Diary from Dixie* in 1905, nearly forty years after the events it described. Mary Chesnut was in a particularly strong position to observe the Confederacy as it rose, fell in defeat, and disintegrated. Born into a well-known South Carolina family, she also married into one of the most prominent families of the South. As was customary for the scion of such a family, her husband, James Chesnut, Jr., entered politics, becoming a U.S. senator in 1858 and serving throughout the war as a chief aide to the Confederate president, Jefferson Davis, whose wife was one of Mary Chesnut's closest friends. Stationed close to the heart of the Confederacy—she was in Washington as the nation divided, in Charleston for the firing on Fort Sumter, and in the Confederate capital of Richmond, Virginia, during much of the war—Chesnut kept an extensive journal filled with notations about the people and events that came to her attention.

Though a keen and often detached observer of her class and culture, Mary Chesnut still held the attitudes of the planter elite. Her faith in the righteousness of the Confederate cause never wavered, and although she condemned slavery as a curse that had brought her society to its destruction, she viewed blacks with the racial and paternalistic condescension common to her class. But Mary Chesnut was only partly an insider. Intelligent, well-educated, and informed, she was nonetheless excluded from the masculine world of power and politics. Even while basking in the social attention her femininity bestowed on her, she resented her position on the periphery of things. Her journal gave her a vicarious sense of participation and superiority, as she gazed down on the masculine world and condemned and criticized its folly and hypocrisy.

*A Diary from Dixie* was fashioned in the 1870s and 1880s from a deliberate reworking of the original journals. Mary Chesnut began to think of herself as a writer only after the war. She wrote partly to try to help recoup the family fortunes, partly to relieve the pain of the collapse of her world, and partly out of a compulsion to write about the South that once had been. She first tried her hand at fiction, writing but never publishing three novels before turning to her Civil War journals as the source for her "big book" about the South and the Civil War.

Filled with gossip, romance, and the ordinary events that happen even in wartime, Chesnut's book retained the day-to-day randomness of a true diary. At the same time, it possessed the coherence and sense of theme and direction that only hindsight and Chesnut's conscious literary intentions could give it. The result was an extraordinary document about the Civil War but strongly shaped by Reconstruction. Her work kept alive the pain of the South's defeat, a pain made all the more intense by the social and psychological devastation that followed in the wake of the Confederacy's collapse. Throughout the *Diary,* life goes on, but the war keeps intruding, with its death, uncertainty, and destruction. A sense of sadness and loss begins to punctuate the book, a sense that in spite of the righteousness of its cause, the Confederacy is doomed and civilization is ending.

Edmund Ruffin, an early and vehement secessionist, who had been chosen to pull the lanyard that opened fire on Fort Sumter, made a final entry in his diary: "I here proclaim my unmitigated hatred to Yankee rule and the perfidious, malignant, and vile Yankee Race." Then he placed the muzzle of his gun in his mouth and pulled the trigger with a forked stick.

The final push to the bloody end had made clear what the decisive year of 1863 had already suggested. This was a war unlike any previous war. The Civil War has been called the first modern war, for good reasons. It was the first railroad war, transporting unprecedented quantities of troops and supplies over unprecedented distances. While Sherman conducted his siege of Atlanta, sixteen trains rushed him 1,600 tons of supplies each day. In addition, the huge armies—ten times the size of any previous units—using new technologies of destruction—trench warfare, Gatling guns, repeat loading rifles—had brought about an unprecedented kind of mass slaughter. As Walt Whitman wrote in 1863, "The heart grows sick of war after all, when you see what it really is— every once in a while I feel so horrified and disgusted—it seems to me like a great slaughterhouse and the men mutually butchering each other."

But what more than anything else set the Civil War apart from earlier wars was its character as a total war. Wars traditionally had been fought by professional armies, which jockeyed for territory until some kind of negotiated settlement was reached. Partly because of the new technologies of war and partly because each side was fighting for a principle it would not compromise, the Civil War became the first total war in modern times. It pitted not just two armies, but two societies—each by the end fully mobilized for the effort—against each other. Victory came not with the taking of territory but with the total destruction of the other society's capacity to fight. Sherman grasped the brutal logic of total war. As he put it, as he embarked on his march to the sea, "We are not only fighting hostile armies, but a hostile people. We must make old and young, rich and poor, feel the hand of war." And victory and defeat were themselves total: a destroyed South held on until it was forced into unconditional surrender. At the end, the Confederacy was in no position to negotiate a peace—it surrendered because it could no longer carry on.

## THE WAR AND SLAVERY

After four long years, the war had once and for all determined that the American republic could not be divided. But the society that had to be reunited was very different from the one that had split apart in 1861. As Lincoln had written to a Southern Unionist in early 1864, "the nation's condition is not what either party, or any man, devised or expected." The Emancipation Proclamation had formally ended slavery in the Confederacy, and the Thirteenth Amendment, proposed by Lincoln in 1864 and ratified in early 1865, had made freedom universal. But well before these acts and well before hostilities ended, the institution of slavery had started to fall apart, due to the "friction and abrasion" of war. By the end of 1861, runaways to the Union armies were treated as "contraband" of war, rather than returned to their masters. As early as 1862, the Northern fleet had captured the Sea Islands off the Carolina and Georgia coasts, and the slaves there had been freed. Masters tried to keep news of the approach of the Northern armies and the progress of the war from their slaves. But slaves devised ways of getting the news anyway. In Forsythe, Georgia, a slave who was charged with bringing the newspaper to his mistress always showed it to the local black preacher before he delivered it. House servants often overheard their masters talking and returned to the quarters with information about the whereabouts of the Union armies. More than once, a master awoke to find that many if not all of his slaves had slipped away in the night to become "contraband." As it marched through Georgia, Sherman's army became a veritable army of liberation (somewhat ironically, since Sherman himself had not op-

FREED BLACKS IN CHARLOTTESVILLE, VIRGINIA

A major problem after the war was the future of the former slaves. Slavery ended without any clear sense of what was to take its place. All over the South, freedmen drifted to the cities in search of work or simply to test their new found freedom. *(Culver Pictures)*

posed slavery and was deeply prejudiced against blacks). After the collapse of the Confederacy, actual freedom came by direct announcement to the slaves by former masters, the grapevine, or federal officials.

By the summer of 1865, most slaveholders had relinquished their slave property. But they still held onto the attitudes that had justified holding the blacks in bondage. They thought of blacks as childlike people, whom they had fed, clothed, housed, and cared for. And most had convinced themselves that their own slaves were loyal and happy, content with the lot to which their race had consigned them. They thus had great difficulty even imagining blacks as anything but a dependent and subservient people. Masters were perplexed, angered, and even hurt when their

slaves (often led by personal or house servants who had been considered most loyal) left them, refused to work, or stole tools and food.

The response of the ex-slaves to their new status was similarly confused and complex. Word of emancipation penetrated many places slowly and often in a garbled way. A few slaves wondered if emancipation meant that they now belonged to "Masr Linkum." Their situation was very confused. When slavery ended, there was nothing definite to take its place. The freedmen possessed a number of agricultural and other skills. But they were a people suddenly released from bondage, with few personal possessions and no money, property, or housing. It was not at all clear what they should do, where they should go, or how they could feed, clothe, and shelter themselves. Some set off for places from which they had been sold, hoping to reunite with their families. Others stayed where they were, working for their former masters or for nearby planters. Others, essentially refugees of war, roamed about and flocked to Union encampments in search of food, shelter, and protection.

In spite of all the confusion and uncertainty, the ex-slaves possessed a clear and definite idea of the difference between slavery and freedom. They asserted their sense of freedom in subtle ways. A rural and agricultural population tied to land and place, most were reluctant to leave areas that they regarded as home. But, refusing to stay in quarters that reminded them of their previous situation, they often moved to huts scattered around their former master's lands. Some moved to a neighboring planter's land to demonstrate that the tie to their former master had indeed been broken. For many, simply the act of moving, whatever the distance, was a gesture of liberation, a deliberate exercise of the choice and freedom that had been denied them under slavery. Many blacks resisted contracting for their labor, a refusal many whites condemned as a sign of laziness and irresponsibility. But many freedmen were suspicious of anything that seemed to bind them and their labor to any white man. Possession of their labor had been one of the essential marks of their enslavement. Indeed, many thought themselves justified in taking food, tools, and mules from their former masters as payment morally due them for their previous labor. But land was probably the most important token of freedom—a parcel of land that was their own. Again and again, blacks during Reconstruction pleaded for land, "forty acres and a mule," that would enable them to establish their independence and set up households where husbands and wives could work for themselves and rear and protect their children.

Reunion required more than just returning the seceded states to full and equal participation in the nation. It also meant reconstructing a society in which slavery no longer existed and determining what kind of freedom the ex-slaves would have. Lincoln had begun to plan for the aftermath of war well before the end of the fighting. He hoped to restore political relations as quickly and with as little animosity as possible. On December 8, 1863, he issued a proclamation specifying that whenever voters equal to 10 percent of the eligible voters of 1860 took an oath swearing future loyalty to the Constitution, the Union, and the acts freeing the slaves, a state could set up a republican form of government and resume ordinary political operations. (As blacks had not been eligible to vote in 1860, Lincoln's proclamation excluded black suffrage.) The Republican leaders in Congress wanted a much tougher procedure, one that would guarantee what they considered true loyalty to the Union. In July of 1864, Congress passed the Wade-Davis Bill, which Lincoln vetoed. The bill required action by 50 percent of the eligible electorate. More important, it contained provisions for an "ironclad" oath—a pledge of past as well as future loyalty—which was designed to bar all former secessionists and Confederate officeholders from political participation.

Lincoln was not unmindful of the troubling question of the freedmen, nor was he unaware of the tricky relationship between race and the politics of reunion. But just as he had initially subordinated slavery to the task of preserving the Union, he now placed highest priority on reestablishing normal political relations. He thought Reconstruction could be best achieved if the question of the freedmen was separated from the process of political reunion: If the ordinary political machinery was reestablished, the nation would be better able to work out what the freedman's place in American society should be. Lincoln had always been reluctant to push for civil and social equality for blacks, partly because of his awareness of the depth of American racism and partly because he shared some of that prejudice. Still, at the time of his death, he had begun to work on the problem of the freedmen and on the politics of that problem. When Louisiana drew up its constitution in 1864, he urged the governor to consider giving the vote to "some of the colored people," especially "the very intelligent and those who have fought gallantly in our ranks." (Altogether nearly 178,000 black troops, many of them ex-slaves, served in the Union armies.) On March 3, 1865, he signed a bill creating a Freedmen's Bureau. The bill gave federal protection and aid to ex-slaves and contained a limited provision for giving them land, a provision that looked forward to the possible establishment of a landholding black yeomanry.

# RECONSTRUCTION: 1865–1877
## Presidential Reconstruction Under Johnson

Lincoln's successor, Andrew Johnson, fully intended to carry out the policy Lincoln had begun. But he operated at a severe disadvantage. As is the case with most vice presidents, Johnson was chosen with no expectation that he would ever be president. He was selected because he was a former Democrat and a staunch Union man from the border state of Tennessee. These very attributes, plus the fact that he had once owned slaves, heightened Republicans' suspicion of him and made them all the more eager to keep control of Reconstruction in the hands of Congress. In addition, he lacked the political power Lincoln had amassed through his adroit dispensing of favors and patronage. Even more important, Johnson lacked the stature—the legitimacy—Lincoln had acquired as the head of state who had seen the Union through to victory and the first president since Andrew Jackson to win reelection. And even with all these assets, Lincoln had run into stiff opposition to his approach to Reconstruction.

Congress was not in session when Johnson took office, and he proceeded to carry out his own plan for Reconstruction by executive action, without consulting the Republican leaders of Congress. Here, too, he partly followed Lincoln's example. Lincoln had jailed opponents to the war, ended slavery, and instituted a draft—all by ex-

ANDREW JOHNSON

When Tennessee seceded in June 1861, Johnson—alone among Southern senators—refused to resign and join the Confederacy. Lincoln appointed him military governor of Tennessee. His staunch Unionism and his effectiveness in restoring civilian rule to Tennessee made him a logical choice as Lincoln's running mate in 1864. *(Culver Pictures)*

ecutive action. He had launched Reconstruction by proclamation and vetoed the Wade-Davis Bill because he opposed its more stringent conditions and thought Reconstruction was properly an executive function. So Johnson charged ahead. He renewed the promise of amnesty to most ex-Confederates, and he set three conditions for a rebel state's reentry into the political system: the state had to nullify its ordinance of secession, accept the Thirteenth Amendment, and repudiate all Confederate debts. Johnson insisted that the states had never legally been out of the Union and hence retained the power to set their own rules on who could vote. He also assured Southern leaders that Congress was constitutionally bound to accept these governments. Under the leadership of many ex-Confederates, the South moved quickly. When Congress came back into session in December, it was presented with a fait accompli: all but Texas had set up state governments firmly under the control of former slaveholders and Confederate leaders and had sent senators and representatives to Washington to claim their seats in the new Congress.

Johnson and most white Southerners thought political reconstruction was substantially complete. Johnson's major goal was political reunion. He was unconcerned about the freedmen. He rescinded General Sherman's Special Field Order of January 1865, which had set aside a 30-mile strip along the South Carolina coast to be distributed in 40-acre plots to the freedmen, and ordered the land returned to its previous white owners. But the planters also wanted to create a society as close as possible to the antebellum South, a goal in direct conflict with the freedmen's aspirations for land and independence. (After Johnson's reversal of Sherman's order, one freedman declared, "they will make freedom a curse to us, for we have no home, no land, no oath, no vote.") As soon as the ex-slaveholders found themselves regaining local power, they moved rapidly to reestablish their economic and social dominion, to return the freedmen to a position of social subordination and keep them as a cheap source of plantation labor. Mississippi, South Carolina, and Alabama enacted Black Codes (the other states followed step in early 1866), which severely restricted black freedom. Some codes barred blacks from jury service or testifying against whites; others restricted them to agricultural labor; still others forbade them from renting land or carrying firearms, or imposed curfews on them. The most far-reaching codes, however, were the vagrancy laws, under which unemployed blacks who could not pay their fines for vagrancy could be bound out to work for whomever paid the fine.

To many in the North, the new South that Johnson's Reconstruction had ushered in seemed frighteningly similar to the old South. Most of the ex-Confederates seemed right back in power. They filled the state legislatures. And the former vice president of the Confederacy, six former cabinet members, nine generals, and more than fifty members of the Confederate legislature had been elected to the national Congress by the reconstructed states. Moreover, the Black Codes seemed to have reestablished slavery under another name. As the *Chicago Tribune* thundered, "We tell the white men of Mississippi that the men of the North will convert the state of Mississippi into a frog pond before they will allow any such laws to disgrace one foot of soil over which the flag of freedom waves." Northerners were divided over what they wanted out of Reconstruction, and few were eager to grant equality to blacks. (Twelve Northern states still refused to give the franchise to blacks.) Still, they had opposed slavery, fought and won a war that had come about partly because of slavery, and they did not want to see it restored under some new guise. But most upsetting of all, those who had led the rebellion—those responsible for the terrible war—refused to acknowledge defeat. Mississippi had rejected the Thirteenth Amendment, South Carolina refused to nullify its ordinance of secession, and members of the old slavocracy demanded seats in Congress. It seemed as if Reconstruction was about to deprive the North of the victory for which so many of its men had died.

When the new Congress returned to Washington, it refused to seat the senators and representatives from the former Confederate states. It moved to take Reconstruction policy into its own hands and set up a Joint Committee on Reconstruction headed by two strong-willed radical Republicans, Representative Thaddeus Stevens of Pennsylvania and Senator Charles Sumner of Massachusetts. They believed that the Reconstruction of the nation would not be completed until the revolution in Southern society brought about by the end of slavery was completed. For Sumner this required granting full citizenship and political rights to the freedmen, while for Stevens it involved using government lands and confiscating the plantations of the old planter aristocracy to give the freedmen the land to establish themselves as independent farmers. Even the moderate members of Congress were alarmed by what was happening in the South: unless there was "some legislation by the nation for his protection," Senator Trumbull of Illinois insisted, the ex-slaves would be "abused and virtually re-enslaved."

Concern for the freedmen was not the only thing that motivated Republicans in Congress. Johnson's Reconstruction threatened them with the loss of their political power. With the end of slavery, Southern representation in the House of Representatives would be increased by about twenty seats, since for purposes of apportionment, a slave had been counted as only three-fifths of a person. Republicans feared that the exclusion of Southern blacks from the vote would ensure the election of unreconstructed rebels, who would league together with pro-Southern Democrats and drive the Republicans from power. Black suffrage might be essential for the establishment of any real freedom for the ex-slaves, but it also seemed essential for keeping the Republicans in power. In fact, it was not until the Republicans began to lose power in the North in 1870 that they passed the Fifteenth Amendment, granting suffrage to black males in the North and the South.

## Congressional Reconstruction

But Stevens and Sumner were not yet in control of Congress. Moderates like Senator John Sherman of Ohio were still in the ascendancy. They did not want to throw out the governments organized under Johnson, but they did want to give some protection to the freedmen. The Congress enacted two pieces of legislation. It extended the Freedmen's Bureau, the agency that had been set up to help the transition out of bondage by providing relief, setting up schools, and helping freedmen find employment. It also passed a Civil Rights Act that extended the rights of citizenship to the ex-slaves and gave federal courts jurisdiction over all cases involving those rights. President Johnson promptly vetoed both acts. The

moderates then countered with the Fourteenth Amendment, a complex measure designed to give some basic protection to the ex-slaves in a form that the moderates hoped the South would accept. The amendment contained the basic features of the Civil Rights Act, but it also reduced the political power of the old Southern elite by barring from public office anyone who had ever sworn fidelity to the Constitution and then participated in rebellion. At the same time, the amendment did not directly require black suffrage; it only threatened to reduce Southern representation if blacks were not permitted to vote. Nor did it contain any provision for the confiscation or redistribution of lands. It was clear, however, that the Republican Congress would not accept any state back into the Union that did not ratify the amendment.

President and Congress were now at complete loggerheads. Johnson denounced the amendment and even urged Southerners to reject it. He decided to take the issue of Reconstruction directly to the voters in the upcoming congressional elections. Contrary to custom, Johnson went on the political hustings, denouncing the Republican Congress and further polarizing the issue. But his campaign was a disaster, and the voters overwhelmingly repudiated his policies. The Republicans, now increasingly under the influence of Sumner and Stevens, won more than two-thirds of the seats in both houses, enough to override any presidential veto.

Most of the members of the newly constituted Southern legislatures were firmly opposed to the Fourteenth Amendment, which would remove many of their members from office. But white Southerners were also angry and felt a deep sense of betrayal. Many had complied with Lincoln's and Johnson's requirements in good faith, only to have new and harsher conditions imposed on them in what seemed like an all-too-familiar resurgence of Yankee tyranny. Amid fiery denunciations of fanatical South-hating Republicans, all the Southern states except Tennessee rejected the Fourteenth Amendment, further infuriating the Republicans in Congress. "The last one of the sinful ten has flung back into our teeth the magnanimous offer of a generous nation," was how Representative John Garfield of Ohio saw it. It was now two years after the end of the fighting, and North and South were further from reconciliation than ever. In his last major speech, Lincoln had pleaded for Americans to "bind up the nation's wounds": two years of Reconstruction politics had only poured salt on them.

## Radical Reconstruction

An angered Republican Congress came to Washington in December of 1866 determined to impose a new, harsh style of Reconstruction on a dismayed and angered South. The radicals now held full power and they brooked no opposition. When the Supreme Court issued a ruling that seemed to challenge the validity of the military courts of the Freedmen's Bureau, they reduced the size of the Court, depriving Johnson of the chance to make any appointments to the Court. When in 1868 the Court seemed about to challenge the Reconstruction Acts the radicals had passed, they took jurisdiction over such matters away from the Court. And the radicals tried to remove Johnson from office for violating the Tenure of Office Act, by which it had tried to keep him from firing people opposed to his policies. The impeachment attempt failed by one vote.

In the spring and early summer of 1867, the radical Republicans drew up a plan of military reconstruction. Lincoln and Johnson had argued that since secession itself was illegal, the Confederate states had never really been out of the Union. But the radicals insisted that by rebelling, the states had "forfeited" their statehood, committing "state-suicide" as Sumner called it. Congress accordingly declared the Johnson governments illegal and divided the conquered South into five military districts. The commander of each district, with the aid of the army, would prepare the states for readmission by registering all adult black males and all white males not dis-

CHARLES SUMNER

The leader of the Radical Republicans in the Senate, Sumner was unwavering and uncompromising in his beliefs. In one memorable debate, his opponent chastised him, saying, "But you forget the other side." Sumner replied, "There is no other side!" *(Culver Pictures)*

enfranchised under the provisions of the Fourteenth Amendment. All voters were required to take a stringent oath of loyalty. Once legitimate voters had been certified—approximately 700,000 blacks and 650,000 whites were registered under these provisions, and probably between 100,000 and 200,000 whites were disenfranchised—the usual steps for setting up a state would take place. Then, if Congress accepted the state's constitution and the state legislature passed the Fourteenth Amendment, the state would be readmitted to the Union. By June of 1868, seven states, all clearly under the control of Republican-dominated "Reconstruction" governments, were accepted back into the Union; and by early 1870, the remaining states were also admitted and the Union was formally restored.

For three years, much of the drama of Reconstruction had taken place in Washington. But as the states returned to the Union under the radical formula, the battle shifted to the South. The North finally had "reconstructed" states it could accept as legitimate, full-fledged members of the Union. But to many white Southerners these governments were never legitimate, and they were determined to do whatever it took to undermine them. To them, radical Reconstruction was an unmitigated nightmare, and it left a century-long legacy of bitterness. There was, first, the tyranny—the imposition by military force of governments and rulers that they themselves would never have chosen. It was a long-standing American axiom that government rested on the consent of the governed, and Southerners had certainly never consented to the kinds of governments that military Reconstruction forced on them. But to most white Southerners, the greatest of the "horrors" of radical Reconstruction was that it subjected them to "Negro rule."

The "Negro rule" of radical Reconstruction was a myth. In no state did blacks dominate or control the government. There was not a single elected black governor, and only in South Carolina was there ever a black legislative majority. Moreover, the range of ability, education, and competence among black officeholders was not wildly different from the range among most white officeholders in the North or South. The Reconstruction governments certainly contained corruption, but they were no more corrupt than their "lily-white" counterparts before or after the war. Although black suffrage was essential for keeping these regimes in power, their electoral base, especially in the beginning, extended beyond the ex-slaves. Many former Whigs, Southern Union men, and antisecessionists initially allied themselves with the new Republican governments. Many whites in nonslaveholding regions who had always resented the rule of the planter elite voted for and participated in the Reconstruction governments. These governments were in many ways reform governments. But they spent comparatively little time trying to achieve social equality between whites and blacks. Instead, they concentrated on such things as public education and eliminating the undemocratic features of the antebellum political system, by which the planter elite had maintained its dominion—things that benefited poor whites as well as the freedmen.

## "Redeeming" the States

But this is not how the former slaveholders and old planter elite saw radical Reconstruction. Illiterate black field hands who could vote while former planters could not, blacks who held office, "uppity" ex-slaves who mocked their former masters, black soldiers who now patrolled whites—all these things in the eyes of the former slaveholders turned radical Reconstruction into "Black Reconstruction." "Negro rule" became the galling symbol of all the horrors of radical Reconstruction, of all they had lost, of the defeat they had suffered and the degradation they now felt. They struck back against the Reconstruction governments with all the means at their disposal. They appealed to white supremacy to draw support of the poorer whites away from the Republicans, casting themselves as saviors who would "redeem" the South from the twin specter of black rule and Yankee domination. In states like Tennessee, Virginia, and North Carolina, where white voters held a clear majority, the "redeemers" gained control by 1871. For the most part they relied on the ballot box for victory; but in some areas they used intimidation and violence against blacks and their allies.

Where the racial balance was even or blacks held a majority, the battle for control was often violent. Scalawags (white Southerners who collaborated with the Yankees) and carpetbaggers (whites from the North) were ostracized and boycotted. Blacks were threatened with loss of jobs, credit, and access to lands for sharecropping. Secret organizations like the Ku Klux Klan were set up. Striking at night, dressed in robes and hoods, they beat, mutilated, and often murdered their

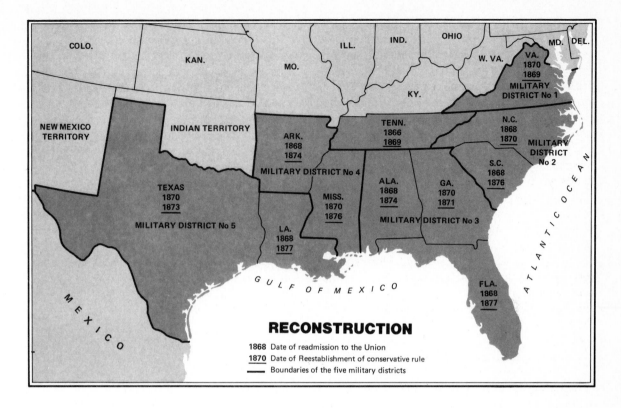

RECONSTRUCTION

**1868** Date of readmission to the Union
<u>1870</u> Date of Reestablishment of conservative rule
—— Boundaries of the five military districts

victims. Directing their attacks mostly against scalawags and black leaders, they tried to terrorize blacks into withdrawing from political activity. The campaign of terror shocked Northerners and a number of Southerners. Two "force bills" and a Ku Klux Klan Act were passed by Congress, and in 1871 President Ulysses S. Grant initiated federal prosecutions in Mississippi. But the laws were unevenly enforced and violence continued. "White legions," semimilitary organizations that intimidated whites into voting Democratic and forcibly kept blacks from voting, helped redeem Texas, Arkansas, and Alabama. As the 1875 Mississippi election approached, whites were determined to keep blacks and Republicans away from the polls, and the governor feared a blood bath if he used black militia to oversee the elections. When he asked for federal help, the Grant administration refused, declaring that, "the whole public are tired of these annual autumnal outbreaks in the South." The Demo-

crats swept to power, aided by the white legions, and Mississippi too joined the ranks of the redeemed.

## The End of Reconstruction

By 1876 only Louisiana, South Carolina, and Florida remained unredeemed. Even there the hold of Reconstruction was precarious, dependent on the continuing presence of federal troops. The election of 1876 removed this prop, largely because most Northerners (at best minimally interested in the welfare of the ex-slaves) no longer cared very much about what was happening in the South. In his inaugural address of 1869, Ulysses S. Grant called for "peace," which most Northerners took to mean relief from the turmoil of Reconstruction politics. The election of 1872 indicated how rapidly Northern concerns were shifting. Many liberal Republicans who had been staunch in their concern for black rights, including Charles Sumner, turned against the Republican party and supported the Democratic nominee, Horace Greeley, himself an old Whig-Republican, who focused his campaign largely on the corruption of the Grant administration. By the mid-1870s, Northerners were more preoccupied with the politics of corruption and agrarian discontent, and with the problems of inflation, tariffs, and railroads, than with Reconstruction.

The election of 1876 resulted in a bizarre deadlock between Rutherford B. Hayes, the Republican nominee, and his Democratic opponent, Samuel J. Tilden. In exchange for the disputed electoral votes of South Carolina, Florida, and Louisiana, Hayes, who had narrowly lost the popular vote to Tilden, promised to remove all remaining federal troops from the South, thus putting a symbolic end to the Reconstruction that in all essential respects had already come to an end.

The end of Reconstruction did not mean a sudden end to all black gains or rights. Blacks continued to vote and even to hold a few offices, and they fought hard to preserve their schools and to hold onto whatever land they had. But continuing intimidation, white unity, and the indifference of the North isolated the ex-slaves politically and made their rights increasingly vulnerable. In his second inaugural address, Lincoln had linked the survival of the Union to the fate of the slaves. Slavery had ended and "the mighty scourge of war" was lifted; but twelve years of Reconstruction had made it clear that white Americans were far from ready to make good on the promise of emancipation.

# SUGGESTED READINGS, CHAPTERS 21–22

## ABRAHAM LINCOLN

The literature on Abraham Lincoln is voluminous. Benjamin Thomas, *Abraham Lincoln* (1952), is a good single-volume biography; it is somewhat surpassed by Stephen B. Oates, *With Malice Toward None: The Life of Abraham Lincoln* (1977). David Donald, *Lincoln Reconsidered* (1958), and Richard Current, *The Lincoln Nobody Knows* (1951), provide refreshing perspectives on Lincoln as a politician. Edmund Wilson, *Patriotic Gore* (1962), treats Lincoln's mystical attachment to the Union and his deepening religious sentiments during the war. David Potter, *Lincoln and His Party in the Secession Crisis* (1942), remains the best study of the subject. John Hope Franklin, *The Emancipation Proclamation* (1963), is a succinct history of how the document came about; and Allan Nevins, *Lincoln and the Gettysburg Address* (1954), is a solid account of that famous oration. Ralph Borreson, *When Lincoln Died* (1965), is a detailed account of Lincoln's assassination and funeral. T. Harry Williams, *Lincoln: Selected Speeches and Letters* (1960), is an excellent sampling of the president's own writings.

## UNION VS. CONFEDERACY

James G. Randall and David Donald, *The Civil War and Reconstruction,* 2nd ed. (1961), remains a valuable guide to the period as a whole. James M. McPherson, *Ordeal by Fire: The Civil War and Reconstruction* (1982), is the best overall treatment of the subject and contains a superb bibliography. David Donald, ed., *Why the North Won the Civil War* (1960), is a readable and provocative set of essays giving major reasons for the Union victory. Allan Nevins, *The War for the Union,* 4 vols. (1959–1971), Bruce Catton, *This Hallowed Ground* (1956) and *Centennial History of the Civil War* (1961–1965), and Douglass Southall Freeman, *R. E. Lee,* 4 vols. (1934–1935), provide full, readable accounts of the military history of the Civil War. T. Harry Williams, *Lincoln and the Radicals* (1942), argues that Lincoln and the radicals were in continuing opposition;

whereas Hans L. Trefousse, *The Radical Republicans* (1968), stresses their cooperation. Emory L. Thomas, *The Confederate Nation* (1979), is a good single-volume treatment. Charles Ramsdell, *Behind the Lines in the Southern Confederacy* (1944), discusses the internal political conflicts within the Confederacy.

George Frederickson, *The Inner Civil War* (1965), and Edmund Wilson, *Patriotic Gore* (1962), provide superb discussions of the intellectual impact of the war. Bell Irvin Wiley, *The Life of Johnny Reb* (1943) and *The Life of Billy Yank* (1952), describe the life of the ordinary soldier on both sides. Benjamin Quarles, *The Negro in the Civil War* (1953), remains a valuable study of black participation in the war. Ralph Andreano, ed., *The Economic Impact of the American Civil War* (1962), contains a number of important articles assessing the economic dimensions of the war. James L. Roark, *Masters Without Slaves* (1977), analyzes the plight of Southern planters during the Civil War and Reconstruction.

## RECONSTRUCTION

John Hope Franklin, *Reconstruction After the Civil War* (1961), Kenneth M. Stampp, *The Era of Reconstruction* (1965), and W. E. B. du Bois, *Black Reconstruction* (1935), are valuable general treatments of Reconstruction. Herman Belz, *Reconstructing the Union* (1969), is a solid treatment of national policy; W. McKee Evans, *Ballots and Fence Rails* (1966), is a superb study of the politics of Reconstruction on the local level in North Carolina. LaWanda Cox and John Cox, *Politics, Principle, and Prejudice* (1965), and William Gillette, *The Right to Vote* (1969), treat race and politics in North and South during the period. Eric McKitrick, *Andrew Johnson and Reconstruction* (1966), is a thorough study of early presidential Reconstruction. William S. Mc-

Feely, *Grant* (1981), is the best study of Grant's presidency. William S. McFeely, *Yankee Step-Father: General O. O. Howard and the Freedmen* (1968), is a useful study of the Freedmen's Bureau. Allan Trelease, *White Terror* (1967), analyzes the role of the Ku Klux Klan and white terrorism in defeating Reconstruction. C. Vann Woodward, *Reunion and Reaction* (1951), and William Gillette, *Retreat from Reconstruction* (1980), describe the end of Reconstruction.

## LIFE DURING THE CIVIL WAR AND RECONSTRUCTION

The story of blacks in Reconstruction is explored in several works. The most notable are Joel Williamson, *After Slavery* (1966); Thomas Holt, *Black over White* (1977); Willie Lee Rose, *Rehearsal for Reconstruction* (1964); and Leon Litwack, *Been in the Storm so Long* (1979).

Collections of documents include Frank Moore, ed., *Rebellion Record,* a twelve-volume compilation put together in the 1860s and reprinted in a modern edition in 1977; Francis T. Miller, *The Photographic History of the Civil War,* 10 vols. (1957), is the most extensive of the many collections of Civil War photographs. Frank Freidel, ed., *Union Pamphlets of the Civil War* (1967), provides a valuable collection of Northern writings. See also Harold Hyman, ed., *The Radical Republican and Reconstruction* (1967). C. Vann Woodward, ed., *Mary Chesnut's Civil War* (1981), and Robert Myers, *The Children of Pride* (1972), provide invaluable insight into Southern life during the war. Rupert S. Holland, ed., *The Letters and Diary of Laura M. Towne* (1970), is a superb collection of letters from a young woman who went to the South Carolina Sea Islands to teach the freedmen.

# 23 ▪ Massacre at Wounded Knee

There was a confusion about names—there almost always was when Indians were involved. Most whites called the tribe the Sioux. But this name was just a French abbreviation of what some of the tribe's enemies had called them. They called themselves Dakota.

There was more than one Indian name for what whites called Wounded Knee Creek, on the Pine Ridge Reservtion in South Dakota. Also, whereas some people called what had happened at Wounded Knee Creek a battle, others called it a massacre. Even the man who rode out from reservation headquarters to Wounded Knee had two names. One was an Indian name, Ohiyesa. One was a white man's name, Charles Eastman. He was a Sioux, but he had been educated in white schools in New England. In fact, he was a doctor of medicine.

But there was no confusion about what Charles Eastman saw on that bright New Year's Day morning in 1891:

> On the day following the Wounded Knee massacre, there was a blizzard. On the third day it cleared, and the ground was covered with fresh snow. We had feared that some of the wounded Indians had been left on the field, and a number of us volunteered to go and see.
>
> Fully three miles from the scene of the massacre, we found the body of a woman completely covered with a blanket of snow, and from this point on we found them scattered along as they had been hunted down and slaughtered. When we reached the spot where the Indian camp had stood, among the fragments of burned tents and other belongings, we saw the frozen bodies lying close together or piled one upon another. I counted eighty bodies of men, who were almost as helpless as the women and babes when the deadly [gun] fire began, for nearly all their guns had been taken from them.
>
> Although they had been lying in the snow and cold for two days and nights, a number had survived. Among them I found a baby of about a year old, warmly wrapped and entirely unhurt. Under a wagon, I discovered an old woman, totally blind and helpless.

**BIG FOOT**

The body of Big Foot, the leader of the Sioux band that was massacred at Wounded Knee, waits, frozen, for the burial party of whites shown in the background. He is wearing mostly white man's clothing, and his body has wrenched itself into a half-sitting position, partially covered with the light snow that fell after the massacre. *(The Bettmann Archive)*

Eastman began to load the few survivors into wagons to return to the agency (reservation headquarters), where he had set up a small hospital. Two groups of white men stayed behind at Wounded Knee. One was a troop of the U.S. Seventh Cavalry. The other was a group of about thirty white civilians who had agreed to bury the dead, at a charge of two dollars a body. They found the body of the chief of the Indians, an old man named Big Foot, frozen half sitting, half lying down. Ill with penumonia, he had been lying on a blanket on the winter ground when the shooting started.

It took until the next day to dig a big, open grave. Then the bodies were gathered. Under an unusually strong January sun, the grave diggers sweated; many worked in their shirtsleeves. They stacked 146 dead Indians—128 men and women and 18 children—in the pit. Then, while the cavalrymen stayed out of sight, the civilians gathered in a half-circle around the grave to have their photograph taken. For the photographer, they held their rifles, not shovels. Then they shoveled dirt in over the bodies. When the diggers and the cavalry rode away, nothing was left at Wounded Knee but the fresh dirt of the grave and the charred poles of the Indian tepees that had been put up only a few days before. The battle, or massacre (it was really some of both), was over.

Wounded Knee was the last and most tragic moment in a long, difficult, and often ugly process: the conquest of the Sioux Indians. The conquerors were the white citizens and blue-coated soldiers of the United States. The process began before the Civil War. At that time the Sioux were a powerful tribe, probably numbering well over 20,000. They hunted on millions of square miles of the plains west of the Missouri River.

The Sioux resisted the invasion of white miners, farmers, and ranchers. They fought often, and they usually won. In the summer of 1876 they won two astonishing victories. At Rosebud Creek, in what is now Montana, they attacked a large column of cavalry and infantry and forced the soldiers into a retreat. Then, just a few days later, the Seventh Cavalry, with General George A. Custer commanding, attacked a large Sioux camp on the Little Bighorn River, just a few miles from Rosebud Creek. Custer divided his force, and the Indians killed Custer as well as most of the Seventh, one of the most experienced cavalry units operating in the West.

But there were too many other soldiers. Though the Sioux were never defeated, their surrender was inevitable. In 1877, just a year after "Custer's last stand," the great war chief Crazy Horse led many of his followers onto a reservation that had been recently set aside for the Sioux. Crazy Horse was murdered a short time later. Some of his people fled to Canada to join the other outstanding Sioux leader, Sitting Bull. About 2,500 Sioux then tried to survive in Canada. But hunger and cold—and the fact that white people had slain most of the buffalo—finally drove them back to the reservation. In 1881 Sitting Bull surrendered—"came in," as it was said. This was the end of a golden age for the Sioux, one that had lasted more than a century.

Originally, before white Europeans had come to North America, the Sioux had lived very much like the Indians of the eastern seaboard. Their territory was not the open plains of the Dakotas, but the woods and lakes of Minnesota and Wisconsin. There, they had built permanent bark houses, used canoes, and hunted only small game. They had also farmed. This life was disturbed by indirect contact with white civilization. The Sioux were driven out of their woodlands and onto the Great Plains by another tribe, the Chippewas. The Chippewas had come into contact with the French in Canada and had obtained guns in trade for furs. The guns gave the Chippewas an overwhelming advantage, and the Sioux had had to retreat to the west and south, out onto the Great Plains.

But what began as a painful retreat soon turned into a triumphant new life. Gradually, the Sioux themselves obtained guns. They also discovered another European "import," the horses descended from the mounts the Spanish had brought into Mexico and the Southwest. Together, these European tools—the horse and the rifle—transformed Sioux culture. For the first time, they could hunt buffalo. The plains were transformed from a barren, hostile environment into a hunting paradise. The buffalo herds became a source of meat, clothing, and shelter. The old bark houses gave way to hide-covered tepees that could be moved from one hunting area to another. This nomadic life brought the Sioux into contact (and conflict) with other plains tribes. Hunting and warfare became the central focus of the Sioux economy and culture. For men, status in the tribe became dependent on skill and bravery in hunts and skirmishes. To a Sioux man, the tools of the hunt—his ponies, his rifle, his bow and arrows—were everything. The rituals of hunting and warfare gave meaning to his life. Any work that was not part of hunting, like preparing hides or drying meat or gathering berries, belonged to women. By the early part of the nineteenth century, the new society the Sioux had built on the plains was confident, prosperous, and expanding. They hunted all the way from the Missouri River to the valleys of the Little Big Horn Mountains on the eastern edge of the Rockies.

But, almost as soon as this civilization was established, it was challenged. The whites, with their cannon, their railroads, their plows, and their reservations, eventually destroyed the Sioux way of life. The whites slaughtered buffalo by the thousands, until practically none were left. Then the whites insisted that the Sioux live again in permanent houses. Government rations of beef, flour, and beans substituted for the hunt. It did not help much if a kindly agent sometimes allowed the men to "hunt" their twice-monthly ration of cattle. Games like this could not replace the old life. The authority of warriors and chiefs had depended on their skill in violent and dangerous activities. Reservation life was, above all, peaceful. The white agents even forbade the most holy annual ritual of the Sioux, the Sun Dance. And they insisted, too, that the men of the tribe could have only one wife.

What was happening was simple and, from the Sioux point of view, tragic. They had been defeated by a much more powerful and complex society. Some of them—the "nonprogressives"—might resist in a few ways. They could reject the cotton shirts and trousers of the white man and continue to wear Indian clothing. They could insist on wearing their hair in the traditional long braid. But resistance could not revive the old life. They had long ago accepted some of the white ways and tools. The horse and the rifle had been useful in the old life. But the government, with the "Great Father" president at its head, had plans for the Sioux that were utterly at odds with the old ways.

American policy was aimed at one long-range goal—to make each Indian family into a self-supporting, farming unit. In the old life, the tribal band, not the family, had been the basic social unit. The band moved, hunted, ate, and worshipped together, and families tended to merge imperceptibly with the common life of the band. The white vision saw each family gathered in its own log house, wearing white people's clothes, gathered around its own, private fire (the white person's stove) and, preferably, worshipping the white God instead of the old Sioux god, Wakan Tanka. To well-intentioned reformers in the East, this meant "raising the Indian to civilization." To many whites in the West, it meant a final end to the Indian as a barrier to westward expansion.

For the Sioux, all of this meant a divided world. Even those who wanted to cooperate most, the so-called "progressives," lived a double life. A man might put on white clothes; might plow and harvest, have only one wife, and send his children to white schools. But still there was the old life, alive in memory but dead in fact. George Sword, for example, was a progressive. He was even a member of the Indian police force the agents used to help keep order. But George Sword's description of his religious beliefs captures the painful division of loyalty that existed in the minds of even the most "civilized" Sioux:

> When I believed that Wakan Tanka was right, I served him with all my powers. In war with the white people, I found their Wakan Tanka superior. I then took the name of Sword, and have served their Wakan Tanka according to the white people's manner.
>
> I became chief of the United States Indian police, and held the office until there was no trouble between the Sioux and the white people. I joined the church and am a deacon in it and shall be until I die.

But all this Christianity and "progress" has not erased the old ways in George Sword. He was still a member of the Oglala band of the Dakota tribe, and his spirit might find itself in the Sioux's heaven, not the whites':

> I still have my Wasicun [ceremonial pouch] and I am afraid to offend it, because the spirit of an Oglala may go to the spirit land of the Dakota.

This divided consciousness, unable to choose finally between the old and the new, the Indian and the white, touched every area of life for the reservation Indians. To the whites who watched them, the Indians seemed almost like children in their confusion. In fact, the Sioux men, especially, had been deprived of their adult roles in the hunt and battle. So their maturity *was* at stake.

One of the whites' main hopes for destroying the old Sioux culture was to educate a new generation in white schools. They took numbers of Sioux children away from their parents and put them in distant boarding schools. The Sioux reaction was mixed. They could hope that this process would make their children's lives better. But there was the inevitable resentment, too, the feeling that their children had been, in effect, kidnapped by the whites.

Even when the white schools were close to home, the Sioux sent their children to them reluctantly. When a new school was opened at Pine Ridge, Sioux parents brought their children in on the first day, but they stayed outside the building, milling about, curious and frightened. Their fears were increased when the white teachers pulled down the shades, so no one could see what was happening inside. Suddenly, a gust of wind blew one of the blinds aside for a moment. The Indians got a glimpse of something that filled them with horror. A white woman was holding one Sioux boy while another woman cut his hair. The whole meaning of the reservation experience came quickly into focus. In the old life, a Sioux male's long braids were a symbol of his manhood. Here were white women scissoring away, symbolically, the tribal badge of masculinity. The Sioux parents, alarmed and outraged, charged into the school and took their children out.

Only at odd moments and in ineffective ways did the Sioux resist the relentless white pressure on their old ways. The whites controlled the Indians' sources of food, blankets, fuel, housing. The whites even controlled the ownership of an Indian's individual plot of land. The Sioux, like other American Indians, did not have a clearly defined concept of private property—especially private property in land. But they could see plainly that their survival depended on the mysterious white concept of land ownership. To lose the land would be to lose everything. Finally, the whites had one ultimate threat: the cavalry that was still stationed in forts scattered all around the Great Plains.

The deep conflict between Indian and white ways came to the surface in 1883, when a Senate investigating committee visited the Sioux. Sitting Bull, who had been one of the Sioux leaders at the Battle of the Little Bighorn, came to testify. But the chairman would not recognize Sitting Bull as chief. Sitting Bull got up and left. All the Indians followed him. But several of the progressive Indians returned to plead with the committee to use its influence with the Great Father to get better treatment for the Indians. Soon even Sitting Bull swallowed his hurt pride and returned to apologize.

Then Sitting Bull gave a remarkable account of what defeat had meant to the Sioux. They had been wealthy in their own terms, with land, ponies, and buffalo aplenty. In one lifetime the white man had reduced them to poverty.

> Whatever you wanted of me I have obeyed. The Great Father sent me word that whatever he had against me in the past had been forgiven and thrown aside, and I accepted his promises and came in. And he told me not to step aside from the white man's path, and I am doing my best to travel in that path. I sit here and look around me now, and I see my people starving. We want cattle to butcher. That is the way you live, and we want to live the same way. When the Great Father told me to live like his people, I told him to send me six teams of mules, because that is the way the white people make a living. I asked for a horse and buggy for my children; I was advised to follow the ways of the white man, and that is why I asked for those things.

Sitting Bull's ideas were a little confused, at least by white standards. But he summed up neatly the dilemma of the Sioux. He was still proud of himself and his tribal ways. He resented the whites' failure to understand this pride. But another side of him recognized defeat and was prepared to plead with the whites not for less civilization but for more. In Sitting Bull, and in almost all the other reservation Indians, pride, resentment, hunger, and begging were so intermixed that a meaningful pattern of life was almost impossible.

The situation was the same among all the Sioux. During the 1880s the Indians were gradually becoming "civilized." But the hunger and anger were just below the surface. Some crucial event or idea was all that was needed to bring the conflict with the whites back into the open, tip the scales one way or the other, and offer the Indians a clear choice between the old life and the new.

A new idea did come, and from an unpredictable direction. In the summer

SITTING BULL—TWO VIEWS

The first photograph shows Sitting Bull dressed in the costume he wore in traveling circuses. His face is that of a brave warrior and leader of his people. His eyes are unflinching and his expression grave, but his costume is a purely white version of Indian dress. The second photograph, of Sitting Bull and his family, was taken on the Dakota reservation, not in a white circus. It shows the other side of Sitting Bull's personality—frightened, confused, and shy of the camera. This is a family that has been very nearly broken in spirit by defeat and reservation life. *(left—Library of Congress; right—U.S. Signal National Archives)*

of 1889—about a dozen years after Crazy Horse had surrendered his band of hostiles—the Sioux began to hear rumors of an Indian messiah (or savior) who had come to earth in the West. They had learned enough of Christianity on the reservation to understand the alien notion of a messiah. If it were true that a messiah had come to save the Indians from the whites, surely it was worth investigating, they thought.

The Messiah was said to be at the Paiute reservation at Walker Lake, Nevada. Three of the six Sioux reservations[1] selected important men to make the trip west. It was about a thousand miles away—farther than almost any of the Sioux had ever traveled. Pine Ridge Reservation sent eight men,

---

[1] One so-called Great Sioux Reservation had been created in 1868. It consisted of about 43,000 square miles in what is now South Dakota, and it was administered from several agencies on or near the land. In 1889 the Sioux territory, much reduced in size, was broken up into six separate reservations—Pine Ridge, Rosebud, Lower Brule, Crow Creek, Cheyenne River, and Standing Rock.

including Kicking Bear, who was to become the most effective disciple of the new Messiah. One of the men from Rosebud was Short Bull. The Cheyenne River Reservation, with a smaller population than either Pine Ridge or Rosebud, sent one man.

The eleven Sioux started west by train. Railroads had by then penetrated all the major Western areas, and Indians hopped freight cars with little or no opposition from the white railroad men. When the Sioux reached Wyoming, they found that other tribes—Cheyennes, Arapahoes, Bannocks, and Sho-shonis—had also sent wise men to seek the Messiah. The whole group then traveled south to Walker Lake. There the Paiutes gave them wagons to complete the pilgrimage. Soon they were in the presence of the Messiah.

His Indian name was Wovoka, his white name Jackson Wilson. He was about thirty-five years old. He was Paiute, but he had grown up close to a white ranching family named Wilson. (They gave him his English name.) The Wilsons were a religious family. From them Wovoka had learned in some detail how Jesus had controlled the wind and the seas, how he had promised eternal life to his followers, and how other whites had crucified him. Wovoka was apparently the son of a Paiute shaman, or medicine man.[2] One day in 1889, when he was ill (and perhaps delirious) with a high fever, there was an eclipse of the sun. This led him to believe that he had been taken up to heaven. After talking with God, he had been returned to earth to bring salvation to the Indians.

Wovoka's doctrines were a fairly straightforward Indian version of some of the basic teachings of the New Testament. In a sermon to some visiting Cheyennes he summarized his new faith:

> You must not hurt anybody, or do harm to anyone. You must not fight. Do right always.
>
> Do not tell the white people about this. Jesus is now upon the earth. The dead are all alive again. I do not know when they will be here; maybe this fall or in the spring. When the time comes there will be no more sickness and everyone will be young again.

In a simplified way Wovoka was telling his disciples that the dead would be resurrected soon. The earth would tremble; a new earth would cover the old. But true believers need not be afraid, because they would soon enjoy perfect life, youth, and health. In the meantime, the Indians should live in peace with the whites.

> Do not refuse to work for the whites, and do not make any trouble with them until you leave them. When the earth shakes, do not be afraid, it will not hurt you. That is all. You will receive good words from me again some time. Do not tell lies.

Wovoka gave the visiting Cheyennes some clay for making the sacred red paint of the Paiutes. Symbols drawn with it were signs of their salvation.

---

[2] Almost all American Indians relied on shamans, men or women who were thought to have supernatural powers such as being able to foretell the future or cure the sick.

Then he advised them: "When you get home, you must make a dance to continue five days. You must all do it in the same way."

This was the famous Ghost Dance from which Wovoka's new religion soon took its name. During the five days it lasted, men and women sang certain songs and went into hypnotic trances. It was during the dance that Indians were supposed to be able to visit their departed relatives in heaven.

When Short Bull returned to South Dakota, he gave his version of the Ghost Dance religion to his excited Sioux audience. The tone was much more militant than Wovoka's. Short Bull promised punishment for those who refused to be converted—just as the Christian missionaries promised damnation for those who rejected their Messiah. He also promised victory over the hated and feared soldiers for those who wore holy shirts into battle. The shirts were supposed to protect wearers from the bullets of the whites.

> If the soldiers surround you, three of you, on whom I have put holy shirts, will sing a song around them, then some of them will drop dead. Then the rest will start to run, but their horses will sink into the earth. The riders will jump from their horses, but they will sink into the earth also. Then you can do as you desire with them. Now, you must know this, that all the soldiers and that race will be dead. There will be only five thousand of them left living on the earth. The guns are the only things we are afraid of, but they belong to our father in heaven. He will see that they do no harm.

It was not only Short Bull who brought back this interpretation from the visit to Wovoka. A similar version of the Ghost Dance faith emerged on all the Sioux reservations during the summer of 1890. The Sioux were offered a new ritual, the Ghost Dance, and a new faith, which held that the whites would soon be buried in the earth and the Indians would once again own the plains. There is no way of knowing how sincere Short Bull was. Nor is there any way of knowing whether Sitting Bull—who soon became a disciple of the Ghost Dance—really believed in the coming resurrection. Most of the Sioux probably rejected the Ghost Dance and decided to continue along the whites' path. For many, though, the religion of Wovoka offered great hope for the return of the old life and the end of their humiliating captivity. There can be no doubt that large groups of Sioux did accept the Ghost Dance.

Agents on all the reservations tried to stop the dances, using Indian police. But, time and again, the dancing Sioux refused to be cowed. They threatened their own police with rifles, insulted the agents, and began to behave like the Sioux of the 1870s. The agents reacted in various ways. When the police failed to make the Sioux obey, some of the agents refused to issue rations to those Indians who were active Ghost Dancers. At least two of the agents asked for federal troops. One, a new agent at Pine Ridge, was so incompetent that the Indians named him Young-Man-Afraid-of-Indians. White newspapermen, always hungry for a sensational news story, began to write about "hostile" Sioux. And white settlers in the Dakotas began to demand protection from the government.

Finally, after a tug of war between the Department of the Interior and the

**WOVOKA**

Wovoka, or Jackson Wilson, was the Paiute who apparently originated the Ghost Dance religion. His ideas were a blend of Native American legends and Christianity. He asked his followers only to dance the Ghost Dance and to await the resurrection of their dead ancestors. *(Smithsonian Institution/ National Anthropological Archives)*

A GHOST DANCE

During a Ghost Dance, which might last up to five days, the Sioux were apparently able to enter into a type of trance. Believers in the new religion thought that they actually could visit their dead during these trances. The complicated relationship between white and Indian cultures in the lives of these people is suggested by the fact that the women dancers are wearing factory-made print dresses. *(Smithsonian Institution / National Anthropological Archives)*

Department of War in Washington, the government authorized the army to send infantry and cavalry onto the reservations. This move brought about the first real confrontation since 1876 between the Sioux and the dreaded bluecoats. On November 20, 1890, cavalry and infantry units occupied Pine Ridge and Rosebud. A few days later the entire Seventh Cavalry arrived at Pine Ridge. This was Custer's unit, and it included many veterans of the Little Bighorn.

The effect on the Sioux of the appearance of the troops was overpowering. Instead of retreating to the outer edges of the reservations, most of the Indians at Pine Ridge and Rosebud immediately left their cabins and camps and gathered around the agency buildings. They pitched their tepees in rambling confusion and hoped that they would not be suspected of any wrongdoing. It was as though the only way to be safe from the rifles and cannon of the army was to be right under the noses of the officers and agents.

Thus the arrival of the army segregated the Indians. Those who wanted peace with the whites—those who had the good sense to be afraid—had gathered at the agencies. Only the most militant of the Ghost Dancers, led by Kicking Bear and Short Bull, decided to hold out. They were gathered along the creeks not far from the Pine Ridge Agency—at Medicine Root, Porcupine, and Wounded Knee.

About a week after the cavalry's arrival, several hundred of the militant Indians broke for open country. They plundered the farms of the peaceful Indians who had fled to the agencies, and they raided the agency cattle herds for beef. Then about 600 warriors and their families struck out for a low plateau at the northwest corner of Pine Ridge. This was known as the Stronghold. Here the Indians had grass, water, cattle, ponies in large numbers, and plenty of guns and ammunition. They announced that they intended to stay all winter, dancing, and then see what the spring brought.

Fortunately, the officer in command at Pine Ridge decided to be cautious. He sent one messenger after another to the Stronghold, promising that there would be no punishment if the Indians surrendered and returned to the agency. In turn the Indians had to agree to give up the Ghost Dance and return the cattle and other things they had taken. The messengers were badly treated, but some of the men at the Stronghold wanted to surrender. It seemed clear that sooner or later the Indians would disagree among themselves and the threat of uprising would be broken. The situation at Pine Ridge settled into a stalemate, with neither side ready to force a confrontation.

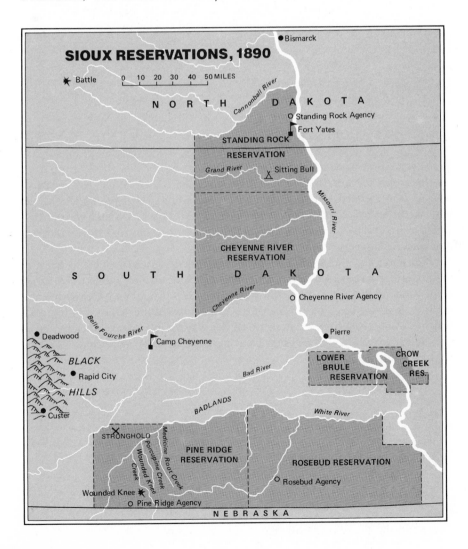

**SIOUX RESERVATIONS, 1890**

★ Battle

0  10  20  30  40  50 MILES

● Bismarck

N O R T H    D A K O T A

*Cannonball River*

○ Standing Rock Agency

▶ Fort Yates

**STANDING ROCK**
**RESERVATION**

*Grand River*    ✕ Sitting Bull

*Missouri River*

**CHEYENNE RIVER**
**RESERVATION**

*Cheyenne River*

○ Cheyenne River Agency

*Belle Fourche River*

● Deadwood

▶ Camp Cheyenne

● Pierre

**BLACK**

● Rapid City

**HILLS**

*Bad River*

**LOWER**
**BRULE**
**RESERVATION**

**CROW**
**CREEK**
**RES.**

↗ Custer

**BADLANDS**

*White River*

✕ STRONGHOLD

*Medicine Root Creek*

*Porcupine Creek*

*Wounded Knee Creek*

**PINE RIDGE**
**RESERVATION**

**ROSEBUD RESERVATION**

○ Rosebud Agency

Wounded Knee ★

○ Pine Ridge Agency

N E B R A S K A

S O U T H    D A K O T A

KICKING BEAR

Kicking Bear was one of the Sioux who traveled to California to seek out the prophet Wovoka. He gave the Ghost Dance doctrine a much more militant interpretation than Wovoka had, creating divisions among Indians and alarm among some whites. *(U.S. Signal Corps / National Archives)*

Now the scene of the action shifted north to Standing Rock Reservation, where Sitting Bull kept his camp. The nonprogressive Indians regarded Sitting Bull almost reverently. He was probably not as great a war chief as Crazy Horse had been. But Sitting Bull had held out against the whites longer than any other Sioux leader. And his people believed that he had extraordinary powers as a medicine man.

The agent at Standing Rock was James McLaughlin, a tough, fair, and experienced agent. For years he had struggled to gain moral leadership of the Indians, and for years Sitting Bull had stood in his way. McLaughlin had been looking for a way to break Sitting Bull's hold over the nonprogressive Indians at Standing Rock. When Sitting Bull took up the forbidden Ghost Dance, McLaughlin decided that arresting him would be the best course. McLaughlin wanted to delay the arrest until winter, when the Indians stayed indoors to avoid the bitter cold and to rest. The agent also believed that the arrest should be made by the Sioux Indian police, not by the cavalry units stationed near the agency at Fort Yates.

In November 1890, McLaughlin began to enlarge his Indian police force. He ordered them to keep a close watch on Sitting Bull's camp and make certain that the old chief did not leave.

In mid-December McLaughlin learned that Sitting Bull had been invited to the Stronghold, where he would join the Pine Ridge and Rosebud Sioux under Short Bull and Kicking Bear. The agent was determined to stop Sitting Bull from taking his group to Pine Ridge. He knew that a stalemate had developed there, and he felt that Sitting Bull's presence might be enough to tip the scales toward open warfare between the Sioux and the cavalry. So McLaughlin ordered Sitting Bull's arrest. He commanded the Indian police, who were led by an experienced lieutenant, Bull Head, to sneak into Sitting Bull's camp at dawn on December 15. They were to arrest the chief and bring him into the agency.

Bull Head and the police met the command with mixed feelings. Most of them were progressives. They prayed to the white man's God before starting their mission. But the thought of Sitting Bull still brought back memories of the great days of the Sioux. One of the police, He Alone, whose white name was John Lone Man, later remembered the way he felt when the orders were read and translated to the police. (The English here is the work of an educated relative of his.)

I'm simply expressing my viewpoint as one who had reformed from all the heathenish ways, formerly one of the loyal followers of Chief Sitting Bull. But ever since I was about ten years of age, I had participated in a good many buffalo hunts and fought under Sitting Bull. But the most important fight I took part in was the Custer fight. After this fight I still went with Sitting Bull's band to Canada. Even after Sitting Bull was returned to Standing Rock Reservation, I remained in his camp, where I tamed down somewhat. We all felt sad.

The police gathered in the early evening of December 14 and passed the night telling war stories. Then, just before dawn, Bull Head ordered He Alone and the thirty or so other police to get ready.

Sitting Bull's camp stood on the north bank of the Grand River. The police, circling from the east, crossed the river to cut off any possible escape southward toward Pine Ridge. Soon they could see Sitting Bull's log cabin. In front of it stood the very tall tepee that was the headquarters for the Ghost Dance. Sitting Bull's two wives, his son Crow Foot, and several other children and relatives lived in the cabin. Other tepees were scattered around it. The police paused for a moment, then crossed the river again. He Alone recalled:

> We rode up as if we attacked the camp. We quickly dismounted, and while our officers went inside we all scattered around the cabin. It was still dark, and everybody was asleep, and only dogs greeted us.
> Bull Head knocked at the door, and the Chief answered, *"How, timahel hiyu you."* [All right, come in.]
> Bull Head said, "I come to arrest you. You are under arrest."
> Sitting Bull said, *"How.* Let me put on my clothes and go with you."
> When Sitting Bull started to go with the police, one of Sitting Bull's wives burst into a loud cry which drew attention. No sooner had this started, when several leaders were rapidly making their way toward Sitting Bull's cabin. Bear That Catches, particularly, came up close saying, "Now, here are the metal breasts[3] just as we had expected. You think you are going to take him. You shall not do it."

By now the entire camp was up and angry. The police might still have been able to arrest the sleepy Sitting Bull if Crow Foot, his seventeen-year-old son, had not intervened. Sitting Bull had been grooming Crow Foot to be a chief, filling his youthful head with tales of courage in battle. As He Alone described it, Crow Foot upset the delicate balance of fear and anger:

> Just about this time, Crow Foot got up, moved by the wailing of his mother and the remarks of Bear That Catches, and said to Sitting Bull, "Well, you always called yourself a brave chief. Now you are allowing yourself to be taken by the metal breasts."
> Sitting Bull then changed his mind, and said, *"Ho ca mni kte sni yelo."* [Then I will not go.]
> Lieutenant Bull Head said to the chief, "Come now, do not listen to any one."
> I said to Sitting Bull, "Uncle,[4] nobody is going to harm you. Please do not let others lead you into any trouble."
> But the chief's mind was made up not to go, so the three head officers laid their hands on him, pulling him outside. By this time, the whole camp was in commotion. Bear That Catches pulled out a gun from under his blanket and fired into Lieutenant Bull Head, wounding him. I ran up toward where they were holding the chief, when Bear That Catches raised his gun. He pointed and fired at me, but it snapped [misfired]. I jerked the gun away from his hands and laid him out. It was about this moment that Lieutenant Bull Head fired into Sitting Bull while still holding him, and Red Tomahawk followed with another shot which finished the chief.

There was more shooting, and soon the Ghost Dancers ran for a line of trees. After a time the police took shelter in Sitting Bull's cabin. The inner

---

[3] "Metal breasts" was a reference to the policemen's badges.

[4] Indians often used words like "Uncle" and "Father" as terms of respect.

walls of the cabin were unfinished but were hung with strips of brightly colored sheeting, sewn together and tacked to the walls. Suddenly, one of the policemen noticed a movement in a corner, behind the sheeting. He Alone raised the curtain:

> There stood Crow Foot, and as soon as he was exposed to view, he cried out, "My uncles, do not kill me. I do not wish to die." Lieutenant Bull Head said, "Do what you like with him. He is the one that has caused this trouble." I do not remember who fired the shot that killed Crow Foot—several fired at once.

Just after Crow Foot was killed, the cavalry units from Fort Yates arrived. The remaining members of Sitting Bull's band scattered toward the south.

He Alone and the rest of the Indian police went home filled with the confusion that was so much a part of reservation life. He Alone performed a Sioux ritual. He built a small shelter and dropped hot stones into water to create a steam bath "that I might cleanse myself for participating in a bloody fight with my fellow men." Then he burned all the clothes he had worn to Sitting Bull's camp. Next, He Alone set out to perform a white man's ritual:

> The next day, I took my family into the agency. I reported to Major McLaughlin. He laid his hand on my shoulders, and said, 'He Alone is a man. I feel very proud of you for the way you have carried out your part in the fight with the Ghost Dancers.' I was not very brave at that moment. His comment nearly set me acrying.

Four Indian policemen died at Sitting Bull's camp. Two more (including Lieutenant Bull Head) would soon be dead of their wounds. One of them, Shave Head, asked McLaughlin, "Did I do well, father?" McLaughlin nodded. Shave Head went on:

> Then I will die in the faith of the white man, to which my five children already belong. Send for my wife, that we may be married by the Black Gown [priest] before I die.

Shave Head's wife came, but too late. The next day, the six dead Indian police were buried. A squad of bluecoats fired honorary volleys over the graves, and taps were blown.

At least eight of Sitting Bull's followers had died. Their bodies were left where they had fallen. Only Sitting Bull was buried. A few moments after completion of the ceremonies for the Indian police, Sitting Bull's body, in a plain coffin, was lowered into a grave in the Fort Yates cemetery. The only people who watched were three officers, serving as official witnesses, and the four guardhouse gravediggers.

None of Sitting Bull's followers was present at his burial. Most of them—about 400—had fled south and west from the Grand River camp. The authorities at Standing Rock had a number of nightmarish ideas about what might happen next. The Standing Rock Ghost Dancers might join Chief Big Foot on the Cheyenne River, where the dance had been in full swing for weeks. On the other hand, the frightened Sitting Bull group might strike out for the Stronghold, where Short Bull and Kicking Bear still held out. Or they might set Big Foot in motion toward the Stronghold too, with terrible results. News of the death of Sitting Bull, likely to spread like prairie fire, could ignite the entire Sioux reservation system.

Agent McLaughlin immediately sent friendly scouts to find Sitting Bull's band. Upon finding them, the scouts were able to persuade over half of them to return to the Standing Rock Reservation. Some of those who simply scattered sooner or later also went back to their homes around Grand River. The rest—fewer than a hundred—headed south to join Big Foot.

They reached a camp that was already nervous and confused. Big Foot had been a great chief. But he was old now, in his seventies, and his control over his band was slipping. The band's medicine man, Yellow Bird, was a fanatical Ghost Dancer. Many of the young braves were ready to bring about their hoped-for victory over the whites. There were about 200 in the band, and all of them were aware of mounting pressure from the white soldiers.

The War Department had ordered Big Foot's arrest, on the false theory that he was almost as large a source of potential trouble as Sitting Bull had been. An observation camp, Camp Cheyenne, had been established by the cavalry just a few miles up the Cheyenne River. Infantry units from the east were trying to cross the Missouri River, which was partially ice-covered.

For several days Big Foot wavered among various alternatives. At one point he was convinced by messengers from the cavalry to go to the Cheyenne River Agency. But many of his young men wanted to go to the Stronghold instead. Big Foot had also been invited by the Pine Ridge Chiefs to go there to settle the troubles. He had a great reputation as a diplomat, and he was offered a hundred ponies to heal the split between the "friendly" Sioux and the Ghost Dancers at Pine Ridge. Most of the time, however, Big Foot seemed to want only to stay put at his own camp and wait.

Finally, for reasons that are difficult to guess, Big Foot made his decision. He would go to Pine Ridge, make peace, and accept the gift of ponies. What he did not realize was that leaving his reservation when the whites were so frightened of a Sioux "uprising" would make him a fugitive "hostile" in the eyes of the military. Almost immediately, new orders went out for Big Foot's arrest. His band was to be disarmed and their horses taken. Then they would be marched to the railroad and sent to Omaha—far away from their own reservation lands. Big Foot never understood that this was the army's plan. He assumed that he was going to Pine Ridge on a mission of peace.

Big Foot's band left camp on December 23, under the cover of night. As soon as the officers at Camp Cheyenne realized that the old chief had gone, a desperate series of cavalry units started patrolling the line between Big Foot's camp and the Stronghold. But the chief passed east of the patrols. The band moved very slowly, for Big Foot had caught pneumonia. He rode in a wagon without springs. Soon Big Foot was bleeding from his nose. And it was bitterly cold for the old man. At one point, in a pass through a steep wall along the Bad River, Big Foot's men had to dig out a road for the wagon.

Big Foot managed to reach Porcupine Creek, only about thirty miles from the Pine Ridge Agency, without being sighted by the army. He sent men ahead to tell the Sioux he was coming.

On December 28, five days after starting south, Big Foot's band was finally "captured" by the Seventh Cavalry. When the Indians and cavalry met, there was a tense moment. The cavalry formed a skirmish line and brought up cannon. Big Foot's braves formed a battle line in front of his wagon. But then the cavalry commander came forward. He and Big Foot shook hands, and the chief accepted an "escort"—going, he thought, to Pine Ridge. Together, the cavalry and the Indians made their way to a trading post at Wounded Knee Creek.

The officer in charge had wisely not tried to disarm the Sioux, and he let them keep their horses for the trip. He even transferred Big Foot into an ambulance wagon. When the two groups reached Wounded Knee, the Indians were issued rations. The rest of the Seventh Cavalry came from Pine Ridge to join the patrol. The Indians pitched their tepees in a low hollow near a ravine that led into the creek. There were 102 men and 230 women and children. The soldiers—a total of about 500—camped on a rise just to the north. Armed sentries surrounded the Indians, but on the whole everything seemed peaceful enough.

Soon the Indians settled down and the cavalry—except for the ring of sentries around the Indian camp—went to sleep. Only a few officers, veterans of the Little Bighorn disaster, stayed up late. They celebrated over a keg of whiskey someone had brought from the agency.

The next morning Colonel James Forsyth, commander of the Seventh Cavalry, asked all the men of Big Foot's group to gather in a council between the tepees and the cavalry encampment. The sentries remained in place. The rest of the cavalry units drew up, mounted, around the Sioux men and their camp. Forsyth asked the Indians for their weapons.

Big Foot tried diplomacy. From his ambulance bed he quietly advised his men to give up the bad guns but hide the good ones. Soon Forsyth sent twenty of the Indians to the tepees to bring the guns. Meanwhile, however, the Sioux women (who understood the value of a weapon) had hidden the rifles that the Sioux had bought, stolen, or taken in battle. The Indians returned to the council with only two old, broken cavalry carbines.

Forsyth heightened his search. He placed a line of troops between the Sioux braves and their camp and sent his own men into the tepees. But this search uncovered only thirty rifles, most of them old and useless. This left one other real possibility: the Sioux were hiding their rifles under the blankets they kept draped over their shoulders against the cold.

By now the situation was very delicate. Forsyth ordered Big Foot brought out on his blanket. The medicine man, Yellow Bird, was dancing around, chanting Ghost Dance songs, urging the young braves to be firm. In the tepees women were hastily packing, ready to run.

Suddenly, one Indian, Black Coyote, pulled a rifle from his blanket and began to shout, holding the weapon over his head. He was probably deaf and, by the Indians' own testimony, a little insane. Two soldiers grabbed him and struggled for the rifle. It went off, firing overhead. In what may have been a signal, Yellow Bird threw a handful of dust into the air. Several braves pulled rifles from their blankets and aimed at the cavalry. "By God, they have broken," an officer shouted. The Indians fired, and at about the same moment came the command "Fire! Fire on them!"

No one could stop what happened next. Big Foot was quickly killed. Cavalry carbines ripped into the group of Sioux men. The bullets that did not find a Sioux body passed on across the ravine into the tepees. Women ran this way and that, followed by children. Some of the Indians broke toward the creek, where they were cut down by waiting cavalrymen. Others ran into the ravine.

Corporal Paul Weinert manned one of the Seventh Cavalry's small, rapid-firing cannon on the hill. Like the other cavalrymen, he was surprised when the firing started. But within a moment or two, he was caught up in the battle, pumping shots angrily wherever he saw moving Sioux:

> All of the Indians opened fire on us. Lieutenant Hawthorne ran toward me and was calling, when suddenly I heard him say, "Oh, my God!" and then I knew he had been hit. I said: "By God! I'll make 'em pay for that," and ran the gun into the opening of the ravine. They kept yelling for me to come back. Bullets were coming like hail from the Indians' Winchesters. I kept going in farther, and pretty soon everything was quiet at the other end of the line.

Corporal Weinert was a soldier with a sophisticated weapon. The experience of Catching Spirit Elk, a Sioux who had surrendered his rifle, was almost the opposite of Weinert's:

> Then followed firing from all sides. I threw myself on the ground. I then jumped up to run toward the Indian camp, but was then and there shot down, being hit on my right leg, and soon after was shot again on the other leg. When the general firing ceased, I heard an interpreter calling out, saying the wounded would be kindly treated. I opened my eyes and looked about and saw the dead and wounded all around me.

Some officers did what they could to prevent women and children from being shot down. But the Indians (at least those who still had weapons) were fast and accurate with their repeating rifles, and the soldiers sometimes fired at anything that moved. When the artillery on the hill opened up on the Indians in the ravine, the shells exploded on all without regard to age or sex. Apparently, too, some of the soldiers broke ranks and chased down fleeing Indians. These were the bodies Charles Eastman found miles away from Wounded Knee.

The actual battle lasted only a few minutes and the cavalry's mopping-up

**BURYING THE DEAD AT WOUNDED KNEE**

Several days after the massacre, a party of about thirty white men, armed with shovels and rifles, went to Wounded Knee to bury the Sioux dead. They were paid $2 a body, a total of a little less than $300, for their work. But they also got to pose for publicity photographs like this one. *(Nebraska State Historical Society)*

only a short time longer. About 150 braves rode out from Pine Ridge, too late and too few to help their comrades. The cavalry gathered their own dead (25) and wounded (39) and returned to the Pine Ridge Agency. They took some of the wounded Sioux with them and left the rest on the field. There were at least 146 Indian dead—about half of them men. Some bodies were probably taken away during the next two days, before Eastman's party arrived to rescue the living and bury the rest. All in all, probably 200 Sioux and whites had died.

Wounded Knee was followed by a few small skirmishes. But soon Pine Ridge was pacified. The Stronghold Indians had given up while Big Foot's band was on the march. The Ghost Dance was over. Spring came and went, but the earth did not cover the white man, as the Messiah had promised. Paul Weinert, the cannoneer, received a Congressional Medal of Honor for his part in the action at the edge of the ravine.

A small white church was later built at the Sioux mass grave, on what came to be called Cemetery Hill. In 1903, with the help of missionaries, the Indians put up their own small monument, burying Wounded Knee in the past.

This monument is erected by surviving relatives and other Ogalalla and Cheyenne River Sioux Indians in memory of the Chief Big Foot Massacre, Dec. 29, 1890. Col. Forsyth in command of U.S. troops. Big Foot was a great chief of the Sioux Indians. He often said, "I will stand in peace till my last day comes." He did many good and brave deeds for the white man and the red man. Many innocent women and children who knew no wrong died here.

# Settling the Last Frontier

There is nothing unique about the history of the Sioux. It is true they resisted the whites longer and more ferociously than most other Indians, east or west. And they were the only tribe that, inspired by the Messiah's new religion, developed a militant resistance to reservation life. But despite these differences, they were finally defeated in a manner typical of the way in which white Americans subdued all the Indians.

The defeat of the Sioux and the other plains Indians was just one part of the history of continental expansion. White Americans had begun moving west in the 1830s. In the decades after the Civil War, this movement increased in speed and recklessness.

## THE LAST WEST

Until the 1840s, America had a clearly drawn frontier. It was possible at each census before then to draw a zigzag line from north to south showing how far settlement had advanced in each decade. But after the Mexican War this was no longer true. The drift of pioneers into Oregon, the settlement of Texas and Utah, and the discovery of gold in California created isolated pockets of white settlement thousands of miles beyond the old frontier line near the Mississippi. By the early 1850s, it was evident that the Pacific Coast would be settled fairly quickly, organized into territories, and carved into states. California had already been admitted to statehood as part of the Compromise of 1850. Oregon entered the Union nine years later.

Between the Pacific coast and the old frontier in eastern Kansas and Nebraska lay a vast stretch of plains and mountains. It formed an area larger than the whole territory over which Washington governed as president. This region was the last frontier, the last region to be settled by white Americans.

The Great Plains begin in the first tier of states west of the Mississippi River, and extend west to the Rockies. In 1836, the Senate Committee for Indian Affairs declared that the Great Plains were an "uninhabitable region." The Indians there "are on the outside of us, and in a place which will forever remain on the outside." In fact the plains were given an official name, "The Great American Desert." The weather there is dry. There is no water in many of the rivers during most of the year. The land is not covered with trees but with stubborn grass. Only the Indian and the buffalo seemed able to thrive. The Rocky Mountain region also seemed to offer little to encourage settlement. For many years its great peaks and high valleys were the home of only small Indian bands and a few American fur traders.

There were many reasons why this myth that the West could not be settled came to an end. Three of the earliest and most important factors were gold, railroads, and cattle. As miners, railroad men, and ranchers moved into the region, they systematically seized Indian lands. Then came the final pioneers of the last West, the farmers. In 1890, the Census Bureau announced that the frontier no longer existed.

## THE MINING FRONTIER

The discovery of gold and silver had been responsible for the rapid development of California. Miners who reached the Pacific coast too late to find gold easily soon began to drift east over the mountains, looking for new bonanzas. In 1858, prospectors found gold near Pike's Peak in Colorado. Soon people were pouring into new, ramshackle towns like Denver, Pueblo, and Boulder. Their covered wagons proclaimed "Pike's Peak or Bust!" A year after the first strike, about 100,000 people—mostly men without their families—had moved into the area. Like most other Western gold and silver strikes, the Pike's Peak boom did not last. The earliest prospectors soon raked off the surface gold. The remaining precious metal was buried deep in the mountains,

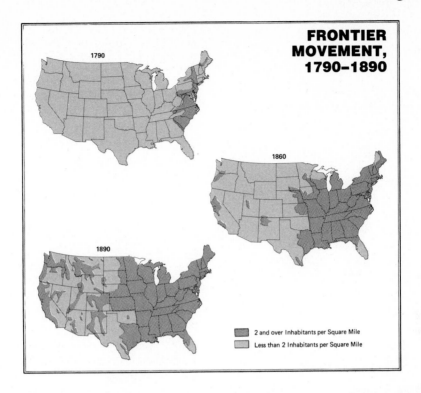

**FRONTIER MOVEMENT, 1790–1890**

1790

1860

1890

2 and over Inhabitants per Square Mile
Less than 2 Inhabitants per Square Mile

where it could be mined only with expensive machinery that individual miners could not afford. Within three months in 1859, the population of the Colorado goldfields dwindled to about 50,000. But enough men stayed to create a pocket of white settlement in the mountains.

A similar process was under way farther west, in what is now Nevada. Miners from California found gold near the western border of the region in the late 1850s. In 1859 they discovered the famous Comstock Lode. One of the richest single mines in America, it produced over $200 million worth of gold and silver in the thirty years following its discovery. Thousands of men rushed over the mountains from Sacramento to build nearby Virginia City. Soon the town had five newspapers, a miniature stock exchange, and a horde of prospectors, saloon keepers, prostitutes, and gamblers. A few men became enormously wealthy. Most of the prospectors, however, went away disappointed.

Some miners who stayed found small pockets of loose gold that could be mined with a pan or a sluice, a simple trough that runs water downhill over dirt and loose rocks, washing out the heavy gold dust. This kind of mining, called placer mining, soon washed off the free metal near the surface. This meant that the miner's frontier quickly became a corporate frontier, exploited by mining companies owned by Eastern investors. Within a few years, any successful field soon became an industrial development. And the prospectors scattered again in search of a new discovery and easy pickings elsewhere.

The California Gold Rush that had excited so many thousands of Americans in 1849 was repeated over and over again throughout the West. In the late 1850s a small strike was made in eastern Washington, but it soon petered out. Restless miners headed farther east, up the Snake and Salmon rivers into Idaho. There they built Boise, Silver City, and other new mining towns. By 1861, the start of the Civil War, there were probably 30,000 white men in Idaho.

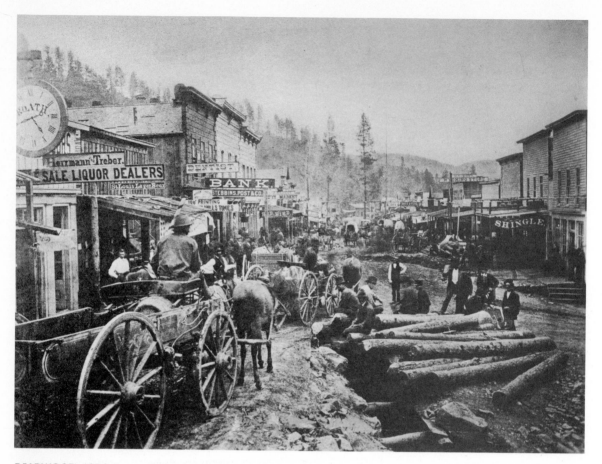

DEADWOOD, 1876

The Plains Indians might win occasional victories over the United States army. But the real menace to their society was not the cavalry but the whites' railroads, farms, and cities. This 1876 photograph shows the bustle of growth in Deadwood, South Dakota, with its liquor stores, dentists' offices, and banks. Against towns like Deadwood, the Indians' teepee villages had little or no hope of survival. *(Culver Pictures)*

During the Civil War—while their countrymen were battling at Bull Run and Chickamauga—white miners moved from Idaho into Montana. There they struck gold and silver at Last Chance Gulch (which later became the city of Helena) and Alder Gulch (Virginia City). By 1863 Idaho had enough citizens to organize as a territory, and Montana followed a year later.

The last Western gold rush occurred in 1874. In the Black Hills of South Dakota, in the heart of the Great Sioux reservation, an army expedition commanded by General Custer found traces of gold. According to a treaty between the United States and the Indians, the hills belonged to the Sioux "forever." For a short time the government tried to prevent white men from entering the Black Hills. But the pressure to find gold was too great. Within two years about 7,000 whites had built Deadwood and Custer City. The Sioux lands had been decisively invaded.

# TRANSPORTATION WEST

The influx of settlers, together with the settlement of Oregon and California, led to demands for quick, safe, and economical land transportation between the settled East and the Far West. Every new mining town wanted to be linked to the rest of the country. People who lived on the West coast wanted an overland route as an alternate to the long sea voyage around South America.

## Trail, Stage, and Pony

The Oregon Trail, Santa Fe Trail, and other routes followed by pioneers in the 1840s and early 1850s were more or less protected by army posts along the way. But they were far from being real roads. Something else seemed necessary.

In 1858 the first stage road was finally cut through the countryside for the Butterfield Overland Express. Its route ran 2,000 miles, from St. Louis south through Indian Territory,[1] then across Texas, New Mexico, and Arizona. The ride was rough and usually very hot; although it took twenty-four days, the overland trip was faster than the sea voyage. Soon other stage and freighting companies were opening additional roads across Colorado and Utah to California.

In 1860 businessmen set up a mail service known as the pony express. Small, lightweight boys, like jockeys, rode big horses (not ponies) in relays between St. Joseph, Missouri, and Sacramento, California. The young riders were able to carry a message across the country in ten days. The pony express prospered for only about a year, however. In 1861 the first telegraph line was put through to the West coast. The time for sending and receiving cross-country messages was then cut to a split second.

---

[1] This region—corresponding roughly to the present state of Oklahoma—was set aside in 1834 for Indians removed from east of the Mississippi. Later, parts of it were reserved for Western Indians, too.

# A Transcontinental Railroad

All these ways of getting people, goods, and information across the country were only preludes to the most dramatic and successful method of all, the railroad. A transcontinental railroad had been a dream since the 1840s—to move people through the West to California. The North and the South, however, had not been able to agree on the western part of the route. The North wanted a line to run from Chicago to San Francisco. The South insisted on a route through Texas to southern California.

The Civil War ended this competition. By seceding, the South lost its right to participate in the decision making. In 1862 Congress settled on a route between Council Bluffs, Iowa, and San Francisco. The same law provided for enormous financial support from the federal government. There would be two companies. The Central Pacific would build east from San Francisco. The Union Pacific (a patriotic name suited to wartime) would go west across Nebraska and Colorado. They were to meet somewhere in the middle. Each railroad would be given a right of way 400 feet wide. In addition, the government would lend the railroads up to $48,000 for each mile of track laid—less for flat country, more for mountain track. Most important, the railroads would be given 6,400 acres for every mile of track completed. In 1864 this land allowance was doubled.

The Central Pacific started building toward the east slowly. The company lacked funds, and labor was scarce. But gradually these problems were resolved. The Lincoln administration cooperated by allowing the railroad to claim flat-country miles as mountain miles, thus entitling the companies to the largest possible federal loans. The labor problem was solved by importing thousands of Chinese. In 1864 the railroad laid only about 20 miles of track, but by 1867 the pace was up to 20 miles a month.

At the other end of the proposed route the Union Pacific also built slowly, at first. But it picked up speed by bringing in thousands of Irish

**EAST MEETS WEST**

In the years after the Civil War, American railroad companies imported thousands of Chinese workers to help finish the rail network in the mountains and deserts of the West. Here, Chinese workers use hand labor to complete a graceful and impressive trestle on the Central Pacific Railroad in the Sierra Nevadas of California. *(Culver Pictures)*

immigrants to lay rails. In 1868 alone the Union Pacific laid 425 miles of track.

In May 1869, after only five years of construction, the two work gangs met at Promontory Point, Utah, just east of the Great Salt Lake. The last tie put down was coated with silver; the last spike was gold. A telegraph operator cabled east and west: "Hats off—prayer is being offered." Then there was a wait of almost fifteen minutes. Again the telegraph clicked. "We have got done praying. The spike is about to be presented." Railroad officials took turns with the hammer; the first blow was a bad miss, but the work was done. The two locomotives eased forward until they touched. The nation celebrated almost as wildly as it had at the end of the Civil War. Chicago's parade was seven miles long. The nation was joined, east to west, across a desert that an earlier generation had believed would never be settled.

During the next fifteen years three more routes were opened across the Rockies. Iowa, Missouri, Kansas, and Nebraska were crisscrossed by rails. In the process, the government gave the railroad companies almost 180 million acres of public land, and it lent them over $100 million. Because of complicated regulations that allowed railroads to delay choosing the land they wanted to keep along their rights of way, they were able to keep great stretches of land for years.

At one point the railroads controlled—at least on paper—almost all of Iowa and Wisconsin. The Northern Pacific, whose route crossed the northern tier of states between Lake Superior and the Pacific, controlled a strip of land larger in area than many European nations. The same kind of situation developed in Arizona and New Mexico. By 1885 the railroads held land totaling almost a sixth of the entire country.

Many of the congressmen and senators who voted these huge grants to the railroads did so in the belief that most of the land in the "Great American Desert" was of little value. The motive behind the first transcontinental lines was not to build a transportation network for the Great Plains and the Rockies but to build a link to the Pacific coast. It took a generation's experience to make clear that the intervening territory was valuable, that it would be settled and farmed. As things turned out, the railroads may have been a very efficient mechanism for disposing of the public lands, at least in some areas. The government's own land policy was confused and often corrupt, and the public interest may, on balance, have been served about as well by the railroad grants as by the government's direct land grant practices.

## FROM BUFFALO TO CATTLE

In any case, the first important effects of the railroads on the Great Plains had less to do with land ownership and cultivation than with animals. The railroads created a new industry on the plains—ranching. Building the railroads not only hastened the destruction of the buffalo herds, it also made possible the systematic exploitation of another set of resources: grass and cows.

Early in the sixteenth century, the Spanish had begun importing European cattle into America. Over the years the cattle had multiplied. Some had escaped and become wild, especially in southern Texas around the Nueces River. These were the famous Texas longhorns—lanky, tough, long-horned, and too dangerous to be captured

**THE GREAT EVENT**

In 1869, the Union Pacific Railroad advertised the first passenger service from Omaha through to San Francisco. The trip took only four days, and avoided "the Dangers of the Sea." Curiously, the railroad's artist chose to emphasize not the train, but a handsome buck in a forest, as though the railroad did not destroy nature but merely passed harmlessly through it. *(Union Pacific Railroad Museum Collection)*

or herded on foot. They roamed at will over the open range, a huge expanse of grass that was part of the public domain. By 1860, there were probably 5 million head of longhorns in Texas.

The Mexicans had learned to rope, brand, and even herd longhorns. In fact, it was Mexicans and not Americans who were the first cowboys. They originated almost all of the tools of the cowboy's trade, from his big hat and kerchief to his tooled leather saddle and boots. Mexico, however, had no real market for beef. The situation was different in the United States.

The Civil War sent beef prices soaring in both the North and the South. The beef herd in the Northern states was smaller at the end of the war than it had been at the beginning. At the same time, the population had grown by more than 20 percent. Thus the demand and price for beef had increased. A man could buy a longhorn steer in Texas for as little as $3. The same steer in Chicago was worth ten times as much.

## The Long Drive

By 1866 the Missouri Pacific Railroad had pushed its line west to Sedalia, Missouri, just east of Kansas City. That same year the first large group of Texans drove enormous herds north across Indian Territory to reach the rail line. The men ran into many difficulties. Part of the route passed through dense forests. The longhorns, unaccustomed to woods, panicked and refused to be driven through the trees. The Indians (whose treaty gave them control of all white travel across their land) harassed the cowboys. This early attempt showed, however, that it was possible to herd cattle safely over hundreds of miles to the railroad—and thus to Eastern markets.

Thus began the twenty-year era of the "long drive." As the years passed, the railroads extended farther west. New cattle towns replaced Sedalia. Among them were Abilene (probably the most successful), Wichita, and Dodge City. Between 1866 and 1888, Texans drove as many as 6 million head of cattle over the grasslands to Kansas.

For those who succeeded, the profits of the long drive were enormous. Cattlemen claimed that as much as 40 percent profit per year was not unusual. Like the miner's frontier, the cattleman's bonanza soon attracted thousands of eager Easterners. Each usually had a few hundred dollars and a dream of running a vast ranch. Like the prospectors, most of the would-be ranchers were disappointed. Many of them either returned home or switched to another line of work such as running a store or saloon.

The long drive, despite the romantic myth of the cowboy it fostered, was a business. It required capital if it was to succeed on a big scale. In the end only the lucky few who had been there first (like the prospectors in California or Nevada) became "cattle barons." In the long run, it was Eastern and European investors, with enough capital to buy and move large herds, who controlled most of the industry.

## The End of the Open Range

The long drive had a brief existence. Gradually, people north of Texas realized that, as the railroads came closer, it made sense to breed and feed cattle nearby instead of driving them up from Texas. During the 1880s, the long drive from Texas was replaced by an even wilder cattle bonanza in other plains territories to the north. In 1860, there were no cattle at all in the northwestern plains, and there were only a few in Kansas and Nebraska. By 1880, Montana, the Dakota Territory, Wyoming, and Colorado had great herds, totaling almost 4 million head.

But the days of the open range, when cattle wandered on public land from one spring to the next, could not last long. The cattle industry soon found itself in a situation faced earlier by tobacco and cotton growers—overproduction. Rapid expansion led to an overstocked range. The grass could not support so many cattle. The increased supply also caused prices to fall. Between 1885 and 1886 the price of a steer dropped from $30 to $10. The following winter on the plains was the bitterest in memory. Thousands of cattle

THE LAST FRONTIER
c.1860-1890

+++ Railroads
···· Cattle trails
⚒ Mining sites
🐃 Cattle raising areas after 1880

0    100    200    300 MILES

starved and froze to death. The cattle bonanza was over.

## THE DEFEAT OF THE WESTERN INDIANS

The miners, railroaders, and cattlemen brought about the final chapter in the conflict between whites and Indians. It was a conflict older than Jamestown and as dark as any aspect of American history. The whites cloaked their actions with high-sounding expressions like "civilization against savagery" or "Manifest Destiny." But the facts were very simple: the white men came and took the Indians' lands.

White people in the New World had always regarded the Indians as a "problem." For most whites—whether they were French, Spanish, or English—the Indians were seen either as a people to be exploited through trade or slavery or as a barrier to westward expansion. A few whites sympathized with the Indians and did what they could to protect them from the worst aspects of white civilization. But even to those who were sympathetic, helping meant teaching the Indians to "adjust to civilization."

The Indians might be a "problem" for the whites, but for the Indians the whites meant disaster. At stake for the whites was only the delay of continental expansion for a generation or so. The stakes for the Indians were much higher. They were in danger of losing their culture, their freedom, their identity as human beings, and, in many cases, their lives. This was true from the time Cortés invaded Mexico, through Bacon's Rebellion and the removal of the Cherokee and other tribes westward,[2] down to the final conquest of the tribes of the West.

## Advantages of the Whites

White people's ways were overpowering to the Indians. In the first place, the whites' methods of dealing with the environment were totally unlike those of the Indians. Some Indians farmed a little.

---

[2] In the 1830s the federal government forced the so-called Five Civilized Tribes—the Cherokees, Chickasaws, Choctaws, Creeks, and Seminoles—to move from the Southeast to Indian Territory. The Indians suffered so much on the trip west that the journey became known as the Trail of Tears.

GULLIVER'S TRAVAILS

This 1886 cartoon was adapted from Jonathan Swift's *Gulliver's Travels*. It shows a helpless Cherokee nation, tied down, like Gulliver, by Lilliputian Americans. The courts cut his hair, the missionaries drain his brains, the railroads steal his shoes. In the background, the government is shown trying to manage other tribes. But it is like the old woman who lived in a shoe and has so many children she doesn't know what to do. *(The Bettmann Archive)*

But the whites were able to cultivate vast stretches of land, first with teams of mules or oxen, then with machinery. Some Indians, like the Navajos, made ornaments out of silver or gold. But the whites came for gold and silver in droves. Big new towns and frightening machines and explosives changed the face of the mountains and valleys of the Rockies. The Indians hunted wild animals, which seemed numerous enough to last forever. But the whites killed off the wild animals, fenced in the range, and raised great herds of cattle instead.

These were the main weapons of the whites—farming, mining, and ranching. Along with these the whites brought strange powers and "medicine" that made the Indians' situation hopeless indeed—the railroad, machine guns and cannons, and the telegraph.

Another weapon of the whites against the Indians was something they did not use on purpose—indeed, the whites feared it themselves. This was disease. Smallpox, measles, and other sicknesses may have wiped out as many as half the Western Indians before any significant number of whites even arrived in their territory. The germs traveled with traders and so preceded actual white migrations by decades. The Indians had no inherited resistance or immunity to many diseases of the whites, since the germs had been "imported" from Europe. Indians died by the band and even by the tribe from sicknesses that only made most whites uncomfortable.

Finally, the whites had an advantage that probably counted more than anything else—numbers. They poured west by the thousands. In one change of seasons, between one Sun Dance and another, the whites seemed able to throw up towns like San Francisco, Denver, or Deadwood—towns with populations larger than the whole Sioux nation.

One by one, the tribes of the Great Plains, the California-Intermountain area, and the Northwest coast were made to realize that the whites were a force they could neither understand nor control. Some groups, like the Sioux, the Kiowas, and the Apaches, fought back. They were sustained by their myths, their magic, and their hatred of the cavalry that invaded their villages, shooting men, women, and children. But in the end, all the tribes were defeated. Only something as unusual as the Messiah's Ghost Dance could convince the Indians—and only a few at that—that there was any way to combat the enveloping white civilization.

## Dealing with the Tribes

From the beginning, United States policy toward the Indians had been contradictory. On the one hand, the government treated tribes as independent nations with whom it could make treaties. On the other hand, Indians were not citizens but wards of the government, subject to federal control. In addition, the American nation was growing with incredible speed. Again and again, government aims that seemed practical in one decade were obsolete ten years later.

In California and Oregon, and in the frontier regions of the Rockies, relations between whites and Indians were poorly controlled by the government. Groups of whites simply drove the Indians out, murdering many of them in the process. The Indians of California suffered especially. They had settled around Spanish missions and learned farming and various crafts. After the Spanish missions were closed down in the 1830s, the Indians were defenseless against the greedy whites. In the ten years after the Gold Rush of 1849, some 70,000 of these mission Indians died from starvation, disease, and outright murder.

On the Great Plains, whites might band together to attack Indians. But the government and its army played a much larger role in keeping the peace there than it did farther west. After 1850, the history of Indian-white relations settled down to a fairly steady rhythm of treaties, uprisings, war, and new treaties. The Indians were always the losers. Even when they won the battles, they lost in the making of the treaties.

This process began in 1851 at Fort Laramie on the Oregon Trail. To protect the trail, the government called hundreds of Indian leaders together and persuaded them to agree not to bother the wagon trains crossing their territory. Each tribe accepted boundaries to its hunting grounds. In return, the government promised to leave them in peace.

These agreements left the Indians in possession of almost all of the Great Plains. But, accepting boundaries laid out by Washington opened the door to a new government tactic—getting each tribe, by a separate treaty, to give up part of its lands. By 1865, the Indians had given up all of Kansas, most of Nebraska, the central half of Utah, and almost all of Texas.

## The Sand Creek Massacre

Much Indian land was surrendered peacefully, in return for promises of peace and annual shipments of government supplies, called annuities. But in 1861 in Colorado, a government attempt to move Cheyennes and Arapahoes onto a small reservation at Sand Creek resulted in the Indians waging a three-year guerrilla war. In 1864, the leader of the warring Indians, Black Kettle, tried to make peace with the whites. The army and the territorial government refused. The unyielding commander of the Colorado militia, Colonel John Chivington, told Black Kettle: "My rule for fighting white men or Indians is to fight them until they lay down their arms and surrender."

Black Kettle led his people to a camp at Sand Creek, where he hoped to be left in peace. But the Indians woke on November 29, 1864, to find 1,000 of Chivington's militia surrounding them. The militia rushed the camp, shooting at everything that moved. When the "fight" was over, 450 Indians were dead. Only about 50 had escaped the massacre. The next year the Cheyennes and Arapahoes had to sign a new treaty. It forced them to leave their Colorado plains for a barren corner of Indian Territory.

## Negotiations with the Sioux

The Sioux fared better, at least for a time. Their agreement at Fort Laramie in 1851 gave them one of the largest hunting areas in the West—most of

the Dakota Territory and the region around the Powder River in eastern Wyoming and southern Montana. But by 1865 miners had crowded into Montana at Bozeman, Virginia City, and Helena. These towns soon demanded a road connecting them with the Oregon Trail. This road would cross the Yellowstone River, skirt the Sioux hunting areas around the Big Horn Mountains, and cross directly over the valley of the Powder River.

In the summer of 1865, the cavalry moved into the area to construct forts and begin work on the road. A Sioux chief, Red Cloud, led his people in a two-year attack on the road and the forts. And in 1868 the government made a new treaty that seemed to give the victory to Red Cloud. The road was abandoned. But the Sioux, in return, had to agree to a reservation that included only the Dakotas west of the Missouri—the so-called Great Sioux Reservation. According to the treaty, they could still hunt in the Powder River country. For the first time, however, they had accepted a reservation to replace the large domain that their 1851 treaty had recognized.

The commission that made the 1868 agreement with the Sioux dealt with other plains tribes in the same way. Reservations were created in Indian Territory for the southern groups—the Kiowa, Comanche, Arapaho, Cheyenne, Osage, and Pawnee tribes. Between 1868 and 1874 the northern tribes—Crow and Blackfoot, Shoshoni and Mandan—also accepted new, restricted reservations. By 1876, the plains Indians had given up over three-fourths of the land they had held under the Fort Laramie Treaty.

## The Battle of the Little Bighorn

The policy of concentrating Indians on reservations was applied once again in the Black Hills area of South Dakota. The treaty of 1868 guaranteed the Tetons complete possession of the Black Hills. But in 1874 rumors of gold led to a reconnaissance of the area by a military column of the Seventh Cavalry under Colonel George Custer. Custer's men found gold, and the result-

# Chief Joseph

*(Culver Pictures)*

Hinmaton-Yalaktit was his name—"thunder coming out of the water and over the land." He was a chief in the tribe the whites called Nez Percé—"pierced nose"—because of their habit of wearing nose ornaments made of shells. Joseph was his white man's name, and before he was taken captive he did two things. He fought the most brilliant and sustained military campaign against the United States Army ever waged by any American Indian leader. And he made the most poignant and famous surrender speech any American Indian ever delivered.

In 1863, the Nez Percé ceded most of their lands to the United States and agreed to live on a small reservation in Idaho. A renegade portion of the tribe, however, refused to recognize the treaty. For ten years, the government did not try to enforce the treaty, and all the Nez Percé had to do was fend off individual white squatters. This was the situation when Joseph, at age thirty-three, became chief after his father's death in 1873.

In 1876, the government decided to enforce the treaty and move the "renegade" Nez Percé onto the Idaho reservation. A group of Joseph's warriors, almost certainly without his blessing, went on a rampage and killed twenty or so white settlers. Reluctantly, Joseph was drawn into a situation in which he knew final victory was impossible. He decided to strike out for Canada.

The force Joseph led into the mountains contained fewer than 200 fighting men, who had to protect and care for about 600 women and children. But Joseph was able to lead this group on a superb retreat that covered more than a thousand miles of difficult wilderness. He ran when he could and fought when he had to. In August 1877, he defeated the cavalry in a desperate struggle on the Big Hole River in Montana. Finally, Joseph got his people into the Bear Paw mountains, only thirty miles from Canada.

Joseph thought he had won, and stopped to allow his dozens of wounded and helpless followers to rest. But he was overtaken by a force of cavalry, and had to decide, and quickly, whether to run, to surrender, or to fight. He chose to fight, and kept the cavalry at bay for five days. On October 5, he surrendered his beaten force: 87 men, almost half of them wounded, and about 350 women and children. To this broken remnant of the Nez Percé, Joseph made his speech:

I am tired of fighting. The old men are all dead. [My brother] who led the young men is dead. It is cold, and we have no blankets. The little children are freezing to death. My people, some of them, have run away to the hills. No one knows where they are. I want to have some time to look for my children and see how many I can find. Maybe I shall find them among the dead.

Hear me, my chiefs. From where the sun now stands, I will fight no more forever.

Joseph and his people were taken first to Kansas and then to Indian Territory, where many of them died of disease. A few were eventually returned to Idaho. But Joseph never went home. He was moved to a reservation in Washington state, and he lived to visit a new "Great Father" in Washington, D.C., Theodore Roosevelt, in 1903. Joseph died in 1904, at the age of sixty-four. The official cause of death was entered as a broken heart.

ing rush into Deadwood and other mining towns made conflict between the Sioux and the whites inevitable.

The Grant administration tried for a time to hold the prospectors back. The army even removed some of them. But finally the government gave in and allowed the prospectors to enter the Black Hills "at their own risk." The next step was as cruel and illegal as any the government ever took against the Sioux. To prevent clashes between the miners and the Indians, Washington ordered all the Sioux to report to reservation agencies. Any who remained outside would be considered automatically "hostile" and liable to attack. Many of the Sioux obeyed the order. But about 8,000 of them defied the government and gathered in the area of the Big Horn Mountains for their annual summer encampment and Sun Dance.

In June 1876, the army launched powerful forces of infantry, cavalry, and artillery against these Indians. One column, marching north from the Platte River, met Crazy Horse at Rosebud Creek on June 17. The army was beaten back in fierce fighting. Crazy Horse returned to the Sioux camp at the Little Bighorn River, where 8,000 Teton Sioux had gathered—the most powerful single force of Indians the army would ever face. Another army column advanced from the east. On June 25 the Seventh Cavalry, again under Custer's command, rode foolishly to the attack. The Sioux killed almost all of Custer's force in the most famous (and, from the white point of view, perhaps the most stupid) Indian battle in American history.

Another cycle of treaty, war, and new treaty was about to be completed. Within a year, the Sioux were forced to give up their important Black Hills area. They were now forced onto a reservation covering only the central part of South Dakota, between the Missouri River and the Black Hills. But their troubles were not over. A railroad was pushing toward the reservation, and the remaining Sioux stood in its path. Farm-

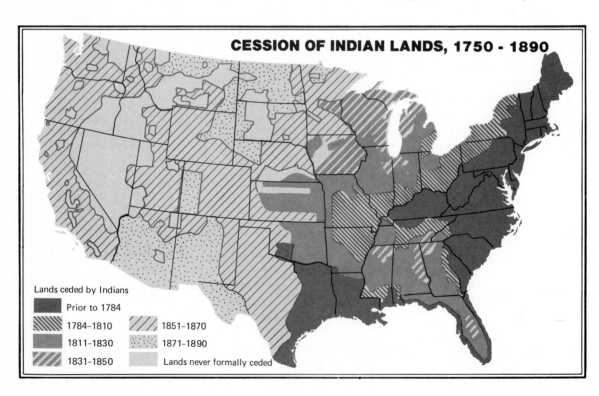

**CESSION OF INDIAN LANDS, 1750 - 1890**

Lands ceded by Indians

- Prior to 1784
- 1784-1810
- 1811-1830
- 1831-1850
- 1851-1870
- 1871-1890
- Lands never formally ceded

ers and ranchers were also beginning to look longingly at the land that the Sioux still held.

## A Changing Indian Policy

The idea of private property is so deeply rooted in white society that it is sometimes difficult to grasp the Native Americans' concept of land "ownership." Most tribes looked on the land in more or less the same way that fishermen look on the sea—as a place to hunt. No Indian thought of himself as owning a piece of the land. He might own his horses, his weapons, his tepee. But the land itself was the "property" of the whole tribe, to be used communally and protected from other tribes.

When the various tribes of the plains agreed to give up their land, they did so as tribal units, not as individuals. When they accepted their "reservations," too, they accepted them as tribes, not as individual property owners.

Reformers, most of whom lived in the East, believed that private property was an essential feature of "civilization." To break the Indians' old, communal concept of land, the reformers proposed that the reservations be divided into lots and given to the Indians in "severalty"—that the Indians be treated as "several" or separate individuals. Westerners, anxious to exploit the Indians, agreed with this proposal. Their enthusiasm was a result of some simple arithmetic. If every Indian family was given an individual farm, a lot of reservation land would be left over. There simply were not enough Indians, in most tribes, to "fill" the reservations. The remaining land could become available to whites.

This new policy became law in 1887 in the Dawes Severalty Act. The next year, after much argument, some trickery, and probably some bribery, the whites persuaded the Sioux to accept the new plan. The one big Sioux reservation could then be broken down into five smaller ones that were, all together, less than half as large in area as the original. The same policy was applied to the other plains Indians. One after another, the

tribes settled for 160 acres per family. One after another, they realized that this meant giving up about half their tribal lands. The resulting demoralization provided a fertile ground for the new Ghost Dance religion. No matter what the intentions of the whites who wrote and supported the Dawes Severalty Act, it was a disaster for the Indians. In 1887, Indians had held about 130 million acres of land in the United States; by 1930, after forty years of the Dawes Act, the total had been reduced to less than 50 million acres.

With the new policy came even stronger efforts to convert the Indians to white civilization—to make them "walk the white man's road," as Sitting Bull put it. These efforts hardened the conflict in attitudes between the progressive Indians, who accepted the new ways, and the non-progressives, who clung to the old ones. The division was dramatized when Sitting Bull was arrested by Indian police from his own tribe. Even after the "reforms" of the 1880s, American policy toward the Indians was a calamity. They were reduced to a condition in some ways worse than that of the freed slaves in the South.

## FARMING ON THE PLAINS

Mining, railroads, and cattle ranching had created a scattered pattern of settlement on the Great Plains and in the Rockies. Miners gathered in towns that were separated by hundreds of miles. Railroads created towns but only along their rights of way. And ranchers needed only a few cowhands to handle even very large herds. The actual white settlement of the plains had to await the slower migrations of farmers away from the Mississippi and onto the dry grasslands.

## The Homestead Act

The pace and pattern of settlement depended very much on government encouragement. In its youth, the Republican party had been the party of "free soil," which meant both agriculture without slavery and free land for any American. One of the first measures promoted by the Lincoln administration was the Homestead Act of 1862. According to this law, any citizen (or any immigrant who had taken the first step toward becoming a citizen) could claim 160 acres of public land, just by paying a fee of $26–34. If he "lived upon or cultivated" the land for five years, the land became his, free and forever. If the homesteader did not want to wait five years, he could pay for the land at $1.25 an acre and own it after six months.

The Homestead Act resulted in over half a million claims, totaling 80 million acres. But if its purpose was to award most of the public lands of the West to simple farmers, it was a failure. Much more land was given to railroads and states or sold directly to speculators than was ever acquired by small farmers.

Moreover, many of the homestead claims were phony. By law it was possible to transfer ownership at any time to any other person or corporation. So, for example, a rancher could have each of his hands claim a homestead and then (for a small bribe) transfer ownership to the ranch. Any land speculator could do the same, just by paying a bribe to a stranger passing through.

## Other Land Acts

Congress made the situation worse by passing several more laws that promoted corruption and the robbery of public land. First, in 1873, came the Timber Culture Act, which allowed a homesteader (or a rancher or speculator) to claim an additional 160 acres if he would plant trees on 40 of the acres. In 1877, Congress passed the Desert Land Act, which allowed an individual to claim 640 acres of land if he would begin irrigation. Under the law, ranchers took up section after section of land, especially in the Southwest, since they needed it for grazing cattle. They had their friends swear that it was irrigated (even if they

had only poured a bucket of water on it in the presence of their "witnesses").

Even more corruption resulted from the Timber and Stone Act of 1878. This law applied to forest land that could not be farmed but that was highly profitable for timber. Under this law, any citizen or immigrant could purchase up to 160 acres of Western forest for $2.50 an acre. Lumbermen used the same tricks that ranchers and other speculators used. They imported sailors, prospectors, and others to buy land and then sign it over to a company for a small fee. And since one good log sold for about $2.50, every tree but the first from any acre of land was pure profit. Under these laws, over 20 million more acres of potentially valuable public land fell into the hands of corporations and speculators.

## Hardships and Solutions

Despite the fact that many of the profits went to land speculators and big corporations, Western lands were opened to the American people. Though they might have to pay $10 an acre to a speculator instead of getting homestead land virtually free, from the government, farmers moved out onto the plains anyway. The majority came from the states bordering the Mississippi. Most of the rest were immigrants. Almost no workers from Eastern cities made the trip west. But the men and women who did settle on the plains performed a monumental task. In the thirty years after 1870 they brought more land under cultivation than had been cleared and plowed by all the generations of farmers from the settlement of Jamestown to the Civil War.

These farmers confronted problems that they had not met farther east. They found that their old ways of plowing and planting would not work. For one thing, rainfall was scarce, rivers often ran dry, and the water table[3] was low.

---

[3] The water table of an area is the supply of water within the ground.

**WAGONS ROLL WEST**
What whites thought of as the settlement of the plains depended on a great migration of farmers, with their wagons, families, livestock, and tools. Here, a massive wagon "train," guarded by cavalrymen, moves across the rolling country west of the Missouri River. *(National Archives)*

Farmers had to haul water from long distances or collect it in holes when it did rain. New well-digging machinery, invented in the 1880s and 1890s, however, enabled people to dig deeper wells. And steel windmills made it easier to pump the water up. Plains dwellers also developed dry farming. This technique—by which a farmer covers a plowed field with a blanket of dust—conserves the moisture in the soil.

Another problem on the plains was lack of wood. Farmers living there often made their first homes from cakes of sod. For fuel they burned old hay or dried cow dung. Fencing was a special

problem until the invention of barbed wire in the 1870s.

A farm family soon learned that, while 60 acres of land could support them farther east, five times as much was needed on the plains. Plowing, planting, and harvesting extensive acreage were greatly aided by the invention of mechanized farm equipment (see Chapter 26).

Nature seemed to do things on a grand scale on the plains. In summer the wind blew hot, and twice as hard as in the East. In winter blizzards howled down out of the mountains, burying homes and killing livestock. Tornadoes, dust storms, and plagues of locusts and grasshoppers were frequent.

Dry years drove thousands of farmers back east. Many of those who stayed barely survived. In the end, though, farmers turned the plains into the world's most efficient area for producing wheat, corn, and other grains. By 1880, American flour—like American beef and pork from the same area—was being exported in great quantities all over the world.

In all this the Indian was, of course, the great loser. The whites' successes on the plains did seem to prove what white Americans had always believed—that the Indians could not make "proper" use of their environment because they lived too much with it and not enough from it.

The white man was able to exploit even the tough plains environment, to draw from it enough food to feed not only most of the United States but part of the rest of the world, too. The Indian, in contrast, had been willing to settle for the little he needed to maintain his way of life. A full century was to pass before white Americans began to ask themselves seriously whether the Indian's way was not somehow at least as good as theirs. Only one thing was certain: in his "primitive" way the Indian had respected nature more. He had never viewed his world as an object to be owned, changed, and exploited. This, at least in part, was what the battle at Wounded Knee was all about.

# SUGGESTED READINGS, CHAPTERS 23–24

## WOUNDED KNEE

Robert M. Utley, *The Last Days of the Sioux Nation* (1963), is a scholarly, balanced, and readable story of the gradual collapse of Sioux society under white pressure. Stanley Vestal's biography *Sitting Bull* (1957) is useful, as is C. M. Oehler, *The Great Sioux Uprising* (1959). James Mooney was an anthropologist who did extensive field work among Western Indians during the period. He collected his observations and many of the Ghost Dance songs in *The Ghost Dance Religion and the Sioux Uprising of 1890* (republished in 1965).

## THE MINING AND CATTLE FRONTIERS

A great beginning is to read Mark Twain's uproarious but informative *Roughing It* (1872). On the gold-mining areas, a somewhat dated but still usable book is G. C. Quiett, *Paydirt: A Panorama of American Gold Rushes* (1936). A more modern and general discussion of the various mining frontiers is R. W. Paul, *Mining Frontiers of the Far West* (1963). These three books are useful treatments of the cattle frontier: E. E. Dale, *The Range Cattle Industry* (1930); J. B. Frantz and J. E. Choate, *The American Cowboy, Myth and Reality* (1955); and Lewis Atherton, *The Cattle Kings* (1961).

## THE FARMER'S LAST FRONTIER

The most approachable story of the way the public lands of the United States were made available for settlement and exploitation is R. M. Robbins, *Our Landed Heritage* (1942). B. J. Hibbard, *A History of the Public Land Policies* (1924), is an old but still usable treatment. On farming, the most careful general discussion is F. A. Shannon, *The Farmer's Last Frontier* (1945). More readable is Gilbert C. Fite, *The Farmer's Frontier* (1966). J. A. Malin, *The Grasslands Agriculture of North America* (1947), is technical but important. The impact of the railroads can be followed in G. R. Taylor and I. D. Neu, *The American Railroad Network* (1956).

## THE DEFEAT OF THE WESTERN INDIANS

Dee Brown, *Bury My Heart at Wounded Knee* (1955), is a sometimes moving, not always accurate book. Nevertheless, it still is an excellent place for the student to begin reading. F. G. Roe, *The Indian and the Horse* (1955), discusses the intimate and important relationship of the Western Indians to a new animal "tool." The most general and reliable scholarly discussion of the gradual ruin of Native American civilization and culture is R. K. Andrist, *The Long Death: The Last Days of the Plains Indians* (1964).

# 25 · The Hay-market: Strike and Violence in Chicago

My Dear Virginia,

      We have had a week of trial and anxiety on the great subject of disturbances in our main factory—the serious labor troubles we have encountered—a great "strike," and all the resulting derangement of our relations—old and pleasant as they were—with our workmen.

      Trouble has come to hundreds of families in consequence; hatred and fierce passions have been aroused; and an injury has resulted to our good name.

      It began with a few molders and went on, one force operating on another, until 1,200 men went out, part of them by intimidation and part of them led by ignorant and blind passion. It ended by our conceding the terms demanded.

      What a sore heart I have carried these days!

          Your Devoted Mother

This letter was written by a bewildered woman in her early seventies to her daughter. The writer, Nettie Fowler McCormick, was the widow of Cyrus Hall McCormick. An ambitious and ingenious Virginia farm boy, McCormick had made millions of dollars from the invention and manufacture of the reaper, a machine that harvested crops mechanically. He opened his Chicago factory, the McCormick Harvester Works, in the 1840s. It was the largest producer of harvesting machines in the world.

  Nettie McCormick had always paid close attention to the family business. Now, just a year after her husband's death, a stable and profitable enterprise seemed to be falling to pieces before her eyes. At first, she remembered, her husband had known all of the original twenty-three workmen by name. He had worked alongside them in the little Chicago factory. Even when, after a few years, there were about 200 workers producing over 1,000 reapers a year,

**CYRUS HALL Mc-CORMICK**

McCormick invented the first successful reaping machine in 1834. He turned his invention into a booming business in Chicago by using sales techniques like installment credit. *(International Harvester Co. Historical Archives)*

**NETTIE FOWLER Mc-CORMICK**

The wife of the Mc-Cormick Company's founder had trouble grasping the reasons for the discontent of the workers at the plant in the 1880s. *(International Harvester Co. Historical Archives.)*

he could still name those who had been with the company for any length of time.

As the business grew, relations with the workers had become more difficult. During the Civil War, when labor had been scarce and prices had jumped every week, there had been many strikes or threats of strikes. McCormick had been forced to agree to one wage increase after another. But after the war ended, McCormick was able to cut wages in the plant five times in five years.

During the two decades after the Civil War, the McCormick Company had grown rapidly. In 1884, when Cyrus McCormick died, the main factory covered dozens of acres. Its modern machinery, including two huge steam engines that supplied power for the whole factory, covered 12 acres of floor space. On these floors, about 1,300 men put in six 10-hour days a week. They turned 10 million feet of lumber and thousands of tons of iron into about 50,000 reapers a year. And these machines were making possible an agricultural miracle in the United States.

For the McCormicks, the result was money and status. In 1884, the company showed a profit of 71 percent. The family lived in a great mansion staffed with servants. They had invitations to the "best" Chicago homes, counted other wealthy people among their friends, sent their sons to Princeton, traveled luxuriously, and supported carefully selected philanthropies. Nettie Fowler McCormick had ample reason to be concerned about "our good name."

She had some reason to carry a "sore heart," too. The McCormick workers had always seemed contented enough. Nine out of ten of them were Germans, Norwegians, or Swedes, and most lived in the neighborhoods just west of the factory—neighborhoods built by the McCormicks—with Swedish and German street names. All this made the strike of 1885 difficult for Nettie Fowler McCormick to understand. Perhaps her husband's death was part of the problem. But McCormick's was still a family business. Her son, Cyrus McCormick II, had taken over the presidency, and other members of the family had always held important positions in the company. What had happened, then, to the "old and pleasant" relations with the workmen?

The problem had to lie, the McCormicks believed, with some small, misguided minority within the plant. And the most likely candidates for this role were clearly the molders. Ethnically, the molders were a distinct group. Almost all of them were Irish—"fighting Irish," as one plant official called them. And they had a tight, successful craft union, Molders Local No. 233. This union had been making trouble for the McCormicks for twenty years. There were only about ninety molders, but their operation was crucial to the manufacture of reapers. They could bring production to a complete standstill, and they had successfully used the power of this threat several times. Every time old Cyrus McCormick had tried to cut wages, the molders had been the first to resist.

The strike of 1885 had its origins in a decision by the new young president of the company to cut wages again. In December 1884, he had announced a 10 percent pay cut throughout the work force—except for the molders, who were to be cut by 15 percent. At first, there was quiet. Even the molders appeared to accept the reduction. But they were only biding their time until production reached its annual peak in the spring. In March of 1885, the molders demanded that the wage cut be restored to them. When McCormick refused, the molders came out on strike. And, to the McCormicks' alarm, some of the other workers followed them out.

McCormick was anxious to prove himself. To break the strike, he sent telegrams to McCormick salesmen all over the Midwest, asking them to send strikebreaking molders to Chicago. He even had these workers listed on the company payroll as "scabs"—the union term of insult for nonunion workmen who replaced striking members. The newcomers were housed inside the plant in a barracks listed in the company records as "scab house."

But McCormick's efforts to break the strike did not work. The "scabs" could not be trusted. Early in April, these two revealing telegrams were sent from company headquarters to salesmen in Iowa and Illinois:

> To Tom Braden, Agent, Des Moines, Iowa: Out of the lot of men you sent us yesterday, but two of them showed up in Chicago. We find it not safe to ship these critters at our expense unless nailed up in a box car or chained.

> To J. F. Utley, Agent, Sterling, Illinois: The gentleman you sent to us as a molder did not remain over an hour or two until he packed his valise and skipped. We took special pains to get him into the Works by his riding with Mr. McCormick in his buggy. If you are able to do so, try and collect back his Rail Road fare.

Just a week after Cyrus McCormick had sneaked this unreliable scab into the plant, hidden in the president's own buggy, the strike reached a climax. On April 14, with the police scattered all over the city to patrol a local election, strikers attacked McCormick workers outside the plant. McCormick—like many other companies of the period—had hired a small private army of the Pinkerton "detective" agency to maintain peace. A wagon loaded with Pinkerton men and a case of Winchester repeating rifles tried to enter the plant gate. The strikers set upon the wagon and burned it, and the rifles disappeared into the crowd. The captain in charge of the few Chicago police still in the area did nothing. His name—O'Donnell—was as obviously Irish as that of any molder.

The violence confirmed the McCormick family's opinion of the "fighting Irish" molders. If twenty years' experience were not enough, the Pinkerton agents' secret reports confirmed what the family had long suspected: They were the victims of an ethnic conspiracy. Just after the violent episode of April 14, one Pinkerton "detective" submitted this report.

> The assault on the Pinkerton police during the strike of last week was urged by Irishmen, who are employed at McCormick's as molders and helpers. These Irishmen are nearly all members of the Ancient Order of Hibernians [an Irish social fraternity] who have a bitter enmity against the agency.

To the Pinkertons, it seemed clear that the molders were actually supported by their fellow Irishmen on the police force:

It looks somewhat strange that these men at McCormick's could have police protection. On each occasion, the police stood by during the assaults and made no effort to stop the outrage.

Once, during the strike, a group of molders had attacked a group of nonunion workers outside the plant gate. The police, according to Pinkerton reports, had this time not merely stood by but had actually chased and arrested the Pinkerton men who were trying to restrain the molders:

> The police made the utmost speed in calling a patrol wagon, which followed the Pinkerton men and arrested them! The men who made the arrests were treated by the strikers in saloons, and from their talk and insinuations, the police urged the mob to more violence by saying the Pinkerton men were sons of bitches, no better than scabs, there to take the bread out of women and children's mouths.

After the molders' triumphant April 14 attack on the Pinkertons, Cyrus McCormick went looking for help and advice. He appealed first to the mayor, Carter Harrison. But Harrison remembered full well that the McCormicks had consistently opposed him in local politics. He politely advised the young industrialist to give in to the molders' demands. McCormick then turned to what he hoped would be a more sympathetic listener, old Philip Armour, head of a large meat-packing company and a veteran of many labor troubles. But even Armour told McCormick that the molders had won. There seemed to be no choice. McCormick offered to give back to the molders 5 percent out of their original 15 percent pay cut. But they refused this, and he ended by restoring the whole 15 percent.

To both Cyrus McCormick and his mother, their defeat at the hands of a few Irishmen was a painful mystery. But it was a mystery that had to be solved. Cyrus wrote to his mother as he mulled over the problem:

> The whole question of these labor troubles is vast and important and throws more new light on a department of our manufacturing interests which we have not hitherto studied with sufficient depth and understanding.

But to this twenty-five-year-old, who had only two years earlier been taken out of Princeton to run the plant, "depth and understanding" were limited to one fact and one conclusion. The fact was that a handful of disaffected molders could bring the entire McCormick enterprise to a standstill. The conclusion was that such a situation must be avoided in the future by making the skills of the molders unnecessary. He wrote his mother:

> I do not think we will have a similar trouble again because we will take measures to prevent it. I do not think we will be troubled if we take proper steps to weed out the bad element among the men.

McCormick went to work at once to "weed out" the offending Irish molders. He focused his efforts on a daring technological gamble. During the summer of 1885, the summer following the strike, the McCormick Company

**THE REAPER WORKS**

This company picture of the McCormick plant exaggerated the factory's size a little. But it did suggest the strategic location of the city at the junction of railroad, lake, and river transportation. In the nineteenth century, smoke was a symbol of progress and a national blessing—the thicker and blacker, the better. *(International Harvester Co. Historical Archives)*

bought a dozen new pneumatic molding machines. They were supposed to perform mechanically most of the foundry tasks that the skilled molders had always done by hand. The machines were expensive, and they were experimental. No one knew whether they would work. McCormick hoped that they would enable the company to rid itself once and for all of the troublesome molders.

In August, the McCormick foundry was closed for two months so that the machines could be installed. The closing was not unusual, since reapers were manufactured seasonally—much like automobiles are today, with a new model season every fall. August and September were always light months at the harvester works. But when the foundry reopened for fall production, not one molder who had participated in the spring strike was back on the payroll.

McCormick seemed to have won a complete victory. All he had done was spend a vast sum of money on the new machinery. A few months after the machines went into operation, he wrote his mother triumphantly that the machines

> are working even beyond our expectations and everybody is very much pleased with the result. Two men with one of these machines can do an average of about three days work in one. Add to this fact that we have only nine molders in the whole foundry (the rest are all laborers), and you can see what a great gain this will be to us.

But McCormick was being more optimistic than he should have been—probably to reassure his anxious mother. Actually, there were troubles with the machines. In October, the McCormick Company complained to the manufacturer that the castings turned out by the pneumatic molding device were too brittle to use. And in November, Cyrus McCormick was called home from a trip to New York because of a crisis in the foundry. He wrote in his diary for Wednesday, November 11: "Telegram from mother urging come home at once about molding machines—probably failure. Critical situation."

The machines were fixed, but even when they worked they seemed to require an endless amount of labor to keep them functioning. Before the machines were installed, the total wage bill in the foundry was about $3,000 a week. After the machines had been in operation for about six months, foundry wages totaled $8,000 a week. Most of the labor was common, unskilled work. But gradually the company had to hire additional new molders to supervise the work. Economically, the machines were a complete failure.

Still, the new technology had broken the molders union at McCormick. And the union was unhappy. The leader of the molders was a veteran union man named Myles McPadden. He devised a new scheme that was much more dangerous to the McCormicks than the old union, with only ninety members. If there was to be no molders union, then McPadden would simply organize all the other workers in the plant into one union or another. The workers were discontented, so the time was ripe. By February of 1886, he had succeeded in organizing every major group of workers in the plant. The skilled workers—blacksmiths, machinists, and so on—joined the Metalworkers Union. McPadden encouraged the others to join the Knights of Labor, a general, nationwide union. Only 300 of the 1,400 McCormick workers remained nonunion. The lines of a new strike battle were shaping up clearly.

During this time McCormick, too, was busy. After his frustrated attempt to enlist Mayor Harrison's help, McCormick had gone to some lengths to make peace with the powerful political leader of the city. In every election before 1885 the McCormicks had opposed Harrison. After that year they supported him. As a result, Captain O'Donnell, the Irish police official who had been sympathetic to the workers in the spring of 1885, was replaced. The new man in charge of the area where the works were located was Police Inspector John Bonfield.

Bonfield had a reputation as a tough antilabor cop. He had once literally beaten his way through a crowd of strikers, shouting a slogan for which he became famous: "Clubs today spare bullets tomorrow." If there was going to be trouble in 1886, McCormick could count on the police in a way impossible a year before.

In mid-February 1886, a union committee representing all three unions—the Knights of Labor, the Metalworkers, and the Molders—presented McCormick with a series of demands:

> First, that all wages of laboring men be advanced from $1.25 to $1.50 a day. Second, that all vise hands[1] be advanced to $2.00 a day, and that blacksmith helpers be advanced to $1.75. Third, that time the men spend in the water closet [the toilet] not be limited as heretofore. Fourth, that, inasmuch as the molding machines are a failure, the preference should be given the old hands. The scabs in the foundry must be discharged, and a pledge given that no man would be discharged for taking part in a strike.

The company offered to meet some of the demands, but not the fourth, which must have made Cyrus McCormick furious. The unions rejected the offer and called a strike.

Before the strike was scheduled to begin, however, the company announced a complete shutdown of the plant for an indefinite period of time. Union pickets started marching near the plant, but they were kept away by 400 city policemen, now under Bonfield's command. To show its gratitude, the company served free hot meals to the police, with Cyrus McCormick sometimes personally pouring the coffee.

After two weeks the works were reopened, but only to nonunion employees. There was a loyal holdover force of only eighty-two men. The company furnished them with pistols. McCormick hoped they would lead an enthusiastic rush for jobs. But only 161 men showed up the first day. The second day was not much better. Once again the company's agents scoured the region for workers. Gradually, the company's situation improved a little. McCormick was willing to sacrifice almost half a year's production in order to settle the union question once and for all.

For the men on strike the situation was just as important. If they lost, their future at McCormick (or any other manufacturing plant in the city) was dim. As March turned into April, families got hungrier and tempers hotter. The explosion McCormick had avoided the year before by giving in to union demands now looked inevitable.

The situation at McCormick was complicated by the fact that during the spring of 1886 there were strikes all over Chicago. On May 1, all the unions in the city began a general strike for the eight-hour day. This was one of the largest and most heated labor actions in American history. The strike at McCormick merged with the more general agitation, involving thousands of skilled and unskilled workers from plants all over the city.

---

[1] "Vise hands" refers to workers who used a vise, a tool for holding metal being worked. They had a skill and were, therefore, to receive higher wages than the "laboring men," who were unskilled workers.

Then, on May 3, two days into the strike for an eight-hour day, a lumber workers union held a mass meeting to hear an address by August Spies, a radical labor agitator. The meeting took place on Black Road, just a short distance from the McCormick factory. Some McCormick men were at the meeting, even though none was a lumber worker.

The McCormicks had been so desperate for workers that they had already granted the eight-hour day (with ten hours' pay) to their scab workers. So, at 3:30, two hours before the former 5:30 closing, the bell at the plant rang, and the strikebreaking workers streamed out of the plant. The striking union men at the meeting watched the strikebreaking workers leave the plant on their new short schedule.

The sight proved too much. Several hundred men, some of them McCormick strikers and some of them lumber workers, mobbed the scabs leaving the plant, driving them back inside the gate. The strikers began to smash windows, unleashing anger that had been building for months. About 200 policemen, under Inspector Bonfield, were there. Suddenly, they began firing their revolvers into the crowd, forgetting Bonfield's slogan about using clubs to spare bullets. When the noise died away, two workers lay dead and several others had been wounded.

August Spies, who had been addressing the meeting of lumber workers near the McCormick Works, followed the crowd and witnessed the violence that occurred. The next day, in the newspaper office where he worked, he heard that a mass meeting was scheduled at Haymarket Square to protest the shootings at McCormick. A circular announcing the meeting was being printed in both German and English when Spies arrived at the paper.

Spies agreed to address the meeting, but he insisted that the final line in the circular be omitted. About 200 of the circulars had already been printed, but the line was removed from the rest. Few of the 20,000 circulars that were finally distributed on the streets of Chicago contained the threatening reference to arms.

August Spies was not, strictly speaking, a workingman. He might best be described as a radical journalist. At the time of the Chicago troubles he was thirty years old and the editor of the *Arbeiter-Zeitung,* a German-language newspaper with a radical viewpoint. He was also the business manager of an organization called the Socialistic Publishing Society, a propaganda organization of a small political party known as the Socialist Labor Party.

From time to time Spies had been in trouble with the police. Only a year before, during the McCormick strike of 1885, he had angered the police by intervening in the case of a poor German servant girl. She had been arrested by the police and held in jail for several days. When Spies and the girl's mother went to the jail, they discovered that the girl had been molested repeatedly. Rather than keep quiet, Spies swore out a warrant for the police sergeant in charge of the jail. He lost the case for lack of evidence, but he became well known to the Chicago police.

Spies was, in short, a politically active radical who did not hesitate to

## Attention Workingmen !

### GREAT

# MASS-MEETING

## TO-NIGHT, at 7.30 o'clock,

### AT THE

## HAYMARKET, Randolph St., Bet. Desplaines and Halsted.

**Good Speakers will be present to denounce the latest atrocious act of the police, the shooting of our fellow-workmen yesterday afternoon.**

## Workingmen Arm Yourselves and Appear in Full Force!

### THE EXECUTIVE COMMITTEE.

THE CALL TO THE HAY-MARKET

This poster was prepared to call a meeting to protest the shooting at the McCormick factory. August Spies insisted that the final line, calling on the workers to come to the square armed, be omitted before the poster was circulated.

condemn people in positions of authority. He was also a committed socialist politician. Furthermore, he hoped that the rally at Haymarket would attract enough people to fill the square, which could hold about 20,000.

Spies reached Haymarket Square late, at about 8:30 on the night of May 4. He must have felt disappointed. No meeting was in progress, and there were only about a thousand people scattered around the square. The other main speaker, a socialist named Albert R. Parsons, was nowhere in sight. Spies climbed on a wagon, sent someone to look for Parsons, and began his talk. He was a good speaker, and soon the small crowd became enthusiastic:

> The fight is going on. Now is the chance to strike for the oppressed classes. The oppressors want us to be content. They will kill us. The day is not far distant when we will resort to hanging these men. [Applause, and shouts of "Hang them now" came from the crowd.] McCormick is the man who created the row on Monday, and he must be held responsible for the murder of our brothers! [More shouts of "Hang him!"]

Spies went on in the same vein for about an hour, trying to rouse his working-class audience to anger and a sense of solidarity against their "oppressors." Then someone announced that Albert R. Parsons had been found. Spies turned over his wagon rostrum to the second speaker.

The crowd had been waiting for Parsons, for he had a reputation as a spellbinder. Unlike Spies and many other Chicago socialists, he was a native American. Born in Alabama in 1848, Parsons came from a family whose ancestry went back to 1632 in New England. He was a self-trained printer in Texas before the Civil War. During the war he fought for the Confederacy in a Texas artillery company. After the war Parsons became converted to socialism and moved to Chicago, the center of working-class politics in the United States.

Like Spies, Parsons was not a worker at all but a political journalist. He edited a radical workingmen's paper called *The Alarm*. The Haymarket rally was just one more in a long series of political speeches for him. His speech was much like that of Spies but slightly stronger in tone:

> I am not here for the purpose of inciting anybody, but to speak out, to tell the facts as they exist, even though it shall cost me my life before morning. It behooves you, as you love your wife and children—if you don't want to see them perish with hunger, killed or cut down like dogs in the street—Americans, in the interest of your liberty and independence, to *arm*, to *arm* yourselves!

### THE HAYMARKET TRAGEDY

Newspapers and magazines had a field day with events in the Haymarket. This engraving was published with the title "Anarchist Riot." It shows the workers and their leaders as a wild-eyed mob, firing into the police ranks. And it pictures the police advance as resolute and orderly, which was not the case. *(Library of Congress)*

Here again there was applause from the crowd and shouts of "We'll do it! We're ready!"

What Parsons and Spies did not know was that the crowd was full of police detectives. Every few minutes one or another ran back to a nearby station house to report what the speakers were saying. Waiting in the station were almost 200 policemen, fully armed, and under the command of none other than John Bonfield.

Parsons and Spies probably did not notice Mayor Carter Harrison in the crowd, either. Only the mayor's presence had kept Bonfield from breaking up the meeting. As Parsons finished, the mayor left; it was obvious to him that everything was peaceful. It was almost ten o'clock and rain was in the air. Most of the crowd, too, began to drift off as the third speaker, Samuel Fielden, began to talk.

Suddenly, 180 policemen (a group almost as large as the crowd itself) marched into the square and up to the wagon where Fielden was speaking. One of the captains turned to the crowd and said: "In the name of the people of the State of Illinois, I command this meeting immediately and peaceably to disperse." After a moment the police captain repeated his order. The crowd was already starting to melt away (it was almost 10:30 by now). Fielden had stopped speaking and was climbing down from the wagon platform. "We are peaceable," Fielden said to Bonfield.

At that moment, without any warning, a dynamite bomb was thrown (it is not known from where or by whom) at the police. The fuse burned for a second or two after the bomb struck the ground. Then it went off with a deafening roar. Screams split the air as people ran in all directions. A number of policemen lay on the ground, one dead and the others wounded. Quickly, the police re-formed their ranks, and some of them began to fire into the crowd. Other policemen waded into the confusion swinging their clubs. The uproar lasted only a minute or two. Then suddenly the square was empty.

In addition to the dead policeman there were seventy-three wounded, six of whom died later. Four civilians were killed, and the official reports listed twelve as wounded. The twelve were those who had been too badly hurt to leave the square. Probably several times as many limped or struggled home and never became official statistics.

**THE HAYMARKET TRAGEDY: ANOTHER VIEW**

This representation of what happened in Chicago in 1886 is probably more accurate than the one on page 526. It shows workers fleeing, none firing at the police. And it shows the bomb killing both workers and the policemen who were beating them with nightsticks. *(Culver Pictures)*

Like most riots, the Haymarket affair had been short. And, considering what could have happened, very few people were hurt. But the incident occurred on the heels of trouble at the McCormick plant, in the midst of the strike for an eight-hour day, with 80,000 Chicago workingmen off the job. Thus the Haymarket bomb touched off a near panic in the city and much of the rest of the nation. Thousands of respectable citizens convinced themselves that a dangerous conspiracy of anarchists, socialists, and communists was at work to overthrow the government and carry out a bloody revolution. One of the leading business magazines of the day, *Bradstreets'*, spoke for thousands of Americans when it said of the Haymarket incident:

> This week's happenings at Chicago go to show that the threats of the anarchists against the existing order are not idle. In a time of disturbance, desperate men have a power for evil out of proportion to their numbers. They are desperate fanatics who are opposed to all laws. There is no room for anarchy in the political system of the United States.

Also important was the fact that many people had been frightened and angered by a recent flood of immigration from Europe to America—and many of the "anarchists" were also foreigners. Not only in Chicago but all over the nation, newspaper editorialists and public speakers demanded the immediate arrest and conviction of the alien radicals who had conspired to murder honest policemen and subvert law and order. The result was a swift and efficient series of illegal raids by the Chicago police. They searched property without warrants. They imprisoned people without charging them and threatened potential witnesses. All in all, the authorities arrested and questioned about 200 "suspects"—probably none of whom had anything at all to do with the bombing.

In this heated atmosphere, fueled by journalists who whipped up unreasonable fears of an anarchist conspiracy, a jury met to determine if indictments could be brought against anyone for the violence. It decided that although the specific person who threw the bomb could not be determined, anyone who urged violence was a "conspirator" and as guilty of murder as the bomb thrower. On the basis of this decision, another jury met and indicted thirty-one persons on counts of murder. Of the thirty-one, eight were eventually tried, all of them political radicals. Most had not even been present at the Haymarket bombing.

The effect of the Haymarket Affair had now become clear. What had begun weeks before as an ordinary strike at the McCormick Works had been transformed into a crusade against political radicalism, most of which was said to be foreign in origin. Only Parsons and Samuel Fielden were not German or of German descent. The names of the other six would have been as natural in Berlin or Hamburg as in Chicago: August Spies, Michael Schwab, Adolph Fischer, George Engel, Louis Lingg, and Oscar Neebe.

In one way or another, all the defendants had some connection with the labor movement and with political agitation for revolution. Several of them were anarchists, though their ideas about anarchism as a philosophy were vague. They might as well have called themselves socialists, as several of them did at one time or another. In general, they were intellectuals. Their jobs were connected with radical journalism in either the English- or German-language press. They did not all know one another, but by the time their trial was over, most of them were probably "comrades," a word they used more and more in the months ahead.

On the other side of the battle were all the forces of law, order, and authority. True, some agreed with Mayor Harrison that the Haymarket meeting had been peaceful, that the whole idea of a conspiracy was a false and legally incorrect notion. But most of Chicago society (including even many elements of the labor movement) favored a quick conviction and the hanging of all eight defendants. The judge who tried the case, the prosecuting attorney, most business leaders, almost all the local clergymen—almost everyone who had anything to say in Chicago—were convinced even before the trial began that the defendants were guilty. Moreover, most of Chicago's leading citizens, and their counterparts in the rest of the country, agreed that the trial was a struggle to the death between American republicanism and foreign anarchism. The entire established order of American society, with very few exceptions, was determined to make an example of the "conspirators."

The Haymarket trial began on June 21, 1886. The first three weeks of the seven-week trial were spent selecting a jury. Under Illinois law, the defense had the right to reject a total of 160 jurors on peremptory challenges—that is, without having to discuss a juror's qualifications and abide by the judge's decision. As one prospective juror after another was called, it became clear that most of them were extremely prejudiced against the defendants. The defense attorneys quickly used up their 160 challenges. They then had to show cause for turning down a juror and depend on the judge, Joseph Gary, to rule fairly. Again and again, plainly biased jurors were accepted by the judge—whose own prejudice against the defendants became apparent as the process went on. The result was a jury composed of twelve citizens who obviously wished to hang the defendants.

In his opening statement, prosecuting attorney Julius Grinnell set the tone of the entire trial:

> Gentlemen, for the first time in the history of our country people are on trial for endeavoring to make anarchy the rule. I hope that while the youngest of us lives this will be the last and only time when such a trial shall take place. In the light of the 4th of May, we now know that the preachings of anarchy by these defendants, hourly and daily for years, have been sapping our institutions. Where they have cried murder, bloodshed, anarchy, and dynamite, they have meant what they said. The firing on Fort Sumter was a terrible thing to our country, but it was open warfare. I think it was nothing compared with this insidious, infamous plot to ruin our laws and our country.

It was obvious that this would not be an ordinary murder trial. The defendants would be judged by their words and beliefs. A ninth "conspirator," Rudolph Schnaubelt, had fled. The prosecution would try to prove that he had thrown the bomb. The next step would be to convict the other eight of conspiracy, which would carry the same penalty as murder itself. And they would be convicted by the fact that they had made speeches and written newspaper articles urging violent revolution. Day after day the prosecution offered evidence about the defendants' beliefs, their writings, and even pamphlets they had supposedly helped to sell.

The prosecution had weak cases against the individual defendants. They were able to prove that one of the defendants, Lingg, had actually made bombs. But Lingg was a stranger to most of the others, and he had not even been at Haymarket Square. Parsons, Spies, Fischer, and Schwab had left the square before the bomb was thrown. George Engel proved that he had been home drinking a glass of beer with his wife. In the end the prosecution's case rested on a theory of "general conspiracy to promote violence." No evidence of a single violent act was brought into court that could withstand even the mildest cross-examination by the frustrated defense attorneys.

After four weeks of testimony the jury retired. The jury members had been instructed by Judge Gary in such a way as to make conviction almost inevitable, and they needed only three hours to discuss the matter. After this short deliberation the jury filed solemnly back into the courtroom. It was ten o'clock, August 19, 1886, when the foreman read the verdict.

> We the jury find the defendants Spies, Schwab, Fielden, Parsons, Fischer, Engel, and Lingg guilty of murder in the manner and form as charged, and fix the penalty at death. We find Oscar Neebe[2] guilty of murder in the manner and form as charged, and fix the penalty at imprisonment in the penitentiary for fifteen years.

Years later Judge Gary recalled that "the verdict was received by the friends of social order with a roar of almost universal approval."

Before they were sentenced, each of the defendants made a speech to the court. Spies spoke for all of them when he said, in a German accent that he had never lost:

> There was not a syllable said about anarchism at the Haymarket meeting. But "anarchism is on trial," foams Mr. Grinnell. If that is the case, your honor, very well; you may sentence me, for I am an anarchist. I believe that the state of classes—the state where one class dominates and lives upon the labor of another class—is doomed to die, to make room for a free society, voluntary association, or universal brotherhood, if you like. You may pronounce the sentence upon me, honorable judge, but let the world know that in A.D. 1886, in the state of Illinois, eight men were sentenced to death because they believed in a better future.

There were appeals, of course, first to state courts and then to the Supreme Court of the United States. One by one the appeals failed. Then there were pleas to the governor of Illinois for mercy, and the sentences of Fielden and Schwab were commuted to life. Lingg, the bomb maker, who was probably half mad, committed suicide in jail—using dynamite set off by a fuse that he lit with his jail-cell candle. The other four condemned men—Engel, Spies,

---

[2] Oscar Neebe was the youngest defendant; almost no evidence had been presented against him. Most of the jury's three-hour deliberation was devoted to this case.

**"THE VOICES YOU STRANGLE TODAY"**

On November 11, 1886, three months after one of the most unfair verdicts in American history, Albert Parsons, August Spies, George Engel, and Adolph Fischer were hanged by the state of Illinois. Victorian refinement required that the victims be put into robes to hide two things: that they were tightly tied up and that most people who are hanged lose muscular control and soil their clothing.

Parsons, and Fischer—were hanged on November 11. As the four stood on the scaffold, ropes around their necks and hoods over their heads, Spies broke the deep silence by shouting: "There will come a time when our silence will be more powerful than the voices you strangle today!"

At the McCormick Works the situation had returned to normal months earlier. On May 7, 1886, three days after the Haymarket bombing, Cyrus McCormick was able to write in his diary: "A good force of men at the works today, and things are resuming their former appearance." Three days later, taking full advantage of the public outrage over the "devilish plot," as McCormick called it, at Haymarket Square, the McCormick Works quietly resumed the ten-hour day. On Monday, May 10, McCormick wrote: "Things going smoothly. We returned to 5:30 closing hour today, instead of 3:30."

# The
# Industrial
# Revolution

This chapter examines the creation of a new social and economic system in the United States: the industrial order. In some sense, industry is as old as human society. People have always made things—tools, weapons, clothing, and so on. But beginning in the eighteenth century, their ability to make goods began to increase rapidly. The so-called industrial revolution that resulted originated in England and spread quickly to the rest of Western Europe and to the United States. By the time of the Civil War, this revolution was well under way in North America, fed by inventions like the steam engine, the cotton gin, and the reaper. After the war, industrialization altered the basic patterns of life in the United States even more drastically.

Everything had to be changed, since every element of this new system had to hang together. Raw materials, like coal and iron for making steel, had to be found and developed. Cheap transportation, like railroads, had to be available to bring these materials to factories and to take finished products from them. Workers had to be hired to operate the factories. And agriculture had to be improved so that fewer and fewer people would be needed to grow more and more food. More and more machines were needed to provide a livelihood for more and more factory workers, who would in turn make still more machines. Nothing could happen at all unless everything else happened—and in the proper order. Every factory functioned as part of a chain of invention, materials, transportation, and workers.

The McCormick Harvester Company, for example, was only part of a complicated series of events and machines. The reapers made at the McCormick Works enabled farmers on the Great Plains to produce unheard-of quantities of grain. Some of this grain was milled into flour for bread eaten by people like McCormick's molders. Other farm products fed cattle, which were slaughtered in big cities at factories owned by men like Philip Armour.

The new transcontinental railroads were necessary to take the reapers west and bring the flour and beef east. Since there were not enough workers to lay the new rails, Irish and Chinese were encouraged to immigrate. The McCormick plant, too, was tended by more than a thousand immigrants. And it was German immigrants who were the main victims of the Haymarket riot. The city of Chicago itself was a new kind of city, built around railroads and factories, in a way that no other American city had ever been built—a great barracks for the workmen at dozens of factories like the McCormick Works.

In building the industrial system, the United States was transformed. It had once been a nation in which nine out of every ten people lived on farms or in rural communities. By the end of the nineteenth century, it was the world's most productive industrial nation, and one of the most urban. The landscape had been remade. The people had been changed, too. There had always been immigrants to the United States. But new industries attracted different types of immigrants in greater numbers. In the end, the daily lives and even the language of Americans were changed. New words like "telephone," "subway," "scab," and "millionaire" became common speech. They signaled just how deep and complete the change had been.

## TECHNOLOGICAL CHANGE

Few of the men and women who made or watched the industrial revolution understood its complexity. Most of them probably regarded it as a product of technological change—the invention of new types of machines or the improvement of existing ones. Certainly one of the most obvious changes of the nineteenth century was that many things that had once been done slowly by hand were now being done rapidly by machine.

# An Agricultural Revolution

Agriculture was a prime example of the replacement of hand labor by machine power. The most striking introduction of new agricultural technology took place on the Great Plains. On these flat and treeless expanses, plowing, planting, and harvesting could be done on a scale that would have stunned colonial settlers and even most plantation owners of the Old South. But what happened on the plains was just an extreme version of what went on in all areas of American agriculture: the industrialization of the farm.

At first, the new machinery was fairly simple. McCormick's earliest reapers, built before the Civil War, were small. They were drawn by one horse and worked by one or two men. Another invention—a steel plow that could cut deeper and faster than the old iron plow—was a further small step. But gradually the new technology gained force and speed. Reapers were soon equipped with automatic binders that could fasten grain into bunches mechanically. The single steel plow was soon modified into a multiple, or gang, plow that could cut several furrows at one time.

Soon other new machines appeared. One could plow and plant at the same time. Another, the combine, added to the reaper a mechanical thresher, which could separate grain from stalks. A combine could move quickly through a wheat field, gathering wheat, separating the grain, and leaving behind only waste to be plowed under in the spring. The machine accomplished its work without a single human hand touching the earth, the wheat plants, or the finished grain.

During most of the nineteenth century, new

AN AGRICULTURAL VISTA

Even without steam engines or gasoline motors, giant commercial farms were able to harvest wheat fields with industrial efficiency. These machines, sometimes drawn by as many as thirty mules, cut and threshed the wheat, hauling the grain away and leaving a field of stubble at day's end. Here, each machine is tended by only two men, plus a third to drive the mules. (*The National Archives*)

machinery was still driven primarily by animals. Some steam engines were used, but the final mechanization of farms had to await the gasoline-driven tractor in the twentieth century. Still, even before the tractor, the life of the American farmer had been fundamentally altered by technology. Farming gradually came to resemble the running of factories, in which a product for sale was processed and made ready by machinery. Sooner or later, almost every step in all but a few kinds of agriculture was mechanized.

The result of the mechanical changes in agriculture was to double and redouble the volume and pace of food production. In 1840, it took more than three hours of human work time to produce a bushel of wheat. By the 1890s, the time had been cut to ten minutes. In 1840, a bushel of corn required almost five hours of labor, from planting to final processing. By the 1890s, the time had been cut to forty minutes.

Hand in hand with the reduction of hours was a marked decrease in the number of farmers needed to produce food. Mechanization made it possible for a tiny minority of Americans to feed all the rest. Those who left farms were then free to work for the railroads and in oil fields, iron mines, factories, and offices—hurrying the process of industrialization along.

The area of land under cultivation doubled between the Civil War and 1900. And the new lands were usually well adapted to the use of machinery. The net result of the agricultural revolution was an enormous abundance of food.

## Improving Rail Transport

The agricultural revolution depended not only on new technology on the farms but also on new methods of carrying food from the farms to the cities—that is, railroads. It was railroads that brought Wyoming beef, Kansas wheat, and Louisiana rice to the table of a McCormick molder. Without the new railroad network built after the Civil War, the mechanization of agriculture would have been meaningless.

Railroads, like farms, benefited from new technological developments. The principle of the steam engine remained the same. But almost every other mechanical aspect of railroading changed drastically during the generation after Appomattox.

The old railroads had used iron rails, small and dangerous wood-burning engines, and tiny, rickety coaches and freight cars. The new lines used steel rails that would last for many years without cracking or rusting. Steel rails could support almost twenty times as much weight as iron, so larger engines and cars could be used. Freight cars increased in weight from 10 tons to over 100 tons. The typical pre–Civil War engine had weighed about 20 tons. By 1900, some locomotives weighed as much as 300 tons. The coal-burning locomotive became a giant source of power that could pull huge freights over the most difficult grades efficiently and safely.

Railroad mileage increased dramatically. In 1870—even after the completion of the first transcontinental line—there were only about 40,000 miles of track in the United States. By 1900, there were almost 200,000 miles. This total was greater than the entire railroad mileage of Europe, including Russia. Other inventions like the telegraph and the electric signal made it possible to control complicated traffic patterns and freight yards.

The trains and tracks of 1900 were as dramatically different from those of 1850 as today's jet plane is from the wobbly aircraft of the 1920s. Railroads were the new giants of the landscape, transforming the process of moving food, objects, and people from one place to another.

## MANUFACTURING

Taken by themselves, the technological changes in agriculture and the railroads would have meant little. They were important only in their relation to other parts of the new industrial system. In this system, manufacturing was the crucial center.

By 1900—a little more than a century after

AN INDUSTRIAL VISTA

For millions of Americans, industrial growth was not a miracle but a misery. The steelworkers who lived in these crowded houses and walked along these dirt streets to the Pittsburgh mills often worked twelve hours a day, seven days a week. *(International Museum of Photography at George Eastman House)*

George Washington had taken the presidential oath—the United States was the leading manufacturing nation in the world. Many factors made this possible. Americans found new beds of coal. They discovered iron ore in Michigan and Minnesota. They opened oil fields in Pennsylvania, the Ohio Valley, and the southern Great Plains. These raw materials and new energy sources fed the new factories of Pittsburgh, Chicago, and dozens of other cities. Mechanized agriculture made it possible for millions of people to move to cities to work in industrial plants. A high tariff kept down competition from foreign manufactured goods. Most important of all were the new machines and processes that enabled Americans to produce so much so quickly.

## The Steel Industry

Steel was very close to the heart of the new economy. It is stronger than iron, more resistant to rust, and easier to shape or mold. People had been making small quantities of steel for centuries, but the process was slow and difficult, since it depended on hand labor. In the 1850s an Englishman, Henry Bessemer, invented a converter that could turn iron into steel by blowing a blast of hot air through the molten iron. The process was spectacular to watch, sending a brilliant shaft of sparks and smoke skyward. The economic results were just as startling. For the first time it became possible to produce steel cheaply and in massive quantities.

The combination of the Bessemer converter, the demand for steel from the railroads and other industries, and the discovery of additional sources of iron ore and coal created a new industry. In 1870, the United States produced only about 77,000 tons of steel. By 1900, production had increased to over 10 million tons a year—an increase of more than 1,300 percent. Pittsburgh became the first (and is still the largest) of the steel towns. But eventually cities like Birmingham, Alabama, and Gary, Indiana—built almost entirely around the steel industry—sprang up in what had until then been open countryside.

## Other Industries

What happened in steel was repeated in dozens of other industries. The sewing machine and other inventions made it possible to manufacture shoes and clothing on a mass scale. Steam-powered mills using steel equipment could cut lumber, or grind wheat, or print newspapers with a speed and efficiency no one had dreamed of earlier.

Another new industry grew up based on electricity. The foremost American in this field was the versatile Thomas A. Edison. Throughout the late nineteenth century, a stream of inventions poured from his laboratories: the phonograph, the first practical electric light bulb, the storage battery, the dynamo, the electric voting machine, and the motion picture camera.

An industry also developed rapidly around the discovery of oil and new ways of refining it. Oil yielded kerosene for lamps and stoves. Heavier oils lubricated the motors of the new technology. Beginning around 1900, it became important as a source of gasoline for the internal combustion engine (see Chapter 36). This vast new industry simply had not existed in 1800.

A revolution in communications began in 1876, on the hundredth anniversary of the Declaration of Independence. In that year a young inventor named Alexander Graham Bell exhibited the first working model of the telephone. At first, the telephone was purchased only by individuals who wanted to communicate between two specific locations, like a house and a factory or office. But soon there were enough phones in use to create the first telephone exchange. It was opened at New Haven, Connecticut, in 1878. Other cities and towns followed suit.

Soon cities began to link up with one another. The first intercity telephone line joined New York and Boston in 1884. New York and Chicago were connected in 1892. By 1915, when a line opened between New York and San Francisco, it was possible to place calls between any two cities in the nation.

The magnitude of what was happening to the United States can be measured only in statistics. In 1869, the value of American manufactured

ALEXANDER GRAHAM BELL

Bell was probably the most inventive man of his age. Here, he is demonstrating his telephone for an attentive, if somewhat grim, audience. The other striking nineteenth-century invention involved in this photograph is the camera. *(Culver Pictures)*

goods was about $1.5 billion. By the end of the century, the figure was more than $4.5 billion. In 1869, about 2 million workers ran American shops, mills, and factories, and the market value of the average person's yearly work was about $940. By 1900, when almost 5 million men and women worked in industry, the market value of their average yearly product had almost doubled, to nearly $1,800.

By the 1890s, the United States had more steel, more rails, more electric trolleys, more telephones, and more electric lights than any other nation in the world. To accomplish all this, Americans mined more metal, cut more lumber, dug more iron ore, and pumped more oil than any other country.

# THE GROWTH OF "BIG BUSINESS"

Technology and manufacturing were crucial in making the United States an industrial nation. But new methods of organizing industry and business were also vital.

## The Factory System

At the beginning of the Civil War, most Americans who worked in industry were employed in small mills or shops—a tailor shop, for example, or a blacksmith's or harnessmaker's. In 1870, when the revolution in industry was already under way, the average industrial plant still had only eight employees. A median plant (one halfway between the largest and the smallest) had thirty workers. By 1914, the average plant had twenty-eight workers, and the median 270. In 1870, no factory in American employed over 1,000 workers. By 1914, several had over 10,000 workers.

What was occurring, in other words, was a change that went beyond the technology of production. The change was nothing less than a parallel revolution. The factory was replacing the traditional small shop.

In a traditional shop (or in the home manufacture of items like cloth or soap), work centers on the person. Power is supplied mainly through human toil. The same worker is involved in all stages of production, from spinning thread, for example, to weaving the final cloth.

The idea behind a factory (first introduced into England in the late eighteenth century) is very different. Work in a factory centers on a machine. Power is mechanical, not human. Parts are nearly identical, and so they are interchangeable. Most important is the division of labor. Each worker specializes, performing only one step in a chain. He or she may never touch or see the raw material. He or she may never see or handle the final product. The result is mass production—manufacturing large numbers of articles in standard shapes and sizes.

Factories are inevitably larger than shops. They cost more money to build and equip with machinery. And more capital is needed in order to enter and compete in almost any line of business. As the factory system grew, then, so did the size of companies.

## Changes in Organization

Growth in turn demanded changes in the organization of business. Mass production required a sizable investment. This made it difficult for family firms to be truly competitive. So, large corporations gradually replaced companies owned by one family or a few partners.

The corporation is an old idea. The Virginia Company and the Massachusetts Bay Company were both seventeenth-century corporations. The idea is as simple as it is old. If many people invest in an enterprise by buying "stock" in it, the company can grow much larger than if it is funded by only a few individuals. If the company fails, each investor has lost only the value of his stock. He cannot be held personally responsible for any of the corporation's debts.

Just as there had been a few American factories before the Civil War, so had there been cor-

# ECONOMICS AND HISTORY

## The Haymarket: Fixed and Variable Costs

The two Cyrus McCormicks, father and son, confronted two different economic realities. For the older man, living in the early period of industrialization, profit depended very much on the costs of labor and material. His capital investment—the money he spent on land, buildings, and a few simple machines—could be relatively low. The main expense was the hand labor and the wood and iron that went into each reaper he manufactured. He would make money or lose mon⁄y according to a simple formula. The total cost of his land, buildings, and machinery (his fixed costs) plus the cost of labor and material (his variable costs) had to be added and put on one side of the ledger. Then, on the other side, he could put the total number of reapers sold, multiplied by their average price. This was income. Subtract fixed and variable costs from income, and what remained was profit.

His son used exactly the same simple formula. But something had changed drastically. For the son, the way to profit most was to increase the investment in expensive buildings and machinery—that is, to increase capital investment. If he installed a great steam engine to mechanize the factory, he could turn out many more reapers with the same number of workers, thus lowering his labor costs for each reaper manufactured. His "pneumatic molding machines" were just such a capital investment, whose long-term purpose was to reduce the cost of labor.

Cyrus senior ran a company that was relatively labor-intensive, compared to his son's more capital-intensive operations. And the experience of the two men in the market economy could become very different as a result of the differences in their patterns of costs. The capital-intensive nature of the son's operations made his possibilities of profit much greater than his father's. But he also had to face much more severe losses in times of depression.

Let us suppose that Cyrus senior spent $50,000 every year in capital costs, and that his son spent four times as much, $200,000. The father might have had to spend, say, $800 in labor costs for each reaper he produced. But the son, with his more elaborate factory and machines, might be able to reduce labor costs to $200 per reaper. Suppose, for the sake of the example, that the price of reapers remained constant at $1,000. Under these conditions, the two men, father and son, would break even at the same point—if each sold exactly 250 reapers in a year. Cyrus senior would have spent his $50,000 in fixed costs plus the labor cost of $800 per machine for 250 reapers, $200,000. His total costs would add up to $250,000. He would have made back that $250,000 by selling 250 reapers at $1,000 each. The son also would have laid out $250,000: $200,000 in capital costs plus $50,000 in labor costs ($200 each for 250

porations. But their number increased greatly after the war. The corporation became the standard way of organizing business, just as the factory became the characteristic method of organizing production.

Mass production required not only corporate investment. It also demanded that each firm market its product efficiently on a broad regional or national scale, instead of selling just locally. To remain in business, a corporation had to create

reapers). Thus his total costs would exactly equal his father's, and each would have broken even in the market.

But—and here was the apparent miracle of industrial capitalism—suppose the market expanded and could now absorb 1,000 reapers. Cyrus senior could meet the demand in only one way: By hiring more workers to do the hand labor needed to produce 1,000 reapers, he would have to increase his labor costs to a total of $800,000. But if he could hold his capital costs at $50,000, he could have an income of $1,000,000 (1,000 reapers sold at $1,000 each), and his costs would still total only $850,000. He would have made a relatively handsome profit of $150,000.

But what of Cyrus junior under the same market conditions? What is the effect, now, of his great steam engines and his pneumatic molding devices? His labor costs for 1,000 reapers, at $250 for each reaper, will total $250,000. His fixed costs are $200,000. His total costs, then, are $450,000. But his sales have generated $1,000,000. So his profit is a whopping $550,000—almost four times what his father could have made by selling the same number of reapers.

On the other hand, though, Cyrus junior faces the possibility of more staggering losses. What if the market collapses or a competitor takes sales away, and only 100 reapers can be sold in a year? The father's arithmetic would go like this: fixed costs, $50,000; labor costs, $80,000; total costs, $130,000. Income: 100 × $1,000: $100,000. Total loss: $30,000. The son's figures would look like this: fixed costs, $200,000; labor costs, $20,000; total costs: $220,000. Income: $100,000. Total loss: a staggering $120,000.

The more capital-intensive industry became in the late nineteenth century, the greater were the opportunities for profit—as long as the market continued to expand and production could be regular and rapid. But trouble in the market, either from competition or from a general economic slowdown, spelled heavier losses than an older, labor-intensive, system would have experienced.

Of course, increased possibilities for profit and loss were not the only consequences of the increasingly heavy capital investment in American industry. As production became more heavily mechanized and rates of production rose, it also became possible to lower prices. With lower prices, a firm like McCormick might hope to generate more sales demand for its reapers, or to drive competitors out of the market. But this pressure on prices could have the effect of convincing several firms that competition was disastrous and that getting together to control prices was the answer. In this way, firms that were capital-intensive were under very strong pressure to join trusts, pools, or some other form of monopoly.

On the other hand, heavy capital investment could put extreme pressure on wage rates. In hard times, when sales fell, expensive machinery like the pneumatic molding machines just sat there, eating up money. It could be better to run them, even at a partial loss, just to pay part of the fixed costs. This meant the company had to try to get workers to accept the lowest possible wages so that as much income from sales as possible could be used to handle the fixed costs of business. This, obviously, was the general strategy the McCormicks pursued during the months leading up to the strike and the Haymarket bombing.

effective distributing and selling divisions. It also had to buy raw materials on a large scale. Ideally, in fact, it would purchase its own source of materials—for example, a forest for a paper company, or an iron mine for a steel mill.

In other words, mass production made it profitable for a company to invest in all the stages of its industry, from original materials to final sales. Economists call this phenomenon vertical integration. It involves a firm not only in manufacturing but in all the other stages and phases relating to the business. An oil company that owns wells, pipelines, and refineries, and has its own sales force, is fully integrated. It is freed from dependence on any other economic unit—except, of course, customers.

## Competition and Consolidation

The new industrial order brought a new kind of competition into the American economy. Before the era of mass production, small shops and mills had catered to limited territories. They competed only where one territory bordered on another. But large corporations needed large markets to absorb their massive outputs. Thus a number of companies might find themselves competing for the same customers.

To win a big market, a corporation might advertise heavily. It might hire high-pressure salesmen and reward them with big commissions. But the most obvious way to win a market was to cut prices. A large company with efficient factories and lower production costs could force competitors into bankruptcy simply by lowering prices beyond the point where the smaller firms could stay in business.

In one industry after another, a few corporations gradually emerged as the leading firms. Each was too large, efficient, and powerful to be driven out of business by the others. Each was too small to be able to control the whole market. When this happened—and it happened sooner or later in most industries—the firm usually entered a period of intense competition. But most American businesses did not welcome such competition and tried to find ways to avoid it.

Railroads led the way. Railroad owners had witnessed the havoc and ruin that could be created when one railroad waged a price war with another. By a process of trial and error, the railroads worked out private agreements among themselves to control freight rates. Railroads also developed a system of grouping their customers in "pools," with each line "entitled" to a certain

share of the total market. Gradually, too, the railroads had become consolidated into a few major lines, each one absorbing dozens of smaller companies. The Pennsylvania and New York Central railroads dominated the Northeast. The Southern Railway controlled much of the South. The Louisville and Nashville line was supreme in the Ohio Valley.

The agreements and consolidations of the railroads became the models for other businesses. Other industries soon copied what railroad leaders had learned and used the economic devices they had developed. Consolidation became the order of the day.

No matter what industry was involved, the process was the same. First, a few large, competing firms would emerge. A period of intense and costly competition would follow. Then firms would consolidate as a way of avoiding competition. During its period of rapid growth, the McCormick Harvester Company was competing with a handful of other large manufacturers of agricultural machinery. In the years after the Haymarket affair, however, the McCormicks began to realize that competition was wasteful and unnecessary. Early in the twentieth century, McCormick merged with its competition to form the huge International Harvester Company, which since then has produced practically all the harvesting machinery manufactured in the United States.

A similar development occurred in the steel industry, which was dominated for almost half a century by a Scottish immigrant, Andrew Carnegie. Carnegie was a classic example of the rags-to-riches success story. At thirteen he came to America with his family and immediately went to work. At eighteen he was a telegraph clerk for the Pennsylvania Railroad. During the quick railroad expansion of the Civil War years, Carnegie realized that iron and steel for rails and bridges were the key to the railroads' future, and that railroads, in turn, were the key to an expanding economy. He saved every cent and invested daringly but successfully. By 1872, he was able to build his own steel plant near Pittsburgh.

# Andrew Carnegie

*(Culver Pictures)*

The most captivating idea in late nineteenth-century American culture was the image of the "self-made man." And, of all the industrial magnates of the day, the man who best fitted the picture was Andrew Carnegie. His life contained all the right ingredients: poor but honest parents, a daring willingness to gamble on innovations, and dazzling financial success.

The full picture, of course, was a little more complicated. Carnegie *was* the son of poor Scottish immigrants. But his parents were skilled weavers who were poor because their craft was already being destroyed by technological innovation when Carnegie was born in 1835. This family of skilled craftsmen had for generations been articulate and politically active. When his parents immigrated to the United States in 1848, Carnegie had the fair beginnings of an education in literature and politics.

Carnegie started as a bobbin boy in a cotton factory in Allegheny, Pennsylvania, where his parents settled. By the time he was thirty, he had made what was then classed as a great fortune: $400,000. The fortune derived from hard work, yes; but it was helped along by a powerful patron who was president of the Pennsylvania Railroad. When this patron was appointed assistant secretary of war in the Lincoln administration, Carnegie accompanied him to Washington as an aide. There, he was in a superb position to learn the crucial role that railroads and iron and steel would play in the new, industrialized economy.

Carnegie's first fortune came from railroading, bridge building, oil, and a series of clever speculations. He had a somewhat ambiguous attitude toward his success. He sometimes seemed to fear that money might destroy his character. In 1868, in a remarkable memorandum to himself, he listed his assets and the income they could produce:

> An income of $50,000 per annum! . . . Beyond this, make no effort to increase fortune. . . . Man must have an idol—the amassing of wealth is one of the worst species of idolatry—no idol more debasing than the worship of money. . . . To continue much longer overwhelmed by business cares and with most of my thoughts wholly upon the way to make more money in the shortest time, must degrade me beyond hope of permanent recovery.

Within five years, in spite of such thoughts, Carnegie was embarked on the creation of Carnegie Steel, which he made into a model of vertical integration and efficiency. When he finally sold his interest in the company to the new trust, United States Steel, in 1901, it was worth $250,000,000.

But Carnegie did try to rescue himself from "idolatry" in a variety of ways. He wrote five volumes of books and essays—a remarkable accomplishment for a man of affairs. He cultivated literary and philosophical friends in both England and America. He also embarked on a program of "scientific philanthropy" that eventually totaled about $350 million, dotting the landscape with what came to be called "Carnegie libraries." Carnegie was not a typical entrepreneur of the period. But his articulateness and his rhetoric of benevolence made him a model for the popular cult of individual struggle, success through fair competition, and enlightened capitalism as the economic basis of American democracy.

Carnegie's company grew with the industry. By 1890, he was producing almost a third of a million tons of steel. By 1900 this amount had nearly tripled. At the same time, Carnegie worked to achieve vertical integration. He bought iron ore deposits, steamers to transport ore on the Great Lakes, and railroad cars to carry it overland—in fact, everything that he needed for making steel.

In the meantime, the process of competition had eliminated all but a few other steel companies. In 1892, the Carnegie Company was reorganized to combine seven other corporations in which Carnegie had acquired a controlling interest. In 1901, the largest steel concerns in the nation were all merged into one great new corporation, the United States Steel Corporation. The power behind this consolidation was another dominant figure of the period, J. Pierpoint Morgan, a New York banker and financier. Morgan spent nearly half a billion dollars to buy out Carnegie and set up this supercorporation. Like International Harvester, the giant company dominated its industry. It produced almost all of some forms of steel and three-fifths of the total steel made in the United States.

An even more stunning example of consolidation brought John D. Rockefeller into control of the oil industry. Rockefeller started out as a poor boy, like Carnegie. He too saved every cent (except for the 10 percent tithe he regularly gave to his Baptist church). Starting with one refinery in Cleveland, Rockefeller by 1872 had created the giant Standard Oil Company.

## The Trust

Rockefeller also created a new device that made it even easier to consolidate an industry—the trust. A business trust is an arrangement in which several companies "sell" themselves to a group of trustees. The companies are paid for with shares in the new trust itself. Only paper changes hands, but the result is a single group of directors who control the operations of several companies.

Through the Standard Oil Trust, the Rocke-

**CAPITAL AND ITS CHAMPION**

One of the favorite subjects for nineteenth-century cartoonists was the trust. Here, Capital brings its newest gladiator to the edge of the ring to introduce the victor. The vanquished at the rear include the "small dealer" and the traveling salesman. *(Culver Pictures)*

feller interests acquired almost total control of the oil industry. The trust could phase out unnecessary plants. It could take full advantage of mass production and distribution techniques to provide most of the kerosene that lighted American lamps and the oil that lubricated American machines. Rockefeller himself summed up adequately the reasons for the trust.

It has revolutionized the way of doing business all over the world. The time was ripe for it. It had to come, though all we saw at the moment was the need to save ourselves from wasteful conditions [of competition]. The day of combination is here to stay. Individualism has gone, never to return.

One by one, the main American industries passed from competition to consolidation. It might occur through giant corporations created by mergers, like International Harvester or United States Steel. Or it might result from the formation of trusts in various industries, from cottonseed oil to sugar to whiskey. By 1900 a few large concerns controlled almost all the major facilities of production and distribution in the United States.

## THE NEW AMERICANS

Industry has always needed people, and the new industrial order needed hordes. The growth in agriculture, railroads, and industry demanded millions of people–both as workers and as consumers.

The American population kept pace with industrial growth. For every 100 persons living in the United States in 1870, there were 126 in 1880, 158 in 1890, 190 in 1900 (and in 1910 a surprising 230!). In one generation, the population more than doubled, from about 40 million in 1870 to over 90 million forty years later.

These were the millions who moved into the Great Plains and the Rockies, bringing about the final collapse of the Western Indians. These were the millions who made or bought McCormick's harvesters, or who built the railroads that carried his reapers into every flat corner of the country where grain could be planted and harvested by machine.

## Shifting Trends in Immigration

These millions, however, were not just more of the same kinds of Americans who had lived here in Jacksonian times. Many of them were "new" people—with different languages, different religions, and different ways of life. Andrew Jackson's "common man" was, most likely, born in America; he was white, Protestant, and a farmer. His parents or grandparents might have been immigrants, but they would probably have come from England or Scotland. When they arrived here, they would have found the language, the ways of worshipping God, and the customs familiar and comfortable.

But the "common man" in New York in 1900 was more likely to be a Jew from Poland or a Catholic from Italy. He lived in a great city and probably had a job in a factory or a business. His English might be poor. His memories of the "old country" would be at least as important to him as his hopes for the new. He represented a social revolution that had accompanied the revolutions in technology, industry, and business—the creation of an urban immigrant working class.

There have been immigrants in America for thousands of years, since people began to cross over from Asia into Alaska. In the hundred years following the American Revolution, the actual proportion of immigrants to the total population did not change much. Two other things happened instead. First, the nature of the immigrant population changed. Second, the immigrants (along with other Americans) began to congregate in great urban centers. These two changes made industrial cities like Chicago the gathering places for a new kind of American: the poor immigrant from a country where English was not spoken and where an Anglo-Saxon Protestant was a rarity.

In 1790, when the United States took its first census under the new Constitution, nine out of ten Americans (except for the struggling black slaves in the South) had English or Scottish ancestors. This pattern changed somewhat with the immigration of the 1840s and 1850s—the "old" immigration—when large numbers of German, Scandinavian, and Irish immigrants began to arrive. However, although their languages might be strange to American ears, most of the Germans and Scandinavians were at least Protestants. And although many native-born Americans resented the Catholicism of the Irish, these immigrants at least spoke English. In 1865, the United States had only about 200,000 inhabitants who had been born in southern or eastern Europe. They were easily absorbed in a total population of about 40 million.

## IMMIGRATION BY REGION, 1860-1920

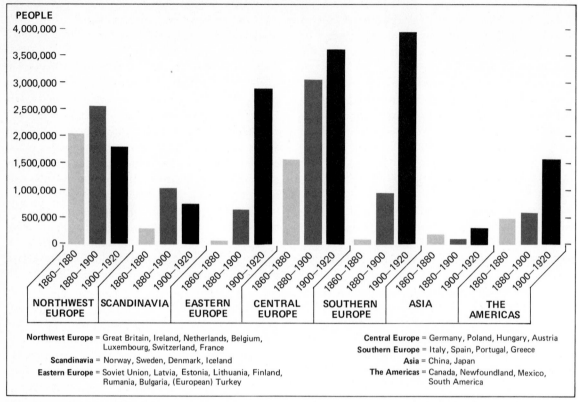

**Northwest Europe** = Great Britain, Ireland, Netherlands, Belgium, Luxembourg, Switzerland, France
**Scandinavia** = Norway, Sweden, Denmark, Iceland
**Eastern Europe** = Soviet Union, Latvia, Estonia, Lithuania, Finland, Rumania, Bulgaria, (European) Turkey

**Central Europe** = Germany, Poland, Hungary, Austria
**Southern Europe** = Italy, Spain, Portugal, Greece
**Asia** = China, Japan
**The Americas** = Canada, Newfoundland, Mexico, South America

By 1914 this picture had changed dramatically. A "new" immigration—mainly from Italy, Russia, and Austria-Hungary—flooded into the United States. Poverty drove many of these people from their home countries. Some men left to avoid the military draft, which discriminated against the poor. Jews wanted to escape the official anti-Semitism of Russia and Poland. Armenians fled from persecutions carried out by the Turkish government. The new immigrants were drawn to the United States by advertisements of cheap steamship transportation, by rumors of free land and golden opportunity, and by a massive propaganda campaign conducted by railroads anxious for workers and for customers to buy up their lands.

Immigration from southern and eastern Europe amounted to only a trickle in the 1860s and

1870s. But by the 1890s, over half the immigrants to America were from southern and eastern Europe. Between 1901 and 1910—the peak decade for immigration in the history of the United States—the proportion of "new" immigrants rose to over 75 percent, as over 6 million Italians, Russian Jews, Hungarians, and other immigrants from southern and eastern Europe poured into the country.

## Reaction to the Newcomers

The strike at McCormick and the Haymarket affair occurred just before the new immigration into the United States reached its peak. But prejudice had already been aroused by the entry of Irish and Germans, and by the beginnings of the influx from eastern and southern Europe. Both the McCormick strike and the trial of the Haymarket "radicals" occurred in an atmosphere of fear and bigotry. The Pinkerton report on the "fighting Irish" molders, and the newspaper comments on foreign "anarchists," make it clear that events in Chicago would probably have been different if they had not taken place at the time of this bewildering flood of immigrants.

The new immigrants were not only different in culture, language, and religion. They also behaved in different ways from those who had preceded them. They moved into a society that was no longer predominantly agricultural and rural, but urban. So they did not fan out onto farms as most of the old immigrants had done. Instead, they followed the lead of millions of other Americans and settled in cities. Two-thirds of foreign-born residents in the United States lived in towns and cities by 1900.

Bewildered and often victimized in America, new immigrants clustered together in their own city neighborhoods, or "ghettos." People from a particular province or even a particular village would move into buildings on the same block, re-creating much of the culture of their Old World homes. As the new immigration increased, so did antiforeign sentiment. Ghetto dwellers earned a reputation among "native" Americans for being clannish, dirty, superstitious, and generally undesirable. They were considered strange, chattering in their old languages, and somehow suited only for city life. Actually, of course, they were no more "natural" city dwellers than were the English who had come to Virginia and Massachusetts in the seventeenth century. They were simply caught in a phase of the industrial revolution—the creation of an urban society.

## Becoming "American"

In the era of the new immigration, the goal of many was still assimilation—to take on the traits of the new society so as to blend with it. But becoming an "American" was not an easy process for most European immigrants in the late nineteenth century.

Real assimilation meant knowing the language. Many immigrant parents made enormous sacrifices to send their children to public school. Mary Antin, a Jewish immigrant, remembered it this way:

Education was free. It was the one thing that my father was able to promise us when he sent for us; surer, safer than bread or shelter. On our second day in the country a little girl across the alley came and offered to conduct us to school. We five children between us had a few words of English by this time. We knew the word "school." We understood. This child, who had never seen us till yesterday, who was not much better dressed than we were, still was able to offer us the freedom of the schools of Boston! No application made; no questions asked; no examinations, rulings, exclusions; no fees.

Learning the language was only one step toward assimilation. Many immigrants joined some kind of voluntary association that brought them contacts with native-born Americans. In cities, the most obvious associations were political parties. They could provide favors, food, and jobs.

"Boss" Richard Croker of Tammany Hall in New York described the work of his machine as dealing with people who

do not speak our language and do not know our laws, yet are the raw material with which we have to build up the state. [The Tammany machine] looks after them for the sake of their vote, grafts them upon the Republic, makes citizens of them, in short; and although you may not like our motives or our methods, what other agency is there by which so long a row could have been hoed so quickly or so well?

Another powerful influence on the new immigrants were those who had preceded them. Some of the earlier arrivals learned English and helped recruit workers from Europe. They sometimes even paid the newcomers' transportation and helped them settle in the cities.

One popular name for such men was *padrone* (an Italian word meaning "patron"). A *padrone* might be paid by an employer for supplying cheap labor, by a political machine for delivering immigrant votes, or by the immigrants themselves for favors. Often the *padrones,* who existed among almost every immigrant group, were ward leaders in political machines, serving as links between the newcomers and the city organizations.

# URBANIZATION

In the ancient world, only two great cities—Rome and Alexandria—had populations of over half a million people. By the time of Columbus, Rome and Alexandria had long ago declined. The only European cities to have reached a comparable size were London and Paris. At the time of the Haymarket affair, however, Chicago had already become a great city. In fact by 1900, the United States had six cities with more than half a million inhabitants.

The process of urbanization was not confined to the United States. All the industrializing nations of Western Europe experienced it too. The factory system demanded high concentrations of workers, and the agricultural revolution made it possible for millions of people to leave their farms—whether in Germany or in Maine.

The United States experienced three great migrations in the generation after the Civil War. One was from the East to the Great Plains and

### AN URBAN VISTA

For the immigrant poor, life in America often began and ended in crowded and dirty slums, like this New York neighborhood. The streets were seldom cleaned, despite the continuing use of horses. For lighting, districts like this one had to depend on storeowners who were willing to install lights and keep them burning through the night. *(Private Collection)*

the Far West. Another was from Europe to America. The third was from the country to the city. Of the three, the movement from farm to city was the most extensive.

In 1800, only about three Americans out of every hundred lived in cities larger than 8,000. By 1900, this proportion had grown 1,000 percent; almost a third of the nation lived in cities of over 8,000. In 1800, there had been only six cities larger than 8,000; by 1900, there were over 400.

This increase was not gradual and smooth. Most of it came in the half-century after the end of the Civil War. During this period, at least 15 million native Americans moved out of farming areas and into cities, and their number was swelled by an almost equal number of new immigrants who settled in cities instead of on farms. Statistics tell the story. Between 1870 and 1900, the total population of the United States increased by about 35 million people. During the same period the urban population increased by about 24 million. The cities had absorbed more than two-thirds of the total increase.

## Technological Factors

A city is not just a collection of people in a small area. Like industry, modern cities were made possible by technological change. In the centuries before the industrial revolution, the size of a city had been determined mainly by the available transportation. It could not be too big, because a person had to be able to walk, or travel by wagon or carriage, to a marketplace or job and back home again. After about 1880, however, cities began to experience a transportation revolution. The introduction of electricity made it possible to replace slow and awkward horse-drawn transport with fast, clean trolleys, elevated trains, and subways. These improvements meant that people could live many miles from their place of work and still be part of a vast city.

Electricity also made it possible to light city streets. Cleveland, in 1879, became the first city

AN EARLY CHICAGO SKYSCRAPER
One of the breakthroughs of the nineteenth century was the steel-frame technique that made possible construction of skyscrapers, like this one in progress in Chicago in 1894. Once the frame was up, the walls could simply "hang" on the outside of the building, since they no longer had to support the structure. *(Culver Pictures)*

to have electric street lighting. Similarly, the introduction of the telephone in the 1880s meant that homes, offices, and factories could be tied together in an almost instantaneous communications network.

At first, city buildings themselves were a limiting factor. Even with the thickest walls, a stone or brick building could not extend higher than fifteen stories. To build a structure even this high, builders had to reduce the size of windows because glass could not support the weight. A second problem was that human legs could tolerate only so many flights of stairs. The first problem was solved by the invention of the skyscraper in the 1880s, pioneered by a Chicago architect, Louis Sullivan. Skyscraper construction—in which walls were hung on steel frames—made possible structures as tall as a hundred stories. Thus more people could be concentrated, level upon level, on smaller parcels of land. The second problem was solved at about the same time by the invention of the electric elevator, which made the tall buildings usable.

## THE INDUSTRIAL SYSTEM

The new industrial system, with its machines and its factories, had some obvious economic advantages. It could produce more goods, with less labor, and at a lower cost. There were some equally obvious disadvantages. The factories were dirty, noisy, and dangerous. And so were the cities where they were built. Factories could produce only standardized goods, lacking the mark of individual craftsmanship. They undercut the skilled worker's control over the pace and intensity of work. And they drove small producers, using simpler methods, out of business.

Many Americans—perhaps even a majority—were convinced that the advantages outweighed the disadvantages. In fact, most Americans seem to have believed that there was something almost inevitable about industrial "progress," something no one could stop even if they wanted to.

## Conditions of Labor

On the other hand, the new system did exploit and oppress many of those who worked in the factories and mills, on the railroads, in the mines, and on the farms. And they knew it. It took no sophisticated economic analysis for a man or woman who worked at a quickened pace from seven in the morning until six at night to understand fatigue. And seven out of ten Americans worked just such a sixty-hour, six-day week—collecting an average of about $10 a week in wages. For others, the situation was worse. In the steel industry, the norm was an eighty-four hour, seven-day week.

The average American worker at the end of the nineteenth century was earning about $450 a year. Everyone understood that a family needed about twice that much to live decently. In fact, about $600 a year was necessary to keep out of deep poverty. The difference, of course, had to be made up with the labor of children and, increasingly, women—all pooling miserable wages to try to put together a passable life.

In addition, the character of work itself was changing. In earlier times, the pace and nature of work had been adjusted primarily to people—to their arms, hands, and tools. But in factories, machinery set the pace, and people had to follow. Skilled workers, especially, understood that the factory threatened their control over the tone and atmosphere of the work place, and that industrial work tended always to become dull, routine, speeded, and intensely bossed.

Working men and women—and even some of the children—responded to these conditions with complaints, protest, and resistance. On the simplest level, they argued and complained in their factories, challenging their bosses' authority and control. They agreed silently among themselves to slow down their efforts, until the machines themselves had to be adjusted to a more relaxed pace. When they could, they quit jobs and moved on to other towns and other factories. They brought effective emotional pressure to bear on foremen, who often shared their ethnic and religious identifications. They managed to insist, in a dozen different ways and in the most desperate situations, on the simple dignity and independence of the working person.

Increasingly, however, it became clear that individual resistance and sabotage were not going to work, and that something more systematic and organized was necessary. And so working people began a generation-long quest for a method of

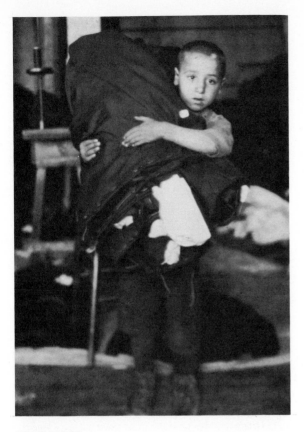

**CHILD LABOR**

Working-class families were usually unable to support themselves on a father's earnings, so others had to take jobs. In many ethnic communities, there was a much stronger prejudice against women working than against children, so boys and girls found themselves in mills and mines. (Often, though, working-class families had no choice but to put women *and* children to work.) One result was the haunting faces of children like this scratched and dazed boy, whose ten-hour-a-day job was to carry mats bigger than he was. *(George Eastman House Collection. Photograph by Lewis W. Hine)*

action that would work; one that would give them shorter hours, better pay, an increased degree of control over work itself, and perhaps even a larger voice in the way the new industrial society was shaped and managed.

## Early Attempts to Organize Labor

One possibility was direct political action: entering party politics, either to support one of the major parties or to find labor candidates. Before the 1890s, neither of the two principal parties were much interested in courting the support of organized groups of workers. So the most active working men experimented with parties of their own. In 1872, a National Labor Reform party tried to nominate a Supreme Court justice, David Davis, for president. But the candidate refused to run on their ticket. In 1876, labor leaders in the East helped to create a National Independent party, but their candidate won few votes, even among workers. A similar experiment in 1880 brought only the same result. Just two years before Haymarket, an Anti-Monopoly party, created in part by labor leaders, was crushed.

With both the Democratic and the Republican parties turning a deaf ear, and with third-party politics offering no hope, it was clear that the only possible path was to organize labor itself, not to engage directly in politics.

In 1866, on the initiative of an iron molder who belonged to the same kind of trade union that was so active in the McCormick strike, the National Labor Union was formed. Its leader, William Sylvis, conceived it as a reform union. It included temperance groups and woman suffrage groups as well as trade union organizations. And it repudiated the traditional last resort of workers: the strike. This union made little or no headway and lasted only about seven years.

A much more promising organization was the Noble Order of the Knights of Labor. The Knights was created in 1869 by a tailor in Philadelphia. Its plan was to organize all workers—skilled and unskilled, farm and factory, male and female, even black and white—in one grand union. In fact, the Knights specifically excluded only four types of people, whom they labeled "parasites": liquor dealers, bankers, professional gamblers, and lawyers. Like the National Labor Union, the Knights of Labor officially discouraged strikes and favored, instead, the "education" of workers and owners.

For a decade, the Knights grew slowly. Then leadership passed to an extraordinarily handsome and magnetic machinist from Pennsylvania, Terence V. Powderly. Powderly dropped an old rule making the Knights' ritual, rules, and membership a fraternal secret. In turn, the Catholic church dropped its official opposition, and membership began to increase. Still, Powderly opposed strikes and talked as though he did not represent workers at all but men who were anxious to become small capitalists: "I shudder at the thought of a strike," he said. We must "give men the chance to become their own employers."

It was, ironically, a strike that skyrocketed the Knights into prominence and into a fantastic rise in membership. Some of the local assemblies decided to stage a wildcat strike against the Texas and Pacific Railroad in 1885. Surprisingly, the railroad settled, and within a year the Knights suddenly had 700,000 members—a tripling of their rolls.

The Knights of Labor was not involved in the McCormick strike of 1886, and only indirectly in the Haymarket affair. But the organization was one of the principal victims of the public hysteria that followed the bombing and shooting in Chicago. Membership began to fall, and when the railroad assemblies were soundly beaten in a second strike against the Texas and Pacific in the same year, the disaster was complete. By 1890, 600,000 men and women had deserted the Noble Order, and it was, for all practical purposes, dead.

Meanwhile, another type of labor organization was building, one that would eventually become the most successful and characteristic in American society. In 1881, a group of craft unions formed the Federation of Organized Trades and Labor Unions. The principles of this organization were clear from the outset. First, it was concerned with skilled workers, not with trying to organize the industrial masses. Second, though reluctantly, they would use the strike as a weapon. Third, they were concerned strictly with wages, hours, and working conditions—not with politics, social reform, or other kinds of "utopian" schemes.

Here was unionism "pure and simple," as the members liked to say. Under the leadership of an immigrant cigar maker, Samuel Gompers, and under a new name, the American Federation of Labor, the organization made steady gains. By

SAMUEL GOMPERS

By the end of the nineteenth century, Gompers, shown here voting, had become the most powerful labor leader in the United States. His conservative American Federation of Labor was winning its contest with other, more radical labor organizations. *(Culver Pictures)*

the end of the century, it had half a million members (and a dozen years later, it would boast of 2 million).

## Strikes and Strikebreakers

Large national unions were destined to be part of American life. But for most people, the "labor question" focused not on unions so much but on a series of spectacular outbreaks of violence that rocked a society which had never witnessed anything of the sort. For a generation—from the 1870s until after the turn of the century—it seemed possible that society might actually be divided between rich and poor, owners and workers, in an increasingly desperate class struggle. This was, in fact, the atmosphere that fed the hysteria of Haymarket. And it was an atmosphere that intensified in every decade.

In 1877, just a year after the nation's centennial celebrations, four large railroads in the East announced a 10 percent cut in wages. The result was a sudden strike that paralyzed rail traffic all over the country. Crowds of workers stopped trains and occupied railroad buildings and roundhouses. In Pittsburgh, especially, the strikers' control seemed to be almost complete. Finally, in July, a frightened federal administration sent troops to "restore order"—that is, to break the strike. There was resistance. Nervous soldiers shot. Angry workers burned. In Pittsburgh a 3-mile-long fire destroyed 160 locomotives and hundreds of freight cars.

Nine years later came Haymarket, less violent and destructive, but just as frightening to those Americans who feared that "radicals" were out to destroy "order."

Then, in 1892, six years after Haymarket, a Carnegie Steel plant at Homestead was struck after the company announced pay cuts. The management asked the Pinkerton company to bring in several hundred armed guards—"goons" and "gun-thugs," the strikers called them. The Pinkerton men came on barges, down the river that ran next to the Homestead plant. The striking workers met them, as heavily armed. Someone fired, and before the guns had stopped several hours later, seven men were dead and many more wounded. In response, the governor of Pennsylvania sent in the entire state national guard, some 8,000 troops, to "restore order." The strike was broken. The men who had remained anonymous enough drifted back to work. The others simply drifted.

Two years later, in Illinois, a similarly angry and violent strike occurred, bringing back memories of Haymarket on both sides. George Pullman, who held a monopoly on the manufacture of Pullman coaches and parlor cars, had built what he boasted was a "model" industrial town near Chicago. Workers lived in company houses, bought in company stores, attended churches built and controlled by the company, and—mostly—worked for the company.

Most of the Pullman workers were members of a militant union, the American Railway Union, led by the greatest of American union leaders, Eugene Victor Debs. A confrontation was almost certain when—in response to a depression—Pullman announced a 25 percent cut in wages, but with no cuts in the rents of company houses or the prices in company stores. The workers struck, and Debs called on all 150,000 members of his union to refuse to move any train with a Pullman coach. Railroads everywhere fired any of Debs's men who refused to handle Pullmans. When this happened, the union called a strike against the offending railroad. In a few days, railroads from Chicago to the West, as well as many in the East, were paralyzed.

Once again, the "solution" was military. The president, Grover Cleveland, sent federal troops into Chicago to "protect the mails," even though Governor Altgeld—who had pardoned the surviving Haymarket defendants—objected. The strike collapsed. Debs went to prison. And Americans on both sides of the struggle seemed to have new evidence that industrial revolution might have more revolutionary consequences than they had at first imagined.

# AMERICAN CULTURE, 1875–1900

Economically and socially, the most important facts about American society in the period following the Civil War were industrialization, urbanization, and immigration. These facts together brought about a change in the landscape that was almost brutally obvious—the crowded, dirty, smoky city, with its alien working class. But people very often did not or *would* not see or acknowledge what was most plain. In their art and architecture, their novels and magazines—in all the areas of their culture—native, white, middle-class Americans seemed determined to ignore the realities of their age. At both the popular and the sophisticated level, middle-class culture seemed almost serene in its lack of awareness of industrial capitalism and its social consequences. To some extent, of course, the practice of ignoring, evading, or denying "reality" is a characteristic of culture in any society. But Americans in the 1870s and 1880s were abnormally, almost absurdly, consistent in their unwillingness to come to terms culturally with the actualities around them.

## Literature

This characteristic of American culture was not confined to the sentimental and quaint books and essays published for a middle-class, primarily female, readership. It was evident in the most talented and sophisticated intellectuals, too. Henry James wrote great novels and stories, as great as any ever published in English. But his subject matter was the elegant and complicated lives of wealthy Americans, usually set in Europe. And even when one of James's heroes was a businessman, as in *The American* (1876), he appeared in the novel only *after* he had made his fortune and arrived in Europe in pursuit of "culture" and an aristocratic French bride.

Henry James was born to wealth, cultivated society, and European travel. Samuel Clemens was born in Missouri into a modestly well-to-do family and spent much of his life scratching for a living as a journalist. As Mark Twain, he wrote about plain people. But his plain people were not immigrants or factory workers. And his settings were the small towns of the Mississippi, where boyish and innocent characters like Huckleberry Finn and Tom Sawyer had their "adventures." *Huckleberry Finn* (1885) was a great novel by almost any standard. But it was hardly a novel that confronted American realities. Samuel Clemens lived in Hartford, Connecticut, a modern city; he was married to the daughter of a coal baron. But the closest he came to an examination of such realities was when he fantasized about the experience a technologically inventive Yankee might have if he suddenly woke up in medieval England, as in *A Connecticut Yankee in King Arthur's Court* (1887).

What was true of Mark Twain and Henry James was equally true of lesser talents. Even when novels were about businessmen—as in William Dean Howells's *The Rise of Silas Lapham* (1884)—the real subject seemed to be not business but high society and romance, and the action occurred *after* the fortune was acquired. Edward Bellamy's *Looking Backward* (1886), one of the most popular novels of the period, was a utopian romance about Boston in the year 2000. The utopia was, in theory at least, highly industrialized, urbanized, and socialistic. And the response of middle-class readers was enthusiastic. But beneath its appearance of relevance to nineteenth-century realities, *Looking Backward* really described a small, pleasant Boston, in which the factories, the poor, and the immigrants had disappeared as though by magic.

In the 1890s, a few books did try to deal with the more sordid aspects of factory and slum life. Jacob Riis's *How the Other Half Lives* (1890) described a slum in vivid language that alarmed his primarily middle-class, native audience:

> Cherry Street. Be a little careful, please! The hall is dark and you might stumble over the children pitching pennies back there. Not that it would hurt them: kicks and cuffs are their daily diet. They have little else. Here where the hall turns and dives into utter darkness is a step, and another, another. A flight of stairs. You can feel your way, if you cannot see it. Close? Yes! What would you have? All the fresh air that ever enters these stairs comes from the hall-door that is forever slamming, and from the windows of dark bedrooms.

Stephen Crane's *Maggie: A Girl of the Streets* (1893) was a darkly realistic account of the way that slum poverty turned innocent girls to sordid lives. But such books came only after decades of industrialization. And they created almost as much scandal as if they had been about sexual perversion. For the most part, writers and other intellectuals provided no insight whatever into the lives and difficulties of the new, alien, urban working class.

On the level of popular culture, the picture

was much the same. A revolution in printing technology had made inexpensive books and magazines easily available, and a flood of popular fiction poured off the new steam-driven presses. But most of the stories and books dealt with rural life or with the doings of chaste and sentimental small-town girls; or they had as their heroes idealized Western cowboys, romantic sailors, or heroic figures from ancient history.

A new type of popular fiction did emerge after the Civil War, the tale of business success. The most successful promoter of the rags-to-riches formula was a Harvard-educated former clergyman, Horatio Alger. His *Ragged Dick: Or, Street Life in New York* (1867) was a sensational sales success. For the next thirty years, under titles like *Jed the Poorhouse Boy* and *Struggling Upward*, Alger sold over 200 million copies of his stories.

Superficially, at least, the Alger stories reflected important economic realities. But the reflection was indirect and distorted. Alger did not deal with the adult, business careers of his heroes. Instead, he wrote coy exercises in moralism, designed to show how Ragged Dick or Tattered Tom, or Poorhouse Jed overcame orphanhood and poverty by saving the drowning daughter of a wealthy, sonless merchant. The books always ended just as their heroes were about to embark on adult careers in commerce. The reader was left to assume that, in their adult lives, Alger's heroes would continue to thrive through a steady application of "pluck."

## Art and Architecture

The practice of turning away from economic and social realities that was so central to the literature of the 1870s and 1880s was equally characteristic of the art and architecture of those decades. The greatest American artist of the period, James McNeill Whistler, painted mostly portraits and nocturnal landscapes. When Whistler did depict a scene of contemporary social or economic activity, the subject was more likely to be European than American.

Most artists confined themselves to painting scenes of nature, domestic life, or portraits of the wealthy in which the sources of wealth were carefully ignored. Winslow Homer, who probably was the second most talented American painter of the period, used his muscular and vivid style primarily on seascapes. When he did paint men at work, they were almost always fishermen in aged boats—an ardently preindustrial subject matter.

Architecture was even more flagrantly systematic in denying the actualities of industrialism. The expanding society of the period required an enormous number of new buildings—campuses for colleges and universities, buildings for banks and corporations, homes and summer houses for new millionaires, railroad stations, and so on. But even the most talented architects were mired in a contest to restore ancient styles. The familiar, reliable Greek and Roman styles that had been so popular since the Revolution were pressed into service again. There was an astonishing revival of Gothic and Georgian, especially in campus architecture. And anyone could stare for days at the largest of the new railroad stations, with their Greek columns or baroque decorations, without gaining any clue as to what the function of the building actually was. In their buildings, as in their novels and paintings, Americans seemed more intent on disguising the industrial revolution than in celebrating it.

## SUGGESTED READINGS, CHAPTERS 25–26

### HAYMARKET

The Haymarket affair cries out for a new treatment. The only readable book on the subject is still Henry David, *History of the Haymarket Affair* (1936). David's sympathies are obviously with the men who were tried for the bombing. But these sympathies did not prevent him from writing a book that is quite fair and balanced.

The strike at the McCormick plant is discussed in Robert Ozanne, *A Century of Labor and Management Relations at McCormick and International Harvester* (1959).

## TECHNOLOGICAL CHANGE

The most curious and interesting study of technological change during this phase of the industrial revolution is an aging book by Lewis Mumford, *Technics and Civilization* (1934). A breezier book is Roger Burlingame, *The Engines of Democracy* (1940). Matthew Josephson, *Edison* (1959) is a fine biographical study of one of the most important innovators of the period. On railroads, see Oscar Winther, *The Transportation Frontier: The Trans-Mississippi West, 1865–1890* (1964). The best general book on agriculture is Fred A. Shannon, *The Farmer's Last Frontier* (1963).

## MANUFACTURING

The basic industries can be approached through these special studies: Peter Temin, *Iron and Steel in Nineteenth-Century America: An Economic Inquiry* (1964); J. F. Wall, *Andrew Carnegie* (1971); Harold Livesay, *Andrew Carnegie and the Rise of Big Business* (1975); Alfred D. Chandler, *Strategy and Structure: Chapters in the History of Industrial Enterprise* (1962); and Ralph W. Hidy and Muriel E. Hidy, *Pioneering in Big Business, 1882–1911: A History of Standard Oil* (1955).

## IMMIGRATION

A very readable introduction to the general subject of immigration is Philip Taylor, *The Distant Magnet: European Immigration to the U.S.A.* (1971). Humbert Nelli, *The Italians in Chicago, 1880–1930* (1970), and Thomas Kessner, *The Golden Door: Italian and Jewish Immigrant Mobility in New York City, 1880–1915* (1977), are two of the better studies of particular immigrant experiences.

## URBANIZATION

The transformation of Boston from a small center with a number of outlying towns into a major city is a model of what happened to American cities during this period. The process can be followed in Sam Bass Warner's fine book *Streetcar Suburbs: The Process of Growth in Boston, 1870–1900* (1962). These three general books are also extremely useful: Howard Chudacoff, *Evolution of American Urban Society* (1975); Zane Miller, *The Urbanization of America* (1973); and Constance M. Green, *The Rise of Urban America* (1965).

## LABOR

A fine place to begin is Herbert Gutman's collection of essays, *Work, Culture, and Society in Industrializing America* (1976). David Brody's study of the steelworkers, *Steelworkers in America: The Nonunion Era* (1960), is one of the best of the works on particular industries. A good brief survey is Joseph Rayback, *A History of American Labor* (1959). The contest between the industrial union and the craft unions is detailed very nicely in Gerald N. Grob, *Workers and Utopia* (1961).

## CULTURE

Henry F. May, *The End of American Innocence* (1959), contains a very readable survey of the cultural life of the last decades of the nineteenth century. On writers, a good introduction is Jay Martin, *Harvest of Change: American Literature, 1865–1914* (1967). One of the most interesting ways to approach the culture of the Gilded Age is through Lewis Mumford, *The Brown Decades: The Arts in America, 1865–1895* (1931). On art and architecture, see Oliver W. Larkin, *Art and Life in America* (1949), and John Burchard and Albert Bush-Brown, *The Architecture of America: A Social and Cultural History* (1966).

# 27 · The Election of 1876

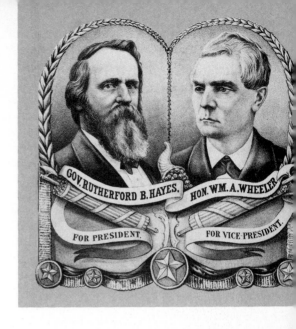

About half a century ago, the novelist Thomas Wolfe thought back to the times of his own father. It was a dull past for him, that world of the 1870s and 1880s, a world of forgotten men: "Garfield, Arthur, Harrison, and Hayes . . . for me they were the lost Americans: their gravely bewhiskered faces mixed, melted, swam together. And they were lost. For who was Garfield, martyred man? Who had heard the casual and familiar tones of Chester Arthur? And where was Harrison? Where was Hayes? Which had the whiskers, which had the burnsides: which was which?"

The problem for Thomas Wolfe was not just one of time. Abraham Lincoln's career lay further back in the past. But Lincoln could never have seemed "lost." Or Jackson or Washington either. The fog that settled over the history of the 1870s and 1880s was a fog of dullness and sameness, with no personalities, no drama, no profound causes won and lost. No Lincolns, Jacksons, or Washingtons.

Wolfe was a novelist, not a historian. But the historians echoed his brooding. They called the politics of the late nineteenth century the "politics of complacency" or the "politics of inertia." They defined it as a period of "uncertainty," or "drift." Little wonder that the bewhiskered faces melt into one another.

But the odd fact is that this period of American political history began with an election that was extremely tense and dramatic. From election day in November of 1876 down to dawn of March 2—less than two days before a new president had to be inaugurated—no one could be sure who would be sworn into office. It was even possible that no one would be, and that a new election might have to be held. Another possibility was that two men would claim the presidency and that the question might have to be settled by force of arms. Except for the crisis of secession following Lincoln's election in 1860, no four months of American political history have seemed more dramatic to the participants than that winter of 1876–1877.

By midnight on election day, November 7, 1876, everything seemed over. In Ohio, the Republican candidate, Rutherford B. Hayes, passed the evening with a few friends and supporters in his home. The telegrams came in, making it clear that he had lost. His wife, Lucy, tried to hide her disappointment. But she lost heart and went upstairs to bed, saying she had a headache. Sometime before 1:00 A.M., Hayes joined her, and they talked for a while the talk of losers: about how defeat was really a good thing, since it meant that their personal lives would be quiet and easy. Their sadness, they told each other, was not that Hayes had lost but that the "poor colored people" of the South would now be abandoned to an administration of Democrats dominated by the ex-rebels of the South. This said, Hayes wrote in his diary, "We soon fell into a refreshing sleep and the affair seemed over."

In New York, the home of the Democratic candidate Samuel J. Tilden, it had rained in the afternoon. But by nightfall, bonfires of celebration lit up the wet streets of lower Manhattan. At Democratic headquarters, the telegrams came in from state after state, promising victory. The politicians all

**HAYES CAMPAIGN POSTER**

This engraving, done by the nation's most successful illustrating firm, Currier and Ives, is filled with the political symbolism of the day. The eagle and the axes are taken from the Great Seal of the United States. The slogan, "Liberty and Union," is from a famous speech by Daniel Webster and is meant to recall the Northern cause in the Civil War. The stars appear as they did on military uniforms during the war. And the horn of plenty at the center suggests that Hayes will bring renewed prosperity. In the midst of it all is Hayes, looking candidly at the voter with an expression meant to convey an incorruptible honesty. *(Culver Pictures)*

knew the formula. If they could win the electoral votes of all the old slave states, and carry Tilden's own New York, then all they needed to do was win any two out of three promising states in the North: Indiana, Connecticut, and New Jersey.

By midnight, the Western Union machines had dotted and dashed the message into party headquarters: The Democrats had almost the whole South. They had New York by more than they had dared hope for. And they had won in all *three* of the other northern states they had needed. Now, even if two Southern states still under federal military "occupation"—South Carolina and Louisiana—were taken from them—they still had won. Tilden's campaign manager, New York congressman Abram S. Hewitt, stepped onto the wet pavements just before midnight and bought a copy of the leading Republican newspaper, the *New York Tribune*. The headline was short and to the point: TILDEN ELECTED.

At Republican national headquarters, in the Fifth Avenue Hotel, everyone except for one clerk had already gone home. A little before midnight, Republican Daniel Sickles—a Union general who had lost a leg at Gettysburg—stumped in, to find only a few gaslights still burning and the clerk putting away the records of defeat. Sickles studied the telegrams. They seemed at first to confirm what the party's chairman, "Zach" Chandler, had decided an hour or so before, when he gave up and went upstairs to his room with a bottle of consoling whiskey.

But Sickles was one of those Republican leaders to whom politics was deeply associated with the war. It was not just to the Confederacy that men like Sickles had lost legs or arms or had suffered in prison camps. It was also the Democratic party that had been their enemy. He would surrender only when the enemy's victory was absolutely certain. As he shuffled the telegrams, they seemed to hold out one tiny hope. If Hayes could win Louisiana, South Carolina, *and* Florida, then he would have exactly the 185 electoral votes needed to claim the presidency.

Sickles knew—as every Republican did—that the vote in these three Southern states had been determined by force and fraud on both sides. Federal troops and marshals, and Republican election officials had done whatever they could to throw these states to Hayes. Democratic crowds and local officials had done whatever *they* had to do to keep black voters from the polls.

If force and fraud were going to prevail on one side or the other, there might still be time to make sure that these states cast their final electoral votes for Hayes.

But if these three states were going to be "saved," the Republican election officials had to be warned to be alert. Sickles, on no authority, drafted telegrams to the three Republican governors: WITH YOUR STATE SURE FOR HAYES, HE IS ELECTED. HOLD YOUR STATE. He signed the name of Zach Chandler, who was asleep upstairs. But did he dare send the telegrams? Just then, Chester A. Arthur, a New York Republican officeholder, wandered in and offered to share responsibility for the decision. Sickles sent the telegrams, Arthur went home to a sick wife, and Sickles also left.

For the next few hours, only a handful of Republican leaders were still awake, and still clinging to their slender hope. Others, like Hayes's Ohio lieutenant, General and Congressman James Garfield, were sleeping the sleep of the defeated, convinced that they had been beaten by a deadly combination of "rebellion, Catholicism and whiskey." Only those were awake who had to be for some reason: William Chandler, a New Hampshire senator, was on a train from his home state to New York. About dawn, he called at the party headquarters to find only the clerk, who gave him the news of Hayes's apparent defeat. Another wakeful Republican was John Reid, who had been at work all night on the dawn edition of *The New York Times*. Reid had been a Confederate prisoner during the war, at a camp of horror known as Libby Prison in Virginia. Like Sickles, he did not forget. And like Sickles, he regarded the Democrats as the party of slavery and rebellion. Reid's determination had kept the *Times* from conceding the election to Tilden. The paper's morning edition bravely said: RESULTS STILL UNCERTAIN.

Now Reid rushed into the Fifth Avenue Hotel with a bit of news he thought might be important. He had just received a telegram from Democratic headquarters asking exactly what the *Times* thought the electoral count would be. Well, if the Democrats were themselves not sure of the outcome, then maybe there still *was* a chance to pull it out for Hayes.

At headquarters, Reid met William Chandler. Reid told his story, and together the two men decided to try to rouse Zach Chandler. They had to beat on the door for a long time, and when he finally appeared, he was in a nightshirt and was thoroughly befuddled. Sleepily, and probably a little drunk, he told the two men to do whatever was "necessary." Back downstairs, Reid and William Chandler sent out more telegrams. The messages to South Carolina, Florida, and Louisiana were about the same as Sickles had sent earlier: CAN YOU HOLD YOUR STATE?

Some hours later, around midmorning, Zach Chandler roused himself, dressed, and did his arithmetic. Leaving Florida, Louisiana, and South Carolina out, Tilden had certainly carried sixteen states, with a total of 184 electoral votes, just one short of the necessary 185. Hayes had clearly won nineteen states, with a total of 166, 19 short of victory. Tilden's forces were claiming all 19 electoral votes from the three disputed Southern states. (Even Hayes and his trusted friend Garfield still believed that Tilden had surely won at least one of the three.) In the face of these facts, Zach Chandler did something audacious. He issued a brief and blunt statement saying, "Hayes has 185 votes and is elected."

The Democrats were astounded. Tilden had won a majority of the popular vote—about a quarter of a million more than Hayes, out of the 8 million votes cast. He had a sizable reported majority in Louisiana: around 9,000 votes. And he seemed clearly to have won in Florida. In South Carolina, things were closer. But Tilden could concede South Carolina if he had to.

There was only one way the presidency could be taken by the Republicans. The small election boards that had to certify election results in South Carolina, Louisiana, and Florida were still controlled by Republicans. And the states

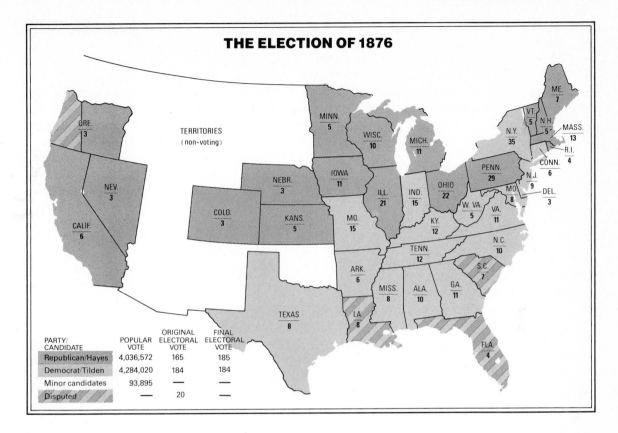

THE ELECTION OF 1876

TERRITORIES
(non-voting)

ORE.
3

NEV.
3

CALIF.
6

COLO.
3

KANS.
5

NEBR.
3

MINN.
5

IOWA
11

WISC.
10

MICH.
11

ILL.
21

IND.
15

OHIO
22

MO.
15

KY.
12

W. VA.
5

VA.
11

TENN.
12

ARK.
6

N.C.
10

S.C.
7

MISS.
8

ALA.
10

GA.
11

LA.
8

TEXAS
8

FLA.
4

ME.
7

VT.
5

N.H.
5

MASS.
13

R.I.
4

CONN.
6

N.Y.
35

PENN.
29

N.J.
9

MD.
8

DEL.
3

| PARTY/ CANDIDATE | POPULAR VOTE | ORIGINAL ELECTORAL VOTE | FINAL ELECTORAL VOTE |
|---|---|---|---|
| Republican/Hayes | 4,036,572 | 165 | 185 |
| Democrat/Tilden | 4,284,020 | 184 | 184 |
| Minor candidates | 93,895 | — | — |
| Disputed | — | 20 | — |

had Republican governors. If those officials threw out enough Democratic votes, they might report a victory for Hayes.

The first step that had to be taken, as both sides quickly understood, was to complete the official count of the votes in the three disputed states. In this process, the election boards had the legal right to challenge and exclude votes where there had been evidence of fraud or coercion of voters. This meant days and days of taking testimony and reviewing sworn statements. And so both parties sent teams of "observers" to the three Southern state capitals, to make certain that the election officials behaved fairly. And it was in this stage of things that something quiet but remarkable began to happen.

As the Republican "observers" went South, they encountered something surprising. They had to deal with Southern elected officials who were above all professional politicians. And so two sets of men began to come together in New Orleans, Tallahassee, and Columbia (just as they had been doing in

Congress increasingly for ten years). These were ex-officers of the Union and of the Confederacy, men who remembered all the violence and the passion of the war, and in whom old hatreds could be roused by a careless remark or discourtesy. But, now, they could not afford to look backward. For they were politicians and lawyers as well as ex-generals and ex-colonels. And this newer side of their personalities demanded order, courtesy, and decorum. And it was this newer, professional side of their lives that began now to dominate things.

General Garfield, one of the Republican observers in New Orleans, scratched into his diary the story of a day in November when a curious group of men took a day off from the political struggle to take a boat trip down the Mississippi to its mouth. One member of the party was General Sherman, who had been the most feared and hated of all of Lincoln's soldiers in the South. The leader of the excursion was the Confederate General P. G. T. Beauregard, who had commanded Southern troops at Shiloh, one of the bitterest battles of the war. Under Beauregard's courtly eye, the visiting Yankees marveled at the river's beauty, at the "vast plantations" and "great orange groves that made the shore beautiful with green and gold." Garfield, who had fought at Shiloh, talked with Beauregard: "He told me, quite fully, the history of the battle in which we were both engaged. It was curious to hear the history of the battle by the rebel commander."

The Democratic observers who went south met "reconciliation" of a different kind from Republican officials in Florida, Louisiana, and South Carolina. (At least they thought they did.) Various Democrats were met with apparent offers from the Republican members of electoral boards to *sell* their state's electoral votes to Tilden. Henry Watterson, a Kentucky Democrat observing in New Orleans, was visited by a man who claimed he had an offer from the two white and two black Republican members of the state's election board. They would sell the election for $250,000—$100,000 each for the two white members, and "$25,000 each for the two niggers."

Watterson apparently did not take the offer seriously. But other Democrats were fooled. Soon coded telegrams were flying back and forth between the three southern states and Tilden's mansion in New York. They never reached Tilden, or even his campaign manager, Abram Hewitt. Instead, they went to Tilden's nephew, William Pelton. One, sent by New York editor Manton Marble from Florida, was decoded by Pelton to read:

HAVE JUST RECEIVED A PROPOSITION TO HAND OVER AT ANY HOUR REQUIRED TILDEN DECISION OF BOARD AND CERTIFICATE OF GOVERNOR FOR $200,000.

Pelton wired back, PROPOSITION TOO HIGH. Marble responded that he had another offer to help rig the vote for only HALF A HUNDRED BEST UNITED STATES DOCUMENTS —$50,000.

All these "negotiations" failed. And the fact is that Marble and Pelton were probably being tricked into dealing with "intermediaries" who had no control over the votes anyway. And as soon as Tilden found out about the telegrams, he put a stop to such dealings on Pelton's part. Marble and Pelton themselves explained that they were convinced the Republicans were stealing the election and were only trying to bribe them into doing the right thing. On their side, the visiting Republican observers were offering federal jobs to Republican election officials once their "duty" had been completed.

The most important fact, in the end, was that both sides were concentrating their attention on the legal process of getting the votes counted and certified. No one said so, but a kind of informal agreement was gradually being reached by the politicians: the election would be decided on the basis of a bundle of legal technicalities. It would be dealt with by lawyers and by politicians, using the quiet skills and devices of their trade.

In all three Southern capitals, the spirit of inducement, legality, and courtesy prevailed. One by one, and in peace, the Republican election boards turned their results over to Republican governors, to be certified and returned to the Republican president of the U.S. Senate. In each case, the result was the same: All nineteen disputed electoral votes were recorded for Hayes. And in each state, Democratic officials refused to recognize the result and sent in contesting results: nineteen electoral votes and the presidency for Tilden.

But the first of many practical compromises had been made: voters and officials in the three Southern states had in effect agreed to leave the final solution in the hands of officials in Washington. During the month between the election and the official casting of the electoral votes of the states, there was no violence in the South, no mobs, no hangings or beatings of visiting Yankees, no challenges to the federal troops that were still posted in the three state capitals.

A curious villain now entered the scene: English grammar—more precisely, the passive voice. The Constitution contains no more cumbersome and creaking piece of machinery than the electoral college—an institution that never meets and exists only as an abstraction every four years. But the framers must have been in an especially wry frame of mind when they prescribed what was to be done with the electoral votes once they were cast. According to Article II and the Twelfth Amendment, the electoral votes "shall be transmitted to the seat of the government of the United States, directed to the President of the Senate" (who is normally the vice president). Then, "The President of the Senate shall, in the presence of the Senate and House of Representatives, open all the certificates and the votes shall then be counted." There it was, the insidious passive voice: "the votes shall then be counted."

But by whom? By the president of the Senate? He was a loyal Republican. By the members of the House and Senate, sitting together? The Democrats outnumbered the Republicans in Congress as whole.

The dilemma was acute. And it could not be resolved on any clear constitutional ground. But such puzzles provide a field day for politicians. Where the rules are not clear, outcomes can be determined by negotiation and compromise. The talents of bluff, swap, and deal now became paramount. The only question was, could some sort of compromise be worked out in time?

**SAMUEL J. TILDEN**

Tilden's was a face hardly likely to inspire passionate support among his followers. It did suggest a capacity for worry or concern. But its most striking feature, given the fashions of the day, was what it *lacked,* for Tilden sported no beard, no moustache, not even elaborate sideburns. And even his hair was much more closely cut than most men's in the post–Civil War decades. *(Culver Pictures)*

If not, then the possibilities would become even more dizzying. President Grant might try to decide who had been elected, and somehow use the army to enforce his choice. The Democratic House might name Tilden president and the Republican Senate might name Hayes. Then whom would the army obey? For men who had lived through secession and Civil War, such possibilities though remote were real enough, especially when some politicians were publicly calling for 100,000 men to come to Washington to settle the matter.

At this point, the personalities and strategies of Hayes and Tilden themselves became crucial. Would either of them *demand* the presidency and exhort their followers to action?

On the face of it, Tilden was the least likely leader of any kind of revolutionary movement. He was a soft-spoken lawyer (but a lawyer whose soft speech had won him a fortune of around $10 million). He was a scholarly bachelor who seemed to love the great library in his Gramercy Park mansion more than the arenas of politics. Like Hayes, he had followed American custom by not campaigning personally. And his quiet habits had been reinforced by a mild stroke he had suffered in 1875. Tilden was beardless in a generation that associated facial hair with the Civil War and military action. Unlike many politicians in both parties, he had not been in the war. In fact, the Republican chairman, Zach Chandler, had assembled a drawerful of signed statements by various nurses and doctors who had treated Tilden, statements that claimed that Tilden was physically "sexless." In a Victorian world where "manliness" was an obsession, there could have been no more profound suspicion.

During the weeks after the election, Tilden played the role of lawyer and scholar. He spent a month doing detailed research on the history of presidential elections. He ignored the pleas of his supporters that he issue a strong statement claiming that he had won. He forbade any mass meetings in his name. He sent telegram after telegram whose first word was "Wait," or "Delay," or "Procrastinate." Democratic leaders who came to him looking for instruction, advice, or practical wisdom on how to handle the crisis went away shaking their heads in disappointment.

Tilden gave his blessing to only one practical action. In Oregon, one of the Republican electors had been a postmaster. The Constitution forbade any federal officeholder from serving as an elector. So, working with the Democratic governor of Oregon, Abram Hewitt devised a scheme to replace the Republican elector with a Democrat. For the rest, Tilden contented himself with quiet, legalistic preparations, making it clear that he wanted no hint of force, fraud, or a mobilized public opinion. In this attitude, Tilden was consistent from beginning to end.

Hayes, on the other hand, was a man divided against himself. In many ways, he was quite different from Tilden. He was a lawyer and a man of some cultivation, but far from being scholarly. He was married and had several children. He had fought for the Union and had even been seriously wounded. He was something of a self-made man and, though very well-to-do, had nothing approaching Tilden's fortune. Above all, Hayes was a man who was deeply committed to being decent and moral. And it was this commitment that established an initial division in his mind about what to do in the disputed election.

On one side, Hayes was convinced that a fair election, with blacks permitted to vote all over the South as the Fifteenth Amendment provided, would certainly have given him a victory. On the other side, however, he had felt all his life that politics was a dirty business, full of fraud and deception. He had managed to avoid being "soiled," and his first reaction to his apparent defeat was to let the election go rather than risk getting involved in a sneaky strategy. His diary wandered back and forth between these two attitudes:

> November 12—We shall, the fair-minded men of the country will, history will, hold that the Republicans were by fraud, violence, and intimidation, by a nullification of the Fifteenth Amendment, deprived of the victory which they fairly won. But we must, I now think, prepare ourselves to accept the inevitable.

> November 27—A fair election would have given us about forty electoral votes in the South. But we are not to allow our friends to defeat one outrage and fraud by another. There must be nothing crooked on our part. Let Mr. Tilden have the place by violence, intimidation, and fraud, rather than undertake to prevent it by means that will not bear the severest scrutiny.

As late as December 3, Hayes believed that Louisiana would probably be decided for Tilden. But he had gradually come to think more realistically. He was looking for a way to have Congress investigate the Louisiana vote, to throw out Democratic ballots: "Should not the whole case be gone into?" (But when Louisiana voted Republican, Hayes steadfastly maintained that Congress had no right to investigate the vote in any state.)

Two days later, a group of Republicans who had been in New Orleans came to Columbus to assure Hayes that he had won Louisiana fairly, without bribery or trickery. The assurances were bland and pious, and Hayes was even a little suspicious. He went around the room asking each man in turn to promise that the result had been "lawful" and "honest." Congratulations began to pour in by telegram and letter. Hayes began to feel more "presidential." I will act, he wrote in his diary, "as Washington would have acted under similar circumstances." From this point onward, he made it clear to his supporters that they were free to make strategies (honest ones, of course) and pursue them in a concerted effort to win the presidency by political means as well as legal. Hayes gave his party an important advantage. The question was, how could they use it?

Hayes's men began to work on a strategy. The Congress whose authority would last until inauguration day in March was divided. In the Senate, the Republican majority was 46 to 29. In the House, the Democrats held the majority: 181 Democrats, 107 Republicans, and 3 who called themselves independents. If thirty-six Southern Democrats could somehow be persuaded to break with their party in the House and vote with the Republicans, then

Hayes could become president with the consent of both houses of Congress.

The idea was bizarre. Why would Southern Democrats suddenly forsake the hatreds of a generation and help elect a Union general as their president?

Against the apparent absurdity of such a notion, Hayes and his strategists could weigh an increasing number of very tempting facts.

First, soon after the election stalemate became clear, Hayes began to be visited by Southern politicians and journalists assuring him of their "good will." They claimed to represent large numbers of Southern political and business leaders.

Second, a plain majority of Republicans were tired of Reconstruction, and convinced that it had ended in corruption and failure. Many Southerners understood this. So a congressman from Mississippi or Tennessee might well be ready to make peace with a changed Republican party.

Third, the Southerners made it clear in everything they said and did that their main concern was to put an end to Reconstruction in the South: to get rid of the hated "carpetbagger" governments that still claimed to rule South Carolina and Louisiana; to see the Union soldiers taken out of the Southern capitals and never returned; and to be free to "handle the color problem" their own way. This goal was much more important to them than the question of who had won the presidency.

Fourth, the Republicans remembered all too well that before 1860, the South had been anything but "solid" for the Democrats. There had been a vigorous Whig party there, led by the same sorts of urban, national-minded businessmen who had now become the backbone of the Republican party in the North. A tantalizing vision began to form in Hayes's mind: maybe the old Whig elements in the South could be pried loose from the Democrats. Maybe a real Republican party could be built in states like Tennessee, Texas, and Arkansas.

But what did Hayes and his supporters have to offer? The answers to this question provided the basis for one of the most famous attempted bargains in American history: the Compromise of 1877.

The bargainers for Hayes were initially a group of journalists and newspaper publishers, headed by three men who were convinced that they might be real kingmakers: William Henry Smith, an old friend of Hayes and the head of the Western Associated Press; Confederate colonel and ex-Whig William Kellar, a Memphis publisher; and Henry Van Ness Boynton, who was the Washington correspondent of a Cincinnati newspaper. With Hayes's apparent blessing, these men began to cultivate contacts with Southern politicians and to work out—or think they were working out—a monumental deal.

Its outlines were these: On his side, Hayes would promise to withdraw federal troops in the South to their barracks and keep them there. He would recognize Democratic governors and state legislatures in the last two "unredeemed" states of Louisiana and South Carolina. And he would appoint at least one Southerner to his cabinet.

On their side, the Southerners would quietly accept the Republican count of the contested ballots from Louisiana, Florida, and South Carolina. And they would "promise" that the blacks in the South would be given their political and civil rights as the constitutional amendments required.

The difficulty with the deal, taken this far, was that it offered nothing to the Southerners that Tilden would not also give them. He would withdraw the troops. He would recognize Democratic governments everywhere. He would appoint Southerners to the cabinet.

Something more was needed.

The Southern politicians were talking a good deal about "internal improvements." In simple terms, this meant nothing more than federal money. Money for reopening harbors that had been ruined during the war. Money for repairing wrecked levees on the Mississippi that had left 28 million acres of prime cotton land exposed to vicious floods. For sixteen years, the Northern states had sucked at the federal treasury. Now, with the South back in the Union, would it get its share? Would the difference be made up? Would the old Confederate states be "reconstructed" in a way their white leaders wanted: with expensive road, harbor, and flood control projects paid for in Yankee dollars? During the war, the North had even begun a railroad to the Pacific, with more than $100 million worth of federal government support— a sum greater than all the federal expenditures for transportation facilities before 1860 combined. Was it now to be the South's turn?

Here Hayes's journalist strategists and would-be kingmakers had a card worth playing. Tilden and the Democratic party were strongly opposed to spending federal money for internal improvements—and had been since the days of Thomas Jefferson. The Republicans, on the other hand, had an impressive record of opening the federal treasury for improvements. And so Boynton, Kellar, and Smith began to propose that Hayes commit himself to a strong program of federal projects of construction and reconstruction in the South. This, they believed, would lure in the thirty-six Southern Congressmen they needed.

The confidence of the negotiators was high because they had a specific project in mind: the railroad to the Pacific that had long been a dream of Southerners in Texas, Arkansas, Mississippi, Tennessee, Kentucky, and Louisiana. It so happened that one of the most restless railroad promoters in the nation, Thomas Scott, vice president of the powerful Pennsylvania Railroad system, had already secured a land grant of 16 million acres for building a road from Texas to the West coast. Companies had already been formed to promote a system of branch lines connecting Fort Worth to New Orleans, Vicksburg, Memphis, and St. Louis. (In fact, Kellar was an officer of one of these companies. And numerous other Southern politicians were officers and board members of the companies.)

Thomas Scott had built a huge reputation as a successful lobbyist. Hayes's journalist friends were awed by the possibility that they might set Scott's forces in motion, divide the Democrats, and make Hayes president with little further ado.

What Hayes understood but his negotiators did not was that the Republicans were no more "solid" than the Democrats. Grant had told his cabinet that he believed Tilden had won. A key Republican senator, Roscoe Conkling of New York, had never supported Hayes. And there were the Republican senators and congressmen from the South—"carpetbaggers" all—whose careers would be ruined if Hayes came in as a result of a bargain with the South. The Republican majority in the Senate was slender. If six men refused to support Hayes, the Senate would be lost. Paradoxically, all the Republican efforts to win the Democratic House would then be defeated in the Senate they supposedly controlled.

And so the bargainers bargained, and Hayes's forces worried about whether they could keep the Republican senators in line. But meanwhile, a quiet process had been going forward that would eventually decide who was to be president.

During the first two weeks of December, both houses of Congress had passed motions to create special committees to study the problem of the election. From the House came four Democrats—including Tilden's manager, Hewitt—and three Republicans. From the Senate came a committee of four Republicans and three Democrats.

From the middle of December to the middle of January the two committees hammered away at their problem, sometimes meeting together and sometimes separately. Their votes were usually along party lines, and it was clear to all of them that they would have to devise a scheme they could all support, or no scheme at all.

What gradually emerged from these committee meetings was the idea of handing the question of the election over to a special body, an Electoral Commission. The committees proposed plan after plan, but what finally won their approval was a cumbersome idea that would, in effect, leave the decision up to one man whose identity could only be guessed at. On January 15, the committees agreed to propose an Electoral Commission with this membership: five members of the House, five senators, and five Supreme Court justices. The House, clearly, would send three Democrats and two Republicans. The Senate would balance off with three Republicans and two Democrats. The committees chose two Supreme Court justices whose past records were clearly Republican and two others with equally clear Democratic loyalties. These four justices were to agree on which remaining member of the Court was to be the fifteenth member of the commission—the decisive member.

Perhaps the most important feature of the proposal was that its findings would be final unless *both* houses of Congress rejected them. In effect, the House and Senate were about to surrender their separate power over the decision. Hayes was upset. Tilden was as close to anger as he came during the entire crisis. But the members of Congress were calm. The politicians in Congress, professionals all, understood that whoever became president now would come in with the weakest possible mandate. The system of power would tilt away from the presidency and back toward Congress, where it had firmly rested during the generation before the Civil War. Control over budgets, patronage appointments, and policy would lie with the senators and

THE ELECTORAL COMMISSION

This astonishing picture purports to show the Electoral Commission taking testimony. Actually, it is a composite picture intended to include the face of every important person who might conceivably have attended any of the sessions. The result is a crowd so densely packed as to constitute a health hazard. The Commission members are shown on the raised bench at the left, and the artist has tried hard to suggest that they and the audience are going about their business with the utmost gravity. *(Culver Pictures)*

the congressmen, not with either Tilden or Hayes. It had simply become more important to name *a* president peacefully than to name any one man.

For the professional politician the important thing was to be able to pursue political interests in an atmosphere of compromise and customary horse trading. To win this, they were prepared to leave the question of the presidency to fate. (At one point, the committees had strongly favored letting the fifteenth member of the electoral commission be chosen by *lot!*)

This became sharply clear when Hewitt went up to New York to explain the proposal to Tilden. Tilden complained that it was a bit late in the day for the Democrats in Congress to consult him. Hewitt's reply was short, but it spoke volumes about the way Congress had begun to look at the presidency: "They do not consult you," he said. "They are public men with their own responsibilities."

Of course, each side could still hope to win, even if the question had been handed over to fate. And the Democrats' hopes were probably higher. Everyone supposed that the fifth justice, and deciding vote, would be David Davis. Davis now called himself an independent, but he leaned toward the Democratic side.

Then, just as the electoral commission was being passed by Congress, came astounding news from Illinois, Davis's home state. The Illinois legislature had just elected him to the Senate. He would resign from the court and refuse to serve on the electoral commission. (Ironically, Davis had been elected to the Senate with overwhelming Democratic support. Neither Tilden nor his supporters had paid any attention, even though they knew that Davis, their best hope for the deciding vote, was a candidate.)

Now the four justices did their duty. They named the least partisan of the remaining justices, Joseph Bradley of New Jersey. Bradley was a Republican, but he had a reputation for fairness.

The electoral commission was, in essence, a judicial body. It even held its sessions in the chamber normally occupied by the Supreme Court. Both parties hired the most talented and famous lawyers they could find. The lawyers presented arguments that lasted day after day on each of the disputed states. Then the commission—like the Supreme Court—went into secret session to hear the opinions of the members and vote on a decision.

A cynical observer might have supposed that everyone except Bradley would simply vote along party lines, and that it would be simpler for that one justice to announce *his* decision. But the commission did not function that way. The arguments were learned. The galleries of the courtroom were crowded to overflowing with the rich, the famous, and the powerful. The commission's members kept an anxious watch over each other. Bradley kept a scrupulous silence.

The first state to be considered was Florida, and the first question was technical but all-important. Congress had left the commission itself to decide one key question: could the commission investigate the people's voting in the contested states? Or were its powers confined to examining the procedures by which the electoral votes had been arrived at and certified? The Democrats, of course, wanted a full inquiry into what had happened in Florida, South Carolina, and Louisiana on election day. The Republicans wanted to examine only what had happened after the election.

On February 6 and 7, after four days of public arguments, the commission met in secret to decide the case of Florida. One by one the members read their opinions—for seven hours on the first day, and five more on the second. One after another, they voted on party lines, until the Republicans had 7 votes. Finally, it was Bradley's turn. Garfield, who was a member of the commission, wrote in his diary that "All were intent, because B. held the casting vote. . . . All were making a manifest effort to appear unconcerned."

Bradley made this crucial ruling: the commission could not investigate the election itself. It could only determine whether all legal rules had been fol-

lowed in the certifying and casting of the state's vote in the electoral college.
Two days later, the commission ruled that Florida's Republicans *had* followed
the rules, and that the votes of the state would go to Hayes.

There was less than a month to go before the scheduled inauguration of
a new president. One by one, the commission took up the states in question.
One by one, they decided each case for Hayes. Even Hewitt's Oregon trap
failed. The commission simply ruled that the Democratic elector from Oregon
had been appointed through a faulty procedure, and that Hayes was entitled
to all 3 Oregon votes. Every vote was the same: 8 for Hayes, 7 for Tilden.

The game was up. But there were two political instincts still alive that
wanted to keep the play going until the bitter end. One was the instinct of
pure partisanship, best put by a Tilden adviser: "God damn them, they will
beat us and elect Hayes, but we shall give them all the trouble we can."

The second and more practical instinct was Southern. It was clear that
Hayes would win. But it was equally clear that he would like to win gracefully
and come into office on a wave of good will that was as truly national as
possible. This opened a tactical possibility. If the Democratic House could
delay by filibuster and adjournment until the very dawn of inauguration day,
then Hayes would be kept on tenterhooks, practically imprisoned out in
Columbus, unable to adopt the grand style of the president-elect, unable to
make the fine speeches calling for national unity. Perhaps some practical
concessions could still be won.

Now, *after* the decision had been made, the Democrats in the House began
to reject the commission's decisions. It made no practical difference, for the
Senate naturally voted to accept them all. But the House Democrats began a
war of nerves, adjourning from day to day. In corridors and in the hotel suites
of senators and congressmen around Washington, Southern politicians and
Hayes spokesmen began to deal and trade.

Finally, on February 26, a conference took place of a type that Hayes's
journalist-strategists had dreamed of in early January. At Wormsley's Hotel,
five Ohioans close to Hayes met with four Southerners who spoke for the
Democratic parties of Louisiana and South Carolina. A curious bargain was
struck.

Hayes's people made general commitments on his behalf: that there would
be a Southerner in the cabinet, that the president would be "liberal" on the
question of internal improvements in the South. The Southerners made promises that were equally vague, especially that the political and civil rights of
the blacks in the South would be protected by the Democrats, once they were
granted "home rule." Hayes's spokesmen then made it clear that they would
return the army to its barracks and that they would allow the Republican
governments in Louisiana and South Carolina to fall and would recognize
Democratic governors there.

(The Texas and Pacific railroad scheme was not mentioned. Tom Scott
had already presented his request for a subsidy to Congress, and the total bill
was too high—a staggering $200 million. The plan died in committee, with

PHILADELPHIA CENTENNIAL

Somewhat ironically, in light of the stalemated election of that year, 1876 was the centennial year of the Declaration of Independence. The center of national celebration was a great fair, or exposition, in Philadelphia, where independence had been proclaimed. This great crowd is waiting patiently for the doors to open on the first day of the exposition, watched over by the ever-present eagles that were such a favorite symbol of the day. *(Culver Pictures)*

two of Hayes's closest supporters voting against it. It would have to wait for a new Congress, where it had no real chance.)

Here was the most famous back-room deal in the political history of the United States. It was known for generations as the bargain that had put an end to Reconstruction and preserved the political stability of the nation. But it was meaningless as a bargain. Hayes had already decided to confine the army to its barracks in the South. Indeed, Grant had already drawn up an order making this last "magnanimous" gesture to the South. Hayes had already decided on a Southerner for the cabinet, and the politicians all knew it. The Southern Democrats' promise to "protect" black rights could be believed by only the most absurdly naive person—though Hayes stubbornly chose to believe it, since it was the only real alternative to thinking of himself as a traitor to the memories of Lincoln, the war, and the crusade against slavery.

Then what were nine experienced, tough, and even cynical men doing in that hotel room? Why were they sealing a bargain that exchanged nothing for nothing? And why did their deal become monumentally famous overnight and for a century afterward?

The answer is that they were doing what their careers required. They were professional politicians, all. Hayes's representatives all hoped for future cooperation from Southern Democrats in the House and Senate. To get it, the new administration had to keep up the appearance of being approachable and ready to compromise. The Southern Democrats, on their side, needed to convince their supporters back home that they had not simply knuckled under, that they had shrewdly won last-minute concessions from the victorious Republicans. They had done their job and had, by a spectacular bluff game, achieved "home rule" for the South. Or so they wanted it to appear, no matter what the realities were.

For the next five days, the Democrats in the House walked a tightrope. They put up enough opposition to delay the completion of the official count of the electoral votes to the last minute. But they moved along just fast enough to make it clear that the count could be finished on time. They manufactured an atmosphere of crisis that enabled their supporters to believe that they had held out to the last, used every weapon, fought every battle, and lost only to superior force. In fact, they held out until dawn on March 2, when Hayes was finally declared the winner. But the struggle, like the bargain at Wormsley's Hotel, was more show than reality.

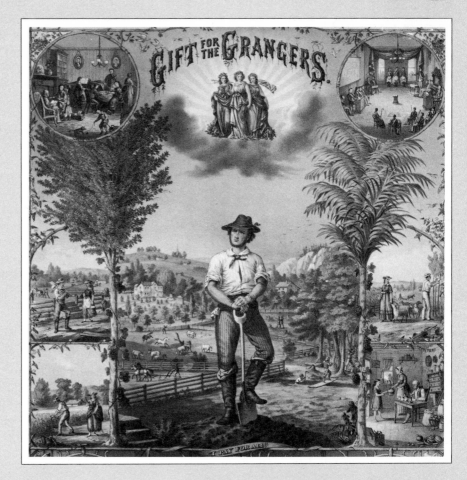

# Politics in a
# Corporate Age

The presidential election of 1872 seemed to signal more years of Republican triumph, and of a vigorous policy of Reconstruction in the South. Grant had come into office in 1869 with a small majority of the popular vote—about 300,000 out of nearly 6 million votes cast. And that slender majority had been made up of black voters in the South. Now, in 1872, Grant swept into a second term with a majority twice as large. In fact, he won 286 electoral votes against only 66 for his opponent. The president and his party seemed to be riding very high indeed. So did their policies—the constitutional amendments giving blacks freedom, citizenship, and the vote; civil rights acts and force bills; Republican control of state governments in the South; and high tariffs and other subsidies for business, industry, and railroads in the North.

Four years later, in 1876, Grant could not win the nomination of his party for a third term—though he badly wanted it. And both parties nominated candidates pledged to *ending* Reconstruction. Something profound had happened between 1872 and 1876, something that not only affected Grant's political career, but that would shape American politics for a generation. The Republican party, which had begun as a movement with a strong ideological thrust, had become a "normal" political institution, less concerned with ideology than with office. In fact, it had become a party that was difficult to distinguish from the opposition Democrats. And for a quarter of a century after 1872, the Republicans and the Democrats would struggle for control of the presidency, of Congress, and of state governments, in a contest that seemed to offer no real choice of policies.

Of course, the Republican party had always had its political side. Many of its leaders, including Lincoln, had been professional politicians, with careers that linked them back to the Whig party of the 1840s. But during the Civil War and Reconstruction, the party professionals had driven to power with a definite program. They might differ among themselves in degree, some more radical than others. But there had been something to be radical *about*. After Grant's presidency, there was simply no Republican position on which any politician could have taken a radical stance, even if he had wanted to.

## THE SLIDE FROM IDEOLOGY

Signals of the change had begun to emerge clearly during Grant's administration. Perhaps the clearest sign was the revelation of a string of corrupt deals that reached into the White House itself. Grant had maintained a public friendship with two of the most notorious speculators in the United States, Jay Gould and Jim Fisk. During 1869, they staged a daring attempt to corner gold—that is, to buy it up—driving its price higher and higher (and the price of corporate stocks correspondingly lower). The solution would have been simple. The president could have begun to sell government gold, flooding the market and bringing the price down. But Grant held off, convincing many people that he was part of the cornering strategy. Only a panicky day on the stock market, known as "Black Friday," in September of 1869, finally forced Grant's hand.

Then, in 1873, came clearer proof of corruption in the administration—though none of the proofs ever touched Grant directly. The Union Pacific Railroad, which had heavy federal subsidies, had been involved for years in a fraudulent arrangement with a construction company known as Crédit Mobilier. Crédit Mobilier was owned by a number of financiers who also owned stock in the Union Pacific. They arranged for contracts between the railroad and the construction company that simply milked the railroad. Since they owned a minority of the shares of Union Pacific, and almost all of Crédit Mobilier, the financiers were the clear winners. The losers were the federal government and the other stock-holders of the railroad.

One of the officers of Crédit Mobilier was a congressman from Massachusetts, Oakes Ames. He began to peddle Crédit Mobilier stock to his colleagues in the House at give-away prices, buying their support. And among those who took the bribes were Grant's vice president, Schuyler Colfax. An investigation eventually exposed Crédit Mobilier, but the administration and the party had been deeply scarred.

Then, months later, another scandal broke. A ring of whiskey distillers had been cheating the government of tax money by submitting false reports. The distillers had bought off several politicians by making large contributions to their state organizations. They had even involved Grant's own private secretary, Orville Babcock.

Everyone seemed to be on the take. In one cabinet department after another, new scandals rolled into the press. And because the Republicans controlled Washington, they were most deeply damaged.

A second sign of change in the Republican party was the rise of leaders in state organizations whose sole interest in politics seemed to be office and power, and for whom political ideas were a nuisance or a joke. Matt Quay in Pennsylvania, Nelson Aldrich in Rhode Island, and Mark Hanna in Ohio were typical. (The Republicans called such men "Stalwarts.") They controlled tightly disciplined party organizations in their states. These organizations in turn controlled the state legislatures. And the state legislatures elected United States senators. So the Senate became the key to and the reward of power. From the Senate, party leaders managed patronage appointments at all levels and kept watch over federal appropriations for "internal improvements" that might benefit their supporters and contributors back home. To such men, the notion that political parties ought to have a mission or purpose higher than power belonged to the old days of the Civil War. One of the most powerful Republican senators, Roscoe Conkling, spoke for them all—Republicans and Democrats alike—when he said

that "Parties are not built by deportment, or by ladies' magazines, or gush."

A third signal that the Republican party had undergone a profound change was the split that developed in it in 1872. Worried about corruption in Grant's administration, a group of Republican politicians met in a separate convention to nominate their own candidate and write their own platform. They called themselves Liberal Republicans, and they were led by high-minded reformers, journalists, and scholars. Their most prominent member was the old radical, Charles Sumner, who now wanted a quick end to Reconstruction, which he felt Grant had transformed into a party-building machine.

Sumner and the other Liberals had, in reality, only one common ground: government ought to be "clean"—controlled not by party patronage but by a civil service system that would make it immune to influence and bribery. They nominated Horace Greeley, the old, fire-eating editor of the *New York Tribune*. The Democratic convention also endorsed Greeley.

The movement failed. Greeley won in only a handful of states. But the emergence of the Liberal Republicans put a marked stamp on presidential politics for the next twenty years. They were independents without a mass base or party organization. In fact, the party leaders caricatured the reformers as "Mugwumps"—a curious sort of political animal, straddling a fence, with its face (or "mug") on one side and its rump (or "wump") on the other. But the Mugwump politicians of the 1870s and 1880s were men of considerable influence. Through reformist editors like E. L. Godkin of the *Nation,* they controlled important magazines and newspapers. Their leaders included men like Charles Francis Adams, who had been Lincoln's ambassador to Great Britain. And they could reach an important segment of the Republican elite through books like *Chapters of Erie,* exposing railroad mismanagement and political corruption, written by Adams's two brilliant sons, Henry and Charles Francis, Jr.

Mugwump independence was a threat to Republicans, a promise to Democrats. It pushed both political parties toward a consistent policy of nominating a special kind of presidential candidate: a man of supposedly spotless moral character and record, who could promise the electorate "good government." The politicos in effect weakened their chances of personally holding the presidency, unless they might come in the side door, through the vice presidency. In return, they maintained control over the Senate, the party machinery, and the all-important system of patronage appointments.

In this respect, the two parties became mirror images of each other. There were some differences during the 1870s and 1880s. The Democrats came to control a solid base in the South, the Republicans in the Middle West. Republicans appealed more to Protestant, native-born Americans, the Democrats to urban Catholic immigrants. The Republicans consistently nominated Union officers as presidential candidates. The Democrats almost always ran governors of New York state, certain that that state held the key to their political fortunes.

But underneath these differences lay a crucial sameness about the parties. Both were very conscious of the necessity of organization, from the ward and precinct level up to the Senate. Both were acutely sensitive to the need for money to mobilize more and more voters. Both succeeded in mustering larger voter turnouts than in the pre–Civil War period. At the presidential level, elections became desperate struggles to win a slim victory. In fact, only one president between 1872 and 1896 won the office with a majority of the popular vote. And this forced both parties into a struggle for swing voters. Democrats and Republicans both tried to occupy a noncontroversial center on major issues at election time, so both had to avoid any position that might generate any sort of division in party ranks.

## THE POWERLESS PRESIDENTS

The net result of all these political forces was to make the presidency an office for men who did not control their own parties and had not been elected on any sort of program they might press through Congress, men whose position was almost that of a figurehead. They might have very strong personal character, as several of them did; but in political terms their position was almost impossible. They entered office to find all the important positions in their administration already sold to win the nomination or the election, all the important legislation controlled by the Senate leadership, and Congress usually divided between a Democratic House and a Republican Senate.

The grave questions posed by industrialization could hardly find their way onto the political stage, where the only issue seemed to be control of the government. Politics had become a kind of serpent, devouring itself, concerned not with economic and social questions, or questions of diplomacy and war, but only with the political process itself. Government had become its own object. A twentieth-century president, Calvin Coolidge, once remarked that "The business of America is business." Any of his predecessors from the 1870s and 1880s could aptly have said that the politics of America was politics.

Soon after his election in 1876, Rutherford B. Hayes announced that he would not run for another term. This, taken together with the way he had won, made him almost powerless. When the Democrats won the Senate in 1878, the administration was even further weakened. Hayes did end Reconstruction—which the Democratic Congress would have done anyway, through its control over appropriations for the military. But for the rest, he confined himself to trying to make decent appointments and to institute a merit system of civil service in some of the federal departments, particularly in the astonishingly corrupt Post Office and Treasury departments.

In fact, Hayes's worst enemies turned out to be not Democrats but the Republican party leaders. The party was divided into the Stalwarts, headed by Conkling, and the "Half-Breeds," who were very much like the Stalwarts but wanted a few concessions to the small "good-government" Mugwump wing of the party. The Half-Breeds

# George Washington Plunkitt

In the late nineteenth century, especially in major cities, elections turned not on issues or even on the personalities of candidates, but on the careful efforts of men whose lives were devoted to two things: getting out the votes on election day and distributing patronage and favors between elections. The most famous political organization in the United States was "Tammany Hall," the Democratic "machine" in New York City.

The Tammany Society was founded in 1789 as a social club for businessmen and bankers. But by the mid-nineteenth century, Tammany had become the city's Democratic Party organization. It controlled the elections of the city's aldermen and representatives to the state legislature. It managed the appointments of the city's bureaucrats. It beat back periodic efforts to reform the city government. And in the process, it profited. Tammany's leaders became rich. Some of them, like the infamous "boss" William Marcy Tweed, went to prison for bribery or theft.

But a more typical Tammany leader was George Washington Plunkitt. He was born in 1842 in an Irish shantytown in Manhattan. He worked his way up in the organization to become an alderman, a state legislator, and a state senator. He died at eighty, a rich man—mostly from investments in real estate. He helped to finance construction of the George Washington Bridge and the American Museum of Natural History.

This was the real Plunkitt of Tammany. A man who knew how to turn the inside knowledge of politics into shrewd real-estate deals that made him wealthy, but who probably never stole anything directly from the public treasury. A man with superb knowledge of the ethnic basis of urban politics, who knew how to organize not just the Irish who were Tammany's original strength, but the newer groups of Jews and Italians. A man who knew, above all, how to deliver the many "favors" his constituents expected.

But there was another Plunkitt, half-fictitious, who fascinated millions of American readers. This Plunkitt was the creation of a journalist named William Riordon. Riordon hung around Plunkitt's "office," a shoeshine stand in the city courthouse, and listened to Plunkitt talk. Riordon then published, in 1905, *Plunkitt of Tammany Hall, a Series of Very Plain Talks on Very Practical Politics.* The book was a masterly blend of cracker-barrel humor, political cynicism, biography, and inside dope. In it, Riordon's readers discovered a man who was a surprising combination of their image of an Irish political hack and their own middle-class moralism.

Plunkitt's "plain talks"—or, at least Riordon's version of them—really constituted a book of advice to young men on how to get ahead, how to go from rags to riches in politics. And his rules were unexpectedly familiar to Riordon's middle-class audience. Don't drink, Plunkitt warned, for it takes a clear head to run a political organization. Be loyal to your friends and to the party. Be modest. Dress plainly. Live in the neighborhood where you work. Be absolutely tolerant of ethnic and religious differences. Work hard: the ward boss must be up early and late, taking care of the legitimate needs of the voters. Never steal: there is plenty of opportunity for "honest graft," so no politician ever needs to take money from the public treasury. Don't be befuddled by abstractions like free silver: a young man must learn to rise above principle sometimes.

Riordon's achievement—and we will never know how accurately he represented the real Plunkitt—was to weld the prevailing myths of the self-made entrepreneur to the image of the political boss. The result was a charming portrait of a man who wanted his epitaph to be one that could have fitted any rags-to-riches hero of the period: "He seen his opportunities and he took 'em."

For President
JAMES G. BLAINE

1884

REPUBLICAN NOMINEES

CAPITOL

For Vice-President
JOHN A. LOGAN

**REPUBLICAN POSTER, 1884**

In 1884, after years of trying, Senator James G. Blaine of Maine finally won the Republican presidential nomination. This poster shows a white plume across the center and is meant to recall a famous speech given for Blaine at the 1876 Republican convention: "Like an armed warrior, like a plumed knight, James G. Blaine marched down the halls of the American Congress and threw his lance full and fair against the brazen foreheads of the defamers of his country and the maligners of her honor." *(Culver Pictures)*

were led by a curiously charismatic senator from Maine, James G. Blaine, whose career had been besmirched by the revelation of railroad fraud. Blaine had written several letters to a colleague in corruption named Mulligan, letters that often ended "Burn this letter!"—an instruction that Mulligan did not obey. For Conkling and Blaine and their followers, Hayes's concern for clean government and for appointments based on merit were the worst kind of nuisance.

The president vainly attempted to get an ap-propriation through Congress to fund the modest Civil Service Commission that had been created during the Grant administration. Finally, in frus-tration, Hayes removed two of Conkling's New York supporters, Alonzo B. Cornell and Chester A. Arthur, from their lucrative federal offices. Conkling fought back by persuading the Senate not to approve replacements for the two men. Hayes could do nothing but submit name after name, waiting for the Senate to turn each of them down, until finally even the senators grew weary and allowed two names to pass.

When the Republicans met to choose a nom-inee in 1880, Conkling and his Stalwart faction supported Grant. Blaine and his Half-Breeds, with Mugwump help, were able to deny Grant the nomination for thirty-five ballots, until the convention finally turned to a noncontroversial dark horse, James A. Garfield, a tried veteran of the House of Representatives from Ohio—and, of course, a Union officer. The Stalwarts con-tented themselves with the vice-presidential nom-ination for the model party professional Chester A. Arthur. The Democrats chose to play dead— or to try to beat the Republicans at their own game. They made the uninspired choice of their own Union general, Winfield Scott Hancock, a man whose military record had created no polit-ical following. The result was a Republican vic-tory but a narrow one, in which Garfield and Arthur won 4,454,000 votes as against 4,444,000 for their opponents.

Garfield was a study in rags to riches, a self-made man. He had been born in a log cabin—a real one—and had managed to become a teacher, then a lawyer and a politician. He had served in Congress since the war years and was apparently a man of honesty. His postmaster general, with Garfield's strong support, unearthed a major fraud in the postal service, and the stage seemed set for another struggle between a reasonably clean president and the barons of the Senate. But before the struggle could reach a climax, Garfield was shot down. On July 2, 1881, after four months in office, he was murdered by an obscure, ambitious, and clearly insane man named Charles

Guiteau, who shouted as he shot: "I am a Stalwart, and Arthur is president!" Garfield clung to
life for three months before Arthur was indeed
president. The new chief executive surprised
everyone by continuing to press the fraud cases
in the Post Office, and by making independent
appointments, as though he were trying to live
down a career as a consummate spoilsman of the
Stalwart faction. He even got a modest civil service law, the Pendleton Act, through Congress
in 1883. The law put only about one federal job
out of ten on a merit system, but it did allow for
future expansion of the number by executive order. (In fact, it put every future president in the
position of being able to appoint supporters to
non–civil service jobs, then, once they were in
place, extending the blanket of protection to them
so they could not be removed. Through this process, by the 1940s, a bare majority of federal jobs
were brought under the Civil Service Act.)

Arthur made no one happy, not Stalwarts,
Half-Breeds or Mugwumps. The convention of
1884 simply ignored him, and turned instead to
the prince of the Half-Breeds, James G. Blaine.
The Mugwumps announced they would not support Blaine if the Democrats were to nominate a
"good-government" man, and the Democrats
obliged them by choosing Grover Cleveland, a
reform mayor of Buffalo and governor of New
York. The resulting campaign was heavily financed on both sides, and consisted mainly of
attacks on the personal character of the candidates. For his part, Blaine was vulnerable because
of the Mulligan letters, and the Democrats could
chant:

> Blaine! Blaine! James G. Blaine,
> Continental liar from the state of Maine!
> (Burn this letter!)

But Cleveland proved to have an unexpected
weak spot. He had accepted responsibility for an
illegitimate child in his youth, so his opponents
could come back with a chant of their own:

> Ma! Ma! Where's my Pa?
> Gone to the White House, Ha! Ha! Ha!

JAMES A. GARFIELD

Garfield won the Republican nomination for the presidency in 1880 not because of any groundswell of support
among voters but as a compromise designed to prevent
the nomination of Grant. Here, he is shown as a model
political leader of the period, staring into the distance with
an expression that is concerned but determined and confident that the future can indeed be conquered. Surely, the
photograph suggests, such a man could not have been
involved in the Crédit Mobilier scandal, even in a minor
way. *(Culver Pictures)*

In November, Cleveland got the better of the
chantings. The election may in fact have been
thrown to him at the last minute. Blaine, at a
reception in New York City, was called on by a
delegation of Protestant ministers. One of them
made a brief speech, in which he accused the
Democrats of being the party of "Rum, Roman-
ism, and Rebellion." Blaine, who had a Catholic
mother, either did not hear the remark or chose
to ignore it. But when it became public, he was
stuck with it. And this slender bit of chance may
have moved enough immigrant and Catholic voters in New York City to swing the election to

Cleveland. Almost 10 million men voted, and Cleveland received only about 20,000 more votes than Blaine. New York State could have given either man the necessary electoral votes for a victory.

Grover Cleveland was a staunch Jacksonian,

**GROVER CLEVELAND**

Grover Cleveland, shown here in a studio photograph, was a shortish, heavy man whose political reputation was built entirely on an honest willingness to say no—to both corrupt party organizations like Tammany Hall and small appropriations meant to relieve farmers ruined by drought. The photographer managed to capture some of Cleveland's determination, along with the conventional brave stare into the distance. On the floor is what appears to be a brass spittoon of modest size. *(Culver Pictures)*

who believed profoundly in laissez faire. The government, he thought, should be a minimal institution, whose main purposes were maintaining law and order and conducting foreign policy. He once vetoed a relief bill to aid farmers who had been stricken by drought, with the observation that the people should support the government, but the government should never support the people. He even did what no president before him had done. He actually read the applications that Union veterans submitted to Congress when they asked for special relief and pension legislation. He vetoed hundreds of such requests—to the fury of the congressmen whose tie to their constituents was heavily dependent on their ability to get such government favors. Congress responded with a bill granting general pensions to *all* disabled veterans—no matter when or how their disability had come about. Cleveland provoked an even more serious storm by vetoing this law.

The president's laissez-faire attitude even extended to one of the sleeping giants of American politics, the tariff. For twenty years or more, the country had had a high Republican tariff, and a system had been worked out for buying support from agricultural states by putting their products—sugar or wool, for example—on the protected list along with manufactured goods. But Cleveland, in the middle of his administration, went to Congress to ask for substantial reductions in tariffs. He was, among other things, embarrassed by a large surplus in the Treasury, a surplus that made it clear that no tariff was necessary for revenue. For him, the meaning of the surplus was plain and outweighed all the justifications for a high tariff that scholars might produce: "It is a *condition* that confronts us," he said, "not a theory."

The Democrats in the House managed to push through a bill making some reductions in tariff schedules, but the measure stalled. For the first time in years, the presidential contest coming up in 1888 would have a statable issue—though a minor one when measured against the more serious questions being posed by industrial development. The Democrats chose Cleveland again. The Republicans turned to Benjamin Harrison of Indiana, who was as unknown as Hayes and Garfield had been, and just as respectable and easy to identify with the cause of clean government. He was the grandson of William Henry Harrison, the Whig president of the 1840s.

But if the parties had a clear issue—high tariffs or low—the voters were not ready with a verdict. Cleveland won the popular vote—though by less than 100,000 out of 10 million. In fact, he was the only presidential candidate of the period to win a clear majority of the total popular vote. But he lost. The electors divided 233 for Harrison, 168 for Cleveland.

Harrison rode into office on a very frail horse. But his Republican Congress behaved as though the party had won a mandate for a great cause. They set out to write the highest protective tariff law in United States history, and they won. The resulting McKinley tariff—named for its sponsor in the House, William McKinley of Ohio—established a level of protection that satisfied every tariff lobby in the nation. But the initiative had come almost entirely from Congress; Harrison himself was as hamstrung by his lack of control over his party as his predecessors in office had been. In fact, he complained after he left office that, "When I came into power, I found that the party managers had taken it all to themselves. I could not name my own Cabinet. They had sold out every place to pay the election expenses." And if that were not enough, he was soon to face a Congress in which his party was crippled. When the results of the congressional elections of 1890 came in, the Republicans had kept only 88 of the 323 seats in the House.

To some extent, the congressional elections of 1890 may have been a referendum on the McKinley tariff. If it was, the answer was clear: McKinley himself was defeated in his home district, and his political career seemed for the moment to be over. But the tariff itself was less the issue than it was the symbol of a range of issues that were struggling to the surface of American political life, a range of issues that focused on the general problem of "monopoly" capitalism, and the failure of governments to take any effective measures to control or regulate it. A few Democrats—even some who had supported the tariff where it protected economic interests in their home states—began to play on the problem of monopoly and to argue that the tariff was designed to protect trusts from overseas competition. They hit a responsive chord. The electorate had become increasingly concerned and frustrated over the apparent inability of their political leaders to do anything about the power of the giant corporations over American life.

In the presidential election of 1892, the Republicans ignored the danger signs and renominated Harrison. The Democrats countered with Cleveland. Once again, as in 1888, the two parties' platforms were almost identical—except for the tariff. The Republicans once more promised to maintain the kind of "protection" provided by the McKinley tariff. The Democrats promised reductions. This time, the swing that had been clear in the congressional voting of 1890 bore fruit for the Democrats. Cleveland won almost twice as many electoral votes as Harrison, and almost a 10 percent edge in the popular voting. More important, the Democrats won majorities in both the House and the Senate. For the first time in a generation, they controlled the executive and legislative branches of the federal government.

The result was disappointing to anyone who had voted for a significant change in policies. Cleveland stood more firmly than ever for his laissez-faire policies, his belief that the government should not "support" any of the people by intervening in their economic life in any significant way. Cleveland did try to push a lowering of the tariff rates through Congress, but even here he failed. The Democrats in Congress would give him only about a 10 percent reduction in the average duties that had been voted a few years earlier in the McKinley tariff. On the surface, at least, the Democrats' surge to power had produced little or nothing in the way of a shift in government policies.

# THE RISE OF THE POPULIST PARTY

But there were straws in the political wind suggesting that some sort of challenge to the prevailing political order of things was building toward a climax. The new tariff included the first peacetime income tax in the history of the United States. The rates were mild—2 percent on all incomes over $4,000, a formula which meant that a sizable majority of Americans would pay no tax at all. But the income tax had been a clear concession to a new and highly visible element in politics, a movement of protest demanding changes that were, from the point of view of the normal politics of the preceding twenty years, almost revolutionary. The political challenge took its clearest and most visible form in the West and the South as an organized movement of farmers, and it finally resulted in the formation of a new political party.·

The movement had roots going well back into the 1870s, and it focused on questions of policy on which the major parties had either taken a weak and tentative stand or no stand at all.

Farmers during the early 1870s—times of prosperity for most of them—had begun to organize themselves into local chapters of the National Grange of the Patrons of Husbandry. The word "grange" was from a medieval term naming a building on a manor where grain was stored. In England, "grange" was a name sometimes given to the farmhouse and buildings of a well-off, "gentleman" farmer. The Americans who first became "Grangers" and "Patrons of Husbandry" were adopting a terminology which suggested that farming was in fact a gentleman's occupation. They met primarily for cultural and social purposes, and used a somewhat elaborate secret ritual. (In these respects, they were very much like the early "Knights" of labor; see pp. 551–552.)

But in 1873, the nation entered the most serious depression in its history, and farmers suffered even more than other Americans. They began to join the Grange in massive numbers—800,000 by 1875—and to redefine its purposes. They formed cooperative grain elevators, stores, milk-processing plants, even factories to make farm machinery and stoves—all in the hope of freeing themselves from the grip of what they clearly understood to be "monopolies." Most of all they turned to politics at the state level, to attack what they felt were the cruel and monopolistic practices of the railroads.

Beginning in 1871, then with even greater success after 1873, the Grangers were able to muster enough votes in the state legislatures of Wisconsin, Illinois, Iowa, and Minnesota, to impose rate regulations on railroad companies. (These attempts at regulation were at first endorsed by federal courts, then increasingly struck down. See pp. 590–591.)

The return of prosperity in the late 1870s reduced both the size and the effectiveness of the Granger movement. By 1880, it had lost 700,000 of its 800,000 members, and it would remain small and inconsequential.

As the 1880s wore on, however, the farmers who raised staple crops—wheat and cotton especially—began to experience a steady and serious drop in the market price for their crops. They began to organize into farmers' "Alliances." In the plains states, they formed the National Farmers' Alliance. In the South, black and white farmers created parallel organizations, the Farmers' Alliance and Industrial Union, and the Colored Farmers' Alliance. By the mid-1880s, the Southern groups had over a million members.

The Alliance movement was even more political than the Grangers had been. The Western group ran candidates under its own party label for state and national offices. In the South, the Alliances tried a different tactic; they attempted to gain control of the securely entrenched Democratic party. In fact, in 1890—the year the Republicans suffered their massive defeats in congressional elections—the Alliances managed to win varying degrees of control over eight legislatures in the South and four in the West. From the South came forty congressmen who had been endorsed by the Alliances against conservative

**GRANGER POSTER**

This 1872 poster captured many of the ideas of the agricultural reform movement known as the Granger Movement. Its main message is that the honest toil of the yeoman farmer is the basis of prosperity: "I pay for all," is the slogan at the center. But the agricultural reality depicted here belonged not to the 1870s so much as to the 1830s. All labor is being done by hand. There is not a single reaper in sight. There is no steam engine, no cotton gin, no railroad line. At the bottom is a dilapidated house of a farmer who failed not because of economic conditions but because of his own "Ignorance" and "Sloth." *(Culver Pictures)*

Democrats and one—Thomas Watson of Georgia—who went so far as to repudiate either a Democratic or a Republican label.

During the next two years, the Alliance leaders planned an even more active challenge to the standing political order. They founded a new party, the People's, or Populist, party. In 1892, delegates representing the Alliances, the Knights of Labor, and other antimonopoly groups gathered at an exultant convention in Omaha to write a platform and nominate a candidate to oppose Cleveland and Harrison.

The Populist platform was a radical document, in the sense that it addressed political and economic questions that had been either kept offstage entirely or dealt with by the federal government in a hesitant and reluctant way. The Populists had three main concerns: public finance, monopoly, and the conduct of politics. They confronted these concerns much more directly than either Republicans or Democrats had been able or willing to do.

For the Populists, public finance boiled down to two questions: the currency and credit. The federal government, under both Republicans and Democrats, had been pursuing policies that led to a restricted supply of currency, or "tight" money, and to equally restricted credit. Both currency and credit had been eased during the Civil War. The Lincoln administration had printed paper money called "greenbacks"—about $450 million worth. At the end of the war, some $400 million worth were still in circulation. The government had also built up a large debt by selling bonds. Most of the bonds were owned by national banks, which had been allowed to make loans to their customers in return for the bonds, to be held by the banks as their "reserve" to pay off depositors. These two policies had resulted in higher prices and easy credit for most farmers.

After the war, the federal government had decided to keep a fixed amount of greenbacks in circulation but to back them with gold. This policy did not create a currency large enough to feed the tremendous economic expansion of the postwar period. So the volume of money in circulation actually was decreasing in proportion to the size of the economy. In addition, Congress in 1873—in what many Populists saw as the "Crime of '73"—removed the silver dollar from the list of money to be coined.

No one had objected at the time, but over the next twenty years the idea took root that the solution to the currency problem was the "free and unlimited coinage" of silver. Cleveland and all the Republicans were "sound money" men—in effect, gold standard men. And so the Populist plank demanding free and unlimited coinage was a direct challenge to the dominant groups of both major parties.

As for credit, the Populist platform of 1892 included a program that would have moved the federal government much further into the credit system. The platform asked for savings banks operated by the Post Office, to give people an alternative to private banking institutions. And it asked the federal government to create storage warehouses for grain and cotton, where farmers might keep their crops when the market price was low. The scheme would have allowed farmers to receive interest-free loans worth 80 percent of the current market price of the crops while they were in storage.

The credit scheme was, when compared with policies then existing, a radical one. But the platform took an even more radical attitude toward the great monopolies the Populists thought were oppressing them. Corporate combinations of all sorts—pools, trusts, holding companies, and mergers—had become a major fact of American life. But Democratic and Republican politicians had responded very little to the growing uneasiness of many of their voters. In a few states, there had been attempts to regulate railroads. But the prevailing attitude of politicians had been one of benign neglect toward, or even support for, corporate growth and integration.

During the late 1880s, some members of Congress had recognized the necessity of making at least a token gesture toward controlling corporations. The result had been two laws that seemed to discourage monopolistic practices—one by regulating them, the other by forbidding them.

The first was the Interstate Commerce Act of 1887. This law created an Interstate Commerce Commission, charged with regulating the railroad industry. The commission was, in theory, to make certain that all railroad rates were "reasonable." The railroads were forbidden to create market "pools" or to discriminate among shippers by giving a lower price to some than to others.

The second was the Sherman Antitrust Act of 1890. In its language, the act was a radical affirmation of the idea that the best economy was one in which there was pure competition. It forbade every "combination" that acted to "restrain" trade, or competition, in interstate commerce.

These two laws had seemed to move in the direction the Populists wanted. But in practice, both turned out to be practically meaningless. It was clear by 1892 that neither was going to provide an effective check on the power of corporations. And so the Populists wrote their most radical plank to deal with the monopolies they believed oppressed them most: the railroads. They demanded, simply, government ownership of all railroad and telegraph companies. As a challenge to the power of other corporations, the platform proposed that the eight-hour work day be made standard in all industries—though this would have been a marked extension of federal power to regulate private businesses and industries.

Experience had taught the Populists that they had no hope but to try to win control over the political process itself. So their platform included demands for significant reforms to the system. They wanted a secret ballot. They asked for a system of initiative and referendum, through which voters could pass laws or repeal them. And they sought to break the stranglehold of the two major parties over the system by providing that senators be elected directly, instead of by the state legislatures.

To run on this platform, the Populists nominated James B. Weaver, who had been a Democrat before the Civil War, then a Republican, now a Populist. In the election of 1892, Weaver won 22 electoral votes. And the Populists won over a million popular votes. About a dozen members of Congress now called themselves Populists.

## DEFEAT OF THE POPULISTS

The stage seemed set for a mighty contest in 1896, to determine whether the People's party would gain full access to federal power for their reform challenge. The drama was intensified by a depression which began in 1893 and was in some ways the most serious the nation had ever experienced. Well over a hundred railroads and four hundred banks failed. Even more important, probably as many as 20 percent of the nation's workers were unemployed—in an era in which there were no programs of relief or unemployment compensation. If the Populists could tap the discontent growing out of the depression and add it to the older and still smoldering complaints that had created their party, then they might expect to play a profoundly important role in the future of American politics.

On their side, the Republicans had just as much reason to expect victory. The depression was, as usual, blamed on the administration. The elections of 1894 had seemed to confirm both Populist and Republican hopes. Taken altogether, Populist candidates collected almost one and a half million votes—a sharp increase over 1892. And the Republicans came out of the election in full control of the House of Representatives—something they had had only twice in the preceding twenty years.

And so the parties approached 1896: the Republicans confident, the Populists excited, the Democrats divided between those who wanted to nominate another Eastern conservative (as the party had done for a generation) and those who wanted to move South or West, to tap the energies of the Populists.

The Republicans nominated William McKinley, author of the McKinley tariff, who after losing his seat in Congress had become governor of Ohio. Behind McKinley stood the man who was, in effect, the head of the party, Marcus A. Hanna, who would manage to raise somewhere between $4 and $15 million for the campaign. (No one probably will ever know the full amount, but it is clear that McKinley's run for the presidency was the first "modern" campaign in terms of the dollars spent. Standard Oil alone contributed $300,000—almost as much as the Democrats spent on their entire effort.) For a platform, Hanna and his party decided on even

**McKINLEY CAMPAIGNS (MORE OR LESS)**

While his opponent Bryan traveled and spoke more than any candidate ever had before, William McKinley stayed home in Ohio, speaking occasionally from his own front porch to carefully chosen crowds. His was a cautious campaign in which the greatest risk was to put the candidate on a rug covering an unstable wicker basket that substituted for a speaker's "stump." But, from the Republican point of view, it all worked splendidly. *(Culver Pictures)*

higher tariffs, solid support for the gold standard, and a vague promise of "prosperity." Nothing was said about the problem of the trusts, regulation of railroads, or the income tax.

At the Democratic convention in Chicago, there was nothing but confusion. The party was divided. On one side was a Cleveland faction that was predominantly Eastern, favored gold, and rejected most of the Populist program. On the other side were Southerners and Westerners who demanded the endorsement of free silver and wanted the party to support at least some of the Populist program—the income tax, for example, and a stronger federal attempt to regulate railroads and corporations. This faction wanted, in effect, to repudiate Cleveland, who had led the party into all three presidential elections since 1884.

To settle the question of the party's position on gold, a debate was arranged, with three men speaking for the gold standard and three for "bimetallism." Surely none of the politicians expected the party to resolve such a problem with speeches. But for once they were surprised. The final speaker for silver, William Jennings Bryan, gave such a masterful address that the convention went into something approaching political hysteria and nominated him for president the next day.

Bryan's strengths were his words and his voice. He could roll out sentences that schoolchildren would be forced to memorize for decades. He ended his address to the convention with a dramatic challenge to the Republicans, a challenge that attempted to identify free silver with the cause of the common man:

> If they dare to come out into the open and defend the gold standard as a good thing, we will fight them to the uttermost. Having behind us the producing masses of this nation and the world, supported by the commercial interests, the laboring interests and the toilers everywhere, we will answer their demand for a gold standard by saying to them: "You shall not press down upon the brow of labor this crown of thorns; you shall not crucify mankind upon a Cross of Gold."

Bryan was a Nebraskan with only two terms in the House of Representatives to his political credit. But he had managed to steal the party and to steal, in the bargain, one of the main planks of the Populists. The Democrats also endorsed the income tax and railroad regulation. This created a painful dilemma for the Populists. Bryan was almost certain to win every state where a Populist would have had a chance against a traditional Democrat. They seemed to have no option but to endorse him and the principle of "fusion" with the Democrats. And so a majority of Populists voted in their convention to accept Bryan as their candidate, preserving a fiction of

BRYAN CAMPAIGNS (MORE)

William Jennings Bryan's strongest political weapon was his ability as a speaker. And his only real hope of victory was to use that skill as often as possible. He traveled and spoke tirelessly but nevertheless failed to carry most of the states he visited. Here in a rare photograph of him in 1896, he is talking to a crowd in Union Square in New York. *(Culver Pictures)*

independence by choosing Tom Watson of Georgia as their vice-presidential nominee.

The Democrats' problem was, in part, money—a problem Bryan attempted to offset by traveling almost 20,000 miles and making more than 600 speeches to audiences that finally totaled in the millions. (In this way, Bryan's campaign was as modern as McKinley's. But McKinley stayed at home and campaigned from his front porch. It would be some time yet before a candidate would conduct a race using both money *and* speeches on an enormous scale.)

But money was only part of the problem. Bryan defined the campaign almost from the beginning as a contest between rural and urban Americans. "Burn down your cities," he said, "and leave our farms, and your cities will spring up again as if by magic; but destroy our farms and grass will grow in the streets of every city in this country." The result was that Bryan won little support from urban workers, even from those who were unemployed or embittered. Hanna, on the other hand, had 120 million pamphlets printed in half a dozen languages, aimed specifically at the urban-industrial-immigrant work force.

Bryan, to no one's surprise, carried the South. He also won much of the electoral vote of the Great Plains and the mining states of the Rockies. But he could not carry states where the Granger movement had been popular in the 1870s—Iowa, Wisconsin, Minnesota, or Illinois. He failed in California and Oregon. And, most important, he did not win in a single state north of the Ohio River and east of the Mississippi. The cities, including most workers, went for McKinley, gold, and high tariffs.

Twice more Bryan would attempt to lead the Democrats to victory, in 1900 and 1908. But he would fail decisively. And with his failure would go the failure of the Populists as a party. They had staked their political future on Bryan and on fusion, and it had failed. They had mounted a serious challenge to corporate power, to laissez faire, and to the political system. They had cried, in effect, "conspiracy" between government and private wealth. (They had even, some of them, blamed "Jews," but in this their attitudes were no more anti-Semitic than those of the leaders of the two principal parties.) They had won a victory of a kind: the Democratic party would never again be quite the same. But the victory had cost them their chance at national power over the long run. The voters and the system of government had returned a negative answer. And the federal courts were, meanwhile, making the negative answer even more definite and ringing.

# A JUDICIAL DEFENSE OF PRIVILEGE

In the courts, particularly in the Supreme Court, the new industrial capitalism found an endorsement that was sure and powerful.

The Constitution did not mention corpora-

tions, or labor unions, or trusts. It had been drawn up by men who would hardly have been able to imagine the scale of the McCormick Company, or of Carnegie's steel works—let alone the billion-dollar realities of the great railroad corporations. And the decisions of the courts affecting corporations during the pre–Civil War period had been about small bridge companies or shipping companies—or even incorporated colleges.

The question now was: How could the Constitution be adapted to the astonishing industrial and corporate developments of the second half of the nineteenth century? What powers did state and local governments have to control and regulate the gigantic new enterprises of the period? How would the brief statement in the Constitution that the federal government had the power to "regulate" interstate commerce be interpreted in an industrial age?

When judges had to decide on the validity of state and local regulation of business, the new legal problem they had to come to terms with was the Fourteenth Amendment. The amendment guaranteed that no state could take away any of the privileges of citizens of the United States. And it extended to the states an old provision—from the Fifth Amendment, in force since 1791—that no person could be deprived of "life, liberty, or property, without due process of law." On the other hand, the courts had long recognized that state and local governments had general "police" powers to control the "persons" in their jurisdictions—including corporations. The question now was: Did the Fourteenth Amendment cut into the police power of the states and municipalities?

This question was put to the Supreme Court very directly in what were known as the *Slaughterhouse Cases,* decided in 1873. A Louisiana law of 1867 had given one slaughterhouse a monopoly of business in New Orleans by simply ordering all competing meat processors to stop doing business in the city.

The Court ruled—by a bare majority—that Louisiana was in the right. The state had followed all the legal forms in creating the law, and so had followed the "due process" requirements of the Fourteenth Amendment. To be sure, the justices admitted, the complaining slaughterers had been deprived of the right to do business. But so long as the state had not violated any legal *procedures,* the law was a valid exercise of the police power. For the moment, the power of governments to intervene drastically in the conduct of business had been upheld, and the application of the Fourteenth Amendment had been confined to the protection of the rights of the ex-slaves.

The efforts of railroads to prevent state regulation of their rates had a similar outcome in the 1870s. In several Midwestern states, farmers' movements gained control of state legislatures and pushed through laws controlling the charges of railroads and grain elevator companies. The railroads went to court, and the question eventually reached the Supreme Court, in 1877, in the case of *Munn* v. *Illinois.*

The companies argued, in effect, that the states were depriving them of rights and property without due process of law. But the Court refused to go along. The justices made a distinction between types of property and ruled that a railroad or a grain elevator was a special kind of property, devoted to a "public use." This "public use" created a "public interest" in the property, so the railroads had to "submit to being controlled by the public for the common good."

For the moment, the railroads had no option but to go back to the legislatures to try to get the rate regulations repealed—which they were able to do in the long run. But there had been dissenting votes—four in the *Slaughterhouse Cases.* And in the next decade, seven new justices would be appointed. Gradually but certainly, the Court would work its way to a new vision of property rights and of "due process of law."

In 1886, in the case of *Stone* v. *Farmers' Loan and Trust Co.,* the Court examined a Mississippi law that had set up a commission with the power to establish railroad rates and fares. The Court upheld the statute but added an important new caution—one that had been absent from the *Slaughterhouse Cases* and from *Munn* v. *Illinois:*

the regulation must set rates that would allow the railroads to make a profit. The problem of regulation was coming to a clear focus on two questions: What was a fair profit for a corporation to expect on its property? And who was going to *decide* what was fair—the legislatures and their commissions? the railroads and other companies? the courts?

The answers came in 1890, in a complicated case known as *Chicago, Milwaukee, and St. Paul Railway Co.* v. *Minnesota.* Corporations, the Court now decided, were not only entitled to *hold* their property, they were entitled to *use* it to make a profit. But the profit had to be "reasonable." And the legislature could not be allowed to decide what was reasonable. "Due process of law" required a *judicial* finding of the reasonableness of regulation.

In 1898, this opinion received a ringing confirmation in the case of *Smyth* v. *Ames.* The Court set aside a Nebraska law that had set railroad rates directly by enactment and not through any commission. The Court made a very lengthy examination of the company's records and found that the rates set by the legislature were "unreasonable" and so constituted a taking of property without "due process of law." The Court had become something new: a type of regulating agency in itself, which would review state and local regulations to determine whether they met the requirements of the "rule of reason."

The occasional efforts of Congress to control corporations and commerce met a similar fate. The Sherman Antitrust Act had outlawed all "combinations in restraint of trade." And if there was a combination that seemed clearly devoted to restraining competition it was the Sugar Trust, a holding company that controlled more than 90 percent of all sugar refining in the United States. But when a federal suit against the company, E. C. Knight, reached the Supreme Court, the Sherman Act was sliced neatly in two. The Court, in *United States* v. *E. C. Knight* (1895), reached the conclusion that the company was not engaged in commerce at all, but in "manufacturing." And since the Constitution did not give the federal government the power to regulate "manufacturing," the company was not subject to federal power. Indeed, according to the Court, "production" of all kinds—in agriculture, mining, and manufacturing—were beyond the reach of congressional legislation.

The Interstate Commerce Act, Congress's second tentative exercise in regulation, was attacked in a slightly more piecemeal way, but the result was no less clear. In 1898, in *Cincinnati, New Orleans, and Texas Pacific Railway Co.* v. *Interstate Commerce Commission,* the Court ruled that the commission did not have the power to establish railroad rates. The justices had already found that rates on interstate shipments could not be controlled by the states. Now they were in effect deciding that such rates could not be set by *any* governmental authority. The force of the Interstate Commerce Act was reduced to two provisions: that the railroads publish their rate schedules, and that they charge all shippers the same prices. The commission itself was becoming, in the words of a dissenting justice, "a useless body for all practical purposes."

In all the important cases of the 1880s and 1890s, the Court had consistently ruled in favor of the arguments of corporations, and against the regulation of business by either federal or state governments. Later judges and historians would come to call the decisions conservative, even reactionary. But there was nothing conservative about them. The Court was not defending any sort of status quo, or protecting legal tradition against innovation. It was *making* innovations, and it was doing so not to protect the past but to accommodate to the present, a present whose main characteristic was change.

In the process, the Court was endorsing a set of social arrangements in which distinctions of wealth and status were becoming more obvious and extreme. This endorsement was clearly expressed in two landmark decisions of 1895 and 1896. In the first, *Pollock* v. *Farmers' Loan and Trust Co.,* the justices struck down the primitive income tax Congress had passed as part of the tariff law of 1894. In the second, *Plessy* v. *Ferguson,* the Court gave its approval for the first time to legal racial segregation.

In the income tax case, the judges were presented with an argument that the tax law violated a constitutional provision that all taxes be apportioned among the states by population. But the argument went further and pictured the income tax as an attempt on the part of the poor to take the property of the rich. The tax exempted all incomes under $4,000. This amounted, according to the argument, to a decision on the part of three-fourths of the people—who would pay no tax—to tax the other fourth. From this, the lawyers pleaded, would inevitably result "communism" and "anarchy." The opinion of the justices was more calm, but they did reject the principle of the income tax outright—and so took away the one shred of legislative success for which the Populists could claim full credit.

In *Plessy* v. *Ferguson,* the issue involved a Louisiana law that required railroads to provide "equal but separate accommodations for the white and colored races" and required white and "colored" passengers to obey the designations. The question was simple. Did this state law deprive citizens—white *or* black—of the equal protection of the laws guaranteed by the Fourteenth Amendment? Plessy was a man who had seven white great-grandparents, and one black. He had been arrested for refusing to leave a "white" railroad car.

In its decision, the Court made a distinction between "political equality" and "social equality." The Fourteenth Amendment, clearly, required that the states respect "political" rights absolutely, without regard to race or color. But the Constitution could not—in matters of race or any other area of ordinary human life—require "social equality." In "social" areas, the legislature was free to pass laws that enforced "the customs and traditions of the people."

A year later, the judges would decide that education, like seating arrangements on trains, was a "social" fact and not a "political" one. And so it would endorse segregated public schools as a proper way to prevent the "comingling of the two races upon terms unsatisfactory to either."

The message was clear. An act of Congress that attempted to make wealthier citizens pay a tax that ordinary citizens did not pay had been struck down. The right of the dominant race to segregate private and public facilities and schools was secure. A string of decisions had turned back even modest attempts to regulate railroads and prevent the formation of trusts and other forms of monopoly. All this, combined with the clear failure of the Populists, seemed to make it certain that the United States could look forward only to a continuation of politics that accepted the privileges of wealth and the power of corporations as an established fact, above any sort of serious challenge.

## SUGGESTED READINGS, CHAPTERS 27–28

### THE ELECTION OF 1876

The classic work on the Compromises of 1876–1877 was published in 1951 by C. Vann Woodward as *Reunion and Reaction: the Compromise of 1877 and the End of Reconstruction*. Today, it should be read alongside the somewhat more Northern-oriented work of K. I. Polakoff, *The Politics of Inertia: The Election of 1876 and the End of Reconstruction* (1973). The difference between the two approaches boils down to a different notion of what is meant by "compromise." In Woodward's version of things, the compromise was a very concrete deal—one that was worked out, literally, in a smoke-filled room in Washington just at the last moment. For Polakoff, the compromise was a settlement gradually reached by the two parties during the months between the election and the inauguration. Two solid studies, from the Democratic and Republican sides, respectively, are A. C. Flick, *Samuel Jones Tilden* (1939), and Harry Barnard, *Rutherford B. Hayes and His America* (1964).

### POLITICAL PARTIES AND PRESIDENTIAL ADMINISTRATIONS

Excellent insights are available in a number of studies of the politics of this period. Among the better ones are David Rothman, *Politics and Power: The United States Senate, 1869–1901* (1966); Ray Ginger, *Age of Excess: American Life from the End of Reconstruction to World War I* (1965); and L. D. White, *The Republican Era: A Study in Administrative History* (1958). A fine study of the 1890s is Paul Glad, *McKinley, Bryan, and the People* (1964), as is Margaret Leech, *In the Days of McKinley* (1959).

### THE POPULIST CHALLENGE

The starting point for the study of Populism is still the general work of John D. Hicks, *The Populist Revolt* (1931), a friendly, comprehensive discussion of the troubles and struggles of Western farmers. It should, however, be read with these three books: Richard Hofstadter, *The Age of Reform* (1955); Norman Pollack, *The Populist Response to Industrial America* (1962), and Walter T. K. Nugent, *The Tolerant Populists* (1963). The finest biography of a Populist leader, and an excellent introduction to Southern politics in the 1890s, is C. Vann Woodward, *Tom Watson, Agrarian Radical* (1938).

### THE SUPREME COURT

The following three books are an excellent introduction to this difficult but important subject: R. G. McCloskey, *American Conservatism in the Age of Enterprise* (1951); A. M. Paul, *Conservative Crisis and the Rule of Law: Attitudes of Bar and Bench, 1887–1895* (1960); and Sidney Fine, *Laissez Faire and the General-Welfare State: A Study in Conflict in American Thought, 1865–1901* (1964). An older and somewhat partisan—but still excellent—book is Benjamin Twiss, *Lawyers and the Constitution: How Laissez-Faire Came to the Supreme Court* (1941).

# 29 · The Lizzie Borden Murders

Thursday, August 4, 1892, 10:40 A.M. At 92 Second Street, Fall River, Massachusetts. An exceptionally hot, sultry morning. Bridget Sullivan, the Irish servant, was busy washing the downstairs windows when her employer, Andrew J. Borden, arrived home from his daily business rounds downtown and started to open the front door. There were two separate locks on the door, and even after Mr. Borden opened them, he was still faced with a bolt, which could be opened only from the inside. Bridget Sullivan knew what was happening, so she stopped her work and went over to the entrance to help her employer. For a moment she had trouble releasing the bolt. As she fumbled with it she muttered in frustration a sound she later reported to be "Pshaw." Her expletive was overheard by the only other person known to be in the house, Lizzie Borden, Mr. Borden's daughter. Lizzie, standing at the top of the stairs leading up from the front hall, laughed.

Mr. Borden entered the house without speaking to Bridget, who resumed her window-washing. Lizzie Borden joined him, and father and daughter spoke briefly with each other. From the next room, Bridget was sure she heard Lizzie tell Mr. Borden that his wife "had a note and had gone out."

After a few minutes, Andrew Borden got up, took the key to his room from its accustomed spot on the dining room mantelpiece, and went upstairs. A few minutes later, he came down again to take a nap. Still dressed in his tie and jacket, he lay down on the couch in the sitting room, his feet resting on the carpet.

As Andrew Borden lay down, the servant Bridget Sullivan moved discreetly into the dining room, to wash the windows there. After a few moments, she was joined by Lizzie Borden. Lizzie was carrying an ironing board, and she began to iron a stack of handkerchiefs. Quietly, she began a conversation with the servant:

593

"Maggie, are you going out today?" Lizzie asked. (Maggie had been the name of a previous Borden family servant, and Lizzie Borden always addressed Bridget by that name.)

"I don't know," Bridget answered. "I might and I might not. I don't feel very well." (Bridget had been vomiting earlier in the morning.)

"If you go out, be sure and lock the door, for Mrs. Borden has gone out on a sick call [to visit a sick person], and I might go out, too."

"Miss Lizzie, who is sick?"

"I don't know. She had a note this morning. It must be in town."

Soon, Bridget finished washing the dining room windows and returned to the kitchen to clean up. She was feeling ill, and she needed to rest. She climbed upstairs to her room in the attic, and without undressing, lay down on her bed. It was too hot to sleep. Soon Bridget heard the clock at city hall, two blocks away, strike eleven. Andrew Borden had now been home for some twenty minutes. Bridget Sullivan continued to lie on her bed undisturbed for ten minutes more—maybe fifteen. All this time, she heard nothing at all from downstairs, no doors opening or closing, no voices talking or arguing, "no sound."

Until 11:10. That was when Lizzie Borden broke the heavy silence and hollered up to her: "Maggie, come down!" Bridget could tell something was wrong. "What is the matter?" she called down.

"Come down quick!" Lizzie yelled back. "Father's dead! Somebody came in and killed him!"

## THE MURDER SCENE

This is a photograph of Andrew J. Borden's body, taken by the Fall River Police Department within a few hours of his murder. Examine the furnishings—comfortable, but shabby and out of fashion. *(Courtesy Fall River Historical Society)*

Bridget ran downstairs and headed toward the sitting room—but Lizzie stopped her; "Oh, Maggie, don't go in," she warned, and then said, "I have got to have a doctor, quick. Go over. I have got to have the doctor." The doctor was Seabury Bowen, who lived diagonally across the street from the Bordens. Dr. Bowen was out on his rounds, however, and after Bridget had blurted the news of the murder to the doctor's wife, she quickly returned to the house.

Once again, Lizzie asked Bridget to go out—this time to find her some companionship. "Go and get Miss Russell," she told Bridget. "I can't be alone in the house." (Alice Russell was Lizzie's best friend: Lizzie had visited her just the previous evening.)

As Bridget went out to fetch Miss Russell, a next-door neighbor noticed that she was walking very fast and looking quite pale. The neighbor, a widow named Adelaide Churchill, peered out through her kitchen window and spotted Lizzie Borden standing by the side door. Opening the window, Mrs. Churchill yelled across: "Lizzie, what is the matter?"

"Oh, Mrs. Churchill, do come over," Lizzie replied. "Someone has killed father!"

Mrs. Churchill rushed over and found Lizzie sitting on the stairs. She put her hand on Lizzie's arm to comfort her; then she asked, "Oh, Lizzie, where is your father?"

"In the sitting room."

Then Mrs. Churchill asked Lizzie a key question: "Where were you when it happened?"

Lizzie's response was the basis of the story she would continue to tell, with variations, over the next year: "I went out to the barn to get a piece of iron. I heard a distressing noise and came back and found the screen door open."

But Mrs. Churchill was more worried about the rest of the Borden family than suspicious of Lizzie's story. She realized that Lizzie's mother, Abby Borden, might be in danger. Where was Abby? she asked.

"I don't know," Lizzie replied. "She had got a note to go see someone who is sick." And she added: "But I don't know but she is killed, too, for I thought I heard her come in."

Now Lizzie changed the subject, and spoke once again of her dead father: "Father must have an enemy, for we have all been sick, and we think the milk has been poisoned. I must have a doctor."

As it turned out, Dr. Bowen had just returned home, learned of the horrifying event, and headed to the Borden house. As a physician, his first thought was of the murdered man. Almost ignoring Lizzie, he went straight to the sitting room to examine the body, which was lying face up on the sofa. He later reported what he had seen.

His face was very badly cut, apparently with a sharp instrument. His face was covered with blood. I felt of his pulse and satisfied myself he was dead. I glanced about the room and saw there was nothing disturbed—neither the furniture nor anything at all . . . . His face was hardly to be recognized by one who knew him.

His brief examination complete, Dr. Bowen moved into the dining room. He kept repeating: "He is murdered, he is murdered." Then he returned to question Lizzie Borden. Had she seen an intruder? he asked. She repeated her story that she had been out in the barn looking for a piece of iron. But now she added an explanation of the fear she had expressed a few minutes earlier about some "enemy": "She said she was afraid her father had had trouble with tenants, and she had overheard loud conversations several times recently."

Meanwhile, Bridget Sullivan had found Lizzie Borden's friend Alice Russell, and the two women returned to the house. Bridget, too, had begun to be concerned about her mistress, Abby Borden. Bridget knew Mrs. Borden well enough to guess where she might be. She knew that there was only one person who would have been likely to ask Abby Borden to come visiting when she was sick: that was Mrs. Sarah Whitehead, Abby's younger sister. So Bridget offered a suggestion:

"Oh, Lizzie, if I knew where Mrs. Whitehead was, I would go and see if Mrs. Borden was there, and tell her that Mr. Borden was very sick."

But now Lizzie repeated her hint that Mrs. Borden might not be out after all, but might be somewhere in the house that very minute. And if she was, then why had she not come downstairs to see what was the matter? "Maggie," said Lizzie Borden, "I am almost positive I heard her coming in. Won't you go upstairs to see?"

Bridget knew very well what it was she might see, and so she refused to do what her mistress asked. She said simply: "I am not going upstairs alone."

The next-door neighbor, Mrs. Churchill, said she was willing to accompany Bridget to the second floor, and the two women started upstairs together. Bridget led the way, so she was the first to spot the second body. It was in the guest room, lying face down, resting on its knees where it had fallen. The two women did not stay very long—they knew who it was and that she was dead. They headed right back to the first floor. Now Lizzie was lying down, as if expecting the dread news. But it was her friend Alice Russell who spoke first, her words tactful, almost delicate: "Is there another?" And it was Mrs. Churchill who answered: "Yes, she is up there."

The police made efforts to find a crazed intruder—but no one ever became a serious suspect. In fact, the possibility of such an intruder almost had to be excluded: too many people had been abroad on Second Street that morning, or watching the street from their windows: if there had been an intruder, he had somehow escaped everyone's notice. Pursuing another avenue of investigation, the police tried to discover whether anyone had sufficient reason to *want* to kill Andrew Borden. And they could come up with no such hypothetical person, either. Andrew Borden may have had trouble with his tenants, as Lizzie had said, but extensive investigation revealed no "enemy" with any real reason to slaughter him and his wife. And robbery could be excluded as a motive: nothing whatever had been taken from the house, and there were not even any signs of a search.

What was troubling was the extreme brutality of the murders. Each victim had been hacked in the skull some twenty times—well after the killer must have known they were already dead. Their deaths were not simply murder—they were slaughter. Whoever killed them was crazy—or filled with consuming rage.

Most unsettling of all, perhaps, was the fact that the two victims had been killed at least ninety minutes apart—Mrs. Borden around 9:30, and her husband shortly after 11:00. This had to mean one of two things: either the murderer had killed Mrs. Borden and then hidden himself without detection somewhere in the house from 9:30 until after 11:00, waiting first for Andrew Borden to return home (whenever that might be) and then waiting for him to fall asleep so that he would not put up a struggle or raise an outcry. Or else the murderer had sneaked into the house, not once but *twice*, totally unseen by neighbors or passersby. But the house had been locked and bolted all morning. And there were no signs of a forced entry.

Every one of these problems and improbabilities simply disappeared with a single alternative hypothesis: that the murderer was not an outsider at all, but a member of the household. Inevitably, then, even as the police dutifully tried to track down all other possibilities, their attention turned toward Lizzie Borden. And they found that the pieces fitted perfectly—almost. Lizzie's guilt could explain the time that passed between the two murders and also the absence of any sign of forced entry or of struggle on the part of either victim. Furthermore, Lizzie's own account of her actions on the morning of the murders—the alibi she told to Bridget Sullivan, Mrs. Churchill, and a variety of police officers—simply failed to hold together. Mrs. Abby Borden had *not* left the house earlier in the morning and then returned. In fact, it turned out that none of her acquaintances was sick that day or had sent a note asking Abby to come visit. No such note was found in the Borden house. Mrs. Borden's sister, Sarah Whitehead, was not sick that day and had not written any note to her sister. Finally, despite extensive and repeated inquiries, nobody ever came forward (either within Mrs. Borden's circle of acquaintances or outside it) to acknowledge having written one. The conclusion became inescapable: there was no such note. Lizzie had invented the story and told it to her father in order to prevent him from looking for his wife—and discovering her bloody corpse.

There were other contradictions in Lizzie Borden's account of her actions between the time her father returned home and the discovery of his murder half an hour later. Lizzie claimed to have gone out to the barn loft soon after her father's arrival—that was the reason she had not witnessed the murder. But she was unable to keep her story straight. To her neighbor Mrs. Churchill, she said she had visited the barn "to get a piece of iron." To another person, she specified that the iron was intended to repair a broken screen on a window. But later, and under oath, Lizzie testified she had gone to the barn because she was planning to go fishing in a few days and wanted "to find lead for a sinker." Most damning of all, a policeman who examined the barn shortly after the discovery of the murders reported that the loft was coated

**ABBY DURFEE GRAY BORDEN**

On the morning of the murders, Lizzie Borden claimed that her stepmother had been about to go shopping for food, clothed in a house-dress. "Won't you change your dress before you go out?" Lizzie allegedly asked, and Abby Borden replied: "No, this is good enough." This trivial exchange reveals the conflict between a fashion-conscious "lady" and a woman who did not need to parade her status by a display of "conspicuous consumption." *(Courtesy Fall River Historical Society)*

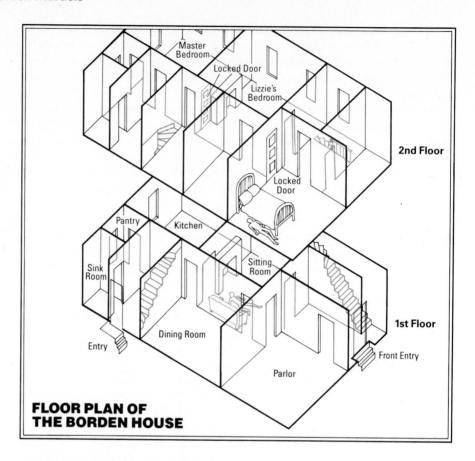

**FLOOR PLAN OF
THE BORDEN HOUSE**

with dust so thick that his footprints were like tracks in the snow—and yet there were no other prints to be found in the place!

The evidence was clear: Lizzie Borden had not been in the barn at all. She had remained in the house the whole time. She must have witnessed her father's killing—or committed it herself.

Lizzie Borden was arrested, charged, and put on trial for the murder of her parents, in the most famous American criminal case of the nineteenth century.

While the evidence against Lizzie Borden was powerful, there were some equally powerful problems that the prosecution faced if it was to put together a case strong enough to gain a probable conviction. To begin with, the evidence against Lizzie was entirely circumstantial: she had neither confessed to the crime nor been seen by any witness to have committed it. Circumstantial evidence was perfectly valid from a legal point of view. However, jurors would have to be persuaded not only that the evidence was airtight but that the defendant was capable of committing murders of such brutality. So the prosecution had to deal with *image* as well as evidence—and that was its most difficult obstacle.

In the first place, Lizzie Borden was female. As her minister put it, "To my mind, it is an impossibility for this girl to have committed the deed." (The minister was not alone in referring to Lizzie as a "girl" rather than a woman, even though she was thirty-two years old.) She was a woman of established character—a church member, a Sunday school teacher, and an active member of the Women's Christian Temperance Union, or WCTU. In fact, the Fall River branch of the WCTU voted to "declare our unshaken faith in her, as a fellow worker and sister tenderly beloved." Even the *Woman's Journal*, a feminist magazine, declared that "The citizens of Fall River who have known Miss Lizzie Borden from childhood are unanimous in their belief of her innocence. She is a solid, substantial young woman of gentle disposition and quiet habits, much beloved by her friends."

Added to the fact that Lizzie was a woman who had lived a respectable life was a closely related point: her family was extremely wealthy. By any standards, her father was a rich man—a member of the single wealthiest and most powerful clan in the city of Fall River. A local newspaper reporter described Andrew Jackson Borden's position in these words:

> He was one of the family of Bordens whose name has always been identified with the growth and business enterprises of the city. No one knows how much money he was worth, but persons who are as well acquainted with his affairs as he would allow them to be, do not hesitate to say that his estate was worth $300,000. He was president of the Union Savings Bank, a member of its Board of Trustees and Investment, a director of the Merchants Manufacturing Company, the B. M. C. Durfee Safe Deposit and Trust Company, the Globe Yarn Mills, the Troy Cotton and Woolen Manufactory and other manufacturing concerns.

It was difficult enough to believe that any woman—even some poor, working-class, immigrant woman—would be capable of committing such a hideous crime as the Borden murders. But it seemed hardly possible to believe it of a woman whose family held such a high position. Lizzie Borden was not only a woman, she was a "lady."

The final difficulty in persuading a jury of Lizzie's guilt was the simplest, and perhaps the most powerful, of all. Lizzie Borden was not accused of murdering some stranger but of killing her own *parents*. She was not only a woman, not only even a "lady"—she was also the victims' own daughter. As her defense attorney put it: "To foully murder her stepmother and then go straight away and slay her own father is a wreck of human morals. Such acts as those are morally and physically impossible for this young woman."

That was the issue, then. The evidence pointed to Lizzie Borden, and to nobody else. But the evidence was all circumstantial, and Lizzie Borden was not the kind of person who seemed capable of committing such a crime. That fact alone might be grounds for "reasonable doubt."

There was only one strategy for the prosecution to follow. It had to convince the jury that Lizzie Borden had a clear and powerful motive to commit the crimes—a motive powerful enough to cut through the doubts inevitably raised by her sex, her background and social status, and her familial role. Lizzie's past history precluded the possibility that she was demented or prone to fits of sudden rage or violence. The second murder had been committed such a long time after the first one that the murders could not have been committed in a sudden act of unpremeditated emotion. The crime had been planned in advance. This meant that the prosecution had to convince the jury that Lizzie had some reason to want her family dead—a reason so long-standing, so deep, that it could overcome all the circumstances that made it so hard to believe she could do such a thing.

The prosecution attempted to undermine with a single stroke all the favorable feeling that had built up around Lizzie Borden. It did so by insisting that Lizzie was not the tender woman or the dutiful daughter she was made out to be, and that her family was not a haven of cordial affection. Instead, the prosecution argued, the Borden household was pervaded by deep and venomous hostility—by "ill feelings" that ran so deep that the family had turned into a "murderous" unit. The hostility between Lizzie and her parents ran so deep that the family had settled into a kind of silent warfare that divided the two generations into armed camps, each eying the other with constant suspicion. As the district attorney put it, "Although they occupied the same household, there was built up between them an almost impassable wall."

It was easy to show that Lizzie had remarkably little to do with her parents. She spent much of her time outside the house, and when she was at home she usually stayed in her bedroom—with the door shut. She rarely bothered to greet her parents when she entered the house. In fact, she hardly ever joined them even at mealtime—instead, she waited until they were finished, and then she ate alone.

But the "impassable wall" that ran through the Borden house was more than a figure of speech. Lizzie and her parents had divided the house up by an elaborate series of "locks and bolts and bars." The "guest room" (the room where Mrs. Borden was murdered) was right next to Lizzie's bedroom, and there was even a door connecting the two rooms. But Mrs. Borden used the guest room for sewing, and Lizzie made sure that the connecting door could not be used. As she reported at the inquest, "It has been locked and bolted, and a large writing desk in my room kept up against it." When Lizzie was asked how she could get from her room to the guest room, she replied: "I have to go to the front hall." (In any case, she said, she was "not allowed in that room.") In the same way, Lizzie could not get to her bedroom by walking up the back stairs—that was her father's territory. "Father's bedroom was kept locked, and his door into my room locked and hooked, too, and I had no keys."

Such arrangements affected the whole household, and the prosecution suggested that they stemmed from the particular hostility that Lizzie Borden felt toward Mrs. Abby Borden. There even seemed to be a plausible explanation for the hostility. Abby Borden was not Lizzie's mother at all, but her stepmother. Lizzie's own mother had died when Lizzie was only two years old, and Andrew J. Borden had married Abby, his second wife, two years later. Abby had now been living in the Borden household for twenty-eight years. Even so, when a policeman on the scene routinely asked Lizzie "if she had any idea who could have killed her father and mother," Lizzie had said: "She is not my mother, sir; she is my stepmother. My mother died when I was a child."

Just a few months before the murders, a seamstress who made clothing for the women of the Borden household had made the mistake of referring to Abby Borden as Lizzie's mother. Lizzie quickly shot back: "Don't say that to me, for she is a mean good-for-nothing thing." That was strong language, and the dressmaker had tried to give Lizzie a chance to take it back (or, perhaps, to say even more):

"Oh, Lizzie, you don't mean that?"
"Yes, I don't have much to do with her. I stay in my room most of the time."
"You come down for your meals, don't you?"
"Yes, but we don't eat with *them* if we can help it."

The pattern of hostility was clear. But what was its basis? The prosecution came up with an incident it argued was an important piece of family history.

Five years earlier, in 1887, Andrew J. Borden had given a piece of real estate to his wife and his wife's sister—the same Mrs. Whitehead who was supposed to have written Abby Borden the "sick note" on the morning of the murders. It was an open secret that Lizzie Borden resented this gift. And there was another open secret about the episode: it was at this very time that Lizzie began to address Abby Borden as "Mrs. Borden." Until then, she had called her "mother."

Behind Abby—behind it all—loomed the figure of Andrew Jackson Borden. It was Andrew who had married Abby, who ran the household, and who more than any other person dominated the life and the imagination of Lizzie Borden. Andrew Borden was a well-known man around Fall River, and something of a local character. He had earned the reputation of being tight-lipped, iron-willed—and notoriously stingy. He was known as a miser— a man who loved to make money, but who hated to spend it. And Andrew's tastes determined the shape of Lizzie's life—a life she had come to loathe.

It was not that Lizzie was short of money. Several years earlier, her father had given her and her sister Emma one of his properties, and the rent from this property had provided Lizzie with plenty of spending money—enough money to buy the nineteen dresses that hung in her closet, and more. When she went out, Lizzie could dress as she wished. But in the house to which she always had to return, she was forced to live in the dark shadow of her father.

The house itself was one of Lizzie's problems. It was not the kind of mansion that Andrew J. Borden could easily have afforded to buy. Most of the wealthy citizens of Fall River had chosen to live in an elegant section of the city, known as the Hill. From this neighborhood, the bankers and mill owners of Fall River could look down on the factories that had made their fortune—and also on the thousands of laborers (most of them Irish or French-

**ANDREW JACKSON BORDEN**

A few months before he was murdered, Andrew J. Borden discussed his future and that of his neighborhood. "Second Street will eventually become an overflow business highway, but it won't be in my time," he told an acquaintance. "I don't like to move off the street in my lifetime." *(Courtesy Fall River Historical Society)*

Canadian immigrants, and many of them children) who worked ten hours or more each day, six days a week, in those same factories, and who lived crowded in nearby tenement houses that were themselves owned by those same wealthy capitalists. Over the previous forty or fifty years, these factory owners and bankers had sold their old houses in downtown Fall River and moved into lavish new mansions on the Hill. Most of Lizzie Borden's wealthy cousins lived there, and so did many people with far less money.

But Andrew J. Borden had never chosen to move up to the Hill. He and his family continued to live downtown, just two blocks away from the bank he owned (and only a few blocks from one of the largest factories in the city). Second Street was one of the busiest streets in the city. His neighbors were a mixed lot of shopkeepers and professional men, many of whom had taken in unmarried working-class boarders to help them make ends meet. One house on the street contained as many as nine boarders. The immediate neighborhood was respectable enough (even though, just a block down the street, a brothel was in open operation!). But Andrew Borden was its wealthiest resident—by far.

What made the situation even more odd was the appearance of Andrew Borden's house. It was a modest structure even in its neighborhood. It was relatively small, and it was more than fifty years old. (There was even a barn in the backyard.) And its two stories were constructed in a style that seemed strangely out-of-date by the year 1892. The house contained no halls or corridors. The only way to reach most rooms in the house (even the bedrooms) was by walking through another room. That was the reason for all the locked doors in the house: because of the structure of the building, there was simply no other way for Lizzie or her parents to ensure privacy.

The house was old-fashioned in other ways as well. For one thing, it lacked most of the "modern" amenities. Fall River had dug an undergound water and sewer system during the 1880s—but Andrew J. Borden had never chosen to have his house connected up with it. There was no indoor plumbing at 92 Second Street. The household got water from a well in the backyard (that was where Bridget Sullivan had filled her pail to wash the windows on the morning of the murders). They urinated into "slop jars" kept in their bedrooms, and defecated in a water closet down in the cellar. A decade or two earlier these had been the standard arrangements. Even in 1892 they would not have seemed unsanitary—merely out of fashion.

The house was furnished in a style that was a generation or more out of date. Police photographs of the bodies of Mr. and Mrs. Borden show some of these furnishings. The glossy black horsehair of the sofa on which Andrew Borden was murdered would have been replaced long ago in more fashionable households by decoratively printed cotton or velvet plush. Mrs. Borden's body lay beside a heavy wooden bedstead with a tall, elaborately carved headboard. It should by now have been replaced by a fashionable metal bedstead. And the carpets in both rooms, running wall-to-wall to cover the wide, uneven floorboards, would have been replaced by smaller throw rugs over narrow, evenly joined, polished floorboards.

**THE BORDEN HOUSE**

Andrew Borden moved here at the age of fifty-one, in 1872, after he had become wealthy enough to retire from the undertaking business. Until then, he had lived with his father in an old and seedy section of Fall River. Even though the new house was modest, even by the standards of its own neighborhood, it was exactly what Andrew Borden wanted. *(Courtesy Fall River Historical Society)*

The house was so embarrassingly old-fashioned that Lizzie Borden's defense attorney felt obliged to confront the issue in his concluding speech to the jury, out of fear that it might provide his client with the necessary motive for murder:

> They say she killed her stepmother and father because that was a house without any comforts in it. Well, gentlemen, I hope you all live in a better way than the Borden family lived, so far as having good furniture and conveniences. Are *your* houses all warmed with steam? Do *you* have pictures and pianos and a library, and all conveniences and luxury? Do you? Well, I congratulate you if you do. This is not a downtrodden people. There are lots of comforts in our country homes. I know something of them, but I remember back in my boyhood *we* did not have gas and running water in every room.

The lawyer's argument was clever. He knew that the jury members were all "old-fashioned" men from the small towns around Fall River, and he was trying to persuade these men that Andrew J. Borden was basically one of them—not a stingy miser, but a man who had remained true to solid old-fashioned country ways. The lawyer summed up his point simply and effectively:

> Andrew Borden was a simple man, an old-fashioned man. He did not dress himself up with jewelry. He carried a silver watch. He was a plain man of the everyday sort of fifty years ago.

Gradually, Lizzie Borden's guilt or innocence had become tied to her father's character. The prosecution wanted the jurors to perceive Andrew Borden as a mean-spirited miser who systematically deprived his household of the most ordinary comforts. The defense wanted them to see him as an old-fashioned man who had courageously refused to surrender to the fads and fashions of the day. The ambiguity was deep and real, and it lay at the heart of the bitter feeling that pervaded and divided the Borden family, and that finally destroyed it. To understand the problem, it is necessary to probe deeper into the inner history of the family—deeper than either side in the trial cared to go.

The Borden clan had seen Fall River grow from a tiny farming village of a few hundred people in 1800 to a dynamic city of 75,000 in 1890. In 1890, it manufactured more cotton textiles than any other city in the entire world. And the Bordens had played an important part in accomplishing the transformation.

At the beginning of the century, a farmer named Borden had owned the rights to operate a sawmill and a gristmill along the powerful stream that gave Fall River its name. With the beginning of industrialization around 1820, these mills had been replaced by the first cotton factories—and farmer Borden's children owned and controlled most of them. As the community began to grow in size and wealth, the Borden brothers took the capital they earned from these factories and shrewdly used it to organize a variety of other economic activities. By 1850, the Borden brothers controlled the banks that regulated the credit system; new factories that produced the dyes and patterns used in the cotton factories and the complex machines that powered them; and even the steamboats and railroads that soon connected Fall River to the commercial centers of Boston and New York City.

Over the thirty years between 1850 and 1880, the Borden brothers consolidated the family grip on Fall River by carefully passing their power into the hands of their own children—nearly twenty of them—and by engaging in a systematic pattern of arranged marriages between those children and the members of another wealthy Fall River clan, the Durfees. The *New York Times* sarcastically described the situation:

> Fall River has been more or less controlled by Durfees and Bordens, who appear and reappear as officers in most of the corporations. Of the Fall River Bleachery, Jefferson Borden is President, Spencer Borden is Treasurer, and Jefferson Borden,

Spencer Borden, Richard B. Borden, Philip D. Borden, and George B. Durfee are Directors. Of the American Print Works, Jefferson Borden is President, George B. Durfee is Clerk, Thomas J. Borden Treasurer, and Jefferson Borden, Thomas J. Borden, George B. Durfee, and W. B. Durfee are Directors. Bordens and Durfees have put their sons, brothers, uncles, sons-in-law, and cousins into office, and permitted them to do nearly as they chose. This is the way the Bordens and Durfees continually break out, like small-pox, in all the industrial enterprises of that city.

From Andrew J. Borden's point of view, one fact about this *New York Times* story would have been particularly striking: his own name did not appear in it even once. But Andrew would have known exactly why not. It was because he was not one of the sons of the wealthy Borden brothers. In fact, he belonged to a different branch of the family. The family had many branches. In 1892, there were no fewer than 128 heads of households in Fall River named Borden—including *four* named Andrew Borden. Andrew J. Borden's grandfather, a farmer, was the *brother* of the man who owned the original sawmill and gristmill. Andrew's father, an unskilled worker who never made anything of himself, was only a cousin of the Borden brothers who "held everything commercial and industrial in their grasp." And Andrew J. Borden himself was only a second cousin of those twenty-odd children whose names "continually break out, like small-pox."

Andrew J. Borden therefore found himself in a curious situation. In a technical sense, it was accurate to describe him (as the local newspaper writer did on the day after his murder) as "one of the family of Bordens whose name has always been identified with the business enterprises of the city." But in real terms, Andrew J. Borden was not a member of that family at all; he was a classic self-made man. He had made his fortune on his own, without any assistance from his ne'er-do-well father on the one hand or his wealthy Borden cousins on the other. A local obituary summed up his career like this: "When he started in life, his means were extremely limited, and he made his money by saving it."

Andrew J. Borden got his start by entering the funeral business—as a casket maker and undertaker. With a single partner and a small gift of cash from his father, Andrew opened the business in 1844, as a young man of twenty-three. The population of Fall River was beginning to increase rapidly in those years of dynamic industrial growth. And a larger population in turn meant that there were more people to die. In this indirect way—and in this way only—Andrew Borden prospered on account of his cousins' banks and cotton mills.

A dozen years after he went into business, Andrew Borden began to invest some of his profits in local real estate and, later, in mill and bank stock. By the time he was fifty, in 1871, he had accumulated enough capital to leave the undertaking business and spend all his time in managing his various investments—which now included a downtown office building that bore his name, and a bank and a cotton mill of which he was president, along with other real estate in and around Fall River. By the time of his violent death at the

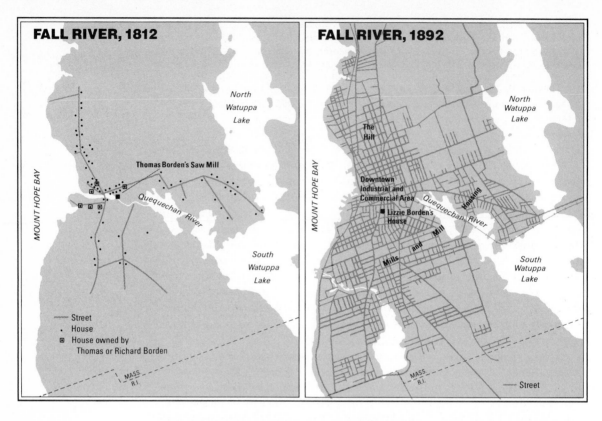

These two maps reveal the intensive growth that Fall River experienced during the nine-teenth century. In 1812, it was a small, quite rural settlement—though even then the Bor-dens were a prominent family. By 1892, it had become a densely populated and industrial-ized city, with well-defined districts. Industrialization and expansion even altered the topography of the area—note, for example, the change in the course of the Quequechan River.

age of seventy-one, the local newspaper was able to claim that Andrew J. Borden was "regarded as one of the wealthiest men in town."

Andrew Borden did all this on his own. To be sure, his luck was good—he lived at a time of opportunity. But he worked long and hard to take every possible advantage of that opportunity. Long before his death, he had a reputation for good judgment and impeccable honesty. His creditors acknow-ledged that he was "safe and reliable," a "good, honest" businessman who stuck to his word and undertook no risky enterprises. His customers and tenants knew him as a man who always drove a hard bargain, but who was "scrupulously upright in all his dealings, and expected the same fairness in others." In his later years, he invariably chose to pay for investments in hard cash, and shortly before his death he told an acquaintance that "the man who didn't borrow lived the most contented life." He believed that it was his character that had made his fortune. He also stressed in the contrast between himself and his wealthy Borden cousins, who had inherited their positions with no effort of their own. He had received no help from them, and he steered clear of them. He remained a loner to the end.

It is not hard to see why. Despite all the money he made, Andrew J. Borden remained an outsider to the Fall River industrial aristocracy. The fact that this aristocracy was dominated by his own cousins and namesakes made his own alienation even more acute. His cousins were the children and grandchildren of wealthy men. They had been raised with all the advantages (disadvantages, Andrew Borden might have said) of inherited wealth. They had been sent to prestigious colleges like Harvard, Yale, and Brown, and early in their lives they had developed fashionable and expensive tastes. One of Andrew Borden's cousins was an accomplished yachtsman. Another bred prize thoroughbred horses. A third was a collector of paintings and rare books. Almost all of them traveled widely, and several owned lavish vacation homes in places like Newport, Rhode Island. They took fully as much pleasure in spending their money as in making it.

In contrast to these industrial aristocrats, Andrew Borden never went to school at all, and to the end of his life he never developed any hobbies or outside interests. As his local obituary tactfully put it, he was "domestic in his tastes, and, although he had considerable leisure time, was rarely to be found where men are accustomed to congregate"—at their clubs or in fancy restaurants. According to the same newspaper, Borden had only a single interest in life: "money getting." To the end of his life, he remained a poor man who had made a lot of money. No wonder that when his cousins chose to build expensive mansions on Fall River's fashionable Hill, Andrew J. Borden never cared to follow them. No wonder that he chose to live out his days in an old-fashioned downtown house without hallways or indoor plumbing.

Lizzie Borden's aspirations were different because her youth was different. Lizzie was Andrew's daughter—but she inhabited a different world. Unlike her father, she never grew up poor. By the time Lizzie was born in 1860, her father's business was thriving, and before she entered her teens he was a rich man. By then, Fall River was an industrial city, and people who had money were living on the Hill. It would have been hard for Lizzie Borden to avoid feeling that that was where she belonged, too. She rarely talked about it (being able to keep her mouth shut was one trait she did pick up from her father), but it seems apparent that she deeply craved to live in the kind of style her father could afford. The nineteen dresses that hung in her closet on the day of the murders provided a vivid display of the deep gulf that divided daughter and father.

The money for Lizzie's dresses came from her father. He gave her gifts of cash and a steady source of income of her own. By his own lights, he was extremely generous toward her and tried to indulge her in satisfying needs he could hardly understand. In the summer of 1890, he even allowed Lizzie

LIZZIE ANDREW BORDEN

Commenting on the Borden case just a few days after the conclusion of Lizzie Borden's trial for murder, one man made the following comment in a letter to a newspaper: "A striking feature of this case is the picture which it gives of life in the Borden household, and presumably in other households in Fall River—and elsewhere. I dare say that this life is so familiar to many people that they are unable to appreciate the meanness and sordidness of it." *(Culver Pictures)*

to take a long vacation in Europe—and he paid for the trip himself. Lizzie had a splendid time abroad. But ironically this taste of elegance and freedom only intensified her revulsion for the household to which she had to return. As the returning ocean liner approached its harbor in New York, in November 1890, Lizzie confessed to her cabin mate that "she regretted the necessity of returning home after she had had such a happy summer, because the home she was about to return to was such an unhappy home." Leaving the house on Second Street altogether was the only thing that would have relieved Lizzie Borden's dread. But her father had no intention of ever doing that.

The silent anger that filled the air at the Borden house reflected something more complex than a gulf between generations. It was also a conflict between social classes.

What could Lizzie do? How could she escape from the prison of her parents' house? The simplest avenue of escape was simply to move out. But Lizzie did not have the money to purchase a house on the Hill. And in any event, moving into a place of her own was unthinkable as long as her parents were alive and she was unmarried. By taking such an unrespectable step, Lizzie would have lost all chance of ever being accepted into the homes and parties of the Fall River upper class.

There was only one way for Lizzie to enter that world—by marrying a man who lived in it already. Only such a marriage would be able to provide her, in a single stroke, with a better house in a better neighborhood, and with the companionship of a person who shared her own values. In short, only marriage could bring her real membership in the class she aspired to join, and real independence from her family.

But now, still single at the age of thirty-two, Lizzie Borden was forced to confront the ever-increasing likelihood that she would never get married. And, with it, she had to confront the likelihood that she would remain in the grubby house on Second Street as long as her father lived. (And Lizzie knew that the Borden males were usually long-lived. Andrew's own ne'er-do-well father, her paternal grandfather, had died only six years earlier, in 1886, at the ripe age of eighty-eight. Andrew Borden himself was in fine health at seventy-one; who knew how long he might survive?) And by then, Lizzie would be past her prime—it would be too late to marry, too late to enjoy the life that was left to her.

It was not that Lizzie had lacked the opportunity to get married. She was not unattractive, and in any case her father was the richest man in her neighborhood. But that was part of the problem: the young men who lived in her neighborhood were shop clerks and laborers—hardly in a position to give Lizzie the kind of life she craved. But on the other hand, it would have been difficult for her (maybe even impossible) to find more desirable suitors. Obstacles were everywhere, and they were insurmountable. Once she made the acquaintance of a proper young gentleman, what could she do? How could she invite him to visit her Second Street home and be entertained by her family? What would her suitor think about a stepmother who might not even bother to change out of her housedress for the occasion? About a neighborhood filled with boardinghouses and immigrants? About an out-of-date house that lacked even a toilet and running water? Lizzie Borden was in a bind, and whichever way she looked at it, her parents were the cause. And now, in the summer of 1892, the hopelessness of her situation, and of her future, was becoming impossible to deny. Lizzie Borden was reaching a point of quiet but total desperation.

On Wednesday, August 3, 1892—the evening before the murders—Lizzie Borden left her house to visit her old friend Alice M. Russell, an unmarried woman in her forties. For many years Alice Russell had been a neighbor of the Bordens on Second Street, but she had recently moved a few blocks away (she was now living on Borden Street). She was probably Lizzie's closest friend, and Lizzie was visiting her friend to confide in her about her confused and desperate feelings.

Much later, at Lizzie's trial for murder, Alice Russell testified for the prosecution about some of the ominous and revealing things Lizzie Borden had said to her. It was a confusing story that Lizzie told, but also an extraordinary one—the closest that Lizzie Borden ever came to disclosing her state of mind on the day just before the death of her parents.

> I feel depressed. I feel as if something was hanging over me that I cannot throw off, and it comes over me at times, no matter where I am.

Lizzie did not (or could not) explain the cause of her depression, but she was vaguely aware that her feelings were affecting her behavior. A few weeks earlier, for example, she had refused an appealing invitation to join a group of her friends who were planning to spend a few weeks on vacation at a seaside cottage in the resort town of Marion, Massachusetts. This was just the kind of opportunity that Lizzie would ordinarily have welcomed, since it would allow her to escape from the oppressive midsummer urban heat as well as from the equally oppressive atmosphere of her family. But Lizzie had refused to join the vacationing party, offering her friends the feeble excuse that she "ought to stay home to see that everything went all right." Things seemed to be getting more and more out of control for her, and she was not sure what was going on. Things were happening within the household, she confided to Alice—things that upset her profoundly, in ways she could not explain.

Lizzie told these things to Alice Russell in rambling, half-coherent fashion. It was unclear to Alice (and perhaps also to Lizzie herself) just which statements described real events, and which were simply expressions of fears or fantasies.

Lizzie talked about an occurrence that seemed simple enough, however unpleasant: "Mr. and Mrs. Borden were awfully sick last night," she said. "They were awfully sick, and I wasn't sick. I didn't vomit, but I heard them vomiting, and stepped to the door, and asked if I could do anything, and they said, 'No'." Was it something Mr. and Mrs. Borden had eaten? Alice asked. Lizzie acknowledged that it might have been the household bread or milk. Then Lizzie offered a bizarre explanation of her parents' illness: "Sometimes," she said, "sometimes I think our milk might be poisoned."

Alice Russell was startled, and she tried without success to convince Lizzie that the Borden family milk could not possibly have been poisoned. But Lizzie would not hear her out. She even went on to make an even more bizarre suggestion—the "poisoning," she hinted darkly, was only the latest in a series of scary events in the household. For example, she now revealed, "the barn has been broken into twice." Alice Russell, trying hard to calm her friend, reassured Lizzie that the break-in must have been nothing more than petty vandalism—nothing to worry about. "Well," Lizzie went on, "they have broken into the house in broad daylight, with Emma and Maggie and me there." And, one night not long before, Lizzie had even seen a strange man "run around the house."

Lizzie was almost certain that these were not random events at all, that they were part of a pattern of conscious hostility on the part of some person who was determined to do nothing less than destroy the entire household: "I feel as if I wanted to sleep with my eyes half open—with one eye open half the time—for fear they will burn down the house over us."

Lizzie seemed unaware that the hostility she was describing was actually her own. But here, at about this point, she unconsciously made a revealing shift in her emphasis. Up to now, she had been speaking of her parents as if they were the innocent victims of an incomprehensible hostility. But now she began to suggest that the hostility might not be incomprehensible after all—that her father had actually *provoked* it by his behavior and manner.

"I feel afraid sometimes that father has an enemy," she began, and told a story (which she would repeat several times the next day, after the murders) of how her father had lost his temper at a prospective tenant who spoke to him in a "sneering" voice about his reputation for money grubbing.

In any event, Lizzie was unable to face the reality of her own hostility. She simply could not grasp a fact that might conceivably have saved the lives of Andrew and Abby Borden: her father's "enemy" was Lizzie Borden herself. "I think sometimes—I am afraid sometimes that somebody will do something to him. *He is so discourteous to people.*" For a few moments, Lizzie Borden came close to acknowledging that her father made *her* feel embarrassed, threatened, and enraged.

As if to explain something about her feelings, Lizzie began to go into detail about what had happened earlier that very day, after Andrew and Abby had gotten sick and vomited. Mrs. Borden had felt concerned, and she told her husband she wanted to send for a physician—Dr. Bowen, who lived across the street (and who would examine her dead body the next day). Andrew Borden did not see the need for professional help, and he scolded his wife for her wastefulness. He told her, as Lizzie recalled, "Well, *my* money shan't pay for it." But Abby had called Dr. Bowen anyway, and when he came over to examine her, Andrew had treated the physician with characteristic rudeness. When she told the story to Alice Russell, Lizzie did not report her father's exact words—but, for once, she directly expressed something of her own feelings toward her father. What Lizzie told Alice Russell was this: "I am so ashamed, the way father treated Dr. Bowen. I was so mortified." It was as close as Lizzie Borden would ever come to identifying *herself* as her father's "enemy."

Never again would Lizzie Borden expose so much of her feelings. Barely twelve hours after her conversation with Alice Russell, Andrew Borden and his wife were killed, and the murders served to restore Lizzie's characteristic poise—and her silence. In the hours after the murders were discovered, and in the days and months of public exposure that followed, the people who observed Lizzie Borden were struck by her extraordinary emotional control. Newspaper reporters often used words like "cold" to describe her manner. She rarely broke down and cried (although at one point during her trial, she fainted—when her father's skull was displayed to the jurors).

Some people even suggested that Lizzie's composure was "unfeminine" and was evidence that she was capable after all of having committed the crimes of which she stood accused. But Lizzie's composure was her characteristic style. It was a style that had developed in years of hiding her feelings behind a façade of cold civility. Throughout the trial, the defense tried and failed to provide evidence that the Bordens had been affectionate with each other (the word they used was "cordial"). Similarly, the prosecution could not show that life in the household had been tempestuous. Even Bridget

Sullivan, the servant who had lived in the house for almost two years, said that she had never seen or heard "any trouble with the family, no quarrelling or anything of that kind." This kind of testimony was damaging to the prosecution's case. But the fact was that Lizzie and her parents had learned to avoid expressing their feelings—just as they had learned to avoid each other in the flesh. There were not only physical locks and bolts that kept the family from invading each other's space, there was also an elaborate, unspoken series of emotional locks and bolts that prevented Lizzie and her parents from expressing either love or hatred, and possibly from even *feeling* the hatred that was always there. Perhaps if these emotional locks had been opened, and if explosions of anger had been tolerated in the Borden household, Lizzie might have been able to express her hidden rage in some fashion less deadly than the form it took on the morning of August 4, 1892. The cold composure that Lizzie Borden displayed to the world at her trial was the hard veneer of lethal civility that pervaded her life. It was almost as if Lizzie had found it easier to confront her parents with an ax than with sharp words.

When Lizzie Borden came to trial in June 1893, she never took the stand in her own defense. The only time she ever testified for the record was ten months earlier, at the private inquest hearing. Her defense lawyers realized that if she were to testify at her trial, she would probably make a poor impression on the jury—and she would be forced to acknowledge the contradictory testimony that she had given at the inquest. Fortunately for the defense, the judges refused to admit Lizzie's inquest testimony into evidence at the trial. (They decided that she ought to have been given the opportunity to have a lawyer present during the inquest, and that anything she might have said on that occasion was therefore legally inadmissible.) The exclusion of Lizzie's inquest testimony dashed any hopes for a conviction that the prosecution might have entertained. So did the presiding judge's final charge to the jury, which was so biased in Lizzie's behalf that one newspaper called it "A PLEA FOR THE INNOCENT."

The jury was out little more than an hour. The panel never seriously entertained the possibility that the defendant was guilty. When it returned, the verdict was "Not guilty." A newspaper described the scene that followed:

> A cheer broke the stillness of the courtroom. Everybody sprang to their feet, and the greatest excitement prevailed, but the woman on whom all eyes were turned sank to the rail, with her face buried in her hands. Lizzie Borden wept as she had not for many months.
>
> Then, in a calm and kindly tone, Judge Mason announced that Lizzie Borden was a free woman at last. The jury came forward to shake hands with Miss Borden.

A few minutes later, Lizzie held a brief press conference in the judge's chamber. She refused to say a word about the verdict, but she did talk about her immediate plans. She simply said: "I want to go home: take me straight home tonight. I want to see the old place and settle down at once."

# Money, Society, and Women

The reporters who interviewed Lizzie Borden a few moments after she was found innocent must have been astonished to hear her say that all she wanted was to go home, "to see the old place," and settle down. But, in fact, she did not settle down in the "old place." Two years later, after the excitement had died down and she received her share of her father's estate, she moved. She bought a mansion on the Hill, and named it, grandly, Maplecroft. Then she changed her name from Lizzie—which was no nickname but her legal given name—to the fancier Lizbeth. She began to buy nice things. Maplecroft got a set of fine china, a lot of elegant furniture, the oil paintings that had been so absent from the old house on Second Street. She also bought five diamond rings and a lot of other expensive jewelry.

Still, her father's investments in real estate and industrial stock continued to grow. Lizbeth Borden died quietly in 1927, at the age of sixty-seven, a rich woman. (She left only one small bequest, to the Fall River Animal Rescue League. "I have been fond of animals," her will explained, "and their need is great and there are so few who care for them.")

Lizbeth Borden got some of the things Lizzie Borden must have wanted. But there were other things she did not get. She never married. She lived a more or less isolated life, with few friends and no invitations to balls or parties, no memberships in fancy women's clubs. She had won her way into the physical world of the Hill. But the murder trial had cost her whatever chance she might have had for access to the Hill's society. She even lost contact with her sister. Her little bequest to the Animal Rescue League was a pathetic testament to her isolation from the social world of human beings.

What Lizbeth Borden did escape was tackiness. She got out of a tacky house, with its slop jars and its grubby basement privy. She got flush toilets and running water. She got away from the embarrassing, old-fashioned horsehair sofa, the barn, and the well on Second Street. Had Andrew Jackson Borden shamed her by carrying a silver watch and not a gold? She would have diamonds and gold aplenty.

The question of Lizzie Borden's guilt or innocence was settled legally by the jury. Most historians have decided the question the other way. She may well have killed her parents. But, on a deeper level, her legal guilt or innocence is irrelevant. What matters most is that her behavior before and after the murders says a great deal about American society at the end of the nineteenth century, particularly about the lives of middle- and upper-class Americans.

Murder, especially one like the brutal ax murder of the elderly Bordens, is a bizarre event that may have little historical significance. But the preoccupations with social class and social status that set the atmosphere for the murder and the trial can tell us a lot about the kinds of ambitions and stresses that "normal," nonmurderous American families labored under. *Whether* Lizzie Borden killed her father and mother might interest a jury or a novelist looking for a plot. *Why* Lizzie Borden might have wanted to kill her parents is a question that takes the case out of the realm of the bizarre and into the realm of history.

## WEALTH, THE NEW GOSPEL

The steel baron Andrew Carnegie, one of the richest men in the world, once visited an American Indian village on the Great Plains. He noticed that the teepee of the chief looked very much like the teepees of all the other men, and he drew what he believed was the compelling lesson. In the modern world of industrial capitalism, Carnegie said, the home of the millionaire was drastically different from the home of the farmer or factory worker. The glaring extremes of wealth and poverty might seem to signal a much more severe exploitation of the poor by the rich than in a "primitive" society like that of the Indians.

NEWPORT MANSIONS

Every American city in the late nineteenth century had its fashionable neighborhoods, like The Hill, in Fall River, Massachusetts, where Lizzie Borden moved after her trial. But no single place in America was as fancy or as pretentious as Newport, Rhode Island, where many wealthy Americans built summer homes— vast Victorian "cottages" like these along Cliff Walk. At the same time, yachting became a popular sport— and means of display—among the rich. And so began a continuing contest for the American shoreline between the wealthy and the rest of the population. *(Culver Pictures)*

But the opulent life of the modern millionaire was really a sign of social progress. He lived a fantastically rich life. But his riches were the result of production. And that same production had made the average citizen wealthy, too. An ordinary family, under industrial capitalism, lived in a style that Carnegie believed would have made any tribal chief, or even any ancient king or emperor, envious.

Carnegie's meditation, which he made famous in a popular essay of 1888 entitled "The Gospel of Wealth," was typical of the attitudes of both wealthy and middle-class Americans in the 1880s and 1890s. One of the most obvious features of their world was wealth. And their awareness of wealth only increased their consciousness of poverty. They were not heartless people. They could pity the poor, especially the "deserving" poor and the children of poverty. They might even try to relieve suffering through philanthropy. But they seldom doubted what they believed were the inevitable twin consequences of

industrial capitalism: the creation of fortunes for a small fraction but of a much better life for everyone else.

## The Monied Class

In 1877, when Lizzie Borden was a teen-ager, Cornelius Vanderbilt died. His will, when it became public, astonished a society that was not yet accustomed to fabulous fortunes. He left an estate worth a staggering $100 million. But by the time Lizzie Borden went to trial, fifteen years later, Americans had become used to seeing newspaper stories about single donations made by men of fortune that almost equaled Vanderbilt's entire estate. By the 1890s, the wealth of men like Carnegie, Rockefeller, and a dozen or so other multimillionaires had become public and legendary. Even more important, there were a hundred millionaires for every well-known multimillionaire. By the 1890s, the United States had, by conservative guesses, well over 3,000 men whose holdings were worth over a million dollars. And there were even more with "moderate" fortunes of several hundred thousand dollars.

Every American city of middling size had its tight cluster of wealthy families. Around these rich people, in every town and city, were grouped a growing number of others who would have described themselves as "well-to-do" or "respectable." Like the truly wealthy, this class of Americans was increasingly an urban fact of life. In 1880, the total value of all rural and urban real estate in the United States was still about equal. Just ten years later, the value of urban real estate had increased twice as much as rural. Even more striking was the fact that city dwellers owned almost three times as much of other kinds of property—furniture, jewels, stocks, bonds, and bank accounts—as rural people did. The average farm family owned about $3,000 worth of such property in 1890. But the average city family owned about $9,000 worth. Since a lot of city people had no money, the average wealth of those who had any at all was far above $9,000.*

## The Preoccupation with Wealth, Display, and Status

This new money was not quiet, discreet, and invisible. The style of the wealthy, from the 1870s down through the end of the century, was one of display. For the very rich and the moderately well-to-do, the purpose of life seemed to be to mount displays of opulence and to make them as visible and imposing as possible. For the multimillionaire, this meant building "cottages" like Marble House at Newport; or houses with dining rooms like that of the Astors in New York; or imposing mansions fronting on Central Park, like the home of Henry Clay Frick, Carnegie's partner in steel.

But even for people of moderate income, in smaller cities and towns, the new style permitted dramatically larger and more pretentious houses. The typical middle-class house of the period was a vast affair, with eight, ten, or even twelve rooms. Cheaper lumber and labor made its vastness possible. New methods of power milling and carving wood gave it opulent woodwork and elaborately decorated mantles and staircases. It had 11-foot ceilings, central steam heat, running water, and gas lights. Soon it would have electricity and a telephone. But the Victorian house of the period, with its turrets and its wrought-iron fences, had one obvious purpose: to be imposing. It was to declare to the world that the family who lived within had achieved the sweet dream of success. This was exactly what the Borden house on Second Street did *not* declare.

The determination to display opulence and grandeur controlled the design and size not just of houses but of all the places the new middle and upper classes might frequent or pass through. Their hotels and restaurants were legendary for their elaborate gilding and marble, their mirrors and vast ceilings. Railroad stations, like the new Pennsylvania Station in New York, were designed to dwarf many a European palace—and many an American government building from the early days of the republic. The Pullman "Palace" cars, in which rich and near-rich Americans traveled, were fantastic studies in conspicuous display.

For the first time, the rich became celebrities—not because of some achievement in war or politics, but simply because of their wealth. To give a dinner at the famous Delmonico's Restaurant in New York, with seventy-two guests and a total tab of $10,000, was enough to make a rich man into a famous one, with pictures and headlines in not only New York newspapers but others around the country. Simply to have and to display money seemed enough to attract attention—and, of course, envy. To return from a ride in Central Park, on beautiful horses, to a mansion facing the park, was enough to attract an admiring crowd. The clatter of hooves, the men in fancy costume, including perhaps a polished top hat, the women in elegant riding costume, with

---

*These figures can be translated into today's dollars by multiplying them by at least seven, perhaps even ten.

PENNSYLVANIA STATION, NEW YORK

Opulence, grandeur, and display—these were the values expressed not only in the private homes of the wealthy but in the public and semipublic architecture of the late nineteenth century; this was the waiting room of the station of the Pennsylvania Railroad in New York. Architects of the time were also careful to design buildings that disguised the purposes for which they were intended. This great room could have served any number of ceremonial functions, but nothing suggests that below the floor was a network of railroad tracks. *(Culver Pictures)*

brilliantly colored silk scarves trailing almost to the street—this was the stuff of which the sweet dream of success was now made. And the public attention was as important as actually having the horses, the clothes, and the mansion in the first place.

Wealthy Americans not only displayed their means, they tried hard to consolidate their position as an upper class—and to make it clear to those who wanted to join them that there were certain definite steps and initiations that had to be passed through. Especially for young men, college now became an important rite of passage. Before the middle of the century, poor boys studying for the ministry had constituted the primary student body of many American colleges. But by the time the century drew to a close, three

things had happened. First, there was a great expansion in the number and size of colleges and universities—from about 60,000 students in the 1870s to almost 200,000 twenty years later. Second, beginning in the 1870s, a number of private colleges for women were established, and many state universities began to admit women. Third, the students were now from a more homogeneous social class, almost all sons and daughters of middle- and upper-class families. Within the colleges and universities, the students heightened class consciousness even further through an array of secret societies, Greek-letter fraternities and sororities, and dining clubs—organizations that had not been a part of college life a generation earlier.

The students' parents were doing the same

**LADIES AT NEWPORT**

During the period between the Civil War and World War I, wealthy women—and many who were not so wealthy—dressed themselves in more and more ornate costumes. Here, two women promenade at an elegant summer garden party in fashionable Newport, Rhode Island. The woman on the left is wearing an outfit (hat, parasol, and all together) that probably weighed some twenty pounds or more. But the sight of the photographer has apparently cheered her up a bit. *(Culver Pictures)*

like, served many of the same functions for middle-class men. There had always been clubs, of course. The Masons was an organization much older than the American republic. The difference now was that the clubs and lodges not only were much bigger, and consisted of many more members, but they were more subtly and elaborately graded signs of class membership.

## The Preoccupation with Manners

The preoccupation with wealth, display, and status gave a peculiar intensity, even desperation, to Americans' concern with "manners." A flood of manuals of etiquette poured from the presses during the decades after the Civil War. These were reinforced by regular columns in the high-circulation magazines of the day, many of which were aimed especially at women: *Ladies' Home Journal, Cosmopolitan,* and *Harper's Bazaar.* As though this were not enough, major newspapers (whose circulation was now leaping into the millions each day), also employed women to write daily columns of advice on good form and "personal" problems.

This tremendous volume of avidly read material was all based on two assumptions. The first was clear and explicit: there was a correct way of doing everything—eating, dressing, talking,

sorts of things. A number of institutions took root in every American town, institutions whose main purpose was to segregate people along class lines. The country club became a regular feature of the lives of the urban middle and upper class. Indeed, most cities of any size would have two or three country clubs, each precisely distinguished from the others along fine but definite lines of status. The same was true of the yacht clubs that seemed to dot every usable harbor on the coasts and lakes. Men joined downtown clubs and women formed an astonishing variety of social clubs of their own. The lodge movement, with its Masons, Moose, Odd Fellows, and the

**THE LADY AND THE GENTLEMAN** *(opposite page)*

This page from an etiquette book—clearly meant for those people who needed elementary instruction—laid down some quite fastidious rules. It advised the ladies, for example, to lift the hem of the skirt when crossing a street. But only with one hand, for "To raise the dress with both hands is vulgar." The manual is uncertain on one point, however. It recommends in general that gentlemen give ladies the inside of the sidewalk when they "promenade" together. On the other hand, it admits that some authorities recommend a different rule: that the lady walk on the gentleman's right, so as to leave her right hand free to carry a parasol. If the lady in the picture had adopted that rule, she would have spared the gentleman from being jabbed in the chest by her parasol. But such were the valiant sufferings demanded of the gentlemen of the day. *(Culver Pictures)*

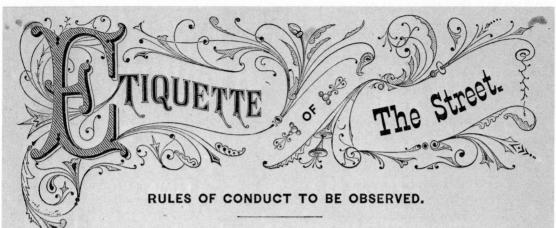

# ETIQUETTE OF The Street.

## RULES OF CONDUCT TO BE OBSERVED.

LADIES and gentlemen, when meeting on the sidewalk, should always pass to the right. Should the walk be narrow or dangerous, gentlemen will always see that ladies are protected from injury.

Ladies should avoid walking rapidly upon the street, as it is ungraceful and unbecoming.

Running across the street in front of carriages is dangerous, and shows want of dignity.

The gentleman should insist upon carrying any package which the lady may have, when walking with her.

Before recognizing a lady on the street, the gentleman should be certain that his recognition will meet with favor.

No gentleman should stand on the street-corners, steps of hotels, or other public places, and make remarks about ladies passing by.

A gentleman may take two ladies upon his arms, but under no circumstances should the lady take the arms of two gentlemen.

Upon the narrow walk, for her protection, the gentleman should generally give the lady the inside of the walk (Fig. 21), passing behind her when changing at corners.

Allowing a dress to trail on the street is in exceedingly bad taste. Such a street costume simply calls forth criticism and contempt from the more sensible people.

A gentleman walking with a lady should accommodate his step and pace to hers. For the gentleman to be some distance ahead, presents a bad appearance.

Should protection on the street be necessary, it is customary for the gentleman to give his right arm to the lady; but if more convenient, he may give the left.

It is courtesy to give silent, respectful attention as a funeral procession passes. It shows want of respect to pass between the carriages while the procession is moving.

Staring at people, spitting, looking back after they pass, saluting people across the street, calling out loudly or laughing at people as they go by, are all evidences of ill-breeding.

The gentleman accompanying a lady should hold the door open for the lady to enter first. Should he be near the door when a lady, unattended, is about to enter, he will do the same for her.

In the evening, or whenever safety may require, a gentleman should give a lady his arm. It is not customary in other cases to do so on the street, unless with an elderly lady, or the couple be husband and wife.

A gentleman will assist a lady over a bad crossing, or from an omnibus or carriage, without waiting for the formality of an introduction. When the service is performed, he will raise his hat, bow, and pass on.

In a street car or an omnibus, the passengers who are seated should strive to give seats to those who are standing, rendering such accommodation as they would themselves desire under similar circumstances.

When crossing the pavement, the lady should raise her dress with the right hand, a little above the ankle. To raise the dress with both hands, is vulgar, and can be excused only when the mud is very deep.

No gentleman will smoke when walking with, or standing in the presence of, a lady on the street. He should remove the cigar from her presence entirely, even though permission be granted to continue the smoking.

Fi. 21. The street-promenade. The gentleman gives the lady the inside of the walk. *

A gentleman should give his seat to any lady who may be standing in a public conveyance. For this favor she should thank him, which courtesy he should acknowledge by a slight bow. In an omnibus he will pass up the ladies' fares.

A true lady will go quietly and unobtrusively about her business when on the street, never seeking to attract the attention of the opposite sex, at the same time recognizing acquaintances with a courteous bow, and friends with pleasant words of greeting.

Swinging the arms when walking, eating upon the street, sucking the parasol handles, pushing violently through a crowd, very loud and boisterous talking and laughing on the streets, and whispering in public conveyances, are all evidences of ill-breeding in ladies.

A lady should have the escort of a gentleman in the evening. A gentleman at the house where she may call may return with her if she goes unattended; gossip and scandal are best avoided, however, if she have some one from her home call for her at an appointed hour.

On the narrow street-crossing the gentleman will allow the lady to precede him, that he may see that no injury befalls her.

Should a lady stop in the street, when meeting a gentleman, it is courtesy for him to stop also. Should his business be urgent, he will apologize for not continuing the conversation, and ask to be excused. Should it be desirable to lengthen the interview, and the lady resumes her walk in the midst of her conversation, it is courtesy for him to turn and accompany her. Should she desire to end the conversation, a slight bow from her will indicate the fact, when he should bid her "good day" and take his leave.

* Some authorities claim that it is most sensible for the lady to walk always at the right of the gentleman, whether on the street or indoors; her right hand being thus free to hold trail, fan, or parasol.

dancing, courting—and that correct way was very likely to be something complicated, unnatural, and slightly European in tone. The manuals were littered with French expressions that seemed to put into words ideas that were a little too subtle or too elegant to be expressed in English. Some things were *très distingué,* which lent them an air of mystery not conveyed by the English "distinguished." Readers were warned of *faux pas,* as though a simple misstep were a dark and disgraceful thing indeed. People who were planning dinner parties might be pleased to learn that host and hostess were no longer expected to carve and serve at the table, that food should be brought to the table by servants. But that information was given an even greater air of elegance when the reader learned that this practice had originated with the Russian aristocracy and was called service *à la Russe.*

The second, somewhat hidden, assumption behind all the books and columns was that a failure to know the right fork, or the proper way to invite a lady to waltz, was a failure of class. The individual whose manners were not in good style—or *bon ton*—had to worry not just about a revealed weakness of personality, or even a lapse of morals. He or she had to worry about being betrayed in class terms, about falling out of "polite society," down into what was now called "the other half."

The world that Lizzie Borden inhabited was a world preoccupied, even obsessed, with wealth and with displays of elegance and manners. Her father was certainly rich enough to afford service *à la Russe.* But he insisted on just keeping plain Bridget. Lizzie, and thousands of other young men and women, pored over newspaper stories of the doings of the wealthy, and over books that laid out impossibly fancy designs of behavior for the proper. In one person, the response might be heightened ambition to have the money and the grand house that lay at the center of the dream of success. In another person, the response might be shame or disgust with the extent to which his or her manners and life style fell short of what was considered correct. In many, the response

was a simple fear of exposure of their rudeness or vulgarity, their lack of "respectability."

One book of manners gave its readers the following example of an elegant conversation. A gentleman has just offered his arm to a lady, to lead her in to table at a fine dinner party.

> The gentleman may say, "We must be careful not to step on that elaborate train," referring to the costume of a lady preceding the pair.
> "Yes, indeed, that would be a mishap. But trains are graceful in spite of their inconvenience."
> Her companion must answer: "Oh! I admire them, of course. Only I have such a dread of stepping on them and bringing down the wrath of the fair wearer on my devoted head."

The proposed conversation may appear comic. But it would have seemed a little bitter to Lizzie Borden, who lived in a house where a dinner party was simply an impossibility. It also suggests something of the discomfort that even the "lady" and "gentleman" had to labor under. She acknowledges that the train is an inconvenience that has to be endured because it is "graceful." He in turn reveals his dread of the wrath that will come down on him if he causes a mishap. If even the men and women in manner-book examples felt this way, their readers can only have been even more anxious.

## UTOPIAN VISION OF THE FAMILY

Americans usually remember the last decades of the nineteenth century as the age of "rugged individualism," when men (almost exclusively *men*) competed in a no-holds-barred contest for individual success. But the sweet dream of success was not really an individual dream. Men experienced life as members of families. And success meant the success of the *family*—clothes and social standing for the wife, education for the children, fine careers for the sons (and increasingly the daughters). The specter of failure was a horror the entire family had to face, not a fear of poverty so much as a horror of losing the vague but urgent sense of being "respectable."

# AMERICAN IMAGES
## Status for Sale

Horatio Alger, the tireless storyteller of the self-made man—or, more precisely, the self-made boy—once had his hero, Ragged Dick, pass by the Palace Hotel in New York. It was magnificent, more magnificent even than the palaces of European nobles. But it was a great "democratic" palace, Alger insisted. Anyone could walk into the lobby, and anyone who had the modest price of a room could luxuriate in its grand, Victorian opulence. Here, to Alger and to his readers, lay the magic of American society. The "average" citizen had open access to elegance, style, and pretension—to all the visible badges of social class and caste.

But how could the truly rich and the well-to-do deal with the fact that people of very modest resources could dress themselves like the wealthy and learn "refined" manners from cheap manuals? One way was to make the clothing of the rich more and more elaborate, their houses larger and even more ornate, their furniture hopelessly grand and gilded. Something like a race developed between the attempts of the wealthy to have a monopoly on the marks of caste, and the capacities of manufacturers and marketers to provide inexpensive facsimiles of these marks at prices many ordinary citizens could afford. No matter how complicated and absurd the clothes of wealthy women became, factories and retailers seemed able to run off and sell cheap versions of them. No matter how shiny were gentle-

**Suspensory Bandages.**

**D 963 Red Cross Suspensory, Army and Navy Style.** Large, medium and Small.

|  | Each. | Doz. |
|---|---|---|
| Cotton, non-elastic | $0.20 | $2.00 |
| Lisle thread, elastic band | .35 | 4.00 |
| Silk, elastic band | .50 | 5.00 |

**D 964 J. P. Suspensory, Single Band.** Large, medium and small.

|  | Each | Doz. |
|---|---|---|
| Cotton Sack | $0.20 | $2.00 |
| English Web Sack | .25 | 2.50 |
| Silk Sack | .35 | 3.75 |

**D 965 O. P. C. Suspensory.** Automatically adjustable and never fails to fit and give satisfaction; for comfort, security, durability and elegance the best in the world. Order by number. Give size, large medium or small.

|  | Each |
|---|---|
| No. 2, lisle | $0.75 |
| No. 3, silk | 1.25 |
| No. 4, all silk | 1.75 |
| No. 5, all silk, fancy colors | 2.25 |

**D 966 Safety Suspensory.** The construction of the Safety secures a perfect self-adjusting, sliding-loop suspensory, which enables the sack to be detached for washing; no buckles on sack. Assorted sizes: large medium and small.

No. 52. Safety, English web sack, elastic band. Each....$0.50 Per dozen........ 4.50

No. 53. Safety, bolting silk sack, elastic band. Each....$0.60 Per dozen........ 5.00

No. 54. Safety, knitted silk sack, elastic band. Each....$0.70 Per dozen........ 6.00

PLATE 1.

All photos on pages 622–628 are from Fred L. Israel, ed., *1897 Sears Roebuck Catalogue* (New York: Chelsea House, 1968).

men's top hats, or how elegant their cotton or linen jackets for the seashore, a man with a dollar to spare could own something very much like them.

Some people were simply out of the contest, of course. No one could mistake the social status of blacks. No one could be confused about the class identity of an immigrant arriving in the United States with a great bundle of possessions. But for a mass of other Americans, even for domestic servants and poor store clerks, the possibility of simulating wealth and status—and the darker possibility that one might not succeed in simulating it—was a central fact of life.

One of the clearest expressions of the dreams and pangs of class anxiety at the end of the nineteenth century was the catalogue—the *Consumers Guide,* they called it, with no apostrophe—of "Sears, Roebuck and Co., Cheapest Supply House."

The two main business notions of the Sears and Roebuck operation, from its beginning in 1895, were low prices and high volume. But these business notions were heavily reinforced with a guiding principle of promotion. The goods being offered for sale, the clothing and the furniture, the canes and the carriages, all were "fine" and "elegant," the "best that money can buy," and "the equal of any available." Page after page of the 1897 catalogue repeated the message: "Fine" was probably the most often used adjective. Then came "choice," "elegant," and even "nobby"—a new bit of slang for belonging to the upper "crust." Even a gentleman's "suspensory" was described as being "for elegance the best in the world" (Plate 1). And the *Consumers Guide* followed the practice of the manuals on manners: It suggested that its products were somehow royal or French, to emphasize their refined character. The "bust developer" offered in one of the largest displays of the catalogue was called the "Princess." The cream that was part of the treatment had been produced by an "eminent French chemist," and the tonic sent along to be taken internally was called the "Fleur de Lis" (Plate 2).

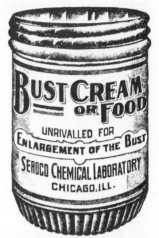
But it was in its sections on clothing that the
*Consumers Guide* insisted most passionately on the
capacity of modern manufacturing and marketing to
obliterate the visible lines of class and caste. Two elegant gentlemen are posed in casual costume (Plate
3). In the background, people are playing lawn tennis and sailing—both the recreations of the very rich.
But the dapper sporting jacket, dashingly striped in
black or blue and white, could be had for anywhere
from 35 to 95 cents. (This was roughly the price of
the work jacket for railroad engineers, on the next
page.) A "Prince Albert Suit," in black worsted, sold
for about $10.00. It came lined in "fine Italian cloth"
(Plate 4). For something more up-to-date, there was
a suit of fine "cassimere," for as little as $6.50—
guaranteed to be "the latest in style for this season . . .
fine tailor made . . . fancy velvet arm shields under

623

PLATE 3.

PLATE 4.

# Mens Black Prince Albert Suits

**We make and sell more Prince Albert Suits** direct to the consumer than all other mail order houses combined and we are prepared to offer values that will mean a saving to you of 25% to 50%. **We can furnish you a double breasted Prince Albert suit,** perfect fitting and equal to anything your local tailor can make, at a saving to you of at least 50%. **We are anxious to get your order** for one of these suits to show you that it is possible for us to furnish the highest class goods at prices within easy reach of all. **Our Prince Albert suits** are made in the very highest style of the art on the latest patterns, cut by expert cutters to fit perfectly, and made by the best tailors we can employ. The linings and trimmings are all of the very finest, and we guarantee every suit to give the best satisfaction. **Sizes run regularly from 34 to 42 inches chest measure,** but larger sizes can be furnished at 20% extra.

**Our terms are liberal.** Any suit will be sent to any address on receipt of $1.00 as a guarantee of good faith, balance and express charges payable at express office. A discount of 3% allowed if cash in full accompanies your order. **Samples of cloth will be sent free on application.**

**Men's tailor made Clay Worsted Double Breasted Prince Albert Suits at $9.80** surely should interest all careful buyers, for a Clay Worsted Prince Albert suit was never before offered at anything like the price.

**We offer a line of Double Breasted Prince Albert Suits at $9.80, $12.00, $14.00, $16.00, $18.00, and $20.00,** and we know that the sale of one suit in a neighborhood will result in the sale of many more.

**No. 4342. Our $9.80 Men's Black Clay Worsted Prince Albert Suit,** a suit that would retail at nearly double our price. Made from a good quality imported **All Wool Black Clay Worsted Cloth,** well lined, trimmed and finished and guaranteed in every respect. **Our Special Price........ $9.80**

**No. 4343. Our $12.00 Men's Clay Worsted Prince Albert Suit,** made from 14 oz. imported all wool black English clay worsted cloth, guaranteed for wear, nicely lined, trimmed and finished and guaranteed in every respect. **Our Special Price................................$12.00**

**No. 4344. Our $14.00 Black Clay Worsted Prince Albert suit,** made from an imported all wool 16 oz. black English clay worsted cloth, finely lined, trimmed and finished and guaranteed in every respect. **Our Special price. $14.00**

**No. 4345. Our $16.00 Black Clay Worsted Prince Albert Suit,** made from 18 oz. imported all wool black English clay worsted, coat lined throughout with fine imported Italian cloth, elegantly trimmed and finished, and guaranteed in every respect. **Our Special Price........................$16.00**

**No. 4346. Our $18.00 Black Clay Worsted Prince Albert Suit,** made from a very fine imported all wool English 18 oz. black clay worsted cloth. This is one of our finest Prince Albert suits. The coat is lined throughout with fine imported black Italian cloth, nicely trimmed and finished, and gotten up first-class in every respect. **Our Special Price . . $18.00**

**No. 4347. $20.00 for our very finest Black Clay Worsted Prince Albert Suit.** The suit is made from our 19 oz. imported all wool black English clay worsted, one of the best English weaves, a goods that we guarantee will never wear smooth, has a very nice soft surface finish. Every suit is made by expert tailors, the coats are lined throughout with fine imported black Italian cloth, nicely trimmed and guaranteed in every respect.

**Our Special Price...........................................$20.00**

No 6    BACK VIEW No 6

624

PLATE 5.

sleeves . . . very dressy" (Plate 5). A man's fancy dress shirt cost a mere 50 cents—the exact price of a work shirt (Plate 6).

Women were promised even more. Their union suits—sold to the slogan "In Union There Is Strength"—had "an air of refinement" (Plate 7). The underskirt that might be put on next was "rich in appearance" (Plate 8). Then came the Venus, "the very latest improved French Corset . . . made of finest Zanella cloth" (Plate 9). After an ornate blouse that might cost as little as 25 cents, or perhaps 47 cents (Plate 10), came the grand suits—"smart . . .

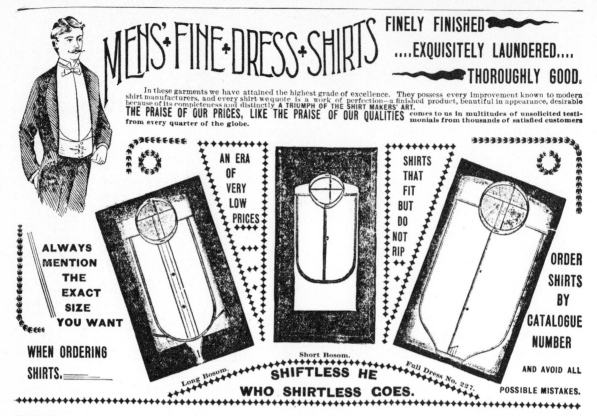

# MENS · FINE · DRESS · SHIRTS

## FINELY FINISHED
## ....EXQUISITELY LAUNDERED....
## THOROUGHLY GOOD.

In these garments we have attained the highest grade of excellence. They possess every improvement known to modern shirt manufacturers, and every shirt we quote is a work of perfection—a finished product, beautiful in appearance, desirable because of its completeness and distinctly **A TRIUMPH OF THE SHIRT MAKERS' ART.**
**THE PRAISE OF OUR PRICES, LIKE THE PRAISE OF OUR QUALITIES** comes to us in multitudes of unsolicited testimonials from thousands of satisfied customers from every quarter of the globe.

AN ERA OF VERY LOW PRICES

SHIRTS THAT FIT BUT DO NOT RIP

ALWAYS MENTION THE EXACT SIZE YOU WANT

WHEN ORDERING SHIRTS.

ORDER SHIRTS BY CATALOGUE NUMBER

AND AVOID ALL POSSIBLE MISTAKES.

Long Bosom.

Short Bosom.

Full Dress No. 227.

**SHIFTLESS HE WHO SHIRTLESS GOES.**

PLATE 6.

PLATE 7.

## LADIES' SUMMER UNION SUITS.
### IN UNION THERE IS STRENGTH.

No. 2953.    No. 2954.    No. 2950.

magnificent ... fancy ... rustling ... very fine." The cost of such a suit, all in wool and taffeta and velvet, was between $4.50 and $8.50 (Plate 11).

It is tempting to smile at the clothes. Nothing seems quite as ludicrous as the costumes of a former generation. But there was a deadly serious point behind it all—a point that Lizzie Borden, and her stepmother, and the servant Bridget would all have grasped well and instinctively. Whatever might be the facts about wealth, income, class, and mobility in the United States, the *appearance* of things was plainly fluid, mobile, and in a certain sense democratic. It was possible (and perhaps even necessary for many people) to go to extraordinary lengths to display wealth. But it was equally possible (and perhaps equally necessary to millions of others) to imitate those displays at discount prices.

PLATE 9.

PLATE 8.

**No. 23678. A Skirt built for wear.** of a fine quality muslin, the embroidery is 10 inches wide and is headed by a cloister of five tucks. The pattern of embroidery is neat and quiet, but nevertheless rich in appearance. Realizing that there are a great many women who still want the class of reliable merchandise on the market years ago, we make a special feature of this skirt. If you want a well wearing skirt order this number. Each........**$1.20**
  Two for.... ......... ........................ 2.30

**No. 23653 French Coutel Corset**; extra long waisted; sateen striped; fitted with unbreakable French wire; trimmed with handsome silk embroidery and heavily flossed, and produces an elegant appearance equaled only by corsets costing double the money. Colors: White, drab or black. Sizes, 18 to 30 only. Price............**95c**
  Extra size in black only; size 31 to 36. Price............**$1.20**

**No. 23654 The Very Latest Improved French Corset**, very highest grade, workmanship and material; made of finest Zanella cloth, extra long waisted, medium size bust and hips, cross boned, high back, beautifully embroidered and finished in every way equal to any corset retailing for $2.65 each; colors, drab or black; size, 18 to 30........**$1.89**

# ladies New Spring and Summer
## shirt waists

24390 50¢

24391 50¢

24392 85¢

24393 58¢

PLATE 10.

# LADIES TAILOR MADE SUITS

## STYLES 1897

24959 $4.50

24965 $6.75

24966 $7.50

24961 $4.50

24960 $4.50

24967 $8.50

24959
24960 24961
Very fine ladies'
suit made of imported
repellant cloth in black,
navy or tan. We make the
suit 24959 Bolero, 24960 Blazer,
24961 Reefer styles. The skirt is
very full; lined throughout with rustling taffeta and bound with velvet. $4.50
24962 Same style as 24959 made of fine serge
in black, blue or green. Jacket all lined with
fine fancy serge. Price............$5.50
24963 Same style as 24960 made as 24962. Price...$5.50
24964 Same style as 24961 made as 24962. Price.....$5.50
24965 Smart Blazer suit made of imported ladies cloth, in
either black or navy, trimmed with braid and small buttons, full
skirt, lined throughout with rustling taffeta, bound with velvet.$6.75
24966 A magnificent Eaton style ladies suit of fancy Scotch mixture, trimmed with fine Hercules braid around bottom of waist and on
sleeves, fancy horn buttons in front, waist lined with changeable silk
serge, full sweep skirt interlined with crinoline and lined with rustle
taffeta, bound with velvet. A fine $15.00 suit for................$7.50
24967 Very Stylish Ladies' Suit, Bolero style, made of blue or black
serge cheviot, newest sleeves, outer jacket trimmed all around with
black mohair and silk, mixed gimp and lined with changeable silk.
Very full skirt trimmed as illustrated. Skirt lined with rustling
taffeta and interlined with crinoline, bound with velvet. Very
rich. Price............$8.50

## SPECIAL OFFER.

WE WILL SEND ANY of these fine tailor-
made suits C.O.D., **SUBJECT TO
EXAMINATION**, on receipt of
$1.00, balance with express
charges to be paid upon examination and approval.

3 PER CENT. OFF
for full cash
with order.

## SOLD ONLY BY SEARS ROEBUCK & Co. incorporated Chicago.

PLATE 11.

In fact, the American dream of success was in many ways a family dream. It was a dream that money might buy enough ease and comfort, enough space and privacy within the home, to make the family a place of harmonious refuge from a world of striving, competition, and ambition. If people could get enough money, the dream promised, then their human problems within the home might be solved. Strife between husbands and wives, anger and resentment between generations—all might disappear once there were goods enough, rooms enough, servants enough. For wealthy and well-to-do Americans, the ideal family had gradually become a truly utopian vision of sanctuary from a lonely, dangerous, and corrupt world.

This utopian vision of family life lay behind the astonishing support that Lizzie Borden got from middle-class and wealthy Americans during her trial. In Fall River, there was an immediate assumption among "respectable" people that she was innocent, that she could not have committed such a deed, since she was a *lady*—not just a woman. As Lizzie Borden became a celebrity in newspapers and magazines around the country, this kind of support broadened and became even more insistent. The reasons had little to do with the facts of the case. They had to do with the profound commitment that "respectable" Americans had made to the relationship between wealth and family happiness. They had assumed that money, honestly earned, could lead only to the good life, to family circles that were quiet and loving. In a very real sense, this *was* the American dream. For the men and women who read about the Borden murders, Lizzie *had* to be innocent. To admit otherwise was to admit that the dream was false, that even Andrew Jackson Borden's wealth could not buy the kind of family they wanted.

## The Middle-Class Woman's Burden

The utopian vision of family put a great deal of emotional pressure on all those Americans who entered the struggle for "respectability." But it probably bore most heavily on middle-class women. Some of them were interested in political causes like getting the right to vote. A small but increasing number were looking for professional careers, attending one of the new women's colleges or one of the state universities that had become coeducational. Various kinds of jobs were becoming "respectable" options for young middle-class women: nursing, teaching, being a librarian or a stenographer or even a clerk in a fancy city store. But for a large majority of women in the white middle class, "respectability" meant staying at home, being a mother, and perhaps—at most—getting involved in church work, women's clubs, or a reform movement like temperance.

These were the women who carried the difficult burden of translating money into comfort, decorum, and elegance at home. And their task was defined in ways that made it extremely trying. For one thing, they were expected to present themselves to the world as models of purity and innocence. Even their clothing seemed designed to shut them off from contact with the world. In the 1870s, the heavily corseted "wasp" waist, which enclosed women in an armor of bone or spring steel, became fashionable among the middle class. Then, about a decade later, came the bustle, heaping layer upon layer of heavy cloth between women and the world. In fact, the most marked characteristic of women's dress was becoming its heavy, complicated, encasing nature. A standard "walking costume" of the 1880s required a strip of cloth 2 feet wide and 45 feet long—a total of 90 square feet. Lizzie Borden, before her parents were murdered, had many elaborate dresses hanging in her closet—as though clothes were the one way she could break through her father's determination to be tacky. And she had sometimes quarreled with her stepmother because the older woman seemed as indifferent to clothing as Mr. Borden was to his house.

But even when they were properly dressed, women had to worry even more than men did about doing all sorts of things the "right" way.

**COLLEGE WOMEN**

During Lizzie Borden's lifetime, American women began to attend colleges and universities, mostly in small private colleges for women only or in coeducational state universities. Here, obviously posed for the camera, a class of young ladies in Washington, D.C., all dressed in black, shows how they study even such scientific subjects as geography and physics without losing their "femininity." *(Culver Pictures)*

For men, in their working lives, there was a simple test of what was right: Did it help get and keep a job? Did it increase profit in the long run? But women were more at sea in a world where social standing seemed to depend on elegance and etiquette, where every detail of life was prescribed, and where a single misstep might lead to disgrace. One manual of manners for the period even tried to prescribe the precise replies a woman ought to make to every kind of letter or note. In a "Letter Refusing a Donation to an Old Ladies' Home," one should write "I am compelled to contribute only to such objects as have my warmest sympathy." Then there was a "Letter Congratulating a Friend upon Finding a Lost Child": "God Bless Essie." Social care and caution seemed to know no limits, with every conceivable situation demanding a rule. There was

even a proper "Answer to a Letter of Condolence on the Loss of a Limb": "Hoping to see you soon, maimed as I am." The book was published in 1888. One can only speculate what its author might have suggested a few years later as the proper way to answer a "Letter of Condolence upon the Ax Murder of One's Aged Parents."

Of course, for most women, most of the time, such detailed prescriptions were unnecessary. But there was no way to escape the sense that there were rules governing what was proper in "good society" for every kind of occasion, and that failure to know those rules doomed a woman and her family to being cast down into "the other half."

Even more important was the fact that the doings of the very rich were relentlessly written up in newspapers and magazines, and paraded as models of "taste." There had always been fancy ladies, members of one kind of aristocracy or another. But now they had become public celebrities. With what mixture of awe, envy, and confusion could a young woman of Lizzie Borden's social class read the *New York Times* description of the costume Mrs. William Kissam Vanderbilt wore to a very famous ball she held in 1883?

> Mrs. Vanderbilt's irreproachable taste was seen to perfection in her costume as a Venetian princess. The underskirt was of white and yellow brocade. The figures of flowers and leaves were outlined in gold and lined with Roman red. Almost the entire length of the train was caught up at one side forming a large puff. The waist was of blue satin covered with gold embroidery; the dress was cut square in the neck, and the flowing sleeves were of transparent gold tissue. She wore a Venetian cap, covered with magnificent jewels, the most noticeable of these being a superb peacock in many colored gems.

It is difficult to measure the emotions of even a single individual, much less of an entire social class or group. But the levels of tension and anxiety among middle-class women in the 1880s and 1890s must have been extremely high. One of the most popular woman writers of the day asked, in 1880, "What is this curious product of today, the American girl or woman?" Her answer was tentative, but a little frightened: "She does not yet understand herself. The face of today is stamped with restlessness, wandering purpose, and self-consciousness." Isabel A. Mallon, who wrote a phenomenally successful "advice" column in the *Ladies' Home Journal,* put the problem this way ten years later, in 1890: "The great fault of the girl of today is discontent. She calls it by the more magnificent sounding name of ambition, but in reality she is absolutely restless and dissatisfied with whatever may be her position in life."

Two serious writers of the period wrote brilliant and chilling stories of the plight of middle-class, middle-aged women. The first was *The Awakening,* published in 1899 by Kate Chopin. The second was *The Yellow Wallpaper,* by Charlotte Perkins Gilman, which was first printed in 1892.

Kate Chopin's heroine is Edna Pontellier, a woman of intelligence and acute sensitivity, married to a wealthy Creole businessman in Louisiana. The social and physical setting in which she moves is lush, picturesque, and even interesting. But she has a vague, powerful sense that her life is incomplete. She considers leaving her husband for another man but discovers that her lover thinks of her as "his" just as much as her husband does. She ponders the possibility of simply having an affair with some experienced, gentlemanly rogue. But that prospect galls. She talks to friends and to a doctor, but no one has any sort of workable advice. Edna Pontellier becomes increasingly despondent. Even the children she wants to love come to seem a trap and a burden to her. Finally, in a curiously indecisive way, she swims naked, out too far to survive, and dies with pink memories of innocent girlhood floating through her mind.

The nameless heroine of *The Yellow Wallpaper* shares Edna Pontellier's vague and powerful sense that she is trapped in an unsatisfying life. She too is married, and to a man of obvious "breeding" and success, a doctor. But she is being gnawed at by depression and anxiety. Gilman paints a classic picture of the way insanity creeps into the life of a woman who feels imprisoned by her marriage, her family, her social position. She begins to imagine that a strange woman is trapped in the vines that decorate the yellow wallpaper in her room. She starts refusing to leave the room, and as the story ends, she is convinced that *she* is the woman in the wallpaper, where she can now hide forever, creeping invisibly around and around the room.

Both of these stories are about women who, superficially, have nothing to complain of. Both seem to have satisfied every conventional ambition for success. Both are surrounded by men who are far from cruel. Their husbands are rich or near-rich. Both women have "help" aplenty and well-behaved children. But both are cut off from any serious use of their intelligence or their

# Susan B. Anthony on Trial

(Culver Pictures)

In the second half of the nineteenth century, a determined minority of women were interested in reforms of several kinds. The most determined minority of all agitated and organized for women's rights, including the right to vote.

One of the most tireless and unwavering feminists of the period was Susan B. Anthony. Like many American reformers she was born and brought up a Quaker. In 1835, at fifteen, she became a schoolteacher. But reform was to be her real vocation. She became interested first in temperance—the gateway to reform for many men and women. Then, by the mid-1850s, she was firmly committed to the twin causes of emancipation for blacks and equality for women.

After the Civil War, Anthony and other feminists thought they might win the vote. How could the politicians liberate black slaves and give them the right to vote, and still deny it to their own wives and sisters? The answer came depressingly quickly. According to the Fourteenth and Fifteenth amendments, every person was entitled to all the privileges and immunities of citizenship regardless of race or color. But *not* regardless of sex.

Anthony decided to test the meaning of the amendments. In 1872, she led a group of women to the polls in Rochester, New York, to vote. She was arrested and charged with voting illegally.

During her trial in 1873, the judge would not allow Anthony to testify. Her lawyers, both men, argued that the Fourteenth Amendment, by defining a citizen as *any* person born or naturalized in the United States, made women full citizens. It must be illegal, then, for any state or the federal government to deny any such person, male or female, the full rights of citizenship.

When the lawyers had finished the judge drew from under his robes a written opinion, obviously prepared before he had heard the arguments. He read it and ordered the jury to find the defendant guilty. Then he got ready to pronounce his sentence. But first he asked the traditional question: Was there any reason the defendant could offer why a sentence should not be pronounced?

The question set off a dialogue between Anthony and the judge that he tried over and over again to stop with an order that she sit down and be quiet.

She finally did sit down, but the embarrassed judge then had to ask her to stand again, to receive sentence. She rose.

JUDGE HUNT: The sentence of this court is that you pay a fine of $100 and the costs of the prosecution.

ANTHONY: May it please your honor, I will never pay a dollar of your unjust penalty. And I shall earnestly and persistently continue to urge all women to the practical recognition of the old Revolutionary maxim, "Resistance to tyranny is obedience to God."

Anthony demanded to be punished with the full rigor of the law. But Judge Hunt was not foolish enough to create a martyr, or to invite a powerful appeal to a superior court. He refused to give her the privilege of going to jail for contempt, saying, "Madam, the Court will *not* order you to stand committed until the fine is paid." And so ended the trial of the *United States* v. *Susan B. Anthony.*

talent. They are suffocating in a world that reduces them to social ornaments, a world ruled by a stifling decorum. And for both heroines, life becomes intolerable. One chooses suicide, the other is pictured as actively choosing insanity. Lizzie Borden, whatever her legal guilt or innocence, would have understood.

# THE OTHER HALF

The heroines of *The Awakening* and *The Yellow Wallpaper* were women for whom the domestic ideal had become a stifling, suffocating nightmare. And it is probably true that some middle-class and wealthy women experienced marriage and motherhood as a frustrating round of tedium and despair. But the domestic ideal was kept vital by one simple, inescapable fact: for most women, there was no acceptable alternative.

## Women's Work

There was one possible alternative, of course: work. Lizzie Borden and other women like her could have escaped the confinements of home and marriage by getting jobs. But the alternative was simply not acceptable. The jobs to which women had access in the nineteenth century were even more degrading and poorly paid than the jobs most men could find. For most women, a job was an unpleasant and temporary alternative to domestic life. For some others, it was an inescapable necessity, not a freely chosen way to avoid marriage, home, and children.

Women always had worked in ways for which they were not paid. Before the Civil War, about 2 million black women had worked as slaves, harder than most men. Women worked in their homes, too, whether they were wives, widowed aunts, or daughters. They cooked, they cleaned and sewed, they planted and harvested. But neither slave women nor "homemakers" were counted as part of the work force because they were not paid. On the record, at the time of the Civil War, only about 10 percent of American women held paid jobs, and they constituted only about 10 percent of the work force.

After the war, the unpaid work done by women increased in at least three ways. First, many ex–slave women began not only to keep house for themselves and their families, but also started to "take in" washing, sewing, and other work. They also entered into informal arrangements with white families, coming in to take care of children or to cook. These kinds of arrangements were usually not recorded, so such women did not show up on official records of who "worked" and who did not. Second, the practice of "boarding" increased, especially in American cities. By the end of the century, one out of every five Americans was a lodger in someone else's home. This meant that the women who kept all these houses had additional work to do, work that did not count as a paid job, even though it earned family income. Third, as cities grew, so did prostitution. Tens of thousands of women earned livings in this trade, most of them working now and then and for brief periods. But their work did not count as part of the public record of women's employment.

The amount of unpaid work that many women had to do kept them from seeking paid jobs. But, still, more and more women did find the opportunity—or, more often, the need—to work outside the home for money. In 1870, women constituted about 15 percent of the total paid work force, an increase of about 50 percent from the proportion in 1860. And the figures climbed steadily. By 1910, despite the vast immigration of male workers from Europe and the Orient, women made up 20 percent of the paid labor force. And fully 25 percent of all women worked for money.

For a few of these working women, a job *was* an attractive and hard-won escape from the pressures of marriage and motherhood. But for most of them—as for most men—work was a grinding necessity. The plain fact was that most men, whether they were native-born, immigrants, or blacks, could not support a family on the wages from their jobs. Since almost all Americans lived in families, the difference had to be made up somehow, and when it could not, people had to go hungry. The difference was made up, more often than not, by women. (In immigrant families, particularly, child labor also supplemented family income.)

## Which Women Worked?

The fact that most women worked not because the jobs were more attractive than home, or because they wanted "careers," created a female working population with a peculiar profile. The women who worked were not typical. They were women for whom the domestic ideal was unreached or unreachable. They were black women. They were daughters of immigrants living in urban ghettoes. They were native-born women who were still unmarried and who would quit work as soon as they could.

Black women were probably the women who were most forced to work for wages, even after they married. In 1900, only about 3 percent of the white married women in America earned wages (and this percentage included many women who lived in poor, immigrant families). But among married black women (most of whom lived in stable, two-parent households), more than 25 percent held paying jobs. And the jobs were unfailingly poor. Black women worked in about equal numbers as agricultural laborers in the South and as domestic servants in Northern and Southern cities. The fact that they could always find work as servants caused black women to migrate to Northern cities much more often than black males. A careful and probably accurate census in New York in 1890 found ten black women living in the city for every eight black males.

In most of the families of the new immigrants living in the cities, cultural pressures against wives and mothers working were very powerful. In these families, some of the slack in family income was taken up by children. By 1900, fully a quarter of Americans under the age of fourteen worked for wages. But an even more typical solution to the problem was to send older unmarried daughters into the labor market. In New York, in 1880, the women who held jobs were, typically, young, unmarried, native-born daughters of recent immigrants from Europe. In fact, fully 90 percent of the city's working women over the age of fourteen were single. Seventy-five percent were not yet twenty-five years old. And 90 percent were the daughters of an immigrant father or mother.

## Women's Jobs

What did they do, these women who "chose" jobs? How did they earn the incomes that would almost invariably put them below the poverty line if they had been trying to support themselves, let alone a family?

A few women did manage to have careers as scientists, social scientists, doctors, lawyers, or writers. And, for such women, a career was an authentic alternative to being a wife and mother. When the census takers in 1920 asked professional women—most of whom had begun their careers in the nineteenth century—whether they were married, nine out of ten answered no. But such women were only a minuscule part of the total female population of the United States. The lives of an overwhelming majority were far removed from any recognized or prestigious profession.

During the nineteenth century, two occupations had opened up to women, nursing and teaching. But nursing was still classified as "domestic service" in most areas. And as women moved into teaching, the status of the occupation fell. Salaries had dropped, and very few middle-class men were willing to take teaching jobs. As a result, most women who taught did so in exactly the same way that most white women worked at other jobs: temporarily, until they married. But teaching was not, in reality, a job that could attract middle-class women for even the short term. As late as 1911, the average

**NURSES**

At the turn of the century, there was a concerted effort to transform nursing from a branch of domestic service into a profession. One clue to the transformation was the development of a uniform. But the uniform shown here in a photograph taken just after the turn of the century bore the indelible marks of nursing's past. The apron and the striped dresses could have been worn by any Victorian servant whose work kept her distinct from the family who employed her. And the woman holding the batch of keys could have been any head house-keeper. *(Culver Pictures)*

woman teacher came from a family, usually headed by a skilled worker or a farmer, that earned only about $800 a year. Teachers and nurses may have yearned for gentility, but in economic terms they were no better off than most other Americans who worked for a living.

An increasing number of women went to work in manufacturing. They were an important part of the work force in a few selected industries, like cigar-making, clothing, shoes, and book-binding. But even at the end of the century, only a small number of the industrial workers of the United States were women. And here, too, women tended to work for a few years, until

marriage, at only the worst, most unskilled, and most poorly paid jobs. Industrial work did not provide a reasonable, permanent choice for middle-class women. And even working-class women left the factories as quickly as they could and returned only under the most severe kinds of economic pressure.

More women earned their wages as domestic servants than at any other job. In the last decades of the century, about a million women were working as maids, cooks, or laundresses. (So there were about half as many female "domestics" in 1900 as there had been female slaves in 1860.) They lived at home with parents when they could. But more often they had to accept miserably paid "live-in" jobs. A few of them may have developed affectionate relationships with the families in whose homes they worked. But only a few. The rest were like the Borden household's Bridget: a little resentful, and dreaming of the day they could put away their uniforms and aprons.

The statistical records tell a clear story. The domestics were almost all single (unless they were black). They were young. About half of them were either immigrant women or the daughters of immigrant parents. Another quarter of them were black. And they did not like their work. Around the turn of the century, social scientists—mostly women—began to survey domestic servants, asking them about their working conditions and their attitudes toward their jobs. The answers were plain. Mostly, the servants testified, they missed "respect" and "freedom." As one young woman put it in an interview in the 1890s, freedom was "as dear to women as to men, although we don't get so much of it."

Lizzie Borden knew all these things. She knew that working for a living was not an acceptable alternative to marriage—especially at her advancing age. Marriage was ruled out, at least to a suitable partner, for the simple reason that a well-mannered courtship was impossible. She had no place to go, no home of her own to look forward to, and no other kind of career. Lizzie Borden probably committed murder for reasons that were partly personal and private. But she was also pushed to violence by inescapable facts about the kinds of things a respectable woman could and could not do outside the home.

American women, like American men, lived in a country where faith that hard work would lead to the good life was widespread. For women, this faith was merged with another dream—that economic success would lead to an idealized home and family. But for most workers, men and women, neither the faith in the gospel of wealth nor the vision of a gentle and "refined" family would alter grim reality. And middle-class women probably clung to the ethic of domestic refinement not so much because they wanted to as because they could not reach for that other ethic of work and career. Most of the men who dreamed of becoming "self-made" successes failed. But most women did not even have the chance to fail.

# SUGGESTED READINGS, CHAPTERS 29–30

## LIZZIE BORDEN

Edmund Pearson, *The Trial of Lizzie Borden* (1937), is an abridged version of the transcript of Lizzie Borden's inquest and trial. A good analysis of the case is Robert Sullivan, *Goodbye, Lizzie Borden* (1974), written by a modern lawyer and Massachusetts judge, who attempts to prove Lizzie Borden's guilt. Victoria Lincoln, *A Private Disgrace* (1967), is written by a Fall River native who believes that Lizzie committed the murders in an epileptic fit. Edward Radin, *Lizzie Borden: The Untold Story* (1961), argues that Lizzie was innocent—the murderer was Bridget Sullivan, the family maid. A feminist perspective on the case can be found in Ann Jones, *Women Who Kill* (1979).

## WEALTH AND DISPLAY

Irvin G. Wyllie, *The Self-Made Man in America* (1954), examines the myth of rapid upward social mobility. Stephen Thernstrom, *Poverty and Progress* (1967), tests the reality of upward mobility in one Massachusetts community during the nineteenth century. Harold C. Livesay, *Andrew Carnegie and the Rise of Big Business* (1975), is a biography of one of the most famous self-made men in U.S. history. William Dean Howells, *The Rise of Silas Lapham* (1885), is a novel of the period about social mobility and a family that somewhat resembled the Bordens. Thornstein Veblen, *The Theory of the Leisure Class* (1898), is a classic critique of "conspicuous consumption" by a man who probably shared many of Andrew Borden's values. Arthur M. Schlesinger, *Learning How to Behave* (1946), traces the development of etiquette through American history. Ann Douglas, *The Feminization of American Culture* (New York, 1976), is an analysis and criticism of consumer culture in the nineteenth century.

## WOMEN AND THE FAMILY

Sheila M. Rothman, *Woman's Proper Place* (1978), traces changing ideas and practices from 1870 to the present. Alice Kessler-Harris, *Out to Work* (1982), is a history of working women. A more specialized study of maids like Bridget Sullivan is David M. Katzman, *Seven Days a Week: Women and Domestic Service in Industrializing America* (1978). Ellen Dubois, *Feminism and Suffrage* (1978), is a good account of feminism in the same period. Richard Sennett, *Families Against the City* (1970), deals with the family as a "utopia," and the tensions between private and public lives in the late nineteenth century. Arthur M. Schlesinger, *The Rise of the City, 1878–1898* (1933), provides a panoramic overview of middle-class life, with a very good chapter on the domestic world of urban women.

# 31 ▪ Woodrow Wilson: The Progressive Moralist

Why may not the present age write, through me, its
political autobiography?

WOODROW WILSON, 1889

Beyond the main reading room of the Princeton library, with its marble busts of Presbyterian ministers and college benefactors, the meeting in the Trustees' Room had just begun. The dark oak paneling of the room deepened the solemnity of the occasion. The trustees cast their eyes downward momentarily while Woodrow Wilson, president of the university, delivered a short prayer. Jaw firmly set and eyes flashing, Wilson finished his invocation and turned to the business of the morning—his resignation. Wilson asked for a suspension of the normal agenda of such meetings, which the assembly quickly granted. He requested release from his duties at once, asking only that "the University may go forward without halt or hindrance in the path of true scholarship and thoughtful service to the nation."

Picking up his hat and coat, while the trustees looked on in silence, he strode from the room. The assembled members voted to accept the resignation. Their victory and Wilson's defeat were total. Dispute over the direction of the university, its graduate program, and more important, its tone and commitments had finally sputtered and flared into the open. Wilson had lost a struggle that had been smoldering for several years.

Wilson's morning defeat, however, was more than matched by victory that evening. Addressing an overflow crowd at the Opera House in Flemington, New Jersey, a town noted for peaches, applejack, and rock-ribbed Democracy, Wilson told an enthusiastic assembly: "I feel as if I am between sizes in occupation." Indeed he was. He had resigned from Princeton to accept candidacy for the governorship of New Jersey on the Democratic ticket. As

639

so often in the past, Wilson had turned a personal defeat into a practical and moral victory. Frustrated by opposition to his educational plans, he had set his ambitions and goals higher. More than ever, he felt sure of the slogan that beat in him like a moral pulse: "To be right is the only happiness in this world."

This was the sort of bittersweet moment he had reflected on in a hundred ways before. As he wrote in an unpublished manuscript:

> Men of strenuous minds and high ideals come forward with a sort of gentle majesty as champions of political or moral principle. They wear no armour; they bestride no chargers; they only speak their thoughts in season and out of season. But the attacks they sustain are more cruel than a thousand keen arrows of obloquy. Friends desert them and despise them. They stand alone.

At the same time, Wilson foresaw:

> Masses come over to the side of reform. Resistance is left to the minority, and such as will not be converted are crushed.

In his imagination he thus prefigured his triumph over his opponents.

Woodrow Wilson was the first Southerner to win the presidency of the United States since before the Civil War. He was an inexperienced politician in an age of rough-and-tumble practical politics. But he was also a man who could rebound from defeat: from the defeat of the South, the shock of his thwarted Princeton presidency, the persistent and threatening illnesses he suffered. At every such point he refused to face failure; instead, he reset his aims and purposes on a higher plane. This was a reflex of self-mastery he had learned early in his youth, and it remained a defining characteristic of his personality. As he preached in a baccalaureate sermon during his last year at the university, a man's purpose in life was the successful "mastery of himself, of circumstance, of physical forces, and of human relations, of the spirit that is within him." Only self-interest, narrow greed, or cowardice could defeat him.

Thomas Woodrow Wilson (Tommie to his parents and young friends) was born on December 28, 1856, in the small city of Staunton, nestled in the Shenandoah Valley between the Blue Ridge and the Allegheny mountains in western Virginia. His father, Joseph Ruggles Wilson, had moved there in 1855 to accept a call to preach at the First Presbyterian Church. The move was a serious displacement for both parents, for it tore up their roots in the North and planted them in the very different culture of the antebellum South.

As the Civil War approached, Joseph Ruggles Wilson emerged as a prominent leader in splitting the Presbyterian church into Northern and Southern wings. So important had he become in this schism that in 1861 Southern separatists favoring slavery held their first assembly in his church in Augusta, Georgia, where he had moved.

The early years of Woodrow's childhood in Augusta left memories of devastation: His father's church became a hospital, and his home scarcely shut out the agonies and destruction of civil war. His education postponed, Woodrow did not learn to read adequately until the age of eleven. Nonetheless, family life was warm and intellectually animated. One of four children, he was his father's favorite: "You are my alter ego," the elder Wilson told him once. "You are assuredly my second edition." At the same time he developed a deep dependence on his mother. From these surroundings, he absorbed paternalism to slaves, chivalry to women, and the tone and tenor of his father's faith.

In the Wilson family, religious instruction was reserved primarily for Sunday afternoons, but family relationships were awash with moral sentiment. Woodrow's father, a fine-speaking, impressive man, with a sharp wit that he often aimed at his son, taught a Christianity of stewardship and service. Emphasizing the Presbyterian notion of covenant—God's agreements with mankind that underlay religion and the social order—Joseph Ruggles instilled in his son a need to find religious justification for all his activities. Ambition, hard work, and success in this formula became stages in the struggle to do God's work on earth.

If Joseph Ruggles drew out and encouraged ambition in his son it was partly because he increasingly felt his own limitations. As friend and confidant, the elder Wilson often confessed his own frustrations to his son. Writing in 1880 to Woodrow, he spoke of his mistakes: "My life might have been greatly stronger by being greatly happier. But mistakenly, I have nearly always chosen the dark sides of probabilities at which to look. It will not do. It is irrational. It is sinful even." The senior Wilson advised his son to resist such self-indulgence and choose a purpose: "Make your mind like a needle of one eye and a single point. Shoot your words straight at the target."

Initially, both parents hoped that Woodrow would follow his father into the ministry. In 1873, that seemed a possibility. After experiencing a religious conversion, Woodrow enrolled in Davidson College, a Presbyterian institution for training young boys for the ministry. But separation from his family proved painful. Woodrow was, he remembered: "a laughed-at mama's boy til I was a great big fellow." Suffering from exhaustion, he returned home during the spring semester to resume old, comfortable habits.

The following fall, Woodrow struck out once more for college, this time Princeton University in New Jersey. Correspondence with his parents continued apace over the next several years. He responded to their plea: "Write me freely, my darling," his father said in an 1878 letter, "as to all your feelings, and trust us both, in the future as in the past, with all your secret desires— being *sure* that we are your truest friends."

One subject that both chose to discuss was ambition. For example, in 1877, Joseph Ruggles warned his son: "Dearest boy, can you hope to jump into eminency all at once?" A year later, the father wrote somewhat ambiguously:

Self-consciousness is a torment: was mine at your age; has, often since then, been such. Go out from your personality. Do not regard ego as the Centre of this universe. Reflect: I am not charging egotism upon you.

In 1880, he made his cautions more pointed:

One of the dangers of a young man like yourself—thoughtful, aspiring, conscious of certain stirring of ambition, and anxious to succeed even where success is hardest—one of your dangers arises from the tendency to *look in* too much and too far: to become too subjective: in short to be too self-conscious.

A better method, he continued, "is to grapple with things outward—is to attack and conquer . . . to learn to defy circumstances, even those that seem most adverse."

While at Princeton, Wilson cast off the confines of parental hopes for the ministry. He increasingly expressed his interest in a political career. Thirty years later, addressing the General Theological Seminary of New York, he explained his reasons for abandoning the ministry. He could not judge others according to the uncompromising principles of the church and still love them. This, he confessed, "is one reason why I have kept out of the ministry." Yet the political ideals he adopted remained anchored in the bedrock of religion, far from the deals and smoke-filled rooms of Gilded Age politics. Indeed, what Wilson thought of as politics was, in his mind, a process like religion and like education—in that it thrust the most righteous and upstanding men into positions of leadership. It had very little to do with politics as it was practiced in the late nineteenth century.

In the 1880s, there was little evidence that politics would ever tolerate the sort of moral vision that Wilson had in mind. Party strife, regionalism, factionalism, and self-interest blocked the emergence of the sort of leadership that Wilson envisioned. But then, Wilson's view of politics had always been idealized. He was especially attracted to the British House of Commons and contrasted its tradition of debate with the American Congress and its practice of wheeling and dealing.

Very early on, Wilson thought of ways he might transform American government into an institution of high ideals and serious debate. In his first published article (aside from several sermons printed in his father's paper), he proposed to change the Constitution to accommodate a cabinet system. By making the president and cabinet members of the Congress, he hoped to encourage free and serious debate on large issues. "Only a single glance," he wrote, "is necessary to discover how utterly Committee government must fail to give effect to public opinion."

At Princeton, Wilson experienced a quickening of ambition and development of his oratorical skills. His first and greatest love was debate. He joined the Whig Society, one of the university's two debating clubs. These clubs, encouraged by the administration, were important institutions to prepare students as lawyers, ministers, and politicians. While he did not always win "first mention" in contests, Wilson impressed his fellow students. But

**THE ALLIGATOR CLUB AT PRINCETON**

Woodrow Wilson (with his hat in hand) joined the Alligator Club while a student at Princeton. Later as president of the university, he attempted to abolish the social clubs for engendering an undemocratic spirit. *(Library of Congress)*

he wanted to institute his own program of debates, something closer to the British House of Commons, where young men could dispute the political questions that concerned them. Consequently, he founded a smaller society, the Liberal Debating Club—a more or less secret society that considered such issues as the Civil War and the ideal length of terms for congressmen.

Wilson also learned about molding public opinion during his stint as editor of the *Princetonian* in 1878. As well as writing most of the editorials himself, he contributed football stories, accounts of baseball games, and book reviews. Religious ideas and points of theology rarely preoccupied him, but he nonetheless crusaded against two Victorian bugbears: impropriety and vulgarity. Students in physical education class, he wrote, "wore too scanty shirts in the gymnasium." Rowdiness, noise, and unseemly conduct by Princeton students pricked his attention. But more than anything, Wilson urged baseball and football teams on to better organization, coaching, and performance. For these efforts he was elected president of the Baseball Association and a director of the Football Association, formed to oversee the institution of football at Princeton.

At the same time, young Wilson's political views began to emerge with some force. As a loyal Southerner and devoted Democrat, he supported a low tariff on foreign manufactured goods. When he found himself chosen to defend universal suffrage (including votes for blacks) during a final debate between the two leading societies, he refused. He would not compromise his principles by supporting this proposition.

Yet Wilson did not consider entering politics when he graduated from Princeton. There was nothing in vote getting, bargaining, and party caucuses that inspired him. So he decided to devote himself to the law. Here, perhaps, his interest in the structure of government could find honest expression.

Wilson's decision was something of a compromise between the need to find an occupation and his widening ambition for leadership. He began his studies at the University of Virginia in October 1879. This was a wise choice. Virginia boasted a fine faculty, a commitment to hard work, and a tradition that reached back to Jefferson, founding father of the university. Wilson worked hard, but he nonetheless succumbed to the enticements of extracurricular activities. He entered the Jefferson debating society, sang in the choir, joined Phi Kappa Psi fraternity, and spent much of his time courting Harriet Woodrow, his first cousin. But when Hattie realized his serious intentions, she broke off the liaison.

Much of the time, Wilson was thinking about the nature of government and outlining the arguments he later put into *Congressional Government,* published in 1885. Other ideas began to emerge, notions that appeared in his first historical work, *Division and Reunion,* published in 1893. A series of brilliant speeches before the Jefferson society won him Virginia's Orator's Medal—in effect a second prize, behind William Cabell Bruce, a budding young politician who went on to a distinguished career in Maryland politics. Wilson, discouraged, and perhaps angered by the choice, nevertheless accepted his prize.

The following fall term was to be his last. The young law student returned to classes and an active round of debating and club activities, but declining health and spirits discouraged him. Bored with law, now fancying a literary career, and distressed over the thwarted romance with cousin Hattie, he left Virginia abruptly and returned home. It was a pattern he had established at Davidson earlier, and one that renewed his spirits.

During the year at his parents' home in Wilmington, North Carolina, Wilson continued to study law and worked on improving his literary style and speech with his father, an ever-ready critic and adviser. Restless and much improved physically, Wilson decided to try law again, and he obtained his degree from Virginia in 1881.

Quickly tiring of the law, however, Wilson abandoned his new profession before he had proven himself. "In a word," he wrote, "my ambition could not be fulfilled at the bar; the studies for which I was best fitted, both by nature and by acquired habit, were not legitimate in a law office." Recognizing his mistake, he struck out in a new direction. He enrolled at Johns Hopkins University in September 1883, in history. At the same time, he was stirred by a new romance, Ellen Louise Axson, a "demure little lady" who caught his eye and heart in April. The daughter of a local pastor, Ellen encouraged his attention, and the two engaged in a long and friendly correspondence. In his letters, Wilson confessed his ambitions and his strong passions. Ellen had begun to replace his parents as his principal confidant.

Wilson chose Johns Hopkins at a time when that university was becoming a model of national scholarship. Its revolutionary new forms of graduate education and its brilliant young faculty made it a pioneer in developing new notions about the origins of American institutions. Wilson joined a founding generation of historians who set the style, methods, and interpretations of the new profession. He worked hard but chafed at the boredom and small scope of his studies.

Politics still fascinated him most, and he began to construct his book *Congressional Government.* Not always original and sometimes laboriously written, the book still marked a new facility with language. Wilson's public presentation of ideas was beginning to acquire force. Moreover, the argument he made favoring parliamentary government had become, more than ever, an appeal for the kinds of literary and debating skills at which he excelled.

Yet a month after this book appeared, Wilson was despondent. A successful author and only twenty-nine years old, he judged himself a failure. As he wrote to Ellen: "I do feel a very real regret that I have been shut out from my heart's *first* primary ambition and purpose which was to take an active, if possible, a leading, part in public life and strike out for myself, if I had the ability, a *statesman's* career." He had an unfulfilled "passion for interpreting great thoughts to the world; I should be complete if I could inspire a great movement of opinion."

Once more Wilson decided to abandon his studies. This time, however, he did not return home but considered a teaching position at Bryn Mawr College. His father encouraged this move and urged him to see it as a first small step: "How greatly I wish it had pleased God to open for you a door very different and much larger than this. Yet perhaps you need the discipline of such narrowness, to enable you to show the stuff of which you are made." Wilson accepted the position and pressed Ellen to marry him. On June 24, the couple were wed in Augusta, Georgia. Loosening the bonds of his parents, he now found a new source of comfort in his wife.

The fledgling women's college at Bryn Mawr, founded in 1885, hired Wilson to lecture in history and political science. While at Hopkins, he had written to Ellen that he could best express "whatever influence I might be able to exercise . . . through literary and non-partisan agencies." Bryn Mawr was a bitter disappointment. But during his three years there, he saw his family expand with the birth of two daughters, he continued to publish works on political science, and he completed his Ph.D. at Hopkins. When an offer came to move to the men's college of Wesleyan in Middletown, Connecticut, he seized it.

The next two years were momentous, with a widening scope of influence and national attention. Wilson taught history, but his book *The State,* published in 1889, and articles in prestigious academic journals and influential magazines like the *Atlantic Monthly* were more concerned with politics. In

1890, he received a call from Princeton to teach jurisprudence and political science, and moved with his wife and three daughters to the famous New Jersey university.

Quickly establishing himself on campus—students flocked to his courses—Wilson began to realize some of his dreams of leadership. He idealized Princeton. It was a perfect society to him, democratic in the sense that those who gained admission could rise, carried by their abilities, to the heights of influence and success. Its gradations and distinctions indicated merit, not privilege. Professors and seniors were "the leading citizens of the little community. They are self-selected," he wrote. In Wilson's mind, this was a vision that never dimmed.

Politics also began to interest Wilson more. No longer so attentive to theories of government reorganization, he had begun to shift his interest to questions of administration and public policy. By the beginning of the great depression of 1893, he spoke more warmly of reform—on a limited scale. Although his political instincts were still conservative, Wilson responded to the chaos of unemployment, bankruptcies, and strikes by developing a more fluid approach to political problems.

Wilson's private world also took a new shape during this time. Dependence now shifted from his parents to Ellen. Increasingly absent for speaking engagements, he wrote passionate love letters to her. This private side would have surprised most casual acquaintances, who assumed that the stern, flashing eyes and studied speech reflected an interior of the same austere design. In one of his few moments of public introspection, Wilson discussed the distinction between his inner and outer lives. As he told the National Press Club in 1914: "You may not believe it, but I sometimes feel like a fire from a far-from-extinct volcano, and if the lava does not seem to spill over it is because you are not high enough to see the cauldron boil."

Home provided relief from a public life that demanded repression of such drives. In the shelter of his house, Wilson unbent. He loved limericks, poetry, and nonsense rhymes, and he entertained close friends and family with parodies and imitations of characters. "He would, in fact," one friend remembered, "enjoy telling jokes on himself, but never liked to have them told about him by other people."

Nonetheless, Wilson suffered recurrent episodes of what were probably psychosomatic illnesses: nervous stomach, depression, and headaches. A robust man who enjoyed bicycle riding, Wilson nonetheless drove himself beyond his capacities. In May 1896, at the age of forty, he suffered a slight stroke, the first evidence of the vascular disease that would ultimately kill him. Although the episode was mild, he suffered numbness in the first and second fingers of his right hand which did not disappear until the next spring.

Wilson's reaction to this secret weakness was (after a European vacation) to rededicate himself to work of even greater seriousness and scope. His denial of fragile health fitted a boyhood pattern of rejecting defeat or frailty by finding and attaching himself to a higher, selfless cause, following his father's advice to "grapple with things outward." To many observers, he turned more

**WOODROW WILSON AND FAMILY, 1912**

Despite his great love of public life, Wilson relished privacy and the comfort and good spirits of his wife and three daughters. *(Library of Congress)*

serious, more dedicated, more committed. If anything, Wilson's disease strengthened his need to find a forum for moral leadership and statesmanship.

At about this time, Wilson wrote an essay entitled "When a Man Comes to Himself." He spoke of a moment of self-recognition that comes to every man as he moves from self-interest to belief in a higher cause:

> He comes to himself after experiences of which he alone may be aware; when he has left off being wholly preoccupied with his own powers and interests and with every petty plan that centers in himself; when he has cleared his eyes to see the world as it is, and his own true place and function in it.

The forsaking of private, narrow interests, he continued, and acceptance of a cause, brought rebirth as a public man.

> It is for this reason that men are in love with power and greatness: it affords them so pleasurable an expansion of faculty, so large a run for their minds, an exercise of spirit so various and refreshing; they have the freedom of so wide a tract of the world of affairs.

Clearly, Wilson had begun to think of himself in a larger leadership role. He had submerged his self-concern in ambitious dreams of a larger cause. At the same time, he had begun to think of commitments beyond the classroom and a scope wider than the bound volumes of history that he wrote. He had begun to cast his eyes beyond the role of popular teacher and leader of young men. As one faculty member described him, "His driving force would brook no opposition."

From 1890 to 1902, he traveled across the country giving over 100 inspirational addresses on democracy, patriotism, religion, liberty, and leadership. "I can't imagine why I consent to do this sort of thing," he wrote to his wife, "but such is your husband—hungry—*too* hungry—for reputation and influence."

By the turn of the century, Wilson had emerged as a candidate to replace the current Princeton administration. Wilson first clashed with Francis Patton, president of the university, in 1893, over the honor system. Patton criticized the system, which he said was unworkable and open to abuse. At a faculty meeting, Wilson rose to the challenge and defended the system as the very heart of the university. His eloquence persuaded the assembly, and the system stood. By 1902, other issues had arisen. Dismayed at the decline of academic standards and obstacles to several of his pet projects, Wilson allied himself with younger faculty members and sought support from the Princeton board of trustees. Together, this opposition ousted Patton. Wilson was appointed in his place.

Granted wide powers to reorganize the university, Wilson moved to change instruction and raise standards. He was determined to make Princeton the ideal intellectual and moral community he dreamed it could be. His basic program was a preceptorial system based partly on the British tutorial system at Oxford and Cambridge. This and other schemes were expensive but adventurous. He called for new buildings, an endowment for tutors' salaries, and general staff salary increases. To finance these projects, he had to raise over $12 million. Important as he knew it was, he found great difficulty and embarrassment in approaching alumni or corporation directors. He could not bear to lobby, hat in hand, for gifts from the wealthy. Fortunately, his plans were saved by a special fund-raising committee of board members. By 1905, the preceptor plan had been accepted and implemented, and Wilson hired an outstanding group of young men to live and work closely with students.

With such reforms, Princeton grew in national prestige, although admissions fell because of more selective standards. Wilson believed that his mission was to make Princeton a national university. In his inaugural speech to the university, he had declared: "We are here to serve our country and mankind, and we know we can put selfishness behind us." Princeton would provide the nation with training in "practical religion." Somewhat later, Wilson put it this way:

> The whole Princeton idea is an organic idea, an idea of contact of mind with mind—no chasms, no divisions in life and organization,—a grand brotherhood of intellectual endeavor, stimulating the youngster, instructing and balancing the older man, giving the one an aspiration and the other a comprehension of what the undertaking is,—of lifting, lifting, lifting the mind of successive generations from age to age.

Despite this succession of achievements, these were not entirely happy years. Family illnesses, the death of Ellen's brother and his wife in 1905 in a freak accident, and overwork may have contributed to Wilson's second serious stroke in 1906. Awakening one morning in late May, he found he had become blind in his left eye. Doctors advised immediate and permanent rest—even retirement. Disguising his infirmity, Wilson spent the summer recuperating in England. He gradually regained some of the vision in his affected eye. And he rejected thoughts of resignation and invalidism. He returned to Princeton a transformed man, more committed to work and leadership than ever, and less tolerant of opposition.

When Wilson returned, he plunged into a fight that he believed would save the soul of the University. He had by now completely submerged private setback in a cause of public regeneration. Princeton had long had eating clubs, to which most students belonged. During his years as a student, Wilson had joined the "Alligators," one of the more exclusive of these establishments. Recently however, the clubs had moved into large, elegant quarters. Wilson was shocked by the frivolity, the drinking, and the luxury of these student organizations. The clubs, he concluded, diverted students to think only of the "social question." They introduced factionalism and degraded university life. Social ambition had become "too strong for individual honour." Nothing could be more remote from Wilson's educational philosophy, and he determined to replace the clubs with more democratic, on-campus activities.

Wilson's solution, called the quadrangle plan, proposed to divide the campus into "quads," resembling the colleges of Oxford and Cambridge. Freshmen, sophomores, juniors, and seniors would each live together, rather than mixing in exclusive clubs. "The fight is on," he declared in 1907, "and I regard it, not as a fight for the development, but as a fight for the restoration of Princeton. My heart is in it more than it has been in anything else, because it is a scheme of salvation."

Wilson's plan stirred powerful opposition. Wealthy alumni who fondly remembered their eating club days opposed the plan. They found sympathetic allies, like ex-President Grover Cleveland, on the board of trustees. This opposition plus the estimated costs of the plan made the whole board pause. Wilson, when he saw that his plan might be rejected, reacted angrily. He believed that wealth and privilege were blocking fulfillment of his most cherished educational ideals. Finding the opposition well entrenched, he took his case to the Princeton alumni. Again he traveled around the country, making his case in a series of rousing speeches against the narrow-mindedness and selfishness that he believed were standing in his way. But the board remained unmoved by his efforts.

Nonetheless, Wilson's speeches and his growing prestige had given rise on campus to talk that he might seek high political office. Princeton seniors sang a satiric verse on the subject in 1908:

> Here's to Woodrow, King Divine,
> Who rules this place along with [Dean] Fine,
> We hear he wants to leave the town
> And try for Teddy Roosevelt's crown.

WILSON AND CARNEGIE AT PRINCETON, 1906

The great industrialist and philanthropist Andrew Carnegie was one of many wealthy patrons whose contributions Wilson solicited while president of Princeton. A university of the importance and prestige of Princeton depended heavily on the generosity of such men to undertake innovations in graduate and undergraduate education. *(Culver Pictures)*

One of the principal enemies to the quad plan had been Andrew West, dean of the graduate school. A portly, elegant man, with fine manners and a good instinct for in-fighting, West emerged as leader of the opposition to Wilson. He too had a plan to transform Princeton. But unlike Wilson, he carefully nurtured a base of power among the trustees. West wanted to relocate the graduate school off campus, where students might, in the midst of leisure and comfort, continue their studies. Wilson fought this notion. It was, after all, a plan that would effectively turn the graduate school into a social club. Wilson had an alternative. He wanted to keep the graduate school on the campus, subject it to his administrative control, and integrate its students into the intellectual life of the university.

In various ways, the graduate school fight between Wilson and West merely continued the quad system struggle. West organized a major segment of the trustees and found wealthy outside benefactors to finance his plan. Wilson made several efforts to raise funds for his plan, even visiting the industrial pioneer Andrew Carnegie in his castle in Scotland. But to no avail; West proved to be the better organizer. Working from the inside, he blocked Wilson's efforts. Attempts to compromise the two plans failed, for there was no way to compromise the philosophies—or the power struggle—behind them.

Realizing that he had been rebuffed on campus, Wilson transformed his fight into a national campaign among Princeton alumni. In his speeches, he reached out to castigate his enemies in harsh terms. The men of great industrial and banking fortunes who served on the board of trustees were acting like a "House of Lords," he railed. The struggle, he maintained, had larger overtones: it involved a national crusade for democracy and against privilege.

Wilson made these points especially sharply in a speech to a bewildered gathering of Princeton alumni in Pittsburgh in April 1910. The *Pittsburgh Dispatch* reported that the alumni gathered to sing college songs, toast the college and old friends, and relive school days.

But Wilson, the last speaker at the affair, jolted "the jolly grown-up college boys" with his sharp remarks. He had come to raise questions about the survival of Princeton, American society, and the state. Striking a tone of high seriousness, he declared:

> The colleges are in the same dangerous position as the churches. I hope that the last thing I will ever be capable of will be casting a shadow on the church, and yet the churches—the Protestant churches, at least—have dissociated themselves from the people. They serve the classes, not the masses. They serve certain strata, certain visible uplifted strata, and ignore the men whose need is dire.
>
> The colleges are in the same class, looking to the support of wealth rather than the people.

This intolerable situation, Wilson continued, had evoked an outcry for the moral regeneration of American society from top to bottom. It even extended to the political parties, which were "going to pieces." Inevitably, the forces of regeneration, he told his shocked audience, would come from the

> mass of obscure men, not from the handful of conspicuous men; it is to that mass of obscure men that it [the nation] must look if it is to live. And we should cry out against the few who have raised themselves to dangerous power, who have thrust their cruel hands into the very heartstrings of the many on whose blood and energy they are subsisting.

Wilson's radical-sounding speeches won him no converts among Princeton alumni. His strategy could not overcome the clever politicking of Dean West, who by early 1910, controlled the votes of most of the trustees. And while Wilson had turned his cause into a larger crusade—to save Princeton and the nation, to create an "absolute democratic regeneration in spirit"—he had also risked losing everything, including his presidency of the university.

By late spring, Dean West had won. The trustees decided that the graduate school would be off campus. But by this time, Wilson's thoughts had turned elsewhere—to state politics. Already mentioned as a possible candidate for governor in 1908, Wilson seemed even stronger to state Democratic bosses in 1910. In June, several leaders visited him and offered him the nomination. They also spoke of a possible presidential bid two years later.

After a week of consideration, Wilson consented, and the machine ground into operation. Crushing any opposition, party leaders secured his nomination over the objections of several reform groups. But Wilson hastily mended his fences. He campaigned for electoral reforms and began to speak of his support for labor unions. He won election in November and began the most reform-minded administration in New Jersey for decades. His presidential race was just two years away.

Much had changed in Wilson's political ideas since he first expressed them as a youth in his early debates and articles. Still an unredeemed Southerner, he retained his belief in a low tariff, his commitment to economic individualism, and his sense of racial superiority. Despite his fiery rhetoric, he was still a conservative, ambiguous about labor unions. He was hostile to large corporations and monopolies, but he remained suspicious of too much government regulation of the economy. Nevertheless, he was poised to plunge into the mainstream of reform. He had begun to change his mind about William Jennings Bryan, the Populist-Democratic candidate for president in 1896, whom he had once considered a dangerous radical. He shared two key principles with other reformers: He increasingly agreed about the need to shape public opinion to bring it to bear upon large social and economic questions of the day. And he increasingly thought of the executive branch as the focus of an activist national government. Here was the best locus for his concept of inspired leadership.

In fact, Wilson's political philosophy had come to rest upon one key question: the worth of the leader. It was an old question in a new guise:

### WILSON AS GOVERNOR OF NEW JERSEY, 1912

Woodrow Wilson's meteoric rise to the presidency was aided by his widely noted victory in the New Jersey governor's race of 1910. Although he held public office for only two years before he was elected president in 1912, he learned leadership in the bitterly fought academic politics of Princeton University. *(Library of Congress)*

WOODROW WILSON RIDING TO THE 1921 INAUGURATION
Wilson, accompanying President-Elect Warren G. Harding to his inauguration in 1921, shows the ravages of cardiovascular disease. After his stroke in 1919, Wilson's participation in the day-to-day functioning of government was minimal. *(Library of Congress)*

He stands for himself. And the final verdict with regard to him will be based upon the answer to this question: is he serving himself alone, or is he serving the public interest?

Thrust into national leadership by special circumstances, Wilson had done much to prepare himself for this position. At every crucial point in his life he had rejected defeat and limitation, turning to a larger, more extensive cause of moral and national regeneration. The nation had come to accept and expect this definition of its progressive politicians, as men whose moral vision outweighed the problems they faced. Wilson had nourished this ideal since childhood. He was the sort of man demanded by the political fashion of the day: stern, moralistic, reformist, and a shaper of public opinion. Shortly after he had been forced out of Princeton and been elected as governor of New Jersey, one of the Princeton preceptors he appointed came across him, sitting deep in thought at the Princeton Junction railway station. "You appear to be revolving a deep problem in your mind," said the young man. "I am thinking about leadership," Wilson replied.

# Progressivism: Defining a Public Interest

The movement that thrust Woodrow Wilson into the White House in 1913 and followed his leadership for eight years began almost two decades before in the moral and political awakening of a broad group of reformers called progressives. This diverse coalition of men and women emerged primarily from the ranks of the new urban middle class. Drawing upon traditional ideas of democracy and an intense but secular Protestantism, they worried deeply about the contradictions of their society. They puzzled over the contradictions between self-interest and social interest, between progress and poverty. Steeped in nineteenth-century concepts of self-help, stewardship, and the work ethic, they were surprised and troubled by the unexpected by-products of industrial growth. The obvious success of the economic system—its productivity, invention, and urbanization—had a threatening, dark side: poverty, exploitation, and violence. Industrial development degraded work and initiated cycles of economic boom and bust, violent strikes, and political instability. The Victorian economic ethic, based on saving, investing, and individualism, had spawned a generation of business leaders whose greed made a mockery of the precepts that had justified their wealth and success.

In a justly renowned article published in 1889, Andrew Carnegie, self-made millionaire and steel and iron entrepreneur, reflected on his society that had grown rich and poor at the same time. Competition, he wrote in his essay "The Gospel of Wealth," made a few men like himself very rich, but many other people poor. Since competition also stimulated the marvels of productivity, he would certainly not oppose it. But its social effects demanded attention. As he put it, finding "the proper administration of wealth" would "bind together the rich and poor in harmonious relationship." But could it be done? In a word, Carnegie had raised the question that most worried progressives: Could industrial progress and economic individualism continue without degenerating into violence and class warfare? Was a social gospel possible?

The depression of 1893 helped precipitate the forces that created progressivism as a national movement. This deep economic downturn shook millions of workers from their jobs. Unemployment rose from around 3 percent in 1892 to over 18 percent two years later. Gross national product (the estimated sum of goods and services produced by the economy) fell by 12 percent in 1894 and did not recover until 1897.

A measure of the depression's seriousness was the social unrest to which it gave rise. In the spring of 1894, this burst into an angry disturbance in Washington, D.C. Led by Jacob S. Coxey, an Ohio businessman, a small army of supporters dubbed the "Commonweal of Christ" marched to the capital to ask for a public works bill to end unemployment. Although it posed no threat, the group was attacked by police and Coxey was jailed.

A far more threatening labor incident began with a strike at the Pullman Palace Car Company in Chicago, in May 1894. Sparked by falling wages and management opposition to unions, the strike took on national significance in June (see p. 553). Alluding to the events later that summer, Woodrow Wilson remarked: "Every one knows that the relations—even the legal relations—now existing between capitalists and laborers are seriously amiss."

Why were these relations frightening to so many observers in the 1890s? There are, essentially, two answers. The industrial system encouraged the organization of powerful private institutions: corporations and labor unions that seemed pitted against each other in a ruthless struggle for power. Surely, it was assumed, society itself would be the loser in such strife. Second, the private, unregulated industrial system had created untold hardships for millions of Americans through unemployment and injury.

# CORPORATIONS VS. UNIONS

## Corporations Organize

The most powerful economic institutions of the early twentieth century were corporations. Many of them were assembled in the waning days of the 1893 depression and in the first few years of the twentieth century. Their object was to control markets, raw materials, and labor. By 1900, about two-fifths of total American manufacturing capital and two-thirds of railroad trackage were concentrated in the hands of large combines and corporations. Ten of the largest holding companies (that is, corporations that owned other operating companies) had assets of more than $100 million; the greatest of these, U.S. Steel, controlled over $1 billion. Such concentrations of power touched off controversy from almost the moment they appeared. In 1890, Congress passed the Sherman Antitrust Act, intended to prevent monopolies from restraining trade and competition. But business circumvented the act and, aided by the courts, turned the Sherman Act against labor unions.

Some capitalists ignored the adverse publicity. But others believed they had to act to deflect criticism of their private power and fortunes. Some like Andrew Carnegie also recognized a larger social responsibility. The successful businessman, Carnegie suggested, should administer his wealth for the good of society. Carnegie acted on his own advice and endowed over 2,000 free public lending libraries during his lifetime.

Carnegie's charitable gifts exemplified the development of professional philanthropy. But this money was not intended for the unemployed or the poor. Instead, most was given to encourage culture or to fund scientific or social research or educational projects. As Carnegie put it, his gifts provided "ladders upon which the aspiring can rise." During the first half of the twentieth century, universities also acquired large endowments from such wealthy donors. Several important institutions, such as Stanford in 1889, were founded by men with large fortunes. Universities hired

professional fund raisers and used fund drives to expand their educational offerings. It was this process that snagged Woodrow Wilson in a bitter fight over the disposition of gifts to Princeton in 1910.

Indeed, the manipulations that Wilson encountered in his fight with the Princeton trustees revealed the shortcomings of modern philanthropy. In many cases, philanthropists wished to control the use of their gifts. In others, philanthropy became a device to turn criticism away from questionable business practices. John D. Rockefeller, whose reputation for ruthless competition was national, used charitable giving to improve his public image. In 1889, he began a series of large donations to the new University of Chicago. In 1891, he hired Frederick T. Gates, a Baptist clergyman, to oversee his donations. But such philanthropy did not prevent criticism; instead, it made the very act of giving suspect. Journalists and politicians denounced Rockefeller's motives, calling him a "robber baron" and "spoiler of the state," and his gifts "tainted money." Obviously, philanthropy itself was not enough.

In response to the 1893 depression and mounting sympathy for labor unions, corporations formed two important new organizations: The National Association of Manufacturers (NAM) in 1895 and the National Civic Federation (NCF) in 1900. The NAM, especially after 1903, pushed the "open shop" movement—a movement devoted to preventing unions from forming. Particularly directed against the American Federation of Labor (AFL), this drive gathered strength in the West, where affiliated organizations sprang up to defeat union drives or prolabor legislation.

The NCF adopted a much less confrontational approach to industrial strife and unions. Ralph Easley, its driving force, had been deeply affected by the Pullman strike of 1894. He believed that business had to negotiate with unions to prevent class warfare. Persuading Samuel Gompers of the AFL and John Mitchell of the United Mine Workers to join Ohio Republican political boss Mark Hanna and a group of financiers, businessmen, and academics, Easley created an organization devoted to moderate labor legislation.

## Unions Organize

Unions were obviously the weaker force in the struggles of the 1890s. The problems that they sought to overcome were legion: poverty, industrial accidents, strikes and lockouts, exploitation. For almost all factory workers, wages were low and industrial accidents frequent. Average wages for nonfarm employees hovered around $500 a year in this period. To earn this amount in manufacturing, the average worker gained about 26 cents an hour with 56 hours of work per week. While wages were low, industrial accidents were common, particularly in the key railroad sector. In the deadly year of 1907, 610 passengers, 4,534 railroad employees, and 6,695 workers in railroad shops lost their lives.

Before they sought to unionize an industry, labor organizers knew they would confront tough employer opposition. Employers possessed an arsenal of legal tactics to discourage unions. They could demand a "yellow-dog" contract, allowing dismissal of any worker who joined a union. They assembled blacklists of workers who sympathized with unions, and they hired scabs to cross picket lines. Often they could persuade a friendly court to declare a strike illegal. As a last resort, employers could hire small armies of detectives, spies, and bodyguards to break up union gatherings.

Other obstacles to unionization came from the nature of the American working class. Increasingly, industrial workers were eastern and southern European immigrants. Divisions by language and national origin made organization difficult—a circumstance that employers often exploited.

Despite these factors, substantial unions emerged toward the end of the nineteenth century. The most important and lasting of these was the American Federation of Labor (AFL) founded in 1886 by Samuel Gompers of the Cigar Makers Union. Consisting primarily of skilled craft unions, the AFL grew rapidly in the 1890s. Gompers, an English immigrant and one-time Marxist, guided his union through thirty-five years of strife and conflict. Although he gave up his belief in class struggle, he remained deeply suspicious of politicians and legislation. Gradually he developed a philosophy of voluntarism, or union independence from political parties and government intervention. Anxious to avoid the socialist unionism sweeping Europe, he devoted the energies of the AFL to rewarding its friends and punishing its enemies. By 1900, the union had increased its membership to 400,000.

The dangers and exploitation in industrial work also bred radical organizations. The most important of these, the Socialist Party of America, was formed in 1901. Eugene Debs, of Terre Haute, Indiana, leader of the American Railway Union, epitomized the movement. Enormously popular, Debs addressed audiences across the country in speeches laced with discussions of class struggle and promises of the coming Christian brotherhood, under which the people, not the capitalists, would own the means of production.

The Socialist party, along with the revolutionary Industrial Workers of the World (IWW), which it helped to found, grew rapidly during the progressive era up to World War I. In 1912, when it presented a serious challenge to Wilson, it had 118,000 dues-paying members, 1,200 public officials, and 300 socialist periodicals. With strength, especially in old Populist strongholds of the Southwest, socialists created a movement dedicated to an "international socialist commonwealth—God's Kingdom." Although it eventually broke with the Socialist Party, the IWW also grew rapidly. It achieved important, though temporary, successes in widely noted strikes such as the textile strike in Paterson, New Jersey, in 1913.

## THE PROGRESSIVES

Facing substantial industrial turmoil and large new power blocks in the economy, middle-class reformers tried to develop a program and philosophy of national public interest. They believed that government could solve the problems raised by unregulated competition and industrial struggle. As reformers, they were critical of both sides: owners and unions. They intensely disliked the selfish moneyed interests and feared the organized power of monopolies. Perhaps even more, they distrusted the industrial labor force of newly arrived immigrants. Many worried that labor unions or socialist organizations would challenge the basic tenets of American capitalism. Like Woodrow Wilson, they proposed to create a reformed society, guided by moral principles, in which all of the contending interests would share the benefits.

The forerunners of the progressives, the Mugwumps (see Chapter 28), appeared first in the sedate halls of Harvard University and the gentlemen's clubs of Boston. These genteel reformers bolted the Republican party in 1884 to vote for Grover Cleveland, the Democratic candidate. They put principle above party and supported reform of the electoral system and, above all, honesty in government enforced by civil service reform. On issues of labor rights, they remained conservative; to them, reform began and ended with good government. However, they did will to the next generation of reformers a commitment to national reform and an invitation to the respectable classes to enter politics.

The Mugwumps also bequeathed a tone of moralism and high-mindedness that progressives like Woodrow Wilson shared. The Protestant churches in particular paid special attention to the developing evils of the industrial system. Led by Baptist minister Walter Rauschenbusch and Congregationalist Washington Gladden, ministers and churchmen advocated a new social Christianity. This "Social Gospel" proclaimed that Jesus had taught a social ethic, not individualism as conservative theologians preached. Proposing good works, these men sought greater and greater social cooperation. Many of them entered local good-government campaigns and crusades to regulate industry.

The intellectual climate in American universities and colleges also lent itself to new ways of thinking about society and government. Much as Princeton had done under Wilson, other prestigious American universities like Johns Hopkins, the University of Chicago, Harvard, and the universities of Wisconsin and Michigan hosted new intellectual movements that swept away the cobwebs of nineteenth-century conservative individualism. The development of sociology, which underscored the importance of social engineering as the legitimate function of the state, was one such movement. Perhaps the most profound thinker of the era was Thorstein Veblen. A difficult writer and an eccentric personality, Veblen authored several remarkable sociological works. The best known was *The Theory of the Leisure Class* (1899). In it he satirized the "conspicuous consumption" of the American middle and upper classes. In its stead, he called for the cultivation of the "instinct of workmanship," which he deemed a more natural and creative human impulse.

Veblen's attack on wastefulness and class consciousness was seconded in the philosophical and educational writings of John Dewey. Dewey belonged to a group of important American philosophers, called pragmatists, who stressed the effectiveness and efficiency of ideas rather than their religious or traditional origins. Dewey constructed a philosophical system that emphasized the possibilities for growth, change, and increasing control of the environment. In education, he emphasized the importance of work and experience. To him, education meant placing the child in an environment where he or she could understand the process of change and social evolution. Hence the school, in Dewey's educational plans, became the center of society and a force to rejuvenate the community. It would, he hoped, help narrow distances between social classes and strengthen American democracy.

Civic reformers also provided an important practical ingredient of progressivism. These city dwellers were often appalled by the powerful coalitions of urban politicos and immigrant voters, and they organized to wrest control of cities like

# Frederick Winslow Taylor

(Bettmann Archive)

The change from rule-of-thumb management to scientific management involves, however, not only the study of what is the proper speed for doing the work and a remodeling of the tools and the implements in the shop, but also a complete change in the mental attitude of all the men in the shop toward their work and toward their employers. The physical improvements in the machines necessary to insure large gains, and the motion study followed by minute study with a stop watch of the time in which each workman should do his work, can be made comparatively quickly. But the change in the mental attitude and in the habits of the three hundred or more workmen can be brought about only slowly.

These words, written by Frederick Winslow Taylor in his book *The Principles of Scientific Management,* represent a curious variant of progressive reformism. Taylor, who was both a hero and a villain to the public, was an enthusiast for corporate and industrial reorganization. He was one of the first—and certainly the most notorious—of modern efficiency consultants. His works were cited by some as a bible for industrial reorganization. To others, his writings appeared to be evidence of a management conspiracy to speed up production and lower wages.

Born in 1856 in Germantown, Pennsylvania, Taylor was educated in Europe and at private schools before entering Harvard Law School. Finding study and preparation too strenuous for his eyes, he shifted to engineering. While working as a manual laborer for Midvale Steel Company, he took a mechanical engineering degree from Stevens Institute of Technology. Over the next decades, he secured scores of patents for inventions, primarily in machine tool development.

Taylor was intrigued, and not a little distressed, by the organization of work at Midvale, and he set out to change it. He developed a work time and motion study system. Quite literally this meant observing and timing (with a stopwatch) the individual motions of a worker, and then studying ways to economize effort and eliminate all unnecessary motions, thus speeding production. In addition, Taylor designed new tools and suggested new minimum production quotas, new shop arrangements and incentive wages. The whole system was designed to increase efficiency. But it required complete cooperation from workers and management— something that Taylor generally failed to achieve.

Taylor's emphasis on efficiency and increased wages, plus his own reform intentions, placed him within the ranks of the progressive movement. Nonetheless, he was bitterly criticized for his exaggerated claims and, most particularly, for his treatment of workers as if they were no more than robots. When he died in 1915, his fame was widespread. Motion studies had become common in industry. But his hoped-for change in mental attitudes toward work had not occurred.

JOHN DEWEY

John Dewey's writings provided a philosophical foundation for the progressive faith in institutional reforms. His theories of education also profoundly altered teaching practices, particularly in urban schools. *(Culver Pictures)*

New York, St. Louis, and Minneapolis from the control of the bosses. The good-government movement received national attention with the founding of the National Municipal League in 1894. The achievements of this movement were exemplified by Tom Johnson of Cleveland, Ohio. Johnson had earned a fortune as an inventor, steel mill owner, and operator of streetcar railways. Elected mayor of Cleveland in 1901, Johnson pushed through several impressive municipal reforms: a new garbage disposal system for the city, a low-cost municipally owned electric company, meat and milk inspection, and park and street building. He also attacked organized gambling. Johnson quickly earned a national reputation. In the words of Lincoln Steffens, Cleveland was the "best governed city in the United States," and Johnson's was "the greatest movement in the world today."

Other urban reformers focused on overcrowded living conditions, poor diet, and the ravages of poverty. Tuberculosis, typhoid fever, influenza, and other contagious diseases were sweeping American cities, fueled by overcrowding, poor sanitation and hygiene, and contaminated food.

A key figure in developing reform ideas—ideas that blamed poverty on social institutions, not just on individual weakness—was Jacob Riis. Riis, a Danish immigrant and journalist for the *New York Evening Sun,* was appalled by the conditions he encountered as a police reporter. In 1890, he published his widely acclaimed *How the Other Half Lives.* Using the new technique of photographic half-tone reproduction, Riis stripped the privacy from poverty. Camera in hand, he led his readers on a grim tour of New York's slums. Other reformers focused their attention on the unregulated and filthy workplace.

## Women and Progressivism

Women contributed to progressivism in a variety of ways. Roused by a fear of disease and shoddy products, and desiring to protect their families, middle-class Americans, especially women, organized consumer groups in the 1890s. The General Federation of Women's Clubs (1890), the National Congress of Mothers (1896), and the Consumers League (1899) hoped to safeguard American homes by improving conditions in the factory.

Women were also heavily represented in the settlement-house movement, which began in 1886 with the establishment of the Neighborhood Guild (later the University Settlement) on New York's lower East Side. Probably the most famous settlement was Jane Addams's Hull House, opened in 1889. Addams expressed many of the ideals of the late Victorian reformers who peopled the progressive movement. Well educated, with a sensitive social conscience, she rejected the roles

**SETTLEMENT HOUSE WORKERS**

Julia Lathrop, Jane Addams, and Mary McDowell (left to right) were three important settlement house workers in Chicago. Besides ministering to the needs of slum residents, they worked to secure national reforms such as woman suffrage. *(Library of Congress)*

open to her: marriage, teaching, or nursing. Instead, she helped to create something new: the profession of social work. Hull House, a mansion near the slums of Chicago, became a residence for women who, like herself, sought a useful profession. Addams and her fellow workers plunged into daily life in the slums, working for local garbage disposal, public education, and child labor laws. (The 1910 census reported that hundreds of thousands of children between the ages of ten and fifteen were employed, many of them in factories and mines.) Hull House also offered a distinctive program to nearby immigrants. The residents taught nutrition and cooking, art and literature. By the turn of the century, the settlement included a gymnasium, boys club, auditorium, and library, making it an institution almost as large as the University of Chicago.

But a large segment of woman reformers felt that their own rights were as much at stake as the welfare of immigrants and child laborers. Although women organized many of the important reform movements that constituted the larger progressive mood, they were still unable, by law, to vote in elections, except in some statewide contests. The women's movement in America had a long and varied history. Beginning in the mid-nineteenth century, the movement pushed a variety of aims, from the abolition of slavery to the prohibition of alcoholic drinks. But in the early twentieth century, it concentrated on obtaining the suffrage.

Many reformers—men and women—believed that extension of the vote was essential to the creation of a responsible public spirit. By adding the moral weight of women to the electorate, they assumed that it would be easier to legislate national reforms. Some suffragists, like one who identified herself as Mrs. George Bass, appearing before the Senate in 1915, declared that woman's duty to family should be expanded to become a sort of social motherhood: women wanted the vote because they required it to continue "the business of being a woman."

For those women opposed to the vote, the logic was reversed. As Mrs. A. J. George of the National Association Opposed to Woman Suffrage told Congress that suffrage would destroy woman's special character. She explained: "The Woman-suffrage movement is an imitation-of-man movement, and, as such, merits the condemnation of every normal man and woman." The vote, she concluded, would condemn women to jury duty, protection of life and property, and quite possibly, military service.

Like other reformers of the progressive era, the suffragists turned to the national government for remedies. They sought an amendment to the Constitution. Finally, toward the end of the period, they persuaded Congress and the president to support their initiative. The Nineteenth Amendment was passed by Congress and three-quarters of the states during World War I. It was declared in effect in 1920.

## Progressivism as a Movement

Like Jane Addams's social workers, urban reformers and Social Gospel ministers shared a feeling of identity with the victims of society. As Woodrow Wilson put it in 1909, a man of the people "felt beat in him, if he had any heart, a universal sympathy for those who struggle, a universal understanding of the unutterable things that were in their hearts and the unbearable burdens that were upon their backs."

Progressivism became a movement by establishing a national audience for reform ideas and a program that stressed social and political solutions to individual misfortune. Men like Woodrow Wilson became expert in gathering public

support for their reforms. But much of the attention to reform came from a new sort of journalism, called muckraking. The technological revolution in printing that occurred in the 1890s enabled large-circulation magazines to lower prices to a dime an issue and begin printing photographic features. Newspaper chains owned by William Randolph Hearst adopted an aggressive investigative journalism. Vying for public attention, journals such as *Cosmopolitan, Munsey's Magazine,* and especially *McClure's* began to expose corruption and corporate ruthlessness. For example, *McClure's* in late 1902 published the first installment of Lincoln Steffens's attack on urban corruption, "The Shame of the Cities." At the same time, it included the first of several articles by Ida Tarbell on the history of Standard Oil. Almost overnight, the company became a symbol of corporate greed and monopoly.

Other journalists, taking their cue from these successful articles, began investigations of other sordid elements of modern life: poverty, corruption, and exploitation. In 1906, reporter David

**THE *HOLBROOK* CARRIES THE SUFFRAGE TORCH**

The campaign for woman suffrage took many forms designed to attract public attention and support. Civil disobedience and hunger strikes were eventually added to more traditional spectacles and parades. *(Library of Congress)*

Graham Phillips even attacked the Senate in his series "Treason of the Senate." Phillips's accusations aroused the ire of Theodore Roosevelt. In an April speech, Roosevelt denounced journalists who raked the muck and never lifted their eyes from it. The name "muckraker" stuck.

By the early twentieth century, progressivism had begun to emerge as an important political force stressing industrial regulation and a new social ethic. The problems of industrialism, immigration, poverty, social violence, and corruption were widely recognized. And middle-class reformers had begun to advocate a larger role for government to balance the contending interests of capital and labor. They had begun to articulate a vision of society controlled by men (and women) of good faith who had an acute sense of the public interest. The shape that public interest would take would depend partly on Woodrow Wilson and partly on the other leading political progressive of the era: Theodore Roosevelt.

## Theodore Roosevelt

Everything in Theodore Roosevelt's background seemed to have prepared him for his aggressive and expansive years in the presidency, which he sometimes called the "bully pulpit." Roosevelt brought a keen mind, unexcelled vigor, a talent for publicity, and a love of politics to the office. He also displayed a Victorian sense of social duty, manliness, and culture.

He was born on October 27, 1858, into a wealthy and established New York family. His father, whom he immensely admired, was a gentleman banker with broad interests in social reform and charities. Suffering from delicate health, asthma, and poor vision, young Theodore evoked his parents' concern. They planned long trips to the country and European vacations, and hired tutors to educate their son at home. But it was a strenuous body-building regimen that Teddy began after the age of twelve that enabled him to overcome his physical weaknesses. This success dramatically affected his personality. It

made him in a sense a "self-made" man, despite his wealth. It added energy to his efforts and confidence to his ambitions. At the same time, however, it tinged him with excess. Too much self-confidence sometimes became arrogance. And failure could be devastating.

Roosevelt resembled other men of his class who entered politics during the progressive era. Educated at a private preparatory school and then at Harvard, he believed firmly in laissez-faire economics, charity for the poor, and respectable government. Like Woodrow Wilson, he tested other careers before he entered politics. Like the Mugwumps, he had an upper-class background, but unlike them, he made the transition to progressivism, developing and changing with the clash of events.

Roosevelt rose through the ranks of the Republican party by loyally supporting party candidates and pursuing modest reforms. He earned a reputation as a civil service commissioner and later as police commissioner of New York City. In 1896, when William McKinley won the presidency, the Republicans rewarded him with the position of assistant secretary of the navy, an appointment he relished.

Roosevelt pushed enthusiastically for a larger navy. When war broke out in April 1898 between the United States and Spain, he quit his position and rushed to organize a cavalry regiment. Telegraphing Western governors for men, he assembled and outfitted a band that became known as the Rough Riders. His major enemy was time. Spain was so weak it might crumble before he could reach the battlefield. The Spanish obliged, however, and held on long enough for Roosevelt to lead a frantic charge up Kettle Hill near San Juan Ridge in Cuba on July 1, 1898. As he wrote in his *Memoirs,* "I waved my hat and we went up the hill with a rush."

Roosevelt's exploits delighted the newspapers and helped win him the nomination for governor of New York. The hero of San Juan Hill squeaked through the election by about 18,000 votes. In his first term as governor, he pushed through civil service reform and a tax bill on corporations. And he promoted an investigation of a state insurance scandal. When the Republicans renominated McKinley in 1900, Roosevelt stood in line for the vice presidency. Republican bosses who disliked him helped steer him into this position. They reasoned that Roosevelt could do no damage in this powerless and dead-end job. Stumping the country for his ticket, Roosevelt helped deliver a huge majority for the Republicans: 292 electoral votes to 155 for William Jennings Bryan.

The bosses were right. At first, Roosevelt had little to do. But on September 6, 1901, while visiting the Pan-American Exposition in Buffalo, New York, McKinley was struck down by two shots fired by anarchist Leon Czolgosz, and he finally succumbed on September 14. Roosevelt was president.

Roosevelt immediately announced that he would continue McKinley's policies. But in fact he moved first to ensure his own position in the party. He also initiated a series of moves to consolidate power in his office, dramatically increasing its influence and importance. Thus, as progressivism moved into the White House, Roosevelt began a transformation of the executive branch. During his presidency, Roosevelt actively campaigned and lobbied for legislation that he favored and increasingly acted as a broker among the organized national interest groups that were clamoring for or resisting reform, attempting to create what he called a "Square Deal" for the American public.

Roosevelt's first administration established new guidelines for the behavior of American corporations. In 1903, Congress passed the Elkins Anti-Rebate Act, which prevented railroads from charging special low rates to favored customers. Congress also established a Bureau of Corporations under the new cabinet-level Department of Commerce and Labor. This agency perfectly fitted Roosevelt's philosophy of business regulation. The bureau could control business behavior through its power to investigate and publicize its findings about corporate concentration and monopoly.

The president took other unusual steps to in-

PRESIDENT THEODORE ROOSEVELT IN ASHEVILLE, N.C., 1902

Part of Roosevelt's skill as a politician depended upon his ability to sway crowds of voters. A masterful campaigner, he, as well as other progressives, took their reform message to the people. *(Theodore Roosevelt Birthplace Association)*

tervene in the economy in the public interest. The first occasion came in 1902 during the long anthracite coal strike. In this bitter clash between mine workers and coal operators, Roosevelt leaned toward the miners. The nation demanded action as winter came. The president pushed for arbitration, against the stubborn opposition of the operators. Labeling them unreasonable, he fought to save them "from the dreadful punishment which their own folly would have brought on them if I had not acted."

Roosevelt finally persuaded the owners to accept arbitration. Workers returned to their jobs, and in early 1903 a commission granted some but not all of their demands. The judgment raised wages by 10 percent and established a conciliation board. But the miners did not win union recognition. In fact, the biggest winner was Roosevelt. He had helped end the strike and had moved labor relations to the level of federal responsibility.

Roosevelt earned the reformer's mantle in another well-publicized action. In 1902, his attorney general, Philander C. Knox, instituted a lawsuit under the Sherman Act to dissolve the Northern Securities Corporation. The company typified what Roosevelt considered a "bad" corporation. Certainly he did not oppose bigness or consolidation. But a corporation that existed only to secure a monopoly was another matter. The Northern Securities Corporation resulted from a compromise between two giant railway systems (the Union Pacific–Northern Pacific and the Great Northern) fighting to control rail access to Chicago. The courts decided that the consolidated company must be dissolved, and in 1904 the Supreme Court upheld this decision. Roosevelt was elated at this and other successful trust-busting suits.

With a reputation for activism and good marks earned for his intervention in the coal strike, Roosevelt won the Republican nomination in 1904. He soundly defeated the Democrats in November and then began a more aggressive legislative program. The railroads continued to be a special concern. They were the nation's biggest business and the favorite target of muckrakers.

Roosevelt actively supported a new regulatory law, the Hepburn Act, named for its sponsor, Congressman Peter Hepburn of Iowa. Passed into law in 1906 after a difficult fight, the act expanded the federal Interstate Commerce Commission and added to its authority. Congress granted the commission power to regulate express companies, sleeping car companies, bridges, ferries, terminals, and oil pipelines. Most important, the agency was granted the power to lower shipping rates that it considered excessive.

Roosevelt also responded to calls to regulate consumer products. Two pioneering measures were passed by Congress in 1906: Spurred by a broad campaign against adulteration of drugs and cosmetics and shocked by the gruesome details of the slaughtering industry revealed in Upton Sinclair's novel *The Jungle,* Congress agreed to the Pure Food and Drug Act in June and the Meat Inspection Act in July. The second of these acts, championed by progressive Senator Albert J. Beveridge of Indiana, provided federal inspection for meat sold in interstate commerce. Together, the acts set up the structure to regulate a wide variety of consumer products. In many cases, the affected industries supported this legislation, which, in effect, meant a government stamp of approval for their products. The result was reform that satisfied many reformers, consumers, and businessmen. It was a model of Roosevelt's commitment to executive intervention, compromise, and reform in the national public interest.

The president's other substantial accomplishments came in the withdrawal of public lands from unregulated exploitation. No preservationist or sentimentalist about wildlife, Roosevelt believed in conserving land for a variety of uses: parks, timbering, and mining. Working with Gifford Pinchot of the U.S. Forest Service (a part of the Agriculture Department), Roosevelt set aside about 150 million acres of public land for restricted use. And he supported reclamation legislation that created dams and irrigation projects. (But when Congress canceled executive power to set aside land in 1907, Roosevelt quickly withdrew a final 16 million acres.) He called this policy of preserving resources the "principle of stewardship."

From 1906 through 1908 in particular, Roosevelt supported other important progressive reforms: extension of the eight-hour day to railway workers, termination of child labor in the District of Columbia, and a minimum wage. Although Roosevelt was not able to persuade Congress to act on these measures, they reveal Roosevelt's deepening commitment to federally sponsored social reform and his greater adherence to progressive goals.

Yet in other areas that deeply affected millions of Americans, Roosevelt was inactive. The progressive era saw racial tension, sweeping attacks on the voting rights of black Americans, and rigid segregation in the South. Even some black leaders, most notably educationist Booker T. Washington, publicly embraced a theory of racial separation. Sympathetic to Washington's theories of gradual black self-improvement, Roosevelt appointed several black politicians to patronage jobs early in his presidency. He personally opposed lynchings and disfranchisement, and he even invited Washington to dine at the White House in 1901. But he did little to improve race relations generally. As he told students at Tuskeegee vocational school in Alabama in 1905: "The race cannot expect to get everything at once. It must learn to wait and bide its time."

## Taft

In 1908, Roosevelt initiated a course of action that ended with his bitter split from the Republican party in 1912: He kept his promise not to run again for president in 1908 and selected William Howard Taft as his successor. Only superficially was Taft a good choice to follow Roosevelt. A staunch party man with few political debts to pay—except to Roosevelt—Taft would have preferred an appointment to the Supreme Court. He was an able administrator but an unimaginative leader. Taft was also unsure about his legislative goals and unsympathetic to the growing band of progressive congressmen in his own party. He lacked their commitment to using government as an arbitrator between contending economic interests. During his four years in office, he relied more and more on conservative Republicans, with whom he shared a natural affinity.

Taft's victory in 1908 came partly because of Roosevelt's aggressive campaign for him. But the presidency was his own. Roosevelt, in a gesture of self-advertisement, sailed off after the inauguration on an African safari to stalk "dangerous game." The new president had to find his own way in the political jungle of Washington.

Taft's cabinet appointments disappointed progressive senators but pleased House Speaker Joseph Cannon, a stalwart Republican conservative.

PRESIDENTIAL EQUESTRIAN POSE
President William Howard Taft sits astride a horse in front of the Executive Office Building in Washington, D.C. *(Culver Pictures)*

With Senate leader Nelson Aldrich, Cannon and Taft agreed to seek a lower tariff. The president called Congress into special session in March 1909. The House managed to pass a somewhat lower tariff bill, but the Senate actually proposed increases. In a conference committee meeting the two houses compromised. When Taft signed the law in August there were 654 decreases in rates and 220 increases. The legislation also raised a tax of 1 percent on corporate profits above $5,000. Although Taft proclaimed the legislation a victory—the best revision ever passed by Republicans—progressive congressmen complained that the president had caved in to special manufacturing interests.

Progressives supported other presidential initiatives, however. For example, Congress passed the Mann-Elkins Act in 1910 placing telephone, telegraph, and wireless companies under the jurisdiction of the Interstate Commerce Commission. Congress also established a postal savings bank system. In addition, Taft's administration initiated ninety antitrust suits against large corporations. One of these secured the break-up of Standard Oil. Another, however, against U.S. Steel, seemed an indirect attack on Roosevelt: Roosevelt had given tacit approval to a giant merger of U.S. Steel and the Tennessee Coal and Iron Company during the deep recession of 1907; Taft's action implied that Roosevelt had done wrong. Other presidential initiatives helped establish administrative reform: a new Children's Bureau and a separate Department of Labor. Taft also supported the Sixteenth Amendment to the Constitution, legalizing the income tax, and the Seventeenth Amendment, establishing the direct election of senators.

This was an impressive legislative record but no proof of leadership among Republicans. In fact, Taft's hold on the party gradually weakened. Opposition came from two sources: congressional progressives and Roosevelt. By the midterm election of 1910, the Republicans were badly split. Taft encouraged conservatives to challenge progressives. But the effort backfired. Democrats won the House, and together with progressives, they also controlled the Senate. Early in January 1911, meeting at Wisconsin senator Robert LaFollette's Washington residence, progressives formed the National Republican Progressive League—with the assumption that LaFollette would be the candidate in 1912.

LaFollette's chances dimmed, however, when Roosevelt bounded back on stage. Never content to sit on the sidelines, the ex-president was furious at Taft's "betrayal." Taft, he said, had taken a narrow view of the presidency: "Most able lawyers who are past middle age take this view," he added disparagingly. Worse, Taft had forced Gifford Pinchot, Roosevelt's ally, out of office in 1910 in a fight over conservation policy: Taft's secretary of the interior, Richard A. Ballinger, had approved the transfer of several federal sites to private development. Pinchot, still in the Forest Service, had opposed the transfer and taken his case to the public. Forced to choose between the two men, Taft had fired Pinchot.

## The Election of 1912

The 1912 election brought progressivism to center stage in American politics, and reoriented both principal parties. The groundswell of progressivism split the Republican party. The Democrats shifted away from their Western leader, William Jennings Bryan, to choose the urban progressivism of Woodrow Wilson. And Eugene Debs challenged conservatives and progressives with his socialist proposals.

By February 1912, Roosevelt had stormed into the presidential race. Entering primaries where he could, he piled up significant convention votes, but not enough to control the party machinery. Taft's forces engineered a narrow—but hollow—victory. Roosevelt's delegates withdrew and called for a new party. Meeting in Chicago in August, the new Progressive party nominated Roosevelt at a meeting that joined shrewd politics and revivalism. The delegates, with banners flying, broke into hymns.

Roosevelt's platform promised direct primaries, legislative initiative and referendum, recall of judges, woman suffrage, an end to child labor, the eight-hour day, and a federal trade commission. The candidate's "New Nationalism" was designed to centralize control of the economy in the executive branch. And Roosevelt received important financing from wealthy capitalists like George Perkins, a power in the National Civic Federation.

Taft was odd man out. He defended his administration but did little active campaigning. The race pitted Roosevelt against Wilson. But Roosevelt could not overcome the effects of the Republican split. Wilson won over 6 million votes, Roosevelt over 4 million, Taft about 3 million, and Debs almost 1 million.

# ECONOMICS AND HISTORY

## The Federal Reserve System

The Federal Reserve system, established by legislation in 1913, is the principal monetary instrument of the federal government. However, it is neither a wholly privately owned nor a wholly federally controlled agency. Instead, it is a quasi-independent government corporation in which member banks and the federal government share a partnership. In practice, it may operate more or less independently of both. This semi-independence derives from the operation of the system. The president, with the advice and consent of the Senate, selects a seven-person Federal Reserve Board, with one appointee designated as chair. Since these terms last for fourteen years, with few grounds for removal, presidents have little control over the board, and member banks have practically none.

The system itself is divided into twelve regional Reserve Banks, to which private banks apply for membership. The regional Reserve Bank is, in effect, the banker for private banks. As such, it performs three essential functions. It holds the reserves of the member banks and allows them to lend the excess that they retain. It operates to control the supply of money available for loans. In this way, it affects the pace of economic activity and the rate of inflation. Furthermore the Federal Reserve system returns cash, based on deposits, to member banks when they require it to supply to customers.

The key purpose of the Federal Reserve system is to expand or contract the money supply available for loans. It does this by multiplier effect, as the following example shows:

If bank A has deposits of $1,000,000, it is required to send 20 percent (or $200,000) to the Federal Reserve Bank; the balance of $800,000 it may retain and lend. If the $800,000 is loaned to a construction company, the transaction does not take the form of bags full of cash. Instead, the company receives a line of credit for $800,000. As the company requires money, it draws on its account by check. These checks in turn find their way into other banks, as the company pays its debts. If all of these checks go to one bank, bank B, then bank B will have acquired new assets of $800,000. It too must send 20 percent (or $160,000) to the Federal Reserve, leaving it with $640,000 in assets. It may now lend this money to another company. Through this sort of multiplier effect, assets worth $1,000,000 can be transformed into $5,000,000 worth of loans.

However, if the Federal Reserve system is to control the expansion and contraction of the economy, it must have the power to regulate this multiplier effect. It has three basic means to accomplish this. Although it has rarely done so, it may change the percentage of deposits that must be placed in reserve. For example, it could raise the reserve requirement to 25 percent. Bank A would then have only $750,000 to lend, which would translate eventually into only $4,000,000 worth of loans.

A more common means of control is to change the discount rate. When member banks are short on reserves they often borrow from the Federal Reserve system. The amount charged for this transaction is called the discount rate. By raising or lowering this rate, the Federal Reserve system signals its desire to expand or contract lending.

The third and most commonly used method of control is called an "open-market operation." In this case, if the Federal Reserve system wishes to expand the money supply, it may purchase U.S. treasury bonds on the open market. It pays for this purchase with a Federal Reserve check, that is, a check drawn on the Reserve bank and not on a private commercial bank. If, for example, the treasury notes are worth $1,000,000, the bond seller will receive a Federal Reserve check for this amount. If the bond seller deposits the $1,000,000 in bank A, bank A will deposit 20 percent of it ($200,000) in the regional Federal Reserve and then may lend the remaining $800,000—which may again be multiplied up to $5,000,000. In effect, the Federal Reserve system has created money! Of course this process may be reversed, with the effect of shrinking the money supply and economic activity.

Thus the Federal Reserve system is a national instrument to carry out monetary policy. Although it cannot control whether or not customers will borrow money, it can control the rate at which they borrow. Sometimes its policies have either a delayed or an oblique effect on the economy. Nevertheless, it is the federal government's principal instrument for creating a favorable climate for economic activity.

## PROGRESSIVISM ACHIEVED

Woodrow Wilson brought a special kind of leadership to the White House. His sense of purpose and commitment was unyielding. He believed that his cause was also the nation's. Sympathetic to the plight of the "masses of men," and distressed by the arrogance of wealth, Wilson supported many of the progressive causes. But the new president's vision also had its bounds. His progressivism spoke nominally for the underprivileged. And his vision of government—like his ideal of Princeton—consisted in the exercise of leadership by meritorious gentlemen.

Having proclaimed a "New Freedom" in the election, Wilson set about to institute it. Congress, both houses now firmly Democratic, prepared to help him. Wilson aimed first at eliminating corporate monopoly and other obstacles to competition. He strongly believed that the restoration of competition would liberate business talent and prevent the excesses of the greedy few. But proposing competition was easier than establishing it. Quickly, Wilson accepted reform projects more in tune with Roosevelt's New Nationalism. By the end of 1916, he had begun to advocate centralized executive power and federal economic regulation. And he put these ideals into practice after 1917. When America entered World War I, Wilson began a limited experiment in national economic and social planning.

Wilson appointed a cabinet to represent the various geographic and ideological wings of the Democratic party: Bryan as secretary of state, William B. Wilson, former official of the United Mine Workers as secretary of labor, and William G. McAdoo, from Georgia, as secretary of the treasury. Like Taft, Wilson began with the tariff and a special session of Congress. But Wilson worked skillfully for lower tariff rates. When lobbyists and conservatives tried to stop him, he took his case to the public. Wilson relished the fight; and as so many times in the past, he was convinced that it pitted principle against special narrow interests. He won the struggle. The new law, the Underwood tariff, lowered rates by about 15 percent and attached a small income tax to make up for lost revenues.

Banking also demanded reform. Since the financial panic of 1907, Congress had debated the issue. Two solutions emerged. The first, proposed by Arsene Pujo, representative from Louisiana, attacked private banks. The second called for a national banking system controlled by private banks. Wilson steered toward the second position. The resulting Glass-Owen Act of December 1913 established a new federal banking system. It consisted of twelve regional banks controlled by a Federal Reserve Board appointed by the president. Local banks which joined the system could borrow from the Reserve banks. And the Federal Reserve system could expand or contract credit by lowering or raising the discount rate it charged member banks for loans.

Trusts, monopolies, and corporations were also a primary concern of the new president. Wilson's New Freedom had promised decisive action to unclog competition. But the problem was not simple. Wilson recognized this and gradually moved away from trust busting to a regulatory approach. Passed in September 1914, the Federal Trade Commission Act, which he supported, incorporated features of the Roosevelt Bureau of Corporations. The commission of five members, appointed by the president, could investigate business combinations and issue "cease and desist" orders where combinations acted illegally. Another law, the Clayton Antitrust Act, passed a month later, defined antitrust policy more sharply and assured labor that it would not be prosecuted under the Sherman Act.

The second half of Wilson's first term saw reforms aimed at curbing the excesses of labor exploitation. Adoption of these progressive reforms marked a significant (and often controversial) expansion of federal power. Wilson was under considerable pressure from progressives, and he acted. In 1916, he supported the Keating-Owen child labor bill, which banned child labor (under the age of fourteen) in interstate commerce. (But in 1918, the Supreme Court declared the law unconstitutional.) Wilson also supported the Adamson Act which set an eight-hour day for railway workers and established, by example, a standard for other industries to follow. He supported a workmen's compensation bill for federal employees. He also initialed the Federal Farm Loan Act of 1916, which provided loans for farmers using their land and improvements as security—thus enacting legislation similar to proposals long supported by the Populists.

One of Wilson's most controversial acts endeared him to progressives but drew the ire of conservatives. He nominated Jewish lawyer and activist Louis Brandeis to the Supreme Court in 1916. The American Bar Association and influential political and social leaders were outraged. Nonetheless, working with congressional progressives, Wilson secured the appointment. Acts such as these demonstrated the power of Wilson's leadership.

Although Wilson broke important ground by making the first appointment of a Jewish American to the Supreme Court, he followed the inclinations of his Southern heritage when it came

### LOUIS D. BRANDEIS

Brandeis's appointment to the Supreme Court in 1916 was noteworthy for several reasons. He was Jewish—the first person of his faith to win this high office. And he was widely known for his successful advocacy of progressive social reform legislation. *(Culver Pictures)*

to black Americans. Wilson did nothing to defuse the explosive racial situation in the South. He did nothing to prevent the disfranchisement of Southern blacks by means of poll taxes or literacy tests. Indeed, his record was worse than the benign neglect of the Republicans. A firm believer in segregation, he allowed his cabinet to segregate federal jobs and downgrade or fire black employees. Wilson's defense of his actions suggest the limitations of his progressivism. Writing in 1913, he said:

> It is true that the segregation of the colored employees in the several departments was begun upon the initiative and at the suggestion of the heads of departments, but as much as in the interest of the negroes as for any other reason, with the approval of some of the most influential negroes I know, and with the idea that the friction, or rather the discontent and uneasiness, which had prevailed in many departments would thereby be removed. It is as far as possible from being a movement *against* the negroes. I sincerely believe it to be in their interest.

By 1916, Wilson had achieved party unity around his program of regulation and reform. The Republicans, still smarting from the split of 1912, nominated Charles Evans Hughes for president. Roosevelt supported him. Despite numerous advantages, Wilson won only a close victory. Progressives and peace advocates had perhaps provided the margin of victory.

Ironically, although the issue of peace had helped carry the election of 1916, it was the issue of war that preoccupied Wilson's second term. Europe exploded in 1914, as the major powers rushed into battle. When the United States was drawn into the conflict in 1917, Wilson turned to progressive ideas of regulation, creating an unprecedented system of planning and control of the economy. The demands of war accelerated the tendency of the executive branch to control the American economy. And Wilson gained considerable power to effect such changes through such legislation as the Overman Act of 1918, which strengthened the president's power to reorganize executive agencies.

During the war, Wilson also extended his commitment to progressivism by advocating, as he had previously refused to do, votes for women. In September 1918, he urged the Senate to approve a constitutional amendment to grant suffrage to all Americans regardless of sex. He cited the "unusual circumstances of a world war."

Yet by supporting restrictions on free speech and empowering a vast public relations campaign to sell the war to Americans, Wilson kindled doubts about his leadership. Did he not see that others might have a valid, if different, sense of the public's interest? Was it sufficient to be confident in a righteous cause?

Quite possibly political writer Walter Lippmann was right about Wilson—and progressivism—when he said:

> That, I believe, is the inner contradiction of Woodrow Wilson. He knows that there is a new world demanding new methods, but he dreams of an older world. He is torn between the two. It is a very deep conflict in him between what he knows and what he feels.

# SUGGESTED READINGS, CHAPTERS 31–32

## PROGRESSIVISM

The literature on progressivism is both extensive and fascinating. One fine and very readable general account is Robert Wiebe, *The Search for Order, 1877–1920* (1967). A very different view of progressivism that stresses corporate interest in reforming the most flagrant and dangerous social injustices is James Weinstein, *The Corporate Ideal in the Liberal State, 1900–1918* (1968). Geoffrey Blodgett examines the politics and ideology of the forerunners of progressives in *The Gentle Reformers: Massachusetts Democrats in the Cleveland Era* (1966). Progressivism on a state level is skillfully reconstructed by David Thelen in *Robert M. LaFollette and the Insurgent Spirit* (1976). As a national movement, progressivism developed because of publicity and journalistic exposés. Louis Filler, *The Muckrakers* (1976), is a revised edition of the classic work on reform publicists.

## MOVEMENTS

In some respects, progressivism was the sum of contemporary social movements. One of the most important of these was prohibition. Jack S. Blocker, Jr., *Alcohol, Reform, and Society: The Liquor Issue in Social Context* (1979), discusses this very significant movement in relation to other reform programs. Women played a key role in prohibition, but, increasingly during the era, they also concentrated on securing the vote. Aileen Kraditor, in *The Ideas of the Woman Suffrage Movement* (1981), recounts the arguments for and against woman suffrage. An essential element in this turbulent era of reform was widespread interest in socialism. James Green's fine work, *Grass-Roots Socialism* (1978) documents the extensive socialist movement that grew up in the American Southwest during the progressive era. Reform inside the factory was, in many respects, as extensive as social reform at large. Daniel Nelson in *Frederick W. Taylor and the Rise of Scientific Management* (1980) examines Taylor's management ideas and their relationship to progressivism. Intellectuals as well as workers, managers, and politicians were deeply affected by the swift changes of the opening century. Christopher Lasch, *The New Radicalism in America, 1889–1963* (1965) contains an outstanding discussion of new attitudes toward the self and society.

## PRESIDENTS

The two commanding political figures of the progressive era were Theodore Roosevelt and Woodrow Wilson. George E. Mowry, *Theodore Roosevelt and the Progressive Movement* (1946) is a fine older work and a good beginning place for the study of the Roosevelt presidency. Of all the political leaders of the era, Woodrow Wilson has received the closest scrutiny. Arthur S. Link set the standards for this scholarship in his excellent *Woodrow Wilson and the Progressive Era, 1910–1917* (1954). John M. Mulder, *Woodrow Wilson: Years of Preparation* (1976) is a careful and fascinating study of Wilson's early years. A new and ingenious medical and psychological study of Wilson is Edwin Weinstein, *Woodrow Wilson: A Medical and Psychological Biography* (1981).

# 33 · Tarzan, Symbol of Empire

The cruel black ape named Terkoz threw Jane Porter across his back and leapt into the jungle, swinging his giant body from tree to tree. Closely behind him followed Tarzan of the Apes, his every sense tuned to the almost invisible trail of his enemy. For a civilized man this task would have been impossible, for in cities, survival no longer depended on the senses. Civilized man had become weak and soft. His powers of sight and smell had atrophied:

> as have the muscles which move the ears and scalp merely from disuse.
> The muscles are there, about the ears and beneath the scalp, and so are the nerves which transmit sensations to the brain, but they are under-developed because they are not needed.
> Not so with Tarzan of the Apes.

Overtaking his quarry in a small clearing, Tarzan challenged the ape to battle. Cast aside, Jane saw the two hurtle toward each other, the giant ape's fangs searching for Tarzan's neck. She felt a strange sensation rising in her— "horror, fascination, fear, and admiration," as she

> watched the primordial ape battle with the primeval man for the possession of a woman—for her.
> As the great muscles of the man's back and shoulders knotted beneath the tension of his efforts, and the huge biceps and forearm held at bay those mighty tusks, the veil of centuries of civilization and culture swept from the blurred vision of the Baltimore girl.

Tarzan dispatched his brutal enemy with a thrust of his knife to the heart. Jane rushed to her savior. Tarzan, following his instincts "smothered her upturned, panting lips with kisses." Then, just as suddenly, Jane recovered herself and pushed Tarzan away. But the ape-man did not understand. He knew only that he had won a female in battle, so he "took his woman in his arms and carried her into the jungle."

The two shortly arrived at another clearing, where the giant ape tribe to which Tarzan belonged frequently held their councils and frenzied death orgies. Tarzan realized that he had won this woman in a fair fight. He could now claim her as his mate . . . and yet he hesitated.

> Now, in every fiber of his being, heredity spoke louder than training.
> He had not in one swift transition become a polished gentleman from a savage ape-man, but at last the instincts of the former predominated, and over all was the desire to please the woman he loved, and to appear well in her eyes.
> So Tarzan of the Apes did the only thing he knew to assure Jane of her safety. He removed his hunting knife from its sheath and handed it to her hilt first, again motioning her into the bower.
> The girl understood, and taking the long knife she entered and lay down upon the soft grasses while Tarzan of the Apes stretched himself upon the ground across the entrance.

This scene at the heart of Edgar Rice Burroughs's great adventure novel *Tarzan of the Apes* pitted civilization against wilderness, heredity against environment, and culture against the jungle. It was an old and well-worn convention in American literature to have a hero confront nature and savagery barehanded. But in the early twentieth century, Burroughs could not imagine this confrontation occurring in the American West or in the forests of the Great Lakes. Instead, he wrote about an Englishman and situated his tale in Africa, a site about which he knew practically nothing. Except that Africa, like many other obscure places of the world, had suddenly become the final battleground for European imperialist struggles and, for Burroughs and many Americans of the early twentieth century, a last frontier for explorers and adventurers.

Burroughs placed his novel in the midst of this colonial struggle. The action begins as the British Colonial Office sends John Clayton (Lord Greystoke) and his wife to investigate terrible conditions in a British West African colony. A neighboring colonial power (Belgium) had been recruiting natives to police its ruthless exploitation of ivory and rubber workers along the Congo River. Lord Greystoke intends to intervene, but he never reaches his destination. He and his wife are caught in a deadly struggle aboard their ship between a dictatorial captain and bloodthirsty sailors. When a mutiny breaks out and the captain is murdered, Lord and Lady Greystoke are set on the African shore—marooned on the edge of the jungle.

The odds against their survival are enormous, but the couple struggle nonetheless. Their only happiness is the birth of a son. But after a year of this fearful existence, marauding giant apes murder them, leaving their two corpses in the jungle cabin they have constructed. But a different fate awaits their infant son. A female ape snatches up the living infant, depositing the

**THEODORE ROOSEVELT IN AFRICA**

For many Americans, including President Roosevelt, Africa offered the risks, excitement, and rewards of encounter with untamed nature. The press, in stories, sketches, and photographs, delighted in recording Roosevelt's exploits during safaris. In this painting, the President strikes a pose as Lord of the Jungle. *(Library of Congress)*

body of her own dead baby in the crib. She secrets the human child back to the ape tribe, where she determines to raise him as her own.

The apes name this human child Tarzan, meaning "White-skin" in their language. Kala (a word meaning "black" that Burroughs borrowed from Hindi), his adopted mother, protects him from the jealousies of the other apes. He grows swiftly in wisdom and strength, adopting the language and customs of the apes.

Tarzan's education—carefully and extensively described by the author—blends heredity and environment. Tarzan learns jungle lore and languages and becomes a fierce fighter. But time and again, he is drawn back to the cabin where his parents died. There he discovers two weapons: a discarded knife and human knowledge. Poring over books filled with "little bugs" (letters), he teaches himself to read:

> Tarzan of the Apes, little primitive man, presented a picture filled, at once, with pathos and with promise—an allegorical figure of the primordial groping through the black night of ignorance toward the light of learning.

With his knife and his self-schooling, Tarzan is able to outfight and outsmart the strongest male apes. Eyes flashing, fists beating his breast, he boasts to the ape tribe: "I am Tarzan. I am a great killer. There be none among you as mighty as Tarzan."

Burroughs endows his jungle hero with many remarkable qualities: intuition (which enables him to discover he is a man), strength, endurance, and physical beauty. But Tarzan's most important quality is his moral vision, derived from the interaction of his heredity and environment. Unlike the apes or the other vicious predators—Sheeta the Leopard, Histah the Snake, Sabor the Lioness—Tarzan consciously acts as a representative of mankind. Unlike the animals, he kills for more than food. But unlike other men who wander into the jungle, he possesses no greed.

In the long process of recognizing his humanity, Tarzan comes also to realize that he is destined to rule the jungle. This recognition begins when he sees that he is different from the apes. It grows sharper when he first encounters other men—black Africans. To him they are strange and repellent. They are cannibals, driven out of their lands by colonial soldiers. Burroughs describes their appearance in lurid prose:

> Across their foreheads were tattooed three parallel lines of color, and on each breast three concentric circles. Their yellow teeth were filed to sharp points, and their great protruding lips added still further to the low and bestial brutishness of their appearance.

One of them, the son of the cannibal king, encounters Kala, Tarzan's ape mother. He fatally wounds her with a poisoned arrow and then escapes as the apes rush after him in revenge. Tarzan, swifter and smarter than his ape companions, pursues him back through the jungle toward the native encampment.

As he swings through the trees, Tarzan suddenly understands what prey he is chasing: a man. And yet, he realizes, not a man like himself, but a black man. Tarzan allows the native to approach the village. He suddenly lassoes him from a tree and yanks him off the ground. Tarzan then leaps down and dispatches him with a thrust of his knife. His mother has been avenged and the law of the jungle obeyed. But should he take the next step? Should he eat this victim? Tarzan finds that he cannot:

> All he knew was that he could not eat the flesh of this black man, and thus hereditary instinct, ages old, usurped the functions of his untaught mind and saved him from transgressing a worldwide law of whose very existence he was ignorant.

But Tarzan is not through with the natives. Moving closer to the village, he discovers the secret of their poisoned spears and arrows. And the natives discover the body of the king's son. So frightened are they that they leave arrows and food outside their camp as an offering to their unseen enemy. Tarzan willingly accepts this tribute. Having established his lordship over all of the other residents of the jungle, Tarzan now rules man too.

Now truly lord of the jungle, Tarzan encounters different sorts of men. The first of these are pirates, whose evil faces reflect their cruel intentions: "They were evidently no different from the black men—no more civilized than the apes—no less cruel than Sabor." But other humans come ashore too, and Tarzan recognizes in them something different—namely, his own identity.

Mutiny is once more the catalyst of the action. On the shore, near the abandoned cabin, a group of villainous pirates abandons a party of treasure hunters that includes Jane Porter and her father, Archimedes Q. Porter; Esmeralda, their black maid; Porter's assistant, Samuel T. Philander; and William Cecil Clayton, Tarzan's own cousin. Civilization invades the jungle again.

At first Tarzan is bewildered by these creatures. They are helpless and weak. Professor Porter and Samuel Philander immediately wander off into the jungle. They quickly lose their way and, thinking they are north of the cabin, strike out to the south.

> It never occurred to either of these impractical theorists to call aloud on the chance of attracting their friends' attention. Instead, with all the assurance that deductive reasoning from a wrong premise induces in one, Mr. Samuel T. Philander grasped Professor Archimedes Q. Porter firmly by the arm and hurried the weakly protesting old gentleman off in the direction of Cape Town, fifteen hundred miles to the south.

They do not go unobserved, however, for Numa the Lion quietly pads after them. As Porter and Philander engage in a pompous debate over the virtues of Moorish culture, Numa comes into view. Porter notes the approach of "a mere quadruped of the genus *felis*" and then resumes his argument. Frightened, but still declaiming in stilted, academic speech, Philander interrupts to suggest that they postpone their discussion "until we may attain the enchanting view of yon *Felis carnivora* which distance proverbially is credited with lending." Despite the "unseemly haste," "most unbecoming to men of letters," they race away, the professor's coattails streaming and shiny silk hat bobbing in the moonlight. Tarzan, who has also been following, rescues them from the clutches of Numa and drags the two "highly respectable and erudite scholars neck to neck" back to the cabin.

Other examples abound of civilized man's inability to cope with the jungle. Esmeralda the maid is especially inept. Her reaction to danger is to mispronounce words, roll her eyes, and faint. Thus when Terkoz the giant ape steals Jane away from the cabin and drags her through the jungle, Esmeralda cries out to the others: "I thought it was the devil, but I guess it must have been one of them gorilephants. Oh my poor baby, my poor little honey."

While Tarzan is rescuing Jane from Terkoz and leading her to the bower, a landing party of French soldiers puts ashore at the cabin. They have come to rescue the marooned group. They also bear the horrifying news that the sailors of the ship that abandoned the Porters had been unable to steer the ship without a captain and a navigator. Desperate for food and drink, the mutineers had fallen on two of their own number, leaving their bodies devoured "as though by wolves."

After relating this terrible story, the commander of the French forces, Lieutenant D'Arnot sets off into the jungle with several soldiers to find Jane. Of course he does not know that she is safe with Tarzan. He travels only a short distance before he is attacked by cannibals, who drag him off to their camp. They seek revenge against white men—all white men—who have invaded the jungle:

> To add to the fiendishness of their cruel savagery was the poignant memory of still crueler barbarities practiced upon them and theirs by the white officers of that arch hypocrite, Leopold II of Belgium, because of whose atrocities they had fled the Congo Free State—a pitiful remnant of what once had been a mighty tribe.

As the cannibals prepare to murder D'Arnot, Tarzan suddenly appears and snatches the French commander from their bloodthirsty grasp.

Tarzan then carries the wounded D'Arnot to safety. As the Frenchman gradually recovers, the two communicate by writing notes to each other. But Tarzan demands to be taught to speak a human language, and the lieutenant obliges him. Thus the king of the apes learns French. At last, when D'Arnot has recovered, he and Tarzan return to the cabin. They discover that Jane (whom Tarzan had earlier returned to her father), Clayton, Professor Porter, and the rest of the party have embarked on a French ship, en route to America.

Tarzan vows to follow Jane, but first he must travel with D'Arnot back to the nearest French outpost. There the jungle hero acquires civilized manners. In two short months he becomes "Monsieur Tarzan," a "handsome Frenchman in immaculate white ducks." As he learns the ways of society, Tarzan also realizes more clearly than ever that he belongs in the forests, not in the drawing rooms of his fellow men. For him the jungle is a complex society, as various and complicated as any human society. Speaking of lions, he tells his amazed friends at the French outpost: "There is as much individuality among the lower orders, gentlemen, as there is among ourselves."

It is when he accepts a wager to hunt a lion, naked and armed only with his knife and rope, that he finally comes to understand that civilization means enslavement. The jungle is freedom:

> Civilization held nothing like this in its narrow and circumscribed sphere, hemmed in by restrictions and conventionalities. Even clothes were a hindrance and a nuisance.
> At last he was free. He had not realized what a prisoner he had been.

As Tarzan returns with the body of a dead lion draped across his shoulders, he realizes something else about civilization:

> It had become evident to Tarzan that without money one must die. D'Arnot had told him not to worry, since he had more than enough for both, but the ape-man was learning many things and one of them was that people looked down upon one who accepted money from another without giving something of equal value in exchange.

Thus it is that Tarzan, more sophisticated and wiser, finally makes his way to America. There he rescues Jane once more, this time from the clutches of a man who has insisted that she marry him to redeem a debt of her father's. He also plucks her out of a forest fire in Wisconsin. Nonetheless, she refuses to marry Tarzan. She has given her word to his cousin Clayton, the presumed heir to the title of Lord Greystoke, and "a man with social position and culture such as she had been taught to consider as the prime essentials to congenial association."

The novel ends with one further twist—which is also the basis for further adventures. Tarzan learns that he is the rightful heir to the title of Lord Greystoke. Fingerprints found in the cabin of his parents in Africa reveal his noble heritage.

Edgar Rice Burroughs composed this splendid tale of adventure and exploit over the winter of 1911–1912 in Chicago. Writing on the back of letterhead stationery from his bankrupt dry-goods store in Pocatello, Idaho, he completed the story in a few months of intensive work and sent it off to *All Story* magazine, a journal that featured serialized adventure stories. An immediate success, the story was republished as a novel in 1914. After that, the character of Tarzan took on a life of its own. The book was made into a movie in 1917 and was followed by more than thirty-five other Tarzan adventure films in subsequent years. The jungle world that Burroughs created lived through the sequels he wrote and the groups of loyal fans who organized Tarzan clubs and wrote publications discussing the strange world that Burroughs had described. Tarzan achieved a special place in American culture, and through this fictional character, Burroughs became possibly the most widely read author of the century.

How did this remarkable story come from the pen of a thirty-seven-year-old failed businessman, cowboy, and gold prospector? Burroughs himself provided a powerful clue. As he said, it was a story of personal escape:

> My daily life was full of business, system, and I wanted to get as far from that as possible. My mind in relaxation preferred to roam in scenes and situations I'd never known. I find I can write better about places I've never seen than those I have seen.

At another time he remarked:

> Perhaps the fact that I lived in Chicago and yet hated cities and crowds of people made me write my first Tarzan story.

The life that Edgar Rice Burroughs sought to flee in his fiction had, indeed, been a bitter disappointment, and his desire to escape it and give full expression to his imagination is altogether understandable. Burroughs was born in Chicago on September 1, 1875, into a prosperous middle-class family. His father, Major George Burroughs, a Civil War veteran, had risen to become vice president of the American Battery Company, which manufactured storage batteries. The youngest of four brothers, Edgar sought to emulate the adventurous careers of the male members of his family. But he also showed an early interest in reading, writing, and poetry.

This division between adventure and culture marked Burroughs's education. Never an outstanding student, he found school tiresome and confining. Like other young boys, he dreamed of the frontier: the Wild West of Indian fighting, gold prospecting, and sudden fame and fortune. His restlessness became apparent early, and it increased with age. The demands of school and then of finding a career were increasingly interrupted by extended periods that Burroughs spent in the West. But Burroughs also had to face a reality that caused him bitterness and then despair. The West was never quite what he imagined it to be; it was as easy to fail there as in the East.

One of Edgar's first memories of school caused him a good deal of shame and embarrassment. In the midst of the sixth grade, his parents took him out of public school and placed him in Mrs. K. S. Cooley's School for Girls on Chicago's West Side. They did so because of a diphtheria epidemic then sweeping the public schools. Mortified to be attending a girls' school, Burroughs was immensely relieved when his parents enrolled him in Chicago's Harvard School in 1888. Earning indifferent grades in traditional subjects like Latin, Greek, and algebra, he quit the school abruptly in mid-1891. It is not clear why his parents agreed to this move, but obviously his studies had not been successful. Edgar was delighted to begin again. And this time his parents placed him in the elite boarding school Phillips Academy, in Andover, Massachusetts.

Before entering Phillips, however, young Burroughs traveled west to Idaho for a short time to join two of his brothers in their livestock business. The first of many trips west, this one introduced him to life on the range. He spent much of his time fetching mail or supplies by horseback from the nearest railroad junction. No doubt this experience kindled his desire to return to the frontier once he finished his education. It appealed to his adventurous spirit, his love of heroism, and his admiration for the free-spirited life of the frontier.

For the time being, however, Eastern schooling was more important. Settling in at Andover when the fall semester began, Burroughs made numerous friends (he was elected class president). But his academic progress was slow. A few of his submissions to the school's literary magazine, the *Mirror,* were published during the winter of 1892, but he paid little attention to his studies. At the beginning of the second term, Phillips Academy sent him home.

Burroughs's parents at this point decided to call in a firmer hand to end this education by fits and starts. They sent Edgar to the more disciplined atmosphere of military school, choosing the academy at Orchard Lake, Michigan. Here, Burroughs finally finished his education. After a difficult beginning, the young student settled down. The new commandant of the school was Captain Charles King, a strict disciplinarian as well as a noted author of Western novels. He supplied just the mixture of inspiration and firmness that Burroughs needed.

While at Orchard Lake, Burroughs became an accomplished horseman and a member of the football team, playing quarterback and ultimately serving as captain. But even in his last year—and despite the leadership of King—Burroughs had troubles. For "neglect of duty" he was reduced in military rank and confined to his quarters.

Burroughs graduated in June 1895 with no clear prospects and no fixed ambition. He had shown himself indifferent, even rebellious, toward authority. Yet military life attracted him. So his family tried to secure his appointment to West Point Military Academy. His brother arranged Edgar's preliminary selection as a candidate under the sponsorship of the congressman from Idaho, but he still had to pass the entrance examination. Of the 118 young men to take the test on June 13, 1895, only 14 passed—"I being among the one hundred and four" who did not, recalled Burroughs.

Almost twenty years old and without any immediate prospects, Burroughs accepted an offer to return to Orchard Lake as assistant commandant in charge of cavalry instruction. He also taught geology, although he had no particular training or aptitude for the subject. Unfortunately, he found these duties onerous. Unhappy at the distance between himself and the young cadets of the academy, he decided to resign in the spring. He hoped for a career in the real military.

In May 1896, Burroughs joined Troop B of the Seventh U.S. Cavalry, assigned to Arizona. Perhaps he joined the cavalry because he had visions of becoming an army hero and a great Indian fighter, but the reality of duty was dreary and monotonous. He was ill much of the time and deeply offended by the petty tyranny of his officers. After three months, he became desperate, pleading in letters to his father for help. He wanted either a discharge or a transfer. Finally, in March, the army released him on medical grounds. Turning in his uniform, he headed north to help his brothers move a herd of cattle to the railhead for shipment. This accomplished, he returned to Chicago.

At home, Burroughs's extreme restlessness and indecision increased. For a short time he considered a career as a political cartoonist and satirist, and he enrolled in drawing classes at the Art Institute of Chicago. Then, abruptly, he withdrew and went to work in his father's battery factory. But he had no intention of remaining there permanently. He also began an active courtship of Emma Centennia Hulbert, daughter of a Chicago hotel owner. But without a job or prospects, Burroughs could not contemplate marriage.

Once more the West beckoned as a place to seek his fortune. So in early 1898, Burroughs left for Pocatello, Idaho, to join his brothers. Almost immediately after he arrived, war broke out between the United States and Spain over Cuba. When Burroughs heard that Theodore Roosevelt wanted volunteers for a cavalry regiment of Rough Riders that he was organizing, he rushed to enlist. But Roosevelt sent a personal note of rejection, and Burroughs sat out the brief war. For a second time his military career had been thwarted.

Burroughs's next enterprise was merchandising. With money borrowed from one of his brothers, he purchased a stationery store in Pocatello in the early summer of 1898. Momentarily enthusiastic, he stocked up on American flags—to meet an anticipated patriotic outburst—and cheap novels and mag-

**EDGAR RICE BURROUGHS**

Burroughs often dressed in military or cowboy garb and used the fortune he earned as a writer to buy a California ranch, which he appropriately called Tarzana. His fiction, however, dealt with Africa, Venus, and Mars—rarely with the disappearing American frontier of his day. *(Edgar Rice Burroughs Estate, Tarzana, California)*

azines. But by fall, he had become discouraged, and losing money, he sold out his interest.

Now his bitterness at personal failure and at not being included in the war against Spain became vocal. He wrote an angry satiric poem on the Philippines, one of the spoils of the war. The United States had just acquired these populous Asian islands from the Spanish. Rudyard Kipling, whose jungle tales Burroughs had read, addressed a poem to the United States called "The White Man's Burden," in which he spoke of sacrifices that imperialist nations (such as the United States had recently become) had to make to uplift other races. To Kipling, this was a burden: the white man's burden was to bear the hostility of ungrateful natives—"your new-caught, sullen peoples."

Burroughs's poem, "The Black Man's Burden, A Parody," also dealt with imperialism—the events by which the United States acquired the Philippines as a protectorate. But Burroughs attacked this American adventure in the Pacific. To him, the white man's burden was in fact the weight of colonialism and exploitation imposed upon the black man:

Take up the white man's burden;
    'Tis called "protectorate,"
And lift your voice in thanks to
    The God ye well might hate.. . .

Take up the white man's burden;
    Poor simple folk and free;
Abandon nature's freedom
    Embrace his "Liberty"; . . .

Take up the white man's burden;
    Take it because you must;
Burden of making money;
    Burden of greed and lust. . . .

Peruse a work of Darwin—
    Thank gods that you're alive—
And learn the reason clearly:—
    The Fittest alone survive.

Abandoning his short and unsuccessful career in merchandising, Burroughs turned again to ranch work with his brothers. The following summer, however, he returned to Chicago and employment with his father. He also claimed Emma Hulbert as his bride and the couple married in January 1900. Although marriage added to his responsibilities, Burroughs still could not settle on a career. Three years later, scarcely advanced in his work and barely able to make financial ends meet, Burroughs turned west. This time, he took his wife to join his brothers in a new gold-dredging enterprise near Pocatello. For a while he planned this to be his permanent home. Finding themselves in the wilds of the Sawtooth Mountains, Burroughs and his wife had a small cabin constructed by some of the mining company employees. (In another guise, this cabin reappears as the jungle hut built by Lord and Lady Greystoke in the opening scenes of *Tarzan of the Apes*.)

But the cabin in the mountains was not to be a permanent home for the couple. Burroughs grew restless with the hard work and boredom of mining. When the gold company failed in 1904, he and his wife abandoned the wilderness and moved to Salt Lake City, Utah. There he took temporary employment as a railroad detective, but depressed by his low wages, he again pulled up stakes and returned home to Chicago. He had to auction his furniture to pay for the tickets.

The next jobs Burroughs took in Chicago merely underscored his predicament. He worked as a salesman for John Lawson Stoddard's travel and photographic lectures, which he sold door-to-door. He briefly sold electric light bulbs to Chicago janitors and then candy to drugstores. In 1906 he attempted one final escape through military service and inquired about enlisting for duty in the Philippines or in China. Finally he found relatively steady employment at Sears, Roebuck and Company, where he rose to become manager of the clerical department.

Despite his advancement at Sears, Burroughs abruptly quit his job in 1908. His prospects, however, were worse than ever. The next few years were among his most difficult, bleak and poverty-stricken. Several enterprises failed: a patent medicine business selling Alcola (to cure alcoholism) and partnership in a business school to train traveling salesmen. Burroughs's spirits could hardly have been lower. He had failed at everything—a career in the military, the search for quick wealth on the frontier, and countless business schemes. In 1908, he wrote a bitter poem that lashed out against the poverty that threatened him and his dreams of success.

> *Poverty!*
> Accurst and cursing
> Thou Drab of Sin and Vice and Misery;
> Thou spur to Fortune.
> From thy shrunk womb a Lincoln springs.
> Engulfest thou a thousand who might have Lincolns been.

Three years later, he had made little progress. In 1911, after a brief, unsuccessful attempt to peddle pencil sharpeners, however, he made a decision that finally and permanently altered his life. As a niece recalled, "He was selling pencil-sharpeners for a living when he first talked himself into writing. He threw down an *All-Story* magazine in disgust one day and said, 'If I couldn't write a better story than that I'd go jump in the lake.'"

The story that Burroughs wrote in this challenge to himself was "Under the Moons of Mars," which he sold to *Argosy* magazine. This was his first fictional adventure, and he took it up with some obvious misgivings. He did not feel at ease seeking his fortune in the literary world. So he chose a curious pen name—Normal Bean (meaning normal head or perhaps normal being)—as if to underscore the hesitations he felt about a normal man of his age writing adolescent fiction.

Burroughs began the story with a short prelude that had obvious parallels to his own life's struggle to find a fortune. But the real adventure begins exactly where these parallels end. The hero, John Carter, a Civil War veteran from the Confederate side with neither money nor profession, travels west to prospect for gold, accompanied by another soldier. They stumble upon a remarkable vein of gold quartz. But unfortunately, a group of renegade Indians chases them from their strike and into an obscure cave. As the Indians approach for their final kill, Carter is suddenly transformed and conveyed to Mars, where he begins a remarkable adventure.

This device of removing the hero out of the American West and into an imaginary land had been employed by Frank Baum in his popular story *The Wizard of Oz,* published in 1900. As authors, both Baum and Burroughs found that the real West lacked the drama and imaginative possibilities they wished for their stories. Thus they created new fictional worlds.

**LORD OF THE JUNGLE**

The illustrations and covers for Burroughs's novels and stories often featured seminaked men and women in suggestive poses. Most of the stories, however, concentrated on adventure, with relations between the sexes guided by a strict and puritanical moral code. *(Culver Pictures)*

Burroughs sold his story, but this single fictional work did little to solve his permanent financial problems. So he took a job with *System* magazine, eventually heading their service bureau. Half a legitimate advice service and half a purveyor of hokum, *System* replied to queries from businessmen about reorganizing their companies. Burroughs certainly had wide business experience. As much as any man of his day, he was driven by the desire to succeed. As much as anyone, he believed in the American myths of mobility and success. But there was an irony to his giving advice to others, for almost every one of his enterprises had ended in failure.

His one small success in writing, however, inspired him to try a new project. This was "The Outlaw of Torn," set in medieval Europe. Despite three rewritings, Burroughs could not sell the manuscript, and so he turned to another project, the story he eventually called *Tarzan of the Apes.* This remarkable novel brought the author what he had vainly sought for many years: fame, financial reward, and success.

Because the story seemed to have emerged from nowhere, critics have long wondered about its origins. Burroughs himself recalled a number of sources that stimulated his imagination:

> As close as I can come to it I believe that it may have originated in my interest in Mythology and the story of Romulus and Remus. I also recall having read many years ago the story of a sailor who was shipwrecked on the Coast of Africa and who was adopted by and consorted with giant apes. . . .

Then, of course, I read Kipling; so that it probably was a combination of all of these that suggested the Tarzan idea to me.

Many elements of the author's readings, from Kipling to Charles Darwin, can be found in Tarzan, but the story also grew, as an imaginative projection, out of his own life. Burroughs steadfastly denied any larger implications or purposes to this work of fiction or any other that he wrote. For him, writing, as he recounted it, was a business enterprise. He even kept a scrupulous count of the number of words he composed per hour and per day—an act of business introspection that Benjamin Franklin would have heartily approved. Each of his settings, in his Tarzan stories and in his science fiction romances, was foreign to his readers—and to his own experience.

Yet underneath these disguises existed familiar worlds and common ambitions. A failure in the real world, Burroughs succeeded in his imaginary realm of fiction. Unable, himself, to attain success through hard work (in fact, unable to work hard and consistently at anything except fiction writing), Burroughs invented worlds where work had no real function. The jungle was a place where natural virtue triumphed, where society could not hold a good man down. Burroughs dismissed civilization as "effeminate" and "sentimental." Poverty and cruelty were its characteristics. Still, Burroughs did not reject the success ethic: Tarzan rose through the ranks of the ape tribe to become its leader. But Tarzan achieved this position because he deserved it. At another time and in another society—such as America of 1912—he might have failed, much as Burroughs himself had failed.

Society, in Burroughs's disparaging view, represented greed, overrefinement, and social disorders that were symbolized by mutinies, piracy, and exploitation. For most of his readers, these were common views. Countless novels and tales in American popular literature were also set at the fringes of civilization, where urban culture clashed with primitivism. Like James Fenimore Cooper, his great predecessor of the 1830s, Burroughs was not quite sure what to make of this encounter. He created a jungle full of animals, men, and the outposts of other societies, just as Cooper had filled his colonial forests with Indians and French soldiers. The jungle and the forest are both places of sudden violence, danger, and opportunity. They are also worlds threatened by exploitation and disruption imposed upon them by European empires. If the jungle and the forest are by some measure superior, they are still under constant assault by civilization.

Despite his obvious distaste for civilized worlds, Burroughs was no reformer. The jungle world he imagined boasted of no equality. Its hierarchical order of men, apes, lions, and other animals was maintained by violence. Whatever perfection it possessed lay in the fact that natural distinctions existed. Tarzan, wrote Burroughs, "was no sentimentalist. He knew nothing about the brotherhood of man."

Nor really did Burroughs. The author bitterly attacked the Belgians for their atrocities against the natives of the Congo Free State. Yet with all his sympathy for natives and other exploited residents of the jungle, racial distinction remains the most critical factor in this imaginary social order. Despite white scoundrels, pirates, murderers, and cowards from the civilized world, Tarzan remains loyal to his own heritage. Reluctantly, he picks up the white man's burden and imposes order at the margin where civilization encounters wilderness. That is where Tarzan happily went "his bloody way scattering virtue and sudden death indiscriminately and in all directions."

Burroughs repeated this successful adventure formula in at least twenty-five Tarzan sequels. Few were as rich as the original, however, in social commentary or biographical parallels. But in 1918, the author's life intersected with his fiction once again in a particularly direct way. World War I had been raging for three years when the United States was finally drawn into the conflict in 1917. Like another aging soldier, Theodore Roosevelt, Burroughs tried to enlist. But his years counted against him. He did finally manage to get an appointment with the Illinois Reserve Militia, but it was far away from the trenches of France.

So once again, Burroughs bent reality into fiction. In his story, *Tarzan the Untamed* (originally titled, *Tarzan and the Huns*) Burroughs waged imaginary war against the Germans. The battlefield is East Africa. Germans, marching through British territory, come upon Tarzan's large jungle estate. With the master away, Lady Jane greets the German troops, who then turn on her and burn and pillage the property. They abduct her, leaving an unrecognizably

**BURROUGHS ON LOCATION, 1933**

Burroughs visited the filming of *Tarzan the Fearless*. A number of American actors played Tarzan in the many films based on his character. The best known of these leading men were Buster Crabbe and Johnny Weissmuller. Here, Burroughs is chatting with actress Jacqueline Wells, who played Tarzan's love in this movie. *(Culver Pictures)*

burned corpse in her bedroom. Tarzan returns, sees the carnage, and vows vengeance, which he deals out in particularly brutal ways.

In this story, Burroughs repeats all the elements of the original formula: an imperial struggle, repeated scenes of violence, capture and escape, torture and black baiting. He invents strangely evolved creatures—in this case an insane yellow race of humans who breed lions for meat. But perhaps most noteworthy is Burroughs's vehemence against German *Kultur* (culture). In his private war against Germany, Tarzan also raged again against civilization:

> In reality he had always held the outward evidences of so-called culture in deep contempt. Civilization meant to Tarzan of the Apes a curtailment of freedom in all of its aspects—freedom of action, freedom of thought, freedom of love, freedom of hate.

Thus the myth that had once served Burroughs so well as a means to escape the humdrum life of Chicago and his repeated failures on the frontier was now pressed into service for the Allied cause in World War I. In ridding the African jungle of fictional German villains, Burroughs, as much as any man, was doing his part to make the world "safe for democracy," and to define what that democracy meant. His success and his destiny were now the nation's.

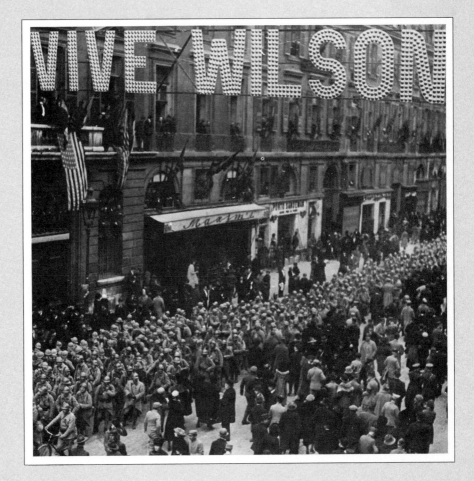

# Imperialism
# and Progressive
# Foreign Policy

cles to success. Gone were Indians and outlaws, replaced by strange new evolutionary races and cultures and the agents of European imperialism.

**F**ew of the hundreds of thousands of Americans who eagerly read *Tarzan of the Apes* in 1914 would have paused to ask if the novel had any larger implications. It appealed to them because it was a great adventure story set in a land of outlandish creatures and involving preposterous coincidences. Nothing could have been further from their own lives than this escapist fiction. Distance and strangeness are part of the charm of this kind of writing. Yet historians have long been aware that popular myths and fiction can be important documents, which, as much as anything else, reveal the deeply held convictions of a society.

*Tarzan of the Apes* is an important document because it is the fictional solution to a problem—one that Edgar Rice Burroughs faced in his own life and one that the nation was beginning to experience in its relationships with other nations. This was the problem of competition in the modern world. Burroughs lived his life in pursuit of two fundamental American beliefs about competition—the sorts of beliefs common to thousands of advice tracts and inspirational stories of the day. Each suggested a sure route to achievement and success. The first advised cultivation of the self: the self-made man would rise to fame and fortune because he was prepared morally and intellectually to seize opportunity when it appeared. The second route to success lay in the West, where opportunity was most plentiful. Pursuit of adventure on the frontier was supposed to bring financial reward to the hardy individual. Edgar Rice Burroughs was as prepared as any man of his age to follow either path to success, but, until *Tarzan,* he failed at both.

His response after many years of indecision and frustration was to revise the myths of success by moving their setting. He eliminated society and replaced the frontier with the jungles of Africa. He also identified new challenges and obsta-

## THE MYTH OF AMERICA'S DESTINY

Burroughs's shift in setting mirrored a similar shift in American attitudes toward the rest of the world during his time. After about 1896, the United States increasingly looked outward, toward the acquisition of an empire and then, warily, toward active participation in the conflicts between European nations. Every step of the way was accompanied by hesitation and debate over two issues: How should Americans treat the peoples of undeveloped countries that they encountered? and Should the United States become permanently involved in alliances and covenants with European nations? If America was to remain the unique civilization that so many writers had proclaimed it to be, then these problems demanded a resolute answer.

Edgar Rice Burroughs's response was a fascinating one. He too worried about such questions. He had written an angry rebuke to Kipling about picking up the white man's burden in the Philippines. He peopled his fictional jungles with villains drawn from the most aggressive imperialists of Europe: the Belgians in the Congo and, later, the Germans during World War I. Burroughs solved the problem by making Tarzan unique. He created a hero who ruled this dangerous, competitive world. But Tarzan, unlike all of the other inhabitants of the jungle or any of the European intruders, remained pure—like the American-style self-made man, uncorrupted either by civilization or by savagery. And he was the son of an aristocratic English lord. His destiny, determined by inheritance and evolution, and sharpened by confrontation with the frontier, was to preside over all the other different and lower beings.

A great many Americans at this time were influenced by the idea that America had a special destiny in the world born out of a combination of its European, principally Anglo-Saxon, racial and cultural heritage and its experience as a frontier civilization. Of course most of them would not have recognized it in Burroughs's jungle parable, but their ideas about the mission of the United States were similarly born out of the feeling of belonging to a unique society. It is these ideas that give Burroughs's myth of success its special importance and convinced Americans that they were duty-bound to try to set the world right.

The United States picked up the burden of empire with some reluctance. The nation was a late entrant in the race for empire. It quickly acquired a string of colonies and protectorates, but then withdrew from the contest for more dominions. However, it did not retire from the scene; its overseas ambitions merely assumed a different form. In the Western Hemisphere, Americans began a series of interventions in the affairs of Latin American countries that continued, sporadically, for several decades. And by 1917, the United States held the balance of power in one of the gravest conflicts in human history.

These events inspired a new national self-consciousness. They gave rise to new ideas about national power, to a belief that because of its history and culture the United States was uniquely fitted to guide the destinies of other nations. Yet these events also aroused doubts. Would America's new activist role in the world forever compromise the special and unique qualities of life in the New World?

Such questions found their way into popular literature like *Tarzan of the Apes* as well as into serious political discourse. Indeed, a great many Americans were talking about the nation's destiny in terms of world leadership. Of course words like "leadership," "destiny," and "mission" had always been part of the American political vocabulary. In the mid-nineteenth century, writers and politicians often spoke of the nation's Manifest Destiny to populate a continent bounded by two vast oceans, on the east and the west, and by two different cultures, to the North

and the South. But with that geographic destiny fulfilled in the 1890s, with most of the fertile land already occupied and millions of new immigrants pouring into cities of the East and Midwest, the idea of Manifest Destiny acquired a new meaning. American institutions of political democracy and economic mobility still seemed superior to the class-conscious societies of Europe. But many Americans wondered how this superiority could survive.

Frederick Jackson Turner, a historian at the University of Wisconsin, in a celebrated and influential essay about the American spirit, summed up the effects of the frontier on American society and offered a vision of continued expansion. Turner asserted that American democratic institutions came from the frontier experience. As settlements pressed across the continent, civilization and wilderness repeatedly intermingled. Savagery refreshed society, and civilization tamed the wilderness. Thus Americans had progressed in a westward trek for almost 300 years.

When he described his "frontier thesis" at the Chicago Columbian Exposition in 1893, Turner, just as Burroughs would later, used the language of popularized evolutionary theory. Struggle and competition on the frontier, he wrote, created a survival ethic of individualism and democratic cooperation. But the historian issued a warning. The frontier, he said solemnly, "has gone and with its going has closed the first period of American history."

Would there be a second, equally rich period of American history? Movement, restlessness, and a desire for opportunity still remained the essence of the American spirit. As Edgar Rice Burroughs's life illustrates, the lure of the West had not died. It drew thousands of young men onto what remained of the frontier. Many failed, but the dream of fleeing the work-a-day cities of the East remained irresistible. Perhaps some Americans could find escape in the fictional heroism and new frontier worlds of popular fiction like Burroughs's. But could the nation survive the loss of energy and creativity that had once come from opening up new frontiers?

Turner did not think so. Nor did he believe that the nation could survive unless it continued to expand economically. So he advised continued expansion in world trade. In effect, the world was to become America's economic frontier. Many of his contemporaries agreed with Turner that the 1890s represented a watershed in American history. With the frontier officially closed and, westward expansion blocked by natural and cultural boundaries, the only feasible economic expansion lay overseas in trade or empire. But there were dangers. Could America avoid falling into the traps that ensnared Spain, Britain, and France in costly colonial ventures? Would America's new activism in the world economy mean entangling alliances with European powers?

Those American policymakers who advised a new activism—a new foreign policy—believed that American society would survive because of its cultural superiority. They believed that America was a nation of Englishmen purified by the encounter with the frontier. Long implicit in American thinking, this theory of Anglo-Saxon supremacy emerged full-blown in the early twentieth century. Many Americans believed that an English background bestowed a special racial heritage. America would survive world competition because of its superior racial stock, culture, and high principles. Nor was this thinking confined to a few diplomats or politicians. As the popularity of *Tarzan* illustrates, it was a myth that found a huge audience among all classes of Americans.

American cultural supremacy was the argument Theodore Roosevelt used to justify America's policy of Indian removal in his book *The Winning of the West*. "It was wholly impossible," he wrote, "to avoid conflicts with the weaker race unless we were willing to see the American continent fall into the hands of some other strong power." Progressive senator Albert Beveridge of Indiana, speaking of America's destiny, called the nation, "the purest race of history." "Fellow Americans," he proclaimed in 1898, "we are God's chosen people." Even William Jennings Bryan, who opposed acquiring colonies, solemnly spoke of the nation's mission "to liberate those who are in bondage."

## THE REALITY BEHIND THE MYTH

The men who developed America's new foreign policy at the turn of the century subscribed to the notion that the nation had a special destiny. Most believed in the superiority of the Anglo-Saxon "race." Some based their position on Social Darwinism, a popular translation of evolutionary theory into a proclamation of the right of the "fittest" individuals and the strongest nations to rule over others. Many were influenced by the ideas that Turner had enunciated in his "frontier thesis." But they were also hard-headed realists. They recognized the political and economic benefits of an activist foreign policy. They realized that the United States had to begin to exercise more power in the world because its position among nations had become preeminent.

The most profound changes in America's world position were economic. In 1877, the United States struck a favorable balance of trade (more exports than imports). Forty years later, during World War I, the nation became a world creditor, owing less to other nations than it had lent out. This evolution toward financial independence reflected a dynamic economic growth. Rapid development in the 1880s and 1890s greatly increased the percentage of manufactures in American exports. This, in turn, focused the interest of American industrialists on maintaining and increasing overseas markets.

Much of the increased American economic activity abroad came in the form of investments, especially in underdeveloped nations. In Mexico, for example, by 1910, about 1,100 American firms held about $500 million worth of investments. In effect, American capital controlled most of Mexico's railroads and a large share of its ranching, lumber and paper industries, and banking. United States companies also dominated Mexican mining and oil extraction.

During the progressive era, exports consti-

## AMERICAN EXPORTS BY VALUE AND DESTINATION: 1896–1924

| Year | Total* | Canada | Cuba | Mexico | UK | France | Germany | China |
|---|---|---|---|---|---|---|---|---|
| 1896 | $883 | $ 60 | $ 8 | $ 19 | $ 406 | $ 47 | $ 98 | $ 7 |
| 1900 | 1,394 | 95 | 26 | 35 | 534 | 83 | 187 | 15 |
| 1904 | 1,461 | 131 | 27 | 46 | 537 | 84 | 215 | 13 |
| 1908 | 1,861 | 167 | 47 | 56 | 581 | 116 | 277 | 22 |
| 1912 | 2,204 | 329 | 62 | 53 | 564 | 135 | 307 | 24 |
| 1916 | 5.483 | 605 | 165 | 54 | 1,887 | 861 | 2 | 32 |
| 1920 | 8,228 | 972 | 515 | 208 | 1,825 | 676 | 311 | 146 |
| 1924 | 4,591 | 624 | 200 | 135 | 983 | 282 | 440 | 109 |

*Millions of dollars.

Source: U.S. Department of Commerce, Bureau of the Census, *Historical Statistics of the United States: Colonial Times to the Present,* bicentennial ed. (Washington, D.C.: Government Printing Office, 1975), Vol. II, p. 903.

tuted between 6 and 7.5 percent of total American production, but this was a vital part of the nation's commerce. From 1890 to 1914, the share of trade with Latin American and Asian countries increased dramatically. The potential for even larger sales was alluring. Yet success bred worries. Power shifts in Europe and instability in Asia, South America, and Africa increased the aggressiveness of leading European powers. The rapid industrialization and armament of Germany and Japan threatened the dominance of Great Britain. After a scramble for colonies in Africa during the 1880s and 1890s, the major powers looked covetously upon the weak Spanish Empire in Asia. China appeared to be tottering. Even the unruly Latin American republics seemed in danger of intervention by European powers.

Thus the new American foreign policy at the turn of the century was defined in the context of serious challenges as well as opportunities. If industrial nations divided the world into competing, closed empires protected by high tariff walls, United States trade and influence would collapse. If the European nations and Japan insisted on expanding their empires, the United States might be shut out from the world economic frontier. To make matters more urgent, many American businessmen and political leaders concluded during the severe depression of the 1890s that agricultural and industrial overproduction were permanent American problems. They could be solved only by exporting more.

## A NEW FOREIGN POLICY

The men who formulated the new American foreign policy of the progressive era were in fundamental agreement: They insisted that the United States pursue a more active role in the world. They were deeply influenced by ideas and worries about America's destiny. They realized the opportunities and problems created by rapid industrial development. But they disagreed about how far the United States should go toward acquiring a formal empire of naval bases and colonies. This practical question dominated debate over foreign policy at the turn of the century.

The major shift toward a new, activist foreign policy began during the second presidency of Grover Cleveland, in the depths of a depression. Three unsettling events pushed the president toward new policy initiatives. The first was a revolt in the Hawaiian Islands in January 1893. Dominated by American planters, the islands became increasingly important because of the fine port at Pearl Harbor and their strategic position along trade routes to the Far East. Immigration of Chinese and Japanese settlers in the 1880s plus the growing economic importance of Americans

# The Singer Sewing Machine

It will doubtless surprise some readers of this article to learn that the serviceable and homely product of Yankee ingenuity, the sewing machine, is one of the things which has helped to spread the fame of America abroad, or that the symbol of the red S [for Singer] so familiar at home, is one of the things which, wherever his wanderings abroad may take him, is sure to confront the American expatriate with its reminder of the country he has left behind. . . . At whatever places men, in their meetings for trade, have set up their markets; in whatever places the cutter and fashioner of cloth or leather or fur, plies his calling, there the American sewing machine has made its way and is welcome, whether it be in the tent of the desert Arab, the Kaffir's hut in South Africa, or the Norwegian fishing village near the Arctic circle.

To quote another traveler's words, this time those of an American missionary speaking of his labors among the tribesmen of Arabia: "I have never yet been in an Arab town without finding Singer sewing machines among people who have never seen the word of God and who have never heard the gospel of Jesus Christ."

*Sewing Machine Advance,*
Chicago, September 1908

The Singer Sewing Machine Company, founded in 1850, was, by the first decade of the twentieth century, an extraordinarily successful American enterprise. In 1913, it had almost 6,000 branches in the United States and abroad, with over 60,000 salesmen. Besides its special marketing program, it operated branch factories in Canada, Scotland, Germany, and Russia. Although other nations manufactured sewing machines, American companies dominated the world market, with Singer taking the largest share. Its machines seemed to be everywhere. As John

Reed, an American war correspondent during the Mexican Revolution, wrote of a Mexican home: "In one corner was a big iron bed, and in the other a Singer sewing machine, as in every other house I saw in Mexico."

The Singer company prided itself on its aggressive salesmanship and favorable publicity. It offered a wide range of manually operated machines and attachments, and easy access to repair and replacement parts. Company employment policy stressed paternalism. Singer instituted a "civil service" so that "every workman knows he can rise if he has merit." The company paid a family man a slightly higher wage and encouraged young men of good character to apply for work. There were also company sports programs and social activities. Singer did not, however, tolerate labor unions.

A slogan, picturing the sewing machine as "the great civilizer," reiterated the company belief, and the American assumption, that the export of Yankee know-how would transform the world.

There were, however, other views of this American dominance of world markets. During the Spanish-American War in 1898, newspapers in Madrid called for a boycott of Singer products. One paper accused Singer of being an "immense octopus whose tentacles encircle Spain and crush it, snatching from it the savings of its workers in order to aggrandize the miserable, iniquitous, cowardly, disgusting North American nation." During World War I, Germany placed Singer's branch companies under government control. And by 1919, the communist government in Russia had nationalized the large Singer plant and sales outlets in that country.

ZULULAND.

**SINGER IN SOUTH AFRICA**

The caption to this advertising card from Singer read, "This is a fertile, well-watered country of South Africa, on the Indian Ocean, and forms a part of the region known as Kafraria. The native Zulus are a fine warlike people of the Bantu stock, speaking the Bantu language. The language extends over more than half of Africa and is one of great beauty and flexibility. The Zulu bids fair to be as forward in civilization as he has been in war. Our group represents the Zulus after less than a century of civilization. Worth wins everywhere. Our agent at Cape Town supplies both the European and native inhabitants of Zululand, The Transvaal, and Orange Free State with thousands of Singer Machines." *(Library of Congress)*

led native Queen Liliuokalani to assert her powers. But the white settlers in Honolulu, supported by the U.S. minister to the island, John L. Stevens, overthrew the queen and asked for American annexation.

When Cleveland entered office in 1893, he faced a decision to accept or reject annexation. He refused, angrily saying that the revolt was "dependent for its success upon the agency of the United States." Cleveland desired trade and influence in Hawaii, but he was reluctant to annex the islands as a colony of the United States.

A second crisis developed in South America in a dispute between Great Britain and Venezuela

that challenged the Monroe Doctrine. The Monroe Doctrine of 1823 had provided a motto for American foreign policy: no further encroachment by Europeans in the Americas. The British navy had generally supplied the shield for this policy. Now, suddenly, the British themselves threatened a Latin American republic.

The dispute was a longstanding one about the boundary between Venezuela and the British colony of Guiana. At stake was the Orinoco River, a large navigable river whose upper reaches tapped trade and gold prospecting areas of Venezuela. Cleveland supported Venezuela's claims and pressed Britain to submit the dispute to ar-

**QUEEN LILIUOKALANI OF HAWAII**

Queen Liliuokalani ascended the throne of the Hawaiian Islands in 1891. Her attempts to assume wider powers persuaded American residents on the islands to demand annexation by the United States in 1893. *(Hawaiian Public Archives)*

bitration. On July 20, 1895, Secretary of State Richard Olney demanded that the British negotiate. In his message he reminded Britain of America's power: "Today the United States is practically sovereign on this continent."

When the British response came, it was curt and inflammatory. No arbitration and no Monroe Doctrine. Cleveland's next move edged the United States toward war. He sent a message to Congress on December 17, 1895, calling upon the nation to resist the "willful aggression" upon Venezuelan rights. Talk of war flared but then subsided quickly. Already overextended elsewhere, the British agreed to arbitration.

No sooner had the Venezuelan crisis ended than a rebellion flared in Cuba that quickly became the center of American attention. One of the last outposts of the crumbling Spanish Empire, Cuba had gravitated into the U.S. economic orbit. American exports to the island reached $24 million in 1893, larger than to any other Western Hemisphere nation save Canada, and larger than all of America's Asian trade. In February 1895, Cuban rebels demanded independence. Too weak to enforce order, Spain still insisted that the rebels surrender. As fighting spread, American-owned sugar plantations and mills suffered from arson and looting. The whole structure of American investments on the island—$50 million worth—hung in the balance.

At first Cleveland sympathized with the Spanish, and he never wavered from his desire to see the rebellion end. But continued violence eroded his patience. Moreover, Cuban rebels gathered significant support in the United States. Many Americans became openly sympathetic to their cause after Spanish General Valeriano Weyler introduced martial law and his "reconcentration" policy. Begun in October 1896, this policy pushed thousands of peasants into the cities to depopulate the countryside. But Weyler miscalculated, and thousands of Cubans died of starvation and disease in crowded city quarters. Newspaper publishers William Randolph Hearst and Joseph Pulitzer, who knew how to provoke sympathy (and circulation), played up the brutality of this policy. Like their progressive counterparts, the muckrakers, these "yellow journalists" discovered the importance and malleability of public opinion.

Under the circumstances, Cleveland could only increase pressure on Spain to end the rebellion. He was not prepared to go to war over Cuba, yet he defined peace in the rebellious colony as key to American interests. Thus when he left office in 1897, he passed on to William McKinley, the new president, the task of protecting America's interests in this explosive situation.

McKinley's inauguration brought a new group of foreign policymakers to power. They were more willing to push ahead in places where Cleveland had been reluctant. The most prominent of these new men was Theodore Roosevelt, the new assistant secretary of the navy, although other members of the group were also important: Senator Henry Cabot Lodge of Massachusetts, diplomat John Hay, historian Brooks Adams, and Admiral Alfred Thayer Mahan.

Although their views differed somewhat, most of the new men agreed with the strategic proposals outlined by Mahan in his book *The Influence of Sea Power upon History* (1890). Mahan proposed an export and investment empire based on naval power. His tactics centered upon building a Panama Canal, acquiring protective bases around it, and then colonial stepping stones across the Pacific to Asia. This would ensure American trade and influence in Latin America and the Orient. These goals, Mahan proclaimed, were far greater than mere national self-interest. "Every expansion of a great civilized power," he wrote, "means a victory for law, order, and righteousness." Overseas empire was America's destiny.

Spain was the major obstacle in America's route to empire when McKinley entered office in 1897. Senator Henry Cabot Lodge expressed what many in the administration, as well as many other Americans, believed about Spain. Using language that might well have been written by Burroughs in deploring European imperialism, Lodge wrote that the Spanish were a people who "stood for bigotry and tyranny as hideous in their action as any which have ever cursed humanity." Spain also held the important islands of Puerto Rico, and Guam and the Philippines in the Pacific.

The new president hoped to avoid direct intervention in Cuba. But unlike Cleveland, he committed himself to a more expansionist foreign policy, including acquisition of the Virgin Islands and Hawaii, and eventual removal of all vestiges of European colonialism from the Western Hemisphere. His first priority was to end the divisive pressure on domestic politics and the economy caused by the Cuban rebellion. So he stepped up pressure on the Spanish. In June 1897, he called on Spain to end its "uncivilized and inhumane conduct." Again in the fall, he warned the Spanish not to seek allies among the European powers.

As Spain moved from one inept policy to another, the United States pressed its case harder. By the end of 1897, the two nations were on a collision course. The Spanish minister to Washington, Enrique De Lôme, in a letter to a friend in Cuba, referred to McKinley as "weak and a bidder for the admiration of the crowd." The letter was intercepted and published February 9 in the *New York Journal*. Sensationalists needed no more evidence of Spanish duplicity.

A far more serious event on February 15 almost ignited war. The U.S. battleship *Maine,* anchored in Havana harbor in Cuba, exploded mysteriously. Of the 350 officers and seamen aboard, 260 perished. Although the perpetrators of the act (if indeed there were any) were never

**ANTI-SPANISH PROPAGANDA**

Portrayals of Spanish authorities as brutal murderers in journals and newspapers in the United States helped incite American public opinion in favor of war against Spain in 1898. *(Culver Pictures)*

captured, many Americans blamed the Spanish authorities. Once again, the sensationalist press bristled with cries of war.

As pressure on Cuba increased, the United States flanked the Spanish Empire in the Pacific. Assistant Navy Secretary Roosevelt ordered Commodore Dewey to anchor his fleet at Hong Kong. In the event of war, he was to destroy the Spanish navy in the Philippines. In late March, McKinley again demanded an end to hostilities in Cuba, proposing an immediate six-month armistice and American mediation. Spain accepted part of the proposal and hedged on the rest. Both nations prepared for war.

McKinley decided to ask Congress for a declaration of war on April 11, 1898. He gave a number of reasons, but they all revolved around one assumption: peace in Cuba was necessary to the domestic tranquillity of the United States. As

he said, there was an "intimate connection of the Cuban question with the state of our own Union." But the president refused to side with the rebels; his intent was to end the rebellion. "Final military victory for either side seems impracticable," he concluded. America's purpose, in other words, was to preserve order in an area where U.S. interests were involved. On April 19, Congress declared war; and one day later it proclaimed the Teller amendment renouncing any intention to annex Cuba.

Enthusiasm for the war ran high. After voting, congressmen burst into song, harmonizing "Dixie" and the "Battle Hymn of the Republic." Much of the popular poetry of the day underscored this feeling of enthusiasm and unity. The opposing blue and gray of the Civil War were reunited in a splendid struggle against decadent Spain. As a *Baltimore News* poet rhymed in 1898:

### THE WRECKAGE OF THE *MAINE*

The tragic sinking of the U.S.S. *Maine* in Havana harbor in March 1898 killed 260 men aboard the naval vessel. Nonetheless, war with Spain did not come for two more months. *(Library of Congress)*

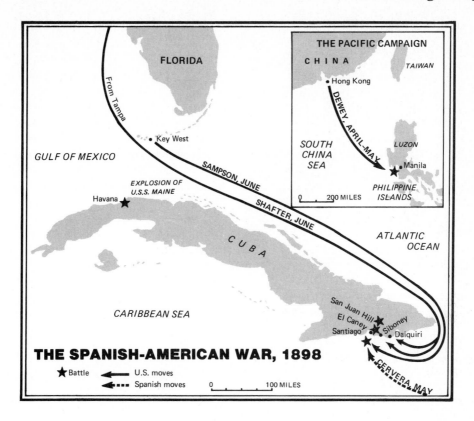

THE PACIFIC CAMPAIGN

CHINA

TAIWAN

• Hong Kong

DEWEY, APRIL-MAY

SOUTH
CHINA
SEA

LUZON

★ •Manila

PHILIPPINE
ISLANDS

0    200 MILES

FLORIDA

From Tampa

• Key West

GULF OF MEXICO

SAMPSON, JUNE

SHAFTER, JUNE

EXPLOSION OF
U.S.S. MAINE

Havana ★

C U B A

ATLANTIC
OCEAN

CARIBBEAN SEA

San Juan Hill ★
El Caney ★ ★ Siboney
Santiago ★ ★ • Daiquiri

★

CERVERA, MAY

**THE SPANISH-AMERICAN WAR, 1898**

★ Battle        ← U.S. moves
         ←--- Spanish moves        0          100 MILES

Those who wore the blue and gray,
And they'll fight for common country,
And they'll charge to victory
'Neath the folds of one brave banner—
Starry banner of the free!

For many Americans this was a romantic war, a chance for a man to prove his heroism and courage. Undoubtedly such thoughts entered the mind of Edgar Rice Burroughs when he tried to join up with Roosevelt's Rough Riders. But the conflict was over in less than four months. American casualties were slight—only 385, although deaths from disease and other hazards pushed the total to 2,446.

In Asia the war began as a naval operation. Dewey, as ordered, steamed to the Philippines in late April and discovered the Spanish fleet huddled under shore batteries in Manila Bay. Dewey ordered an attack on May 1. Passing before the harbor and pouring fire into the motionless ships, Dewey's forces devastated the Spanish fleet. The Americans sustained no casualties at all. When the smoke cleared, Spanish rule over the islands had practically ended. The city of Manila surrendered on August 13. Elsewhere in the Pacific, U.S. forces took Guam Island on May 10. And Congress annexed Hawaii in early July.

By the time Spain sued for peace in August, the outlines of an American empire existed: a protectorate over Cuba, with claims to Puerto Rico, Guam, and the Philippines. Hawaii and the port of Pearl Harbor now belonged to the United States. The question that remained was, Should the United States annex the Philippines? The islands lay thousands of miles east of America. They were peopled by what Commodore Dewey called "little brown men." To hold them meant fighting Filipino nationalists. Here was a problem that required rethinking the whole history of

**EMILIO AGUINALDO, PHILIPPINE REVOLUTIONARY**

For nationalists such as Aguinaldo, the fight for Philippine independence only intensified after the United States became master of the former Spanish colony in 1898. American troops required almost four years to subdue the insurrection he led. Independence was finally granted in 1946. *(Culver Pictures)*

American foreign relations. To take the islands meant embarking on colonialism. It meant holding and keeping whole territories and peoples in subordination to the United States. McKinley weighed these factors carefully. He agreed that a naval station at Manila was highly desirable. But he doubted it could be defended without holding the island of Luzon and perhaps all of the Philippines. If the United States moved out, on the other hand, European powers such as Germany seemed prepared to move in. McKinley made his decision after a night of prayer. He decided it was America's duty to "Christianize" the islands. The president forwarded his demands to the peace negotiations; Spain had no choice but to cede the islands to the United States in the Treaty of Paris, signed in December 1898. America had, reluctantly, picked up the "white man's burden."

Filipino insurgents, led by Emilio Aguinaldo, believed that the Treaty of Paris merely changed the guard. Unpersuaded of America's expressed intentions, Aguinaldo and his army launched an insurrection in early February 1899 against American occupation forces. For the next two years the U.S. army fought the rebels. Finally, in March 1901, the rebel leader was captured, although sporadic fighting continued into 1905.

American tactics combined force with persuasion. The military campaign was brutal and much more costly than the war against Spain had been. Tens of thousands of Filipinos died. On the other hand, William Howard Taft, heading the Philippine Commission, improved administration after 1900. Taft pushed for order and reform, for the building of schools and roads, and for the provision of sanitation and health facilities. In 1902, under the Philippine Organic Act, the islands gained a constituent assembly and limited self-government.

## Results of the War

America plunged deep into colonialism when it took the Philippines, and this decision touched off a furious debate about the meaning of the new foreign policy. Two major groups emerged: the imperialists and the anti-imperialists. But these designations are somewhat misleading. Both sides agreed that America should intervene in areas of American interest. Both wanted a dynamic international trade. But there were real differences.

The imperialists generally favored acquiring colonies. They believed that these new territories could be administered by the United States without any serious compromise of tradition or the American Constitution. The anti-imperialists, led by Grover Cleveland, William Jennings Bryan, Andrew Carnegie, Civil Service reformer Carl Schurz, together with a host of reformers, argued against keeping the Philippines. They drew a dividing line through American history. In the first period—up to 1899—they praised legitimate continental and territorial expansion. But taking the Philippines meant European-style colonialism. How, asked Carl Schurz, could the United States absorb populations "incapable of becoming assimilated to the Anglo-Saxon"? For Bryan, principle overshadowed questions of race. America's mission was to liberate, "not place shackles upon those who are struggling to be free."

Most of the anti-imperialists believed that trade could be increased without colonies. They wanted a limited number of bases—a strategic empire—but not the Philippines. As many as 30,000 Americans joined the Anti-imperialist League and almost prevented passage of the peace treaty. And by 1913, they had reversed the initial victory of the imperialists regarding the formal possession of colonies. The new president, Woodrow Wilson, agreed that the Philippines should eventually be granted independence.

The Spanish-American War had other serious effects. It moved the United States closer to the sort of entangling alliances it had traditionally avoided. In the late nineteenth century, Great Britain faced a loss of its world predominance and looked around for new friends. The swift rise of Germany in Europe had upset the balance of power. Britain moved to court the Americans. After the near-collision in Venezuela, Britain strongly supported U.S. claims against the Spanish. In return, the United States expressed sympathy for England in its bitter colonial war in South Africa with the German-backed Boers.

The new informal alliance of Anglo-Saxon nations paid off handsomely. Britain supported American efforts to retard Japanese, German, and Russian efforts to carve protectorates out of the Chinese empire. Secretary of State John Hay's brash "Open Door" notes of September 1899 and July 1900 demanded that European powers stop partitioning China and that they treat all nations equally in their spheres of interest. This, he hoped, would prevent the collapse of China and the exclusion of American commerce. The British agreed in principle. Other nations were far less compliant, but China did manage to avoid being partitioned by the contending European nations.

Probably more significant, Britain agreed in 1901 to the Hay-Pauncefote Treaty, which canceled prior agreements for joint U.S.–British

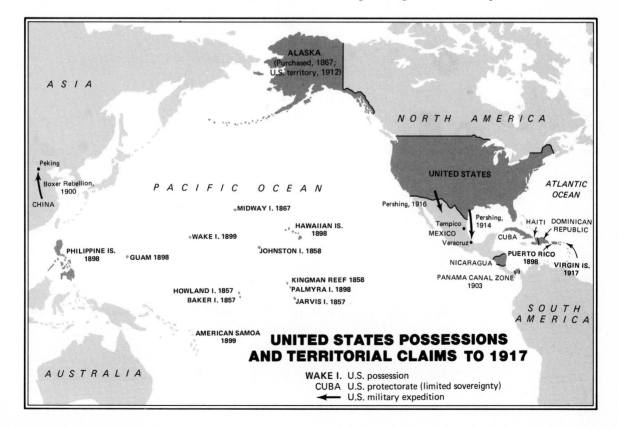

**UNITED STATES POSSESSIONS AND TERRITORIAL CLAIMS TO 1917**

WAKE I.  U.S. possession
CUBA  U.S. protectorate (limited sovereignty)
⟵  U.S. military expedition

construction of a canal across the Isthmus of Panama. The treaty freed the United States to dig the canal alone. As Hay wrote of it, the developing American-British friendship was "a sanction like that of religion which binds up to a sort of partnership in the beneficent work of the world."

# U.S. POLICY IN LATIN AMERICA, 1901–1916

## Roosevelt and the Panama Canal

When an assassin's bullet brought Roosevelt into the White House in 1901, it elevated to power America's leading advocate of an activist foreign policy. But Roosevelt's actions disclosed that even he believed foreign policy had important limitations. By 1901, most of the pieces of an American empire had already fallen into place; only the Panama Canal remained to be built—

"By far the most important action I took in foreign affairs," wrote Roosevelt.

By securing the independence of Panama and an American monopoly for a canal, Roosevelt reached into someone else's yard and plucked the ripest fruit. Panama had been the northernmost—and most troublesome—province of Colombia. Its greatest natural asset was favorable terrain for a shipping canal. Roosevelt encouraged Panamanian rebel leaders, who declared their independence in late 1903. The president ordered naval vessels to protect the fledgling government, and almost immediately afterward the United States signed a treaty with Panama. The new nation granted the Canal Zone to the United States plus exclusive rights to construct a canal. In exchange, the United States paid $10 million to the new republic.

Possession of the Canal Zone and a network of bases and possessions focused American attention on the perennial instability of Latin America. In December 1904, Roosevelt issued his corollary

**THE PANAMA CANAL UNDER CONSTRUCTION**

The enormously costly and difficult canal across the Isthmus of Panama was completed in August 1914. Engineers not only had to subdue the jungle to construct a vast, artificial waterway; they also had to fight against debilitating diseases such as malaria and yellow fever. Shown here is one of the many spillways that had to be built as part of this massive project. *(Culver Pictures)*

to the Monroe Doctrine. The situation of economic chaos and potential foreign intervention he described in Central America was acute. Speaking of the need to preserve "civilized society," the president declared that he would intervene in any country to restore order and decent government. If a nation "keeps order and pays its obligations," it need not fear the United States, he said. But if chaos invited foreign interference, America would intervene. Roosevelt backed up his statement with action in 1905, when he sent troops to the Dominican Republic to force it to pay its international debts.

## Taft and "Dollar Diplomacy"

As president from 1909 to 1913, Taft continued most of Roosevelt's policies but under a new name: Dollar Diplomacy. He did not use this title to sound crass; he merely wanted to downplay the use of force. But like so much else in his administration, good intentions tripped over a bad choice of words. Taft left much of his policymaking to Philander C. Knox, the new secretary of state. Knox reorganized the State Department into more efficient regional and topical divisions. Overt interventions in Latin America continued—in the Dominican Republic again, and in Honduras and Nicaragua. The purpose was to enforce order and security in areas around the Canal Zone. Taft's other purpose was to increase American economic dominance in the area. As he told Congress in 1912, he intended to support "every legitimate and beneficial enterprise abroad." He also worked hard to open European development consortiums in China to American investors.

## Wilson and Mission Diplomacy

Taft's administration bridged the empire-building years of McKinley and Roosevelt with the mission diplomacy of Woodrow Wilson beginning in 1913. Wilson's assumption of the presidency brought leading anti-imperialists to power. With William Jennings Bryan as secretary of state, Wilson invoked a high moral tone in foreign relations. But much had changed since the debate over the Philippines. The United States had acquired an empire and the Panama Canal. It had established an informal alliance with the British. Involvement in the affairs of Latin American republics had increased. Wilson did not intend to undo any of these achievements, but he did commit his administration to what he believed was a responsible exercise of power.

When Wilson assumed office, ideas about America's world destiny were very much in the air. Anglo-Saxon cultural consciousness, based on pseudo-scientific theories of racial superiority, combined with traditional notions of moral mission to create a special American sense of purpose. These notions informed Edgar Rice Burroughs's tale of Tarzan's reluctant acceptance of the white man's burden. Burroughs had uncovered an enormous popular audience prepared now to imagine the jungles of Africa as the proper arena for enacting the struggle for success once reserved for the American frontier. They readily accepted a view of the world as filled with social rebellion, insurrection, and imperial struggle. They could also be convinced that America's mission, like Tarzan's, was to "scatter virtue" in this world. They would not be surprised to read, later, of Tarzan's exploits against the Germans during World War I.

Under Woodrow Wilson, the United States pursued a diplomacy that the president believed would set new standards for international behavior. The next eight years proved the possibilities and limitations of this hope. When Wilson became president, the problems that had launched America's new foreign policy had grown more complex. The balance of power in Europe had continued to swing away from Britain; there were new rebellions in the nonindustrialized world; and American economic and political interests abroad had increased significantly. By 1917 these problems had helped draw the United States into World War I.

At first, Wilson hoped to wean American foreign policy away from the interventionism of his two predecessors. But he did not give up the idea that it was America's responsibility to act to suppress chaos. Nor did he wish to retard the growth of American trade and investment. This placed him in something of a dilemma. For example, he sympathized with the goals of the social revolutionaries in Mexico, but he intervened in that nation when he thought events were headed in the wrong direction. Although he found Dollar Diplomacy distasteful, he nonetheless worked to protect American trade and investments abroad. He desired to prove America's right to moral leadership, but he convinced some critics that such aims were delusive or, worse, hypocritical.

In October 1913, Wilson proclaimed a new Latin American policy: "Human rights, national integrity, and opportunity," he declared, "as against material interests—that, ladies and gentlemen, is the issue which we now have to face." In China, he terminated Taft's attempts to bring Americans into investment consortiums with European powers. And he supported Secretary of State Bryan's efforts to win international treaties of arbitration to prevent war. As a gesture, Bryan had several old swords belonging to the War Department melted down and fashioned into miniature plowshares, which he presented to the president and his cabinet.

The symbolism was clear, but the policy proved more difficult to shape, particularly in the Western Hemisphere. From the first days of his administration, Wilson faced increasing problems with Mexico. Under the friendly regime of Porfirio Díaz up to 1910, American capital had flowed into Mexico. This had had two important effects: It gave control of much of the Mexican

**THE U.S. CAMPAIGN AGAINST PANCHO VILLA, 1916**

In order to retaliate against Mexican revolutionary leader Pancho Villa for his raids across the American border, General John J. Pershing led an expeditionary force 300 miles into Mexico. Pershing never did capture Villa, but the American presence in Mexico greatly complicated U.S. relations with that country. *(Library of Congress)*

economy to Americans. And economic development increased the social strains, which in turn precipitated the Mexican revolution. When it broke out in 1910, therefore, the revolution had serious implications for U.S. policy.

Although Wilson wanted the revolution to pursue democratic goals, he could not guide or control it. At first he tried nonrecognition as a means of convincing Mexican revolutionaries to moderate their policies. When this failed, Wilson intervened militarily. Responding to what he interpreted as an insult to the nation, Wilson ordered the seizure of the Mexican port of Vera Cruz in April 1914. Eventually General John Pershing led an American expeditionary force into Mexico during the spring and summer of 1916 to capture a Mexican troop led by Pancho Villa that had attacked across the U.S. border. At this point, however, Wilson backed off and withdrew American soldiers. But for dire events in Europe, Wilson might have intervened further. Nevertheless considerable damage had been done. American-Mexican relations suffered for many years. With the best of intentions, Wilson had made a bad situation worse.

# THE UNITED STATES AND WORLD WAR I

## American Neutrality

The increasingly desperate war in Europe curtailed Wilson's Mexican adventure. World War I began in late July 1914. Like the gears of a giant machine, the iron-cast alliances of Europe engaged the British, French, Italians, and Russians (the Allies) against the Germans, the Austro-Hungarian Empire, and Turkey (the Central Powers). Other nations joined the struggle, but, the key battlefields developed in northern France and western Russia. After overrunning neutral Belgium, German troops poured into northern France, outflanking French defenses. By the end of 1914 the war had bogged down in fixed positions along a line that moved only with enor-

mous sacrifices. Until 1917 and the defeat of Russia, additional offenses in the West gained little new territory for either side.

Once the war began in 1914, American economic power and trade became a major prize in the contest between the Allies and Germany. Both sides hoped to use American economic resources to their own advantage. In such a world it was extremely difficult for Wilson to maintain American neutrality, but he tried. On August 19, 1914, the president appealed to Americans to remain "impartial in thought as well as in action." He promised that the United States would not be drawn into the conflict. Inevitably, his stance enraged Theodore Roosevelt and Henry Cabot Lodge. Owen Wister, like Burroughs a popular writer, addressed the following scornful lines to Wilson in early 1916:

> Not even if I possessed your twist in speech,
>   Could I make any (fit for use) fit you;
> You've wormed yourself beyond description's reach.

Try as he might, Wilson could not control events, nor did most Americans remain neutral. Many believed that Germany had ruthlessly crushed neutral Belgium. They despised German militarism and feared their new weapons such as submarines and poison gas. On the other hand, the British angered the United States with their attempts to control American policy. And much of the large American-Irish community rooted for defeat of the English.

Wilson's greatest problem became protection of American trade and commerce. In late August 1914, the British navy initiated an economic blockade of the Central Powers and announced it would search ships for contraband. Most of the goods that the Germans wished to import and the Americans hoped to export were on the banned list. Strict enforcement of the blockade caused periodic breaches between the British and the Wilson government, particularly in the fall of 1915 and the summer of 1916.

The British tried to appease American objections while they vigorously pressed their economic strangulation of Germany. Skillful diplomacy and a large increase in British purchases of American goods made the policy work. For example, when the British placed cotton on the contraband list in 1915, they simultaneously bought American cotton to make up for the lost trade. In 1914, the value of American trade with Britain was about $600 million annually. By 1917, it had increased to over $2 billion. Smaller to begin with, German trade fell to almost nothing in 1917.

In effect, Wilson accepted the British blockade. The Germans, therefore, had to choose. They could let British-American trade flourish, or they could block it and risk sinking American ships. Germany tried at first to impose a blockade against the British Isles. Its only effective weapon was a fleet of submarines. Although no match for naval vessels on the surface, these U-boats wreaked havoc on undefended merchant ships.

For two years, the Germans pursued an intermittent policy of sinking merchant ships. But they dared not use their full powers for fear of forcing the United States into war. This possibility loomed in May 1915 when, without warning, a German U-boat sank the passenger ship *Lusitania*. Although carrying some war materiel, the ship had 2,000 passengers aboard. Struck by a torpedo, the ship floundered and sank; 1,200 persons, including 128 Americans, perished.

Rejecting any excuses or explanations, Wilson demanded that the Germans immediately end their attacks on merchant ships. William Jennings Bryan, rather than send this ultimatum, resigned as secretary of state. His successor, Robert Lansing, was far more antagonistic to the Germans. But the crisis died down by summer, when the German government promised to refrain from attacking passenger ships.

The next serious confrontation occurred in the spring of 1916 when a U-boat sank the *Sussex,* an unarmed Channel steamer. This time Lansing sent an ultimatum to Germany. Either stop attacking "passenger and freight carrying vessels" he warned, or the United States would break diplomatic relations. Germany retreated. In the meantime, America and the Allies moved closer, as Wilson allowed the British and French to borrow large sums of money from American bankers.

By the winter of 1916–1917, the Germans had decided they could win the war quickly by attacking all shipping to the Allies. They had opted for war with America. An exacerbating factor had been publication of an intercepted note from Alfred Zimmermann, the German foreign secretary, that spoke of an alliance with Mexico—with recovery of Texas, New Mexico, and Arizona as part of the agreement—which infuriated American public opinion. Then on February 1, 1917, Germany declared unrestricted submarine warfare against shipping. Three days later the United States severed diplomatic relations.

## War and Peace

Wilson had always made it clear that in or out of the war the United States desired a hand in settling the peace. This was the essence of his mission diplomacy. On January 22, 1917, he informed the Senate of his goals: peace without victory, the spread and support of self-government in Europe, freedom of the seas, and world disarmament. He also outlined an organization that would later become the League of Nations.

### DEFENSE EXPENDITURES BY SERVICE: 1895–1920

| Year | Army | Navy |
|------|------|------|
| 1895 | $51,805,000 | $28,798,000 |
| 1899 | 229,841,000 | 63,942,000 |
| 1903 | 118,630,000 | 82,618,000 |
| 1907 | 149,775,000 | 97,128,000 |
| 1911 | 197,199,000 | 119,938,000 |
| 1915 | 202,060,000 | 141,836,000 |
| 1919 | 9,009,076,000 | 2,002,311,000 |

Source: U.S. Department of Commerce, Bureau of the Census, *Historical Statistics of the United States: Colonial Times to the Present,* bicentennial ed. (Washington, D.C.: Government Printing Office, 1975), Vol. II, p. 1114.

# AMERICANS AT WAR

## World War I

World War I began in the Balkans, the most politically volatile area of Europe; it infected two tottering empires, Russia and Austria-Hungary; and it quickly spread to the most advanced industrial nations. Since the 1870s and the swift industrialization of Germany, Europe had embarked on an arms race, with each side fearing isolation and encirclement. Germany formed the Triple Alliance with Austria-Hungary and Italy. France signed an agreement with Russia and then an *entente cordiale* ("friendly understanding") with Great Britain. Competition between these two groups of nations had world-wide ramifications. Germany sought to overcome Britain's predominance in international trade and to acquire the colonies and naval bases befitting a modern imperial nation. Rivalry between these two powers inevitably came to involve other industrial nations, including the United States.

The war broke out along the explosive edges of Austria-Hungary and Russia. Austria-Hungary sought to repress Slavic nationals, who were supported by Russia in areas bordering the Ottoman Empire (present-day Turkey), Greece, and Rumania. On June 28, 1914, a member of the Serbian nationalist group "Black Hand" assassinated Archduke Francis Ferdinand, heir to the Austro-Hungarian crown. Austria declared war, the Russians (supported by France) mobilized, and Germany declared war on Russia on August 1 and on France on August 3. Britain entered the war against Germany on August 4.

Even before its official declaration of war, Germany had initiated what it planned to be a rapid, fatal blow to France. On August 1, German troops, in accordance with the Schlieffen plan (named after the former chief of staff Count Alfred von Schlieffen) attacked. Disregarding treaties, Germany poured troops through neutral Belgium and toward northern France, hoping to trap the bulk of the French army up against heavy German defenses that lay along the northeastern borders of France. Then, with France knocked out of the war, the German armies could shift rapidly by railroad to battle the Russians.

To the dismay of the French and the British, the Schlieffen plan worked well. Belgium reeled and collapsed under the hammer blows of the advancing German armies. British troops rushed to northern France. By early September, German armies had occupied important areas of northern France. The Allies chose this moment to counterattack along the Marne River. The battle raged from September 5 to 12, resulting in 500,000 casualties. Despite its indecisive result and lack of a clear winner, the German advance now stalled; France was spared. German plans had not anticipated the resilience of the French and British armies nor the logistical difficulties of supplying and commanding an extensive force over long lines of communication. Now the war settled down to a stalemate, disrupted by intermittent bloody thrusts to secure limited territory. Both sides constructed elaborate networks of trenches and defensive positions ringed with barbed wire and separated from each other by a "no man's land."

The relative immobility of the forces in France was influenced by the technology available to each side at the time. The principal weapons, artillery and the machine gun, exacted a terrible price in manpower but could not, in themselves, turn the tide of

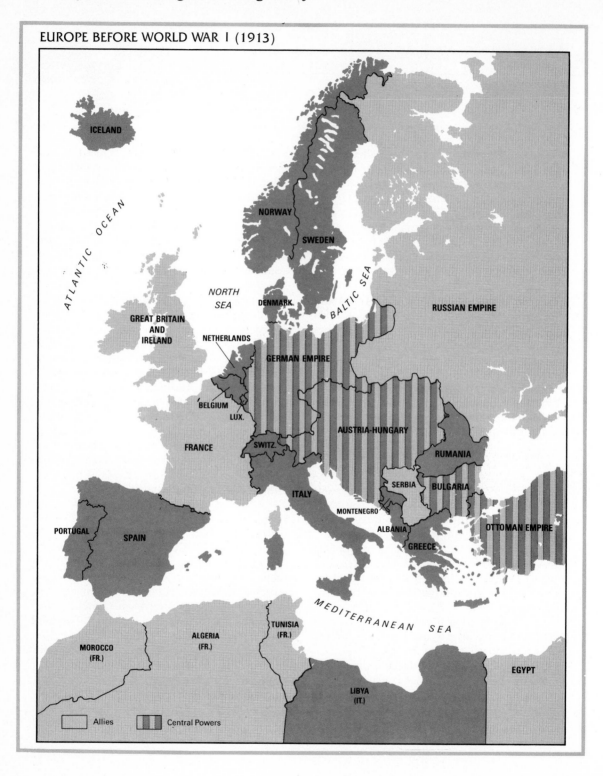

EUROPE BEFORE WORLD WAR I (1913)

battle. Mounted cavalry, which had always been important in earlier wars, proved ineffectual. New weapons like tanks and airplanes were too few to be decisive. Understandably, each side sought tactics or new weapons that might tip the balance. The Germans developed and employed poison gas, which they first used in 1916. And to overcome their inferior naval position, the Germans deployed submarines, which effectively attacked British shipping.

On the Eastern front, the Germans were more effective because they excelled in equipment, training, and command. Joined by the Ottoman Empire and Bulgaria, Germany and Austria (the Central Powers) inflicted huge losses on the Russians. Despair, disorganization, starvation, and revolution stalked Russia. The czar was desposed in March 1917,

and the Bolsheviks took power in November. In mid-December, Russia signed an armistice with Germany, whose troops were now freed for a final push on the Western front.

Despite this stunning victory, Germany was still overextended. Its allies, the Turks and the Austro-Hungarians, suffered discouraging defeats. More serious was the tight economic blockade around Germany enforced by the British navy. Consequently, the German general staff decided in the winter of 1917 to try one last, decisive assault. First, the submarine fleet was ordered to attack all Allied and neutral ships sailing to and from Britain and France—a move that precipitated U.S. entry into the war. Then, in the spring of 1918, the Germans initiated a massive ground offensive, hoping to win the war be-

## U.S. PARTICIPATION IN ALLIED OFFENSIVES, 1918

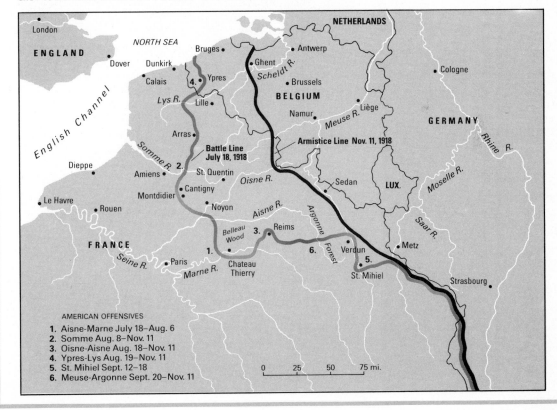

AMERICAN OFFENSIVES
1. Aisne-Marne July 18–Aug. 6
2. Somme Aug. 8–Nov. 11
3. Oisne-Aisne Aug. 18–Nov. 11
4. Ypres-Lys Aug. 19–Nov. 11
5. St. Mihiel Sept. 12–18
6. Meuse-Argonne Sept. 20–Nov. 11

0    25    50    75 mi.

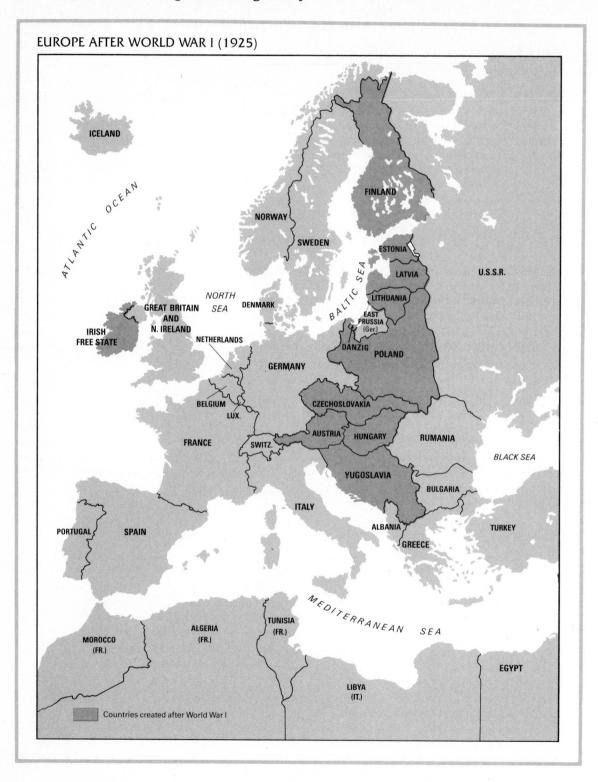

EUROPE AFTER WORLD WAR I (1925)

ICELAND

ATLANTIC OCEAN

NORWAY

SWEDEN

FINLAND

ESTONIA

LATVIA

LITHUANIA

U.S.S.R.

NORTH SEA

BALTIC SEA

DENMARK

EAST PRUSSIA (Ger.)

DANZIG

POLAND

GREAT BRITAIN AND N. IRELAND

IRISH FREE STATE

NETHERLANDS

GERMANY

BELGIUM

LUX.

CZECHOSLOVAKIA

FRANCE

SWITZ.

AUSTRIA

HUNGARY

RUMANIA

YUGOSLAVIA

BLACK SEA

PORTUGAL

SPAIN

ITALY

BULGARIA

ALBANIA

GREECE

TURKEY

MOROCCO (FR.)

ALGERIA (FR.)

TUNISIA (FR.)

MEDITERRANEAN SEA

LIBYA (IT.)

EGYPT

Countries created after World War I

fore American manpower could tip the scales against them. After a declaration of war in April, the United States rushed troops and supplies to the front and also helped to suppress the German submarine attacks.

In five offensives, lasting from March through July, the Germans broke through at several points. Paris came under attack by long-range artillery. But a counteroffensive by the Allies in mid-July turned the Germans back. Aided by fresh American troops and materiel, the Allies initiated the second battle of the Marne. Exhausted German troops reeled in the face of a successful fall offensive by the Americans, British, and French. Germany's ambitions were shattered.

After a revolution in November, a new German government signed an armistice on November 11. Germany, Austria-Hungary, and the Ottoman Empire watched, helplessly, as the Allied powers redrew the maps of Europe and the Middle East. Even at the end of the Paris Peace Conference in 1919, Europe still lay devastated, with transportation, industry, and agriculture in shambles, governments in turmoil, and over 14 million persons dead.

Thus when German attacks on U.S. shipping forced the nation into war early in the spring of 1917, Wilson had already anticipated how the final peace treaty might be drawn.

The declaration of war was passed by an overwhelming majority of the Congress: 82 to 6 in the Senate and 373 to 50 in the House. American troops did not reach the front until the latter part of 1917, but the navy and merchant marine rushed to protect trade routes to England and France. In 1918, the Germans tried for a quick, decisive victory. They struck five times between March and July. Successful in some respects, these moves ultimately exhausted and disheartened the German troops. Over the summer and fall, the Allies struck back. By this time, fresh American troops had entered the contest. After a final offensive in September, the Allies advanced sharply and the Germans retreated. By November, Germany had been routed. On November 11, 1918, the two sides signed an armistice and maneuvering for a peace settlement began. These were Wilson's most glorious and tragic moments.

Early in January 1918, Wilson had publicized his peace proposals—the Fourteen Points. Some of these—such as the return to France of Alsace-Lorraine and independence for the peoples of the Austro-Hungarian and Turkish empires—coincided with Allied aims. But others did not. For example, freedom of the seas and removal of trade barriers could be construed as an attack on the British Empire. Among all the points, the proposed League of Nations to guarantee world peace was most important to Wilson, although some Allies viewed it with indifference.

The president traveled to Europe in early 1919, a hero to the huge crowds who greeted him. But in the peace negotiations he had no real power to impose his demands upon the Allies. Thus he compromised: punitive territorial and economic measures to be exacted from the Germans; the German protectorate of Kiachow in China to be transferred to the Japanese. He did, however, win on the League of Nations. On June 28 the Germans, under duress, signed the treaty in the splendid Hall of Mirrors at Versailles Palace outside Paris. Although something of a personal victory for Wilson, the negotiations had taken a heavy toll. One observer remarked: "I found him looking utterly worn out, exhausted, often one side of his face twitching with nervousness."

Wilson brought the treaty back to a deeply divided and war-weary America. The Democratic party had lost control of Congress in 1918, and Henry Cabot Lodge, an opponent of the treaty and the League of Nations, now headed the Senate Foreign Relations Committee. To such opponents, the treaty, and especially the League of Nations, seemed destined to entangle the United States forever in the machinations of Eu-

"VIVE WILSON!"

This electric sign in Paris (which translates as "Long live Wilson!") was part of the hero's welcome accorded to President Woodrow Wilson when he traveled to Europe in 1919 to negotiate a peace treaty. Despite his personal popularity Wilson won only a compromise from America's European allies when he asked for a less harsh and punitive treaty against Germany. *(U.S. Signal Corps, in The National Archives)*

ropean politics. To some, this appeared not to be a fitting culmination of a war to end wars and make the world permanently safe for democracy; it seemed, instead, to risk recurring wars. Moreover, the war had caused enormous strains in American society.

Some of these strains must be blamed on Wilson. He had allowed an overzealous George Creel to wage a vociferous propaganda campaign in favor of the war, using the new Committee on Public Information. Unfortunately, the committee had oversold its case. Attacks on civil liberties also soured Wilson's efforts. The Espionage Act of June 1917 and the Sedition Act of May 1918 effectively outlawed criticism of the American government, its leaders, and its national symbols. Intolerance was also aimed at German-Americans. In areas of large German immigrant populations in the Midwest, local authorities tried to suppress the German language and German culture. Popular writers like Burroughs depicted Germans as degenerate beasts in their fiction. Racial intolerance also flared in this charged atmosphere, erupting in a violent race riot in 1917 in East St. Louis, Illinois, in which thirty-nine blacks and nine whites died.

Attacks on radical political groups were also intense. This "red scare" drew energy from fears of the Russian Revolution of 1917; the organization of revolutionary communist organizations in the United States, which changed the face of American radicalism; and a series of widespread strikes. Socialist leaders like Eugene Debs who spoke against the war were imprisoned. And the government attacked the Industrial Workers of the World, seized their records, and deported many of their members. In this atmosphere of fear and suspicion, it was easy to conclude that America's active participation in the war—its pursuit of the new foreign policy—had resulted in contaminating the nation with the class struggle and the disorders of Europe. It seemed to threaten to compromise American uniqueness.

For a nation worried about such questions, the Versailles Treaty was both too full of idealism and too riddled with compromises. Worse, it tied the United States to a permanent world organization. Wilson demanded its acceptance. Trying to arouse public support, to work around strong and articulate opposition in the Senate, he embarked on a futile speaking tour in late summer in 1919. On September 25, 1919, in Pueblo, Col-

# John Reed

(Culver Pictures)

Soon we were near the battle. In the east, across the vast level country, a faint gray light appeared. The noble alamo trees, towering thickly in massy lines along the ditches to the west, burst into showers of bird-song. It was getting warm, and there came the tranquil smell of earth and grass and growing corn—a calm summer dawn. Into this the noise of battle broke like something insane. The hysterical chatter of rifle fire, that seemed to carry a continuous undertone of screaming—although when you listened for it it was gone. The nervous, deadly stab—stab—stab of the machine guns, like some gigantic woodpecker. The cannon booming like great bells, and the whistle of their shells. Boom—Pi-i-i-e-e-a-uuu! And that most terrible of all the sounds of war, shrapnel exploding. Crash—Whee-e—eaaa!!!

Like the juxtaposition of dreamy romanticism and brutal reality in this passage from his book *Insurgent Mexico,* John Reed's life represented a mixture in suspension of romantic and revolutionary elements. Born in 1887 in Portland, Oregon, John Reed grew up a sheltered and wealthy young man. Until the age of sixteen or so, he was a thin and sickly boy. By the time he entered Harvard College in 1906, however, he had conquered physical weakness. He had also begun to write fiction.

At Harvard, Reed continued his writing, contributing stories and poems to the school's famous publication *The Lampoon.* He also took up with a group of young radicals and socialists. Among them was the future political writer and essayist, Walter Lippmann. By the time Reed graduated, he had become an accomplished prose stylist, although certainly not the poet that his classmate T. S. Eliot was.

Like another famous Western writer of his day, Jack London, Reed thirsted for experience to give his prose the hard edge of realism. For a young man, the best way to find experience was in travel. Although he voyaged first to Europe, he quickly set his sights on New York, his "enchanted city."

Living in Greenwich Village, which was still a quaint, cheap backwater of the city, Reed plunged into the district's bohemian life, with its all-night discussions, passionate love affairs, and revolutionary politics. A friend of many of the century's young experimental painters and poets, Reed himself turned more and more to journalism. But this was not the typical journalism of his day. He insisted on being part of what he observed, on merging himself into revolutionary struggles, such as the one in Mexico, that seemed to be breaking out across the world.

So this poet and revolutionary trudged along the lines with Pancho Villa, the radical general of the Mexican Revolution, sending back dramatic articles describing the struggle. In 1917, Reed found himself in Russia, a participant in and recorder of the events of the Communist Revolution. This account he published in a famous and controversial book, *Ten Days That Shook the World.* In 1920, he died in Moscow, victim of an influenza epidemic, still a romantic . . . and a revolutionary . . . buried in the wall of the Kremlin as a hero of the Russian Revolution.

orado, he renewed his vision of America's destiny: "We have accepted [the truth of America's moral vision] and we are going to be led by it, and it is going to lead us, and through us the world, out into pastures of quietness and peace such as the world never dreamed of before."

These were the words of a man who saw not just a dream of world peace but perhaps also his own final peace. The next day he collapsed, and he never fully regained his old vigor. The Versailles Treaty languished in Congress; Wilson refused to compromise on the League, and the Senate refused to accept the treaty as written. The dream of putting the world in order receded.

Picking up the burden to set the world right was easy enough for the writers—and readers—of popular literature to imagine. The power of the myth of America's uniqueness and mission could inspire historians, patriots, and dreamers. The variant of this myth that Edgar Rice Burroughs created in 1911–1912, on the eve of America's assumption of mission diplomacy, was—like the new foreign policy itself—a new way of envisioning America's role in the world. But the cold reality of war forced Americans to ask the hardest question of all: Was America really unique, or was this idea just a national fiction?

## SUGGESTED READINGS, CHAPTERS 33–34

### DIPLOMATIC HISTORY

The field of American foreign relations at the turn of the century has recently undergone a rich and fruitful debate. The best early works in the field established the outlines of American diplomatic history. Samuel Flagg Bemis, *The Latin American Policy of the United States* (1943), is a classic study of the intricacies of diplomacy. Dexter Perkins, *A History of the Monroe Doctrine, 1867–1907* (1955), traces the development of American attitudes toward other Western Hemisphere nations. Charles S. Campbell's *The Transformation of American Foreign Relations, 1865 to 1900* (1976), provides an excellent, balanced, and updated account of American foreign policy in this period.

Much of the dispute over the meaning of America's foreign relations was initiated after the publication of William Appleman Williams, *Tragedy of American Diplomacy,* revised ed. (1962). This work began a critical re-evaluation of the motivations and accomplishments of foreign policy. Another principal work in this vein is Walter LaFeber, *The New Empire: An Interpretation of American Expansion, 1860–1898* (1963). LaFeber explores the economic and ideological impulses that triggered the American quest for empire. An excellent study in this tradition that focuses on the Orient is Thomas J. McCormick, *The China Market: America's Quest for Informal Empire, 1893–1901* (1967).

### IMPERIALISM

A key problem to emerge in the debate over foreign relations was the meaning of imperialism and the degree to which American policy makers shared imperialist ambitions. Thomas G. Paterson, ed., in *American Imperialism and Anti-Imperialism* (1973), presents the writings of imperialists and anti-imperialists as they debated such questions as acquisition of the Philippines. The best examination of the leading participants in the debate is in Robert L. Beisner, *Twelve Against Empire: The Anti-Imperialists, 1898–1900* (1968). In connection with this issue, a fascinating and influential document is Alfred Mahan's *The Influence of Sea Power Upon History* (1957). Ernest R. May, in his thoughtful *American Imperialism: A Speculative Essay* (1968), offers a different view of the origins and nature of the imperialism debate at the turn of the century.

### LATIN AMERICAN POLICY

American foreign relations in the progressive era related largely to Latin America. Theodore Roosevelt helped establish a new foreign policy toward America's southern neighbors. A good place to begin study of Roosevelt is John Morton Blum, *The Republican Roosevelt,* 2nd ed. (1977). A lively and interesting account of the Spanish-American War is Frank Freidel, *The Splendid Little War* (1958). P. Edward Haley, *Revolution and Intervention: The Diplomacy of Taft and Wilson with Mexico, 1910–1917* (1970), untangles the complicated and very important relations of the United States with Mexico prior to World War I.

# 35 · Lindbergh's Flight

The captain was a little man, dapper and very French. But he sought a big prize: $25,000 for the first man to fly an airplane from New York to Paris. His name might sound somewhat strange—even funny—to American ears: René Fonck. But his reputation was formidable. He had been the youngest French air ace in the Great War of 1914 (as World War I was known until World War II). Without being seriously injured himself, he had shot down at least seventy-five German planes. In a war that had turned the new aviators into overnight heroes, Fonck's reputation for skill, courage, and "dash" was probably greater than that of any other pilot. Now, in the summer of 1926, he was preparing for a flight that could make him an even greater hero, both in France and in the United States.

Compared with any of the planes Fonck had flown during the war, his new silver-colored craft was huge. Like most of the other large aircraft of the day, it had three engines and two wings—a biplane, it was called. Its large cabin was equipped for a crew of four: a pilot, a copilot, a mechanic, and a radio operator. The problem that Fonck faced was simply getting the plane off the ground with enough fuel to fly the 3,600 miles to Paris. All summer he tested the plane in New York, gradually increasing the gasoline load for each test.

At daybreak on September 21 Fonck's plane was pulled onto the east-west runway at Roosevelt Field, a small airport on Long Island. The wind was blowing from the west, as it almost always does after dawn on Long Island. So Fonck would take off from east to west. To get the plane off the ground he and his crew would have to attain a speed of 80 miles an hour. One by one, the engines were turned up to their maximum power. The blocks were pulled away from the wheels, and the plane began to move. It lurched slightly, having over 2,000 gallons of gasoline aboard, and chased its own awkward shadow down the dirt runway.

When the plane passed the halfway point on the small airstrip, it did not have the speed needed for takeoff. The small crowd of onlookers waited for Fonck to cut power. But something had gone wrong, either with the pilot or with his controls. The plane simply roared on. The runway ended. The plane took a sharp, short drop into a gully, then exploded and burst into flames. Somehow Fonck got out, and so did his navigator. But the copilot and the radio operator burned to death.

Despite the crash, the man who had offered the $25,000 prize—Raymond Orteig, a Frenchman who managed two hotels in New York—announced that his offer still stood. For a while Fonck's crash made headlines and kept alive the idea of a New York–Paris flight. Late in February 1927, others began to announce that they would make the flight. It was soon obvious that a real contest was developing. It would not be merely a battle between one airplane and the ocean but a race among several aviators and their planes. The stage was set for what the public began to sense would be the greatest thrill of the decade.

By the end of March 1927 there were four serious contenders. One was the *America,* a plane piloted by Admiral Richard E. Byrd, who had gained fame as the first man to fly to the North Pole. Byrd was backed with over $100,000 from a wealthy New York merchant. His three-engined plane, with a wingspan of over 70 feet, was huge by the standards of the day. It seemed to have the best chance.

A second entry was another trimotored craft, the *American Legion,* named after and supported by the veterans' organization. It too was backed with $100,000. Unlike Fonck's plane and Byrd's *America* the *American Legion* carried only two men. A third entry was a plane known as the *Columbia,* a single-winged, single-engined craft. The *Columbia* would soon set the world endurance record by flying for over fifty hours. Finally, there was a French entry, a single-engined biplane called the *White Bird.* Its pilot and copilot, a pair of French aces from the Great War, planned to make the flight in reverse—from Paris to New York. The *White Bird* was said to have the most powerful gasoline engine ever put into an airplane.

By mid-April the weather had warmed up enough to make flight over the North Atlantic seem possible. On April 16, Commander Byrd took his *America* up from a New Jersey airport for its first test flight. Byrd and three crewmen tested the plane for a few hours and then brought it down for its first landing. The heavy landing gear touched ground smoothly. But almost at once there was a sound of splintering wood and wrenched metal. The *America* flipped over and skidded to a halt on its back. All four men managed to escape. Byrd had a broken wrist, and two of the other crewmen were badly hurt. They would not be able to fly again for weeks.

Ten days later the *American Legion* was in Langley Field, Virginia, undergoing its last test flight. The plane had flown well in earlier attempts. But both its designers and its pilot knew it was too heavy. To find out whether the plane could make the Paris flight, the pilot and copilot decided to fly it from Virginia to New York with a full load of gasoline. The takeoff was slower than usual. For a moment it seemed as if the plane would not clear a line of trees at the end of the runway. To avoid them, the pilot banked to the right a few degrees. The slight turn was too much. It upset the delicate balance of the plane. The *American Legion* slid downward into a wet marsh and turned over. The pilot and copilot were trapped inside the cabin that filled first with gasoline fumes and then with water. By the time rescuers came wading through the marsh, the two men were dead.

Four men had been killed and three others hurt, and the race over the Atlantic had not yet begun. On both sides of the ocean, in America and in France, newspapers stirred public excitement to a high pitch. Surely one of the planes would make it sooner or later. But no one knew what might happen next or who might be injured or killed. The race to Paris had the competitive excitement of a World Series or a heavyweight championship fight. And it had the danger and drama of war. In the United States, the race gained as much importance in the public's mind as had the war of 1898, the sinking of the *Lusitania,* or the declaration of war in 1917. In France the excitement was heightened by the memory of Fonck's crash. Moreover, the entry into the contest of two other young ace pilots from the Great War, Charles Nungesser and Francis Coli, held great promise. Both had been wounded a total of twenty-six times in air combat. Between them they had won almost every medal that their government could award.

At dawn on May 8, Nungesser and Coli took off for New York from Le Bourget airport near Paris. A great crowd gathered to watch the two heroes and their *White Bird.* Nungesser got the wheels off the ground, but too soon. The *White Bird* dropped back down on the runway with a thud. Finally, it gathered speed and left the ground almost two-thirds of a mile down the long strip.

The next morning, American newspapers reported that the plane had been sighted over Newfoundland. Paris celebrated with an excitement that almost matched that on the day of the armistice. Nungesser and Coli had dropped their landing gear over the ocean to save weight and lessen wind resistance. New Yorkers watched the harbor where the Frenchmen hoped to land and keep afloat until they could be reached by waiting boats. But the *White Bird* was never seen again. In France the celebrations quickly came to a shocked end.

The death toll in the New York–Paris race had reached six in less than a year. The world's most experienced pilots—backed by large sums of money, flying the best airplanes that modern technology could provide, with the most powerful motors ever developed—had all failed.

The man who was finally going to win the race to Paris had been reading every newspaper report he could find on all the airplane tests, takeoffs, and crashes. When Fonck's plane burned, Charles Lindbergh was flying airmail between Chicago and St. Louis. When Byrd and the others announced that they would enter the competition, Lindbergh was in San Diego supervising the construction of a new plane for himself. When Nungesser and Coli took off from Paris, he was waiting in San Diego for the weather to clear over the Rocky Mountains and the Great Plains, so he could fly east to St. Louis. From there he would go on to New York to make his attempt.

Lindbergh had only $2,000 of his own money, carefully kept for him by his mother in Detroit. He was only twenty-five years old. He looked even younger, so that almost everyone called him a boy. Worst of all, he decided on what struck everyone as a suicidal idea: to make the flight in a single-engine plane with only himself in the cockpit. He had been able to persuade some St. Louis businessmen to back him to the extent of $15,000. But this was a small sum compared to the support that Byrd's group and the *American Legion* had. Still, late in the summer of 1926, just before Fonck's crash, Lindbergh had come to an almost religious conviction that he could make the Paris flight.

At first Lindbergh tried to negotiate with several large aircraft companies. He was turned down. No one wanted to risk a company's reputation on an insane stunt like flying from New York to Paris alone. Then Lindbergh sent a plain but daring telegram to Ryan Airlines, a small, little known factory in California:

RYAN AIRLINES, INC.                          FEB. 3, 1927
SAN DIEGO, CALIFORNIA

CAN YOU CONSTRUCT WHIRLWIND ENGINE PLANE
CAPABLE OF FLYING NONSTOP BETWEEN NEW YORK AND
PARIS. IF SO PLEASE STATE COST AND DELIVERY DATE.

Surprisingly, the answer came quickly. The small company could build the plane, and it could do so for the amount of money Lindbergh had at his disposal. But it would take three months, the telegram said. Lindbergh answered:

RYAN AIRLINES                                FEB. 5, 1927
SAN DIEGO, CALIFORNIA

COMPETITION MAKES TIME ESSENTIAL. CAN YOU
CONSTRUCT PLANE IN LESS THAN THREE MONTHS.
PLEASE WIRE GENERAL SPECIFICATIONS.

Again the company answered quickly, making as much of a guess as a calculation. It could build a plane capable of carrying 380 gallons of gasoline at a cruising speed of 100 miles per hour, with an engine rated at only 200 horsepower. (This was less than half the power of the big engine that had taken the *White Bird* out over the Atlantic. It was also much less than the

**BEFORE THE FLIGHT**

This publicity photograph of Lindbergh and the *Spirit of St. Louis* was taken some time before the flight. Lindbergh may have been shy, but he fully understood the need to publicize his daring effort. And he knew how to emphasize the solitary nature of his flight by posing himself and his plane as though they were partners. *(National Air and Space Museum, Smithsonian Institution)*

power supplied by the three engines of Byrd's great *America*.) Most important, the company promised to have the plane ready in time.

By the last week in February, Lindbergh was in San Diego working out the details on his plane. Neither Lindbergh nor the engineer who designed the plane knew how far it was to Paris. They drove to the San Diego public library to measure off the distance on a globe with a piece of string. Lindbergh remembered it this way:

> "It's 3,600 miles." The bit of white grocery string under my fingers stretches taut along the coast of North America, bends down over a faded blue ocean, and strikes the land mass of Europe. It isn't a very scientific way of finding the exact distance between two points on the earth's surface, but the answer is accurate enough for our first calculations. The designer was making quick calculations in pencil on the back of an envelope. "Maybe we'd better put in 400 gallons of gasoline instead of 380," he concludes.

Lindbergh's project was simple, almost amateurish: hastily drafted telegrams, bits of string stretched across a public-library globe, figures on the back of an envelope, and "maybe" calculations. But with no more detailed or expert plans, he decided to go ahead.

The mechanics and carpenters at Ryan started work at once on the plane that Lindbergh would call the *Spirit of St. Louis*. They built it almost literally around the pilot. The narrow, simple cockpit was just large enough to hold Lindbergh's tall, skinny body (and then only if the overhead ribs were hollowed out a little to make room for his head). In the end the plane would be only about 3 feet taller than Lindbergh himself. Moreover, it would have a smaller engine than any of the other planes in the race. But this was the secret of Lindbergh's plane—simplicity. He would build the smallest, simplest plane possible, a machine designed with only one purpose: to carry enough gasoline for the trip. Everything else—comfort, safety, complicated navigating equipment—would be sacrificed to save weight, weight that could be turned into gallons of gasoline.

On April 26, the day the two pilots of the *American Legion* were killed in Virginia, the *Spirit of St. Louis* was finished. Two days later, Lindbergh was ready for his first test flight. He squeezed himself into his seat in the cockpit. He could touch the sides of the fuselage with his elbows. To the front, the cockpit was blind. Shiny metal sloped all the way up from the engine to the top of the wing. There were only two side windows and a glassed-in skylight overhead. For takeoffs and landings he had to lean out of one of the side windows. But the plane was designed for only one important takeoff and landing. The rest of the time, over the Atlantic, there would be nothing to see but ocean, clouds, sun, and stars.

Directly in front of Lindbergh's face was a small cluster of instruments—an air-speed indicator, a turn-and-bank indicator, a fuel-flow meter, a compass, and one or two others. The plane carried a pitifully small survival kit containing a rubber raft, a flashlight, a canteen of water, some matches, and string. Surrounding the cockpit were nothing but gasoline tanks. One tank rested in the nose between the pilot and the engine. Another lay behind the cockpit in the fuselage. And there were more tanks in the wings overhead. There was no radio, no heater to provide warmth at freezing altitudes, no sextant for navigational sightings, not even a parachute. The *Spirit of St. Louis* was built to carry only gasoline—over a ton of it, as it turned out, weighing more than the plane and the pilot put together.

To Lindbergh, as he walked onto the sunny runway in San Diego, the *Spirit of St. Louis* was a thing of beauty and awe:

What a beautiful machine it is, resting there on the field in front of the hangar, trim and slender, gleaming in its silver coat! All our ideas, all our calculations, all our hopes, lie there before me, waiting to undergo the acid test of flight. For me, it seems to contain the whole future of aviation.

"Off! Throttle closed."

I'm in the cockpit. The chief mechanic turns the propeller over several times.

"Contact!"

He swings his body away from the blade as he pulls it through. The engine catches, every cylinder hitting. This is different from any other cockpit I've been in before. The big fuel tank in front of me seems doubly large, now that I'm actually to fly behind it.

I signal the chocks [blocks in front of the wheels of the plane] away. The *Spirit of St. Louis* rolls lightly over the baked-mud surface of the field.

The *Spirit of St. Louis* moved very quickly. Its tanks were almost empty for this first test flight.

The tires are off the ground before they roll a hundred yards. The plane climbs quickly, even though I hold its nose down. There's a huge reserve of power. I spiral cautiously upward. I straighten out and check my instruments. I circle over the factory, watching little figures run outdoors to see the machine they had built actually flying overhead. I rock my wings and head across the bay.

During the next week Lindbergh tested the *Spirit of St. Louis* for speed, control, and, most important, takeoff under load. More and more gasoline was filtered by hand into the tanks for each run. With a load of slightly over 300 gallons the plane took off easily. But continued landings with large loads were dangerous. Lindbergh decided to stop the tests.

The *Spirit of St. Louis* had needed a little more than 1,000 feet of runway to take off with 300 gallons. From this and other data, the Ryan designers made a theoretical calculation that, fully loaded with 400 gallons, the plane would need 2,500 feet of hard runway. Rather than tempt fate, as the crew of the *American Legion* had done by testing with a full load, Lindbergh decided to trust the plane and the designers' arithmetic. He was ready. And he knew Byrd's *America* had been repaired and was undergoing final tests. The *Columbia*, too, was ready. Both planes were poised on Long Island. Time counted more than tests.

But time seemed to work against Lindbergh. A big storm blanketed the western United States, moving with painful slowness eastward. Lindbergh had to wait several days until the rain and clouds had moved east. On the evening of May 10 he began the first leg of his trip, from San Diego to St. Louis. He flew the 1,500 miles in record time. It was the longest nonstop solo flight ever made. Then, after a night's sleep, he headed for New York.

Lindbergh arrived on Long Island on May 12. He had set another record for the fastest transcontinental flight in history. The crews of Byrd's *America* and the *Columbia* came over to shake his hand and wish him luck. There was a crowd. Newspaper photographers and reporters pushed and shoved their way to Lindbergh, shouting for pictures and answers to their questions. A crowd of people climbed to the roof of a small building next to the hangar where Lindbergh parked the plane. Their weight caused a wall to collapse. Something new and strange was happening to Lindbergh. The newspapers and the public were making him into a hero, almost a myth.

Even without Lindbergh, the New York–Paris contest had all the elements of an exciting publicity event: death, drama, and competition. But Lindbergh's entry into the race added new elements. He was going alone, thus he

INSIDE THE *SPIRIT OF ST. LOUIS*

The cockpit of Lindbergh's plane was a model of stripped-down efficiency. The wicker seat may have been uncomfortable, but it was lightweight, and weight was Lindbergh's main concern. The plane had only side windows, so the pilot could not see much—for most of the flight, though, there was nothing to see. In any case, the most important thing Lindbergh had to watch for was ice on the wings. *(Culver Pictures)*

could become an object of hero worship in ways that the crews of the other planes could not. He was tall, thin, blue-eyed, and handsome in a boyish way. And along with his youthful good looks went other personality traits that soon endeared him to the newspapers. Above all, he was modest, shy, and simple.

All these traits combined to present a picture of an innocent young man ready to dare the impossible, alone. Lindbergh was the honest, plain-spoken, cowboy-like young man from the West. He was a modern David challenging the Eastern Goliaths, with their money, their experience, their financial backers, and their head start. In short, he was an underdog. The *Spirit of St. Louis*, too, was simple and seemingly innocent compared with the other planes in the race. It was a sentimental favorite.

Lindbergh could not leave his hotel room without being mobbed by people anxious to touch him "just for luck." And the newspapers played his story for all it was worth. They nicknamed him "Lucky," "The Flyin' Fool," or just "Lindy." (He had always been "Slim" to his friends.) All the hero worship that the Americans of the 1920s usually reserved for baseball players like Babe Ruth or movie stars like Rudolf Valentino was now showered on the twenty-five-year-old airmail pilot. The worship was made more serious by the fact that "The Flyin' Fool" was doing something real and dangerous, not merely hitting baseballs or posing for motion picture cameras.

In most ways this public personality created for the new celebrity was only a myth. Lindbergh may not have had Byrd's $100,000, but he had finally obtained solid backing from St. Louis businessmen. And even if the *Spirit of St. Louis* was smaller than the other planes, it was still a sophisticated piece of machinery, created by advanced technology. It was a little silly for newspapers to write of Lindbergh and his plane as though they were a cowboy hero and his beloved horse.

Nor was Lindbergh's background as simple as the newspapers tried to make it appear. He came from a well-to-do, educated family. His father had been a congressman. Lindbergh had been to college for a time and held a commission as captain in the Army Air Service Reserve and the Missouri National Guard. He had been chief pilot for the airmail company in St. Louis. He was, despite his youth, an experienced professional pilot, flying an advanced aircraft.

But there was just enough truth to the mythical picture to make it stick. It probably infected Lindbergh somewhat, too. He had always been a bit wild, even though he was shy. Cars, motorcycles, ice boats—anything that involved speed—had always fascinated him. When he was just twenty he dropped out of college to learn to fly. He bought his first craft, a war-surplus plane, even before he had made a solo flight, and he almost crashed it on his first takeoff.

Lindbergh had barnstormed all over the West, crashing regularly and surviving only with luck. He had walked on airplane wings while in flight and done dangerous parachute jumps for one aerial circus after another. Four times he had been forced to parachute for his life from planes that had collided, run out of gas, or gotten lost at night.

All this—combined with Lindbergh's shyness and boyishness, his faith in himself and his plane—did smack of something supernatural and mythical. So the hero worship that began almost as soon as he reached Long Island was probably inevitable. At times the publicity and the public attention irritated Lindbergh. Reporters went so far as to burst into his hotel room without knocking to discover what kind of pajamas, if any, he wore to bed. But the irritation could not overcome the excitement. Lindbergh was becoming, even before takeoff, a national hero.

The *Columbia* was scheduled to take off on May 13, the day after Lindbergh reached Long Island. But the weather was closed in over New York and the North Atlantic. The same storm that had delayed Lindbergh in San Diego was making its slow progress north and east. So the *Columbia* had to wait. Lindbergh was able to test and tune his engine, to check and recheck every instrument. A noisy crowd that sometimes numbered over a thousand gathered around the hangar to watch him. By May 16 he was ready. As far as he could tell, Byrd was ready too. In the *Columbia* organization there was a legal quarrel over who would be the pilot. One of the men who had trained for the flight had secured a court order preventing the plane from taking off without him. But the court order could be lifted at any minute. So there seemed to be a real chance that two or possibly even three planes would take off from Roosevelt Field on the same morning.

The storm persisted for three more days. Then, on the evening of May 19, the forecast called for clearing skies. Though it was not clearing rapidly, Lindbergh made his decision. He would fly, even if it meant taking off into a rainy sky from a muddy field. He bought five sandwiches "to go." A few hours later the *Spirit of St. Louis* was towed to the west end of the Roosevelt Field runway. Lindbergh had decided to take off before dawn. Not far behind the *Spirit of St. Louis* was the scorched area, marked by a bent propeller stuck into the ground as a tribute, where Fonck's plane had burned.

Slowly, carefully, mechanics strained five-gallon cans of gasoline into Lindbergh's plane. The tanks were oversized. They had a capacity of 450 gallons instead of the 400 that the designers had planned earlier. Lindbergh decided to fill them to the brim, even though it meant a dangerous overload for the takeoff. In the hangars of the *America* and the *Columbia,* there was only darkness and silence. No one else was going to fly.

As he looked over the situation, Lindbergh wondered whether he should go. He was overloaded with gasoline. The field was muddy. The wheels of the *Spirit of St. Louis* sank into the earth as though warning him that flight was out of the question. The wet weather affected the engine, which turned about thirty revolutions per minute slower than it should have at full power. Worst of all, the process of getting ready took so long that Lindbergh lost the night wind. By the time he was ready to fly, the breeze had shifted to his back, creating a tailwind of five or six miles per hour. This meant he would need even more speed on takeoff.

Lindbergh's only guidelines were the San Diego tests. They had demonstrated theoretically that he should be able to take off in 2,500 feet on a hard runway with no wind and with full engine power. At the end of the Roosevelt Field runway were a ditch, a tractor, some telephone wires and then a hill with a line of trees. He had to clear them all. He considered towing the *Spirit of St. Louis* through the misty rain and mud to the other end of the runway to get the help of the wind. He thought about postponing the flight altogether. But he decided to go.

Lindbergh looked around at the crowd that had gathered to watch. Nearby there were the mechanics, the engineers, several policemen, all looking into the dark cockpit at his pale face.

Their eyes are intently on mine. They've seen the planes crash before. I lean against the side of the cockpit and look ahead, through the idling blades of the propeller, over the runway's glistening surface. I study the telephone wires and the shallow pools of water through which my wheels must pass. A curtain of mist shuts off all trace of the horizon. Sitting in the cockpit, in seconds, minutes long, the conviction surges through me that the wheels *will* leave the ground, that the wings *will* rise above the wires, that it *is* time to start the flight.

I buckle my safety belt, pull goggles down over my eyes, turn to the men at the blocks, and nod. Frozen fingers leap to action. I brace myself against the left side of the cockpit and ease the throttle wide open.

The *Spirit of St. Louis* feels more like an overloaded truck than an airplane. The tires rut through mud as though they really were on truck wheels. Even the breath of wind is pressing me down. The engine's snarl sounds inadequate and weak.

A hundred yards of runway passes. How long can the landing gear stand such strain? I keep my eyes fixed on the runway's edge. I *must* hold the plane straight. Pace quickens—the tail skid lifts off ground—I feel the load shifting from wheels to wings. The halfway mark is just ahead, and I have nothing like flying speed.

The halfway mark streaks past. Seconds now to decide. I pull the stick back firmly, and—*the wheels leave the ground!* The wheels touch again. I ease the stick forward. Almost flying speed and nearly 2,000 feet ahead. The entire plane trembles. Off again—right wing low—pull it up—ease back onto the runway. Another pool, water drumming on the fabric [covering the fuselage]. The next hop's longer. I could probably stay in the air, but I let the wheels touch once more.

The *Spirit of St. Louis* takes herself off next time. Full flying speed. The controls taut, alive, straining—and still a thousand feet to the telephone wires. If the engine can hold out one more minute. Five feet, twenty, forty. Wires flash by underneath. Twenty feet to spare!

Green grass below—a golf links. People looking up. A low, tree-covered hill ahead. The *Spirit of St. Louis* seems balanced on a pinpoint, as though the slightest movement of controls would cause it to topple over and fall. Five thousand pounds suspended from those little wings. Five thousand pounds on a blast of air.

Now I'm high enough to steal glances at the instrument board. The earth inductor compass needle leans steeply to the right. I bank cautiously northward until it rises to the center line—65 degrees—the compass heading for the first 100-mile segment of my great-circle route to France and Paris. It's 7:54 A.M. Eastern daylight time.

Back in San Diego, when Lindbergh and the designer of the *Spirit of St. Louis* had measured the distance of the flight across a library globe, the string had made a straight line between New York and Paris. But on a flat map, where the lines of latitude are straightened out into parallels, the route had to bend into an arc known as a great circle. The route Lindbergh would take curved north and east from New York, up the east coast over Cape Cod, then out over the ocean to Nova Scotia. Lindbergh planned to change his course every hundred miles (about one hour's flying time in the *Spirit of St. Louis*). He would head a few degrees farther south and east across the southern coast of Newfoundland and then out over the North Atlantic.

As Lindbergh flew up the coast on this route, people waited on streets and housetops to watch him pass. Despite the fact that his navigating equipment was primitive, he managed to reach the Nova Scotia coast only a few miles off course. Every hour excited messages were telephoned to New York giving details of his progress. In the twelfth hour of his flight, Lindbergh passed over St. John's, Newfoundland, then out over the ocean:

I come upon it suddenly—the little city of St. John's, after skimming over the top of a granite summit. Farther ahead, the entrance to the harbor is a narrow gap with sides running up to the crest of a low coastal range. Twilight deepens as I plunge down into the valley. It takes only a moment, stick forward, engine throttled, to dive down over the wharves (men stop their after-supper chores to look upward) and out through the gap. North America and its islands are behind. Ireland is 2,000 miles ahead.

CHARLES AND ANNE MORROW LINDBERGH
After he became famous, Lindbergh married the daughter of a wealthy stockbroker. He and his wife never freed themselves from the publicity that had brought them together in the first place. This became an even more cruel fact after they lost a child to a kidnapper in one of the most celebrated crimes in American history. *(Culver Pictures)*

Throughout the flight Lindbergh faced the ever-present dangers of engine failure, storms, and the possibility of a structural weakness in the *Spirit of St. Louis* itself. But between Newfoundland and Ireland there were two additional dangers. The first was sleep. Lindbergh had not slept all the night before his takeoff. During the next night and the day after, as he flew over the ocean, he fought back the terrible temptation to close his eyes for just a few seconds of rest. Despite its virtues, the *Spirit of St. Louis* was not a very stable plane. Lindbergh knew that if he relaxed his hold on it for more than a moment, he might crash. He had to hold his eyes open with his hands. Once he even had to hit himself full force in the face to keep awake.

The second danger was ice. This hazard hit Lindbergh suddenly after he had climbed over 10,000 feet, trying to clear a bank of clouds about 200 miles east of Newfoundland. He was suddenly aware of being cold himself. (He had left the glass out of the side windows of the *Spirit of St. Louis,* hoping that the fresh air and engine noise would keep him alert.) Cold? He jerked himself wide awake. If *he* was cold, what about his plane?

Good Lord! There are things to be considered outside the cockpit! How could I forget! I jerk off a leather mitten and thrust my arm out the window. My palm is covered with stinging pinpricks. I pull the flashlight from my pocket and throw its beam on a strut. The entering edge is irregular and shiny! *Ice!*

I've got to turn around, get back to clear air—quickly!

Lindbergh fought the urge to turn quickly. He knew that if he did, the ice on the wings might cause the plane to go out of control. Instead, he eased the *Spirit of St. Louis* around in a long, slow curve back toward Newfoundland.

> I throw my flashlight [beam] onto the wing strut. Ice is thicker! Steady the plane. Everything depends on the turn indicator working till I get outside the cloud. Just two or three more minutes.
>
> My eyes sense a change in the blackness of my cockpit. I look out through the window. How bright! What safety have I reached! I was in the thunderhead for ten minutes at most, but it's one of those incidents that can't be measured by minutes. Such periods stand out like islands in a sea of time.

After this brief but dangerous encounter with the night sky, Lindbergh picked his way cautiously toward Ireland and dawn. (Since he was flying west to east, into the sunrise, he was experiencing the shortest night of any man before him in history.) He sipped cautiously at the quart canteen of water. For the rest of the time he just flew his plane, waiting for moonrise, then sunrise, then landfall. He later recalled the twenty-eighth hour of his flight.

> I keep scanning the horizon through breaks between squalls. Is that a cloud on the northeastern horizon, or a strip of low fog—or—*can it possibly be land?* It looks like land, but I don't intend to be tricked by another mirage. I'm only sixteen hours out of Newfoundland. I allowed eighteen and one-half hours to strike the Irish coast.
>
> But my mind is clear. I'm no longer half asleep. The temptation is too great. I can't hold my course any longer. The *Spirit of St. Louis* banks over toward the nearest point of land.
>
> I stare at it intently, not daring to believe my eyes, watching the shades and contours unfold into a coastline. Now I'm flying above the foam-lined coast, searching for prominent features to fit the chart on my knee. I've climbed to 2,000 feet so I can see the contours of the country better. Yes, there's a place on the chart where it all fits—Valentia and Dingle Bay, *on the southwestern coast of Ireland!* I can hardly believe it's true. I'm almost exactly on my route, closer than I hoped to come in my wildest dreams back in San Diego. What happened to all those detours of the night around the thunderheads? Where has the swinging compass error gone?
>
> Intuition must have been more accurate than reasoned navigation.
>
> The southern tip of Ireland! On course, over two hours ahead of schedule; the sun still well up in the sky, the weather clearing!

Now it was easy. So easy that Lindbergh himself fell into the temptation of making a myth out of his own achievement:

> I'm angling slowly back onto my great-circle route. I must have been within three miles of it when I sighted Ireland. An error of fifty miles would have been good dead reckoning under the most perfect conditions. Three miles was—well, what was it? Before I made this flight, I would have said carelessly that it was luck. Now, luck seems far too trivial a word, a term to be used only by those who've never seen the curtain drawn or looked on life from far away.

After Ireland the landmarks appeared rapidly—a lighthouse, the coast of England and the coast of France, "like an outstretched hand to meet me." For

PARIS WELCOMES LINDBERGH

At 10 P.M. the *Spirit of St. Louis* came to rest on the runway at Le Bourget airport just outside Paris. A huge crowd gathered, ready to rush onto the field to greet the man who overnight had become the epitome of a "real American." *(National Air and Space Museum, Smithsonian Institution)*

the first time Lindbergh felt hungry. He ate one of the sandwiches, stale and dry now, that he had bought in New York. He picked up a series of beacon lights marking the route between London and Paris. Then the city rose before him. He circled the brightly lit Eiffel Tower and then turned northeast to look for Le Bourget. "You can't miss it," he had been told. He was like a tourist.

It was almost ten o'clock at night in Paris. Lindbergh was confused by an incredible number of lights around the dark spot where the airport ought to be. A factory, he thought. He did not know that he had suddenly become the most famous man in the world. Thousands of Parisians had rushed out to the airport to greet the American flyer. The roads leading to Le Bourget were jammed with cars with headlights blazing.

Finally, Lindbergh was able to pick out floodlights showing the edge of a runway. He dragged the field once, flying low over it to check for obstructions—a tractor or maybe some sheep let out to crop the grass, he thought. He brought the plane in as carefully as possible, as though he were teaching a student to fly. The plane felt sluggish. By his own guess he still carried a lot of gasoline. His own reflexes seemed slow. Lindbergh had never landed the *Spirit of St. Louis* at night. He glided in at an angle so he could peer out of his side window.

It's only a hundred yards to the hangars now. I'm too high, too fast. Drop wing. Left rudder. Careful. Still too high. I push the stick over. Below the hangar roofs now. Straighten out. A short burst of the engine. Over the lighted areas. Sod coming up to meet me. Careful. Easy to bounce when you're tired. Still too fast. Tail too high. Hold off. Hold off. But the lights are far behind. Ahead, there's nothing but night. Give her the gun and climb for another try?

The wheels touch gently. Off again. No, I'll keep contact. Ease the stick forward. Back on the ground. Off. Back, the tail skid too. Not a bad landing, but I'm beyond the light. Can't see anything ahead. The field *must* be clear. Uncomfortable, though, jolting into blackness. Wish I had a wing light, but too heavy on the takeoff. Slower now, slow enough to ground-loop safely. Left rudder. Reverse it. The *Spirit of St. Louis* swings around and stops rolling, resting on the solidness of earth, in the center of Le Bourget.

I start to taxi back to the floodlights and hangars. But the entire field ahead is covered with running figures!

**THE HERO IN NEW YORK**

Lindbergh probably became a more famous celebrity, more quickly, than any American ever had. Here, in a nighttime parade in New York City, he is welcomed home among the crowds, the fanfare, and the flags that followed him everywhere. *(Culver Pictures)*

# A "New Era"

When Lindbergh completed his ground loop at Le Bourget and turned to taxi back to the lighted area around the hangars, all he could see was a running crowd. About 100,000 Frenchmen had broken through police lines to rush onto the field, almost hysterical over this new hero. All day, the transatlantic cables, the newspapers, and radios had been full of news of the flight. And for hours before Lindbergh landed, Parisians had been fighting heavy traffic to drive out to Le Bourget to greet this "Flyin' Fool."

As soon as the *Spirit of St. Louis* touched down, the crowd rushed the plane. Lindbergh was afraid (as he was to be for months, whenever he made announced landings anywhere in the world) that the people would lose their heads and run into his spinning propeller. When he tried to climb out of his cramped cockpit, the crowd grabbed him. For a long time, he could not even set foot on French soil, but was passed through the crowd, from shoulder to shoulder. In the din, he shouted for a mechanic, someone to protect the plane; but no one could hear or understand him.

In the log he kept of the flight, Lindbergh made this brief, slightly bitter entry: "May 20, Roosevelt Field, Long Island, New York, to Le Bourget Aerodrome, Paris, France. 33 hours. 20 min. Fuselage fabric badly torn by souvenir hunters." The first part of the entry, the flight, was what was significant to Lindbergh. But the second part, the half-crazed hero worship of the crowd, is just as important to understanding the full significance of what Lindbergh had done and become. In Paris, but even more in New York and dozens of other American cities, Lindbergh was adored. From the time he landed at Le Bourget, his life was not his own. People crowded around wherever he went. They stole his hats in restaurants. He could not keep shirts, or even underwear, because laundry employees swiped them for souvenirs.

More than any other man of his generation Lindbergh captured the imagination of his contemporaries. Newspapers printed more stories about him and his flight than they had about the death of President Wilson. More people—4 million the police said—turned out to see him in a New York parade than had even come out to look at any president. Something about Lindbergh and his feat touched a deep and responsive chord in the America of the 1920s.

On the face of it, there was no overwhelming reason for Lindbergh's fantastic fame. As a matter of cold fact, his flight had proven nothing—except that a superb pilot, blessed by some luck, could fly a specially built airplane 3,600 miles. The *Spirit of St. Louis* could carry no passengers and no cargo. In fact, Lindbergh had refused to carry even one pound of mail, though he was offered $1,000 to do so. Lindbergh was not even the first man to fly the Atlantic. Eight years earlier, in 1919, a British dirigible had done it *twice*. That year, too, an American seaplane had crossed from New York to England, landing several times on the ocean. And in the same year, two pilots had made it nonstop from Newfoundland to Ireland, to win a prize of $50,000—double Lindbergh's prize. For a variety of reasons, when Lindbergh made his flight in 1927, almost no one seemed to remember these earlier feats, while "Lucky Lindy" quickly became a household word.

The causes of Lindbergh's incredible celebrity have to be found outside his actual accomplishment. They lie in deep changes that had occurred in American society. Americans were excited about Lindbergh for reasons that had more to do with them than with him. They projected more significance into the event than it really had. When masses of people experience such excitement, they tend to see historical actors as demons or heroes. They oversimplify the world and thus make some new kind of sense out of their own lives. This process often has very little to do with reality. Lindbergh became a symbol. His contemporaries saw in him what they wanted to see, making him into a sort of mirror for the technological and social changes that had transformed American society in the twentieth century.

# REACHING A MASS AUDIENCE

One of the reasons for Lindbergh's rapid rise to fame was the publicity he received from the press and the radio. Since the 1890s, the newspapers of the United States had been increasing in number and circulation. They competed fiercely for the attention of the public. This expansion of newspapers was only part of an important revolution in communications that began in the nineteenth century and still continues today.

One by one, new inventions brought people's lives closer together. These included the telegraph, the telephone, the phonograph, the camera, the radio, and the motion picture. They created a world in which whole nations and continents could share almost simultaneously in distant events. Lindbergh's flight was covered intensely by the press, which transmitted its stories over telegraph and telephone lines. Lindbergh was also photographed mercilessly. His activities were recorded both in newspaper photographs and in the newsreels that accompanied the early silent motion pictures. Hour-by-hour reports of his famous flight were transmitted on the radio—an invention that had come into use only a few years before. As soon as Lindbergh landed in Paris, the news was flashed back to the United States by transatlantic telegraph cable.

In many ways, Lindbergh the hero was the creation of mass communications. He was the first celebrity to have the full advantage of every modern form of communication except television. (Television did not come into wide use until after World War II.)

## The Communications Revolution

The revolution in communications began with the telegraph, which linked California and New York more than half a century before Lindbergh's flight. During the same period, newspapers began to attract a mass audience. The telephone, too, contributed to the rapid and widespread circulation of information. In the first part of the twentieth century the number of telephones in use

skyrocketed, from a little over 1 million in 1900 to more than 10 million in 1915. By the time Lindbergh took off for Paris, practically every middle-class American home had its own telephone.

But the communications revolution did not gather full speed until the invention of the radio. The principle of wireless transmission of sound was almost as old as the telephone. In 1887, a German scientist had proved the existence of electrical waves in space. He speculated that they might be turned into signals. An Italian inventor, Guglielmo Marconi, applied the theory to wire-

### SELLING COMMUNICATION

This salesman for the Radio Corporation of America (RCA) is doing what he can to put this middle-class mother and her children in touch with the New Era. The car parked off to the left of the porch is very likely his, too. The product he is selling (probably with the option to buy on installments) was known as a "Radiola." The suffix "-ola" was one of the treasured marketing devices of the 1920s and survives today in a number of popular brand names and expressions, such as Motorola, Mazola, and payola. (RCA)

less transmission of telegraph signals in 1896. From then on it was only a matter of assembling the appropriate tubes, transmitters, and receivers.

In 1920, Americans heard their first commercial radio broadcast. The station was KDKA in Pittsburgh, and the program was a news report on the 1920 presidential election. Soon after that, the winner of the election, Warren G. Harding, installed a radio set in the White House. Gradually, Marconi's invention was transformed from a toy into a commercial reality. By the time Lindbergh made his flight to Paris, an estimated 10 million sets were in use in the United States, almost one for every telephone.

Two other inventions, the phonograph and the camera, furthered the revolution in mass communications. Thomas A. Edison found a way of capturing and recreating sound that was to make music available to millions at an instant. George Eastman's perfection of the camera made it possible for newspapers to include pictures on their pages.

All these changes allowed millions of people to participate indirectly in events they were not able to witness in person. In other words, these developing communications facilities had created a potential public that could take part in any happening, frown at any villain, worship any hero.

## A Middle-Class "Public"

The new public that celebrated Lindbergh's flight with such enthusiasm should not be confused with the whole nation. Lindbergh's fame was primarily a middle-class phenomenon. He was, in some ways, a media creation; and the media that made him catered primarily to white, well-to-do citizens. Even newspapers catered mainly to a middle-class audience. Radios and telephones were the property of the middle class almost exclusively. In 1927, the phonograph and the camera were still alien novelties to many millions of poor Americans. Whole great subpopulations—blacks, many poor white farmers, millions of immigrants in the cities—were practically excluded

from the new "public" that the mass media helped create.

Eventually, of course, the new inventions (and the television sets that completed the communications revolution) would become the common property of almost every American, rich or poor. But in the 1920s, and for some time after, they were still middle-class conveniences. If Lindbergh was a symbol of popular values, they were not necessarily values that belonged to all of America. They were the beliefs and hopes of white, middle-class citizens. At the time, it was easy and tempting for the members of this restricted "public" to believe that they *were* America. Most of them would have agreed quickly with the American ambassador to France, who said that Lindbergh represented "the spirit of our people." Similarly, the *New Republic,* a magazine with a small, highly educated audience, could say confidently that Lindbergh "is US personified." But the ambassador and the *New Republic* spoke carelessly. The "people" and the "US" they referred to were in fact only the public defined by the media.

As for the others, the majority—the poor, the blacks, the immigrants—there is no way to know what (if anything) they thought about Lindbergh. In all likelihood, if they noticed Lindbergh at all, it was only for a moment and with no special sense of identification with him or his feat. Like most of the cultural content of the Roaring Twenties, the Lindbergh phenomenon occurred mainly within the very class from which he had come. In fact, he may have served the need of this class to believe that it really did possess the spirit of the whole nation.

## THE MACHINE AND THE MAVERICK IN A TECHNOLOGICAL SOCIETY

Americans were fond of calling the period after World War I the New Era. Much of what they meant by the phrase was summed up symbolically in Lindbergh's airplane. The New Era was

# AMERICAN IMAGES
# People and Machines

During the summer of 1893, Henry Adams—historian, politician, essayist, and descendant of two presidents—traveled to Chicago to view the World's Columbian Exposition. Set in an artificial lagoon skirting the city's lakefront, the great fair presented the visitor with a unified vision, a "great White City" of display halls, fountains, and walkways. Adams was deeply moved by this unity of design and structure of molded and painted terra cotta and masonry. The fair proclaimed confidence, pride of accomplishment, and faith in the future. "Chicago," he wrote, "asked in 1893 for the first time the question whether the American people knew where they were driving."

PLATE 1.   In spite of its themes of progress and belief in the future, the World's Columbian Exposition at Chicago in 1893 consisted almost exclusively of buildings whose classical architecture evoked the past. The only exception was the Transportation Building, shown here. Its recurring arches celebrated motion and must have reminded most visitors of railway tunnels. *(New York Public Library/Picture Collection)*

Yet Adams foresaw a more uncertain future than the planners of the fair. As he thought about the exhibits of modern machinery, particularly the dynamo capable of generating electrical current, he sensed serious contradictions. For Adams, the dynamo was a symbol of power and force operating in ways that would drastically transform American society—for better or for worse. But he could not be sure which it would be.

Adams's choice of the dynamo to symbolize the modern age was a brilliant one. Quietly transforming energy into power, the dynamo represented one of the most potent machines of the era. Likewise, Adams's uncertainty over the machine-dominated future was farsighted. During the next forty-five years, up to World War II, machines dramatically reshaped American life, work habits, transportation, the shape of everyday objects, even toys. They made consumer items available that had been only dreamed of previously. But in the midst of this amazing transformation, artists, writers, and ordinary citizens sometimes wondered where the machine was leading.

Part of the wonder of the new machine age of the 1890s derived from a special machine perfected during the era. This was the camera. In use during the mid-nineteenth century for portraits and posed public events, the still camera was gradually improved. In 1895, a miniature portable camera using roll film, the "Brownie," brought cameras out of the studio to become a permanent and indispensable part of the home. Motion pictures became practical after Thomas A. Edison invented the 35 mm camera in 1889. Further developments shortly thereafter made it possible to film and develop longer motion pictures. By the second decade of the twentieth century, a huge new industry had sprung up, first in New York and New Jersey and then, after World War I, in Los Angeles.

The effect of the camera in refocusing America's vision and image of itself, cannot be exaggerated. People and places—the faces of political leaders, celebrities, relatives, and friends; the silhouettes of na-

PLATE 2.   The hand-held camera had become commonplace and almost indispensable by the 1920s. It made possible a permanent record of family and leisure activities of millions of Americans. *(The Bettmann Archive)*

PLATE 3.   By the 1930s, photography was securely established as an art form and a means of social commentary.  Margaret Bourke-White, one of the foremost photographers of the period (see also "American Images: Women—The War and After," Plate 1), took this picture of flood victims in Louisville, Kentucky, in 1937—a startling and grimly ironic reminder that not all Americans reaped the benefits of the Machine Age. *(Margaret Bourke-White, LIFE Magazine, © 1937 Time, Inc.)*

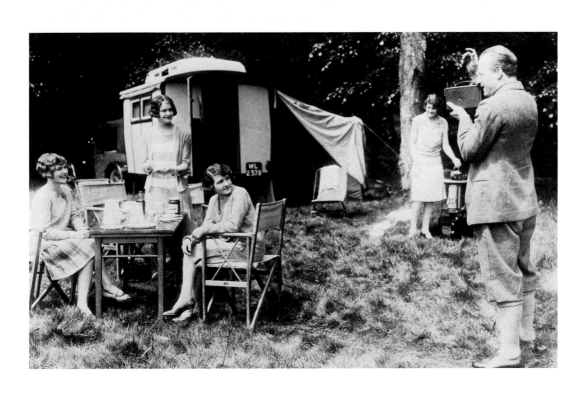

WORLD'S HIGHEST STANDARD OF LIVING

There's no way like the American Way

tional parks and monuments; the skylines of New York and Chicago—became familiar to everyone. By World War I, photography had also presented the nation with poignant pictures of the victims of exploitation and poverty, adding weight and authority to the proposals of the progressive reformers. By the 1930s, photography had earned a secure place as a public art form. Pictures carefully recorded the suffering of the Great Depression. Photographers such as Margaret Bourke-White became celebrities. Beginning in 1936, *Life* magazine provided millions of Americans with a weekly display of some of the finest contemporary photography.

One favorite subject of photographers and artists was machinery and objects transformed by machinery. With such images, they explored the contradictory attitudes of society about machines. Machines provided the energy to tame nature and transform the countryside. They created great man-made

PLATE 4.    Murals—such as *Detroit Industry* (1933) by the great Mexican artist Diego Rivera, a detail of which is shown here—were used to decorate public buildings during the 1930s. Very often, they emphasized the workings of industry and the shapes and sights of urban life. *(The Detroit Institute of Arts)*

Energy Consumption, 1890–1940 (in thousands of horsepower)

|  | 1890 | 1900 | 1910 | 1920 | 1930 | 1940 |
|---|---|---|---|---|---|---|
| Work animals | 15,970 | 18,730 | 21,460 | 22,430 | 17,660 | 12,510 |
| Factories | 6,308 | 10,309 | 16,697 | 19,422 | 19,519 | 21,768 |
| Mines | 1,445 | 2,919 | 4,473 | 5,146 | 5,620 | 7,332 |
| Railroads | 16,980 | 24,501 | 51,308 | 80,182 | 109,743 | 92,361 |
| Merchant ships | 1,124 | 1,663 | 3,098 | 6,508 | 9,115 | 9,408 |
| Sailing vessels | 280 | 251 | 220 | 169 | 100 | 26 |
| Windmills | 80 | 120 | 180 | 200 | 200 | 130 |
| Electricity | 447 | 1,350 | 6,228 | 17,050 | 43,427 | 53,542 |
| Automobile | — | 100 | 24,686 | 280,900 | 1,426,568 | 2,511,312 |

SOURCE: U.S. Department of Commerce, Bureau of the Census, *Historical Statistics of the United States: Colonial Times to the Present,* Bicentennial ed. (Washington, D.C.: Government Printing Office, 1976), Vol. II, p. 818.

monuments like the Chicago skyscrapers. They transported people and commodities from shore to shore, from Canada to the Gulf, in only a few days. They increased productivity and made possible a multiplicity of new goods that transformed the home, the factory, the farm, and the workplace. For some, the machine was not only awe-inspiring, it was beautiful—a source of patterned motion that increasingly affected modern art and design.

Nonetheless, the machine (as it had in the nineteenth century) also represented darker forces: filth and pollution and exploitation. Linked to an uncompromising search for profits, the machine seemed to empower the greedy and to condemn children, women, and men to long hours of alienating work and short, weary lives. This was the subject of a good deal of literature, art, and photography through the period. Some social critics even wondered: Were human beings losing control of life to the machine? Were people becoming mere extensions of machines?

However the machine was evaluated, it changed every element of American life—from the shape of everyday objects like knives and forks, glassware, furniture, and clothing to the design of automobiles, trains, buildings, and ships. During the 1920s and

PLATE 5. This remarkable photograph, *The Steamfitter,* by Lewis Hine, suggests a point that many artists and writers made during the 1920s. In order to work at his machine, this man is forced to bend his body to the contour of the tank. Was the fate of all mankind, many Americans wondered, to be shaped by machines? *(International Museum of Photography at George Eastman House)*

THE SIX-CYLINDER FOUR-DOOR TOURING SEDAN

OLDSMOBILE ~ 6 AND 8

PLATE 6.   The shape of objects changed dramatically during the early twentieth century. Tools, housewares, furniture, houses, office buildings—all were streamlined to emphasize the sense of motion suggested by industrial progress. Trains and cars were made to *look* as if they traveled speedily; a woman's scarf boasts stylized cars flying through the clouds; handcrafted tableware was designed to look as if it were machine made. *(Train—The Bettmann Archive; Oldsmobile, scarf, tableware—New York Public Library/ Picture Collection)*

PLATE 7. Perhaps the most influential American architect of the early twentieth century was Frank Lloyd Wright. His houses and interior designs helped to create the streamlined look of the period. *(The Metropolitan Museum of Art, Purchase. Bequest of Emily Crane Chelbourne, 1972. Installation through the generosity of Saul P. Steinberg and Reliance Group Holdings, Inc.)*

PLATE 8. The 1939 New York World's Fair was a kind of summary of 1920s and 1930s attitudes toward the machine. The futuristic globe and spire seem to symbolize the limitless possibilities of industrialism and modern life. *(The Bettmann Archive)*

1930s, a great many ordinary objects were transformed by streamlining. Trains, cars, smoothly curving buildings, rounded arches, graceful high-flying bridges—all testified to designers' dreams of a pleasant and completely functional future. By the time of the New York World's Fair in 1939, the streamlined "World of Tomorrow" had anticipated future cities of glass and steel, with geometric shapes and machine-inspired designs. Unlike the Chicago Fair of 1893, the façades of buildings were themselves a kind of mechanical display. Gone were the ornate decorations of 1893, as well as the contradictory vision that Henry Adams had sensed. And yet the vision was contradicted—by the poverty and depression that plagued the late 1930s and by the approach of a second world war, just a few months away, in which mechanized force would contribute to the greatest destruction in human history.

above all a machine age, a triumph of advanced technology. Compared with a modern jet or a moon rocket, the *Spirit of St. Louis* was a very primitive machine. But to millions of Americans of the 1920s it was the final and glistening outcome of the industrial and technological revolution that had begun in the preceding century. It symbolized what they believed was happening in the United States: the creation of a new kind of civilization, a miracle of progress in which every barrier to human comfort and achievement would be broken by industry and invention.

The United States of the mid-1920s was much more thoroughly industrialized than it had been at the turn of the century. Total steel production, for example, quadrupled during the period between the death of McKinley and Lindbergh's flight to Paris. The total value of all manufactured goods increased about eight times in the same period. The number of people engaged in agriculture declined to about one-fourth of the total population. American cities grew at an astounding pace. By 1930, three years after Lindbergh's flight, 40 percent of the total population of the United States lived in twenty-five large metropolitan centers. In short, Lindbergh appealed to a society that was overwhelmingly industrial and urban, and fundamentally dependent on machines and factories.

## Electric Power and Assembly Lines

In some ways the New Era was an extension of the revolution in industry that had occurred after the Civil War (see Chapter 26). The factory system had continued to expand. New and more complex forms of machinery had been developed to produce more and more goods. But if the basic trends were the same, there were some new elements too. The New Era, to a far greater extent than the old, was powered by electricity and organized around assembly lines.

In 1870, when the industrial revolution was making its first powerful impact, steam and water were used equally to drive industry. Steam continued to be the main form of motor energy in industry until about 1917. But steam had its drawbacks. It was the introduction of electricity that made possible the extraordinary advances in industry that took place in the 1920s.

Again, the basic inventions belonged to the nineteenth century. Within the ten-year period from 1877 to 1887, the dynamo for generating electricity and the motor for converting it into motion were both perfected. This was largely the work of Thomas Edison. During these same years, Edison's incandescent light was introduced into homes and streets. In 1882, the first commercial electric power station, the Edison Illuminating Company, was built in New York.

While electric lighting brightened life in offices, houses, and streets, the electic motor helped transform industrial production. In 1900, electric motors provided only one-twentieth of the power used in American industrial plants. By World War I, this figure had increased to about one-third. When Lindbergh flew to France, just ten years later, electricity provided almost two-thirds of the total industrial power in American factories and mills. Between 1870 and 1920, the amount of raw energy used by American industry, measured in horsepower, increased by well over 1,000 percent!

The development of the moving-belt assembly line also had far-reaching effects on industrial production. Assembly lines were first introduced on a large scale by Henry Ford at his automobile plant in Michigan in 1913. The principle was a simple one. Workers were placed in a row in the order of sequence of their jobs. As the product (in this case the automobile) moved past him, each man performed his assigned task. The idea might be simple, but the savings in time and motion were dramatic. Each worker, using a specialized tool to perform a small task, could now produce much more in a given day. Ford's assembly line was copied by dozens of other industries. By the middle of the 1920s, it was a standard technique.

ALL IN A DAY'S WORK

The Ford plant in Detroit was a miracle of productivity. Assembly-line methods cut the time needed to produce these chassis from more than twelve hours each to less than two hours. In this photograph, one day's chassis production is shown. The question was, who was going to buy all these cars? The answer, in part, lay in installment credit: because of it, consumption rose much faster in the 1920s than the real incomes of working people. Sooner or later, there would be a reckoning. (Ford Archives)

## Effects of Mechanization

The industrial revolution continued. The changes brought about by the electric motor and the assembly line made the lives of most Americans in 1927 very different from their lives a generation or two earlier. More and more, the ways in which people lived and worked were determined by machines and technological innovations. More and more, mechanical devices replaced human energy and skill.

This process of mechanization had two deep effects on American society. First, it made modern Americans more conscious of the efficient use of time and effort than any other people in the history of the world. Second, it threatened to standardize life by reducing the area of imagination and individuality in people's daily working environment. The celebration of Lindbergh was connected to both these consequences.

In planning his flight, Lindbergh was almost ruthlessly efficient. The *Spirit of St. Louis* was a nearly perfect machine. It was designed to perform one simple task in the most effective way, with a minimum of wasted energy. Like a machine in a modern factory, the plane represented the harnessing of energy to a carefully designed instrument for the performance of a rigidly defined task. Much of what Americans admired in

Lindbergh was precisely what they admired in their own society—his technological achievement.

But there was another side to Lindbergh. He was a maverick. Some of the pet names the newspapers gave him, like "The Flyin' Fool" and "Lucky," made his daring seem more important than his technical skill. Lindbergh seemed to go against the trend toward standardization of life in the New Era. He represented individual imagination, as well as engineering and piloting skill. A large part of Lindbergh's fame probably rested on this contradiction. His flight was both a triumph of technology and a victory for individual daring.

## WHEELS AND WINGS: THE MOTOR AGE

The development of electricity had a powerful effect not only on industry but also on American home life. New inventions like the electric washing machine and refrigerator (which utilized small, inexpensive motors) changed the working and eating habits of American families. And a dozen other smaller electric appliances—from toasters to thermostats for home furnaces—helped usher in the American consumer's vision of a New Era.

# Henry Ford

(Culver Pictures)

As much as any other single factor, automobiles caused the dramatic change in American life in the twentieth century. Yet the man who did the most to put the nation on wheels, Henry Ford, disliked the change. The older he grew, the more fondly he looked back on the America of his youth. He valued its rural base, Puritan work ethic, and simple pleasures.

Life began for Henry Ford on a farm near Dearborn, Michigan, on July 30, 1863. Early in his life two traits became apparent: he loved machinery, and he hated farming. He was a born tinkerer. By the time he was thirteen, he could disassemble and reconstruct a watch. He was forever fixing his father's farm machinery and his mother's household appliances. When he ran out of things to repair at home, he repaired the watches, clocks, and machinery of neighbors.

As soon as he could, he left the farm for Detroit to become a machinist. He quickly learned his trade and was soon a well-paid, highly skilled workman. In his spare time, he worked on a gasoline buggy in an old brick shed behind his home. By 1896, he was able to drive it through the hole he had knocked out of the shed wall. Mounted on four bicycle wheels was a two-cylinder, four-horsepower engine. Mounted on that was a buggy seat. To steer it he used a curved stick like the tiller on a boat.

From this awkward beginning, Ford built a billion-dollar industry over the next fifty years. But as he grew from home-shop tinkerer to industrial tycoon, he never really changed his boyhood attitudes. They remained those of an agrarian Populist of the 1880s and 1890s.

As a result, Henry Ford was a mass of contradictions. While he professed a firm belief in the value of the individual workman and of hard and useful work, he developed an assembly-line process that was truly dehumanizing. He broke down each of the jobs involved in making a car into its tiniest steps. Consequently, a workman did only one thing—like tightening a single bolt—all day long. Ford was even proud of the fact that 43 percent of the jobs in his factories could be mastered in no more than one day.

While he was an expert businessman, as shown by his development of an enormous personal fortune and a vastly profitable corporation, Ford disliked many aspects of capitalism. He had an abiding mistrust of bankers and moneymen.

And while he continued to turn out millions of cars, making Americans a highly mobile and rootless society, he romanticized the stable, well-rooted small-town life. He so loved nineteenth-century rural America that he spent twenty years constructing a reproduction of the community he grew up in— Greenfield Village. There, skilled artisans worked at jobs that had long since been taken over by assembly lines.

Henry Ford died an old man of eighty-four, puzzled and unhappy with the people and the world he had done so much to transform.

## Perfecting the Automobile

The largest change in American social life was brought about by the gasoline engine. The basic principle of the internal combustion engine was understood by the middle of the nineteenth century. The principle was simple. Instead of burning fuel externally to convert water into steam, the internal combustion engine burned fuel in an explosive way inside a chamber. The force of the explosion was then used to drive a piston or a rotor. The first internal combustion engine was built and operated in the 1860s in France. Power for the new engine was available in the form of gasoline, a "waste" product in the making of kerosene, the basic fuel oil of the nineteenth century.

It was only a matter of time, then, until someone perfected the engine, mounted it on a "horseless carriage," and so created the automobile. No one, however, could have begun to guess at the end of the nineteenth century just how rapid the development of the automobile would be. Nor could they foresee the range of consequences it would have on the ways Americans lived.

The first man in the United States to build a workable automobile powered by a gasoline engine was probably Ransom E. Olds. (His rickety machine was the forerunner of the present-day Oldsmobile.) Five years later, in 1895, Henry Ford put together his first car. The new machine was noisy, unreliable, and expensive. Still, a few Americans were willing to pay the price and stop their ears against the noise. By 1900, there were about 8,000 of the curious new machines operating in the country.

But Ford was not so much an inventor of the automobile as an inventor of a style and a method of production. In the early years of the century, Ford began simplifying the automobile. He cut away every fancy decoration and convenience that had been adapted from the luxurious carriages of the day. Moreover, he reduced costs by turning out standardized, mass-produced machines. The results were astonishing. In 1907, the average price of an automobile was over $2,000.

The next year, Ford introduced a model selling at only $850. By 1914, he was able to cut the price to a little over $500. By the mid-1920s, Ford was selling his assembly-line Model T for less than $300. The car was similar in many ways to the *Spirit of St. Louis*. It was the simplest machine possible, designed to do a plain task in the most efficient way.

Other automobile makers began to imitate and compete with Ford. The result was an exploding new industry. By the 1920s, the manufacture of automobiles was by far the largest consumer products industry in the United States. It employed tens of thousands of workers at large and growing factories centered in Detroit. The automobile had a remarkable impact on other industries, especially steel and rubber, which provided the raw products for the assembly lines. The oil industry also underwent a major expansion. The automobile turned gasoline into the main stock-in-trade of the petroleum companies.

## Life in the Motor Age

The most obvious impact of the automobile was not on industry but on American social life. By 1927, Ford had made 15 million cars. About 20 million American families owned an automobile. The immediate result was that horses and other draft animals disappeared from the landscape and the streets.

But the automobile had other, less obvious and predictable effects. First, the automobile encouraged Americans to move farther and farther out of the cities, into the suburbs. From about the time of Lindbergh's trip to Paris, the "lure of the suburbs" attracted more and more middle-class Americans. Second, cars and buses transformed American education, especially in small towns and farm areas. The school bus made it possible to consolidate school districts into larger units. Gradually the simple one-room schoolhouse, with one or two teachers for all the grades, disappeared.

Finally, the automobile, the truck, and the bus

began a process that would take another thirty years to complete: the near destruction of the railroads—the principal technological innovation of the nineteenth century. At first, in the 1920s and 1930s, the car and the bus cut mainly into the railroads' local traffic. But as roads and engines improved, the competition became more and more severe. As for freight, the trucking industry began to compete for what had been almost a railroad monopoly. The train, with its mighty steam engine, had been the great symbol of the industrial revolution up to the 1920s. By the middle of the twentieth century, much of the railroad industry was ailing and unprofitable, no longer able to survive as a private enterprise.

In the long run, the automobile proved to have unwanted as well as unpredicted consequences. Among these, the modern decay of central cities was the most serious. Gradually, large sections of cities like New York, Boston, and Chicago became the slums of the poor, who could not afford suburban homes. Also, although no one in Lindbergh's day could have predicted it, the automobile caused a major problem of air pollution. Smog resulted from the exhausts of millions of cars and trucks burning hundreds of millions of gallons of gasoline every year.

To most Americans, though, the automobile was an unquestioned miracle. To those who could afford it, it meant freedom to move at will through the city or the countryside. It also provided status, as manufacturers introduced more elaborate models, some costing ten times as much as Ford's Model T. And the automobile meant adventure. Middle-class Americans could get behind the wheel of a powerful, complicated piece of machinery—just as Lindbergh had climbed into the cockpit of his machine—and be off on an exciting journey of motion and speed every day. Like Lindbergh, too, Americans went beyond a concern with efficiency and practicality to a romantic affection for their machines. They polished them, paraded them, and gave them pet names like the "old bus," the "flivver," the "tin Lizzie," and the "merry Oldsmobile." Despite its defects, Americans loved the car.

## Development of Air Transportation

For the first quarter of the twentieth century, the automobile had the greatest social and economic impact on America. The development of the aircraft industry and airline passenger service did not become truly important until years after Lindbergh's flight. But the airplane was in many ways more thrilling than the automobile. (This was why Lindbergh and other pilots could make a living in the 1920s barnstorming across America in their aerial circuses.) Like the automobile, the airplane depended on the small, powerful, and efficient gasoline engine.

The first men to fly a real airplane were Orville and Wilbur Wright. In 1903, they camped at Kitty Hawk, North Carolina (a location they chose because it had strong and steady winds, plus a great expanse of beach), with a primitive biplane. It had a tiny gasoline engine, which turned two push-type propellers. The first successful test flight came in December, after a series of dangerous and frustrating failures. This first flight lasted a little less than a minute, and covered only about 800 feet. But the Wright brothers were soon experimenting with larger planes and engines. In 1909, after six years of work, they sold the first plane to the United States Army.

World War I brought about a dramatic spurt in design sophistication, not only in the United States but in Europe. The new planes had larger and better engines, and a much more rigid construction than the Wrights' original. The war also romanticized flight and created a new type of military hero, the "aviator." Lindbergh, then, was able to capitalize not only on advances in technology but on a new image of the heroic and daring "ace."

The main civilian use of the airplane was shipping mail. The government began service in 1918. Later, private companies (like the one Lindbergh worked for in St. Louis) took over the service. The operation was dangerous. A majority of the pilots were killed in crashes during the early years. But by the mid-1920s, there was regular, all-weather airmail service between most major cities in America.

Lindbergh's flight, combined with the introduction of larger airplanes like Byrd's *America,* did more than any other single event to encourage the growth of air transportation. Lindbergh had faith in the future of aviation. Soon after his return to America in 1927, he began a flying tour of the country to promote airmail and air transportation. By 1930, just three years after his solo transatlantic flight, there were forty-three domestic airline companies, operating over 30,000 miles of flying routes.

# NEW MANNERS AND MORALS

All these changes—the development of mass communications, the expansion of industry, the introduction of a new technology—brought about another revolution. This revolution marked a dramatic difference in the manners and morals of the American people. Americans of the 1920s knew they were living a time when the world was undergoing rapid change. They coined new words and phrases—like the "Roaring Twenties," the "lost generation," and "flaming youth"—to describe what was happening to them. Americans were adopting habits and moral standards that their parents found shocking and offensive.

## A Revolution for Women

At the center of the revolution in manners were women. The revolution that would change women's lives did not begin in the 1920s. During the first two decades of the twentieth century, many middle- and upper-class women had adopted new patterns of behavior (including divorce) that broke the traditions of nineteenth-century Victorian America. But because of the impact of World War I and the influence of books, radio, and advertising, the trend started at the turn of

the century began to affect ever-widening circles of women. By the 1920s, the revolution was in full bloom.

Politically, women were new creatures. After decades of agitation, they finally won the right to vote, with passage of the Nineteenth Amendment in 1920. But this new political role was only a small part of the emancipation of women. The new woman of the 1920s wanted to do every-

### SMOLDERING YOUTH

Many Americans of the 1920s were intensely conscious of the changing ways men and women behaved toward each other socially and sexually. At the center of the supposed changes was the "flapper," the young woman scantily dressed, hatless, with bobbed hair, at home with alcohol, frankly provocative, and carefully posing in ways designed to seem altogether natural. In truth, the consciousness of change probably ran considerably ahead of the changes themselves. This cartoon of 1927 wildly exaggerates the degree of public nakedness most women were willing to risk—or most men to accept. *(Culver Pictures)*

THE AMERICAN FLAPPER - 1927

thing. "Everything" included many more opportunities than her mother had had.

She was much more likely than her mother to attend college. She might go to work, too. By 1930, 10 million women were employed in the American labor force. This new experience of education and work increased the number of women who were likely to remain single, or, if they did marry, to get divorced. The divorce rate in 1930 was twice what it had been before the war. This did not mean that marriages were more unhappy. It meant, instead, that women were less likely to put up with a bad marital situation. They would demand their freedom instead.

There was an even more obvious revolution in the way women dressed. The ideal that gradually emerged in the decade of Lindbergh's flight was that of the "flapper." She wore her dress short—above the knees rather than at the ankle. And the dress was not only shorter, it was made of thin material, designed to move with her body as she walked or danced—designed, too, to give an occasional glimpse of thigh above the hemline. The flapper discarded the corsets that her mother had worn, and dispensed with the bustle, too. She put on much more make-up and perfume, and jangled with much more jewelry at her neck and wrists. In advertisements and in movies, and in real life, too, she was likely to pose with a cocktail in one hand and a cigarette in a long holder in the other—the essence of a new "sophistication."

Like Lindbergh, though, the flapper and the "liberation" she symbolized were a middle-class phenomenon primarily. College, careers, divorce, and emancipated dress still touched only a minority of American women. Even though the suffrage now belonged to every woman, in practice, voting was primarily confined to middle-class women. For the rest, life continued to be quite confining. And when women did leave the home to take jobs, they still suffered from a systematic discrimination in wages and opportunities. In the final analysis, the flapper, like Lindbergh, had a significance that was more symbolic than real.

# The Jazz Age

The new woman was part of a changing culture. A freedom of action and belief unheard of before seemed to go hand in hand with the triumph of industrial technology, with its prosperity and sense of unlimited possibilities for life. Both men and women listened to new music—jazz—and danced new steps. Instead of formal waltzes and other Victorian dances, they moved to the fast Charleston and the Black Bottom. They also

### SIMPERING YOUTH

Dancing was one of the main preoccupations of the popular culture of the 1920s. White people appropriated, and drastically modified, black dances just as they did black music. (They managed to do this, usually, with no apparent change in their racial attitudes.) Here, a young couple are shown doing the Charleston. The effect they are striving for in this staged photograph is one that combines open sexuality with youthful innocence; and their own highly patterned intimacy is mixed with an awareness that they are not so much dancing as they are performing for a public. To accomplish this, they (or their photographer) have made a deal: Bob will look intently at Bev; but Bev will look ever so cutely at us. *(Culver Pictures)*

**BESSIE SMITH**

One of the effects of the communications revolution was to turn previously obscure musicians and singers into public celebrities and art forms that had been folk music into commercial properties. This was particularly true for black artists and their music. Bessie Smith, shown here dressed in the ideal movie-queen costume of the period, made the blues into a form that managed to combine superb talent with commercial success. As a phenomenon, the celebrity was nothing new. But there were more of them than ever before, their variety was more striking, and their fame more instantaneous and widespread. *(Bettmann Archive)*

danced close together in the slow fox trot. Many older Americans were shocked by these changes. But these dances became part of the new culture, sweeping their way through high-school gymnasiums and college campuses across the country.

The sexual ideas of Americans were changing, too. The ideas of the Austrian psychologist Sigmund Freud on sex began to be discussed at the dinner table and in the polite magazines of the middle class. Words like "bitch" appeared in novels published by respectable publishers and read by respectable people. "Petting" and "necking" became part of the everyday vocabulary of magazine readers and even ministers. In the movies, sex became a major box-office attraction. Stars like Theda Bara and Clara Bow appeared on the screen in thin clothing, locked in long, passionate embraces with their leading men. When Clara Bow was advertised as the "It" girl, hardly anyone needed to ask what "It" meant.

Americans drank more, too. Despite prohibition (see p. 768), liquor was easy to obtain. And since liquor was illegal, millions of Americans became technically criminals on an almost daily basis. Probably half of the respectable, middle-class families in the nation had their regular bootlegger. Terms like "bathtub gin" and "speak-easy" became part of the national language. Especially in colleges, drinking became a regular pastime of the "flaming youth" of the decade.

## The Search for Innocence

As their own lives became more and more confused, Americans began to celebrate innocence. In their movies and sports they created simple, naive heroes who were guided by straightforward codes of justice and virtue. The most popular type of movie hero of the decade was the cowboy, a symbol of innocent, preindustrial man. And the most popular movie star of the period, Rudolf Valentino, played roles that put him on horseback in a country far removed from Fords and factories and modernity. It was no accident, too, that the

**RUDOLF VALENTINO**

Valentino, shown here dressed for his role in *The Sheik*, was the most popular male movie idol of the 1920s. Valentino and his directors emphasized the curious intensity of his apparent passions, using stares like the one he has adopted for this publicity photograph. But they also armed him to the teeth, with knives, swords and bullets, whenever his roles allowed for it. The resulting effect of violence and lust was made acceptable partly by the fact that he often played some sort of foreigner from a culture distant in time and place. In such realms, any fantasy could seem appropriate, even to the most conservative middle-class movie goer. *(Culver Pictures)*

greatest sports hero of the decade, George Herman Ruth, was nicknamed "Babe."

Lindbergh stirred the deep urge of people to believe in innocence. His youth, honesty, and simple determination made him seem much purer than the public that worshipped him. Lindbergh did not smoke or drink. He displayed no interest in women, at least at the time of his flight. And his boyish face looked out at the world through clear blue eyes. They seemed to say that everything was still the same, that the world had not lost its innocence after all.

## Illusions of Disillusionment

In the midst of all this change and confusion, intellectuals offered very little help. Beginning in the 1890s, intellectuals in America had produced a remarkable body of literature on the workings of society. In the 1920s, a new generation of intellectuals began to turn out a profusion of superb novels, plays, and essays—as rich a cultural flowering as the country had ever produced. But their work embodied a marked shift away from a concern with social and political problems. With a few exceptions, the new writers either ignored society altogether or viewed it as the enemy, to be mocked or damned.

All in all, the viewpoint of the writers of the 1920s fits Malcolm Cowley's description quite well: "Society was something quite alien . . . a sort of parlor car in which we rode, over smooth tracks, toward a destination we should never have chosen for ourselves." This self-conscious sense of alienation from social structures and purposes governed the literary culture of the decade. It was what prompted the idea that the writers of the period belonged to a "lost generation." The result was a rush of great art that pointed in no particular social direction whatever.

The dominant theme of the writers of the 1920s was disillusionment. Their heroes and heroines usually entered their novels, plays, and stories caught up in some sort of innocent faith—in religion, civilization, progress, freedom, or the like. But, typically, this faith was broken by experience, and the outcome was a ripping away of old illusions. In the typical novel of the decade, the illusions were not replaced by any working new beliefs, but instead by a brooding sense of mistrust and disappointment, and a curious kind of boredom with the world.

The first great subject for disillusionment was the war and the mistaken peace that followed.

Several of the best young writers cut their teeth on the war experience—William Faulkner, Ernest Hemingway, John Dos Passos—and for most of them, the conclusion was simple: the war had proved the bankruptcy of what people called "civilization." Hemingway summed up the experience in a story called "Soldier's Home," about the shattered illusions of a veteran named Krebs: "Krebs acquired the nausea in regard to experience that is the result of untruth or exaggeration." The same logic governed Maxwell Anderson's popular *What Price Glory,* e. e. cummings's *The Enormous Room*—a hilarious book on his arrest and imprisonment in France—and the two war novels of Dos Passos, *One Man's Initiation* and *Three Soldiers.* The only way to escape the "nausea" brought on by the war was to make what Hemingway called "a separate peace."

Actually, when looked at carefully, the American war novels were not so much about the war at all, but about what the writers thought lay behind the war: technology, bureaucracy, and propaganda. For people like Faulkner or Dos Passos, the war was not so much a subject as a dramatic metaphor. In many of Hemingway's books and stories of the 1920s—*A Farewell to Arms* (1925) and *The Sun Also Rises* (1926) among them—the war was only the most violent phase of modern civilization. It merely brought into sharper focus the cruelty and inhumanity that were an inherent feature of contemporary social life.

When the writers looked at peacetime subjects, the result was much the same. Sinclair Lewis's riotous parody of the consciousness of a Midwestern businessman, in his novel *Babbit,* was just as "disillusioned" as any war novel. In *Winesburg, Ohio,* Sherwood Anderson looked behind the drawn blinds of a small town with exactly the same sense of alienation and distaste. Dos Passos's voluminous novel, *1919,* made little or no distinction between war and peace. All in all, the writers of the decade agreed with the judgment of the poet Ezra Pound that Western civilization was "an old bitch gone in the teeth." Another

poet, T. S. Eliot, summed up the attitude in the title of his most popular work of the period, *The Waste Land.*

For many, the only solution seemed to be expatriation. In *The Sun Also Rises,* Hemingway portrayed the aimless confusion of American and British intellectuals in Paris. And for those who did not actually leave the country, there were other forms of withdrawal. William Faulkner— probably the best writer of the period—techni-

### THE FITZGERALDS, 1927

No writer was more closely associated with the idea of flaming youth than F. Scott Fitzgerald. Indeed, no American writer did more to help invent it. But for this photograph he chose to pose with his wife Zelda and daughter Scottie as the ideal family. Scottie is caught "candidly," looking right at the photographer and saying something. But Fitzgerald himself is looking benignly down at her with the patient and loving smile of a doting father. *(Culver Pictures)*

cally, stayed stubbornly in Mississippi. From that vantage point, he wrote social novels, but they were novels about a rural society whose problems were hardly those of an industrial and urban society. In novels like *The Sound and the Fury* (1929), Faulkner resorted to disarmingly traditional and innocent solutions to human problems—honesty, decency, and even simple modesty. At times, he even seemed to propose religious faith as the only authentic alternative to meaninglessness in modern life.

The writer who best caught the spirit of the "Jazz Age"—as he called it—was F. Scott Fitzgerald. *This Side of Paradise* (1920) rocketed him to a precocious fame. But his reputation was quickly confirmed by *The Great Gatsby* (1925). Fitzgerald's characters inhabited a world of money and sophistication. They were literate and articulate, young and dashing. They drank and smoked and danced their way toward disaster. They were a curious mixture of innocence and disillusionment.

Jay Gatsby, easily Fitzgerald's most characteristic hero, was in some ways a cynical man. He was a criminal who had become extraordinarily wealthy and had invented a false and cultured identity for himself, complete with a great mansion on Long Island. But there was another side to Gatsby, very like Lindbergh. He was a boy from the Midwest who had read Benjamin Franklin, worked hard for "success," and dreamed an innocent dream—that he might find and marry the girl he had loved as a youth. It was this dream, this "romantic readiness," that made Gatsby "great." And if the naive dream led only to corruption and murder, that seemed to Fitzgerald to capture the inner meaning of his generation's experience.

In a sense, Gatsby and Lindbergh were opposite manifestations of the same heroic figure. Both were simple in the midst of complexity, daring in a world that had become increasingly routine and bureaucratic. Both were driven by a private conviction that had little or no social significance. The difference was that Fitzgerald's hero ended in failure and death; Lindbergh won success and fame and married the daughter of a wealthy financier.

# SUGGESTED READINGS, CHAPTERS 35–36

### LINDBERGH

The most engaging way to begin reading about Lindbergh's feat is to start with his own story, written years after the flight, *The Spirit of Saint Louis* (1953). There are two intelligent modern biographies: Kenneth S. Davis, *The Hero: Charles A. Lindbergh* (1959), and Walter S. Ross, *The Last Hero: Charles A. Lindbergh* (1968).

### COMMUNICATIONS

The following books are helpful discussions of the new media: David M. White and Richard Averson, *Sight, Sound, and Society* (1968); Ronald Gellatt, *The Fabulous Phonograph* (1965); Beaumont Newhall, *The History of Photography* (1964); Erik Barnouw, *A Tower in Babel:* *A History of Broadcasting in the United States to 1933* (1966); and Frank Luther Mott, *American Journalism* (1962).

### TECHNOLOGY

A workable introduction to the new technology of mass production is Sigfried Giedion, *Mechanization Takes Command* (1948). Henry Ford's career may be tracked in the exhaustive and sympathetic study by Allan Nevins and Frank E. Hill, *Ford*, 3 vols. (1954–1962). But the more interesting approach is through the writings of some of the molders of technological change, such as Henry Ford, *My Life and Work* (1922), and Wilbur Wright and Orville Wright, *Papers* (1953).

## POPULAR CULTURE

Two classics from the period, the first charming, the second influential, are Frederick Lewis Allen, *Only Yesterday* (1931), and R. S. and H. N. Lynd, *Middletown* (1929). An interesting study of the definition of a generation is Paula Fass, *The Damned and the Beautiful: American Youth in the 1920s* (1977). William Henry Chafe, *The American Woman* (1974), is a plausible place to start reading on women in the 1920s. Two interesting and usable books are Harold Seymour, *Baseball*, 2 vols. (1960–1971), and Edward Wagenknecht, *Movies in the Age of Innocence* (1962).

## INTELLECTUALS

Two classics from the period are Malcolm Cowley, *Exiles' Return* (1934), and Edmund Wilson, *Axel's Castle* (1931). The two best books on the literary history of the period—though both must be used very cautiously—are still Alfred Kazin, *On Native Ground* (1942), and Frederick Hoffmann, *The Twenties* (1955).

# 37 ▪ Defeat of the Bonus Marchers

T he witness shifted nervously but stood his ground. Having waited a long time to testify, he was not going to be put off. Without formally addressing the committee or saying so much as a polite "Gentlemen," he began: "My comrade and I hiked here from nine o'clock Sunday morning, when we left Camden. I done it all by my feet—shoe leather. I come to show you people that we need our bonus. We wouldn't want it if we didn't need it."

The witness was Joseph T. Angelo, veteran of World War I. He was addressing a committee of the House of Representatives of the United States Congress in 1931. The committee was hearing witnesses testify about a controversial matter: the immediate payment of a "bonus" to all the veterans of the war. The country was in the third year of a depression, and the bonus would pay about $1,000 each to over 3 million veterans and their families.[1] It would, in fact, be the greatest program of direct relief for the poor ever undertaken by the federal government.

For six days officials of the Republican administration testified. President Herbert Hoover was opposed to the bonus. The testimony of government officials reflected this opposition. A few congressmen and one or two officials of veterans' organizations spoke out for the bonus. But they were outnumbered by a long string of bank vice presidents, insurance executives, and other businessmen. The testimony was dull. It was full of statistics designed to prove that the bonus would bankrupt the federal treasury and bring about a dangerous inflation.

---

[1] Congress had set up the bonus (a combination of life insurance and a pension) in 1924. It was not due to be paid until 1945, except to the heirs of veterans who died earlier.

But now for the first time an ordinary veteran, with no job, a hungry family, and a plain man's English, was testifying. Before Angelo had finished, the committee and the audience were stirred to a mixture of laughter, admiration, and stunned confusion.

> I have got a little home back there [in Camden, New Jersey] that I built with my own hands after I came home from France. Now, I expect to lose that little place. Last week I went to our town committee and they gave me $4 for rations. That is to keep my wife and child and myself and clothe us; and also I cannot put no coal in my cellar.

Here, in the poor grammar and tired face of the witness, was the whole meaning of the depression that had begun in 1929. Angelo said he spoke for hundreds like himself in New Jersey. But he spoke, too, for millions all over the country who had not worked for a long time, who stood in bread lines, and who built the shacks in the shabby little towns they wryly called Hoovervilles.

But Angelo was also a veteran. So he spoke from his experience of the two most important events in his time—the war that people still called the Great War and the depression they were beginning to call the Great Depression. There was no economic theory or political philosophy in his testimony. He was just a hungry man who had fought in France.

> All I ask of you, brothers, is to help us. We helped you, now you help us. My partner here has a wife and five children, and he is just the same as I am. He hiked down here at the same time with me, and our feet are blistered. That is all I have to say. And I hope you folks can help us and that we can go through with the bonus. We don't want charity; we don't need it. All we ask for is what belongs to us, and that is all we want.

Some of the congressmen were confused. Others were curious. Following the custom of congressional committees, they began to question the witness:

MR. FREAR: What is your business?
MR. ANGELO: Nothing. I am nothing but a bum.
MR. FREAR: You say you have not worked for two years?
MR. ANGELO: I have not worked for a year and a half. But there is no work in my home town.
MR. RAINEY: You are wearing some medal. What is it?
MR. ANGELO: I carry the highest medal in America for enlisted men, the Distinguished Service Cross.
MR. RAINEY: You have a Distinguished Service Cross? What is that for?
MR. ANGELO: That is for saving Colonel Patton.

George S. Patton was already a well-known army officer. (In World War II he would become one of the most famous and controversial of America's generals.) Congressman Rainey continued the questioning and pressed Angelo for details. Angelo responded with a startling tale. He had been part of a 305-man unit attacked by German machine guns in the Argonne Forest in 1918.

When the battle was over, he said, most of the men were dead. Colonel Patton was wounded, and only he—Angelo—was left standing. Then Angelo showed the committee a tiepin made from a bullet he said was taken from Patton's leg in France. Neither the tiepin nor the medal had ever gone to "Uncle," Angelo's pet name for the pawnshop that had swallowed up most of his other possessions.

The afternoon was wearing on, but Angelo had roused the attention of the committee members and the audience as none of the other witnesses had. So the congressmen began to ask about his life. As Angelo answered, the audience sometimes laughed, sometimes applauded. He told them of working in a DuPont plant, making munitions for the British before the United States entered the war. When Congress declared war in 1917, he enlisted at once. But he was almost rejected because he weighed a mere 107 pounds. Only after ten doctors had examined him and a general had watched him do a handspring and jump a table was he accepted.

Then, obviously agitated, Angelo wound up with another statement:

> I can make money. I can make lots of money. Now, I could go bootlegging. It is just the same way I could have went to France and I could have run out on my outfit. Which is the best, to be a live coward or a dead hero?
>
> When this was put on me, brothers, I wasn't worried when I went through. I don't have nothing to worry about. I wasn't married, and I got a wonderful sendoff when I went to France. My father throwed me out. [Laughter.] And when I came back, I went home to my father. I saw a big, fat woman sitting in the seat. I knowed her from next door. I said, "She is the last woman you want on earth. Pop, what is she doing here?" He says, "That is my wife." I says, "Oh, My God!" She says, "Get out of here," and that was my welcome home, and I got out. [Laughter.]
>
> So, folks, I tell you all I will say to you is, help us through with the bonus. That is the best answer for you folks to give to the fellow at home. Don't forget me for a job. [Applause.]

Joe Angelo was three things: a veteran, a bum, and a victim of the most serious economic depression in American history. In each of these roles he was not just an individual grappling with purely personal problems. He represented over 4½ million soldiers (about half of whom had actually been sent to Europe) suddenly discharged into civilian life in 1918 and 1919. These veterans organized—like other veterans in America's previous wars. More than a million joined the new American Legion and the Veterans of Foreign Wars. They thought of themselves as a special type of citizen, with a special claim on their country's gratitude.

As a bum, Angelo also spoke for countless people, many of them veterans, who had worked unsuccessfully at one job or another but mostly drifted through the 1920s. Naturally, the depression added millions of new "bums." Angelo, who had not been able to find work for a year and a half, was only one of a great, restless mass of unemployed. When he appeared before the congressional committee, at least 5 million men and women were classed as unemployed. Probably another 5 million were able to find only part-time work. Almost every second worker in America had his or her wages cut after the stock market crash of 1929. Few people could doubt in 1931 that unemployment was one of the most serious problems the United States had ever faced.

Joe Angelo's instinct was to turn to Washington for help. On his walk from Camden, he had met other small groups of veterans with the same idea. The unemployed, the veterans, and the bums (often one man, like Angelo, was all three) were looking more and more to the federal government for relief. They had one fairly good chance of getting help from a reluctant Congress and a stubborn president—payment of the bonus. This, in Angelo's words, was "the best answer for you folks to give."

Angelo wanted $1,000 immediately, instead of waiting until 1945 to collect a larger amount. This was the heart of an issue that was about to create the most dramatic crisis of the depression—the massing in Washington of a "Bonus Army." Behind the crisis lay the old task of writing a final chapter to the World War and the new, complicated task of dealing with the depression. But for the marchers in the Bonus Army, the problem was quite simple: When and how would they be able to collect their bonus in full?

Veterans could already borrow money against the promise of the government to pay. Over 2 million had taken out loans that averaged $100 each—just enough to pay a back grocery bill, buy some coal for winter, or meet a medical emergency. But veterans everywhere were beginning to ask for ten times more, the payment of the entire bonus. And they found some sympathetic ears in Congress. Representative Wright Patman of Texas introduced a bill to authorize printing almost $2½ billion in new paper money to pay the bonus. As time passed there was more and more talk of the bonus, not only in Washington but wherever knots of hungry veterans gathered.

In November 1931 a group of veterans left Seattle to ride freight trains to the capital. All over the country others were doing likewise. A movement began that would shake the Hoover administration.

For two years the president had been telling the nation that the depression was not so serious and would soon end. Administration officials had always played down unemployment statistics. They portrayed the crisis as a temporary economic slump that would cure itself. Meanwhile, Hoover kept to his principle that the federal government should not provide direct relief to poor individuals. The veterans who were hitchhiking and jumping freight trains headed toward the capital were not so sure of their principles. Certainly they lacked the president's political experience and skills. But they knew that they needed the bonus.

In May 1932, 300 men from Portland, Oregon, left for Washington in a group. They called themselves the Bonus Expeditionary Force—a play on the name of the American army in France, the American Expeditionary Force. They elected a leader, Walter F. Waters, once an army sergeant, then foreman in a fruit cannery, now unemployed. They rode freight cars east and, by late May, reached East St. Louis, Illinois. There they tried to hop new trains going

## STARTING FOR WASHINGTON

In June 1932 this group of several hundred veterans from New York moved into the passenger yards of the Baltimore and Ohio Railroad in Jersey City, New Jersey. The men hoped to take over a train, which would carry them to Washington, where they could press their demand that the government pay them the bonus it had promised they would receive. *(UPI)*

farther east. When railroad police told them to leave, they began to break up trains by uncoupling cars. They also soaped the rails in some places, making it impossible for engines to move.

The state called for its national guard to drive the veterans away. A scuffle occurred, but no one was hurt badly. The marchers were soon on their way again—in national guard trucks that Illinois had provided in return for their promise to leave the state peacefully. But, most important, for the first time, the Bonus Army had won the attention of the newspapers and the public. Other veterans soon followed suit.

The scene was repeated everywhere. Merchants and mayors, railroad officials and governors, found it easier to supply trucks or boxcars than to stop the veterans. Thus a steady stream of bonus marchers was pouring into Washington. Each group had a leader or two, and their purpose was the same. They were in Washington to demand their bonus, even if they had to wait there until 1945 to get it.

One man deeply interested in the veterans' cause was Pelham D. Glassford, a West Point graduate and the youngest American in the World War to become a brigadier general. In 1931, Hoover appointed Glassford superintendent of

Washington's police force. So he would have to deal with the Bonus Expeditionary Force in the capital.

Glassford hoped that the Bonus Army either would not come or would go home quickly. But, when the marchers arrived, he became sympathetic and helpful. He regarded them as "his boys." He assigned them quarters in abandoned buildings on Pennsylvania Avenue The location was at the heart of official Washington, between the White House and the Capitol.

At Glassford's suggestion, also, the marchers made a "muster," or list of their groups, to make it easier to track down criminals and keep out the "reds" and radicals. Gradually, the marchers formed companies and then regiments. They elected Walter Waters, leader of the Portland group, as commander of the Bonus Expeditionary Force. He appointed junior officers and divided the men into companies named after states. Soon, the Bonus Army had a structure of command like the regular army.

Glassford's original decision to let the marchers camp along Pennsylvania Avenue was based on his hope that few would come. Soon it was obvious that the Bonus Army was much too large and dangerous (and embarrassing to the administration) to be in the center of things. Glassford sent most of the marchers to a new campsite a few miles southeast of Capitol Hill. The place was Anacostia Flats, a muddy landfill near the forks of the Potomac and Anacostia rivers. There, about 6,000 veterans built a shabby but orderly camp, with shacks and tents arranged in winding rows.

At Anacostia Flats the veterans tried to recreate their old army life. They woke to bugles, conducted roll calls, and had inspections. A company of men was assigned every day to "KP." Waters exercised strict discipline.

Other aspects of camp life were more relaxed. Some men had brought their wives and children. The Salvation Army set up a post office, a library, and a recreation room. Glassford managed to borrow some field kitchens and other equipment. He supervised the distribution of food donated by Washington citizens, American Legion posts, and others. At one point Glassford gave several hundred dollars of his own money to buy food. There was even a newspaper to keep the veterans informed about the progress of bonus legislation in Congress.

By June 6, 1932, the veterans were ready for their first direct action. About 7,000 left their separate camps around the city and lined up neatly in six "regiments" to parade through Washington. The men felt fairly hopeful as they moved along. The Patman bill, which was in the House, seemed as if it would pass soon. The rumors that they were controlled by communists, spread by some politicians to smear the Bonus Army, were not given much credit. Best of all, their parade had drawn a crowd of about 100,000; mostly Washington clerical workers. Every time another company with its American flag passed, the crowd applauded.

Shortly after dark the long line of march reached a circle near the Capitol. (They were forbidden to pass the White House or go to the Capitol itself.) Orders were given to fall out, and the marchers broke ranks to walk quietly back to Anacostia. They had heard that in less than a week the House would

VETERANS ON PARADE

In July 1932 the Bonus Army held this shirt-sleeve parade from the Washington Monument, shown in the background, to the Capitol. The marchers maintain their ranks and files in good order and are absolutely in step, in spite of the lack of a band. They are obviously trying to emphasize both their military skills and their patriotism. *(Wide World Photos)*

vote on the bonus bill. If it passed both the House and Senate and was signed by Hoover, most of the veterans could collect the thousand dollars needed to get their hungry families through another depression year.

The parade was simply a beginning. Veterans kept coming to Washington—the police estimated a hundred every hour. On June 15, when the House passed the bill, there were probably 15,000 veterans, plus some of their wives and children, scattered around Washington. Anacostia Flats was crowded, but new shacks kept going up. By now the ex-soldiers had stripped half the city of every stray board or door, every spare piece of tin or canvas. One man moved a burial vault onto the flats and took up residence in it. The camp was about level with the river, and had to be protected by a levee. When it rained, mud was a foot deep. But the Bonus Army kept building.

Obviously some kind of crisis might soon develop. Health officials predicted a typhoid epidemic. Waters predicted victory if 100,000 more veterans arrived. Hoover's advisers predicted that communists would take over the Bonus Force.

The Bonus Army and the administration were both waiting for the Senate to vote on the Patman bill. Hoover was sure he would win. The House elected in 1930 was Democratic. Since it was the first body of politicians to graduate from the depression, it was full of representatives who had recently promised their constituents direct action. But only a third of the Senate had been elected in 1930. The majority were still firmly Republican and loyal to the president. Both houses were striving for a July adjournment. (It was an election year, and everyone wanted to get home to campaign.) The administration hoped that the Bonus Army would simply disappear after the Senate voted and Congress adjourned.

On July 17 the Senate would debate and vote on the bonus. Waters commanded his marchers to go to the Capitol and fill the galleries, steps, and grounds. By noon, there were 10,000 marchers in and around the Capitol.

Inside, the Senate debated. Men would leave the galleries every few minutes to report to the marchers out on the steps. Opponents of the bill argued Hoover's position on what should be done about the depression: the government ought to cut spending, not spend more. Direct relief to individuals was not a federal responsibility. Recovery would come as large banks, businesses, and railroads regained their health. Then jobs would become available, and the economy would escape from radical tinkering.

Many senators supporting the bill argued that since the veterans were hungry and would be able to collect the bonus in thirteen years anyway, they should have it now. But one or two senators gave a more complicated justification for the bonus. In a depression, they insisted, the government should spend money, not save it. If the government printed 2½ billion new dollars for the bonus, the money would swiftly circulate. The veterans would be only the first to gain. The stores where they spent their payments would get the money. These stores, in turn, would order more goods from wholesalers and manufacturers. So every bonus dollar would become a dollar in motion, moving through the economy and stimulating all business. Naturally, when the depression was cured, the government would stop deficit spending—that is, spending more than it raised in taxes. The economy would return to normal. The government would only "prime the pump" with its paper dollars. The happy results would then be automatic.

Though the argument went on, it soon became clear that only a political miracle could save the bonus. The Senate was much too conservative to experiment with such legislation. Even some of the liberal senators who usually opposed Hoover questioned the bill. What was needed, they said, was a general bill for relief of all the unemployed. Veterans should receive no special favors.

Finally, after eight o'clock, someone came from the galleries and whispered to Waters. The bill had lost decisively, 62 to 18. Waters climbed the steps and turned to face the largest body ever gathered in Washington to demonstrate for a cause. The marchers had been waiting for hours, and for a moment it seemed as if they might riot. Marines were stationed nearby, just in case. Members of the administration wanted to ready machine guns, but Glassford persuaded them not to. Waters shouted: "Comrades![2] I have bad news. Let us show them we can take it on the chin. Let us show them we are patriotic

---

[2] This was an old term from the war, not a communist greeting.

Americans." There was a muttering from the crowd. Then a gigantic roar came from 10,000 throats. Waters pleaded for calm:

> We are not telling you to go home. Go back to your camps. We are going to stay in Washington until we get the bonus, no matter how long it takes. And we are one hundred times as good Americans as those men in there who voted against it. But there is nothing more to be done tonight.

The situation was tenser than any in the capital since the Civil War. Ten thousand disappointed people, who had kept good discipline for weeks, were ready to break and mob the Senate. Waters played a final card to keep order: "I call on you to sing 'America,' " he shouted. After a few false starts, the men obeyed. Gradually, the song gathered strength.

The emergency was over, at least for the moment. The singing died out, and bugles sounded assembly. The men milled about, looking for their outfits for the march back to camp. It was dark now, and the nervous men waiting in the White House and the Capitol could take a deep breath. The bonus was dead, at least until Congress reconvened in December, after the presidential elections.

But the Bonus Army did not disappear. The government issued reports that the men were leaving. The Bonus Force and the police reported, however, that new recruits were arriving about as fast as old ones left. Estimates of the size of the force issued by the government, the police, the newspapers, and

**IN CAMP AGAIN**

At their Washington campsites, the Bonus Marchers tried to maintain military order. Among other things, this meant setting up kitchens to cook and to serve large groups of men. Here, one ex-soldier ladles out a dish of food for another. The stove is a trench, covered by a steel beam, with a rude chimney at the cook's left. *(Culver Pictures)*

the Bonus Army itself varied widely. At its largest, the Bonus Army probably numbered just under 20,000 men. Membership shifted constantly; perhaps as many as 50,000 veterans were in Washington at one time or another during June and July of 1932.

The government offered to lend the marchers train fare or gas money to leave town, plus seventy-five cents a day for other expenses. Many veterans simply took the money and stayed in town. Others used it to recruit new members. Thus a month after the Senate had defeated the Patman bill, there were about as many marchers as ever. The police estimated 15,000 people, two-thirds of them now crowded into Anacostia Flats.

By July, with no hope of a bonus from Congress, the veterans' mood soured. Their newspaper published more militant calls for action. Waters began to allow the small group of about 150 communists to eat occasionally at the Anacostia mess. (He had always thrown them out before.) He even began to talk about a permanent organization of veterans in politics, which he would call "Khaki Shirts," in imitation of the "Brown Shirts" that Adolf Hitler had organized.

In the White House, too, opinions were getting stronger. After the Senate had defeated the bonus, the president decided the marchers had no business squatting on government land. He also decided they were not truly patriotic veterans asking for relief. Instead he believed they had been:

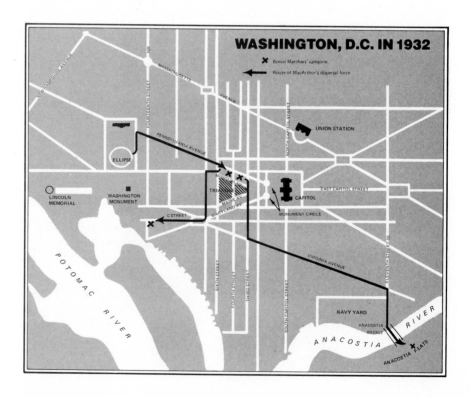

### ON THE CAPITOL STEPS

The high point of the Bonus March was probably this scene on the steps of the Capitol. Inside, while the veterans wait, the Senate is debating the Patman bill, which would have given them early payment of the bonus they had come to ask for. The bill's defeat nearly triggered an angry confrontation between the veterans and U.S. Marines, who had been called out to keep order. *(Wide World Photos)*

organized and promoted by the communists, and included a large number of hoodlums and ex-convicts determined to raise a public disturbance. They were frequently addressed by Democratic congressmen, seeking to inflame them against me.

The differences grew sharper, the summer hotter, and tempers shorter. On July 16, the most serious incident so far broke out at the Capitol. Congress was about to adjourn. Waters ordered his men to make one last symbolic demonstration. By midday, nearly 7,000 Bonus Marchers were at the Capitol. Their mood was much uglier than a month before. Senators and congressmen crowded near every window to watch. Even Glassford lost his nerve.

Glassford ordered Waters taken into custody and moved to the basement of the Capitol. When the veterans saw what was happening, they stopped cheering Glassford and began to boo and jeer. "Waters! Waters!" they shouted. Glassford was forced to bring the Bonus Army's commander onto the platform. After a short, harsh exchange with Glassford, Waters tried to calm his people. Then he ordered them to move to the middle: "Use the center steps. But I want you to keep a lane open for the white-collared birds, so they won't rub into us lousy rats. We're going to stay here until I see Hoover!"

The demonstration was clearly dangerous. Several congressmen came out of the Capitol to speak to the demonstrators, trying to cool them off. Finally the Speaker of the House, John Nance Garner, agreed to meet with Waters and a committee of his aides inside the building. Garner handled the situation well. He made a few empty promises of help and was photographed with Waters. When the conference was over, Waters went back outside and ordered his followers to their camps. For a second time an extremely touchy and potentially violent situation had been controlled.

In the White House, however, tempers were also growing shorter. Hoover had just been renominated by the Republicans to run for a second term. The Democrats would meet soon to nominate Franklin D. Roosevelt, then governor of New York. Hoover knew the campaign would be rough. But he knew he would win if he could overcome the widespread idea that he was responsible for the depression.

A favorite tactic of Hoover's closest associates was to picture him as the firm opponent of all kinds of radicalism. Unfortunately, the Bonus Army was the most visible kind of radicalism. Hoover had always opposed the bonus. Now he and his advisers decided to move firmly against the veterans. Some even hoped for an incident. Then it would appear that the government had to defend its very life against a radical insurrection.

### THE PRESIDENT'S CAMP

Herbert Hoover opened a rest camp for himself in The Raridan, Virginia, not far from Washington. To meet his new neighbors, Hoover held a lawn party, where he is shown chatting with one of the guests. Behind him stands another Virginia neighbor wearing riding jodhpurs. *(Culver Pictures)*

A few days after Congress had adjourned, the administration decided to move. The tensest point in Washington was the two square blocks on the south side of Pennsylvania Avenue, just a block from the Capitol and a mile from the White House. The buildings here were part of a triangle of structures that had been condemned to make way for a government building program. All over the triangle, veterans had camped in and around vacant and half-demolished structures, eyesores that embarrassed the administration. On July 21, on instructions from the Treasury Department, the commissioners who governed the District of Columbia (and were directly responsible to the administration) ordered the veterans to evacuate the two blocks. For various reasons the order was not carried out at once. But Waters told his people to be ready to leave. Glassford was locating another site farther away, where they could take their few possessions and settle again.

Finally, at about 10:00 A.M. on July 28, Treasury officials accompanied by Glassford and his police entered the area. The veterans began to evacuate the buildings and their makeshift shanties, leaving behind everything that they could not carry or push along in small carts or baby carriages. Everything went peacefully, though a few veterans had to be taken out under arrest. Before noon the first building was empty. In the meantime, a large crowd of Washington citizens had gathered to watch. Their sympathies were divided between the police and the veterans.

Then, a little past noon, veterans from other camps filtered into the area, mixing with the crowd. One group came to stage a formal demonstration. Paul Anderson, a journalist, described what happened next:

> At noon, three bonus men, one carrying a large American flag, started across the block, followed by several hundred. When the leaders encountered a policeman, he grabbed the flag. There was a scuffle, and one of the marchers was hit on the head with a night stick. He wrested it from the officer and struck the cop, and there was a shower of bricks from the buddies in the rear. It looked like an ugly mess, but the cops kept their heads, and no shots were fired.
> Glassford dashed into the heart of the melee, smiled when a brickbat hit him on the chest, and stopped the fighting. Within two minutes, the veterans were cheering Glassford.

For another half hour the police continued their work. The veterans were leaving the buildings, but they stood around outside, many on big piles of bricks. No one is certain what happened next. Some witnesses said a policeman tried to clear veterans out of a building that had not even been ordered vacated. They resisted. Another observer said that a policeman started climbing some makeshift stairs, lost his balance, and fell. In a panic he pulled his revolver and began to fire wildly into a crowd near him. General Glassford gave what may be the most accurate account:

> I was about twenty yards away from the building when I heard a commotion. I went to the second floor. One officer had started up the steps, and near the rear, I heard some say, "Let's get him!"

VETERANS AND THE POLICE

A group of Bonus Marchers try to defend their tents against the advancing police. The
Bonus Army was one of the few organizations in America that was more or less integrated
racially, and the group shown here includes at least a couple of determined blacks. The most
intense struggle seems to concern whether the marchers or the police have a better right to
the flag. *(Culver Pictures)*

As he started up the steps, bricks started falling on him [Glassford was not
certain whether the bricks were being thrown or were just falling], and as I leaned
over the railing above, I saw him fall and draw his gun, firing two shots.

Other policemen also started shooting. Then veterans began to throw
bricks at every policeman in sight. Again Glassford acted quickly to prevent
a vicious riot. He ran outside, shouting, "Stop that shooting!" The firing
ended, and the bricks stopped flying. Ambulances rushed to take away the
injured. One policeman was hurt seriously by a brick. One Bonus Marcher
was dead; another died later of gunshot wounds.

The battle of the Bonus Army might have ended here. Glassford had the
situation in hand. The veterans were moving out of the buildings as they had
been ordered. On the whole they were reluctant but still willing to cooperate.
Waters had supported Glassford every step of the way. Within another hour
or two, evacuation of the two blocks would have been complete. But the
administration also had decided to act. Hoover had ordered the chief of staff
of the army, General MacArthur, to bring troops into the city to restore civil
peace.

The troops—about 500 at first, then later over 1,000—formed up behind the White House. They came armed with bayoneted rifles and heavy blue canisters of tear gas. There were cavalry with sabers, a machine-gun squadron, several infantry companies, and even a half-dozen tanks. MacArthur put the troops under the command of General Perry L. Miles. But as he later wrote, "In accordance with the President's request, I accompanied General Miles." With MacArthur was his aide, Major Dwight David Eisenhower. And in the cavalry was George S. Patton (who had no way of knowing that Joe Angelo had come back to Washington and was out in the troubled city with about 12,000 of his buddies, waiting).

At about four o'clock the cavalry led the way, the iron shoes of their horses clattering on the asphalt of Pennsylvania Avenue. Then came tanks, more cavalry, the infantry, and the mounted machine gunners. They rode, walked, and rumbled up to the triangle, pushing the crowds back and surrounding the buildings. Without any conference or hesitation the troops (who wore gas masks and carried fixed bayonets) began to throw tear-gas bombs into the buildings. They were going to clear the entire area.

The veterans did not resist. A few hung back and had to be jabbed at with bayonets. Mostly they stumbled out of the area and toward Anacostia. MacArthur, who also had tears streaming down his face from the tear gas, ordered most of his men to herd the veterans south. Another detachment moved west, to attack the small, separate camp of the communist group.[3] Suddenly, it became clear that the general intended to clear the entire District. In the triangle, smoke began to rise. There, the troops had set fire to the shacks, tents, and scattered belongings of the Bonus Army.

MacArthur's forces kept pushing the straggling veterans before them with bayonets and sabers. The sun was going down behind them. Ahead lay the drawbridge to Anacostia. The Bonus Army's rear guard hurried across the bridge at about sunset. Waters had already given the order to evacuate Anacostia and had sent word to MacArthur asking for time to move women and children out of the camp. On the flats about 7,000 men were scurrying around, trying to keep order in a forced retreat.

From the time the troops first appeared, the Bonus Marchers gave no resistance. They booed, they swore—but they moved. MacArthur left his tanks north of the river and paused before Anacostia Flats for an hour before sending the infantry. But when they went onto the flats, the soldiers threw gas everywhere. Stragglers were treated very roughly. The soldiers then set fire to the camp. (Many of the veterans had already put matches to their borrowed army tents.) Next they moved out of the camp to the nearby area where many of the veterans still stood watching their shacks burn. As the troops rushed up the hill, which was not federal property, they continued to throw tear gas. One woman, whose baby had actually been born since the Bonus Army's arrival, told this story:

**MACARTHUR AND EISENHOWER**

The command of the military force that finally chased the Bonus Army out of Washington was in the hands of General Douglas MacArthur, shown here on the left, with his aide, Dwight David Eisenhower. MacArthur insisted that the Bonus Marchers were a fundamental threat to the government. *(UPI)*

---

[3] Communists in this camp included James Ford, their candidate for vice president. On July 31 the *New York Times* ran a front-page article quoting the communists. "We agitated for the bonus and led the demonstration of the veterans in Washington." However, the communists were never the Bonus Force's prime movers.

The troops came up the hill, driving the people ahead of them. As they passed by the house [where the woman was staying], one of them threw a tear-gas bomb over the fence into the front yard. The house was filled with gas, and we all began to cry. We got wet towels and put them over the faces of the children. About a half an hour later, my baby began to vomit. I took her outside in the air and she vomited again. Next day, she began to turn black and blue.

A few days later the baby died—the third and last fatality of the battle of the Bonus Army.

The day after the action was a time for summing up. The White House and other administration officials issued statements. MacArthur gave his version in a press conference:

That mob was a bad-looking mob. It was animated by the essence of revolution. They had come to the conclusion, beyond the shadow of a doubt, that they were about to take over either the direct control of the government, or else to control it by indirect methods. It is my belief that had the President not acted today, he would have been faced with a grave situation. Had he let it go on another week, I believe that the institutions of our government would have been severely threatened.

To this version of the threat posed by the Bonus Force, MacArthur added that it was the veterans who had burned their own shacks in the triangle.

Another kind of summing up came from Joe Angelo, who told a newspaper reporter his story. He was at Anacostia Flats, watching a group of infantrymen in gas masks overrun the shack he had been living in. They were urged on by a tough, confident cavalry officer. Angelo blinked the burning tear gas out of his eyes and recognized George S. Patton. Then, like the rest of the Bonus Army, he ran. Soon he was back home in Camden, from where he had started his long hike to Washington a year and a half before.

# Prosperity, Depression, and New Deal

Most of the Bonus March veterans who went to Washington were as politically innocent as Joe Angelo. Some of their leaders had a little political knowledge—only the tiny fraction who were communists thought they understood the basic problems of American society and sought a revolutionary solution. But the great rank and file of the marchers were simply caught in a web of circumstances they did not understand or want.

The marchers' experience was defined by the two great events they had participated in, the Great War and the Great Depression. Between lay the decade of the 1920s, the "Jazz Age." But most of the marchers had experienced only a little jazz. Like most Americans, they had passed through a curiously contradictory decade. On the one hand, American society of the 1920s was characterized by tremendous innovations—some technological, other social. But, alongside all the newness and experimentation, the 1920s had been a decade of profound, sometimes violent conservatism. Both in formal politics, centered in Washington, and in the informal politics of organized movements, the keynote had not been innovation but restoration.

Conservatism in politics received a kind of endorsement from the economy. The 1920s was a period of apparent prosperity. In some sectors, in fact, the economy virtually underwent a "boom." And this prosperity made it appear to many Americans that the country had returned from the distortions of progressive reform and war to "normalcy." It took the Depression to show that normalcy was an illusion, and that the 1920s had contained profound distortions of its own.

## A TIDE OF REACTION

For millions of Americans, the uncertainties of modernity, the wave of progressive reforms, and the moral crusade of the war were all extremely unsettling. Even before the war was over, millions of people had already decided that change had gone too far, that the republic was in desperate danger of losing its stability and virtue. For some, the threat was simple: the country was being overrun by foreigners and by "foreign" political ideas. For others, the problem was alcohol, and the loose life associated with it. Still others viewed blacks as the principal threat. For many, the danger lay in the growing number and power of Jews and Catholics. Some complained about the inroads new scientific ideas were making on "traditional" values and beliefs.

Not every American participated, by any means, but a large and very active segment of society—especially in the South and the Midwest—joined in a series of movements and organizations to save their country from what were seen by them as the perils of change. Sometimes, the results were merely quaint—as when the sale of alcohol was forbidden by an amendment to the Constitution. Or when schoolteachers were prosecuted for explaining Charles Darwin's theory of evolution in their classrooms. At other times, however, the results were more serious, even tragic, as when dozens of blacks were lynched by mobs, or hundreds of immigrant "radicals" were hounded in court and even sentenced to die for their supposed crimes. This was part of the character of "normalcy," the opposite and darker face of the "Jazz Age."

## The Red Scare

The conservative reaction focused sharply on radicalism. The Russian Revolution, which had brought the communist government of the Bolsheviks to power, was followed by communist uprisings in Germany and Hungary. These developments created an atmosphere of fear in the United States. Many people, including a number of powerful leaders in federal and state governments, believed that a communist conspiracy was at work among them, ready to "radicalize" the country.

In 1919, a series of spectacular strikes and the

outbreak of political sabotage fed the fear. In the spring of that year, two small groups of anarchists attempted to bomb the homes and offices of a number of government officials and businessmen. The bombs, most of which were sent through the mails, were probably the work of mentally unstable persons. Certainly they had nothing to do with the tiny organized Socialist and Communist parties of the country.

In fact, the bombers were incompetent. Most of the bombs were never delivered because they did not have enough postage. One bomb only damaged the house of its intended victim, but it blew the bomber himself—an Italian anarchist—to bits. Another, addressed to a Georgia politician, was opened by his maid (a black worker, not a capitalist). She lost her hands as a result. But the bombings did convince many people that revolution was at hand.

One of the people who was most convinced was Woodrow Wilson's attorney general, A. Mitchell Palmer. Like Wilson, Palmer was a liberal and a strong antiradical. The attorney general also had his eye on the Democratic nomination

of 1920. So he used the "red scare" to make his department the center of the action. He obtained a special appropriation for hunting down radicals. With the money, he formed a new antisubversive division of the Justice Department, headed by J. Edgar Hoover.

Beginning in November of 1919, the Justice Department conducted a series of raids against radical groups, seeking out suspected communists at union meetings, at Communist party headquarters, and in their homes. The most spectacular of the raids, which came on New Year's Day, 1920, resulted in the arrest of 6,000 people. In the end the Palmer raids led to the conviction of only a handful of citizens, most of them for minor crimes. Immigrant aliens, who were Palmer's main target, suffered more; about 600 were eventually deported, mostly to the Soviet Union.

Palmer's campaign created an atmosphere of near hysteria among many Americans. It led to one tragedy that did more than any other single event of the 1920s to divide Americans of different political beliefs. In 1920, two Italian anarchists were arrested in Boston on a charge of robbing

**SACCO AND VANZETTI**

Here, in 1927, Nicola Sacco and Bartolomeo Vanzetti enter the courtroom to make their last plea for justice. Some recent evidence seems to show that at least one of them may have been guilty of the crime he was charged with. But no amount of new evidence can set aside the fact that they were unfairly tried and unfairly convicted. *(UPI)*

a shoe company and murdering two of its employees. Their trial soon became a political event, a test of the established authority against political radicalism. The trial was unfair. Even the judge privately referred to the defendants, Nicola Sacco and Bartolomeo Vanzetti, as anarchists.

But in the political climate of the red scare, Sacco and Vanzetti were convicted and sentenced to death. The process of appeals was long and unsuccessful. Finally, in 1927, the year of Lindbergh's flight, both men were executed in the electric chair. To the small number of American liberals and radicals of the 1920s, Sacco and Vanzetti were the century's greatest martyrs. They were modern counterparts of the victims of the Salem witch trials and the Haymarket affair. But to most Americans, they were just Italian radicals who had been properly punished.

The bonus marchers of 1932 had to contend with the lingering effects of the red scare. They were accused of being communists, and of serving as tools in a foreign conspiracy. When Douglas MacArthur marched on their camp at Anacostia, he did so in the belief that he was protecting the country from a powerful revolutionary movement. The irony was, however, that the marchers themselves accepted much of the ideology of "Americanism" that underlay the red scare. Their response to the charge that they were communists was to insist on their own patriotism, and to point proudly to their record of military service. Most of the marchers were probably just as devoutly anticommunist, just as insistent on their own "100 percent Americanism" as their critics.

The red scare also made it possible for those Americans who feared immigrants and their ethnic and religious differences to restrict immigration. In February 1921 (over the veto of President Wilson) Congress passed a law that limited immigration, especially from countries in southern and eastern Europe. According to the law, the number of immigrants from a country in any given year could not exceed 3 percent of the number of people of that nationality who were already in the United States in 1910. In 1924, the law was

made even more restrictive. Quotas would now be based on resident population in 1890, immigration limited to 150,000 a year after 1927, and Asians totally excluded. The effect of the laws was to end, almost at once, the flow of immigration.

## Prohibition and Reaction

Like the red scare and the movement for immigration restriction, the prohibition of alcohol in the 1920s had its roots in the progressive period. In 1919, the states had passed the Eighteenth Amendment, which empowered Congress to prohibit the sale of alcoholic beverages. The amendment marked the victory of a long campaign of temperance. It provided another rallying point for conservative, small-town Americans. They divided society into the "drys" and the "wets" and opposed any politician who did not favor prohibition.

The prohibition movement failed to stop Americans from drinking. In most cities, people continued to drink whiskey in speakeasies. The sale of bootleg whiskey was controlled largely by organized gangs of criminals. Gangs like the one led by Al Capone in Chicago bribed public officials and policemen to cover up their operations. But for most conservative Americans, prohibition was above all a moral crusade. It was an issue they could use to split their countrymen into two camps: one composed of decent people, the other of riffraff.

Another conservative campaign of the 1920s was the attempt of many Protestant Americans—again, especially in the South and the Midwest—to prevent schools from teaching dangerous or "un-American" ideas. In several Southern states this crusade was aimed mainly at the idea of evolution. The notion of biological evolution was an old one. It became scientifically respected in the nineteenth century through the work of Charles Darwin. By the 1920s, practically every scientist in the world believed that animals, including man, had evolved over a long period of time. But this seemed to many people to go against the fundamentals of their religion. They saw it as a challenge to the biblical story of creation.

Several state legislatures forbade their schools to teach the doctrine of evolution. In 1925, John Scopes, a schoolteacher in Dayton, Tennessee, decided to challenge the law. He was arrested, and his trial became almost as much a spectacle as the trial of Sacco and Vanzetti.

Scopes was defended by the most famous criminal lawyer in the United States, Clarence Darrow of Chicago. William Jennings Bryan led the prosecution. Bryan, an aging but still powerful leader of millions of fundamentalists, stood ready to smite the forces of modernism. He was humiliated on the witness stand by Darrow. Reporters from every major American newspaper—and several European papers—covered the trial.

Scopes lost the case and was fined $100. The Tennessee law stayed on the books. But after the Scopes trial, the direction of education in the South and elsewhere shifted away from Bryan's intellectual conservatism toward the acceptance of modern science. Bryan's crusade, like many other conservative movements of the 1920s, was only a temporary victory over twentieth-century ideas and social habits.

## The Ku Klux Klan

The most spectacular conservative movement of the 1920s was the Ku Klux Klan. The Klan, which had all but disappeared after Reconstruction, was reorganized in 1915 in Georgia. Its membership grew slowly until the war was over. Then, taking many of its cues from the red scare, the Klan began to gain support. Much of its strength still lay in the rural South and Southwest. But there was a new element in this second growth: now, millions in the Northern states, many of them city dwellers, joined this bizarre organization. At one time or another, about 5

THE KKK ON THE MARCH

The Ku Klux Klan is shown here, in 1926, in one of its favorite kinds of moments. The robed Klansmen are marching publicly and openly, declaring to all the world their patriotic purposes and determination to save the country from a host of perils. And yet, even in this aggressively public setting, the marchers preserve the air of secrecy, mystery, and ritual that is so important to many of its members. (Culver Pictures)

million Americans took up membership and donned the white sheets that were the uniform of the Klan. The strongest Klan state was not in the South at all but in Indiana, where the organization appeared for a time to control even the state government.

The Ku Klux Klan was a marginal, fringe organization. It attracted only the most conservative citizens. The white robes and hoods, the secrecy and the rituals, the burning of crosses in the night, demanded considerable dedication from its members. They had to be able to stomach a good deal of violence and torture. And they had to be able to tolerate a large element of the ridiculous—as in the titles of Klan officers, like "dragon," "kleagal," or "kludd." Nevertheless, the Klan was still able to elect one of its dragons governor of Indiana, able to march openly in Washington in 1925, and able to control the Democratic presidential nomination in 1924.

In the long run, the Klan—like the prohibitionist movement and the fundamentalist attempt to prevent the teaching of evolution—was destined to lose. Blacks would not be lynched in great numbers forever, the freedom to drink alcohol would return, new scientific theories would get taught, eventually. But in the political atmosphere of the 1920s, it was possible for millions of Klansmen, and millions of other conservatives who did not join the organization, to convince themselves that their victory was close at hand, that the country would be saved, after all.

## THE POLITICS OF CONSERVATISM

The political instrument of salvation, restoration, and "normalcy" was to be the Republican party. As the war ended, the Republicans could see as plainly as anyone else that there was a change in the atmosphere. The policies of reform and military crusade, on which Woodrow Wilson and the Democrats had built their success in national politics, were clearly going to fall into disrepute. The Republicans met at Chicago in their national

convention of 1920 full of hope. They were still the majority party, they knew. And no Democrat on the horizon represented a real threat to the election of a Republican president. Wilson's illness, the failure of the League of Nations, the doings of A. Mitchell Palmer—all had helped to disorganize the Democrats.

The only question seemed to be whether the Republicans could unite on a candidate. The convention deadlocked for six ballots. Then, a few party leaders huddled in one of the most famous "smoke-filled rooms" in American history and chose a surprise candidate—Warren Gamaliel Harding, senator from Ohio.

## Harding

Harding was a small-town newspaper publisher and politician, reminiscent of the Republican style of the late nineteenth century. He had risen carefully through the party system in Ohio to become a senator. His political virtues were, primarily, loyalty to the organization and a discreet silence on most issues. A handsome but simple man, he was puzzled by complicated issues like taxation, the tariff, and foreign affairs. He was "one of the boys," who enjoyed a night of whiskey and poker with his cronies. He had never proposed an important law or policy, nor made an important speech, in his whole career. But he had a face that voters wanted to trust. And the people who ran the party knew they could trust him, too. He was a party regular. He would not have any strange ideas about regulating business or supporting labor unions; nor would he propose any odd reforms. He was, in a word, conservative.

For vice president, the Republicans nominated Calvin Coolidge, another small-town politician. Coolidge had first won a national reputation as a tough antilabor man during the strikes of 1919. When Boston's police organized as an AFL local and went out on strike, Coolidge was governor of Massachusetts. Without attempting to settle the strike peacefully, he sent armed troops into Boston. The protest of Samuel Gompers, the

# W. E. B. Du Bois

(Culver Pictures)

William Edward Burghardt Du Bois (1868–1963) had one of the most extraordinary and creative careers of any modern American writer or intellectual. During his nearly ninety-six years, Du Bois was a black student at Harvard, a poet, a novelist, a journalist, a reformer, a New York intellectual, a founder of the Pan-African movement, and, at the end, a communist and an expatriate.

Du Bois began his life in Massachusetts. Intellectually talented, he made his way through Harvard and did some graduate work in Germany to earn a prestigious Harvard Ph.D. His initial career choice was to be an academic. He taught at Wilberforce College in Ohio, at the University of Pennsylvania, and then at Atlanta University.

But his writing and his move to the South drew him gradually away from academic life and into the politics of race. His first book, *The Philadelphia Negro* (1899), was not only a superb exercise in academic sociology but a passionate recognition that the "Negro problem" could be solved only when blacks chose no longer merely to imitate whites but instead to cultivate a new attitude of respect for what they were as blacks.

In *The Souls of Black Folk* (1903), Du Bois pressed the point further. The prevailing program of reform among blacks had been devised by Booker T. Washington. But Washington's plan, as Du Bois saw it, proposed only that blacks should accept white society as they found it and seek gradually to work their way into it, from the bottom up. Du Bois believed this plan would not work—partly because of white resistance, which he viewed as determined and even violent. Washington's program was flawed in other ways also. It did not recognize that blacks were different, that many of the black "souls" of which he wrote were kindly, gentle, submissive, and generous, and that it would be fatal merely to toss such souls into the white world of competition, materialism, and greed.

These ideas, combined with an increasing number of violent acts against blacks in all parts of the United States, led Du Bois into political activism. He was one of the founders of an organization called the Niagara Movement, dedicated to a more militant defense of black rights. Du Bois wrote a series of resolutions that voiced the sense of crisis that gave form to the movement, a sense of no progress. "Stripped of verbose subterfuge and in its naked nastiness, the new American creed says: fear to let black men even try to rise lest they become the equals of the white. And that in the land that professes to follow Jesus Christ. The blasphemy of such a course is only matched by its cowardice."

In 1910, in league with a large number of white reformers and intellectuals, Du Bois formed the Niagara Movement into a new organization, the National Association for the Advancement of Colored People. He was for many years the editor of the association's magazine, *The Crisis*. But Du Bois had been losing faith in the capacity of white society ever to accept blacks as blacks. He left teaching and moved into Harlem. He helped found the Pan-African Congress during the peace talks in Paris in 1918. And at the age of ninety-six, he renounced his United States citizenship, announced his membership in the Communist Party, and moved to the African state of Ghana, where he died.

AFL president, was met with one of Coolidge's most famous quasi-grammatical retorts: "There is no right to strike against the public safety, anywhere, anytime."

Coolidge was less a party regular than Harding, but he was even more conservative in matters of policy. Except for his odd flair for terse statements, he was a lackluster man with a crabbed countenance, a striking contrast to Harding's open handsomeness. In any case, no one at the Republican convention thought that they were choosing anything but a vice president.

The Democrats nominated a lackluster candidate of their own, James M. Cox. However, they tried to spice up the ticket with a dashing young New Yorker, Franklin D. Roosevelt. Roosevelt had served as assistant secretary of the navy under Wilson. The convention hoped the Roosevelt name would attract voters who remembered his cousin Theodore. But probably no Democratic ticket could have won in 1920. The voters wanted a change. Sixty percent of them voted for Harding. They also sent large Republican majorities to both the House and the Senate, making it one of the most complete victories in the history of American national politics. Harding carried every state outside the Democrats' solid South and cracked even that by winning Tennessee. The repudiation of Wilson's New Freedom seemed complete.

## Return to Normalcy

Harding took office with a slogan that coined a new word. He said the country needed a "return to normalcy." No dictionary defined "normalcy," but almost every American probably knew what the president meant. Harding believed that there had been too much experimentation, too many attempts to regulate the economy and the working lives of Americans, too much speculation about new diplomatic arrangements such as the League of Nations. Normalcy meant letting things take their natural course—not interfering in the decisions of businessmen or in the complex affairs of other nations. Normalcy meant, in short, a return to simpler times and uncomplicated politics.

Harding's relaxed conservatism was not a well-defined policy. Rather, it was a wish for fewer policies and less activity by the government. For his cabinet, the president chose people sympathetic to the practices of industrial and business leaders. His most important appointment, in fact, was Secretary of the Treasury Andrew Mellon, a Pennsylvania industrialist who owned the only important company then making aluminum in the United States.

Mellon helped to shape the small amount of legislation that the Harding administration presented to Congress. His pet bill was one cutting the maximum income tax on the wealthy from 65 percent to 25 percent. (Congress at first reduced the limit to only 50 percent, but Mellon later got most of what he wanted.) He also proposed, and got from Congress, much higher tariffs on imports, a policy that benefited American business and industry by limiting foreign competition.

## The Ohio Gang

Specific legislation was less important in Harding's conservative administration than its general relaxation of federal controls over business. Harding did not try to tear down the established regulatory agencies, like the Interstate Commerce Commission or the Federal Reserve Board. Instead, he merely appointed persons to these agencies who were so friendly toward corporations that they administered the law gently or not at all. And Harding named as his secretary of commerce Herbert Hoover, who had made a fortune as a mining engineer and investor.

Hoover was clearly the most distinguished of Harding's appointments. He had made an enormous reputation during the war as head of the federal Food Administration. Unlike most of his colleagues in the Harding administration, Hoover was a thoughtful man, with a fairly clear-cut ideological position. He was a promoter of what he called "individualism." His central faith was that private enterprise, left to its own devices, could end poverty and usher in a "new era" of prosperity and progress.

To Hoover, the modern corporation was, ultimately, an instrument of social justice. Capitalism had, he believed, emerged from its nineteenth-century youth into a mature period of development. In this new maturity, corporations would be less concerned with sheer competition for profits and more determined to produce goods efficiently. In the process, the corporations would also contribute a great deal of what Hoover called "service" to society—technological innovation, education, the redistribution of income, and so on, until ignorance, poverty, and disease were banished.

The role of government, Hoover believed, should be to help this process along by providing information and assistance to businesses, not to hinder them through wasteful and inefficient regulation. This was the logic that Hoover applied as secretary of commerce. And this was the logic he would later bring to the White House.

Unfortunately, Harding also brought to Washington a group of friends who soon became known as the Ohio Gang. Some held seemingly harmless positions, like Old Doc Sawyer, a doctor in less than good standing with the medical profession. Old Doc became the White House physician, with the rank of army brigadier general. Other Ohio Gang members were given more important positions, such as attorney general and secretary of the interior.

After two years in office, Harding, who was personally honest about money, began to realize that his appointees were stealing and peddling influence. In the spring and summer of 1923, two administration officials committed suicide while being investigated. In June, Harding began a long vacation in the West. As he left, he complained to a journalist, "My God, this is a hell of a job. I have no trouble with my enemies. But my friends! They're the ones that keep me walking the floor nights!"

Two months later, in California after a trip to Alaska, Harding suffered what Old Doc Sawyer called food poisoning. Harding now had to pay in person for this political appointment, for Sawyer was wrong. The president had suffered a heart attack instead; on August 2 he died. In a way, Harding was lucky. He was mourned by his countrymen almost as much as Lincoln had been. He was spared the knowledge of a new scandal that would later become almost synonymous with his name.

Albert Fall, Harding's secretary of the interior, had finagled Interior Department control of oil reserves set aside for the navy. There were two large reserves, at Elk Hill in California and at Teapot Dome in Wyoming. Private oil interests were willing to pay almost any price to drill the land. And they did.

Two oil company executives, Edward L. Doheny and Harry F. Sinclair, gave and "lent" Fall almost a half-million dollars in return for secret leases allowing them to drill on the reserves. The secret leaked out faster than the oil. The government managed to cancel the leases, but Fall went to prison for a year. He was the first cabinet officer in American history to be put behind bars.

## COOLIDGE AND BUSINESS

When Harding died, Vice President Calvin Coolidge became president. Though privately a talkative man, "Silent Cal" as Coolidge was called, spoke very little in public. He kept most of Harding's appointees and basically followed his predecessor's policies for the rest of the term. As the 1924 election approached, there was little doubt about what the Republicans would do. Their convention enthusiastically nominated Coolidge.

The Democrats experienced a struggle between two wings of their party. One represented the rural South and West, the old Bryan supporters. They were at least as conservative as the Republicans. The other wing was newer and based in the Northern cities. It was made up

### HARDING AND COOLIDGE

Warren G. Harding and Calvin Coolidge, president and vice president, were the personal symbols of the "return to normalcy" after World War I. Harding's style, as suggested by his clothing in this picture, was a trifle sporty for a president—but in keeping with the tone of the 1920s. Coolidge, on the other hand, was a man of unrelieved dourness, both of expression and of dress. *(National Photo Co., courtesy of the Library of Congress)*

mostly of "wets" (opponents of prohibition) and depended heavily on the support of immigrants (many of them Catholics or Jews). After 103 ballots the convention settled on a compromise candidate, John W. Davis.

Coolidge was conservative. But so was Davis, who was associated with the firm of J. P. Morgan. Once more the time seemed right, as in 1912, to try a third party. The Progressive candidate was Robert La Follette, now nearly seventy but still a fiery opponent of business interests. He did well. Although Coolidge won the election easily, with 15 million votes, La Follette managed to get almost 5 million votes, and he carried Wisconsin's electoral vote. Davis and his badly split party could muster only 8½ million votes, less than a third of the total.

Coolidge's second term in office was a continuation of the conservative policies of the earlier years, but without the scandals of 1921–1923. Mellon and Hoover still exercised great influence. The new administration went on supporting high tariffs, low taxes on corporations and the wealthy, and a hands-off policy on trusts. It had an essentially do-nothing approach to farm problems and a negative attitude toward labor as well. The entire conservative politics of the 1920s was summed up in Coolidge's most famous sentence: "The business of America is business."

Still, the president was popular, and doubtless he could have been nominated for a second full term and won. But his second most famous sentence was: "I do not choose to run." Coolidge may have meant simply that he would accept a draft. Still, for once, "Silent Cal" had spoken too soon and said too much. The Republicans took him literally and turned to Herbert Hoover, the most prestigious official in the administration.

## The Democratic Challenge of 1928

The Democrats partially healed their old split, hoping for victory. Governor Alfred E. Smith of New York won the nomination easily. Smith and Hoover were almost perfect contrasts. Hoover was conservative, even gloomy. He dressed in neat blue suits and was the perfect representative of stability and efficiency. Above all, he opposed any extension of federal power over private enterprise (unless, as with tariffs, federal power could be used to help business.)

Smith, on the other hand, was a happy, talkative, cigar-chomping Irish American politician. He wore a brown derby and checked suits and talked with an urban twang. During the campaign, Hoover accused Smith of socialism because the New Yorker favored federal ownership of electric power-generating facilities.

However different their personalities and political backgrounds may have been, Smith and Hoover actually ran on very similar platforms. To head his campaign, Smith chose a Republican executive from General Motors, a man who had in fact voted for Coolidge in 1924. And in a variety of other ways, the Democrats strained to capture the political center by hewing to a very conservative policy line. On the surface, at least, the election was a contest between personal styles and religious convictions.

Smith's Catholicism got most of the publicity. Some of the charges were merely nasty, as when the Methodist bishop of Virginia referred to Smith as "this wet Roman Catholic chamberlain of the Pope of Rome." But even literate, liberal Protestant newspapers and magazines were concerned. The *Christian Century,* one of the most popular Protestant journals, said that Smith's victory would be the victory "of an alien culture, of a mediaeval Latin mentality, of an undemocratic hierarchy and of a foreign potentate."

Smith's stand on prohibition also alarmed many voters. Hoover called prohibition a "noble experiment," and it may have been this stand, not Smith's religion, that won Hoover powerful support in the South and Southwest. Smith, on the other hand, was a publicly announced "wet," who believed that prohibition was not only a failure, but an act that unfairly deprived urban workers of their modest pleasures.

In the end, Hoover won what appeared to be a landslide. With 58 percent of the popular vote, he almost equaled Harding's record. In fact, because the turnout was unusually heavy, Hoover amassed 21 million votes—more than the combined votes of Coolidge and La Follette in 1924. In the process, Hoover cut deeply into the traditionally Democratic South, where he carried Virginia, Tennessee, North Carolina, Florida, and Texas.

But there was another side to the election, an aspect that was almost lost in the apparent landslide. Smith had made some gains, too. Although he had won fewer electoral votes than any Democrat since 1872, Smith had succeeded in taking two Eastern states, Massachusetts and Rhode Island. This was an indication of a powerful new source of support that the Democrats might be able to capitalize on later—support from immigrants and the children of immigrants in Eastern cities. In 1924, Coolidge had swept all twelve of the largest cities in the nation, and by a large margin. In 1928, Smith won more urban votes than Hoover.

Despite this straw in the wind, however, the Republican ascendancy was still in full swing. Hoover could look toward the inauguration and the future with confidence. The powerful and profitable industrial system, watched over at a discreet distance by a sympathetic government, did seem to be ushering in an era of unprecedented prosperity for millions. So it looked in the winter of 1928–1929.

## BOOM AND BUST

On the surface, at least, the 1920s was a decade of great prosperity. Progress seemed inevitable as more and more cars, radios, washing machines, and other goods poured off assembly lines. More workers were producing more goods than ever before. The United States seemed to have created an economic miracle.

American buyers and investors were confident. The New York Stock Exchange, where the economy's pulse seemed most vital, enjoyed an amazing boom period after 1923. Sales on the Exchange quadrupled between 1923 and 1930. As sales increased, so did the prices of stocks. Americans were on an investment binge. The total amount of money kept in stocks and bonds increased faster than any other economic factor during the period (much faster, for example, than the actual production or sale of goods).

Much of the new investment was made on credit. According to the rules of the New York Stock Exchange, investors could buy stock by putting some money down and owing the rest to their brokers. These "brokers' loans" showed how little of the investment rush was real money and how much was pure speculation. By 1927, almost $4 billion was still owed on such loans. The whole structure of the stock market was rickety.

Such investment was really a form of gambling. If a stock cost $10 a share and an investor expected it to go up, he could buy a share and wait for the price to rise. In fact, for his $10 he could buy ten shares, one for cash and the other nine on loan. When the stock went up, he could sell his shares at the new price, pay off his broker, and pocket the difference in cash. There would be a problem, though, if the stock went down. Then, when the broker's loan was due, the investor might have to sell not only his ten shares of stock but other assets as well. If the stock market fell too low, he could be ruined.

Year after year, the gambles paid off. More and more ordinary people, with only small amounts of money to invest, began to play the market. The prospering economy appeared to justify their confidence.

## A Warped Economy

But this prosperity was very unevenly distributed through the population. There were large pockets of people throughout the country who did not share it at all. Blacks in both the South and the North did not benefit much. Nor did most farmers, whose lives had long been difficult.

The problems of farmers were especially difficult. In the second half of the nineteenth century, an agricultural revolution had provided the foundation for industrial expansion. Then, during the war, farmers had prospered because of high demand and government supports. The end of the war brought a sharp drop in the demand for exports, and an end to federal aid. At the same time, something odd happened in the domestic market. Improvements in diet slightly increased the demand for vegetables and fruit. But

at the same time, the demand for cereal grains dropped, partly because men released from heavy labor by machines needed fewer calories. In addition, the prevailing Victorian ideal of a sturdy, almost fat figure for men and women had given way to a new slender image of the ideal American male and female.

At the same time, farmers were trapped by the high-volume, technologically sophisticated agriculture that had made many of them successful during the preceding two generations. In wartime, especially, they invested heavily in expensive machines, and they continued to do so even after the demand for their crops had fallen off. In the 1920s, in fact, the number of working tractors on American farms quadrupled.

The effect of these changes was to cause farm prices to drop and production to increase. In 1920, the income of farmers represented about 15 percent of the total national income. By 1929, this proportion had fallen to only about 9 percent. Several million farmers were driven off the land. They drifted to the cities or joined the ranks of the bums who made up a portion of the Bonus Army. Those who stayed in farming very often lost ownership of their land and had to become either tenant farmers or hired hands.

One solution to the problem was government intervention. Grain farmers, especially, supported a scheme that would guarantee farmers a "fair" price for their crop. The scheme involved two things. First, a tariff on imported foodstuffs was needed to prevent foreign producers from taking advantage of an "artificially" high price on the American market. Second, the domestic price of grain needed to be set at a level that was the average for the ten years preceding 1914. The result would be "parity," or a kind of rough equality of agricultural prices and other prices. Under the sponsorship of a senator from Oregon, Charles McNary, and a congressman from Iowa, Gilbert Haugen, a bill providing for parity for grain crops was introduced in the 1924 Congress, but it was defeated in the House.

Two years later, in a bid for Southern support, the McNary-Haugen Bill was broadened to include cotton, tobacco, and rice. In 1927, it passed both houses of Congress but was turned back by a Coolidge veto that could not be overridden. The next year, 1928, Congress again passed the act, but President Coolidge once more exercised his veto power. The principle of parity would have to wait until well after the crash of 1929.

For industrial workers, the situation was a little better. Real wages—the actual purchasing power of earned dollars—rose during the decade by over 20 percent. And some corporations began to behave a little like Herbert Hoover's model, with programs of "enlightened" capitalism. Sanitary and safety conditions were improved in some of the more modern factories. Some companies started pension funds that gave workers a tiny share in the stock of the corporations that employed them. But the major purpose behind these "progressive" practices was to undercut the growth of industrial unionism. The AFL, meantime, pursued a very cautious policy throughout the decade. The failure of strikes in 1919 and several succeeding years made many workers hesitate to join even a conservative union like the AFL. The outcome was a decline of about 15 percent in union membership, despite an increase in the total number of factory workers.

Those at the outer edges of the industrial system—blacks, most women, the many underemployed recent immigrants in the cities—simply did not participate in the prosperity of the decade. Such "soft" spots in the economy led to a very serious distortion. Technological innovation increased productivity rapidly. The question was, simply, How would the increased production be absorbed? Who would buy the washing machines, the cars, the clothes, all the products of a sophisticated industrial system? The total quantity of goods for sale was increasing much faster than the population. Either wages would have to rise dramatically, so that workers would have more money to spend on all the things being made, or prices would have to fall, so that everyone could afford more. Otherwise, the gap between production and sales would grow until inventories were clogged with unsalable surpluses of consumer goods.

But businessmen generally raised wages less than they should have. They also kept prices high. In the short run, their measures meant higher profits—and higher profits for corporations meant the price of their stock rose. They could either invest the profits in still larger factories and produce still more goods. Or they could invest them in stock and heat up the stock market even more. Many corporations did both.

The result was a warped economy. The amount of goods being produced ran far ahead of the people's power to purchase them. Sooner or later an adjustment had to be made. Otherwise, factories would have to close until the surplus cars, clothes, tools, and other items could be bought. For a time the problem could be avoided in two ways. The surplus products could be sold, on credit, to people who could not really afford them. A family could pay for a car, for example, over two or three years. Or the surplus could be exported to foreign countries. But both credit and exporting could help a distorted economic system only briefly.

## The Stock Market Crash

These facts were difficult to see. On the surface, the economy had never looked better, and Americans continued to bet on the future by speculating in stocks. In 1928, the average price of industrial stocks increased by about 25 percent. An investor who bought, say, $1,000 worth of stock in January could sell it in December for $1,250. He could then pocket the $250 profit or invest it in some new gamble. Most speculators did the latter.

Then, after a few rumblings and warnings, the bubble burst. The stock market was not a sure indicator of the country's economic health. In 1929, reality finally caught up with it.

In September, the most popular index of stock prices stood at 452. Two months later it was 234. What this meant, in plain terms, was that the market value of stocks on the Exchange had been halved. Most of the holders of the $4 billion in brokers' loans were ruined. So were many of the brokers. On the worst day of all, "Black Tuesday," October 29, the market index fell 43 points. Other days were almost as bleak and ruinous. Stock prices continued to slide. They reached bottom in 1932. Then, most stocks were worth little more than a tenth of their cost in September 1929. The Great Depression had begun.

It was difficult then, and still is, for people to understand why the panic on Wall Street should have had any effect on the real economy. The factories were still there, ready to roll out goods. The farms were still there, ready to produce food. All the hands willing to work before Black Tuesday were still there, still willing to work.

But, month by month, the entire economic machine ground down. The stock market crash was the crucial link in the chain of events leading to this breakdown. It caused people to make the grim decision not to buy or invest. So storekeepers sold less. And factories produced less or closed down altogether. Many foreclosed on loans made to others because they needed money to pay off their own loans.

Farmers behind on their payments lost their farms as banks desperately tried to collect hard cash. The banks needed cash because millions of people with savings accounts, frightened now, lined up at tellers' windows to withdraw their money. The banks often could not produce the cash because they had invested or lent it. So even the banks began to fail.

Builders of houses and offices stopped construction because they could not borrow money to continue. Down at the bottom of this tangle were plain workers who, by the millions, received notices that they need not come to work anymore. Their jobs disappeared. Since they could not work, they could not buy; since they could not buy, others could not sell or make goods.

The jobless were not just the old-line poor. Many had been solid, middle-class citizens, such as bank tellers or factory foremen. Others were farmers, who had barely managed to survive

throughout the decade. Now they had lost their farms forever. They moved to the cities, looking for food and work, or they began to drift, looking for migrant workers' jobs. People combed garbage heaps for food for their families. They made soup from dandelions. Mostly, however, they waited in a cold, gloomy fog of despair for something to happen.

## Hoover's Optimism

The question posed by the Depression and symbolized by the Bonus March was simple. Could the federal government be used as a tool for dealing with economic disaster? In the past the answer had been no. Other depressions had been allowed to run their course without any federal attempt to bring early recovery or relieve human suffering. But the Great Depression was by far the worst ever. Now the industrial economy was so large and complicated that its collapse affected far more people. Countless millions were jobless; banks were failing by the thousands; tens of thousands needed food. Something had to be done.

At first the Hoover administration was optimistic. The stock market crash was called a needed adjustment. The economy, Hoover announced, was fundamentally sound. Recovery would be natural and would come soon. Meanwhile, no federal action of any kind was needed.

Surprisingly, most Democrats agreed. In the congressional elections of 1930, the Democrats made prohibition as big an issue as the depression. Nor did the voters heavily punish the administration for its failure to bring about recovery. The Democrats won the House, but the Senate stayed Republican. Hoover was still predicting that a return to prosperity was just around the corner.

But things kept getting worse. In 1929, over 600 banks shut down; in 1930, over 1,000; in 1931, 2,000. For farmers, there seemed to be no bottom. Wheat in 1931 sold for $.36 a bushel, compared to $1.03 in 1929. No one even knew how many people were unemployed by 1932, but guesses ran as high as 15 million. For those who

**DROUGHT AND DEPRESSION**

For farmers in the Southwest, the 1930s brought a cruel mixture of economic depression and drought. Dry years spoiled millions of acres of farm land, especially in Arkansas and Oklahoma. This, in turn, set thousands of "Okies" and "Arkies" on the move to California. The crisis could be relieved only slightly, even when the Red Cross distributed $11 million in food to farmers like these leather-faced Arkansans, lined up in 1930 for their bit of slab bacon, potatoes, greens, and a little canned food. *(American Red Cross Photo)*

still had jobs, pay envelopes grew smaller. By 1932, wages in industry were less than half what they had been in 1928.

As he faced all these facts—or, sometimes, tried not to face them—the president grew gloomy and confused. He tried to stay optimistic in public, believing business confidence was crucial to recovery. In private, however, he was trapped between two different beliefs. A humane man, he did not like to see people suffer. But he still thought that government should not interfere in the economy. Free enterprise would bring the nation back to its feet.

Most important, Hoover believed that the federal government must never give direct relief to the poor, unemployed, and hungry. Direct federal welfare, he thought, would destroy people's moral character. It would make them dependent

instead of healthy, strong personalities. This set of attitudes, which he referred to as individualism, made Hoover seem insensitive and cruel. He became the target of bitter jokes. People named their shantytowns Hoovervilles and called an empty pocket, turned inside out, a Hoover flag. Reluctantly, Hoover decided that the government must act.

## New Federal Powers

Early in 1932 Hoover signed a law creating a new federal agency, the Reconstruction Finance Corporation (RFC). It could lend up to $2 billion to banks, insurance companies, and railroads. These loans, the administration believed, would be used especially by the banks to make other loans to businesses. Businesses would in turn use the money for new construction or to reopen factories. Their moves would create new jobs and save old ones. Thus, eventually RFC loans would end up in the pockets of workers, who would then spend the money and create new demand, resulting in more new production, and so on, in a circle of recovery.

The president also went against his own beliefs by signing another law empowering the RFC to lend relief money to state governments. But the amount of the loans was too small to help much. Pennsylvania, for example, could borrow only enough to provide 3 cents a day to its unemployed workers. Also, the RFC loans to business were far too small to aid the economy effectively. Compared to previous government activity, Hoover's actions were bold experiments in the use of federal power. But measured against what was actually needed, they were too little too late, as the bonus marchers recognized.

# THE NEW DEAL

## The Election of 1932

Herbert Hoover was not a cruel man. His reluctance to meet the crisis of the depression was not a result of hard-heartedness but of confidence. He devoutly believed that the nation's economy was healthy and that it needed only "adjustment."

But the Democratic party was about to nominate a man who was altogether willing to define the depression as a crisis. Franklin Roosevelt had been working diligently for the Democratic nomination for months. By the time the party held its convention in Chicago during the summer of 1932, his nomination was almost a foregone conclusion.

The contrast between Hoover and Roosevelt was striking. Hoover was methodical, somewhat gloomy, and calm. Roosevelt was cheerful, brash, and smiling. He had been stricken by polio in 1921 but had made a ten-year effort, with braces and canes, to look healthy and powerful. One of his main political tools was a wide, exaggerated

grin. And he was ready to present himself as a leader who would not be bound by tradition. He broke precedent by going to Chicago to accept the nomination in person—and doing so in an airplane, not by train.

He quickly made it clear to the cheering delegates that his strategy would be simple and relentless: to define the depression as a real crisis and to flay the Republicans for their failure to meet it:

> Republican leaders not only have failed in material things, they have failed in national vision, because in disaster, they have held out no hope. I pledge you, I pledge myself to a new deal for the American people.

Roosevelt's campaign speeches never made clear just what his "new deal" would be like. He made vague promises that he would relieve suffering, create jobs, and make the economy work again. And this, plus the fact that voters did blame Hoover for causing the depression, was enough to give Roosevelt a smashing victory. He received about 23 million votes, against about 15 million for Hoover. Just as important, the Democrats won large majorities in the House and Senate for the first time in modern history.

On March 4, 1933, Roosevelt took his oath of office with a ringing pronouncement that he would have both the courage to admit that a disaster had befallen the nation and the courage to deal with it. And he seems to have believed that courage was the key to the problem. "Let me assert my firm belief," he said in a bluff, confident voice, "that the only thing we have to fear is fear itself. This nation asks for action, and action *now*."

## Launching the New Deal

Roosevelt's inaugural judgment was a little illogical. For men and women out of work, with hungry children, there was in fact plenty to fear. But what counted was not the accuracy of his sentences but their bravery. And the sentences had to be brave because there was a growing sense of despair and even panic in the nation. Millions of men were roaming the country looking for work. Radios played popular songs like "Brother Can You Spare a Dime?" Every city had its "Hoovervilles" and its bread lines. Middle-class Americans, who might still have their jobs and their houses, were frightened by the plague of bank failures, which seemed to be a sign that the economy had simply, perhaps finally, collapsed.

In fact, the banks were the most immediate problem Roosevelt chose to face. If they did not work, nothing else would. On his last night in the White House, Hoover declared, "We are at the end of our rope." After his inauguration, Roosevelt made it clear that he intended to pull the rope at once. He boldly declared a bank "holiday," shutting down all banks, sound and unsound, until further notice. At least a closed bank could not fail, and the money that was supposed to be in people's savings and checking accounts would still be there. Then, five days after he became president, Roosevelt sent to Congress an Emergency Banking Relief Act. The act empowered the federal government to buy stock in failing banks, providing the cash to pay off its depositors if they demanded their money. Astonishingly, the act passed through Congress in eight hours! The New Deal—whatever it was to be—had begun.

## The Debate over Meaning

Ever since the 1930s, Americans have debated, sometimes in anger, the meaning of the New Deal.

For some, including both partisans and critics of Roosevelt, the New Deal was a kind of revolution. According to this view, Roosevelt's programs broke the normal patterns of politics and economics, and brought radically new federal control and regulation of economic and social life.

For others, the New Deal did not represent much of a departure from the patterns of history. This argument claims that Roosevelt was, in essence, a conservative. His basic motive was to leave the Constitution and the capitalist economy intact. In fact, this picture of Roosevelt's administration is one of a program whose deepest wish was to preserve the American system from the kinds of convulsions and revolutions that had been occurring in Europe since the World War.

Both pictures of the New Deal have a good deal of truth to them, depending on what kinds of comparisons are being made. Compared to other peacetime presidents, Roosevelt does look something of a revolutionary. But when compared to the wartime presidencies of Abraham Lincoln and Woodrow Wilson, Roosevelt's administration seems much more "normal." Looked at as part of a progressive tradition reaching back to Populism, to Theodore Roosevelt's "Square Deal," and to Wilson's "New Freedom," the New Deal looks moderate, even tame. Finally, measured against the dramatic changes the Russian Revolution of 1917 had brought, or the kinds of changes that Benito Mussolini and Adolf Hitler were bringing to Italy and Germany, the New Deal can fairly be described as a program of preservation rather than of change.

The difficulty is that the arguments and the comparisons often assume that the New Deal was a coherent, unified program based on a clear political and social theory. In fact, it was a loose bundle of laws and executive orders that were designed by many men and women. Most of the new policies were established as practical steps to solve immediate problems. There was only one crude idea behind it all: that the federal government's power should be used to meet any national crisis.

What held the New Deal together, in fact, was not a program but Roosevelt himself. And he was a curious, contradictory, and sometimes confused man.

## Roosevelt

Franklin Delano Roosevelt was forty-seven years old when the stock market failed, and he was fifty-one when he won the presidency—young by American standards of the day. But he was

# ECONOMICS AND HISTORY

## Three Types of Budgets

During the 1930s, bitter debate raged over the meaning of the budget deficits created by New Deal spending. One of the active participants in this dispute was former president Hoover. He vigorously defended a policy of moral and economic "restraint" . . . and balanced budgets. He argued that the truths of economic policy were simple and self-evident. As he told an audience in 1935:

> When I was a boy in Iowa I learned some very simple truths about finance. I learned that money does not grow on trees; it must be earned. I learned that the first rule of a successful career is to keep expenditures within the means of paying them. I learned that the keeping of financial promises is the first obligation of an honorable man. And I learned that the man who borrows money is headed for bankruptcy or disgrace or crime.
>
> As I have increased in years and in opportunity to study the affairs of governments I have made a very simple but vital observation. That is that a government should have in financial matters the same standards that an honorable man has.

Hoover's stern demand that the federal government be guided by the same economic rules as each citizen and family echoed a deep and abiding faith in his audiences. It was taken for granted that in matters of finance, families, companies, and governments had to obey the same fundamental rules. Each should borrow no more than it could pay back, for excessive credit was the temptation that led to profligate spending and bankruptcy.

At the beginning of the 1930s, most economic theorists endorsed the ideal of a balanced budget. The analogy between family, business, and national budgets seemed logical and self-evident. During the 1932 election, candidates Hoover and Roosevelt both promised a balanced national budget, on the assumption that business confidence could be restored only by frugal national policies. Yet the experience of the 1930s proved otherwise. First, it revealed important distinctions between the operation of family, corporate, and government finances. Experience showed the role of borrowing, credit, and fiscal measures in promoting economic growth and stability. Most of this experience was translated into economic theory by the English economist John Maynard Keynes, whose ideas challenged the truisms of Hoover and the assumptions of common knowledge.

The operation of debt in family, business, and government budgets is, in some ways, remarkably different. Most personal debts, consumer credit, and loans are incurred to pay for consumption, not to buy assets to generate future income. In the 1930s, in particular, personal debt could be a frightening burden that might be passed from generation to generation. Anyone basing economic theory on an analogy between government spending and household experience could only conclude that a balanced budget and repayment of all outstanding debts are the best policies.

But business debts, even in a time of depression, operate somewhat differently. Corporations and other businesses borrow money to buy materials and machines so as to increase production because they anticipate future profits. Debts and repayments are therefore a normal business expense. There is nothing controversial about taking on new debts before all the old ones have been repaid. Nor does a company gain anything by repaying all of its old liabilities and refusing to borrow any more. Without risk, without borrowing, a company may well fail.

At the federal level, budgets operate in a fashion even more remote from the family model. When the government borrows money, it borrows from the same community that it must repay. The government borrows money from the people. Then it taxes the people so it can pay their money back to them. In a sense the government only borrows from itself.

The impact of debt during the 1930s was not, at first, understood. The New Deal fell into using debt to promote economic recovery as much by accident as by choice. At the beginning of the period, almost no one in the Roosevelt administration even knew of Keynes's theories.

Roosevelt had promised to balance the federal budget. But he had also promised to aid millions of unemployed Americans. He could not do both. By choosing to pour money into relief and employment programs, he unbalanced the federal budget even more than it had been in 1932. The deficit increased from $2.7 billion in 1932 to $3.5 billion in 1936. The result was a partial recovery. By early 1937, this injection of money had helped raise production back to its 1929 level.

Just at this point, however, the bubble of confidence burst. A steep recession began in 1937 and extended into 1938. Employment, business activity, and trade fell off sharply. Why? In part, the reason was Roosevelt's retreat to his 1932 campaign pledge to balance the budget. In 1937 he cut federal expenditures by about 25 percent, while tax revenues rose by about 50 percent. These actions shaved the federal deficit to slightly over $1 billion. The dampening effects smothered economic recovery. Of course, other factors played a role, but the decline in deficit spending helped trigger one of the sharpest recessions in history. The economy was not finally jolted out of its doldrums until the early 1940s, when huge federal deficits (over $40 billion a year) plus large war orders from the Allies generated a full recovery.

John Maynard Keynes's theories explained why the economy responded to deficit spending—and why Hoover's analogies made no practical sense. Keynes's landmark book *The General Theory of Employment, Interest, and Money,* published in 1936, was an unusual piece of economic theory. Rather than begin with abstract models, Keynes sought to understand a specific historical event: the Great Depression. His analysis focused on the unique aspects of this depression. Unlike previous downturns, he argued, this one showed few signs of correcting itself. Nothing in the private economy seemed capable of breaking the lock of unemployment and inadequate investment. Left to itself, the economy might stagnate forever.

The only practical solution, Keynes concluded, was manipulation of the fiscal resources of the state. This meant increased government economic activity, financed by borrowing. The infusion of large amounts of government funds for relief of unemployment and for building roads, bridges, and other projects, would stimulate the economy. Then, if business boomed too much, causing labor and materials shortages and inflation, the government could cut back expenditures, balance the budget, and slow economic activity.

Keynes's theories both explained and persuaded. They explained why the New Deal had almost worked and why it had failed. His theories persuaded many politicians and economists that deficit spending and fiscal measures were essential tools for maintaining the economic health of a nation. They also convinced economists to look more closely for the distinctions between national, corporate, and family finances. They constituted a new common belief—that the national debt need *not* be repaid, that its existence and moderate increase could be useful in regulating and guiding economic growth. These theories became the new orthodoxy of the postwar period.

old enough that his ideas about the world had already been formed, and there is little evidence that the depression changed any of those ideas very much.

He was, in many ways, a very traditional man. He came from a wealthy family of Hudson River aristocrats. He went to exclusive private schools and then to Harvard. He owned a great country estate, where he liked to play at being a gentleman-farmer. In private life, he was a practicing, though not especially devout, Episcopalian. He was also a practicing, though not especially devout, capitalist. And he was a Democrat because his branch of the family were Democrats. Unlike some other great presidents—Jefferson, Lincoln, or Wilson—he was neither a scholar nor

a gifted writer. All in all, he was a suave, smiling, public man; fond of dogs, children, and women; a man whose most striking characteristic was not his lameness but the intensity of his desire to be president.

On the other hand, Roosevelt's sense of personal confidence—combined perhaps with his determined victory over polio—made him open to experiment in a way Hoover could never have been. He was ready to try a variety of things and, if they did not work, to try others. He was also ready to appoint a large number of advisers with ideas of their own. The inner circle, composed heavily of academic economists and social scientists, became known as the Brain Trust. Some of its members did have theories of government and

## FRANKLIN D. ROOSEVELT AT A CCC CAMP

The Roosevelt administration tried to help unemployed young men by creating the Civilian Conservation Corps, a quasi-military group that was supposed to plant trees, improve public land, and otherwise "conserve" the landscape. Here, the president takes lunch out of a mess-plate with a group of uniformed members of the corps. Second from the left is Roosevelt's trusted adviser from the 1920s, Louis Howe. To the president's left is Henry Wallace, who would run for president in a controversial third-party bid in 1948. To Wallace's left is Rexford Tugwell, a member of the "Brain Trust." *(Franklin D. Roosevelt Library Collection)*

the economy. And some were much more radical than Roosevelt and worked to make the administration reflect their wishes.

But the president remained secretive, and even a bit coy, about what he had in mind. As it turned out, Roosevelt seemed to think always in very specific and concrete terms. He was willing to send to Congress a bewildering set of proposals for new agencies and programs, many of which became known by their initials. This gave rise to a popular joke that the New Deal was an alphabet soup. But the master chef—who was also popularly called by his initials, FDR—had no master recipe. This became obvious during the first whirlwind weeks of his administration, which became known as the Hundred Days— after the Hundred Days of campaigning that followed Napoleon's escape from Elba and ended at Waterloo.

## Relief and Stabilization

The New Deal functioned on two very different levels. First, it involved direct efforts to feed people and to calm the economic panic, to achieve what people were calling relief and stabilization. Second, the New Deal program included other measures that were aimed at long-term reform. During the Hundred Days, and for some time afterward, relief and stabilization were the primary goals and concerns.

The simplest approach to relief was to distribute direct aid. The Federal Emergency Relief Act of 1933 distributed billions of dollars to the states, which in turn doled out the money to needy people.

But the most characteristic New Deal solution to hunger and poverty was not a dole but jobs. Roosevelt and his advisers were willing to make the federal government the employer of millions of men and women. The Public Works Administration (PWA), created in 1933, eventually spent over $4 billion, employing people to construct roads, public buildings, and other such projects. In 1935, the PWA was joined by a new agency,

which scrambled the initials a bit. The Works Progress Administration (WPA) employed Americans in every kind of project—from construction, to producing plays, concerts, paintings, and sculpture, to library work and scholarship.

The PWA and the WPA were designed to give people a steady income. But the New Deal was just as preoccupied with the other side of middle-class economic life: property. Some of its most important measures were designed to protect farmers from losing their land and homeowners from losing their houses because of unpaid debts or mortgages. In 1933, a Farm Credit Administration was created, with power to lend mortgage money to harassed farmers. In the same year, a Home Owners' Refinancing Act created a federal corporation to give government-financed mortgages to hard-pressed families threatened with foreclosure of their privately financed mortgages.

Direct relief meant much to the men and women who got jobs in the PWA or WPA, or to farmers who were able to save their land. But Roosevelt's administration was perhaps even more interested in getting the economy stabilized. Calling a bank holiday might help in the short run. But something more was needed to prevent bank failures in the future. Since banks failed because their depositers got frightened and suddenly withdrew all their money, the New Deal solution was simplicity itself. The Glass-Stegall Act of 1933 established a Federal Deposit Insurance Corporation (FDIC). This agency simply stood behind the banks, guaranteeing to pay every depositor his or her money—up to $10,000 for each acount—if the bank failed. Presumably, neither banks nor their customers would have to worry any more about sudden and disastrous "runs" of withdrawals that left the banks' vaults empty.

The same sort of logic lay behind the two programs that were most central to the New Deal—both of which suffered heavily from attacks in the courts. The National Industrial Recovery Act and the Agricultural Adjustment Act, both passed in 1933, were aimed at regulating private industry and farming, respectively, without changing the basically private and capitalistic nature of either.

The National Industrial Recovery Act was, at its heart, simply a repeal of parts of the Sherman Antitrust Act (see page 586). That law, which represented nineteenth-century confidence in the idea—if not the reality—of competition, forbade businesses to get together to set prices. It did not work, at least not very well. The new law recognized this fact and tried to build on it. It set up a National Recovery Administration (NRA), with the mission of encouraging corporations and businesses to work together to set and hold prices and production quotas.

For workers, the new law provided that the companies should agree on uniform wages and hours. And when some businesses were slow to cooperate, the NRA itself established wages and hours for industries. The companies that did cooperate won the right to fly a flag with the NRA's symbol, a blue eagle, as evidence of their civic conscience.

The Agricultural Adjustment Act attempted to deal with the farmers' peculiar problem: when prices fell, they were driven to produce even more food for the market. This simply sent prices further down, creating a spiral of oversupply and falling incomes. The act created the Agricultural Adjustment Administration, with the power to give farmers money *not* to plant crops. The AAA could also buy up "excess" amounts of crops like cotton and wheat, and store them. The goal was to control production and marketing, to drive farm prices back up to the prosperity levels of 1909–1914, a level of parity.

In the short run, at least, the AAA seemed to work, though some of its measures seemed misguided to the men and women rummaging in garbage heaps for scraps of food. The AAA simply plowed under millions of acres of cotton, potatoes, and other crops. It also killed and dumped about 5 million pigs. But the result was apparently successful. In 1933, farm prices stood at about 55 percent of parity. In 1939, the ratio was 90 percent.

# Reforms of the New Deal

Programs aimed at direct relief and at economic stability made up the bulk of the New Deal, at least as measured in new laws. But Roosevelt and his advisers made efforts to introduce other, more fundamental and lasting changes in American life. These reform measures seem mild and timid by comparison to later exercises of federal power. But to many men and women of the 1930s, they seemed innovative, even radical or revolutionary.

One of the most visible of Roosevelt's measures was the Civilian Conservation Corps. The CCC set up camps for unemployed young men, put them into uniforms that looked suspiciously military, and set them to cleaning up parks and planting countless trees all across the country—not only on federal property but on public lands of all kinds. Here was an astonishing, though short-lived, fact: a uniformed federal corps, not an army, working along hundreds of highways and lakefronts, doing things that were far removed from traditional notions of federal responsibility.

A more daring and enduring effort was the Tennessee Valley Authority. The TVA was established to build dams and generate electrical power in the backward, flood-ravaged valleys of the Tennessee and Cumberland rivers. But the responsibilities of the TVA went further: to reforest, to reclaim marginal land, to improve health and recreation for the people of the valleys. Opponents charged that the plan was patterned on "Soviet dreams." But others saw the matter differently. For its supporters, the TVA was a magnificent effort to salvage some of the most economically and socially depressed areas of five states.

The National Labor Relations Act of 1935—popularly known as the Wagner Act, after a New York congressman—was another effort at social reform. The Roosevelt administration used the act to enable the federal government to intervene in relations between labor and capital in a more forceful way than in the past. The Wagner Act made it illegal for an employer to refuse to bar-

THE PICKWICK DAM

One of the proudest—and most controversial—achievements of the New Deal was the creation of the Tennessee Valley Authority. The agency built dams like this one in an attempt to
control the waters that raged every year through the valleys drained by the Tennessee River.
But the TVA also generated and sold electric power, hurrying a social revolution in the hill-
country farms and towns of the area. The power-generating plant is at the end of the dam
on the far side of the river. *(Culver Pictures)*

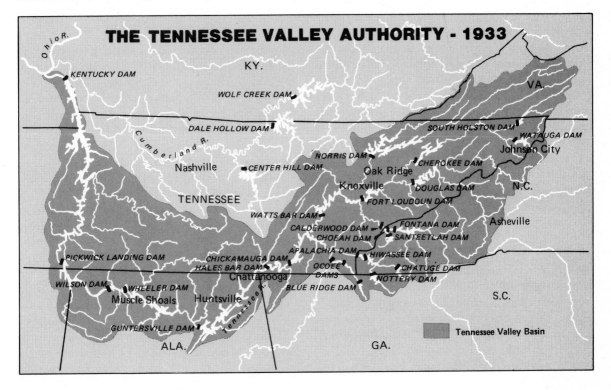

## THE TENNESSEE VALLEY AUTHORITY - 1933

Ohio R.

KENTUCKY DAM

KY.

VA.

WOLF CREEK DAM

DALE HOLLOW DAM

SOUTH HOLSTON DAM

WATAUGA DAM

Johnson City

Cumberland R.

NORRIS DAM

CHEROKEE DAM

Nashville

CENTER HILL DAM

Oak Ridge

Knoxville

DOUGLAS DAM

N.C.

TENNESSEE

FORT LOUDOUN DAM

Asheville

WATTS BAR DAM

CALDERWOOD DAM

FONTANA DAM

CHOEAH DAM

SANTEETLAH DAM

APALACHIA DAM

PICKWICK LANDING DAM

CHICKAMAUGA DAM

HIWASSEE DAM

HALES BAR DAM

OCOEE DAMS

CHATUGE DAM

WILSON DAM

Chattanooga

NOTTERY DAM

WHEELER DAM

BLUE RIDGE DAM

Muscle Shoals

Huntsville

S.C.

GUNTERSVILLE DAM

Tennessee R.

Tennessee Valley Basin

ALA.

GA.

gain with a union chosen by his or her employees. The Wagner Act also outlawed a list of "unfair labor practices" by employers, a list that could be indefinitely extended.

Partly as a result of the Wagner Act, union membership tripled between 1933 and 1939—from about 3 million to over 9 million. And the character of the unions changed too. The American Federation of Labor had organized workers by craft and trade. An employer could then negotiate—if willing to negotiate at all—with a series of separate organizations, each representing a fraction of the company's workers. Now, a more radical vision of unionism gained force: industrial unionism. Industrial unionism was based on the idea that all the workers in a particular industry—steel, say, or automobiles—ought to be organized into one union rather than into a number of small craft unions. The most striking development of the 1930s in labor history was the emergence of the CIO—the Congress of Industrial Organizations.

The organizing leadership of the CIO contained a number of labor radicals and even some communists. But its rank-and-file members were committed to the simple idea that collaboration was as necessary to workers as to corporations, that the only way to achieve fair bargains between workers and industrial giants was through wholesale solidarity among all the workers in an industry. Employers resisted, of course. Bitter battles were fought. A tremendous sit-down strike at General Motors in 1936, in which the workers did not leave the plants but "sat down" at their places, ended in partial victory for the CIO. In 1937, the steel industry (notoriously antiunion for decades) was forced to submit to bargaining with the CIO after weeks of bloody violence.

In the perception of the New Deal, old people needed federal assistance even more than industrial workers. The Social Security Act of 1935 was an attempt to create an insurance and retirement system for American workers. It provided for small "contributions" from workers and their employers to be paid into a common fund. This fund could then pay a pension to men and women

who retired, or benefits if they became crippled and unable to work, or support for their children if workers died prematurely. The payments were small at first. But the Social Security Act was still a long first step in the direction of what critics of the New Deal referred to as a "welfare state."

There were a number of reform possibilities that the Roosevelt administration shied away from. There was no civil rights legislation. There was no attempt to redistribute income through taxation. In fact, there was no attempt to tamper with existing relationships between social classes, between races, or between men and women. His enemies might charge him with "Sovietism," but Roosevelt's own perception of the possibilities of federal action were far from drastic. Some of the young men and women who supported and worked in the administration might hope for more. But that "more" lay well over the historical horizon—beyond further years of depression and then years of total war.

## End of the New Deal

Franklin Roosevelt did everything he could to make the election of 1936 a test vote of the people's confidence in his efforts. And he won smashingly. His Republican opponent, Governor Alfred Landon of Kansas, won only Maine and Vermont. No American president had ever won such a ringing endorsement of such a controversial program of action.

But victory did not bring more of the New Deal. If anything, it brought less. For the New Deal now had to face a set of distressing realities.

The first problem, though minor, was noisy and irritating. A third-party candidate, Congressman William Lemke, had polled almost a million votes in 1936. The vote itself did not matter, but it did seem to be the tip of an ominous political iceberg. Lemke had put together the votes of a number of critics of the New Deal who were demanding more radical action on a number of fronts. Senator Huey Long of Louisiana, an eccentric and fiery figure, was promoting a simple

"Share Our Wealth" plan that held out the promise "Every man a king." A much quieter man, Dr. Francis Townsend of California, had created a movement for more adequate pensions for the elderly, a movement organized into thousands of Townsend Clubs. And an anti-Semitic Catholic priest, Father Charles Coughlin, had used the radio to generate a passionate belief in millions of people that Jews were responsible for the depression and that they controlled the Roosevelt administration. Hindsight makes it obvious that Long, Townsend, and Coughlin had little in common and no chance of success. But their movements raised serious doubts about the workability of the New Deal.

A much more trying problem for Roosevelt, however, was the failure of his efforts to end the depression. The gross national product would not budge. Federal deficits remained high, despite Roosevelt's personal commitment to a balanced budget. Unemployment refused to drop significantly. And no sooner was Roosevelt inaugurated the second time than a new wave of economic panic struck. The depression of 1937—a sort of depression-within-a-depression—shook the confidence not only of many voters but of many New Dealers themselves. The congressional elections of 1938 brought a coalition of Republicans and conservative Democrats to power, a coalition that made it virtually impossible to achieve any new legislative victories.

Finally, Roosevelt had to deal with an increasingly troublesome federal judiciary. In 1935 and 1936, parts of the AAA and the NIRA were ruled unconstitutional by the Supreme Court. Roosevelt became convinced that unless the Court could somehow be changed, the Wagner Act, the TVA, and the Social Security Act would not be safe.

He made a daring move. He proposed a scheme to "pack" the Supreme Court. He suggested that Congress empower the president to increase the size of the Court by one for every justice over seventy years of age.

What followed was a political "Court fight" lasting for months into Roosevelt's second term. In the end, he both won and lost. He won because some justices were frightened into retiring and others into shifting their votes. This change gave rise to one of the finest witticisms of American history, that "A switch in time saved nine." But Roosevelt also lost, in that public opinion seems to have shifted markedly against him. Voters apparently disliked the idea of tampering with the Constitution (though the Constitution is in fact silent on the number of justices who sit on the Supreme Court). The Court fight virtually ended the New Deal. From that point onward, the attention of Roosevelt, and increasingly of everyone else, turned across the Atlantic and the Pacific, to fields of revolution and battle that would soon involve the nation in another world war.

# SUGGESTED READINGS, CHAPTERS 37–38

## THE BONUS MARCH

The only full-scale modern history of the bonus march is Donald Lisio, *The President and Protest: Hoover, Conspiracy, and the Bonus March* (1974). As his title suggests, Lisio is more concerned with what went on inside the Hoover administration than with the bonus marchers themselves. Douglas MacArthur, *Reminiscences* (1964), is an interesting route into the mind of one important participant.

## CONSERVATIVE REACTION

Robert K. Murray, *The Red Scare: A Study in National Hysteria, 1919–1920* (1955), is colorful and readable. The best place to begin reading about Sacco and Vanzetti is still Felix Frankfurter, *The Case of Sacco and Vanzetti* (1962). The best account of Prohibition is Andrew Sinclair, *Prohibition: Era of Excess* (1962). The only book-length story of the Scopes trial is Ray Ginger, *Six Days or Forever?: Tennessee v. John Thomas Scopes*

(1958). On nativism and the Klan, see John Higham, *Strangers in the Land* (1955), and David M. Chalmers, *Hooded Americanism* (1965).

## THE POLITICS OF CONSERVATISM

A fine general history—though an aging one—of the Republican administrations of the 1920s is John D. Hicks, *Republican Ascendancy* (1960). On the Democratic side, see David Burner, *The Politics of Provincialism* (1967). Two unusually sympathetic discussions of the most conservative presidents of the period are Robert K. Murray, *The Harding Era* (1969), and Donald R. McCoy, *Calvin Coolidge* (1967). Burl Noggle, *Teapot Dome* (1962), is excellent. An elegant general book on the 1920s is William Leuchtenburg, *The Perils of Prosperity* (1958).

## BOOM AND BUST

The crash and what brought it on can be approached best through John Kenneth Galbraith's fine little book, *The Great Crash, 1929,* 3rd ed. (1972). The fairest discussion of Hoover's reaction to the onset of the Great Depression is probably Joan Hoff Wilson, *Herbert Hoover, Forgotten Progressive* (1975). The victims of the crash speak eloquently in Studs Terkel, *Hard Times: An Oral History of the Great Depression* (1970).

## THE NEW DEAL

The literature on Roosevelt and the New Deal is vast. The most readable, though thoroughly biased, general account is contained in three volumes by Arthur M. Schlesinger, Jr.: *The Age of Roosevelt: The Crisis of the Old Order, The Coming of the New Deal,* and *The Politics of Upheaval* (1957–1960). Two excellent special studies of crucially important aspects of the New Deal are James Patterson, *The New Deal and the States* (1969), and Ellis Hawley, *The New Deal and the Problem of Monopoly* (1966). A fine, general, and brief book is William Leuchtenburg, *Franklin Roosevelt and the New Deal* (1963). The most ambitious study of Roosevelt, which still covers only the beginning of the New Deal, is Frank Freidel, *Franklin D. Roosevelt,* 4 vols., to date (1952–1973). A fascinating look at radical opposition to the New Deal is Alan Brinkley, *Voices of Protest: Huey Long, Father Coughlin, and the Great Depression* (1982).

# 39 · Hiroshima: The Dawn of the Atomic Era

On a cold day in early spring 1955, a U.S. Air Force plane circled over Mitchell Field on Long Island, New York. Plunging into the turbulence, the aircraft landed and released its cargo: twenty-five young Japanese girls, "the Hiroshima maidens." Disfigured, some crippled, they huddled together, waiting to be taken to Mount Sinai Hospital for surgery to release their limbs, twisted by radiation and burns, and to smooth their swollen and distorted features. They were a fortunate few among the victims of the atomic bomb, brought to the United States by a group of religious workers and concerned citizens. It was a small, private gesture of reparation by Americans for the tragedy of Hiroshima.

Ten years earlier, shortly after eight o'clock on a warm August morning, a U.S. Army Air Force B-29 droned high over the center of Hiroshima. Most of the residents were only vaguely aware of its presence, reminded briefly, perhaps, of an earlier air-raid alert, which had then been followed by an all-clear signal. Most of the twenty-five girls were in the basement of their public school preparing erasers and chalk for classes. Most residents of the city were on their way to work. Other schoolchildren were getting ready to resume their labor of clearing fire lanes in the city. This safety precaution, of pulling down crowded wooden houses and buildings in wide swathes across the city, had become necessary to prevent the fire storms from American incendiary raids that had obliterated whole square miles of Tokyo and other cities. Thus far, Hiroshima had been spared. Built on the flat delta of the Ota River, Hiroshima had become an important manufacturing center for the Japanese war effort. Most of its population lived along inlets connected by bridges, and most of the city was built of wood or other flimsy materials.

On the morning of August 6 the weather was clear. No antiaircraft fire or fighter planes met the American bomber, the *Enola Gay,* as it cruised smoothly toward its mission. Suddenly over target, the ship released its 5-ton bomb and dived sharply to the right. The weapon drifted down slowly on a parachute, giving the plane forty-three precious seconds to escape. Then, shortly before it reached the ground, the bomb's altitude detectors triggered the device.

The burst flashed far brighter than the sun at midday. Waves of concussion pulverized everything at its center, and in an instant, the enormous heat ignited the splintered debris. Inrushing winds thrust smoke and dust 40,000 feet into the atmosphere within two minutes. Still close by, but safe, the *Enola Gay* was buffeted by shock waves. One crew member looked back and remarked that it was "like boiling dust." The B-29 continued on its long trip back to base at Tinian Island. Built on a coral ridge, the airport's six 2-mile runways, constructed especially for heavy bombers, made it the world's largest airport. It had launched the *Enola Gay* and, with it, a new era in world history.

In Hiroshima, the devastation was instantaneous. About 80,000 people were killed or seriously wounded, most by burns, pressure from the blast, or falling buildings. Fires leapt out over the precautionary fire lanes. There was no way to fight them. The explosion had destroyed most firehouses, roadways were blocked, and scores of firemen were dead. Of the city's 200 doctors, 180 were killed or injured; of 1,780 nurses, 1,654 had died or were disabled. Some residents who survived, like Mrs. Futaba Kitayama, working about 2,000 yards from the blast, were terribly burned. Fearing that the bomb contained incendiary powders, she recalled, "I rubbed my nose and mouth hard with a *tenugui* [towel] I had at my waist. To my horror, I found that the skin on my face had come off in the towel." Farther out, people fell sick from radiation poisoning; many more died painfully within weeks. The Hiroshima maidens scrambled out of their collapsed school, some badly burned by fire or radiation. Nothing remained of their classrooms or schoolmates.

Of all the feelings experienced by Hiroshima survivors, perhaps the most universal was shock followed by a protective numbness. The small bomb, the single plane, surprise, and then enormous destruction—the combination wiped out all sense of proportion and disrupted the logic of cause and effect. It left only shock. As a Japanese poet wrote later:

There is nothing for us to sing
Whose eyes are closed,
When we, in tears, gaze through
The clear sky's depths.
We find that all is lost and scattered;
Suppose our brains have turned to ashes,
Soaked in the River Ota, flowing in its blue;

You people,
Believe us;
We find that all is washed away.
What song is there for us to sing whose eyes are closed?
But a song of tears?

NAGASAKI BEFORE ATOMIC ATTACK

Nagasaki, a port city and shipbuilding center, was the target of the second atomic bomb dropped on Japan at the close of World War II. Built on a series of hills, the city was devastated by the single blast on August 9, 1945. *(The Bettmann Archive)*

HIROSHIMA

This picture of devastated Hiroshima captures the bewildering destructiveness of the atomic-bomb raids on Japan. *(UPI)*

Three days later, the United States dropped a second atomic bomb, this time over the city of Nagasaki. Although different in composition from the first, the device had an equivalent destructive force. But because of the hilly terrain and the greater prevalence of concrete buildings, the city sustained somewhat fewer casualties. Still, the general effect was similar: a bewildered population, the breakdown of social services, and a landscape littered with splintered trees, twisted girders and towers, and the debris of what once had been a place of human habitation.

In August the Japanese had been on the verge of surrender—their cities shattered, their navy sunk, and their air force limited to defensive operations. Two days after Hiroshima, the Soviet Union declared war on Japan and marched rapidly into Japanese-held Manchuria. Against overwhelming odds on land, and facing extinction from the air, the Japanese sued for peace after Nagasaki. With their surrender, the war ended on August 14.

The decision to drop the atomic bomb on two Japanese cities had been one of three key decisions relating to atomic energy that American policy-makers had confronted during the war. The first decision was to build the bomb; the second, to use it; and the third, to try to maintain its secrets as an American monopoly after the war. None of these decisions was made lightly; for, as the president, his scientific advisers and administrators, and the few other officials brought into the process knew well, the shape of the postwar world depended on the wisdom of their decisions.

The decision to develop an atomic bomb was, initially, made out of fear that the Germans would create this awesome weapon first. And there was no doubt that they would use it if they acquired it. Germany's *blitzkrieg* (lightning war) invasion of Poland in September 1939 had demonstrated the importance of technological superiority in winning battles. World War II was—as Winston Churchill, prime minister of Great Britain, aptly called it—"a wizard war." By this he meant that inventions were decisive. The opposing nations spurred their scientists to develop weapons that would turn the tide of this desperate struggle. As Albert Speer, the German Reich's minister for armaments and munitions said in 1946, even to the last moment, the German population believed that some new "miraculous weapon" would save them from defeat.

The Americans and the British feared the awesome potential of Germany's pure science and its sophisticated industrial plant. German military tactics, demonstrated in Poland and then in Belgium and France in the spring of 1940, underscored the advantages that military strategy had when harnessed to science and industry. During the war, German science fielded several new weapons, including self-guided rockets and a new jet fighter plane. Had the jet been developed more quickly, it might have reversed Allied air supremacy in the last days of the war.

American and British science was also active in the development of new weapons technology. A new radar system invented by the British helped deflect Hitler's effort to achieve air supremacy over England. Sonic systems to detect submarines, proximity fuses for mines, and a host of other engineering triumphs helped turn the tide of battle in favor of the Allies. None of these accomplishments, however, matched atomic power. Whoever tamed this energy first could command the gods of war.

The American scientific community, led by a distinguished group of European physicists who had fled German and Italian fascism, had good reason to fear German atomic science. In 1938, German scientists had demonstrated the possibility of nuclear fission—the basis for a chain reaction in radioactive material. The practical question was: Could a chain reaction be harnassed and be detonated as a bomb? In March 1939, physicist Leo Szilard (from Hungary) and Enrico Fermi (from Italy) directed successful fission experiments. Deeply worried that the Germans had made similar advances, Szilard went to the world-renowned scientist Albert Einstein. Einstein agreed to sign a letter to President Roosevelt warning him that Germany might be on the verge of developing atomic weapons: "It is conceivable," the letter concluded, "that extremely powerful bombs of a new type may be constructed."

Roosevelt undoubtedly knew little about the scientific basis of this prediction, but he was enough impressed by this warning to appoint a Uranium Committee inside the National Bureau of Standards. By early 1940, he had

ENRICO FERMI

One result of fascism in Italy and Germany was the flood of scientists and intellectuals who sought refuge in the United States during the 1930s. Some of these scientists, like Fermi, conducted crucial experiments that enabled America to construct the first atomic weapons. *(UPI)*

agreed to spend significant sums of money on atomic research, even though the United States remained technically at peace with Germany and Japan. Moreover, he determined that these activities should be pursued in secrecy; only a few scientists and only his closest political associates knew of the project.

In early summer 1941, Roosevelt appointed a larger committee to muster science in the cause of defense. Headed by Vannevar Bush, president of the Carnegie Institute and a noted engineer, this new National Defense Research Committee took over the work of the Uranium Committee. Bush reorganized the uranium group; he added more scientists and removed some of the military representatives. Then, in the spring of 1941, word reached Washington that the British had begun their own atomic program, dubbed MAUD in secret code. The British warned that a bomb was practical and could probably be built in two years.

Spurred to move faster by the British report, Roosevelt pushed through another reorganization during the fall of 1941, this time creating an advisory group called Section 1 and making it part of a recently formed Office of Scientific Research and Development. Section 1 consisted of Bush, James B. Conant, president of Harvard University; Secretary of War Henry L. Stimson; Army Chief of Staff George C. Marshall, and Vice President Henry Wallace. In March 1942, Roosevelt turned the actual building of the bomb over to the War Department, which appointed Brigadier General Leslie R. Groves of the Army Corps of Engineers as officer in charge of the project. By then, it had acquired a new name—the Manhattan Project—and a large, secret budget, hidden even from Congress.

Bureaucratic shuffling, agency reorganization, and new liaison committees signified the growing importance of atomic research. Roosevelt, by his actions, was also tightening federal control over research, giving the military a dominant role in guiding the work. By the time the project ended, it had spent about $2 billion. Over 100,000 people had worked on various aspects of the endeavor at thirty-seven military, scientific, and industrial installations—all to create a device that would cause about 13 pounds of plutonium to release its energy. Yet this work had been accomplished with a degree of secrecy unknown in American history. Even many of the scientists did not know the precise objective of their research.

The project began in earnest in late 1942. General Groves appointed Robert Oppenheimer, a physicist from the California Institute of Technology, to direct the nuclear facility at Los Alamos, New Mexico, where much of the work was completed. In December Enrico Fermi, working in an abandoned squash court at the University of Chicago, created the first self-sustaining chain reaction. Thus by early 1943, American scientists had acquired the basic knowledge and the facilities to develop a bomb. Ironically, at almost precisely the same time, German scientists concluded that an atomic weapon was not feasible. Yet no one knew this for sure. In fact, Arthur Compton, a Manhattan Project participant, reported that the United States worried so much about German atomic progress that "when the Allies landed on Normandy [France] beaches on 6 June, 1944, certain of the American officers were equipped with Geiger counters," to detect traces of atomic weapons.

Secrecy, compartmentalization, and hierarchy characterized General Groves's administration of the project. By dividing up the research and preventing any scientist in the project from having access to more information than was required to answer a specific question, Groves prevented leaks of information. He possibly also slowed the progress of the project. More important, however, he stopped scientists from discussing the larger implications of their work: whether or not a weapon should be used and under what conditions. Furthermore, he angered a number of scientists with his security-conscious rules and bureaucracy.

Groves, however, was not the only policymaker who wanted to hide the project. Bush and Conant hoped to exclude the British, to prevent their gaining atomic weapons. At first Roosevelt seemed to agree; but in the summer of 1943, he reversed himself. At an August conference with Prime Minister Churchill in Quebec, Canada, the president agreed to a full exchange of information. This left only the Soviet Union, America's other principal ally, out in the cold. In fact, the decision not to tell the Russians, while keeping the British informed, became one of the most momentous of the war, for it came to symbolize the lack of trust and cooperation between the opponents of Germany. Apparently, Roosevelt never seriously considered informing the Russians about the project or keeping them abreast of scientific developments. And, as General Groves later declared, "There was never, from about two weeks from the time I took charge of this Project any illusion on my part but that Russia was our enemy."

Although atomic research always aimed at production of a usable bomb, the details of its actual deployment remained uncertain and controversial. Depending on its completion date, a bomb could be dropped on Germany or Japan or both. If one or the other of the Axis powers were knocked out of the war—and by early 1945 Germany was rapidly crumbling—it would have to be used exclusively on the sole enemy survivor, if it were used at all.

In 1944, as the bomb moved from the drawing board stage to construction, several scientists began to discuss the wider implications of atomic power. The decision to use the bomb was implicit in its creation and in the momentum that the Manhattan Project gained in 1944 and 1945. But the decision could have been reversed, and a few of the scientists working on the project or familiar with atomic energy desperately worked for a reconsideration. They recognized that the bomb was more than just a new, powerful weapon. Its development and its use, they contended, would have vast implications in shaping the postwar world. This was a difficult position to take, for the bureaucratic structure governing the Manhattan Project was designed to prevent broad discussions of any sort—especially those that challenged the use of the bomb. Any halt to plans for deploying the bomb would have to come from the very top, from the few civilian leaders like Churchill and Roosevelt who knew the details of the weapon's development.

As the weapon became more of a likelihood in 1944, several scientists became uneasy about the choice of a target. Increasingly it appeared that Germany would not be the victim. That country was rapidly falling apart under the massive attacks from west and east by Allied armies. That left Japan, a nation that could not develop a bomb of its own but that still clung tenaciously to its empire of Pacific conquests. Allied commanders estimated that to knock the Japanese out of the war would require a two-stage invasion of Japan—the first in November 1945 with a landing on the island of Kyushu, and a second, full-scale attack in the spring of 1946. Estimated Allied casualties in the two assaults were placed at somewhere around a million men. If this were the case, then the atomic bomb could prove decisive. But it was also possible that the Japanese would give up before such a costly assault.

Other questions worried scientists as early as 1943. Niels Bohr, a Danish refugee and key theorist in the field of atomic science, firmly believed that atomic information should be shared among all the Allies, including the Russians. If not, he warned, an atomic arms race might develop after the war. In several memoranda to Roosevelt, he urged international control of atomic energy. And he asked the president to inform the Russians of the Manhattan Project. Scientists could help in promoting an

> understanding of how much would be at stake should the great prospects of atomic physics materialize, and in preparing an adequate realization of the great benefit which would ensue from a whole-hearted co-operation on effective control measures.

Roosevelt postponed taking any such initiatives, and so Bohr tried to persuade Winston Churchill. The scientist traveled to England in the spring of 1944 with letters of recommendation and waited impatiently for a meeting with the British prime minister. When it finally occurred, Churchill showed himself hostile to sharing atomic secrets with the Russians. Bohr left the meeting knowing he had failed: "We did not even speak the same language," he later remarked. Other scientists active in the project, such as Bush, eventually came to share Bohr's fears that attempting to maintain a monopoly on atomic secrets would stimulate an arms race between the United States and Russia. But by the end of 1944, Roosevelt clearly agreed with Churchill: the two allies would not share atomic knowledge with the Soviet Union.

By the spring of 1945, the Russian issue had greatly complicated the question of using the atomic bomb. And decision making became even more difficult in April. President Roosevelt died suddenly on April 12, leaving to Vice President Harry S Truman the decision about dropping the first atomic weapon in history. War was racing to a climax in Europe. The new president had to face the hard task of designing a peace in an atmosphere of growing competition with the Russians. Truman had little experience in foreign affairs and he was not aware of the plans or promises Roosevelt had made. Most important, he did not even know about the atomic bomb.

At a White House meeting on April 25, Stimson and project director Groves informed the new president of the weapon about to be placed under his command. Secretly ushered into the president's office, Groves made several points: The United States would soon test an atomic device; the United States and Britain held a monopoly on the world's fissionable materials; the Russians were probably spying on the Manhattan Project. Stimson took a very different tack, warning the new president of the dangers that atomic bombs presented to international diplomacy:

> In the light of our present position with reference to this weapon, the question of sharing it with other nations and if so shared, upon what terms, becomes a primary question of our foreign relations.

Truman's sole initiative at this meeting was to appoint an interim committee to choose targets in Japan.

Once the Germans had collapsed, in early May, Truman turned his attention to formulating a European peace and to ending the war in Asia. Increasingly, these two efforts became intertwined. The president was deeply distressed by news reaching Washington: the Russians, occupying Europe as far west as central Germany, were consolidating their hold on Eastern European countries, including Bulgaria, Poland, Hungary, and Czechoslovakia. And the Japanese, he believed, were preparing to defend their island empire to the last inch. In both situations, the atomic bomb might be important. In Europe, exclusive American possession of a successful bomb might convince the Russians to cooperate with the United States. In Asia, its use might save hundreds of thousands of American and Japanese lives.

Truman had both possibilities in mind when he scheduled a meeting at Potsdam, Germany, with Stalin and Churchill in July. The timing coincided with the first testing of the atomic bomb, the news of which Truman expected to reach him during the conference. As expected, on July 18, word flashed from Alamogordo Air Base, near Albuquerque, New Mexico: a successful explosion with "the brightness of several suns at midday." The president then proceeded to use the news. On July 25, he wrote in his diary:

> We met at 11 A.M. today, that is, Stalin, Churchill and the U.S. President. But I had a most important session with Lord [Louis] Mountbatten and General [George] Marshall before that. We have discovered the most terrible bomb in the history of the world. It may be the fire destruction prophesied in the Euphrates Valley Era, after Noah and his fabulous Ark.

The president then recorded his thoughts about using the bomb:

> This weapon is to be used against the Japanese between now and August 10th. I have told the Secretary of War, Mr. [Henry] Stimson, to use it so that military objectives and soldiers and sailors are the target and not women and children. Even if the Japs are savages, ruthless, merciless and fanatic, we as the leader of the world for the common welfare cannot drop this terrible bomb on the old capital [Kyoto] or the new [Tokyo].

Truman believed that the bomb would save lives and that its use was inevitable, since the Japanese, even after warnings, would not surrender: "It is certainly a good thing for the world," he concluded, "that Hitler's crowd or Stalin's did not discover this atomic bomb. It seems to be the most terrible thing ever discovered, but it can be made most useful."

Truman's private musings contained at least three dubious assumptions or misapprehensions. The first was that it was incontestable that the bomb had to be used. There were strong rumors at the time that the Japanese were on the verge of collapse. On July 18, Stalin informed Churchill of a message from the Japanese emperor suing for peace. With the imminent prospect of a Soviet declaration of war on Japan, surrender—without the use of the bomb—was at least possible. Second, Truman had assured himself that the targets selected were primarily military. This was only partly the case, for both Hiroshima and Nagasaki were cities with large civilian populations. Finally, Truman believed that the weapon could be useful. Perhaps he meant useful to end the war. But possibly he also meant that it would intimidate the Russians.

If making the Russians more cooperative was one purpose of the bomb, it did not entirely work. When Truman hinted to Stalin about the new weapon at Potsdam, the Russian leader replied that he hoped it would be used against the Japanese. The conference resumed and eventually reached certain limited agreements about the shape of the postwar world. But as Truman later wrote:

> What a show that was! But a large number of agreements were reached in spite of the setup—only to be broken as soon as the unconscionable Russian Dictator returned to Moscow! And I liked the little son of a bitch.

By August, Truman had determined not to share any secrets with the Russians, and he was committed to dropping two bombs. Last-minute appeals of atomic scientists to reverse his decision failed to convince him. A committee of Chicago scientists had warned in early June that a surprise attack against the Japanese would initiate an arms race with the Russians. However, Truman's own Scientific Advisory Committee, made up of several eminent scientists, advised using the weapon:

> We can propose no technical demonstration likely to bring an end to the war; we see no acceptable alternative to direct military use.

One last serious attempt to stop the bomb came from Chicago scientists on July 17. Leo Szilard authored a petition and gathered the signatures of sixty-eight other atomic scientists. The document urged President Truman not to drop the bomb:

> The development of atomic power will provide nations with new means of destruction. The atomic bombs at our disposal represent only the first step in this direction, and there is almost no limit to the destructive power which will become available in the course of their future development.

No nation, Szilard concluded, would ever be safe from destruction.

This petition, as well as other serious reservations expressed by other scientists, failed to reach the president. Project director Groves refused to pass them on because "no useful purpose would be served in transmitting either the petition or the attached documents to the White House." And besides, by the time the petition reached Groves, Truman was already in Potsdam. Having built this terrible weapon, and seeing its multiple advantages—in ending the war immediately and in impressing the Russians—Truman, Stimson, and other policymakers were determined to use it.

On July 26, the United States, Britain, and China issued a new warning to Japan and a final demand for unconditional surrender. The proclamation threatened the "utter devastation of the Japanese homeland," but it did not mention the bomb. The Japanese rejected the call, still holding out for preservation of the power and status of the emperor. Use of the bomb had now become irreversible.

On August 6, President Truman in a dramatic report to the nation announced the explosion of the atomic bomb over Hiroshima. "Sixteen hours ago an American airplane dropped one bomb on Hiroshima, an important Japanese army base," he said. Then he described the size and power of the weapon. It was, he proclaimed, "the greatest achievement of organized science in history." It had been built in secret, and it would be continued in secrecy:

## THE CREW OF THE *ENOLA GAY*

Pictured here are Major Thomas W. Farshee, bombardier; Colonel Paul W. Tibbets, pilot; Captain Theodore J. Van Kirk, navigator; and Captain Robert Lewis—the crew of the B-29 bomber that dropped the first nuclear weapon over Hiroshima. *(UPI)*

It has never been the habit of the scientists of this country or the policy of this Government to withhold from the world scientific knowledge. . . .

But under present circumstances it is not intended to divulge the technical processes of production or all the military applications pending further examination of possible methods of protecting us and the rest of the world from the danger of sudden destruction.

Truman's decision to maintain secrecy about atomic research and development was, like the decision to drop the atomic bomb, very much the product of past decisions. Having already excluded the Russians, and believing that sole possession of the weapon would make them more amenable to American wishes for postwar Europe, Truman and his advisers were dubious about sharing America's scientific advantages. But any decision can be reversed, and there were some compelling reasons to do so in this case. In the first place, many scientists argued that there were no secrets. In the words of

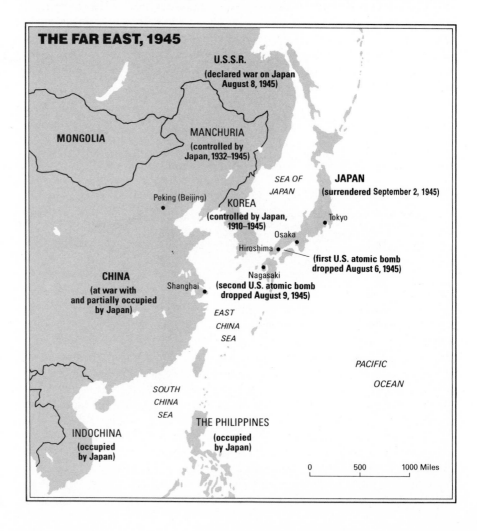

**THE FAR EAST, 1945**

U.S.S.R.
(declared war on Japan
August 8, 1945)

MONGOLIA

MANCHURIA
(controlled by
Japan, 1932–1945)

SEA OF
JAPAN

JAPAN
(surrendered September 2, 1945)

Peking (Beijing)

KOREA
(controlled by Japan,
1910–1945)

Tokyo

Osaka

Hiroshima

(first U.S. atomic bomb
dropped August 6, 1945)

CHINA
(at war with
and partially occupied
by Japan)

Shanghai

Nagasaki
(second U.S. atomic bomb
dropped August 9, 1945)

EAST
CHINA
SEA

PACIFIC

OCEAN

SOUTH
CHINA
SEA

THE PHILIPPINES
(occupied
by Japan)

INDOCHINA
(occupied
by Japan)

0        500        1000 Miles

Albert Einstein, "There is no secret and there is no defense." Second, the administration recognized that Russian espionage was likely to penetrate American security anyway. This possibility was confirmed in September 1945, when the Canadian prime minister revealed details of an atomic spy ring operating in the United States and Canada. Furthermore, to hold scientists captive to the secrets they discovered in their research betrayed the very essence of free scientific inquiry. Finally, there was the possibility of an arms race. As a scientist at the University of Chicago put it in 1946:

> If we seek to achieve our own security through supremacy in atomic warfare, we will find that in ten years the whole world is as adequately armed as we, and that the threat of imminent destruction will bring about a "preventive" war.

These were grave risks: dependence on secrets that might not be safe, excessive government direction and interference in scientific research, and an arms race.

Nevertheless, to Truman, they were risks worth running. By late 1945, he had become convinced that a monopoly on the atomic bomb would allow the United States great flexibility in foreign policy without the cost of a large standing army. On October 27, he declared that American possession of the bomb was a "sacred trust" for humanity. Nonetheless, Truman made at least one serious effort in early 1946 to demilitarize nuclear energy. But the spring of that year was a tense time to formulate a treaty based on mutual trust. In February 1946, news of the Russian spy ring operating from Canada had been made public. And American and Russian foreign policies had both stiffened. Still, a committee in the State Department devised a plan for international control of atomic energy. The group was headed by David Lilienthal, former head of the Tennessee Valley Authority and future head of the Atomic Energy Commission. After serious debate, the committee suggested a scheme in March that would give the United Nations control over the mining, refining, and utilization of atomic raw materials. Each nation, under this plan, could retain control over the peaceful uses of nuclear energy.

Truman endorsed the plan and appointed the elderly financier Bernard Baruch to present the plan to the UN Atomic Energy Commission. Baruch agreed but insisted on the right to make changes. His modifications almost guaranteed a Russian refusal. He proposed total disarmament, not just control of nuclear weapons. His plan included dire punishments for nations who violated the agreement and private, not international, control of mining and manufacture. Finally, he proposed abolishing the Security Council veto in atomic energy matters. The Russians rejected the plan in the summer of 1946. Almost immediately, the United States resumed atmospheric nuclear bomb testing, and the Russians continued their drive to develop a bomb.

Public opinion—which might have contributed significantly to the extended debate about the bomb, atomic secrecy, and the role of science—was splintered, confused, and often anxious. A Gallup poll taken on August 16, 1946, disclosed that about 85 percent of Americans approved the bombings, 10 percent disapproved, and 5 percent had no opinion. In the context of the war's end, this result is hardly surprising. Mixed into the approval were certain strong American beliefs: admiration for science and technology, and a faith in progress. Shortly after the war, David Dietz captured this spirit in his book *Atomic Energy in the Coming Era.* Dietz predicted a plane that traveled more than 1,000 miles an hour and a moon rocket ship powered by atomic chain reactions. He also promised an automobile engine fired by "tiny explosions of Uranium 235." These, he proclaimed, were a few of the "miracles just ahead for mankind in the coming Era of Atomic Energy whose dawn was heralded Sunday, August 5,[1] when the first bomb of atomic energy exploded over the Japanese city of Hiroshima."

Nonetheless, many Americans worried about the bomb, especially after the initial euphoria of the war's end died down. They did not believe General Groves, who told a Senate hearing that radiation poison was "a very pleasant way to die." Church leaders in particular condemned the bomb. Roman Catholic spokesmen denounced the weapon because, contrary to expressed intentions, the explosion did not spare civilians. Thirty-four leading Protestant clergymen sent President Truman a petition calling the bomb an atrocity. In 1946, the Federal Council of Churches of Christ wrote of its anguish at the attack:

> As American Christians, we are deeply penitent for the irresponsible use already made of the atomic bomb. We are agreed that, whatever be one's judgment of the ethics of war in principle, the surprise bombings of Hiroshima and Nagasaki are morally indefensible.

It was not the moral outrage of churches that touched the American public so much as the book *Hiroshima,* written by novelist John Hersey. Hersey traveled to Japan in October and November 1945 and brought back material for an extended article for *New Yorker* magazine. Ordinarily a witty and fashionable periodical known for its sardonic cartoons, the magazine suspended its humor for a single issue in August 1946. It printed no satire, cartoons, or verse, and even excised some of the more inappropriate advertising. The issue sold out four hours after it hit the newsstands. It was subsequently reprinted in fifty newspapers and then became a best-selling book.

Hersey wrote about the bomb in a way that most Americans could understand—through the eyes of six survivors. He clothed bare statistics with the details of the life and death of ordinary people. He captured the essential experience of surprise, nakedness, and numbness before a force that was incomprehensible.

The effectiveness of Hersey's story aroused a response from the bomb's defenders. Hollywood produced a quick propaganda film in 1947, *The Beginning or the End?* showing the president tormented by the fateful decision to

---

[1] Because Japan is on the other side of the International Date Line, the blast occurred there on August 6.

employ the weapon. Some of those who had helped guide the construction of the bomb, like Henry Stimson, wrote articles in popular magazines to defend its use. In the end, most Americans remained convinced that the bomb had been necessary. Neither guilt nor fear of atomic warfare translated into significant opposition to relying on a nuclear monopoly in foreign policy. Instead, the public increasingly worried about keeping nuclear weapons a secret.

In July 1945, just before the end of the war, Vannevar Bush submitted a report entitled *Science—the Endless Frontier* to the president outlining his suggestions for a new relationship between science and the government. The government should coordinate and support broad research programs, he wrote,

> But we must proceed with caution in carrying over the methods which work in wartime to the very different conditions of peace. We must remove the rigid controls which we have had to impose, and recover freedom of inquiry and that healthy competitive spirit so necessary for expansion of the frontier of scientific knowledge.

Bush's worries about government interference and rigidity were well founded, for three major groups were contending for the control of science and atomic research after the war. These included the scientists themselves, the civilian branch of the federal government, and the military. In the end, something of a compromise was worked out, and basic scientific research in the United States evolved into a partnership between scientists and the civilian and military branches of government. But to some researchers, this compromise severely limited their freedom to speak and publish and, above all, to determine the uses of their work. Research in peacetime was too much like research under conditions of war.

In the next several years, three federal institutions were developed to direct and finance scientific research in the United States. The precedent of the Manhattan Project, the commitment to secrecy, and the desire to advance science in competition with the Soviet Union played a significant role in their foundation. The first was the Atomic Energy Commission (AEC), established in 1946, which guided and controlled the development and application of nuclear energy in a variety of military and nonmilitary areas. The National Science Foundation, set up in 1950, became the major institution to fund and direct basic scientific research (some of it relevant to weapons development and much of it not). The third institution was the military administration and funding of large weapons projects by the Defense Department.

The AEC, established on August 1, 1946, had many of the characteristics of the Manhattan Project. Its bylaws prevented international cooperation on atomic energy development, and its employees had to pass an FBI investigation. But tightly run as it was, the AEC represented a significant compromise. Scientists who had balked at tight security and army intereference on the Manhattan Project demanded freedom to do research. Some of these organized the Federation of Atomic Scientists in 1945. This group opposed any efforts to impose direct military control of research. It successfully opposed legislation that would have placed military representatives in a dominant position on the commission.

The question of funding basic scientific research ended in much the same sort of compromise. In his report on science, Vannevar Bush proposed a new agency to underwrite basic research. Run by civilians and scientists, it would direct research in a wide variety of fields, not just those related to military weapons. Although this proposal appealed to scientists, President Truman rejected the plan because it appeared to be independent from federal control. In 1947, when a bill to create an independent National Science Foundation passed through Congress, Truman vetoed it. Lacking close executive branch control, Truman argued, the proposed foundation would be divorced from control by the people "to an extent that implies a distinct lack of faith in democratic processes." What he meant was that government would not have sufficient power to direct and focus the agency's activities.

Unable to agree on the shape of a new science foundation, the federal government forged ahead with funding basic scientific and weapons research. Military planners pushed hard for weapons research. In particular, the Office of Naval Research, created in August 1946, funded large military research contracts. Many universities and corporations were initially skeptical about secret peacetime research; but by 1949, the office had spent more than $20

### THE ATOMIC ARMY

During the 1950s, the United States and the Soviet Union carried on extensive open-air nuclear weapons testing. Frequently, as pictured here, American soldiers were stationed close to the test blast area for training purposes. The risks of such exposure to radiation were, at the time, rarely acknowledged. *(UPI)*

million on 1,200 projects at some 200 institutions. And most of this work was undertaken without public knowledge.

Militarily funded research met the immediate needs of a growing defense establishment, but it did not fill the place of a broader, federally funded science research program. This came, finally, in 1950 with the establishment of the National Science Foundation. The new agency would report directly to the president—a victory for Truman. Its purpose was to fund basic research in the sciences—a victory for scientists. Weapons development would remain primarily under the control of the military.

Thus by 1950, cooperation between scientists, the federal government, and the military had been established. Federal funds were lavished on research in ways hitherto unheard of in peacetime. A mode of operating in secret, yet with some latitude, had been established. Science had become the willing servant of federal policy. But there was a price.

In August 1949, the dream of scientific superiority over the Russians turned into an anxious nightmare, when American scientists detected traces of a Russian atomic blast experiment. The monopoly had been broken. The public and Congress demanded to know how the secrets had been lost. Scientists had often warned that there were, essentially, no secrets, but few had been willing to listen. This was even truer in 1949. In this atmosphere of recrimination and spy stories, President Truman pushed ahead to try for a monopoly on a new super weapon. In January 1950 he accelerated research into a hydrogen bomb. Two and a half years later, the United States tested its first fusion device. By 1954, the Soviets had also tested a fusion bomb. American superiority had evaporated in an arms race in which equality was probably the best that could be hoped for.

Rather than stimulating debate over fundamental issues, the growing stalemate in nuclear terror pushed concern about secrecy and security to a frenzied pitch. Ironically, the most important scientist of the Manhattan Project, Robert Oppenheimer, fell victim to this mood. From the very beginning, Oppenheimer, the physicist who had led the Los Alamos scientists to their triumph, had been viewed suspiciously by military and security experts. Some of his associates in the 1930s had been political radicals, including his wife and his younger brother. But during the years of the Manhattan Project, Oppenheimer always received security clearance. Moreover, Oppenheimer had supported using the bomb. Now, after the war, his independence of mind began to carry him away from established policy, and he began to question some of the assumptions of the arms race.

In 1948, shortly before the Russians exploded their first atomic bomb, Oppenheimer proposed making small tactical weapons. He wanted to develop atomic explosives suitable for use against military targets. He opposed building huge bombs to hold civilian populations hostage. Working for the AEC General Advisory Committee in 1949, he spoke against committing massive resources to developing the hydrogen bomb. Losing this debate, he also earned the suspicion and opposition of scientists who were advocating the

At the height of the Cold War, public consciousness of possible nuclear war was heightened by air-raid drills, such as this one in a New York City office building in 1951. Nonetheless, civil defense spending was reluctantly funded, and public support for extensive precautions did not develop. *(UPI)*

larger bomb, such as Edward Teller. Teller's opposition was well founded, for Oppenheimer had changed many of his views about atomic energy. Shortly after the decision to build a hydrogen bomb, Oppenheimer told a radio audience:

> The decision to seek or not to seek international control of atomic energy, the decision to try to make or not to make the hydrogen bomb, these are complex technical things, but they touch the very base of our morality. It is a grave danger for us that these decisions are taken on the basis of facts held in secret.

As Oppenheimer astutely saw, the decision to build the hydrogen bomb compressed almost every question surrounding atomic energy research into one momentous problem. Secrecy, international control—practically all the elements of the nuclear debate were involved. He decided he could not support such a decision.

By raising these doubts, Oppenheimer lost much of his credibility in atomic policymaking. By 1953, he was rarely being called in for advice. Nonetheless, during that year the doors of secrecy were unceremoniously closed on him, shutting him out of any further research in the atomic field. Outraged by Oppenheimer's apparent change of heart on nuclear weapons, a former staff member of the congressional Committee on Atomic Energy had sent a long denunciation of the scientist to the FBI in mid-1952. The writer said that Oppenheimer "more probably than not . . . was a sufficiently hardened Communist [and] that he either volunteered espionage information to the Soviets or complied with a request for such information." Agency director J. Edgar Hoover reassembled Oppenheimer's clearance file, reworked it, and forwarded the letter and the dossier to the newly inaugurated President Eisenhower. The president acted quickly, barring Oppenheimer from access to all atomic secrets and government research facilities. The scientist was officially notified on December 24, 1953.

Oppenheimer decided to fight the decision, and the AEC set up a special panel to hear his plea. Meeting in April and May of 1954, the three-member board heard thirty witnesses, among them most of the principal atomic scientists of the nation. In late May, the board reported. Oppenheimer was cleared of all charges of disloyalty and espionage; but the panel voted, anyway, to remove his security clearance. The policy became official in late June: the father of the atomic bomb was now permanently barred from further work on atomic energy.

In a sense, Oppenheimer was a scapegoat for an unworkable policy of secrecy. Accused and then cleared of divulging secrets to the Russians, his real crime had been to challenge the policies that he had helped to create during the Manhattan Project. He now discarded the role of government servant and used his reputation as an independent scientist to argue in public

**J. ROBERT OPPENHEIMER AND MAJOR GENERAL LESLIE R. GROVES**

Oppenheimer, the scientific head, and Groves, the military chief, of the Manhattan Project inspect the remains of the tower that held the first atomic test bomb. The total commitment of the United States to be first in producing atomic weapons brought together these extraordinarily different men. *(UPI)*

against the building of the hydrogen bomb. In doing so, he rejected the fundamental premises that had guided the Manhattan Project, the release of bombs over Hiroshima and Nagasaki, and postwar arms research. In 1946, he had argued that weapons development would make the "problem of preventing war, not more hopeless, but more hopeful." Now he had changed his mind. But it was too late. America could not undo the damage of the bombs that had been dropped. It could only treat a few of its victims—like the Hiroshima maidens who came to the United States the following year. Secrecy was now too entrenched in weapons research and deployment to be reversed. Both the United States and the Soviet Union held the power to eliminate civilization in a flash having the "brightness of several suns at midday." Only the equality of mutual terror—the fear of a thousand Hiroshimas—could now prevent the further use of atomic weapons.

The brilliant achievements of American science had thus altered the nature of war and peace. In 1945, after the first successful test of the atomic bomb, Secretary of War Stimson had congratulated science administrator James B. Conant for his work on the project. Conant had replied: "Yes, it worked. As to congratulations, I am far from sure—that remains for history to decide."

# World War
# and
# Cold War

Those three vital decisions—to build the atomic bomb, to drop it on Japan, and then to obscure its scientific secrets in tight national security—can best be understood in the context of a developing cold war between the United States and the Soviet Union. This grim falling out between allies did not occur suddenly. It grew gradually out of the conduct of the war, a long history of U.S.–Soviet antipathy, the antagonistic war aims of West and East, and the remarkable shifts in the world balance of power that the war confirmed. In the degenerating relationship between Russia and America, the bomb was at first only a minor irritant—a symbol of distrust. By 1945, it provided the leverage that the United States hoped to use to modify Russia's postwar behavior. By 1949, it had become a doomsday weapon possessed by both sides in a contest that seemed to have no other logical outcome than the destruction of mankind.

The atomic bomb was also a scientific and technological achievement that represented a vast federal commitment of money and administration. Like winning the war itself, building the bomb required careful planning, centralized authority, and an almost unprecedented intervention of the government into the economic and political life of the nation. After the war, this interference and control persisted—for several reasons. Policymakers continued to believe that the federal government had to take a more activist role in economic planning to prevent the recurrence of depression. Continued confrontation with the Russians led to large peacetime military budgets that required extensive government direction and planning of the economy. And maintaining secrets related to research strongly implied that the federal government might also legitimately investigate and monitor the political beliefs of individual citizens—as it did in the case of Robert Oppenheimer.

## THE WORLD WAR II ALLIANCES

The shape of the cold war developed from the circumstances of the alliance against Germany, Italy, and Japan. In their struggle against the Axis powers, the Americans and British worked closely together. They integrated their military command and supply structures and consulted frequently on strategy. Scientific cooperation was also important, although the United States admitted Britain only as a junior partner in atomic research. Relations with the Soviet Union, on the other hand, were very different. Although an ally after 1941, the Russians were never full partners. Britain's leader, Winston Churchill, feared Stalin's motives. The American president, Franklin Roosevelt, worked hard to win the cooperation of the Russians, but the relationship was never much more than an alliance of convenience. When the war ended in mid-1945, it left a legacy of unresolved problems, economic and political competition, and old hostilities that quickly degenerated into a cold war between the United States and the Soviet Union.

Opposition to Germany and Japan forged the alliance of the United States, Britain, China, and the Soviet Union, but it was a union of desperate partners. In the late 1930s, both Japan and Germany advanced on their weaker neighbors. Japan marched inexorably against China, while Adolf Hitler, the Nazi dictator (Führer), moved rapidly to recoup German losses from World War I. Breaking the Versailles Treaty, Hitler announced German rearmament. In 1936, he marched troops into the Rhineland bordering France. Emboldened by this move, he forcibly annexed Austria in March 1938. He then turned his attention to Czechoslovakia, demanding cession of its German-speaking areas. Clinging to a hope for peace, British and French officials conferred with Hitler at Munich in September. They concluded that a policy of appeasement would slake the thirst of the German dictator, so they agreed to Germany absorbing a substantial part of Czechoslovakia. Hitler conquered the remainder of that nation in March 1939 and then turned on Poland.

KOEHLER
ANCONA

# This is the Enemy

## THE NAZI ENEMY

The image of the efficient, ruthless Nazi enemy haunted American reactions to World War II, both in art and popular culture. *(Collection, The Museum of Modern Art, N.Y., Anonymous Gift, 1942)*

Here, for the first time, Hitler met resistance. The Poles refused to relinquish areas that Germany demanded. As war threatened, Hitler signed a nonaggression pact with the Soviet Union in late August promising to respect Russian claims to territory lost to Poland in 1920. Then on September 1, 1939, German armored divisions and aircraft swept across western Poland while Russians moved into eastern areas of that nation. On September 3, France and England declared war on Germany. But Poland fell in less than a month.

The furious fighting in Poland was followed by quiet, as German and French-English divisions bristled at each other across the fortified eastern reaches of France. Then suddenly in early May,

Germany pounced, crashing through Holland and Belgium in a few weeks and then turning on France. A major contingent of British and French troops retreated to the northern port and beaches of Dunkirk, where they were evacuated by an improvised flotilla of private and navy ships. German troops then quickly crushed the remaining French armies, while Mussolini struck from the south. With no chance of victory, the French surrendered on June 16. German armies occupied the north but let a French puppet government, located in Vichy, administer the south.

Hitler then set his sights on Britain and began an air war to destroy English defenses. The German Luftwaffe began to strike British airfields and aircraft plants in August 1940. Wave after wave of bombers struck the British Isles, but the English fought back, using their new Spitfire fighters, radar, and antiaircraft barrages. By mid-September Hitler realized that his plans had failed and turned east. Moving his legions into Poland, he swept into the Soviet Union in June 1941, breaking the 1939 nonaggression pact. Catching the Soviets off guard, his panzer divisions crashed toward Stalingrad, Moscow, and Leningrad. In July the Russian premier, Joseph Stalin, called for aid from the Allies. By late summer, Moscow itself was besieged.

Roosevelt responded to these desperate events in two ways. He pushed for American rearmament and established close working relations with the British. And he approved plans to initiate research into building an atomic bomb. Although still technically neutral, the United States became the armorer for the opponents of Germany and Japan. In the summer of 1939, the United States informed Japan that it intended to terminate its trade treaties with that nation. Following the invasion of Poland, the president called Congress into session to repeal America's neutrality acts, which made it difficult to trade arms to belligerents. After extensive debate, Congress repealed some of the more stringent elements of these acts.

Following the fall of France, Roosevelt pushed harder for rearmament and direct aid to Britain. Moving around legal obstacles and obstinate public opinion, the administration agreed, in September 1940, to exchange destroyers for British bases in the Western Hemisphere. Most reaction to this agreement was favorable, but an America First Committee was formed to oppose U.S. participation in the war. Led by such celebrities as Charles Lindbergh, the committee galvanized the remaining opposition to war.

In early spring 1941, the United States took a giant step toward more direct involvement with passage of the Lend-Lease Act. The law empowered the president to sell, lend, or otherwise dispose of defense materials to any country deemed strategic to American defenses. The original sum made available for this aid was set at $1.3 billion, but it quickly ballooned. As shipments to Britain increased, so did the risk to U.S. ships that had to cross the submarine-infested waters around the British Isles. Over the summer, the United States began escorting convoys of merchant ships; by fall, the navy had engaged in skirmishes with German submarines.

## THE UNITED STATES ENTERS THE WAR

The Japanese decided the timing of America's entry into the war in dramatic fashion. Over the summer of 1941, Roosevelt announced that he would freeze the assets of the Japanese and end all trade in strategic materials if that nation proceeded to attack the French colonies in Indochina. When the Japanese imperial armies moved in this direction, the president acted. Although the Japanese continued to negotiate, they were secretly preparing a broad attack on U.S., British, and French possessions in Asia. During the summer of 1941, U.S. intelligence broke the Japanese diplomatic code. Intercepted messages pointed to an attack in early winter. On November 27, 1941, Washington warned commanders in the Pacific. Minimum defense steps were taken at the giant naval base at Pearl Harbor, Hawaii, including the fatal bunching together of fighter planes to prevent sabotage.

On December 7, again by decoding Japanese diplomatic messages, the United States learned of an impending attack. Washington sent out alerts to the Pacific, but these failed to reach the commanders in Hawaii on time. Even radar failed to detect the first wave of bombers and fighters that took off in early morning from the Japanese fleet lying secretly about 250 miles north of the Hawaiian island of Oahu.

Three waves of fighters and dive bombers plunged down out of the calm Sunday morning sky. The attack lasted about two hours. When it was over, the Japanese had devastated the navy air force, killed 2,403 Americans (about 1,000 of whom died when the battleship *Arizona* exploded), and sunk or damaged the bulk of the U.S. Pacific Fleet. Other U.S. bases and possessions came under attack. Wake Island fell, and Roosevelt ordered General Douglas MacArthur to move his command from the threatened Philippines to Australia. By May, the Philippines had fallen and the Japanese had taken most of the territory in their master plan. They now turned to menace Australia and India.

Despite these early successes, the Japanese had achieved a precarious victory at best. But their attacks exposed the weak defenses and inadequate planning of American forces in the Pacific. They also inflamed American public opinion. Roosevelt denounced the "sudden criminal attacks perpetrated by the Japanese in the Pacific" and asked for a declaration of war. On December 11, Hitler joined his Japanese ally and declared war on the United States.

Once the United States had entered the war, Roosevelt decided on a strategy of attrition to defeat the Axis powers (Germany, Italy, and Japan). He planned an enormous economic effort in which superior resources, supplies, productivity, organization, and scientific breakthroughs would overwhelm the enemy. This emphasis on weapons, he believed, would minimize American casualties. With this aim in mind, he authorized the secret building of the atomic bomb. His commitment made the factory assembly lines as important as the front lines of fighting men.

The war build-up also meant new federal economic controls. After Pearl Harbor, Congress granted sweeping powers to the executive branch. On January 16, 1942, Roosevelt created the War Production Board. This agency had the power to channel civilian production into armaments manufacture and to contract for the construction of new defense plants. With the massive reorientation of production, the draft of millions of men, and a rise in employment, the United States suddenly faced labor shortages. War orders wiped away the huge unemployment left from the depression. The War Manpower Commission was organized to recruit new workers for the booming defense sector. The largest pool of potential employees was women, and millions of them eagerly took over jobs in aircraft, shipbuilding, and munitions plants. They went to vocational schools and learned trades and skills that transformed their lives. They were crucial in building the vast array of weapons that poured from the factories. They constructed B-29 bombers like the *Enola Gay* that carried the first atomic bomb; they built the tanks and ships that shattered the Nazi armies and the Japanese navy. The other large group of potential workers were Southern blacks. They too were welcomed by the federal government for work in defense plants.

Eventually, full employment and shortages of consumer items like automobiles fueled inflation and labor unrest. The federal government stepped in here too, setting up the War Labor Board in January 1942 to prevent strikes and runaway wages. After several skirmishes with labor, the board established the "Little Steel" formula, worked out first for smaller steel-producing companies. This formula, which applied to other industries as well, placed a limit on pay hikes. Labor disputes did not disappear, but in general, the War Labor Board did much to ease the pressure on wages, and it allowed unions to raise their membership extensively.

Another new agency, the Office of Price Administration, tried to limit price rises by setting maximum prices for standard items. It also ov-

ORDNANCE WORKERS

World War II opened economic opportunities to millions of underemployed workers. Southern blacks and women streamed into defense plants. Black women were employed extensively in munitions factories. *(UPI)*

ersaw the rationing of scarce items such as coffee, canned foods (to save tin), shoes, and gasoline (to save rubber tires). Although many workers earned more money than before the war, there were few goods to spend it on; even a thriving black market could not supply them.

Expansion of the armed services had begun before the United States entered the war. The army had reached 1,400,000 men by July 1941. But after total mobilization, this number moved up rapidly. By 1945, over 8,000,000 men were in the army. (The Women's Army Corps—WAC—reached about 100,000 at this time.) The navy experienced a similar expansion, reaching 3,400,000, with the marines constituting about 500,000 of this total. The air force (administratively part of the army) also expanded rapidly. By the end of the war, about 1,000,000 black

Americans had participated in the various services.

Extensive government control over the economy was matched by increased federal attention to shaping public opinion and preventing possible subversion. In this climate, civil liberties suffered. Of course the military censored news from the front. There was little serious opposition to the war; but even so, the administration overreacted as demands for security and secrecy increased. For example, it brought a group of inconsequential American fascists and right-wing opponents of the war to trial.

Much more serious was the treatment of Japanese-Americans. In early 1942, American com-

### JAPANESE-AMERICAN EVACUATION

Scenes such as these were common throughout California in 1942, as Japanese-American citizens and immigrants were forced to abandon their homes and businesses. Up to 110,000 of them were eventually placed in makeshift internment camps in the central United States. *(The National Archives)*

manders on the West Coast argued that Japanese residents must be removed. This fear of sabotage scarcely concealed a longstanding racial antipathy toward the Japanese in California. (There was no corresponding internment of Japanese residents of Hawaii, where race relations were better.) The military command and the administration in Washington agreed to evacuate all Japanese-Americans, whether citizens or not, in February. By June, over 100,000 had been forcibly removed, their property and jobs stripped away. Most were placed in ten crude army camps and provided with tarpaper barracks, cots, common toilets, and shared bathing and laundry facilities. Many of the internees gained their release before the end of the war, but few ever recovered their farms, businesses, or homes.

For black Americans, prospects were brighter but conditions remained difficult. Black Americans joined the armed forces but were assigned to segregated units. At first they were generally excluded from defense employment opportunities. But A. Philip Randolph of the Brotherhood of Sleeping Car Porters threatened a march on Washington in the summer of 1941 unless equality of employment was offered. This helped persuade Roosevelt to order integration of defense industries. By the end of the war, hundreds of thousands of black workers had found jobs in war production. Despite these gains, however, they continued to suffer discrimination in the work place and in housing. Racial tension often erupted when they took new jobs or moved into new areas. Such was the case in Detroit in June 1943, when a bloody race riot broke out that had to be quelled by troops.

## THE WAR IN EUROPE

While the administration worked to organize production, it defined its strategy to win the war. In practical terms, the United States had disagreements with both of its major allies. Roosevelt opposed Britain's desire to hold on to its vast colonial empire. And he was reluctant to allow the Russians to establish control over the invasion

## AMERICANS AT WAR

## World War II

The military crisis of 1939 had its origins in the economic catastrophe of 1929 and the harsh peace after World War I. The Great Depression, symbolized by the stock market dive in New York in October, signaled the beginning of a long, unnerving, and costly decline in production in most industrial nations. Stock values fell in Germany, England, France, and the United States, while unemployment rose and agriculture stagnated. Production world-wide fell by almost 40 percent, and international trade shrank by two-thirds. In 1930, unemployment in nations that kept such records reached 30 million persons, with other millions uncounted.

The continued depression brought political instability. In the United States, it created the impetus behind the New Deal and the energy to create the modern welfare state. In Europe, the effects were grave. Following World War I, most industrial societies were seriously divided between contending ideological factions: socialists, communists, fascists, and liberal and conservative capitalists. In Italy, in 1922, fascists led by Benito Mussolini forced a change of government, consolidated power, and eventually eliminated democratic rule. Mussolini instituted censorship, curtailed the vote, repressed labor unions, and founded a secret police.

Fascism appealed elsewhere in Latin nations, including Spain, Portugal, and France, where major fascist movements sought power. However, in Germany, fascism achieved its greatest triumph. Led by Adolf Hitler, the National Socialists (Nazis) seized control of the German government in 1933 and, once in power, initiated a virulent totalitarianism. Political parties (aside from Hitler's National Socialists) were abolished, unions were disbanded, and a cruel and effi-

cient secret police, the Gestapo, was established. Hitler then embarked on a broad rearmaments program while Germany muscled its way to dominance in eastern European economic markets. Hitler's aim, as he repeatedly announced, was to establish Germany's preeminence among European nations, by whatever means.

The threat of communism, which Hitler invoked to justify his quest for power, also alarmed other European nations touched by political and economic chaos. France swayed between conservative governments and a socialist-communist alliance called the Popular Front. In the late 1930s in Spain, civil war pitted an elected Popular Front government against fascist revolutionaries. In the Far East, Japan, swept by some of the same economic and political currents, and frustrated in its search for markets and power, initiated attacks against China.

In this unstable world, alliances were valuable but difficult to achieve. Italy and Germany agreed in 1936 to form a fascist Axis, with Japan added later as an ally. For Britain and France, forging military ties was more difficult. One potential ally, the United States, although worried about the advance of fascism, remained officially neutral. The second most powerful nation in Europe, the Soviet Union, represented a force that many in Britain and France detested. Hitler recognized this conflict among potential allies, and he brilliantly exploited it. In 1936, he renounced the Versailles Treaty and fortified the Rhineland. He also aided the Spanish fascists. In 1938, he annexed Austria and began to demand German ethnic areas inside Czechoslovakia. Despite treaties with France, the Czechs were forced to concede large areas of territory—in effect, dooming that nation.

Britain and France feared war and willingly appeased Hitler, hoping to satisfy his desire for expansion. But they miscalculated. After signing a friendship treaty with the Soviet Union in August 1939, Hitler invaded Poland on September 1 and World War II began.

The strategy of the Germans and their European allies in World War II was an extension of World War I plans, carefully revised to avoid failure. The Germans in studying their loss in 1918 realized the importance of mobility and logistics: the ability to deliver firepower rapidly and in massive amounts. Their strategy centered on tanks and mobile artillery with tactical air support.

The Japanese, Americans, and British during the 1930s also studied the successes and failures of World War I—in particular, the problems and potential of landing troops and materiel quickly, under fire, onto hostile shores. The Americans and Japanese also emphasized the aircraft carrier, which proved to be a superb attack weapon, superior to traditional naval vessels because of the striking force of the fighters and dive bombers it carried.

All of the major nations developed air power but with varying success. Germany did not, at first, fully recognize the potential of long-range bombing and tended to use fighters primarily in aid of infantry. The British better understood the potential of long-range offensive air power as well as the need for an effective defense. The Americans also developed long-range weapons, culminating in the B-29 bomber, which dropped the atomic bombs on Japan.

As in World War I, Germany fought a war in two directions, but this time with far greater success. After a lull following the conquest of Poland, Hitler invaded Denmark and Norway. On May 10, 1940, German troops swept through Holland and into Belgium, conquering both nations by May 25. Hitler then sent his armored divisions into northern France. Facing a sometimes poorly equipped army and a divided Allied command, the Germans broke through. British troops pinned up against the English Channel were spared only because Hitler halted his armies to allow his air force to batter the British. The Allies were able to mount a desperate evacuation at Dunkirk while the Royal Air Force fought off the German Luftwaffe.

Hardly a victory, this evacuation saved 350,000 troops; but it left the French to fend for themselves. After only five days, German armored divisions were nearing Paris. The French abandoned the city on June 13. On June 16, the French government—in disarray and retaining only a bleeding remnant of its army—surrendered. The Germans, to save themselves the costs of a total occupation, established a puppet government in southern France quartered at Vichy. Now Hitler aimed at Britain.

Hitler's strategy for the invasion of England hinged upon establishing air superiority. Despite the new British radar system and a valiant defense, he almost succeeded. After sustaining days of bombardment, the British sent bombers to Berlin. Infuriated by this attack on their capital, the Germans shifted their attention to London and away from British defense installations. This decision allowed the British to concentrate their defenses, greatly raising the cost of air attacks. On September 30, the Luftwaffe made its last daylight raid. Hitler had to cancel plans to conquer England.

Throughout the spring and summer of 1941, the Germans and Italians moved against British positions in the Mediterranean and conquered Yugoslavia, Greece, and Crete. Germany's major objective, however, was the destruction of the Soviet Union. Hitler's divisions struck in June 1941, hoping to knock the Russians out of the war before winter. They almost succeeded, advancing hundreds of miles toward Moscow and Leningrad. The Russians suffered over 1,500,000 casualties, with a similar number taken prisoner. The Germans lost about 800,000 men.

**THE BATTLE OF BRITAIN, 1940**

St. Paul's Cathedral stands amid a Nazi air raid. The relentless bombing of London by the German Luftwaffe in the fall of 1940 failed to break the resistance of the population or secure Axis air superiority. The British fought back valiantly and gained the admiration and support of many Americans. *(Library of Congress)*

Despite superior equipment, training, and command, the Germans failed to deliver a decisive blow, and the Russians, with British and American aid, began to rebuild their armies. By December 1941, Hitler's empire was vast; but the short war he had anticipated had turned into a grueling battle of attrition.

In Asia as in Europe, war began gradually through incidents of escalating aggression. Japan, which had long planned the conquest of China, moved against this weaker power throughout the 1930s. Japanese armies captured large areas of Chinese territory but could not eliminate the nationalist forces of General Chiang Kai-shek or the Chinese communists who controlled territory to the north. By 1940, the Japanese had turned toward conquest of the colonies belonging to European nations under attack: France, Britain, and the Netherlands. The only significant powers standing in the way were Britain (now desperately fighting for survival in Europe) and the United States.

Japanese war planners realized the impossibility of outproducing or directly defeating the United States. Their plan called for surprise destruction of the American navy, simultaneous seizure of Southeast Asia and defeat of any counterattacks. They counted on the problem of maintaining long supply lines, and America's low level of preparedness, to discourage the United States.

In November 1941, six Japanese aircraft carriers and supporting ships slipped out of the Kurile Islands and steamed toward Hawaii. Although American commanders anticipated a Japanese attack, they expected it in Malaya or the Philippines. On December 7, 360 planes from the Japanese fleet struck Pearl Harbor Naval Base, trapping a substantial part of the American Pacific fleet at berth. Caught completely by surprise, the Americans fought back but lost three battleships (four others were badly damaged), three cruisers, three destroyers, and over 150 planes. On December 8, the Japanese struck in Malaya and the Philippines and invaded Guam and Wake Island. On December 10, Japanese planes sank the British ships *Prince of Wales* and *Repulse,* leaving only three American aircraft carriers operating in the Pacific.

American strategy, once war was declared in Asia and Europe, necessitated a massive mobilization and military build-up. Since American productive supremacy in Asia was never in doubt, military planners emphasized the critical situation in Europe. Given their commitment to unconditional surrender, the Allies intended not only to defeat Germany and Italy but to destroy fascism. Their first object, however, was to relieve pressure at two critical points: on the Russian front and

ATTACK ON PEARL HARBOR

The U.S.S. *Arizona* sinks following the surprise Japanese air raid on the principal American naval base in the Pacific on December 7, 1941. The Japanese came close to knocking out most of the U.S. fleet in the Pacific. *(Official U.S. Navy Photograph)*

in Northern Africa, where the Germans threatened to seize the Suez Canal. In the latter area, the turning point came at El Alamein, where the British defeated Field Marshal Rommel and his Afrika Korps. On November 8, 1942, American and British troops invaded French North Africa and recaptured Algeria. At about the same time, Russian armies, partly supplied by the United States, began an offensive that finally broke the German siege at Stalingrad.

By late 1942, pressure on several fronts forced Hitler to spread his soldiers and armies. Round-the-clock air attacks against Germany began, and from then on they intensified throughout the war. By May 1943, the Germans had abandoned North Africa. The Russians desperately urged the opening of a second front in France, but the British and Americans preferred the tactically easier invasion of Italy. The Allies took Sicily by August, precipitating the overthrow of Mussolini. On September 3, Italy signed an armistice and switched sides in the war. Nonetheless, occupying German troops effectively stalled the Allies in northern Italy for the remainder of the war. During the winter and spring of 1943, Soviet forces began to capture lost territory and to push the Germans back. Everywhere, the German offensive had ended.

As German front lines in the East and in Italy receded, Hitler began the terror bombing of England, using V-1 and, later, V-2 rockets. This belated attempt to frighten the British public did not, however, stanch Ger-

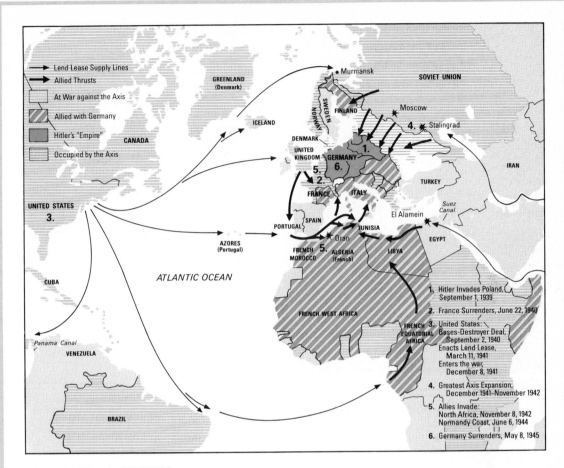

Lend Lease Supply Lines
Allied Thrusts
At War against the Axis
Allied with Germany
Hitler's "Empire"
Occupied by the Axis

GREENLAND (Denmark)
ICELAND
CANADA
UNITED STATES 3.
AZORES (Portugal)
ATLANTIC OCEAN
CUBA
Panama Canal
VENEZUELA
BRAZIL

Murmansk
SOVIET UNION
NORWAY SWEDEN
FINLAND
Moscow
4. Stalingrad
DENMARK
UNITED KINGDOM
GERMANY 1.
5. 6.
2.
FRANCE ITALY
IRAN
TURKEY
Suez Canal
El Alamein
PORTUGAL SPAIN
TUNISIA
Oran
FRENCH MOROCCO 5. ALGERIA (French)
LIBYA
EGYPT
FRENCH WEST AFRICA
FRENCH EQUATORIAL AFRICA

1. Hitler Invades Poland, September 1, 1939
2. France Surrenders, June 22, 1940
3. United States: Bases-Destroyer Deal, September 2, 1940 Enacts Lend Lease, March 11, 1941 Enters the war, December 8, 1941
4. Greatest Axis Expansion, December 1941–November 1942
5. Allies Invade: North Africa, November 8, 1942 Normandy Coast, June 6, 1944
6. Germany Surrenders, May 8, 1945

## THE EUROPEAN THEATER

man losses. On June 6, 1944, after preliminary saturation bombings and barrages, Allied forces landed on the Normandy coast of France with 176,000 troops and vast amounts of equipment. After a series of bitter battles, Allied troops reached Paris in late August. By September, the Allies had rolled up to the borders of Germany. A desperate counterattack in the Ardennes in December 1944 only slowed the American and British advance. Germany now faced invasion from the East and the West. On May 7, Germany surrendered to the Americans and to the Russians.

In Asia, the Japanese tide flowed until the battle of Guadalcanal in late 1942 and early 1943. Although General Douglas MacArthur was forced to abandon the Philippines, American forces recaptured Guadalcanal. Even more significant was the great American naval victory at Midway in June 1942, in which carrier-based planes destroyed four Japanese carriers, effectively blunting Japanese offensive capability. At this point, Japanese war calculations proved entirely false; it was now they, not the United States, who had to protect long supply lines against increasing attacks.

In 1943, the United States seized the ini-

**NORMANDY BEACH, 1944**

Operation Overlord, on June 6, 1944, successfully landed five divisions of Allied troops in Normandy, France. Opening this second front against Germany doomed the Nazi Reich, which fell the following May. *(Acme News Photo)*

tiative in Asia, retaking the Gilbert Islands and knocking out a major portion of the Japanese navy and air force. Despite efforts to invade Burma and India in late 1943, the Japanese were primarily on the defensive. In a series of important naval engagements in the Marianas archipelago during the summer of 1944, Marc Mitscher's fleet turned back an attempt by the Japanese navy to stop the American advance.

In 1944, President Roosevelt chose a plan proposed by General MacArthur to retake the

**IWO JIMA**

This famous photograph of marines raising the American flag on Mount Suribachi on February 23, 1945, marked the capture of the principal part of the island of Iwo Jima. Organized resistance collapsed on March 16. The battle, which was bitter and costly on both sides, gave the United States a major air base that was widely used in the last months of the war. *(The National Archives)*

THE PACIFIC THEATER

Philippines and then assault Japan itself, thus bypassing possible engagements with the bulk of the Japanese army still stationed in China. Another huge naval engagement, in Leyte Gulf in October 1944, destroyed what remained of the Japanese navy. After the Americans retook most of the Philippines, the Japanese Empire was split into two parts.

With naval and air superiority, the United States pried island bases (Iwo Jima and Okinawa) out of Japanese clutches and moved relentlessly toward Japan. Able to bomb the Japanese homeland with long-range B-29's, the American air force finally ended the war in August 1945 by dropping the atomic bomb on Hiroshima and Nagasaki.

routes from Eastern Europe. The president tried to circumvent potential friction through face-to-face encounters with Churchill and Stalin. Several conferences shaped the course of the war and established general principles for a peace settlement. In 1941, Churchill and Roosevelt met and signed the Atlantic Charter, a document that outlined international rights and responsibilities and promised self-determination, free trade, and the abandonment of force after the war. They also agreed to focus on defeating Germany first. Even after Pearl Harbor, this meant that a substantial portion of war supplies went to Britain and the Soviet Union; the Asian war took second place. Churchill and Roosevelt made a second major decision at Casablanca, Morocco, in January 1943. The two leaders agreed to demand unconditional surrender of the Axis powers in order to fix blame for the war on Hitler and Mussolini; no negotiated or partial peace with the fascist leaders would be tolerated.

For the Russians, the immediate and paramount problem was the opening of a second front—by an Allied invasion of France—so as to divert the German armies and relieve the enormous pressure that Hitler had brought to bear on the Soviet Union. The Russians were reeling before the German onslaught, and sustaining huge casualties and losses of territory. A more long-range Russian desire was to gain control of those areas through which the Germans had twice invaded during the twentieth century.

Roosevelt and the U.S. army commander, Dwight Eisenhower, agreed with the proposal for a second front, but Churchill twice convinced Roosevelt to postpone a landing, arguing that preparations remained incomplete. In August 1942, Churchill explained to Stalin why the United States and Britain had chosen to invade North Africa instead of France. Preparations for the attack advanced, and in November 1942, Allied forces landed in French North Africa. At first, French troops loyal to the Vichy government resisted, but Eisenhower negotiated a capitulation with Admiral Jean François Darlan. American and British troops pushed into Tunisia

to engage German forces led by General Erwin Rommel ("the Desert Fox"). By May 1943, the battle for North Africa had ended. Rommel was defeated and a large contingent of his army captured. But Russia still stood alone with no second front in sight.

Once again, in the spring of 1943, the Western Allies postponed the invasion of France. This time the United States and Britain decided to attack Sicily and knock Italy out of the war. Once again, the Russians were angered and suspicious that Britain and the United States wanted them to continue to bear the brunt of the European struggle. Nonetheless, the Allied command went ahead; troops landed in Sicily on July 9, 1943, and took thirty-eight days to conquer the island, although the bulk of the German army escaped into Italy.

This victory led to the fall of the Italian fascist leader, Benito Mussolini. A provisional government signed a peace treaty with the Allies on September 3, and Italy switched sides in the war. On the same day, British and American troops invaded Italy itself, and gradually they pushed a fiercely entrenched German army toward the north. The British and Americans agreed to administer liberated portions of Italy jointly, excluding Russia from any significant participation in shaping postwar Italy. Stalin considered this a precedent for his treatment of Eastern European nations liberated from the Germans by Soviet armies.

The western Allies finally launched the second front, in Operation Overlord, in early June 1944. When it came, it demonstrated masterful planning and execution. Although German defenders expected an attack, they misjudged its location. Allied troops established major beachheads in Normandy, at Utah and Omaha beaches. Landing massive amounts of materiel and troops, and protected by superior air cover, they fought their way inland. By late June the port of Cherbourg was liberated, and then Caen in early July. A counterattack ordered by Hitler failed, and the Germans fell back rapidly. For the Nazis the war was over. The Russian armies, who had turned the tide of battle in late 1942, rushed toward Poland and eastern Germany. Paris fell on August 25, 1944, and the Germans retreated behind the Siegfried Line along the German border. So hopeless was the war that a group of military officers attempted to assassinate Hitler on July 20 to hasten a German surrender.

In early 1945, Eisenhower ordered an offensive, moving into Germany and taking the Ruhr Valley during February and March. The Russians had entered Warsaw on January 17, and on April 13 they took Vienna. On April 30, Hitler committed suicide in his bunker in Berlin. At the last minute, German leaders offered to surrender to the United States, but Eisenhower refused. Germany had made war against all the Allies; Germany would have to surrender to all of them. Russian troops took Berlin. Finally, on May 8, Germany surrendered. The Third Reich ended in flame and ruin. Allied troops finally stopped the murderous regime that in its frenzy had executed millions of Jews, Poles, gypsies, communists, and others.

By May 1945, foreign armies occupied practically all of Europe—from France eastward through Poland and south through Italy. As the Allies had foreseen, this created immense political problems. Churchill, Stalin, and Roosevelt had tried to forestall some of these problems at the Teheran Conference in 1943 and the Yalta meeting in February 1945. Roosevelt tried to restrain British hostility toward the Russians. (He had opposed Churchill's suggestions for an invasion of Germany through the eastern end of the Mediterranean to head off the Soviet forces.) Roosevelt hoped to accommodate Stalin and enlist his peaceful cooperation with the United States after the war. He had come to sympathize with the Russian desire to control the invasion routes of Eastern Europe. And he encouraged Stalin to expect reparations to reconstruct his battered nation. In exchange, he hoped to secure Russian help against the Japanese in Asia. But Roosevelt did little to implement these policies and postponed hard decisions about redrawing European boundaries and reconstructing governments.

By the time of the Potsdam Conference, Germany had been defeated; Roosevelt was dead; and the new president, Harry Truman, had to make the decisions that Roosevelt had put off. Truman was more suspicious of Russian motives; but more important, the United States now possessed

THE TEHERAN CONFERENCE, 1943

At meetings such as this one during the fall of 1943 in Teheran, Iran, Roosevelt (center) met with Russian Premier Joseph Stalin (left) and British Prime Minister Winston Churchill. Roosevelt hoped to use personal diplomacy to overcome the enormous differences in aims among the Allies. (The National Archives)

a workable atomic bomb. However, if the new president hoped this weapon would convince Stalin to compromise, he was mistaken. The most contentious issue was Poland. Occupying Russian forces changed the boundaries of that nation, incorporating eastern portions into the Soviet Union and pushing Poland's western boundaries to the Oder-Neisse line, thus giving them control over territory that had formerly been a part of Germany.

The issue of reparations also separated the Allies. Russia demanded huge compensation from Germany to restore some of the vast industrial losses it had suffered. But the amount and type of reparations could not be settled. Consequently, the Soviets dismantled factories in their zone of occupation and sent them eastward. On the issue of the occupation of Germany, the Allies agreed, after much dispute, to four zones: a Russian zone, including jointly controlled Berlin; a French zone, bordering on eastern France; an American zone in southern and central Germany; and a British zone to the north. But the alliance of convenience had degenerated swiftly into a contest between the United States and the Soviet Union, with each side blaming the other for blocking its legitimate aspirations, and with the atomic bomb playing a crucial role in the strategies of both sides.

## THE WAR IN THE PACIFIC

The war in the Pacific did not involve the Soviet Union until the very last days of the struggle. The chief burden of fighting the Japanese fell to the United States and China, with some aid from Australia and particularly from the British in areas like Burma. Although given a lower priority, the contest was bitter and protracted. American strategy—carried out by General Douglas MacArthur and Admiral Chester W. Nimitz—focused on seizing control of the air and the seas, retaking the Philippines, and then moving from island chain to island chain toward Japan.

By midsummer of 1942, the Japanese advance had slowed. After furious fighting on land and

**THE JAPANESE SURRENDER**

A party of Japanese officials surrenders to the Allies aboard the U.S.S. *Missouri* in Tokyo Bay on September 2, 1945, thus ending World War II. *(U.S. Army Photograph)*

**YOUNG MAO ZEDONG, 1939**

Chinese Communist leader Mao Zedong found his greatest support among peasants and made them the basis for his opposition to the invading Japanese armies and the official Chinese government headed by Chiang Kai-shek. *(UPI)*

sea, the United States held Guadalcanal in the Solomon Islands near Australia. By early 1943, the United States prepared to take the offensive. Gradually American forces moved northward, skipping heavily fortified islands to outflank the Japanese. After several months of battle around the Philippine Islands, General MacArthur finally retook Manila on March 4, 1944.

The island-hopping American forces, now superior against the crippled Japanese navy and air force, took Iwo Jima in early 1945 and the island of Okinawa, near southern Japan, in April 1945. These conquests provided a final, crucial link in the American strategy: bases from which to bomb the Japanese homeland. From air bases on these islands and from Tinian and Saipan in the Marianas, new B-29 long-range bombers began to pound industrial and population centers in Japan. General Curtis E. LeMay took command of the bomber operations in late August 1944 and developed tactics that showed the terrible potential of the new planes. Using incendiary devices, LeMay began systematic attacks on Japanese cities

designed to start fire storms. In March 1945, for example, B-29s destroyed about a quarter of the city of Tokyo. Still the Japanese refused to surrender and prepared for a desperate, even suicidal, defense of their island empire.

Air raids became more spectacular and punishing, until the devastating attacks on Hiroshima and Nagasaki. Faced with obliteration from the skies and destruction of its armies by the Russians, the Japanese sued for peace on August 10. After maneuvering to save the Japanese emperor, the government capitulated on August 14. Final surrender took place on September 2 in Tokyo Bay, aboard the battleship *Missouri*.

The occupation and reconstruction of Japan remained principally an American task. The Soviets were not granted a share in the occupation, although by agreement they acquired important territory in northern China and on Sakhalin Island. By agreement also, Russian armies accepted the surrender of the Japanese north of the 38th parallel in Korea, while Americans administered the area to the south.

A more fundamental Asian problem was China. All Japanese troops in China were instructed to surrender to Chinese leader Chiang Kai-shek. But in northern China, communist rebel forces led by Mao Zedong took power from the Japanese and confiscated their war supplies. Troubled by conflict between these two Chinese factions during the war, the United States tried fruitlessly in 1945 to arrange a cease-fire while continuing to aid Chiang. But in late 1949, Chiang's corrupt and inefficient government was driven out of mainland China to the offshore island of Taiwan by the communists. Nothing short of full-scale intervention by the United States could have prevented this.

# DEMOBILIZATION AND POSTWAR ALLIED COOPERATION

Despite intensifying hostility between the United States and the Soviet Union in 1945, the United States proceeded rapidly to demobilize its war economy and armed forces. Even before Germany's surrender, on May 8, 1945, the Truman administration began to cancel war orders and dismantle economic controls. By the end of 1945, most controls had been lifted and the economy was returning rapidly to civilian production. The American army demobilized under irresistible pressure from GI's and from their families at home. "Bring Back Daddy" clubs sprang up in the United States, and soldiers stationed abroad agitated for immediate release. Troops were brought home and mustered out of the service as quickly as transportation could be arranged. Total personnel in the armed services fell from over 12 million in 1945 to 3 million in 1946 and 1½ million in 1947.

But demobilization did not by any means imply that the federal government had suddenly ceased to intervene in the lives of Americans or in the economy. After a long debate, the Congress agreed to the Employment Act of 1946, which pledged the government to maintain an active role in directing the economy. Government officials also encouraged the shift of women out of the work force. The great and successful experiment in training and employing women was undone almost as fast as it had been achieved. Finally, defense spending and direction of scientific research in such fields as atomic energy required large expenditures and tight federal controls. Continued military production required that hundreds of decisions shaping the American economy be made in Washington. Even in the late 1940s, when defense spending was relatively low, it still consumed over 25 percent of the federal budget. And scientific research increasingly fell under the direction of federal agencies like the Atomic Energy Commission.

Other federal activities profoundly shaped the postwar world. To reward soldiers for their sacrifices, the U.S. government passed a generous bonus for returning soldiers in the form of the Servicemen's Readjustment Act of 1944 (see p. 859). State governments often added their own system of financial rewards and preferential hiring. Over 2 million soldiers used the GI Bill to attend college after 1946. The result was a significant democratization of American higher education.

Many Americans hoped that postwar peace could be maintained by the United Nations, a new institution organized around the wartime alliance against Germany and Japan. The UN Charter, signed in 1945, created two chambers: a Security Council and a General Assembly. The Security Council was made up of five permanent members (Britain, France, China, the United States, and the U.S.S.R.) and ten elected representatives of other nations. The permanent members could veto any Security Council undertaking. The General Assembly consisted of all member nations, each with one vote. But even in creating the United Nations, competition between the United States and Russia erupted. Finally, a compromise on membership was reached: the U.S.S.R. received three votes in the General

Assembly (the Ukraine, Byelorussia, and the U.S.S.R.), and the United States secured membership for Argentina (a profascist power) and ensured the legality of regional alliances like the Organization of American States.

On the trial of war criminals, the Allies remained united. After arresting German leaders in the summer of 1945, the Allies opened trials in Nuremberg in November. Four judges—one each from Britain, France, the United States, and the U.S.S.R.—presided over the hearings. Prosecutors accused Nazi officials of crimes against peace (for undertaking aggressive war), breaches of accepted war conduct, and crimes against humanity in the death camps. The first Nuremberg trial lasted 216 days; on October 1, 1946, nineteen of twenty-two defendants were found guilty; twelve were sentenced to hanging, three to life imprisonment, and four to long prison terms. In addition, the judges declared four Nazi organizations to be criminal in character. In Japan much the same procedure was followed. When all the trials ended in 1949, 2,647 persons had been convicted, with 689 death sentences handed down. The purpose had been to stamp war guilt irrevocably on the German and Japanese leadership and to proclaim wars of aggression to be illegal.

# THE COLD WAR

## Cold War in Europe

Despite agreements between the United States and the Soviet Union, a cold war quickly developed in international relations. On Roosevelt's death in 1945, Truman came into office ill prepared in foreign policy matters yet facing urgent unfinished business. Sentiment to return to prewar neutrality was overpowered by the sense that the United States had to enforce its own interests and goals upon a turbulent world. This meant that the United States remained on a semi-war footing. Naturally, secret weapons research and development became a high policy priority. Just

as inevitably, the federal government retained much of the power over research, allocation of resources, and direction of the economy that it had acquired during the war.

The impetus for military security also generated an atmosphere of insecurity and suspicion. The arms race that had once been directed against the Germans now resumed against the Russians. But the growing sophistication of weaponry only increased the vulnerability that many Americans felt. Every confrontation with the Russians stimulated the arms race and underscored the necessity for secrecy. More and more, these demands for control strained the assumption that a peacetime society ought to tolerate dissent and free and open scientific inquiry. The bitter conflict even convinced some Americans that they should try to define the purposes of their society more narrowly and perhaps exclude from it those who did not appear to agree.

Disputes between the United States and the Soviet Union at first focused on the restoration of Europe. The frightful destruction of war had created economic havoc in Germany, France, and Eastern Europe. Political instability in France, Italy, and Greece brought local communists close to power. In Greece, civil war broke out in 1946 between British-backed royalist forces and communist-supported insurgents. But Great Britain was exhausted by the struggle against Germany and could play only a minor role in Greece. Either the United States or the Soviet Union would fill the vacuum.

To exercise a decisive role in Europe, the Truman administration had to overcome several problems. One was traditional American reluctance to become involved in the problems of European politics. Truman eventually won the support of Republicans for a new activist policy in Europe. A second problem was the rapid disintegration of American military preparedness. The president could not rely on conventional military forces to oppose the Russians in Europe. As a result, the temporary monopoly of the atomic bomb and the defense potential of the American

## FEDERAL RESEARCH AND DEVELOPMENT FUNDS, 1947–1970 (IN MILLIONS OF DOLLARS)

| Year | Total for R&D | For Defense | For AEC* | For NSF† |
|------|---------------|-------------|----------|----------|
| 1947 | 619.5 | 469.3 | 39.9 | — |
| 1953 | 3,106.0 | 2,577.3 | 309.9 | 2.3 |
| 1959 | 6,693.5 | 5,161.6 | 699.8 | 60.4 |
| 1965 | 14,614.3 | 6,796.5‡ | 1,240.7 | 187.2 |
| 1970 | 15,340.3 | 7,360.4‡ | 1,346.0 | 289.0 |

* Atomic Energy Commission.
† National Science Foundation.
‡ After 1962, large amounts of research and development funds were funneled to the National Aeronautics and Space Administration (NASA). Some of these funds, because of their application to missile development, may be considered defense expenditures.

Source: U.S. Bureau of the Census, *Historical Statistics of the United States* (Washington, D.C.: U.S. Government Printing Office, 1975), Part 2, p. 966.

economy were crucial to foreign policy decisions.

At the war's end in Europe, the Soviet Union occupied Rumania, Hungary, Czechoslovakia, and Poland, and in these nations Stalin insisted on governments friendly to the U.S.S.R. In the face of traditional bitterness toward the Russians in these areas, this often meant that only communists were willing to play such a role. And the placement of communists in power contradicted American desires for free elections and wholly independent nations in the area.

Acrimony between Americans and Russians broke out in a dispute over control of Iranian oil resources in early 1946. The Russians had stationed several thousand troops in northern Iran but were eventually compelled to withdraw them. Negotiations at the United Nations over internationalization of atomic energy control failed in the early summer. And the United States rejected a Soviet request for a large loan to help rebuild its shattered economy. As prospects for a comprehensive peace receded, the United States and the Soviets began to create separate political and economic institutions in their German occupation zones.

In these trying times, Americans attempted to understand how the peace of 1945 had become so fragile. In a speech on March 5, 1946, Winston Churchill provided language that seemed to describe what had happened to the world. Speaking of Russian influence in Eastern Europe, Churchill warned that "an iron curtain has descended" across Europe. Probably more influential in defining American policy toward the Soviet Union were ideas authored by George Kennan, counselor at the American Embassy in Moscow. First in a long telegram in 1946 and then in an essay published under the pseudonym "Mister X," Kennan provided a convincing rationale for American foreign policy. He argued that the United States had to "contain" Soviet influence and hope that this action would cause Russia to change internally. A number of American leaders were convinced by this notion of containment, although they often exaggerated its military aspects.

In early 1947, Kennan's principle of containment became a fundamental part of American foreign policy. This occurred in two ways. On March 12, 1947, the president announced the Truman Doctrine, which promised aid to Greece in its struggle against insurgents. Truman argued that the world was divided between two types of societies: Western democratic capitalist nations and Eastern communist nations. The outcome of the struggle between the two sides in Europe, he proclaimed, was "of grave importance in a much wider situation." Truman asked for military assistance for Greece and Turkey, and Congress obliged by voting funds on May 15.

Truman put forward the second stage of his policy in early summer. George Marshall—formerly a general, now secretary of state—proposed a plan of economic assistance for Western Europe. The Marshall Plan, as it became known, promised to revive the economy of Europe and eliminate conditions that communist politicians could exploit. The program even offered economic assistance to the Soviet Union and its allies, but they refused. And Communist parties in Western countries like France demonstrated against the plan. Nonetheless, sixteen European nations eventually agreed to a joint plan for economic recovery, signed in September 1947. Congress funded the project in March 1948.

The Soviets responded to the growing integration of the Western European nations by increasing their control of occupied territories such as Poland, Czechoslovakia, and Hungary. In 1948, with the United States and Western European nations contemplating a military alliance, with the Soviets' former ally Yugoslavia pursuing an independent course, and with the integration of the western zones of Germany to form one single political and economic entity, Stalin acted. After the United States introduced a single West German currency into West Berlin in late June, the Russians clamped a blockade on all ground and water entrances into the city. Truman had to make the next move: either abandon Berlin or force a reopening of supply routes.

The American president chose a third way. He initiated a massive airlift to supply the city. Finally in the spring of 1949, the Russians lifted

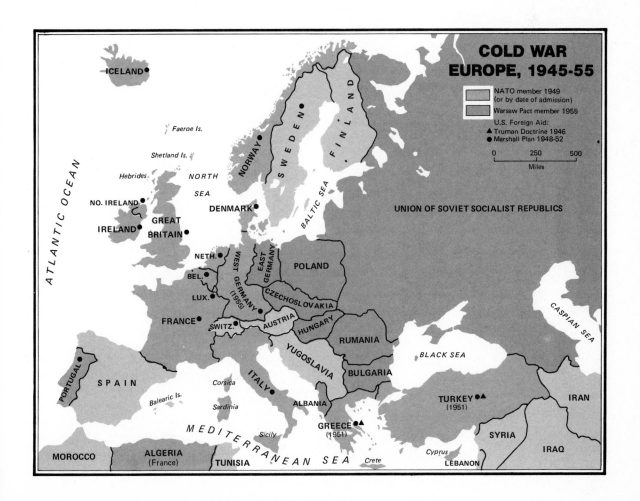

BERLIN AIRLIFT: "OPERATION VITTLES"

Faced with the Russian blockade of Berlin, President Truman might have acquiesced in Soviet control over the divided city, or he might have forced open trade routes by military
means. Instead, he chose a third alternative—the highly successful and dramatic supply of
the American, French, and British sectors of the city by air. *(UPI)*

their ineffective blockade. Not only had Stalin's
tactics failed, but they had helped pressure Western nations into forming the North Atlantic
Treaty Organization (NATO) in mid-1949. Britain, France, Belgium, the Netherlands, Luxembourg, Portugal, Denmark, Norway, Italy, Iceland, Canada, and the United States joined. West
Germany was admitted in 1954. This formal alliance became the mainstay of America's European policy and effectively prevented further de-
terioration of U.S. influence in Europe.

In September 1949, Truman announced that
the Russians had exploded an atomic bomb. The
short-lived American monopoly had been broken. The president ordered American scientists
to begin serious development of hydrogen weapons. In four short years, the peace of 1945 had
degenerated into a new arms race and new entangling alliances.

## War in Asia

The defeat of Chiang Kai-shek in 1949 touched
off recriminations in the United States over who

had "lost" China to the communists. In Asia, the
victory of Mao Zedong created a major new
revolutionary force. In this context, the Truman
administration faced a serious crisis in June 1950.
For two years, the divided sections of Korea had
glowered at each other with increasing hostility.
Separated only by the 38th parallel, two nations
had sprung up: North Korea, supported by the
Russians, and South Korea, dependent on the
United States. On June 25, 1950, North Korean
troops plunged into the south. Truman had to
decide quickly: stand and fight, risking a large-
scale Asian war, or abandon an ally. Because of
withering criticism of his foreign policy and
doubts about the loyalty of some members of his
government, Truman probably had no real
choice.

By the middle of 1953, the first armed confrontation between the United States and communist troops had finally ended. War had been
confined to a small portion of the globe. The
United States and the Soviet Union had avoided
using the doomsday weapons that they now possessed in abundance. But the arms race and the
cold war became, if anything, more serious in a

# AMERICANS AT WAR

## The Korean War

The Korean conflict employed many of the weapons and tactics developed during the total war experience of World War II, but on a limited terrain and for limited goals. This contradiction between potential means and narrow goals meant, for example, that the United States rejected use of the atomic bomb against North Korea and communist China. It meant, also, that each side operated from privileged sanctuaries: the United States from naval and air bases in Japan, and the Chinese from behind their border at the Yalu River on the northern edge of North Korea. The battlefield in Korea, however, witnessed a war that was as bitter and bloody as World War II.

In 1945, as part of the postwar distribution of conquered Japanese territories, Korea was divided at the 38th parallel, with the Russians occupying the north and the United States the south. As the cold war intensified, each section organized as a separate nation. In 1948 and 1949, the Soviet Union and the United States withdrew occupying troops, leaving the two small nations to confront each other. On June 25, 1950, North Korea struck South Korean lines, breaking through easily to seize the capital, Seoul, and then pushed southward to destroy the entire South Korean army. On June 27, President Truman called on Douglas MacArthur, commander of U.S. Armed Forces in the Far East, to support South Korea. The United Nations (with the Soviet Union absent because of a boycott) voted to demand North Korean evacuation and offered supporting troops. Eventually small contributions came from France, Britain, Turkey, Greece, New Zealand, the Netherlands, Belgium, Ethiopia, and others. Most of the troops, however,

**A KOREAN WAR SCENE**

A familiar sight during war on the Asian mainland in World War II and then the Korean conflict: soldiers advanced to the front lines while civilians fled in the opposite direction, carrying what possessions they could. *(UPI)*

were supplied by the United States and South Korea.

Hemmed in by the continued communist offensive, American and South Korean troops clung to the area around Pusan. But on September 15, 1950, the American army took the offensive. At the same time, a surprise amphibious landing near Seoul at Inchon, behind communist lines, broke North Korea's offensive and shattered its army. United Nations troops drove rapidly to the north and crossed the 38th parallel into North

## THE KOREAN WAR, 1950–1953

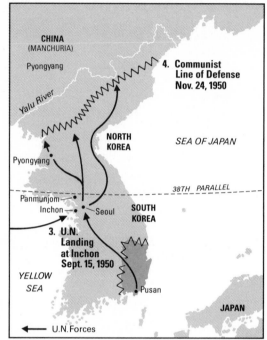

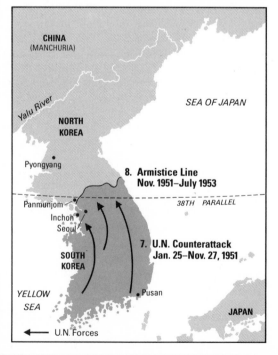

**GENERAL DOUGLAS MACARTHUR**

General Douglas MacArthur was chief of Southwest Pacific operations in World War II, administrator of postwar Japan, and commander of United Nations forces in Korea. Because he disagreed with the limited American objectives in the Korean conflict—and said so publicly—President Truman removed him from command. *(U.S. Army Photograph)*

two fronts toward the border of China. His purpose was to destroy the North Korean army. Disregarding warnings from the Chinese communists, he approached the Yalu River border. On November 25, Chinese troops, ferried across the river, attacked in force, compelling the UN troops to retreat to the 38th parallel. MacArthur's brilliant victory at Inchon was thus undercut by his grave miscalculation.

Offensive and counteroffensive followed. MacArthur's outspoken defense of a wider war brought his dismissal by Truman in April 1951. Costly battles pushed the front back and forth over the 38th parallel until July 1953, when a permanent armistice line was established somewhat north of the original line. For this eventual small exchange of territory there were perhaps 1,500,000 casualties on the communist side and perhaps 450,000 on the UN side (including 33,710 Americans killed in action and several thousand more who died as prisoners of war). In terms of tactics and materiel, the United States navy had completely dominated sea lanes and harassed North Korean coastal installations at will. The United States had also controlled the air over North Korea, although U.S. Saber Jet fighters met stiff resistance from Russian MIG planes stationed at bases inside China.

Korea, capturing the capital, Pyongyang, on October 20.

General MacArthur, after conferring with President Truman, drove farther north on

divided and restless world. Peace was further away than it had been in 1945 when the war ended—and when American scientists had developed a weapon to end all wars.

## Cold War at Home

At home, worry about military secrets and ideological purity increased. Robert Oppenheimer was not the only American to fall under scrutiny during this security-conscious era. In 1950, Julius and Ethel Rosenberg were arrested and convicted of passing atomic secrets to the Russians. (They were executed in 1953.) From 1949 to the mid-1950s suspicion of communism focused on schools, teachers, books, and government workers. Charges of communist infiltration into the government and into the Democratic party became an effective campaign slogan, especially for Senator Joseph McCarthy of Wisconsin. But McCarthyism became a corrosive element in politics because it also fed on the insecurities of Americans who were uneasy about rapid social change. Groups reluctant to accept the admission of labor unions or blacks into the American political consensus sometimes saw the hand of communist conspirators behind these movements. It

# Edward R. Murrow

(UPI)

Radio, if it is to serve and survive, must hold a mirror behind the nation and the world. If the reflection shows racial intolerance, economic inequality, bigotry, unemployment, or anything else, let the people see it—or rather, hear it. The mirror must have no curves, and must be held with a steady hand.

With these words, Edward R. Murrow, shortly after World War II, explained the responsibilities of radio news reporting in America. However, the vitality and incisiveness of the news depended on who held the mirror. When it was Murrow, the result was bound to be brilliant and controversial.

Ed Murrow was born in rural North Carolina in 1908. In 1913, his family moved to Washington state. In high school he joined the debating team. In college, at Washington State University, he worked in the new field of radio. As a result of his election as president of the National Student Federation, he moved to New York City in 1930.

In 1935, CBS hired Murrow to be "director of talks"—that is, head of news features. Two years later, CBS sent him to England as its chief European correspondent This job carried enormous prestige and responsibility. Murrow was the perfect reporter for the disintegrating world situation—from his trenchcoat, to the smoldering cigarette forever dangling from his lips, to a voice that conveyed worldliness and fatigue.

For many Americans, Murrow's was the grim voice of the war. He broadcast the retreat at Dunkirk; he recorded the blitz over London. He flew on a bombing mission over Berlin. When the war ended, he accompanied American troops into the Nazi concentration camp at Buchenwald. Throughout these trying times, his stand was clear. His trademark was informed opinion; his was no world for neutrals.

In 1946, Murrow returned to a desk job with CBS and then became producer of the news program *Hear It Now.* In November 1951, Murrow entered the new medium of television with *See It Now.* This enormously successful show established the general format for other television documentaries and news programs. Murrow appeared weekly, his film clips interspliced with critical commentary. In October 1953, he developed another new format, *Person to Person,* an interview program with celebrities such as Senator John F. Kennedy and movie star Marilyn Monroe.

In March 1954, Murrow ran a critical exposé of Senator Joseph McCarthy. Murrow spoke calmly but acidly about the senator's activities while showing him harassing witnesses at government investigations. McCarthy and his allies were furious. But Murrow's impact and continued popularity contrasted with McCarthy's sudden loss of popularity. In the contest for credibility, Murrow had won.

Nevertheless CBS, its sponsors, and much of the mass media establishment began to frown on Murrow. As television evolved toward quiz shows and situation comedies like *The $64,000 Question* and *The Beverly Hillbillies,* Murrow's tough journalism seemed out of step. A symbol of war and cold war, and a critical roving eye willing to expose America's faults, Murrow lost influence after the early 1960s. He remained greatly admired for his integrity, but he was a man who belonged to an earlier age.

**SENATOR JOSEPH McCARTHY AND THE *DAILY WORKER***

McCarthy used Communist Party publications such as the *Worker* during Senate hearings to cast suspicions on his opponents. Favorable mention in such a publication would often bring charges of disloyalty from the Wisconsin senator. *(Wide World Photos)*

was no accident that segregationists charged that integration was a communist plot or that some Americans feared that the United Nations was communist-dominated.

President Truman saw his task principally as defending the Democratic party against charges of being "soft" on communism. This helps explain his swift, early action on federal employee loyalty. In 1946, he appointed a Temporary Commission on Employee Loyalty to design a security program. Following the commission's suggestions, he asked the attorney general to draw up a list of subversive organizations. He also established federal departmental loyalty boards that checked each employee. Five years later, about 20,000 federal workers had been screened: a little over half had been cleared, 3,000 cases were still pending, 2,500 employees had left service voluntarily, and 400 had been dismissed.

Despite Truman's extensive and even overzealous scrutiny of federal workers, Congress, the Republican party, and a substantial part of public opinion remained skeptical. Between 1945 and 1952 over eighty congressional investigations of communism were held. Many of them explored federal agencies. The most important of these inquiries were held by the House Un-

American Activities Committee (HUAC). Very little legislation emerged from this committee, but it did provide a forum to attack Truman. And some conservative Southerners on HUAC used the committee to charge that integration was un-American.

The principal anticommunist, antisubversive legislation of the era came in 1950 with the passage of the Internal Security Act. The bill required the Justice Department to register the names, finances, and membership of all communist or front groups. All literature from these groups passing through the mail was to be stamped "Communist." Known party members could not obtain passports. Most controversial was a provision to set aside internment camps for suspected disloyal Americans in time of emergency. Truman angrily vetoed the act, saying that it subverted elementary ideas of a free society. Congress thought otherwise and overrode his veto.

The Internal Security Act symbolized Congress's growing initiative on the anticommunist front. In 1948, Alger Hiss, a minor New Deal adviser and well-connected lawyer, had been charged with passing secrets to the Russians in the late 1930s. His accuser was Whitaker Chambers, a self-confessed spy, a man of many aliases, a writer and later an editor for *Time* magazine. Chambers accused Hiss before HUAC and then in public, on NBC's *Meet the Press*. Hiss sued for libel, but in 1950 he was charged with and convicted of perjury. HUAC investigators, led by Congressman Richard Nixon, established a strong circumstantial case to fit Chambers's eyewitness accounts. Truman, Secretary of State

Dean Acheson, and many liberals refused to believe in Hiss's guilt. But their attitude only increased the desire of some congressmen like McCarthy to expose communists in government. By 1952, issues of defense, secrecy, and spying threatened to overwhelm American political discussion. Consequently, the commitment to building more bombs and maintaining secrets was hardly questioned.

# SUGGESTED READINGS, CHAPTERS 39–40

## HIROSHIMA AND THE ATOMIC BOMB

The effect on American society of building and deploying nuclear weapons is difficult to overestimate. Martin J. Sherwin, *A World Destroyed: The Atomic Bomb and the Grand Alliance* (1975), is an insightful account of the creation of the first atomic weapons. Gregg Herken, *The Winning Weapon: The Atomic Bomb in the Cold War, 1945–1950* (1980), details the role of nuclear weapons in policy-making. Of the many accounts describing the effects of the bomb, John Hersey's novel *Hiroshima* (1946) is the most personal and poignant.

## WORLD WAR II AND ITS EFFECTS

For an accessible and comprehensive discussion of battles and strategies during the war, Richard Ernest and Trevor N. Dupuy's *Encyclopedia of Military History*, rev. ed. (1977), is indispensable. Alan S. Milward, *War, Economy, and Society, 1939–1945* (1977), and Richard Polenberg, *America at War: The Home Front, 1941–1945,* (1968) are two excellent discussions of the effects of war on American society. Otis L. Graham, in *Toward a Planned Society: From Roosevelt to Nixon* (1976), focuses on the role of federal economic planning during and after the war. In *Another Chance: Postwar America, 1945–1968* (1981), James Gilbert examines some of the long-range effects of the war.

## THE COLD WAR

The origins of the Cold War have been extensively debated. John Lewis Gaddis, in *The United States and the Origins of the Cold War, 1941–1947* (1972), carefully and comprehensively explores the issues. An excellent account with substantial coverage of Soviet policy is Adam B. Ulam, *Expansion and Coexistence* (1968). Lloyd C. Gardner, in *Architects of Illusion: Men and Ideas in American Foreign Policy, 1941–1949* (1970), sheds considerable light on the complex motivations of American policy makers. The central political figures of the Cold War era have left excellent memoirs. In his *Memoirs*, 2 vols. (1955–1956), President Harry S Truman proves to be a marvelous storyteller and competent defender of his administration. George Frost Kennan, *Memoirs, 1925–1950* (1968), is a brilliant and intriguing account by a key policy-maker and commentator. James MacGregor Burns, *Roosevelt: The Soldier of Freedom* (1970), is a masterful description of the Roosevelt presidency during the war years. James B. Conant, *My Several Lives: Memoirs of a Social Inventor* (1970), is an account by one of the leading figures in the politics of wartime and postwar science.

# 41 · Martin Luther King, Jr.: The Struggle and the Dream

At about one o'clock on the afternoon of May 3, 1963, the public safety commissioner of Birmingham, Alabama, Theophilus Eugene "Bull" Connor, stood next to the city's outgoing mayor, Arthur Hanes. Connor, a fleshy, heavy-jowled man, whose glass eye gave him a peculiar stare, watched the entrance to the Sixteenth Street Baptist Church. Nearby policemen, and farther on a line of police and firemen with high-pressure hoses, backed up by a dog squad with several German shepherds, also waited and watched. They were determined to prevent black civil rights demonstrators from marching. Their commander, Bull Connor, was a national symbol of old-style violent enforcement of race separation. Although this was just one more day in a series of rolling demonstrations that had continued for almost a month, it proved to be decisive. The Reverend Martin Luther King, Jr., leader of the demonstrators inside the church had demanded "promises and action." "We are ready to negotiate," he claimed. "But we intend to negotiate from strength." Connor just as adamantly had promised to arrest every demonstrator, even if it filled every cell in the city jails. King, he scoffed, would "run out of niggers."

Hanes nudged Connor. "Here they come," he said. Connor's men swept back a crowd of about 100 jeering white onlookers and turned on the demonstrators. Police Captain G. V. Evans ordered the emerging group to halt and disperse: "Or you're going to get wet." The first fifty blacks continued to march. Most were young and carrying signs. Suddenly the hoses squirted on. High-pressure water splattered the crowd. Some demonstrators fled. Some fell to the ground, upended by the force of the spray. Others skidded down the pavement, like debris in a gutter.

Now a large crowd of almost 2,000 blacks who had been waiting in nearby Kelly Ingram Park grew restless. Firemen turned their hoses on this more formidable group. Instead of dispersing, however, many in the crowd responded by hurling rocks, bricks, bottles, and chunks of concrete at the police. The situation had reached a breaking point. Connor signaled and his dog squad advanced. The enraged animals snapped at demonstrators, separating them into smaller groups, as other police moved in for arrests. But hundreds of demonstrators retreated into side streets, where they continued to pelt the advancing police. Finally, James Bevel, an assistant of King's, negotiated a quick truce. If the police called off the dogs and shut down the water cannons, he would urge the demonstrators to go home. Gradually the riot subsided, and Birmingham drew back once again from full-scale fighting. But the mask had fallen from Connor's segregation. The next day, in almost every newspaper in the country—and all over the world—one photograph told the story of Birmingham: a snarling police dog, scarcely restrained by an officer, lunging at the chest of a black demonstrator.

The violence in Alabama broke the impasse by escalating the confrontation. In Washington, Attorney General Robert Kennedy issued a sympathetic statement: "These demonstrations are understandable expressions of resentment and hurt by people who have been the victims of abuse and deprivation of their most basic rights for many years." Then he warned King against further marches. But, quite clearly, the federal government had decided to intervene. Kennedy dispatched Assistant Attorney General Burke Marshall to Birmingham to negotiate a settlement between King and the local business community. Connor and Hanes were conspicuously left out of the talks.

Kennedy chose this tactic because of the chaos in Birmingham's government. Connor and Mayor Hanes were still in office only because of stubbornness. In November 1962, the voters of Birmingham had altered the old city government structure that was dominated by Connor. When the new structure went into effect in April 1963, Connor ran for mayor but lost to a milder segregationist, Albert Boutwell. Then, switching tactics, Connor claimed that he and Hanes could not be unseated, whatever the new frame of government. They would serve out their terms of office under the old system. Thus when the new mayor was sworn in on April 15, Connor and Hanes prevented him from taking office. The matter stood, in early May, before the courts.

Connor's use of police power to enforce segregation pushed the situation to a crisis. Extremist elements in Birmingham and from the rest of the state, including the Ku Klux Klan, rallied to the city to support Connor. Some of them pushed for further confrontations, in hopes of a declaration of martial law. To them, anything was better than integration.

In this explosive atmosphere, Burke Marshall began his negotiations with a group of city business leaders. From Washington, President Kennedy stepped up pressure as cabinet members persuaded corporate friends to ask Birmingham's business elite to support a compromise. What King and his forces demanded was not easy to grant: desegregation of lunch counters, restrooms, fitting rooms, and drinking fountains in all downtown stores; job placement for blacks as clerks and salespeople; release of prisoners arrested for demonstrating; and establishment of a permanent dialogue between white and black leaders.

Marshall and his negotiating team raced against a short, sputtering fuse of racial violence. From Saturday, May 4, when he arrived, Marshall met in long sessions with white and black leaders. In the streets of Birmingham, the violence accelerated. King refused to call off demonstrators, even though confrontations with city police had escalated. Complicating matters, Alabama's governor, George Wallace, sent in reinforcements to aid Connor. By Tuesday evening, 575 riot-equipped state troopers were camped out around the city. By late Tuesday night, however, Marshall had hammered out a tentative agreement, and King and his forces called off further demonstrations. The city waited . . . Wednesday, then Thursday, until the final details were worked out. Friday morning King announced the accord. Most of his demands had been met. The back of segregation was broken.

Nevertheless, segregationists tried to disrupt the agreement. Governor Wallace denounced the agreement with "lawless Negroes." He would never, he promised, compromise on segregation. On Saturday night, shortly after a joint Georgia-Alabama Klan rally in Birmingham, a car sped past the house of A. D. King, brother of Martin Luther King. Passengers tossed two dynamite bombs out of the car, blasting the house. Minutes later, four white men threw two more bombs at the Gaston Hotel, where King himself had been staying.

Although these bombings had caused no serious injuries, Birmingham's blacks poured into the streets. Picking up anything handy, they pelted policemen, smashed car windows, and beat up white bystanders. When police reinforcements arrived with the dog squad, the crowd became still more enraged. Even state troopers could not calm the situation. Finally, black leaders persuaded the crowd to disperse. The riot ended, but not before flames had consumed several white-owned businesses in the black section of town. Still, the agreement held. The events made King's words, uttered during the campaign, all the more prophetic: "I stand alone in the middle of two opposing forces in the Negro community. One is the force of complacency. . . . The other force is one of bitterness and hatred and comes perilously close to advocating violence."

Gradually peace returned to Birmingham. The reign of Bull Connor ended on May 23, when the Alabama Supreme Court unanimously certified Mayor Boutwell's election and right to office. The businessmen's agreement was implemented. But racial hatred and white resistance continued. On September 14, white terrorists hurled a dynamite bomb through a window of the Sixteenth Street Baptist Church. It exploded in a crowded Sunday school class, killing four young girls. Twenty other children were injured. In a eulogy sermon, King tried, as he always did, to channel sorrow and shock into something positive: "Their death says to us that we must work passionately and unceasingly to make the American dream a reality."

Birmingham was a grim and inevitable rendezvous for the Southern civil rights movement—a protest movement that had begun almost spontaneously in Montgomery, Alabama, in 1955. The success at Montgomery had been astounding—in no small measure because of King, who was thrust into leadership of the new movement. But Montgomery was also deceptive. It represented only one wall breached, the first battle in a war of attrition against Southern strongholds of segregation. One by one they fell, some in violence, some peacefully. But some, like Birmingham, held out.

King's generalship of this movement was crucial. His strategy was honed in failure and success. He recognized, where others did not, the great energy and moral force of Southern black religion. But he also understood the tenacity of segregation and the ultimate necessity of outside, federal intervention. He realized that integration had to force its way into the American conscience, but without allowing fear to prevail in the white community. This line between vision and threat was a precarious one.

King was a new resident of Montgomery in 1955. He had arrived there just one year earlier—with a new Ph.D. and his wife, Coretta—to answer a call from the Dexter Avenue Baptist Church. King had grown up in Atlanta, Georgia. His father was a prominent minister at the Ebenezer Baptist Church. His mother was the daughter of Ebenezer's previous pastor.

An outstanding student academically, King entered public school and then switched to the private laboratory school at Atlanta University. From there, he attended Atlanta's only black high school, Booker T. Washington. He skipped ninth grade and graduated at the age of fifteen. Like his father before him, he went on to Morehouse College. During this period, he began to think seriously about the ministry. He began preaching at the age of seventeen and shortly thereafter became assistant pastor at Ebenezer.

But at this point, King's career diverged from his father's—which had always been limited to the black community and to black educational institutions of Atlanta. Young King wanted a deeper, wider, more committed education. Thus in 1948, he enrolled at Crozer Theological Seminary in Chester, Pennsylvania, a predominantly white school. During his three years there, he also attended philosophy courses at the University of Pennsylvania.

In his studies, King immersed himself in the social philosophy of Marx, Hegel, and other Europeans, and in the writings of the American Protestant theologian Reinhold Niebuhr. He avidly studied the Social Gospel, an earlier theological movement that stressed working for social justice. He read deeply in the writings of Mahatma Gandhi, the pacifist leader of the Indian revolution against British colonial rule. King interwove ideas from these sources into the fabric of his experience. His developing philosophy brought together his understanding of the economic exploitation of his race, his admiration for nonviolent tactics, and the traditions of Southern black religion as he had experienced them. Could he, he wondered, transform the quiet and accommodating religion of Southern blacks into a force for change? And could he do this without inciting a violent backlash?

When King became a graduate student at Boston University, he did not

**MARTIN LUTHER KING, CORETTA SCOTT KING, AND THEIR FIRST CHILD, 1956**

Despite his growing fame, King always depended upon his wide family network for support and aid. Here, he stands with his wife and first child on the steps of the Montgomery Dexter Baptist Church, his first pastoral position; the capitol building of Alabama is in the background. (©Dan Weiner/Magnum)

yet know the answers. And being a young man, he was often concerned with matters other than philosophy or social change. While working for his doctorate in philosophy, he met a young woman, Coretta Scott, who was studying at the New England Conservatory of Music. He decided immediately that this was the woman he wanted to marry. After their first meeting, he said to her abruptly: "You have everything I have ever wanted in a wife."

For Coretta, the decision was difficult. As her affection for King grew, she was torn. Should she give up a promising career in music and marry a Baptist minister? She finally consented, and the couple wed in June 1953. Coretta joined the Baptist church and put aside her career. In 1954, the Kings accepted a call from the Dexter Avenue Baptist Church in Montgomery. Within a year, King, only twenty-six years old, had become the leader of a bus boycott that initiated the modern civil rights movement.

On December 1, 1955, Rosa Parks, a black woman, exhausted from her shopping and her job as a seamstress, entered a crowded bus in front of the Fair department store in Montgomery to pay the driver. She then got off the bus and walked to the "colored" entrance in the rear, where she boarded the bus again. Finding most seats at the rear occupied, she moved forward and sat down in a row immediately behind the section reserved for whites. The bus resumed its route, stopping again at the Empire Theater. Six white passengers entered the front of the bus, paid and moved back. But there were not enough seats in the white section. Seeing this, the driver called on the nearest black passengers to vacate their places. All of them did—except Rosa Parks. Too tired, or perhaps mindful of earlier incidents of rudeness by white drivers, she refused. James F. Blake, the driver, left the bus and returned with

ROSA PARKS

Rosa Parks, the woman who defied the segregation laws of Montgomery and thus began the bus boycott of 1955, was able to take a front seat on a city bus a year later, after the Supreme Court banned segregated public transit in Montgomery. (UPI)

a policeman, who arrested Mrs. Parks for violating Montgomery's segregation laws.

The incident was not entirely unexpected. Others had previously defied the law, and they had been arrested. But Mrs. Parks was different. She was a well-known figure in Montgomery's black community and a member of the city's National Association for the Advancement of Colored People (NAACP). The times were also different. The Supreme Court on May 17, 1954, in *Brown* v. *Board of Education,* had ruled school segregation unconstitutional: separate could never be equal the Court maintained. On May 31, 1955, the Court had ordered lower federal courts and school authorities to integrate schools "with all deliberate speed."

Yet nothing much had changed in Montgomery or the rest of the South. Few black citizens could vote, although the number of black voters was growing slowly. And the indignities of segregation continued to pervade private custom and public commerce. From birth to death, the races were separated. Hospitals, prisons, and graveyards were divided by race. Marriages across racial lines were strictly forbidden. Swimming pools, golf courses, movie theaters, and airport and railroad waiting rooms were segregated. So were drinking fountains and bathrooms. Stores often served blacks from a back or side door.

Mrs. Parks's arrest galvanized the black community. A group of black women, the Women's Political Council, mimeographed and distributed a call to boycott Montgomery buses. E. D. Nixon, a Pullman car porter and leader of the local NAACP, began to telephone ministers, hoping to persuade them to endorse the boycott. One of those that Nixon called was Martin Luther

King, Jr. On the afternoon of December 5, King accepted leadership of a new boycott group, the Montgomery Improvement Association (MIA).

The initial demands of the group were cautious. They did not ask for an end to segregation. They asked only for courtesy from drivers, equal reserved seating (equal numbers of seats for blacks and whites), and black drivers on predominantly black routes. This modest plan would have made segregation work more harmoniously, not ended it. But after a fruitless meeting between the MIA, the City Commission, and the bus company, a lawyer for the company declared: "If we granted the Negroes these demands, they would go about boasting of a victory that they had won over white people, and this we will not stand for." The lines were drawn hard and fast.

By early winter, both sides had stiffened their determination. But developments among the whites became ominous. The White Citizens' Council, a group devoted to preserving segregation, enlisted thousands of new members, including the mayor and the city commissioners. Abusive telephone calls frequently disturbed the King household. On the evening of January 30, 1956, a bomb blast on the front porch of the King residence, split the porch and shattered windows in the house.

Faced with inflexible opposition to bus integration, the MIA decided to challenge segregation laws through the courts. On February 1, with help from the NAACP, Fred Gray, one of two black lawyers in the city, filed his case in federal court. At the same time a group of white businessmen, the Men of Montgomery, began negotiations with the MIA. Sales in downtown stores

**SEGREGATED SOCIETY IN THE SOUTH**

Throughout the South, public facilities were carefully designated "white" or "colored." This custom persisted well into the 1960s. *(Leonard Freed/Magnum)*

had fallen, and the bus company was losing about $3,000 a day. Finally, in mid-February, elected officials and the MIA leadership met—but without results. The city was now willing to back down, but it was too late for halfway concessions. Now Montgomery blacks demanded equality in bus transport. Weeks of struggle had led them to make deeper demands. In a shifting and increasingly explosive situation, King and other MIA leaders pressed for a more extensive program of integration. There was no other way to retain their leadership.

The city responded with tougher tactics. In late February, King and ninety others were indicted for breaking an old antiboycott law. The trial began on March 19 before Judge Eugene Carter. On March 22, King was convicted and fined $500 or thirteen months at hard labor. His lawyers appealed the decision. Meanwhile the boycott continued. In mid-May, a federal district court declared Alabama's bus segregation laws unconstitutional. The city immediately appealed to the Supreme Court.

As the boycotters stood firm, through the spring and summer, they attracted more and more national and international attention. King spoke several times in the North, and funds raised by outside black congregations and white liberals began to flow into the city. Finally, on November 13, word came. The Supreme Court had declared that Alabama's bus segregation laws were unconstitutional. The boycott remained in effect until December, when the decision was implemented.

For King, the lessons of the fight had been painfully learned. He realized the crucial role of religious leadership in the black community. He recognized too, the tenacious hatred of the segregationists. He understood that nonviolence, to be successful, would require outside intervention. King also gained insight into the problems of leading the presently inert but potentially explosive black population—a dangerous and volatile situation, given a constituency that was unpracticed in politics.

King's success in Montgomery elevated him to national leadership, but his movement remained unorganized, dispersed, and still without an articulate philosophy. He was determined to change this. King knew the old answers and their modern equivalents: the accommodationism of Booker T. Washington, the legal integrationism of W. E. B. DuBois and the NAACP, and the black separatism of Marcus Garvey. None of these strategies had deeply touched the masses of Southern black Christians. King's strategy was to organize his constituency around the black churches. He favored a philosophy that could transform the quiet strength of Southern blacks into an aggressive force for change. The ability of black men and women to suffer, to face indignities impassively, was the foundation upon which he erected his program of nonviolence. And his ultimate goal was clear: integration of black Americans as equals into the full benefits of citizenship.

In early 1957, King, the Reverend Ralph Abernathy and other ministers from the South met in New Orleans to organize the Southern Christian Leadership Conference (SCLC). Headquartered in Atlanta, the group selected King as head. One of King's first strategies was to capitalize on his national

POVERTY IN THE MISSISSIPPI DELTA

Poverty was not restricted to blacks in the 1950s and 1960s across the South. Nonetheless some of the poorest Americans were small black farmers in the cotton belt. (©*Danny Lyon/ Magnum*)

visibility to press for federal legislation. After leading a prayer vigil in Washington, he met afterward with Vice President Nixon in June. The result of this and other pressure was the Civil Rights Bill of 1957, a law that established a Civil Rights Commission to monitor voting rights violations.

King's general strategy was to force immediate change. Using nonviolence, he led masses of demonstrators into confrontation with segregationists. These nonviolent tactics had a special meaning in the American context. When Mahatma Gandhi led the nonviolent movement for Indian independence, he represented a majority of his society pitted against a small, vulnerable British colonial government. Once the Indian masses decided to be independent, probably nothing could stop them. But King had to use nonviolence in a society where blacks were only a minority.

Thus nonviolence depended ultimately on some form of national action—inspired either by agreement with the goals of integration or by fear of the social disorder that might be created by confrontation. King hoped it would be the former, for this would make ultimate accommodation between the races easier. It would also channel the raw anger of the black community. But there were great risks. King recognized that nonviolence would breed disenchantment among blacks who demanded speedy change.

This was precisely the complaint of the young integrationists who later challenged King. In February 1960, white and black college students began sit-ins in Durham and Greensboro, North Carolina, demanding service at the segregated lunch counters of Woolworth dime stores. The movement spread to fifty-four other cities in two months. By mid-April, the Student Nonviolent Coordinating Committee (SNCC) had formed. King maintained cordial relations with the young leaders, but he eventually lost influence over the group.

In the next few years, the desegregation movement spread rapidly, and King struggled to maintain his leadership and a national vision of the goals. From 1961 through early 1962, he supported the "freedom rides" organized by another black group, the Congress of Racial Equality. These rides on integrated buses into the South called national attention to the problem of segregation, particularly in bus stations. The first ride left Washington in May 1961; its purpose was to integrate Southern transportation facilities. The trip was uneventful until the bus carrying the freedom riders was bombed and burned by whites near Anniston, Alabama, on May 14. Other groups that ventured out later were attacked in Birmingham and Montgomery. As these attacks grew, so did national concern. By the end of the month, a freedom ride that left for Jackson, Mississippi, was assigned an escort of the National Guard and army helicopters. Responding to an intolerable situation, the Interstate Commerce Commission in December prohibited segregation aboard buses and in terminals.

A freedom ride to Albany, Georgia, in December 1961 to integrate a railway station marked the beginning of a newer, broader tactic employed by King, but one that also exposed the movement to counterattack and possible defeat. Black leaders in the city called in King to help organize a movement that had been stirred up by the freedom ride. The local SCLC leader hoped to focus protest on the entire race and caste system of the city. As in other Southern cities, public segregation was only symbolic of deeper divisions and exploitation in jobs, wages, social benefits, and political rights. On December 16, King and the Albany leadership organized a march to demand change in all of these areas. Over 700 demonstrators were arrested. King refused release on bond and called for more demonstrators to come to the city.

A temporary compromise was reached two days later. King left jail, and the railway station was integrated. Civil rights leaders were optimistic. But the city had not really budged. All of its parks, libraries, movie theaters, and buses remained segregated. So King and his allies decided to launch a selective boycott against white businesses and the bus company. The city struck back and reneged on an informal promise to integrate the buses.

By July 1962, King faced failure and mounting criticism of his leadership, so he turned to new tactics—civil disobedience to force city leaders to grant SCLC demands. Groups of blacks fanned out across the city to integrate parks, lunch counters, bowling alleys, etc. On July 20, however, a newly appointed federal judge granted the city an injunction against all demonstrations. Simultaneously, thousands of Ku Klux Klansmen gathered outside the city. Tension broke into angry rioting after a deputy sheriff had brutally beaten Mrs. Slater King in Camilla, Georgia. Mrs. King (no relation to Martin Luther) was the wife of an Albany civil rights leader. On the evening of July 24, a group gathered in Albany to protest Mrs. King's beating. Police moved in to break up the meeting. When they did, the long-suffering blacks of Albany reacted, just as King feared they might. Before long, thousands of demonstrators were battling police.

This outbreak of violence deeply distressed King. He had lost control of the movement; his nonviolent tactics had not worked. His first reaction was to pull back and avoid further demonstrations. The Kennedy administration in Washington was profoundly disturbed and embarrassed by events in Albany—but not enough to act. Scores of white Northerners who had poured into the city to bolster the movement were preparing to leave as fall approached. And the segregationists were holding firm. In September, with most white integrationists gone, they initiated selective revenge against local black leaders. Several churches were dynamited. Public facilities remained segregated or closed. The Albany movement had failed.

This setback represented a personal defeat for King. It resulted from poor planning, divided leadership, and inconclusive and uncoordinated tactics. Furthermore, he had failed to engage either national sympathy or, more important, federal support, for his cause. He could either retreat or assault an even more dangerous citadel, Birmingham. It was a risk that threatened the whole movement, for by 1963, Birmingham had become a symbolic center of resistance to integration. The new Alabama governor, George Wallace, elected in 1962, had vowed undying opposition to integration. Birmingham's tough police had a leader pledged to enforce laws that rigidly separated both the public and private lives of Birmingham citizens. As King described it:

> Birmingham is probably the most thoroughly segregated city in the United States. Its ugly record of police brutality is known in every section of the country. Its unjust treatment of Negroes in the courts is a notorious reality. There have been more unsolved bombings of Negro homes and churches in Birmingham than any city in this nation. These are the hard, brutal and unbelievable facts.

King decided to risk failure and violence. He and the SCLC worked closely with local leaders headed by the Reverend Fred Shuttlesworth. They decided that their movement should be clearly focused, well planned and financed, and designed to elicit maximum sympathy from Northern liberals and the federal government. If the city used violence against demonstrators, this would only force outside intervention.

King and the SCLC planned Project C (for confrontation) to be launched during Easter week to disrupt the season's sales. This assault on business was designed to force economic leaders in the city to negotiate with integrationists. Several hundred volunteers worked to train black Birmingham in nonviolent tactics. B-day (the first day of protest) had to be postponed until April 3 to avoid disrupting the local mayoral election. B-day began twelve hours after Albert Boutwell's victory at the polls.

At first it appeared that Bull Connor might also play by the rules of nonviolence. During the first few days, demonstrations and sit-ins occurred without serious incident. Then on April 10, a local judge issued an injunction against all further demonstrations. King decided to break the law and suffer the consequences. In itself, this was an important turning point. Jail meant national attention. But more important, King crossed a threshold by defying a court order. Until now, he had respected such orders. His defiance represented a deeper attack on segregation and the structure that supported it.

On April 12, Good Friday, King and several volunteers set out on an illegal protest march. Connor and his police allowed them to proceed several blocks and then moved in for arrests. Connor arrested King and held him in solitary confinement. He was allowed no calls or visitors. In Atlanta, Coretta waited anxiously for word that did not come. Anything was possible in Connor's jail. So she telephoned Wyatt Walker, one of the Birmingham leaders. Together they agreed that she should call the president.

Coretta's call to Kennedy forced the president's hand. While Kennedy had expressed sympathy for integration, he had done little to push it publicly. But pressure in the North was building for action. Press commentary around the world sharply criticized government inaction in the face of brutality. Coretta tried several times to reach the president at the White House, without success. Then she tried Vice President Johnson, but he too was absent. Finally, a sympathetic operator, sensing her desperation, suggested that she telephone the president's aide Pierre Salinger. He promised to notify Kennedy immediately. A short time later, Attorney General Robert Kennedy telephoned Coretta to promise his help. But he warned: "Of course Birmingham is a very difficult place." Within fifteen minutes the phone rang again. It was King. He was safe.

King's eight days in Birmingham jail were critical ones for him and for the fate of the integration movement. At first he pondered the hope and despair of his situation. As he wrote: "You will never know the meaning of utter darkness until you have lain in such a dungeon, knowing that sunlight is streaming overhead and still seeing only darkness below."

What bothered King more, however, was the fate of the movement he headed. Had he led it into violence and disarray? Were his tactics of challenge, which brought out the bitterest attacks from segregationists, inevitably doomed? Did the violence of Birmingham indicate that the doors to integration might forever remain shut? Was he going too far; was he in danger of losing the vision of racial justice that appealed to whites?

This last question was posed to him by eight Alabama clergymen on April 12. In their "Public Statement Directed to Martin Luther King, Jr.," they wrote: "We are now confronted by a series of demonstrations by some of our Negro citizens, directed and led in part by outsiders. We recognize the natural impatience of people who feel that their hopes are slow in being realized. But we are convinced that these demonstrations are unwise and untimely."

King received the statement while in solitary confinement and almost immediately began his response. At first, he penciled his thoughts on the unprinted edges of a newspaper. When this proved inadequate, he continued his reply on sheets of paper brought in by a friendly black guard. Finally, he secured a pad of legal paper from his attorney. When finished, he dated and titled it: April 16, 1963, "A Letter from Birmingham Jail."

King answered the three charges of the clergymen: that he and his organization were outsiders, that he should be patient, and that his tactics endangered the whole community. His reply was careful but passionate. King realized from the tone of their letter, that the eight clergymen defined him and all blacks as being outside the community of equal citizens. Thus in his response, he tried to find the language and symbols that would find a place for Southern blacks in the community in which they had always lived but to which they had never belonged.

He bristled at the suggestion that he was an outsider. "We are," he said, "caught in an inescapable network of mutuality, tied to a single garment of destiny. Whatever affects one directly affects all indirectly. Never again can we afford to live with the narrow, provincial 'outside agitator' idea. Anyone who lives inside the United States can never be considered an outsider anywhere in this country."

As for the question of patience, King rejected the ministers' advice. "For years now," he recalled, "I have heard the word 'Wait!' It rings in the ear of every Negro with a piercing familiarity. This 'Wait' has almost always meant 'Never.'" How long, he retorted, while African nations had emerged into political sovereignty could American blacks remain "smothering in an airtight cage of poverty in the midst of an affluent society."

King did acknowledge the risks of violence. But he argued that only "creative tension" could push the white majority into negotiation. Breaking the law—the unjust and illegal law of segregation—he continued, was a duty. "In no sense do I advocate evading or defying the law as the rabid segregationist would do. This would lead to anarchy. One who breaks an unjust law must do it openly, *lovingly.*"

If, as King believed, Birmingham represented the risk of failure and violent resistance from a closed community of bigotry, the march on Washington represented a chance to express, before a national audience, the vision of a new American community that King had sketchily defined in his Birmingham letter. The march on Washington in August of 1963, and King's dramatic speech there, represented a high point in the impulse to open America to all its citizens. He succeeded in making integration and equality for blacks the very center of a new sort of patriotism.

King had always recognized the limitations of a Southern movement and an all-black movement. He had long sought allies in the white community—among ministers, political liberals, and labor unions. His strategy was to force Americans to recognize Southern segregation as a national problem. The federal government tolerated the special status of Southern laws. The Democratic party allowed segregationists a veto over presidential nominees as well as over civil rights laws. To break the tentacles of power that radiated out from the South, King had forced federal intervention in Montgomery and then in the bloody situation in Birmingham. But the problem also required a national vision. Change would not come without firm civil rights laws and some national manifestation of solidarity. These were the goals of the march planned for the nation's capital.

At the center of national and international attention (indeed, criticized for this by younger black leaders, who referred to him as "De Lawd"), King tried to turn the "creative tension'" of Birmingham and its accompanying publicity into a broad, national movement. President Kennedy had finally been forced to move—and not just to preserve peace in the South or to deal with a specific injustice. In early June, the president spoke warmly of civil rights. New civil rights legislation in Congress was stalled by Southern opposition. Birmingham and the rest of the South seemed to be a powder keg, ready to explode. Arrests of civil rights demonstrators were shooting upward—they totaled almost 14,000 during the year. In his speech, Kennedy reiterated the proposition that King had enunciated so forcefully in his Birmingham letter:

> We are confronted primarily with a moral issue. It is as old as the Scriptures and is as clear as the American Constitution. The heart of the question is whether all Americans are to be afforded equal rights and equal opportunities; whether we are going to treat our fellow Americans as we want to be treated.

Only passage of civil rights legislation, Kennedy concluded, could solve the crisis.

This was the commitment that King had long sought. But was it enough? Could the movement relent and wait outside the legislative halls for progress? King believed it could not, and together with other leaders—the aging A. Philip Randolph, of the Brotherhood of Sleeping Car Porters and representatives from most of the other civil rights organizations—he planned the march on Washington for late August. As first conceived, demonstrators were to engage in civil disobedience and sit-ins on Capitol Hill. But planners rejected this idea. The march would be a simple demonstration of solidarity for "jobs and freedom" to stir the nation's conscience.

From the beginning, the march was controversial. The president refused to endorse it, although he agreed to meet with civil rights leaders afterward. His wariness only underscored the risks. If there was violence or, worse, if only a small crowd assembled, the damage might be irreparable. But other political leaders were not as hesitant as Kennedy. Mayor Wagner of New York City spoke in favor of the march and proclaimed August 28 "Jobs and Freedom Day." Support from some labor unions was strong: the United Auto Workers (a major contributor to the civil rights movement) and the International Ladies Garment Workers Union (ILGWU) sent representatives. Church leaders and rabbis endorsed the march. The National Council of Churches even prepared box lunches for sale at low prices during the march.

Other leaders and groups were reluctant or even hostile. Former President Truman deplored the demonstration, although he approved its goals. Governor Wallace tried to convince the Southern Governors Conference to de-

**AFTER THE MARCH ON WASHINGTON**

King hoped to secure the cooperation and support of white leaders. Here, following his dramatic speech at the March on Washington, he, Rabbi Joachim Prinz of the American Jewish Congress, veteran civil rights leader A. Philip Randolph, President John Kennedy, and labor leader Walter Reuther (left to right) discussed the need for civil rights action. *(UPI)*

nounce the march. A number of newspapers across the country warned of a possible backlash. They proposed that black Americans seek redress in the Congress and in the courts, not in the streets. At the fringe, Robert Welch of the right-wing John Birch Society accused King of aiming to create a "Soviet Negro Republic," headquartered in Atlanta, with himself as president.

In the face of uncertainties and attacks, planning continued. But at first, response was weak. Silence from the urban black ghettos and the rural South numbed the organizers. Then suddenly, in August, the headquarters of the march was swamped with requests for information and help. Special trains and buses had to be hired. Car caravans were organized. Some set out early on foot. In Washington, predictions of attendance went up and up. More marshals had to be recruited to control the crowd. The demonstration would be enormous.

August 28 was bright and hot; the sort of Washington summer day when humidity and bright light make the stark white government buildings and monuments shimmer in the glare. Marchers began pouring into the city, into Union Station near the Capitol, and into the Fourteenth Street bus terminal. Cars and chartered buses jammed the side streets around Capitol Hill. Diesel fumes and dust stirred up by hundreds of demonstrators hung over the gathering crowd as it moved toward the staging area at the Washington Monument for the march to the Lincoln Memorial.

By one o'clock a crowd of over 200,000 had assembled around the reflecting pool and the grassy approaches to the memorial. Most carried banners proclaiming "Freedom Now" or placards identifying the marcher with his or her hometown, church group, or labor union. The crowd had a look rarely seen at political gatherings in Washington: a sea of black faces set off by white shirts or made somber by the well-worn blue gabardine of Sunday-best suits. Sharecroppers, students, women with broad sun hats, moved in an undulating mass. Fewer in number, but readily visible, were white faces—evidence of the racial solidarity that King had worked for.

The ceremonies began slowly. First, "The Star-Spangled Banner." Then a speech from Fred Shuttlesworth of Birmingham. Then words from Ralph Abernathy and greetings from 1,500 Americans abroad. Then a speech by A. Philip Randolph—a voice of continuity with old struggles and old battles. "We are," he proclaimed, "the advance guard of a massive moral revolution for jobs and freedom. This revolution reverberates throughout the land, touching every city, every town, every village where black men are segregated, oppressed, and exploited."

In the hot sun, the demonstrators shifted from foot to foot and swayed to catch the words carried out to them by loudspeakers. They had come to move and be moved, but so far the words had not done that. John Lewis, the new chairman of the Student Nonviolent Coordinating Committee, spoke angrily about the failure of government, the failure to achieve change. His remarks had been muffled by censorship; Patrick A. O'Boyle, the Catholic archbishop of Washington, had refused to appear at the march if Lewis directly attacked the Kennedy administration. But Lewis made his intent clear. Concerning the pending civil rights bill, he declared, "We support the bill with great reservations, for it is too little and too late." When he had finished, every black speaker shook his hand. Every white speaker on the platform ignored him.

As the speeches continued, some of the demonstrators began to drift back to their cars and buses. The march had been impressive, but they were tired or anxious to return home. Then the gospel singer Mahalia Jackson stood before the microphones. She began to sing an old hymn: "I Been 'Buked and I Been Scorned." As the words rolled out over the crowd, her familiar deep and resonant voice caught and stopped many of those who were departing:

> I'm gonna tell my Lord
> When I get home
> I'm gonna tell my Lord
> When I get home
> Just how *long* you've
> Been treating me wrong

When the echo of the song had died out, the crowd answered back, shouting, waving, screaming, moving tighter together around the memorial.

Then, finally, King rose to speak. When he mounted the rostrum, a burst of applause greeted him. He waited calmly for it to subside, showing no signs of fatigue and the late night he had spent finishing his speech.

He began by invoking the memory and language of Lincoln—and of the emancipation that had been frustrated by a century of racism and segregation:

**THE MARCH ON WASHINGTON**
King addressed a huge crowd of civil rights supporters on August 28, 1963. Standing on
the steps of the Lincoln Memorial, he faced the Washington Monument, symbol of the
foundation of the republic, and the crowd roared approval as he proclaimed, "I have a
dream." *(©Bob Henriques/Magnum)*

"Five score years ago a great American in whose symbolic shadow we stand
today signed the Emancipation Proclamation." He continued:

> When the architects of our Republic wrote the magnificent words of the Consti-
> tution and the Declaration of Independence, they were signing a promissory note
> to which every American was to fall heir. This note was a promise that all men—
> yes, black men as well as white men—would be guaranteed the inalienable rights
> of life, liberty, and the pursuit of happiness.

King directed these words at every American, but particularly at white Americans. He mentioned the three most famous documents of American history:
the Gettysburg Address, the Declaration of Independence, and the Constitution—all of which defined freedom. And yet none of them had extended
freedom to all Americans. King was demanding the payment of an old debt.

He then spoke of the question of caution. Was it time to be tranquil, to
quiet the voice of protest? King firmly rejected this possibility. He called for
new alliances, reaching out to those white Americans who would help. But
he also warned that blacks would never be satisfied while "our children are
stripped of their adulthood and robbed of their dignity by signs stating 'For
Whites Only.' " As a leader, he would not rest until "justice rolls down like

waters and righteousness like a mighty stream." And then he urged, "Go back to Mississippi, go back to Alabama, go back to South Carolina, go back to Georgia, go back to Louisiana, go back to the slums and ghettos of our Northern cities, knowing that somehow this situation can and will be changed."

From the beginning, the crowd had listened, straining to catch each word as it swept through the loudspeaker system. Most were now standing. A few murmured their approval. He had them with him as he returned to his opening words: "I still have a dream. It is a dream deeply rooted in the American dream. I have a dream that one day this nation will rise up, live out the true meaning of its creed: 'We hold these truths to be self-evident, that all men are created equal.' "

King could have stopped then. The speech had been a great one, evoking a vision of hope and the fulfillment of American ideals. The crowd was ready to burst into applause and movement. But he struck deeper. He also had a personal dream to confess: that his own "four little children will one day live in a nation where they will not be judged by the color of their skin but by the content of their character." "I have a dream," he repeated, that "right there in Alabama little black boys and black girls will be able to join hands with little white boys and white girls as sisters and brothers." The crowd roared its approval.

"I have a dream today," he continued, moving out and away from any specific reference to the civil rights movement or the march or his own family. "I have a dream," he continued, quoting the words of biblical prophecy from Isaiah 40:4:

> I have a dream that one day every valley shall be exalted, every hill and mountain shall be made low. The rough places will be made plain, and the crooked places will be made straight. And the glory of the Lord shall be revealed, and all flesh shall see it together.

Every time he repeated the words "I have a dream," the crowd roared in response, moving with him as he revealed his vision. "I have a dream," he shouted again, this time quoting the words of the patriotic hymn "My Country 'Tis of Thee," that someday "all of God's children will be able to sing with new meaning, 'My country, 'tis of thee, sweet land of liberty, of thee I sing.' "

As he finished, King wove these words into a final vision of America— an integrated America, in which the black experience would be the essence and meaning of the national experience:

> When we allow freedom to ring—when we let it ring from every city and every hamlet, from every state and every city, we will be able to speed up that day when all of God's children, black men and white men, Jews and Gentiles, Protestants and Catholics, will be able to join hands and sing in the words of the old Negro spiritual, "Free at last, Free at last, Great God a-mighty. We are free at last."

# An Era of Promise

The civil rights movement that Martin Luther King, Jr., led in triumph to Washington in the summer of 1963 was, in some regards, the culmination of a very old process in American history. Previous groups, such as labor unions and ethnic groups, had demanded and achieved legitimacy in American society. Now after decades of struggle, it was the turn of black Americans to win the rights that others had been granted. Although this struggle was harder and more bitter than any that preceded it, it nevertheless succeeded.

King's triumph was possible because of a political consensus that gradually developed during and after World War II. This agreement was based on three fundamental assumptions about the nature of American society: (1) that an expanding economy would make it possible for all groups to share in the material bounty of the nation; (2) that a fundamental political program could be defined that would satisfy the diverse interests in American society; and (3) that government should be the instrument to achieve these goals of bounty and social harmony.

The origins of this postwar liberal vision lay in the New Deal. In the 1930s, Franklin D. Roosevelt used the federal government to protect millions of forgotten men and women from the hardships of depression. He built a remarkable political consensus to support his programs, a consensus that included farmers, Catholics, urban workers, the solid South, and Northern ethnic groups. Wide as this group was, however, it did not fully embrace American blacks.

In 1944, when Franklin Roosevelt delivered his state of the Union message—what he called his economic bill of rights—there was no evidence that he had black Americans in mind. He spoke of rights for all Americans, regardless of race or creed. But these were words with little force or meaning for black Americans. Indeed what happened between Roosevelt's enunciation of a new program of rights and the beginnings of the civil rights movement in the mid-1950s was that traditional phrases about liberty and equality acquired a new content. They became real for groups formerly left out of the American dream. This was the point of Martin Luther King's speech; he created a new language of equality that really did include all citizens.

But in 1944 this was not Roosevelt's purpose. He was repeating ideas he had voiced in the 1930s, when he had tried to lift the spirits of the unemployed. Now he used the same language to suggest goals for the postwar society. All Americans, "regardless of station, race, or creed," he said, had rights that should be defended by the federal government. These included the right to food, clothing, education, and a useful job. They included the right of every family to a decent home, medical care, and support in times of misfortune or old age.

Had Congress enacted these rights with serious attention to racial, class, and ethnic equality, it would have initiated perhaps the greatest social revolution in American history. But legislators scarcely paid attention to Roosevelt's stirring suggestions. The Democratic majority in both houses had long since ceased to be a liberal majority. A coalition of Republicans and solid-South Democrats could veto any wide-ranging social legislation.

Yet Roosevelt's vision in his economic bill of rights was important. It promised an extension of the basic social programs of the 1930s. With its twin emphases on equality and inalienable social rights, it set an agenda that others—such as Martin Luther King, Jr., then only fifteen years old—would be able to seize upon and transform in the postwar period.

## BACK TO PEACETIME

Roosevelt's immediate plans for postwar society concentrated on rapid conversion to peacetime production. Controls enacted by Congress generally had a time limitation triggered by the end of the war. In late 1944 and early 1945, the economy was set to return to civilian production. There was little momentum to continue New Deal reforms or extend social planning. Yet one piece of legislation, passed to reward soldiers for their combat service and to prevent their reentering the labor force too quickly, profoundly affected the social status of millions of Americans. This was the so-called GI Bill.

This program, enacted as the Servicemen's Readjustment Act of 1944, provided federal subsidies for college attendance and home buying. It provided for the federal government to pay tuition charges as well as a small living allowance to any serviceman with two or more years of duty. And it provided low-interest mortgages for the purchase of homes and businesses. Veterans were also granted preference in federal and state employment. Together, the various federal and state programs to aid veterans amounted to a massive affirmative action program that allowed millions of young men—men who might not otherwise have had the chance—to enter college, purchase a home, or find a job in the public sector.

The GI Bill put millions of returning soldiers to school who otherwise might have joined the ranks of the unemployed. This, plus pent-up consumer demand for products that were scarce during the war, kept the economy booming. The favorable position of the United States in world trade also proved significant. Raw materials and energy supplies were cheap and easily available. Progress in aviation, television, and information systems, plus new inventions and materials, created whole new industries. These factors, along with constant federal intervention in the economy mandated by the Employment Act of 1946, guaranteed important gains in worker productivity, personal income, and gross national product.

# THE TRUMAN YEARS

What Roosevelt would have done to spread this bounty to the groups that did not yet share it will never be known, for he did not live to see the end of the war.

When the president announced that he would seek reelection in 1944, for a fourth term, most voters fully expected him to serve four more years. Nonetheless, when he and the party leaders chose his running mate in 1944 they were, in effect, selecting the next president. Their choice, Harry S Truman, senator from Missouri, proved a controversial one. Truman's qualifications for the vice presidency rested principally on his political support. Labor, represented by the CIO's Sidney Hillman, agreed that he was acceptable. As a border-state senator, he could count on support from Southern Democrats. He also had a good reputation for his clear-headed and tough investigation of war industries. Most significantly, his leading competitors, including the current vice president, Henry Wallace, all had serious liabilities.

## Truman's First Administration

Like any vice president who graduates to the presidency in a crisis, Truman's first problem in the spring of 1945 was to establish command of the office. Although he pledged to pursue Roosevelt's policies, he did not. Nor could he. He lacked Roosevelt's consummate political skill. Moreover, Roosevelt had not really defined a postwar policy except in the vaguest way. So Truman was on his own.

Much of what Truman did during the eight years of his presidency was dictated by his attempts to find and secure a political constituency. He had to hold onto the coalition that Roosevelt had assembled during the 1930s and perhaps try to extend it, particularly to blacks who had migrated to Northern cities during the war in large numbers. Inevitably, he had to compromise among the conflicting interests of this coalition.

Like Roosevelt, Truman planned a rapid reconversion to peacetime production. In the last months of the war, he canceled hundreds of defense contracts. Only two days after V-J (Victory over Japan) Day, he modified controls over prices, wages, and raw materials. In November 1945, he terminated control of wage hikes exer-

**HARRY S TRUMAN**

The new president received documents confirming the Japanese surrender on August 14, 1945, shortly after the second atomic bomb fell on Nagasaki. Without a great deal of experience in foreign relations, Truman had the enormously difficult task of constructing postwar American policy. *(UPI)*

cised by the National War Labor Board. By the summer of 1946, he had reluctantly eliminated many controls over consumer prices. When the Republicans gained control of Congress in the elections of 1946, he eliminated the remaining price controls.

Deregulation of labor controls caused economic stress and brought serious political headaches to the new administration, which counted on unions for support. During the war, organized labor had rapidly increased its membership—from 10 million in 1941 to 14 million in 1945. Wage increases were modest during the war but overtime and fringe benefits pushed up earnings. After the war, labor sought large increases, and management was just as determined to prevent them. The result was an outbreak of strikes as substantial as any in the twentieth century. Walkouts at General Motors and in the oil and steel

industries involved hundreds of thousands of workers. In April 1946, the United Mine Workers went out. Finally, when railroad workers threatened a strike in May, Truman seized the railroads.

This rash of strikes fueled public hostility to unions and energized the successful Republican congressional campaign of 1946. When it met in 1947, the new Republican-controlled Congress pledged to curb New Deal labor legislation. During the first four months of the session, members submitted seventy bills on this single issue. Finally, the Labor Committee chairmen in each house hammered out a compromise law. On the Senate side, conservative Senator Robert A. Taft of Ohio provided leadership. In the House of Representatives, this was done by Fred A. Hartley, Jr., of New Jersey. The resulting Taft-Hartley Bill outlawed the closed shop, in which every worker was required to join a union as a condition of employment. It required unions to file annual financial reports with the Labor Department. Right-to-work laws passed by states were legalized, and the president was granted power to interrupt strikes with an eighty-day "cooling-off" period.

Passed by Congress on June 9, 1947, the bill went to Truman for his signature. Fully aware of the political consequences, he returned the bill with a sharply worded veto message. He denounced the legislation as contrary to the "national policy of economic freedom." It was, he continued, "a clear threat to the successful working of our democratic society." Congress thought so little of his arguments that it overrode his veto the following day. The bill became law.

In practice, the Taft-Hartley Act was not what either side claimed. It neither seriously limited the activities of organized labor nor destroyed democracy. In some ways, it represented the basis for a more permanent peace between management and labor; for while it trimmed the power of unions, it certainly did not seriously limit them. However, the controversy surrounding the act helped to overcome suspicions of Truman in the union movement.

Truman's vigorous defense of labor in his

veto was one key to his successful 1948 reelection campaign. Another was his overture to black voters. Trying to hold on to and expand Roosevelt's electoral coalition, Truman realized that he needed the support of blacks. The steps he took to win their votes were small but significant.

Following the Republican victory in 1946, Truman issued an executive order creating a special Civil Rights Committee headed by Charles E. Wilson, president of the General Electric Company. Other members included representatives from labor organizations and the NAACP. The group was charged with writing proposals to improve the lives of American blacks. Several months later, on October 29, 1947, it submitted its suggestions. These included home rule for the largely black city of Washington, D.C., an end to racial segregation in the U.S. armed forces, protection of voting rights in state primary elections, an end to restrictive covenants in housing sales, a permanent commission on civil rights, and equal treatment in and access to facilities in interstate commerce.

Truman was certainly not prepared to push ahead on each one of these demands. Indeed, it took twenty years, the rise of new leaders like Martin Luther King, Jr., and a social convulsion of extraordinary proportions to realize most of them. But the president did include some of this agenda in his 1948 civil rights message to Congress. And by July 1948, he had started desegregation of the armed services, gradually phasing out all-black combat units. (It was not until October 1954 that the last segregated army unit was abolished.)

## The Election of 1948

Truman's initiative in civil rights earned him support from black leaders and from Democratic liberals, but it splintered his allegiances in the South. Bedrock Southern conservatives revolted against his nomination in 1948. When Northern liberals placed a strong civil rights plank in the party platform, a group of "Dixiecrats" bolted

the party, met in Birmingham, Alabama, to found the States' Rights party, and nominated Governor Strom Thurmond of South Carolina for president.

The Republicans helped Truman hold onto what remained of his coalition by presenting a distinctly conservative alternative. Their nominee in 1948, Governor Thomas Dewey of New York, had earned national praise for his attacks on organized crime. As a campaigner, however, he left much to be desired. Known as a staunch conservative and a foe of the New Deal, Dewey lacked the visible energy, humor, and humanity of Truman. The president's campaign was also aided by a splinter party to the left of the Democratic party. A new Progressive party nominated Henry Wallace, one-time vice president and then Truman's secretary of commerce. Running on a program criticizing Truman's cold war foreign policy and with Communist party support, Wallace actually deflected criticism away from the president. Truman could accurately claim that he represented the political center of the Democratic party—and perhaps the nation.

Truman relished nothing so much as a good fight. Once Congress had adjourned from a special session called during the summer, Truman began an energetic campaign trip by train across the nation. Punching away at the self-confident Republicans, he stressed the continuity between his presidency and the New Deal. The results of the November election proved how successful this strategy had been. He won 24 million to Dewey's 21 million votes. He had held the New Deal coalition together despite some defections in the South. He had also helped lay the political groundwork for federal support for civil rights.

## Truman's Second Administration

Truman began his second term in office with the promise of swift and extensive social reform. His rousing address in Congress on January 15, 1949, called for a "Fair Deal." His words and his program echoed many of Roosevelt's 1944 ideas. He began by defining the purpose of government—to use the nation's wealth "for the benefit of all." This definition implied intervention in the economy to maintain healthy production, and regulation to ensure a fair distribution of goods and services. Specifically, Truman wanted a rise in taxes, repeal of the Taft-Hartley Act, a higher minimum wage, farm price supports, a rise in social security benefits and expansion of the system, a national prepaid medical insurance system, and government construction of more low-cost public housing units.

But the president failed to translate his surprise victory in November into legislative success. Despite a Democratic majority returned to the Senate and the House, the party remained divided over reforms. Medical insurance and Truman's agricultural program fell to intensive lobbying by doctors and farm groups. Repeal of the Taft-Hartley Act could not attain a majority, and the claims of racial minorities were ignored despite the promises of the civil rights plank of the Democratic platform. Thus although civil rights had entered the legislative agenda, it had not yet become a compelling part of it. Only in the extension of social security coverage and in housing did the president achieve major successes. The 1950 amendments to the Social Security Act of 1935 extended coverage and raised benefits. The Housing Act of 1949 mandated construction of 810,000 low-cost units.

Spy convictions and Senator McCarthy's anticommunist crusade also helped weaken Truman in the last two years of his administration. Nothing went well for the president. The war in Korea touched off a constitutional crisis when the commander of the U.S. forces, General MacArthur, openly criticized Truman's policy of limited warfare in 1951. As commander in chief of the armed forces, Truman had no choice but to remove the popular general if he wished to maintain civilian control of the military. In Congress, his Fair Deal failed to generate support. Scandals and accusations of communist influence surrounded the Democratic party. Clearly, Truman had become a serious liability.

# THE EISENHOWER YEARS

## The Shift to the Suburbs

The disintegration of Truman's support came partly from opposition to his leadership and partly from shifts in social structure and demography that began after the war. New Deal rhetoric lost some of its power to galvanize voters, as memories of the depression faded and the new affluence of the 1950s appeared. Much of this affluence became visible in the new suburbs that sprang up around cities. Of course, American cities had long had suburbs, but traditionally these were built out along commuter rail lines. In the 1940s and 1950s, suburbs were connected to central cities by means of new highways. As they proliferated, they tended to depend less on the central city and more on their own booming economies. In effect, suburbs had begun to com-

*THE LIFE OF RILEY*

One of television's early situation comedies was *The Life of Riley,* starring William Bendix and Marjorie Reynolds. The series ran in 1949–1950 and again in 1953–1958. It was one of the few radio programs that made a successful transition to the new medium. *(Springer/Bettmann Archive)*

## MASS-PRODUCED SUBURBIA

These mass-produced homes (available in twenty-seven slightly different designs) were constructed in Lafayette, Indiana, in 1951. Typical of suburban development, they cost about $6,000 each, well within the range of millions of Americans who could enter the housing market for the first time after World War II, thanks to loans to veterans under the GI Bill. *(UPI)*

pete seriously with central cities for industry, jobs, population, and political power.

The suburbs won a quick victory. After the war, most cities lost jobs in manufacturing and trade while gaining modestly in service industries. Employment in all three of these categories soared in the suburbs. By 1960, the central cities had lost almost 300,000 jobs. They were also left with diminished tax bases. Responding to this shrinking opportunity, increasing numbers of affluent or aspiring whites abandoned the central cities. Their places were taken by blacks and Hispanics. In 1950, the black population of central cities was about 12 percent of the total. Twenty years later, the percentage had doubled. (But the proportion of blacks in the suburbs remained about the same.) Political power followed affluence to the suburbs.

If the predominant image of the early 1950s was suburban life, the focus of that image was the family. Newspapers, magazines, radio, movies, and the new medium of television extolled the virtues of family life. Behind this publicity

lay a surprising change in American demographics. After World War II, divorce rates fell sharply and the marriage rate (the percentage of eligible persons who in fact marry) rapidly increased. So too did the birth rate, which shot up from 20.4 births per 1,000 population in 1945 to 25.0 per 1,000 in 1955. This increase reversed decades of decline in the number of children born to American families.

Added to the family-centered and child-centered focus in popular culture and social mores, was an emphasis on leisure living and informality inspired by California. In the postwar world, California's population increased from 5 to 10 percent of the U.S. total. For those who did not live there, the state remained the most popular place to visit. Of all the states in the Union, California exhibited an accelerated and exaggerated version of contemporay social trends. It was the most urbanized (and suburbanized) state. It had the most extensive freeway system. It had a huge modern aircraft and defense industry. Its life styles were the subject of countless Hollywood

## THE BABY BOOM: TOTAL BIRTHS AND RATE PER 1,000 POPULATION

|      | Number of Births | Births per 1,000 Population |
|------|------------------|------------------------------|
| 1935 | 2,377,000        | 18.7                         |
| 1940 | 2,559,000        | 19.4                         |
| 1945 | 2,858,000        | 20.4                         |
| 1950 | 3,632,000        | 24.1                         |
| 1955 | 4,097,000        | 25.0                         |
| 1960 | 4,258,000        | 23.7                         |
| 1965 | 3,760,000        | 19.4                         |
| 1970 | 3,731,000        | 18.4                         |
| 1975 | 3,144,000        | 14.8                         |
| 1980 | 3,598,000        | 16.2                         |

Source: U.S. Department of Commerce, Bureau of the Census, *Statistical Abstract of the United States, 1981* (Washington, D.C.: Government Printing Office, 1981), p. 58.

films and television shows—as well as the backdrop for most advertising commercials. In a sense, California was America's future and a symbol of the new postwar economy and culture.

## The Election of 1952

Some of these changes began to register first in the 1952 election. The Republicans' vice-presidential candidate, Richard M. Nixon, was a congressman from southern California. The mood of the electorate tended toward conservativism, reflecting in part the new priorities of suburban life. More important, the Democratic coalition reestablished by Truman in 1948 began to show some signs of age and strain, as the weight of political power shifted away from the central cities to the suburbs, and from the old industrial East to the new industrial West.

Both sides bitterly contested the 1952 election and, consequently, issues were sometimes lost in the flurry of flimsy and preposterous charges and countercharges. Republican chances appeared very good—but so had they in 1948. However this time, the party's choice of a candidate—General Dwight David Eisenhower—proved to be enormously popular.

Born in 1890, "Ike" grew up in Abilene, Kansas. From the time he entered the U.S. Military Academy in 1911, Eisenhower's life was defined by the army. Mischievous, handsome, and athletic as a student, he rose, rank by rank, to become commander of the allied armies in Europe during World War II.

Eisenhower's lack of civilian experience cost him very little. His position in the army required the exercise of every skill needed by a politician. Furthermore, he owed no political debts. In fact, he had been approached earlier by the Democrats seeking him as a candidate. Thus when he declared his willingness to run as a Republican in 1952, he quickly became the front-running candidate. To heal any breaches in the party, Eisenhower offered the vice presidency to Richard Nixon, a man known for his hard-line anticommunist views and popular with conservatives. The party adopted a relatively moderate platform, but the rhetoric of the campaign charged treason in high places and promised to crusade against communism, corruption, and the war in Korea.

For the Democrats, the choice was not easy. Truman realized his unpopularity but still wanted to play kingmaker. Adlai Stevenson, governor of Illinois, secured Truman's favor and the nomination, but he had an almost impossible task. He had to endorse the previous twenty years of Democratic rule yet declare his independence from Truman. He also had to hold onto the Democratic coalition that was increasingly divided on such questions as civil rights. Unfortunately for him, Stevenson's personality became an issue. Witty and elegant in his speeches, he earned loyal support from liberals. But to conservatives he appeared to be the incarnation of the suspect Eastern intellectual lambasted by McCarthy.

Despite a momentary shock when it appeared that Richard Nixon might have to withdraw because of charges that he had operated an illegal slush fund of campaign donations, the Republicans stayed on course. Nixon convinced most critics that the charges were groundless. After his famous explanatory "Checkers Speech" (named

# AMERICAN IMAGES
## Women:
## The War and After

PLATE 1. Margaret Bourke-White was one of the foremost photographers of the 1930s and 1940s and a pioneer in the field of photojournalism. (An example of her work appears in "American Images: People and Machines," Plate 3.) During World War II, as a correspondent for *Life* magazine, she helped to keep the American public informed about the course of events in Europe and North Africa, often at great personal risk; she was, for example, the first woman to accompany an Air Force crew on a bombing mission. Many other American women went to work during the war (see p. 815), performing functions that were perhaps less dramatic but equally significant. *(Margaret Bourke-White, LIFE Magazine, © 1972 Time Inc.)*

In 1945, *House Beautiful* magazine addressed its female readers in an article on returning soldiers entitled "Home Should Be Even More Wonderful Than He Remembers It." As the author put it: "He's head man again. . . . Your part in the remaking of this man is to fit his home to him, understanding why he wants it this way, forgetting your own preferences."

As this article suggests, the postwar years left women with an ambiguous experience that touched their identity and particularly their social image. During the war, they had been welcomed and even encouraged to enter the labor force in order to take the place of men drafted into the armed forces. Now, though, they were encouraged and sometimes forced to leave. Many of them, however, did not leave—they could not afford to stop working. But most of these women took up jobs that were traditionally labeled "women's work," such as waitressing and nursing. For married women who remained in the work force, this usually involved a double burden: a job from 9 to 5 and housework and cooking afterward. Statistics demonstrate that the percentage of working women shrank after 1945, but did not fall as low as prewar levels. In fact, after the initial drop, the number and percentage of working women resumed a steady increase.

These abrupt changes in women's activities gave rise to contradictory and conflicting pictures of the proper role of women in American society. During the war, the popular press, newspapers, and govern-

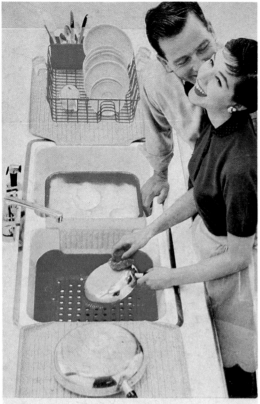

# carefree

PLATE 2. This 1957 advertisement illustrates some of the pressures that were placed on American women in the postwar years and through the 1950s. Not only was the perfect wife supposed to do the housework, she was expected to *enjoy* it—and look her best while washing the dishes. *(New York Public Library/Picture Collection)*

ment publications stressed the contributions of women to the war effort. Of course, there were exceptions. In 1943, particularly, government and the press alike lamented the fate of "door-key" children. These were the unsupervised children of working mothers who returned from school to an empty house and "unfilled hours of loneliness." Generally, however, when women enlisted to work for the duration of the war, their reception was positive. Indeed, during the war, both major political parties endorsed the Equal Rights Amendment, which would have improved wages and job opportunities for women; Secretary of Labor Frances Perkins and the president's wife, Eleanor Roosevelt, declined to support it, however.

After the war, government, business, and labor unions pressured women to return home. Women's magazines were filled almost entirely with articles urging meticulous housekeeping, giving suggestions for improving domestic skills, or pressing readers with new beauty and fashion tips. Eventually this pressure—and the desire of many women to live up to ideals of femininity derived from novels and movies—affected a wide range of behavior. It also led to a "family first" ideology that dominated American culture during the 1950s and gave that period a tone of orthodoxy and conservatism. Whatever else they did, women, according to the new domestic philosophy, should put family above all else. As girls their goal was marriage, and as women their duties revolved around caring for children and maintaining a home.

Statistics suggest that the revived ideology of domesticity was linked to changes in family-related behavior. From 1945 to the end of the 1950s, family stability increased. After a momentary postwar rise, the divorce rate in the United States fell until about 1960; thereafter it increased sharply and then zoomed upward in the 1970s. After the war, the marriage rate also increased. And not only were more persons of eligible age actually married, but the average age for marriage had also dropped. For women, this meant that about half married before

PLATE 3. One important task for women in the 1950s and early 1960s was to raise their daughters to be future housewives. This involved passing on skills in homemaking and careful shopping. *(Ironing— © Lew Merrim/Monkmeyer Press Photo; supermarket— © Sybil Shelton/Monkmeyer Press Photo)*

PLATE 4. Actress Marilyn Monroe was the epitome of one image of women in the 1950s: beautiful, sexy, fragile, and unapproachable—a goddess with a little girl's heart. *(UPI)*

PLATE 5. In the early 1960s—and, in fact, much of the twentieth century—secretarial work was one of a handful of occupations that were widely available to women. Others were nursing, teaching, and food services. (© Sybil Shelton/Monkmeyer Press Photo)

PLATE 6. In the 1950s and 1960s, black women such as Rosa Parks (see p. 844) played major roles in the battle for racial equality. They were joined by many white women—such as this marcher in Selma, Alabama, in 1965—who were not content to be merely model homemakers. From their experiences in the civil rights movement, both black and white women learned lessons that they later applied to their struggle for equality with men. (© Bruce Davidson/Magnum)

the age of twenty. Most significant, the birth rate rose sharply after the war, reaching a peak in 1956. Simply put, this meant that more women were having more babies—thus reversing, temporarily, a twentieth-century trend toward smaller families.

By the end of the 1950s, most of these trends began to shift. The marriage and birth rates declined and the divorce rate increased. The family appeared less stable, and the role of women was no longer clearly defined. Pressure to remain a model mother remained, but women increasingly found such a role irrelevant. The suburban home, touted as the ideal environment in the 1950s, could also be barren. Days spent at home could be boring and empty. Perhaps more important, life styles were changing. Increasing accessibility of birth control devices (the Pill and interuterine devices) made it more possible for women to control reproduction. And economic necessity—the need to pay for the affluent life styles that modern families sought—often required women to work.

As women increasingly entered the job market in the 1960s, they encountered discrimination, the effects of inferior education, and sexism. Learning from the civil-rights movement of the late 1950s and 1960s, some women organized to advance their cause. By 1966, the National Organization of

PLATE 7. The sudden and enormous popularity of the Beatles (see p. 912) focused the attention of youth around the world on the latest British music and fashion. American parents reacted with dismay—and often anger—as their sons' hair grew longer and their daughters' hemlines rose higher. Here, singer Marianne Faithfull prepares to model the new look of the mid-1960s. This style reflected contradictions in the emerging female role. Freed from the constraints of elaborate hairdos, long skirts, and delicate heels, this look expressed not only a spirit of liberation but also a provocative and "natural" sexuality. (© David Magnus/RDR Productions 1983)

PLATE 8. One alternative to the traditional domestic role for women was a career in entertainment. This option was doubly difficult for black women, but by the late 1960s, several young singers, such as Florence Ballard, Mary Wilson, and Diana Ross (left to right)—known collectively as the Supremes—had achieved extraordinary success. (UPI)

Women in the Labor Force as a Percentage of Total Female Population, 1945-1980*

| | |
|---|---|
| 1945 | 38.1 |
| 1950 | 33.0 |
| 1955 | 34.8 |
| 1960 | 37.7 |
| 1965 | 39.3 |
| 1970 | 43.4 |
| 1975 | 46.3 |
| 1980 | 51.6 |

* Male participation in the labor force ranges from about 77 to 80 percent in this same period.

Women (NOW) had organized and began to concentrate its efforts on passage of the Equal Rights Amendment (ERA) to the Constitution; the amendment passed Congress on March 22, 1972. In 1973, the Supreme Court in *Roe* v. *Wade* declared the right of women to secure abortions.

Despite these rulings, there were enormous counterpressures. Many women did not wish to be "liberated" from traditional roles centering on the family. Housewives often felt slighted by the career-oriented rhetoric of the women's movement. Many men resented the attack on their dominant position

PLATE 9.   Like civil rights activists before them, feminists took to the streets in the 1970s to publicize their political aims and their new image. *(UPI)*

PLATE 10. Despite real progress in legal rights and in the workplace, women were still considered by many men to be primarily sex objects. The Miss America pageant (pictured here in 1972) continued throughout the period to celebrate femininity as a blend of bathing beauty, charm, a movie-star smile, and a little bit of talent. *(UPI)*

PLATE 11. One of the most important leaders of the women's movement was Betty Friedan (left). She is shown here with two First Ladies, Rosalyn Carter (center) and Betty Ford, advocating passage of the Equal Rights Amendment to the Constitution. This amendment attracted the support of a great many prominent women in business, entertainment, and politics during the 1970s. *(UPI)*

in the workplace. By 1982, the ERA had been blocked and its life as a proposed Constitutional amendment ended. National agitation to end abortions, control contraception, and regulate sexual behavior of teen-age girls grew quickly. And the conflict over women's roles remained unsettled as even more women entered the labor force.

PLATE 12.   Tennis star Chris Evert, like a growing number of women in the 1970s, did not drop her maiden name when she married, but merely added her husband's name to her own, becoming Chris Evert-Lloyd. Her worldwide fame illustrates the importance to which women's sports rose during this decade. *(UPI)*

PLATE 13.   As more and more women entered the work force, some began to rise to important executive positions. This was particularly true in government work and service industries such as publishing. *(© Leonard Speier 1983)*

"IKE" IN KOREA
President-Elect Dwight Eisenhower toured Korea in December 1952. His campaign for the presidency succeeded, in part, because of promises that he would be able to end the war quickly. *(UPI)*

after a pet dog his daughter had received as a gift), Nixon persuaded the public and Eisenhower that he had done no wrong. When Eisenhower promised to go to Korea, implying he would end the war, the outcome was all but decided. On November 4, Eisenhower won a landslide victory: 33 million votes, to 27 million for Stevenson. The voters also swept Republican majorities into the House and Senate for the first time since 1946.

## Eisenhower's First Administration

Eisenhower's concept of government was a conservative one. He believed in balanced federal budgets and minimal intervention in the economy. But he did not seek to undo New Deal reforms. He hoped, instead, to create a harmonious partnership between business and govern-

ment that would generate prosperity and opportunity. In large measure he succeeded—except in one area. Within American society, the forces that touched off the Montgomery boycott and brought Martin Luther King, Jr., to national prominence proved to be irresistible. Over the rest of the world, the rise of former colonies to independence and the wholesale liberation of formerly subjected peoples brought issues of racial equality to the bargaining tables of international relations. Increasingly in the contest between capitalism and communism, the United States could ill afford to persist in old ways of racial injustice; for at least in part, the outcome of that contest lay in the Third World of black and brown peoples. By the beginning of the Kennedy administration in 1961, such issues had reached the flash point. Would American society finally accept its black members as equal participants? Or would the civil rights movement end in confrontation and violence?

Eisenhower's first priority on assuming the presidency was to defuse the anger and hostility in American society that his election had tapped. The president had to fend off McCarthy, whose attacks had become progressively wilder. At first, Eisenhower treated McCarthy with caution, although he personally disliked the senator's extremism. Eisenhower had caved in to pressure during the campaign and shied away from defending former Secretary of State George Marshall, an old friend, who was under attack by McCarthy. Once in office, he still refused to challenge the senator. But when McCarthy attacked "reds" in the army in the summer of 1954, Congress finally decided he had gone too far and voted to censure him.

On the issue of Korea, the new president acted decisively. Shortly after the election, in December 1952, Eisenhower visited Korea as promised. He renewed talks with North Korea and the People's Republic of China, and by summer, he had achieved an armistice. Thorny questions of repatriating soldiers were finally resolved. After three years of bitter struggle, peace was restored in 1953, but victory had eluded both sides.

In defense policy, the president developed what he called the "New Look" strategy to replace the large conventional military build-up pushed by Truman. This policy projected small, efficient defense budgets, allowing Eisenhower to redeem a campaign pledge to keep budgets balanced. Production would concentrate on sophisticated nuclear weapons and delivery systems—a strategy that would also provide deterrence against attacks from the Soviet Union.

The New Look plan had other implications. It concentrated on rearmament and self-defense for European nations, including West Germany. It did help the president maintain relatively low federal spending, with a balanced budget in three years and minimal deficits in two other years. It also enabled Eisenhower and Secretary of State John Foster Dulles to declare a policy of "massive deterrence." By this, Dulles meant that the United States would employ nuclear weapons against the Soviet Union in case of aggression.

Dulles's grand strategy, however, had two flaws. First, it proved to be part bluster. The commitment to "roll back" communism proved to be a hollow promise; twice, the United States stood by while the Soviets crushed popular movements in Eastern Europe. Second, it was a policy that had little effect on turbulent Third World countries. Policies aimed at securing formal alliances against the Soviet Union had little to offer millions of people struggling to cast off military dictatorships and corrupt oligarchies. When revolutions occurred in the Third World, the American response was often worried and hostile. Lacking a flexible view of the dynamics of social and economic change, the United States frequently intervened secretly to retard or even overthrow such movements. Thus throughout the Eisenhower years, the Central Intelligence Agency (CIA) carried on clandestine operations in such countries as Iran, Guatemala, and Vietnam.

If some Republican conservatives hoped to undo the New Deal welfare state, they were not heartened by the president's domestic program. Eisenhower did agree to legislation that lowered farm parity supports from 90 percent to 70 per-

cent on most commodities. These price supports were designed to guarantee a minimum living standard to farmers, but cutting them slightly did not in any way constitute a return to free market competition. Two other programs actually extended federal spending: a Social Security Act in 1954, which extended coverage to self-employed workers, and a new public housing program. In May 1954, Eisenhower signed a bill to construct the St. Lawrence Seaway—a waterway that would join the Great Lakes to the Atlantic Ocean via the St. Lawrence River. Two years later, the president signed an act to fund a system of more than 40,000 miles of interstate highways. It was the largest public works project in American history.

Inadvertently, Eisenhower initiated activism in an area where he had hoped to avoid change. Early in his administration, the president appointed California governor Earl Warren to be chief justice of the Supreme Court. But he did not anticipate that Warren would lead the Court into a period of social activism that would help redefine and broaden government guarantees of equality and civil rights. The Warren Court's most important decision came quickly, in the case of *Brown* v. *Board of Education* (1954). This unanimous decision revised the language of American democracy. Citing the evidence of experts, the Court rejected school segregation on the grounds that any separation causes psychological damage. In addition the *Brown* decision ratified the commitment of a growing number of Americans to equal rights. Like the GI Bill, it emphasized equality of education as the means to achieve equal citizenship.

For integrationists, the Supreme Court decision fixed their tactics. They could now confront local and state segregationists knowing that ultimately they could depend on the courts. Certainly this did not eliminate the risks they ran, but it did help determine the outcome of the struggle. This was the strategy that Martin Luther King, Jr., applied in the Montgomery boycott two years later and in Birmingham in 1963.

Warren's decision put Eisenhower in a difficult position. The president did not wish to push

# Jackie Robinson

(UPI)

If you do this you will be suspended from the league. You will find that the friends you have in the press box will not support you, that you will be outcasts. I do not care if half the league strikes. Those who do it will encounter quick retribution. All will be suspended and I don't care if it wrecks the National League for five years. This is the United States of America and one citizen has as much right to play as another.

The National League will go down the line with Robinson whatever the consequences.

With this firm statement, Ford Frick, president of the National Baseball League, squelched a strike planned by the St. Louis Cardinals in early 1947. The Cardinals, with support from players throughout the league, had decided to refuse to play baseball on May 6, when the team faced the Brooklyn Dodgers for the first encounter of the season. The reason: the Dodgers had hired Jackie Robinson, a black man, to play first base.

Up to 1947, the National and American leagues were lily white. Even the seating in some ball parks was segregated. The "national pastime" was a white man's sport. There were all-black baseball leagues with talented players, but none had made it yet into the majors.

Quite clearly, hiring Robinson was an experiment. Just out of the army in 1944, Robinson joined the all-black Kansas City Monarchs. In August 1945, he was approached by a scout from the Brooklyn Dodgers. Branch Rickey, the Dodgers' president, had picked Robinson to be the first black player in the major leagues. Rickey hired Robinson and assigned him to the Montreal Royals farm club for the 1946 season. Then, early in 1947, he announced that Robinson would join the Dodgers for the coming season.

Both Robinson and Rickey had prepared for what happened next. Several Southern teammates protested the presence of a black man. Other players proclaimed that Robinson (and by implication all black men) lacked the talent to play baseball. Some opposing teams, like the Philadelphia Phillies, peppered him with obscenities from the dugout when he batted or fielded. Travel for road games proved to be very difficult because many hotels and restaurants refused to serve Robinson or seat him with his fellow players. Robinson had been coached by Rickey to cope with these taunts and insults.

In Boston, however, Robinson reached the breaking point. Fans shouted and cursed at him when he took the field. They also screamed at Pee Wee Reese, the Brooklyn shortstop. Reese was a white Southerner, and the fans taunted him for playing on the same team as a black man. When the shouting became more intense, Reese suddenly left his position. He walked over to first base and put his arm around Robinson. In a loud, clear voice, he shouted: "Yell, Heckle. Do anything you want. We came here to play baseball." The jeering died down.

Gradually, the heckling stopped all over the league. Robinson batted and fielded better than any of his detractors had predicted. His fiery hitting and base running helped the Dodgers to win the National League pennant for the first time in years. In the fall, Robinson was voted "Rookie of the Year." Rickey's experiment in integration, and Robinson's talent, had made it possible for black players in sports to compete as equals.

**THE ARKANSAS NATIONAL GUARD PREVENTS INTEGRATION IN LITTLE ROCK**

In September 1957, Governor Orval Faubus of Arkansas used the state's National Guard to block court-ordered racial integration of Little Rock Central High School. Faced with this defiance and growing threats of violence, President Eisenhower, much against his inclination, sent federal troops to the city to enforce integration. *(Burt Glinn/Magnum)*

desegregation, although he had agreed to integration of the armed forces. During the remainder of his years in office, he refused to speak in favor of school desegregation and never affirmed his agreement—moral or otherwise—with the *Brown* decision. This excessive caution and lack of leadership encouraged some white Southerners to believe that the inevitable would never occur. But they were wrong. Even Eisenhower was finally forced to act. In 1957, he signed a weak but significant civil rights bill. More important, when Governor Orval Faubus of Arkansas tried to stop the integration of Little Rock Central High School in September 1957, the president was obliged to intervene. Faubus disobeyed a court order and installed the National Guard in front of the school to prevent black students from entering. After serious rioting, sparked by the governor's inflammatory remarks, Eisenhower dis-

patched federal troops to the city and appealed for calm. It was a short step, taken reluctantly. But it had enormous implications for the future pattern of civil rights agitation, for it put the federal government on the side of the integrationists.

## The Election of 1956 and the Dawn of the Youth Culture

Eisenhower's congenial and low-keyed administration focused attention and power on his own leadership. Thus his sudden heart attack on September 24, 1955, pointed up how fragile his administration was. He improved rapidly but then suffered a serious attack of ileitis in the spring of 1956, which required intestinal surgery. During neither illness was the president completely incapacitated, but attention nevertheless focused on Vice President Nixon. Viewing him with suspicion, some party regulars openly talked of a new vice-presidential candidate in 1956. But speculation quickly fizzled, and the Republicans renominated Nixon along with Eisenhower.

The Democrats turned once again to Adlai Stevenson, who then allowed the convention to select the vice-presidential candidate. Their choice was Estes Kefauver of Tennessee, a liberal senator with a reputation for racket and crime investigation. But he was unpopular with party bosses, whom he had offended in his investigations.

Another leading (but unsuccessful) candidate for vice president was John Fitzgerald Kennedy, senator from Massachusetts. Kennedy's rise to national attention in the late 1950s signaled the beginnings of a political and cultural transformation that came to fruition in the early 1960s. This new politics emphasized youth and activism.

Beginning in the middle and late 1950s, American culture exhibited changes that began to disrupt the conservative, family-oriented as-sumptions of the immediate postwar period. The suburban culture that only a few years earlier had seemed to settle permanently on American society suddenly showed flaws. Beyond the books and articles that now criticized the smugness and conformity of the suburbs, many suburban children were defying those values. These young people absorbed a new youth culture that differentiated them seriously from their parents. While it too exhibited strong elements of conformism—its customs were organized around rituals of romance, "going steady," and marriage—the new youth culture also had a more restless side, reflected in the emergence of new popular heroes such as movie stars James Dean, Marlon Brando, and Natalie Wood. Dean, in particular, in such films as *Rebel Without a Cause* (1955), captured a mood that rejected the preselected social and sexual roles for youth. His sensitive and emotional acting challenged a stereotyped postwar image of the American male as a military figure complete with crew cut.

Also of immense importance to the burgeoning youth culture was rock-'n'-roll, a new pop-

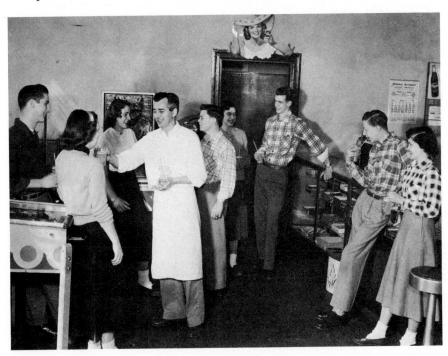

TEENAGERS IN A SNACK BAR

The teenage subculture of the 1950s provided endless fascination—and worry—for the rest of society. New dating customs, dancing, and music reflected the effects of postwar prosperity and new, more permissive methods of childrearing. *(The Bettmann Archive)*

**JAMES DEAN**

Actor James Dean had a brief but brilliant screen career before his fatal auto accident in 1955, during the filming of *Giant*. Dean evoked a good deal of sympathy from teenagers for his roles of anguished and misunderstood youth. *(The Bettmann Archive)*

specific audience segments, and often the most lucrative of these seemed to be youth. Consequently, film companies produced scores of movies in the late 1950s featuring drugs, delinquency, and rock 'n' roll.

In a more subtle way, this generation of teenagers (the first suburban generation and the elder brothers and sisters of the postwar baby boom) seemed adrift and in search of belief. Many of them, although they could not vote, were attracted by John Kennedy—his youthful political style and his glamorous wife. They were not as hesitant as their elders to face a new world of changing social and racial relations.

But in 1956, the political hour still belonged to the moderate Republicans, and Eisenhower

**SENATOR JOHN F. KENNEDY AND JACQUELINE BOUVIER**

Senator Kennedy's marriage to socially prominent Jacqueline Bouvier in 1953 proved to be a great political asset. His political style, stressing action, youth, and glamour, helped make him a prominent presidential contender by the late 1950s. *(UPI)*

ular music that had sprung out of America's urban black ghettos. With dramatic and direct sensuality, this music expressed feelings of love, hate, and other emotions, in ways that delighted teen-agers and appalled their parents, teachers, and religious leaders. Although groups of white artists capitalized on the success and energy of the new sound, its creative origins in the black experience did not disappear. Moreover, with the appearance of Elvis Presley, the new music absorbed energy and inspiration from a long tradition of country music.

The mass media played a crucial role in developing and popularizing this distinctive new youth culture. Magazines such as *Seventeen* informed teen-age girls of changing styles and customs. Recorded music became available to almost every young person because of the mass marketing of long-playing plastic records and because of a dramatic growth in radio stations aimed at the youth market. Hollywood films, once produced for the entire family, increasingly targeted

and Nixon won a dramatic victory, garnering 35½ million votes to Stevenson and Kefauver's 26 million. This endorsement of Eisenhower's administration did not extend to Congress, where the Democrats held on to majorities in both houses. It seemed that the American public wanted moderation at the presidential level and continued activism in Congress.

## Eisenhower's Second Administration

Despite his great personal victory in the election of 1956, Eisenhower faced serious problems in the remainder of his presidential years. Beginning in 1957 and extending into 1958, a serious recession gripped the economy. Unemployment rose from about 4 percent to 7 percent and the gross national product fell back by about 1 percent. Eisenhower refused to apply federal stimuli, and he rejected calls for a tax cut or public works projects. He insisted that the best policy was to allow the economy to correct itself. This stance, added to an influence-peddling scandal that forced the White House staff chief, Sherman Adams, to quit, hurt Republican chances in the 1958 congressional elections. After November, the Democrats controlled the House by 283 seats to 153 and the Senate by 64 to 34. Then, on November 26, the president suffered a mild stroke. He recovered quickly but was left with a slight speech impediment.

Facing a revived Democratic party that claimed to have uncovered a "bomber gap" in 1956 and a public that was shocked when the Russians launched *Sputnik*—the first successful space satellite—in October 1957, Eisenhower had to struggle to maintain his modest defense budget strategy. Pressure to increase defense spending and invest in huge civil defense programs came from all sides. But Eisenhower gave little ground. He did, however, step up funding for space programs and created the National Aeronautics and Space Administration (NASA) in 1958. In September 1958, he signed the National Defense Education Act, which provided about $1 billion in loans and scholarships for the study of mathematics, the sciences, and foreign languages.

In the last two years of his administration, Eisenhower revived attempts to negotiate with the Russians. After the new Russian premier, Nikita Khrushchev, took office in March 1958, he announced a suspension of open-air nuclear testing. The United States followed suit in late summer. Eisenhower's most astute move was an invitation to the Russian leader to visit the United States in the fall of 1959. Arriving on September 15, Khrushchev and his party toured the country, visiting farms, cities, and Disneyland in California. Final negotiations at Camp David, Maryland, set a spring summit meeting for Paris in 1960. The Russian premier's trip had been controversial, touching off scattered demonstrations, but he impressed many Americans with his energy and self-confidence.

Despite its possibilities, the opportunity for rapprochement with the Russians was lost. Shortly before the Paris conference in the spring of 1960, the Soviets announced the downing of an American U-2 aerial reconnaissance plane deep inside their territory. On May 9, one week before the summit meeting, Eisenhower accepted responsibility for the overflight. When the conference began, Khrushchev seemed determined to disrupt it, demanding a personal apology from the president. When Eisenhower refused, the Russian premier left Paris, and negotiations ended.

Perhaps all of these troubles sobered Eisenhower's thinking. As he left office in 1961, he delivered an address to the nation that was more warning than farewell. He underscored the basic themes of his administration. He had tried to keep defense spending down. He had wanted to avoid acrimonious and divisive issues such as civil rights. He had hoped that a stable economy would satisfy those who proposed quick social change. But now he feared a push for larger budgets, more social legislation, and an adventurous foreign policy. He warned the nation of a "military-industrial" complex and a technological power elite that might destroy American democracy:

In the councils of government, we must guard against the acquisition of unwarranted influence, whether sought or unsought, by the military-industrial complex. The potential for the disastrous rise of misplaced power exists and will persist.
We must never let the weight of this combination endanger our liberties or democratic processes.

This final cautionary statement had little effect on the exuberant young politicians about to take office. It seemed misplaced and excessively conservative. The day belonged to a new generation of leaders, to the Kennedys and the Kings. They were determined to face some of the social and economic questions that had been gathering force during the last eight years.

# THE KENNEDY YEARS

## The Renewed Promise

In November 1960, American voters chose a president who exemplified change and action. But John F. Kennedy won against Richard Nixon by only a slim margin. At first, the action he proposed aimed at ending the slump in economic growth of the late 1950s and the impasse in foreign relations that Eisenhower had reached. But the new administration quickly became the focus for social forces that were transforming American society. Young, photogenic, with a richly accented voice, Kennedy radiated self-confidence. He personified an era of rising expectations and growing self-confidence among groups formerly defined as being outside the mainstream of American political life. Together with more and more Americans, he believed that government could bring the nation a fuller and more satisfying life. Government could help correct the injustices of the past and fulfill the aspirations of the present.

Kennedy was simultaneously a tough-minded practical politician and a man of legend. The myths that surrounded him came in part from his wealth and his highly publicized accomplishments. In part they were inspired by his heroism in the navy during World War II. The second son

of Joseph Kennedy, an Irish-Catholic millionaire who was a major contributor to the Democratic party, John grew up to live out the ambitions of his father. Able to move easily and gracefully in the public eye, he won the acclaim and political power that had eluded his father.

Kennedy's nomination and election in 1960 represented a new departure in American politics, and it symbolized the growing political importance of groups once held at arm's length in presidential politics. He was the first Roman Catholic to be elected president—an issue heavily debated in some sections of the country. Some Protestants, like the 9-million-member Southern Baptist Convention, opposed him because of his faith. But his extraordinary proportion of Catholic votes (81 percent) neutralized most of this opposition.

The Catholic issue was just the first of many obstacles to Kennedy's nomination and victory. He also had to satisfy the various constituents of the Democratic party: liberals like Eleanor Roosevelt, labor leaders like Walter Reuther of the United Auto Workers, politicos like Harry Truman, and Southern conservatives. At best this road was tortuous, but Kennedy managed to neutralize his most serious opponents. His record as senator from Massachusetts had not been particularly distinguished, but he made up for this weakness in political attractiveness and energy. Labor was reluctant to support him at first because of his tenacity in investigating the Teamsters Union for corruption. And liberals wondered aloud why he had never opposed Joseph McCarthy. Yet the political organization he built and the support he gathered helped swing the party to him and create an electoral majority.

During the campaign, Kennedy had pledged to get the American economy moving again. This meant, primarily, attacking the current recession, with its high unemployment and low productivity. Like Eisenhower, Kennedy could have waited for natural market forces to pull the economy out of its lethargy. But he had promised action. Moreover, a major element among his advisers subscribed to the general theories of the English economist John Maynard Keynes. They believed that the federal government should, as required, intervene in the economy to expand or contract expenditures. These fiscal measures, based on enlarging or shrinking the federal budget in relation to tax revenues, might temporarily increase budget deficits, but they promised to touch off strong growth that would fill federal coffers later.

Kennedy's advisers were also convinced that the free-market system inevitably left serious problems unresolved. Despite the successes of the Eisenhower years, 39 million Americans or about 22 percent of the population lived below the minimum poverty level set by government economists. Moreover, rapid changes in the economy had left residues of serious unemployment in rural areas of West Virginia, New England, and the South. In the cities, large numbers of working men and women had been left behind by technological unemployment (joblessness due to lack of the skills demanded by new industries). Underlying all of these economic problems was a broad shift in the American economy away from farm and blue-collar employment into jobs in

government and in the service, retail, and communications industries. The private economy, these advisers argued, excluded too many Americans. Only a large new spurt of growth stimulated by the federal government could sweep these eddies of poverty back into the mainstream.

The president was initially very cautious about adopting these ideas, but he eventually accepted the principles behind his advisers' suggestions. His first economic proposals in early 1961 focused on securing supplements to unemployment benefits, increased social security benefits, a higher minimum wage, and relief aid for seriously distressed areas. All of these measures passed through Congress by September. But his proposals for withholding taxes on stock dividends and interest earnings and his attempt to narrow expense-account deductions met stiff resistance. He did succeed, however, in winning larger tax deductions for business investment in new equipment.

Nonetheless, business leaders were distressed by the Democratic administration. They distrusted Kennedy and the growing consensus

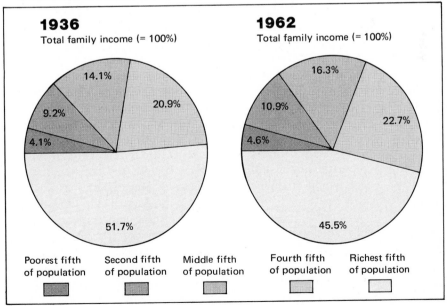

**DISTRIBUTION OF FAMILY INCOME, 1936 AND 1962**

**1936**
Total family income (= 100%)

14.1%
9.2%
4.1%
20.9%
51.7%

**1962**
Total family income (= 100%)

16.3%
10.9%
4.6%
22.7%
45.5%

Poorest fifth of population

Second fifth of population

Middle fifth of population

Fourth fifth of population

Richest fifth of population

among his inner circle of advisers that the federal government should intervene more decisively in economic and social matters. Kennedy was keenly aware of his unpopularity with business, and he tried to mend his fences. In early 1963, he delivered several speeches designed to win business over to a new program of moderate tax reform. His major proposal, however, was a large individual tax cut. This reduction proposed a cut in income taxes that would save taxpayers over $13 billion. Something of a gamble, it passed finally in 1964 and paid off handsomely by helping stimulate a burst of growth that increased tax revenues and narrowed the federal budget deficit.

## Kennedy and Civil Rights

Kennedy's strategy for solving social problems rested upon two tactics. He attempted to stimulate economic growth as a way of bringing underprivileged elements of the population into the mainstream. And he worked to maintain the political support of the diverse coalition that had elected him. But he remained reluctant to employ the power of the federal government to end segregation because of the political controversy it would stir.

During the campaign, Kennedy had called for Americans to dedicate themselves to high principles. This suggested his support for civil rights. But campaign hints proved difficult to translate into action. Initially, the president did little to reverse segregation. In fact, he appointed several men to federal judgeships who were unsympathetic to black rights. On the other hand, he chose several black Americans for ambassadorships. His brother Robert, working quietly in the Justice Department, ordered desegregation of interstate transportation facilities in the South.

Still, pressure mounted to fulfill one specific campaign pledge: his promise to eliminate "with the stroke of a pen" the segregation maintained in federally financed housing projects. The president waited until June 1962 to act—partly because he hoped to create a new Department of Housing and Urban Development and appoint a

black man, Robert Weaver, as head. Too much pressure, he reasoned, would raise the opposition of Southern Congressmen and jeopardize his whole program.

Yet the idealism of which Kennedy spoke so often in public increasingly pushed his administration to do something about the spreading confrontation between integrationists and segregationists. The president had to act in the fall of 1962 to protect James Meredith, the first black student to enter the University of Mississippi, from mob violence. Kennedy had to intervene again in the spring of 1963, during the explosive Birmingham marches, to restrain police violence against demonstrators. These actions deepened resentment against the president in the white South. Gallup polls taken over the summer revealed profound national concern about integration, with a significant group of Americans worried that it was proceeding too fast.

Recognizing the growing momentum and importance of the civil rights movement, Kennedy believed that federal action on a broad scale had become necessary. In early June 1963, two black students tried to enroll at the University of Alabama in Tuscaloosa. George Wallace, governor of the state, stood defiantly in the doorway of the registration hall and read a proclamation denouncing federal interference in his state's business. Facing him, Deputy Attorney General Nicholas Katzenbach, sent by Kennedy, read a statement ordering the governor to end his obstruction of a court order to integrate the university. Confronted by federal power, Wallace stepped aside and the black students enrolled.

As Kennedy moved closer to acclaiming the goals of the civil rights movement, Martin Luther King, Jr., reached the height of his power and influence. During the massive march on Washington of August 28, 1963, King proclaimed a new meaning and content for the old promises of equality and freedom. These words, he declared, now meant for the first time equality and freedom for black men and women. Kennedy did not endorse or attend the march, but he invited its leaders to the White House afterward. A few weeks earlier, he had evoked his own vision of

American citizenship and called for support of a new civil rights bill because, as he told a national television audience: "We face . . . a moral crisis as a country and as a people." Kennedy's bill proposed to end segregation in public accommodations, strengthen voting rights, and speed school desegregation.

Extensive reforms to aid other slighted populations in America made up Kennedy's 1963 legislative package: medical insurance for the elderly and subsidized care for the indigent, aid to education, and a new Urban Affairs Department of the federal government. Toward the end of the summer, he instructed his advisers to begin sketching out legislation for a concerted drive to end poverty. Kennedy thus proposed to move the federal government aggressively into the realm of social reform.

By the fall of 1963, the administration had embraced broad and ambitious new programs to expand the power of the federal government to guarantee the rights and well-being of minority, poor, and disadvantaged groups in America. It was a task worthy of the vision of Martin Luther King, Jr. But it was also, as King himself realized, a difficult task filled with great personal danger.

## Kennedy's Foreign Policy

As in domestic affairs, Kennedy promised activism in foreign policy. Unwilling to rely solely on nuclear weapons to preserve a stalemate between the United States and the Soviet Union, the new president believed that his country should intervene in Third World revolutions. Kennedy hoped that the United States could woo these nations into the Western camp. Or, failing this, he was willing to use military means to support wars against communist insurgents. Similarly, in January 1961, the Russian leader Nikita Khrushchev proclaimed his support for "wars of liberation." Thus, both the Americans and Russians planned to increase their involvement in the unstable politics of the Third World.

Kennedy's policy was based on financial, technological, and economic aid coupled with military intervention. In March 1961, the president announced the Alliance for Progress for South America. This aid program promised assistance to Latin American nations for schools, roads, and health facilities. The president intended to strengthen middle-class elements in Latin America who were sympathetic to reform and who would steer their societies away from military dictatorship or Soviet influence. At the same time, the president announced the Peace Corps—a project to send young American volunteers into Third World countries to aid in agricultural projects and community development.

Both of these programs appealed to young Americans, who took them as symbols of a new and idealistic foreign policy. At the same time, however, Kennedy pushed readiness for military intervention. He encouraged the armed forces to develop plans for counterinsurgency, and he pushed creation of a new, sophisticated strike force for use against guerrillas, called the Green Berets.

Kennedy's first military intervention proved a fiasco. At the end of the Eisenhower administration, Cuban rebels led by Fidel Castro, overthrew Fulgencio Batista, the ruthless dictator of the island. Castro was determined to secure agricultural reform, nationalization of foreign companies, and industrialization. His program brought harsh criticism from American business and the Eisenhower administration. During 1960 the CIA began planning Castro's overthrow, but Eisenhower decided to let his successor carry out the plans. Despite some hesitations, Kennedy approved a landing of American-trained and -supplied counterrevolutionaries. When the landing party moved ashore at the Bay of Pigs, Castro's forces were ready. Most counterrevolutionaries were captured. Leaks to the press and circumstantial evidence linked the Kennedy administration with the invaders. Subsequently Kennedy admitted U.S. involvement.

In October 1962, Cuba was once again the site of international conflict, but this time, the incident involved a direct confrontation between the United States and the Soviet Union. On October 14, U.S. Air Force spy planes photo-

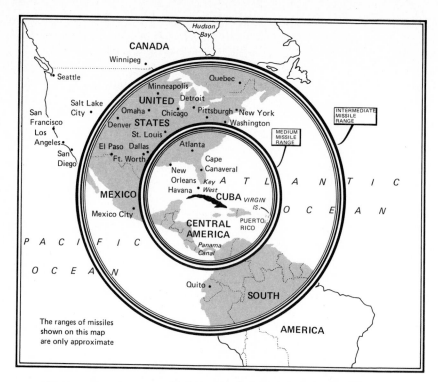

**THE RANGE OF CUBAN–BASED SOVIET MISSILES**

graphed missile sites being constructed in Cuba by Russian technicians. Kennedy was gravely concerned. He could not allow deployment of these missiles, if only because of the intolerable political risks at home. But to destroy them would risk nuclear war with the Soviets. He chose, instead, a public confrontation, declaring a blockade of Cuba to prevent further Russian supply of the missiles. On October 23, the Russians finally agreed to dismantle their bases in exchange for an American pledge not to invade Cuba.

Despite the risks incurred by intervention in Cuba, Kennedy approved stepped-up intervention in the more intricate affairs of Vietnam. At first the president feared that communists would gain control of neighboring Laos, but his attention quickly focused on Vietnam. To Kennedy, Vietnam became a testing ground for his theories

of nation building and counterinsurgency. The president recognized the complexity of the political and military situation in Vietnam. He understood that the division of the former French colony into two entities, one communist and the other supported by the United States, created instability. The communist-led insurgency that had driven out the French was now directed at expelling the Western-supported government in the south. But Kennedy believed that with United States support, the government of South Vietnam, headed by Ngo Dinh Diem could survive.

Nonetheless, American intervention did not work as intended. The Diem government became more unstable than ever. Counterinsurgency could not stem government loss of control over the countryside. Diem spoke of reform, but he isolated himself from the political and religious majorities of the South. The military situation continued to deteriorate because the South Vietnamese army, despite its sophisticated equipment and training, proved unreliable in battle. Opposing revolutionaries—now called the Viet Cong—drew increasing support from the embattled rural population. The whole nation was becoming an armed camp.

By 1962, American advisers had approved more drastic policies: defoliants to destroy jungle cover, napalm, and a "strategic hamlet" program to isolate revolutionaries by moving the peasantry into armed camps. Still the internal political situation was shaky. Diem clung obstinately to unpopular dictatorial policies.

In the spring of 1963, Kennedy signaled his ambassador in Saigon to the effect that the United States would accept a replacement for Diem. However, when Diem was overthrown in November, the violence of the coup shocked the administration. Instead of a new order, corruption and brutality continued to rule South Vietnam. Insurgents operated freely and successfully despite 20,000 Americans troops and advisers. Kennedy himself was growing suspicious of optimistic military and intelligence reports. The struggle had come to a crossroads. The president either had to increase American participation or slow it down and face Republican criticism. As in domestic policy, Kennedy was faced with serious choices. What he would have done will never be known.

### MID-RANGE BALLISTIC MISSILE SITE IN CUBA

Aerial reconnaissance over Cuba on October 23, 1962, indicated that work was proceeding on Soviet-supplied missile sites in Cuba, despite the warnings of President Kennedy and the announcement, a day earlier, of a blockade around the island. On October 27, the Russians agreed to dismantle the bases in exchange for an American pledge not to invade Cuba. *(Wide World Photos)*

# SUGGESTED READINGS, CHAPTERS 41–42

## MARTIN LUTHER KING, JR., AND CIVIL RIGHTS

Richard Kluger's *Simple Justice: The History of* Brown *v.* Board of Education *and America's Struggle for Equality* (1976) details the complex forces and events that converged on the Supreme Court when it delivered its landmark desegregation case. Richard Polenberg, in *One Nation Divisible: Class, Race, and Ethnicity in the United States Since 1938* (1980), provides an interesting perspective for understanding some of the larger issues in American racial and ethnic attitudes. Coretta Scott King, *My Life with Martin Luther King, Jr.* (1969), is stirring and poignant. David Lewis, *King: A Biography* (1978), is far more critical, but ultimately it is a sympathetic portrait.

## THE COLD WAR AT HOME

The issue of domestic anticommunism and the subsequent prominence of Senator Joseph McCarthy began during the presidency of Harry Truman. A good assessment of Truman is Alonzo L. Hamby, *Beyond the New Deal: Harry S Truman and American Liberalism* (1973). A controversial look at the effects of McCarthyism is David Caute, *The Great Fear: The Anti-Communist Purge Under Truman and Eisenhower* (1978). Richard H. Rovere's *Senator Joseph McCarthy* (1959) is a very readable account of the rise and fall of the Senator from Wisconsin.

## THE 1950s

An excellent economic history of the 1950s is Harold G. Vatter, *The United States Economy in the 1950s* (1963). The effects of prosperity during this decade were controversial. One book that set the tone for much of the subsequent criticism of 1950s life styles was David Riesman, *The Lonely Crowd* (1950). *The Affluent Society* (1956), written by the notable American economist John Kenneth Galbraith, details some of the problems of prosperity. On the other hand, David M. Potter, *People of Plenty* (1954), argues that abundance has had a generally positive effect on society.

## THE EISENHOWER ADMINISTRATION

One good place to begin study of the Eisenhower presidency is Herbert S. Parmet, *Eisenhower and the American Crusades* (1972). Recently published material in *The Eisenhower Diaries,* Richard H. Ferrell (ed.), reveal the president to be a very complex and thoughtful leader. Robert L. Branyan and Laurence H. Larson (eds.) have collected important public documents from the era in *The Eisenhower Administration 1953–1961: A Documentary History,* 2 vols. (1971).

# 43 ▪ Chicago, 1968

Giants lived here once. It was that kind of town, thirty years gone, that made big men out of little ones. It was grand for great deeds then, as it is grand for small deeds now.

NELSON ALGREN

Dear Students for a Democratic Society:

I'm twelve years old, and I wish to join the society. Because of the conditions at school your hair must not be two inches above the eyebrow. You must wear white socks. If you wore any other color you'd be punished and this is the reason I want to join the society.

Letter to the Editor,<br>New Left Notes, 1968

## "SURREALISM IN CHICAGO"  *(Dallas Morning News)*

Jerry Rubin mounted the stage at the Grant Park bandshell in Chicago shortly after 4:00 P.M. on August 28, 1968. His arms circling a large, squirming pig, he shouted out, to the delighted crowd of 10,000 student and other demonstrators: "Today is a historic day for America—we are proud to announce the declaration of candidacy for the presidency of the United States by a pig." The crowd roared its approval of Pigasus.

Rubin, with his shaggy hair and unkempt beard, was well known to police guarding the edges of the park. So friends had smuggled the pig through the crowd in a burlap bag from a nearby car. (Earlier in the week, Rubin had tried the same stunt at Chicago's Civic Center, but police had arrested him before he could start his speech.)

Milling around in anticipation, the crowd had already listened to several speakers. Whiffs of tear gas rose from the grass or drifted across from the nearby flagpole area. Only a short time before, police had charged into a group of demonstrators trying to haul down the American flag. Tear gas exploded and police waded through the group flailing nightsticks. Volunteer medics dragged the injured to safety.

David Dellinger, longtime peace advocate and leader of Mobilization, a group that helped organize the demonstration, now rose to address the crowd. He announced a march out of the park, across Chicago's Loop (the business section), to the Amphitheater, where the 1968 Democratic convention was in session. There was no permit for the demonstration, but Dellinger insisted the march was a question of free speech. "This is a peaceful march," he cried. "All those who want to participate in a peaceful march, join our line. All those who are not peaceful, please go away and don't join our line."

A few small groups, some wearing helmets, their eyes smeared with Vaseline to protect against chemical mace and tear gas, broke off. But most of the demonstrators followed Dellinger up the sidewalk of Columbus Drive until they ran up against a solid line of Chicago policemen. The demonstrators stopped and sat down. Dellinger went off to negotiate with the police. But the officials refused to budge: no march would be permitted. Hearing this, the crowd began to clump into thick knots, which then moved around the police line and toward the bridges that led from the park, hoping to make their way over the railroad tracks and into the heart of the city. National Guardsmen standing on the bridges prevented this by firing tear gas. But the demonstrators quickly discovered one unprotected bridge toward the north and raced across it. They poured down Michigan Avenue to the Conrad Hilton Hotel, headquarters for several candidates for the nomination and a symbol of the Democratic convention. The stage was set for a violent battle between police and demonstrators—a battle that shocked the nation and shook the Democratic party to its foundations.

## "YOUTHS FRUSTRATED, BITTER"    (Boston Evening Globe)

The origins of the confrontation in Chicago lay in opposition to the war in Vietnam. The brutal course of this war had battered the presidency of Lyndon Johnson. Early in 1968, a Viet Cong insurgent attack against South Vietnamese and American troops (the Tet offensive) had brought the war into the streets of every city in South Vietnam. Although the Viet Cong fell back with severe losses, the campaign was a debacle for American home-front support for the war. Many Americans concluded, as they watched the nightly accounts and news summaries on television, that the war was neither winnable nor worth the casualties.

The Tet offensive was just one element of a growing political crisis that forced President Johnson from office. Johnson had staked his reputation and fate on winning the civil war in Asia. But after three years of heavy escalation and commitment of American resources to the war, casualties were still mounting with no end in sight. Opposition, particularly within the Democratic party, was growing rapidly. At first it gathered around Senator Eugene McCarthy of Minnesota, who came close to defeating President Johnson in the March 12 New Hampshire presidential primary. Predictions for the upcoming primary in Wisconsin were even bleaker for the president. Thus Johnson in a surprise national television broadcast on March 31 announced his withdrawal from the race.

Nonetheless, Johnson had no intention of bowing out of politics. He remained determined to choose his own successor. He believed that McCarthy was only a marginal threat; the real danger to continuation of his policies was Robert Kennedy, who could rally antiwar support and win approval from Democratic party regulars. As his candidate, Johnson pushed Hubert Humphrey, his vice president. But he made his support contingent on Humphrey's firm commitment to pursue the war in Vietnam to victory.

In late spring, Kennedy's chances for the nomination mounted, as support for McCarthy dwindled and Humphrey failed to arouse much popular support. On June 4, Kennedy won the crucial California primary and seemed well on his way to unseating Humphrey, the party front runner. Then in the early morning of June 5, at a victory celebration in Los Angeles at the Ambassador Hotel, shots suddenly rang out. An Arab immigrant, Sirhan Bishara Sirhan, fired at Kennedy from close range. The injuries were fatal. The candidate died twenty-five hours later. This second murderous attack on the Kennedy family removed the only viable antiwar candidate from the race. Humphrey was as good as nominated.

The Republican party proved even less hospitable to antiwar sentiment, counting on polls that showed a majority of Americans still supporting the war. When Republican conventioneers gathered in Miami, Florida, they had no trouble agreeing to nominate Richard M. Nixon. Nixon opened his campaign to the center and the right—to gather up critics of Johnson and the Democrats, and to take advantage of a growing backlash against civil rights and antiwar demonstrations. He was vague and noncommittal on the issue of Vietnam. He promised to end the war but declined to say how.

For those who opposed the war—and there were significant and visible numbers of Americans who did—there was no place to go: no political haven, no believable candidate, and no welcome from either party. Nor was there a meaningful third-party alternative. Thus when the Democratic party shut its doors to the antiwar movement, it inevitably forced that movement out onto the streets of Chicago.

## "CHICAGOANS AWAIT PROTESTORS WITH TEETH, FISTS CLENCHED" *(Los Angeles Times)*

Although many voters disapproved of the war in Vietnam, it was young people who took to the streets to manifest their opposition. Two groups, in particular, organized and led the Chicago demonstrations: the Yippies and student radicals.

The YIP (Youth International Party), founded in early 1968, dedicated itself to a world revolution led by youth. During late 1967 and early 1968, student protests against the war escalated across the United States. Student movements and crippling strikes also rocked France, West Germany, and other European nations. Many young Americans concluded that they were part of a rising generation destined to change the world. The Yippies capitalized on this sentiment and wove together diverse elements of youth culture: political protest and experimental counterculture life styles. As Allen Ginsberg, poet and troubadour of the movement, described it, it drew together

> younger people aware of the planetary fate that we are all sitting in the middle of, imbued with a new consciousness and desiring of a new kind of society involving prayer, music, and spiritual life together rather than competition, acquisition, and war.

The Yippies formed originally from a group of ex-college radicals living on New York's Lower East Side. They worked at shelters for runaway teenagers and held music festivals and street theater for the growing hippie community and drug culture of that area. During the October 21, 1967, antiwar protest march on the Pentagon in Washington, two future Yippie leaders, Jerry Rubin and Abbie Hoffman, demonstrated their genius for combining politics, culture, and humor. They built the protest into a media event and urged the crowd to circle the huge building to "exorcise" the evil inside. They astutely recognized the enormous importance of such symbolic events. Photographs and newsreels of demonstrators planting daisies in the gun barrels of troops guarding the building brought more attention to the march than did speeches, lobbying, or slogans.

The tone of Yippie protests was mocking and anti-Establishment, but it was not entirely unfamiliar. Indeed, the exploits of Rubin and Hoffman belong to the bittersweet vein of American humor exemplified by the Marx brothers in their best political films—such as "Duck Soup," shot in the 1930s. In a gesture that might have fitted such a film, Hoffman and a group of friends burst into the New York Stock Exchange in August 1967. Standing on the balcony above the bustling Exchange floor, they threw dollar bills over the side. Some of the brokers below them jeered and shook their fists; others scrambled for the bills that floated downward. Those demonstrators who escaped arrest rushed to the front entrance of the building and chanted "Free! Free!" while they shredded and burned dollar bills.

The Yippies decided to organize as a political movement in February 1968. As Hoffman related:

There we were, all stoned, rolling around the floor. . . . Yippie! . . . Somebody says oink and that's it, pig, it's a natural, man, we gotta win. . . . Let's try success, I mean, when we went to the Pentagon, we were going to get it to rise 300 feet in the air. . . . So we said how about doing one that will win.

The purpose of the Yippie organization was to turn the Chicago Democratic convention into a protest. The tactic was to organize a "Festival of Life"—a giant counterculture rock concert to be held simultaneously as the Democrats nominated a candidate for president. As singer and Yippie member Phil Ochs said, "They wanted to be able to act out fantasies in the street to communicate their feelings to the public."

On March 17, at the Americana Hotel in New York, Hoffman, Rubin, Ochs, singer Arlo Guthrie, and others announced further details of their Festival of Life. It would feature a concert with Guthrie, Judy Collins, the Fugs, Country Joe and the Fish, and other popular groups. Leaders promised to cooperate with Chicago officials, to secure proper permits for the concert and permission for the audience to sleep in the city parks. But Mayor Richard Daley of Chicago refused to grant permits for the festival, believing that a tough line would restrict the numbers who came to the city during the convention.

**YIPPIE POLITICAL THEATER IN CHICAGO**

Yippie demonstrations against the Vietnam War were dramatic, outrageous, and effective. Marching under the symbol of death, Yippies marked the "Unbirthday" of President Johnson on August 27 during the Democratic Convention. (© 1969 Roger Malloch/Magnum)

Without permits, several performers withdrew. But the obstinacy of the city suited Yippie purposes. As one flier put it, YIP was a "National disorganization whose sole purpose would be the Theater of Disruption." Accordingly, the Yippies revised their plans. They still planned a concert, but the highlight of their mock celebration would be the nomination of Pigasus for president. This name had a special significance. "Pig" was ghetto slang for policeman. By nominating a pig for president, the Yippies were proclaiming that the United States was a police state.

Through the summer the Yippies tried, without success, to persuade Chicago officials to grant a permit for their festival—although they made no effort to hide their purpose of disrupting the convention. And the list of demands they released was designed to shock, rather than to form the basis for any negotiations. They demanded an end to the war in Vietnam, legalization of marijuana and other psychedelic drugs, freedom for prisoners, the disarming of police, and the abolition of money. As for events of the festival, they "predicted" activities in Chicago that would disrupt the entire city: an "unbirthday" party for President Johnson on August 27, a plan to dump LSD into the Chicago water system, a stall-in on city traffic arteries, the release of greased pigs throughout the city, and the recruitment of "230 hyper-potent hippie males into a special battalion to seduce the wives, daughters, and girlfriends of convention delegates." As the Yippies and their supporters began to converge on Chicago in late August, Hoffman proclaimed: "I use guerrilla theater as a medium for creating what I call blank space. Blank space is where you use media so that the observer, the audience, becomes a participant, becomes involved." But for Mayor Daley and the police and convention officials, the Yippies' agenda was not theater but political warfare.

Far larger than the Yippie group was the contingent of demonstrators that came to Chicago from the more subdued and serious student antiwar movement. The largest of the political action groups, the Students for a Democratic Society (SDS), founded in 1962, refused to participate officially. Its leaders believed demonstrations to be ineffective, and they feared violence from the police. They also wanted to remain separate from any movement that might support Senator McCarthy. Nonetheless, two former SDS leaders, Tom Hayden and Rennie Davis, played leading roles in Chicago. And the days of protest had a profound effect on radical organizations like SDS.

The National Mobilization Committee to End the War in Vietnam (MOB), headed by David Dellinger, was an umbrella organization that included most of the important student radical groups. It was MOB that had organized the 1967 demonstration at the Pentagon. Its leaders occasionally worked with the Yippies, but the Yippies never officially joined it. Their strategy was theater, not serious politics.

In February 1968, MOB opened a Chicago office and chose Davis and Hayden to coordinate activities. Their first job was to secure demonstration permits from the city for a march on the convention. At a planning session held in late March, Hayden and Davis defined their aims. They wanted peaceful, legal demonstrations during the convention. But they anticipated

police violence that would "dramatize to the world the large numbers of people who feel unrepresented, and in fact disgraced and used, by our government's policies on the crisis of Vietnam and racism and the mockery that democracy has become." Hayden hoped that demonstrators would converge on Chicago:

> The final funeral march on the Democratic Convention, beginning as the first ballot is taken, should bring a half a million people demanding a choice on the issues of peace and justice; citizens who have come to "make the democratic process work" by pinning the delegates in the International Amphitheater until a choice is presented to the American people.

MOB leaders agreed that the final march to the Amphitheater would be their central aim. But Johnson's announcement in March that he would not seek reelection put these plans on hold. The violent response of Chicago police to the ghetto riots that erupted after Martin Luther King's assassination in April also gave pause. Mayor Daley had encouraged the police to take stern measures against looters and arsonists. Observers warned that he would also be very tough on demonstrators.

Nonetheless, MOB leaders meeting in Cleveland in mid-July, decided to proceed. They appropriated money for the Chicago office and organized a legal group to help out with arrest and bail problems. Medical groups, including the Committee on Human Rights and the Student Health Organization, were asked to set up first-aid support services. MOB expected trouble.

During the summer, Davis and Hayden still hoped for official permission to march. After several fruitless phone calls and letters, they finally set a meeting with city officials in early August. When the officials stalled on a permit, MOB pressed for a court injunction. But the judge ruled on August 21 that the city was not obligated to issue a permit. The city did make one counteroffer—a location for a march at least 10 miles from the Amphitheater and well away from the business heart of the city. MOB refused this. Finally, during the convention, the city did issue one permit—for the afternoon rally at Grant Park bandshell on August 28.

Quite clearly, the city intended to frighten protesters from coming to the convention by making marches and demonstrations illegal. In part, they succeeded. Chicago officials put MOB leaders in an awkward position. By planning illegal demonstrations, were they not inciting to riot? On the other hand, did they not have a duty to exercise their right to assembly and free speech? The MOB leadership chose to proceed, believing that if violence occurred, it would be initiated by the police. This in turn would discredit the Democratic party and the presidential nominee. David Dellinger promised: "We are not going to storm the convention with tanks or mace. But we are going to storm the hearts and minds of the American people."

Other protest groups decided to come to Chicago during the convention, but they played a minor role. The Black Panthers did not officially join the demonstrations, but their representatives sometimes spoke at meetings. The Panthers, founded in Oakland, California, in 1966 by Huey Newton and

**TOM HAYDEN**

Shortly after the Chicago demonstrations, organizer Tom Hayden was called to testify before the House Un-American Activities Committee. In 1969, he and other organizers of the convention demonstrations were tried for inciting to riot. *(UPI)*

Bobby Seale, were a black power group that advocated self-defense and political coalition with white radicals. Shadowed closely by police agents, Panther leader Seale spoke in Chicago, but the organization generally kept in the background. The black leader who participated most actively in the demonstrations was comedian and civil rights advocate Dick Gregory.

Chicago also attracted large numbers of young McCarthy supporters, who came to demonstrate for their candidate. Originally, they did not intend to join the Yippies or MOB, but many of them crossed over to the radical lines after the first bloody encounters with police. And finally, Chicago drew several literary celebrities, including novelists Norman Mailer, Terry Southern, William Burroughs, poet Allen Ginsberg, and French playwright Jean Genêt.

## "CHICAGO: CITY OF MUSCLE, IN INDUSTRY AND POLITICS" *(New York Times)*

The Democratic party chose Chicago as a convention site partly because of the tough reputation of Mayor Richard J. Daley. Daley was one of the last, old-time city political bosses. He ran Chicago as his own personal fiefdom. Labor unions, the police, and city employees all marched to his tune. If anyone could maintain an orderly city and keep control over local arrangements, Daley seemed the one.

With a firm hand on the convention site in Chicago, the Democratic party was ruled by another firm hand in Washington. Johnson's power in the party remained strong, and he was determined to prevent the convention from adopting either a platform or a candidate that questioned American participation in the war in Vietnam. Thus Johnson prevented Humphrey from accommodating the antiwar forces in the party. He made sure that the credentials committee did not lean toward antiwar delegates in deciding disputed seats. He also insisted that the platform committee write a prowar plank. All of these moves were successful, but they stripped Humphrey of power and a separate identity. In fact, Humphrey had so little influence that when he wrote to ask Daley to grant parade permits to demonstrators, his request went unanswered.

From the beginning, Mayor Daley and his police advisers prepared for a confrontation. They took Yippie "predictions" seriously. In January, the city established a joint planning command with the police department, the mayor's office, the fire department, the U.S. Secret Service, and military intelligence. This committee met every two weeks until August, when it stepped up the tempo of its conferences. One function of the committee was assessment of intelligence gathered by agents assigned to infiltrate MOB and Yippie meetings or taken from publications in the underground press. The committee paid special attention to possible participation by Chicago's black citizens. After the violent riots in April, Daley feared renewed outbreaks. Should white radicals enlist support from the black ghetto, the mayor feared he might not be able to control the city.

Daley concentrated his antiriot efforts through the police task force, which in April had been the backbone of the crackdown on demonstrations and riots in the ghetto. This agency borrowed a large tear gas dispenser from the U.S. Army, which it mounted on a city sanitation truck. And it organized police helicopter surveillance of routes leading to the convention center.

Squads of police were assigned to the two major city parks: Lincoln Park on the north side, which became the demonstrators' headquarters, and Grant Park, across from Michigan Avenue and the railroad tracks, facing the Hilton Hotel. All leave was canceled for the period, and twelve-hour shifts were instituted. The fire department was put on special alert. Police officials also issued special riot equipment to officers: nightsticks, helmets, service revolvers, and disabling mace spray. A number of officers, on their own, purchased plastic face shields to attach inside their helmets. Instructions issued to officers stressed the need to maintain calm, especially while making mass arrests:

> Mass arrests made by police in a helter-skelter manner will serve absolutely no purpose as far as maintaining law and order is concerned. However, arrests made in an orderly and well-planned manner indicate a trained force prepared for such emergencies and will help convey to the demonstrators and the rest of the city that they are dealing with a superior force.

Mayor Daley also asked for support from the Illinois National Guard. Following several weeks of negotiations with the guard, the governor's office, and the U.S. Fifth Army, the governor announced that the guard would be activated. Approximately 5,000 guardsmen were stationed in armories around Chicago by August 23. In addition, 6,000 federal riot-control troops were brought to the city (250 U.S. Air Force C-141 jet cargo planes were assembled to ferry the troops). With about 11,000 reinforcements, Daley and his police force probably outnumbered the demonstrators who planned to come to Chicago.

Security around and inside the convention hall was tight. Barricades prevented any unauthorized persons from approaching the entrance. Police assigned to the inside of the Amphitheater were supplemented by Andy Frain, Inc., ushers generally on duty during Cubs baseball games at Wrigley Field. Entrance would be by ticket only, and delegates would receive new tickets each day. Any delegate or any newspaper or television reporter without proper identification would be removed from the floor or the galleries of the hall.

Mayor Daley also increased security around the city's water system in view of the Yippies' warning that they might dump LSD into the reservoirs. Special police were assigned to the two main pumping stations. Elements of the canine section of the task force guarded filtration plants.

Mayor Daley apparently took one further step to control the protest. An International Brotherhood of Electrical Workers strike, begun prior to the convention, remained unsettled. (It was settled immediately after the convention ended.) Daley intervened enough to ensure that live television coverage would come from the convention itself. But networks were not allowed to set up live coverage facilities around possible demonstration focal points. They could still film, but the film had to be carried to network facilities at the Amphitheater for processing. A story in *Television Digest* on August 26 explained the problem:

> Networks encountered several new labor disputes last week and were told by Chicago police they couldn't park videotape vans on streets outside major hotels. They also are prohibited from locating cameras outside hotels or in windows overlooking streets.
>
> New difficulties brought back into prominence earlier charges that Democrats were deliberately attempting to curb TV live coverage outside Convention Hall. CBS News President Richard Salant saw difficulties as part of "a pattern well beyond simple labor disputes, logistics, and security problems."

The news media also made special preparations for the convention, partly because of these obstacles. Besides the large contingent of reporters and cameramen assigned to the Amphitheater, the major networks, news services, and newspapers like the *New York Times* assigned about 300 reporters and cameramen to follow the demonstrators. Each major news service was handed a special introduction to Chicago published by the police department. It opened: "Welcome, Newsmen! Welcome to Chicago, the City of 'The Front Page,' with an outstanding tradition of competitive journalism. Another tradition has been the excellent rapport between the Chicago police and newsmen." The news services, however, did not anticipate excellent rapport. In fact, they prepared for the worst. The *Washington Post,* for example, issued the following warning in its list of instructions:

> *Tear Gas Protection.* Reporters traveling in areas that have been heavily gassed have encountered significant problems. Each of the cars is now being equipped (in the trunk) with small containers of oxygen, and with watersoaked cloths. The cloths, enclosed in plastic bags, should be used to sponge out eyes and remove the gas from the skin. An additional small supply of oxygen containers will be kept in the radio room cabinet. This style of tear gas protection was decided upon since the Army-type of gas masks would tend to make reporters targets, and are quite uncomfortable to users who are not accustomed to their use.

## "IN THE HALL: BLACK CREPE AND ANGER IN THE STREETS: TEAR GAS AND CLUBS"
*(Washington Post)*

Despite the overwhelming force of the city and its troop reinforcements, and with the press anticipating trouble, the Yippies and the MOB leadership refused to retreat. The city's unwillingness to grant a march permit anywhere near the Amphitheater or to allow demonstrations, plus police refusal to allow anyone to sleep in the parks, meant that almost any action was, by definition, illegal. Thus in the tightly surveyed and tense city, the very act of political protest threatened to become a confrontation.

Neither the MOB nor the Yippie leadership (even if they desired it) had much control over the thousands of young people who began to assemble in the city over the weekend of August 24. MOB did train several hundred

DEMONSTRATORS AND THE ILLINOIS NATIONAL GUARD

During the Democratic Convention, Chicago city police were supplemented by 5,000 National Guardsmen activated by the governor of Illinois. Scenes such as these persuaded many observers that the war in Vietnam was tearing apart American society. (©1969 Roger Malloch/Magnum)

marshals to control crowds during marches, but they proved totally ineffective in the chaotic conditions of police confrontation. Communications between leaders and followers were spotty and often tardy, carried by word of mouth or by fliers pasted to walls. Moreover, the two principal wings of the protest, MOB and the Yippies, had different aims. MOB had a more traditional belief in the effectiveness of demonstrations and protests, hoping to attract attention to their message of opposition to the war. The Yippies also opposed the war, but their vehicle for protest was any public event that brought attention—by shock, anger, or amusement. Under such circumstances, the initiative belonged to the police. They determined the nature and extent of the pitched battles that followed.

The police had the further advantage of an informer close to Jerry Rubin. Posing as a member of the motorcycle gang the Headhunters, Robert L. Pierson, a private investigator employed by the Chicago Police Department, met with Rubin and Hoffman and secretly relayed information about demonstration plans back to police headquarters. In order to convince the Yippies of his loyalty, Pierson had to be active in the demonstrations. As one newsman reported:

> One such hell-raiser—Robert L. Pierson—has indiscreetly told the *Chicago Tribune* (as published August 31) how he gained Rubin's confidence and, to confirm his credentials, threw rocks and bottles, hurled epithets at the police and even participated actively in lowering the American flag and raising a red flag in Grant Park—an action that touched off a police assault.

Those demonstrators who were prepared to brave what they realized could be physical danger headed for Lincoln Park, about 2 miles from the city's center. There, in a large area that separated Lake Michigan from "Old Town"—Chicago's bohemian center—the Yippies set up their headquarters. Many of the demonstrators planned to take advantage of housing offered by nearby residents, but others brought sleeping bags to spend the night in the park.

At about the same time, delegates began to stream into town and fill the hotels in downtown Chicago. The media set up to report on two simultaneous events: the opening of the convention and the first confrontations between police and demonstrators. The two stories became point and counterpoint in the nomination process. As Humphrey's nomination moved inexorably forward, it was increasingly punctuated by events outside the Amphitheater, by the growing tension and violence between police and demonstrators.

Yippie and MOB strategists hoped to keep media attention focused on their protests, and to build support and momentum for the large (illegal) march on the convention center Wednesday evening, the time of the nomination vote. During the weekend and first two days of the convention, television and newspapers were filled with pictures of Yippies—camping in the parks, holding rock concerts and news conferences, practicing *washoi* (linked-arm marching tactics borrowed from Japanese radicals)—and of Allen Ginsberg chanting Indian mantras. On Tuesday, they reported the mock "unbirthday" party for Lyndon Johnson, featuring music by the Holocaust No-Dance Band, songs by Phil Ochs, and speeches by writers opposed to the war.

Yet the high jinks of the Yippies were gradually overshadowed by the violence that occurred nightly in a battle for the parks. Each night, as police swept through Lincoln Park, spraying tear gas and exploding smoke bombs, the atmosphere became more ominous. Demonstrators increasingly fought back and, when forced out of the park, continued their harassment of police from nearby streets. More and more, the police struck and arrested first, and asked questions second. And increasingly, reporters and newsmen were caught in the middle and then on the side of the demonstrators. By Tuesday, many of the reporters and their parent news services were convinced that they were watching a police force riot out of control.

The convention floor was also a battlefield of sorts. Dissenters and antiwar delegates faced the same unfavorable odds. The convention's rules and credentials committees, which had convened a week earlier, evidenced the first sharp encounters. Antiwar delegates pledged to McCarthy challenged Humphrey's forces in an effort to demonstrate that the convention was boss-ridden. They were only partly successful. Surprisingly, Humphrey delegates joined to push through several dramatic changes in the rules relating to Democratic party conventions. They agreed to abolish the unit rule, whereby a state could require all its votes to be cast for the same candidate. And they voted to ask the convention to reexamine its manner of selecting delegates. A Reform Commission was chosen to suggest how these changes might be implemented. But of course, these reforms would not apply to the 1968 convention.

On the question of the platform, however, Humphrey's forces were unbending. They wrote a plank praising Lyndon Johnson's conduct of the war. The minority of the platform committee that wanted to commit the party to a quick end to the war vowed to carry their fight to the convention floor.

## "CHICAGO NOTEBOOK: TERROR IN THE STREETS BILLY CLUBS AND BLOOD IN A NO-MAN'S LAND"
*(Seattle Times)*

On Wednesday, although the convention had not yet nominated a presidential candidate, one outcome of the contest had already been decided. As predicted, Yippie tactics had brought enormous publicity. Action shots, music, wild dress, and extravagant statements were far more interesting than the droning speeches inside the convention. None of this theater of the absurd, however, blunted the point of the demonstrators: They were there to protest the continuing war—and the police were determined to stop them.

As police violence mounted, the nation watched in horror. Newsmen and television commentators increasingly sided with the students. Their photographs and newsclips showed police beating protesters. And police attacks on newsmen only increased the public's partiality. By Tuesday night, protests from major news organizations like CBS began to pour into Chicago city headquarters, demanding that Mayor Daley control the police. Even several Chicago aldermen, usually quiet on such matters, denounced police brutality. As Frank Sullivan, press officer of the Chicago police bitterly put it: "[the demonstrators] are a pitiful handful. They have almost no support. But, by golly, they get the cooperation of the news media."

On Wednesday, the spirit of confrontation even entered the Amphitheater. For a brief time, the convention itself was threatened. As the press increasingly criticized Mayor Daley, he and his aides packed the spectator section of the hall with city workers who waved American flags and signs supporting Daley. On the floor, with the Illinois delegation, Daley watched the proceedings in sullen silence. Late in the afternoon, the convention began debate on the majority (Humphrey) and minority (McCarthy) Vietnam planks. The peace delegates fervently cheered speakers who called for a speedy, negotiated end to the war. But Humphrey's forces were too numerous. When the votes were tallied, the Humphrey-Johnson position on Vietnam had won: 1,567¾ to 1,041¼. The Democratic party was now pledged to support President Johnson's position on the war. This accomplished, the convention adjourned until evening. But many of the delegates remained in their seats. New Yorkers broke into peace songs. The convention band, in reply, blared out the tune "This Will Be the Start of Something Big." Several California delegates moved over to the New York standard and joined in the singing. The band retorted with "California Here I Come" and "Happy Days Are Here Again." Strains of music overlaid shouts of "Stop the war!" as the last stragglers filed off the floor.

At about this time, the Grant Park bandshell demonstration broke up and

David Dellinger tried to lead protesters out of the park. He and other leaders,
however, lost all control when the crowd discovered the unguarded northern
bridge, swarmed over to Michigan Avenue and then ran down the avenue
toward the Conrad Hilton. Now about 3,000 strong, the crowd approached
a police line across Michigan Avenue at East Balboa Drive, blocking their
route. Another police line stretched west of the Hilton on Wabash Avenue.
Guardsmen, newspeople, and television trucks waited in front of the hotel.

When they encountered the police line on Michigan Avenue, several demonstrators began shouting and chanting slogans and insults. Blue-helmeted
officers repeatedly ordered the crowd to leave the street. A few demonstrators
tried to flank police lines by heading west and then south toward the Amphitheater. Most were turned back after brief, violent scuffles. They rejoined
the growing crowd blocked on Michigan Avenue.

Then, at about 7:30, a small contingent of black demonstrators following
a mule train, tried to make its way through the crowd south on Michigan
Avenue and past the Hilton. To do so it had to pass through the demonstrators
and the police lines. This group, led by the Reverend Ralph Abernathy of the
Southern Christian Leadership Conference and including old people and children, had a legal permit to march. A police wedge allowed them through and
they continued south on Michigan and then west away from the hotel.

By this time, the corner of Balboa and Michigan had become an undulating
mass of confusion. Segments of the crowd tried to push forward, shouting
"Pig!" at the police who blocked them. Others tried to sneak through police
lines behind the SCLC demonstrators. The protesters were determined to

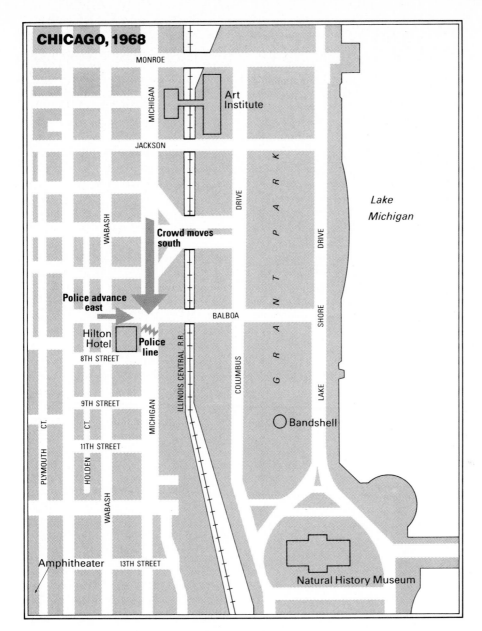

**CHICAGO, 1968**

MONROE

MICHIGAN

Art
Institute

JACKSON

DRIVE

WABASH

**Crowd moves
south**

Lake
Michigan

DRIVE

G R A N T   P A R K

BALBOA

**Police advance
east**

SHORE

Hilton
Hotel

**Police
line**

8TH STREET

COLUMBUS

ILLINOIS CENTRAL R.R.

MICHIGAN

LAKE

9TH STREET

PLYMOUTH CT.

HOLDEN CT.

11TH STREET

○ Bandshell

WABASH

Amphitheater    13TH STREET

Natural History Museum

continue their march toward the Amphitheater. And the police were determined to stop them. Where the two groups butted against each other, violent
incidents flared. In the twilight, police and television floodlights gave the
scene an eerie and ominous quality.

Police again tried to warn the crowd to leave Michigan Avenue. But in
response, a large number of young people sat down in the street. Another
group split off and headed west on Balboa until they ran into an advancing

phalanx of officers with clubs in their hands. The protesters retreated, shouting epithets and throwing rocks and bottles. Police guarding the front of the Hilton were struck by objects hurled down from the front windows of the hotel.

At about 7:57, police advancing along Balboa neared the main body of demonstrators on Michigan Avenue. Suddenly they charged into the crowd, trying to clear the street and grabbing at random to make arrests. Nightsticks flying, they trapped a mass of demonstrators that was so large and hemmed in, it couldn't move. Part of it pressed up against the police line on Michigan Avenue, and these officers, too, began to swing their clubs. Rocks and other thrown objects thudded onto the helmets of police as they advanced.

Reporters and news cameras focused on incident after incident of brutal beatings by the police. Even the deputy superintendent of the police department rushed into the crowd to stop his officers from their attacks. One witness testifying at later hearings on police violence reported a typical beating by police:

> When they caught him, they began to beat him with their nightsticks until he fell to the pavement. They continued to beat him briefly after he fell. Then they dragged him about 30 feet to a paddy wagon.

As the police drove demonstrators back up Michigan Avenue, away from the hotel, a group numbering about 200 pushed through police lines and raced toward the entrance of the Conrad Hilton. Officers attacked the edges of this group using mace spray. They pushed the bulk of the group up against the hotel and the plate-glass windows of its Haymarket Lounge. Suddenly a shattering noise burst above the roar of the crowd. The large window had crashed inward under the pressure, sending several demonstrators sprawling into the lounge among the shards of glass. A squad of police lunged into the bar after them, beating fallen victims and anyone else who looked like a protester.

Outside, the riot continued. The bulk of the crowd, now massed along the side of the avenue on a small strip of park facing the Hilton began to chant: "The whole world is watching!" Indeed it was. Spotlights poured onto the crowd, and television cameras picked out the bloodied, angry, sobbing faces.

Police reinforcements continued to pour in, and they gradually cleared the intersection, arresting anyone who dared enter it. Several units of the Illinois National Guard moved up from the south on Michigan Avenue toward the hotel. Here and there, police struck or arrested a demonstrator, but the battle had ended. Nevertheless, a crowd of about 5,000 remained facing the Hilton, while the police and National Guard occupied the streets.

Back in the Amphitheater, the delegates had reconvened at 6:30 to complete the final business of the convention—nomination of the presidential candidate. The nomination speeches proceeded slowly, and as they did, the

THE BATTLE FOR
MICHIGAN AVENUE

During the short, violent
confrontation in front of
the Conrad Hilton Hotel
on August 28, 1968, en-
raged police charged into
crowds of demonstrators.
The major casualty, how-
ever, was Hubert Hum-
phrey, whose nomination
was associated with vio-
lence and riot. *(UPI)*

delegates gradually learned what was happening back at the Conrad Hilton. Tension inside the hall mounted rapidly. Most of the attention was riveted on Daley. As the delayed films from the riot on Michigan Avenue arrived at CBS headquarters, the director of news gave the go-ahead for a live interview with the mayor. As Daley sat whispering and nodding to the Illinois delegates around him, CBS news intercut scenes of police beating demonstrators and dragging off newsmen for arrest. Then the interview began:

> Dan Rather, standing next to where Daley was sitting, leaned down to talk to him. From the floor Rather wasn't seeing any of the taped material from downtown, of course.
> "Mayor? Sir? Mayor Daley, Walter Cronkite is reporting downtown the police have used tear gas and there is considerable turmoil around the Hilton Hotel."

Daley remained placid. He assured Rather that the police had complete control of the situation. But television viewers at home saw dizzying pictures of soldiers in riot gear, bayonets fixed, advancing on demonstrators; of gas bombs exploding; of Chicago police rushing after protesters, beating them.

During a seconding speech for Humphrey, a Colorado delegate interrupted the proceedings and shouted: "Is there any rule under which Mayor Daley can be compelled to end the police state of terror being perpetrated?" The mayor sat immobile. Then when Abraham Ribicoff, senator from Connecticut and an old Humphrey friend, was placing Senator George McGovern's name in nomination, he abruptly departed from his text. With McGovern as president, he declared, "we would not have these Gestapo tactics in the streets of Chicago!" Mayor Daley leapt from his seat, joined by friends and supporters, cursing and shouting at Ribicoff.

With order restored, the nomination process continued, and Humphrey edged toward victory. At about 11:30 his vote total passed into a majority. Watching back at his headquarters in the Conrad Hilton, the new candidate was surrounded by well-wishers and congratulations. He rushed over to the television set and threw his arms around the screen.

If anything, however, Humphrey had embraced his worst enemy. Television was part of his undoing in the election that followed. Scenes from the riot in front of his hotel had been continuously intercut into live television broadcasting from the convention. Thus the violence, which had ended about 9:00 P.M., seemed to punctuate the whole long process of nomination. There was no way that the new candidate could undo the impression that he had been chosen in the midst of a riot and that he had silently acquiesced in the violence.

## "DEMOCRATS AWAKE TO A PARTY IN RUINS"  *(Washington Post)*

The physical devastation of that Wednesday evening battle for Chicago was serious: almost sixty policemen and many more demonstrators injured, and the Hilton Hotel reeking of gas and stinkbombs, its posh lounge closed for repairs. But the immediate political damage to Humphrey and the Democratic party was far greater. Unable or unwilling to accommodate antiwar sentiment, the convention had chosen a candidate who represented the continuation of bitterly opposed policies. Nominated in an atmosphere of violence and brutality, Humphrey could never generate enough enthusiasm to carry him to victory. Selected behind the closely guarded doors of the Amphitheater, Humphrey was defeated in Chicago's streets and in the nation's media. Much of the press and television commentary concluded that the police had rioted out of control. Despite a spirited defense of his actions and charges that "terrorists" had "set out to destroy the purpose of this national political convention," Mayor Daley was convicted in the press of inciting a riot because he would not tolerate peaceful demonstrations.

In the face of these recriminations, and Richard Nixon's close presidential victory in November, the Chicago demonstrations reverberated through the next year. In October, the House Committee on Un-American Activities convened hearings to discuss possible "connections, if any, of certain leaders of the demonstration with foreign powers." They called Hoffman, Rubin, Davis, Hayden, and Dellinger as witnesses. At the first hearing, Hoffman appeared wearing an American flag for a shirt and was promptly arrested. The committee struggled to maintain a serious atmosphere, but witnesses replied to questions with attacks on the credentials of the members. After several exasperating attempts, the committee gave up.

More ominous, in 1969 a federal grand jury indicted several of the MOB and Yippie leaders under the 1967 Federal Conspiracy Act Law, which made it illegal to cross state lines to incite to riot. The trial began in late September before Judge Julius Hoffman of the U.S. District Court in Chicago. An elderly justice with a reputation for firmness, Hoffman quickly lost both his temper and control of the courtroom. In the riotous days that followed, he delivered blistering attacks on the defense attorneys, prevented defense witnesses from appearing, and openly sided with the prosecution.

Nothing could have better suited the Yippie theatrics of Abbie Hoffman and Jerry Rubin. Once again, they won a media victory. Perhaps Judge Hoffman's worst mistake was to refuse Bobby Seale, a codefendant, the right to independent counsel. When Seale protested and disrupted the court, the judge warned that he had the power to restrain the defendant: "I don't want to do that. Under the law you may be gagged and chained to your chair." When Seale continued to object, the court bound him and refused to let him speak.

The long, ludicrous trial ended in the spring of 1970. The jury returned a guilty verdict on lesser counts than conspiracy, but the judge sentenced Rubin, Davis, Hayden, Hoffman, and Dellinger each to five years in prison. To this he added 175 contempt citations for their behavior in the courtroom. He also ordered the trial lawyers imprisoned for contempt. By piling legal outrage upon legal outrage, however, Hoffman set himself up for easy reversal. When the U.S. Court of Appeals heard the case in November 1972, it reversed the convictions and sternly rebuked Judge Hoffman and the prosecution. Later, most of the contempt charges were also rescinded. This final act of the Festival of Life thus ended with a vindication of the Yippies and a reaffirmation of the rights of protesters.

In one sense, however, the victory was a shallow one. The war in Vietnam dragged on for a further five years to its bloody and chaotic conclusion. The innocence of radical students had died in the Chicago confrontation. Small elements of SDS slipped underground and advocated violence. Other student radicals turned to heavy and fruitless theoretical debates. The thrust of the movement faltered. The Yippies also found their following confused and splintered. Some turned to drugs; others dropped out of politics entirely. Some joined exotic Eastern religions.

One almost unnoticed event of the convention suddenly loomed very large in the next few years. This was reform of the party structure. In 1969, George McGovern was appointed to chair the Democratic Party Reform Commission. His working staff of researchers and writers were young political activists and veterans of the 1968 campaign. Taking the commission across the country for hearings on ways to democratize the party, the staff interviewed representatives of local black movements and women's rights organizations. It concluded that a variety of changes were necessary to eliminate control by political bosses such as Mayor Daley.

Its most radical proposal along these lines concerned quotas—proportional representation for racial and ethnic groups and for men and women. Although the proposal finally adopted was vague, its implications were not: each state delegation to the 1972 convention must have a "proportion of women, minorities, and young people" not less than the proportion of each group in the state represented. In this way, the struggle for Chicago had ended in victory for the demonstrators. They had triumphed over the old Democratic party. Many of them were now on the inside. But the party itself had been crippled and its constituencies bitterly divided.

# The Decline
# of
# Liberalism

The young protesters who clamored to enter the Democratic party convention of 1968, those who shouted their defiance at symbols of authority, were assaulting the foundations of post-war political consensus. The target of their ire, Hubert Humphrey, the candidate nominated by the party to run against Richard Nixon, was a man of impeccable liberal credentials. His record on civil rights stretched back to the 1948 Democratic convention, when he engineered a strong plank on black rights. Throughout the 1950s and 1960s he had championed the cause of organized labor. He stood behind most of the social reforms passed by the Kennedy and Johnson administrations. Yet the Chicago protesters dismissed him with contemptuous cries of "Dump the Hump!" They demanded, instead, a very different sort of politics than that practiced by men like Humphrey.

In the eight short years between the election of John F. Kennedy and the Chicago convention, much had happened to fragment the consensus in American society and to convince a variety of interest groups to repudiate political compromise. The result by the end of the decade was growing acrimony, confrontation, and violence. In 1968, it appeared as if the political center could no longer hold and that politics would splinter into competing ideological groups.

To some extent, the break-up of the liberal coalition of the 1960s occurred because of the rising and unfulfilled expectations of social reform, and the unfulfillable aims and rising costs of the war in Vietnam. The promises of the civil rights movement foundered on white resistance and splits in the black movement. Reformers and elected officials promised more than they could deliver. And from the beginning of the Kennedy administration, through the five years of Johnson's presidency, the war in Vietnam was a constant drumbeat. At first only audible as a kind of background noise, the war eventually drowned out the voices still calling for social reform. By 1968, opposition to the war in Vietnam had all but consumed the impulse to reform, as the war frustrated the expectations aroused in the early years of the decade.

The march on Washington of 1963 represented the high point of optimism that the ideals of King and the practical political sense of Kennedy could be intertwined to achieve major civil rights legislation. It was not optimism, however, but violence and tragedy that eventually persuaded Congress to pass the Civil Rights Act as well as Kennedy's other reform projects.

Late in the fall of 1963, most of the president's program was stalled in Congress. The Civil Rights Act, toughened and amended, languished despite Kennedy's support. The centerpiece of his economic program, an extensive tax cut designed to stimulate production and jobs, remained unpassed. Work had begun in earnest to develop a program to fight large poverty pockets in rural states and urban areas, but hopes of passage of such a program were not bright.

Partly as an effort to win support for his faltering legislation, partly to shore up his presidency for the election one year away, Kennedy embarked on a speaking tour in late November. One of his stops was Dallas, Texas, a center of opposition to his programs. On November 22, Kennedy rode through the center of the city in an open car. Suddenly, shots rang out and the president slumped forward. Two bullets had shattered his skull and throat. John Connolly, governor of Texas, who was sitting in front of Kennedy, was also wounded. The driver of the car sped to a nearby hospital, but the president's wounds were fatal. His administration had begun in a burst of enthusiasm and media attention. Now millions of Americans watched on television the last scenes of its tragic ending—the murder of the accused assassin, Lee Harvey Oswald, and then the Kennedy funeral.

# JOHNSON'S FIRST ADMINISTRATION

It was Lyndon Baines Johnson's genius to turn this tragic moment into triumph. Assuming the presidency, Johnson stood back from the rituals of bereavement, acting to consolidate his power. In some ways this was a difficult task, for Johnson represented a different constituency of the Democratic party. He was a Texan, boisterous and crude in manner. He had mastered the clubroom politics of the U.S. Senate, which had brought him enormous legislative influence during the late 1950s. But most of the Kennedy entourage of advisers and cabinet officers considered him an outsider. Now, suddenly, he was president.

On the other hand, Johnson believed even more strongly than Kennedy had in the power and duty of the federal government to guarantee the rights of marginal or poor citizens. Seizing the stalled legislative program of the Kennedy administration, Johnson vowed to win its passage as a memorial to the slain leader and, perhaps, as testimony to his own right to the presidency. But there was an irony to this. Johnson succeeded in

pressing reform legislation through Congress that dwarfed Kennedy's accomplishments. Yet he could never elicit the enthusiasm that his predecessor did. His legislative triumphs more than fulfilled the New Frontier promised by Kennedy, but he could never win the adulation that Kennedy had inspired.

Johnson grasped the wheel of government firmly. Five days after the assassination he addressed Congress, pledging to continue the policies of Kennedy. By early 1964 his efforts bore fruit. Congress enacted bill after bill: a major tax cut to stimulate the economy; the Economic Opportunity Act, setting up the structure for a "war on poverty"; and, most significantly, a major civil rights act. To push civil rights legislation through Congress meant overcoming strong Southern opposition. Johnson built a majority by calling in debts owed him by other senators. Particularly important was the Republican support he gathered. Convincing the Republican leaders—Everett Dirksen of the Senate and Charles Halleck of the House—ensured victory.

Johnson also did what neither Eisenhower nor Kennedy had done: he adopted the language of

**THREE DEMOCRATS**

In the early 1960s, John F. Kennedy (left), Eleanor Roosevelt, and Lyndon Baines Johnson represented three versions of Democratic party liberalism and the continuity between the New Deal of the 1930s and the pragmatic liberalism of the 1960s. *(Library of Congress)*

## COMPARISON OF WHITE AND BLACK FAMILY INCOME (in constant 1975 dollars)

|      | *White Families* | *Black Families* | *Ratio* |
|------|------------------|------------------|---------|
| 1950 | $7,702           | $4,178           | .54     |
| 1955 | 9,271            | 5,113            | .55     |
| 1960 | 10,604           | 5,871            | .55     |
| 1965 | 12,370           | 6,812            | .55     |
| 1970 | 14,188           | 9,032            | .64     |
| 1975 | 14,268           | 9,321            | .65     |
| 1980 | 20,502           | 12,380           | .60     |

Source: U.S. Department of Commerce, Bureau of the Census, *Statistical Abstract of the United States, 1981* (Washington, D.C.: Government Printing Office, 1981), p. 436.

## THE WAR ON POVERTY: EDUCATION, EMPLOYMENT, AND TRAINING FUNDS, 1960–1980

|                                | *1960* | *1965* | *1970* | *1975* | *1980* |
|--------------------------------|--------|--------|--------|--------|--------|
| Percentage of federal budget   | 1.1    | 1.8    | 4.4    | 4.9    | 5.3    |
| Amount (in billions of dollars)| 1.0    | 2.1    | 8.6    | 15.9   | 30.8   |

Source: U.S. Department of Commerce, Bureau of the Census, *Statistical Abstract of the United States, 1981* (Washington, D.C.: Government Printing Office, 1981) p. 248.

the civil rights movement. On March 15, he appeared before Congress to speak for civil rights. The United States, he demanded, must "overcome the crippling legacy of bigotry and injustice." Delay, hesitation, and compromise were intolerable. Then he paused and repeated slowly and deliberately the most important slogan of the civil rights movement: "And . . . we . . . shall . . . overcome."

The new civil rights act did not end discrimination, but it strengthened voting rights, outlawed segregation in public facilities, increased federal capacity to enter desegregation cases, and bolstered the Civil Rights Commission. When the new tax-cut legislation passed, it worked as anticipated. Economic growth rates increased rapidly in 1964, 1965, and 1966. Unemployment shrank, and the federal budget hovered almost in balance. This economic growth, in turn, helped improve the ratio of black to white family income from .55 in 1960 to .64 in 1970.

The Office of Economic Opportunity (OEO) was largely Johnson's project. The Economic Opportunity Act of 1964 centralized federal antipoverty activities into one comprehensive executive agency. Under its various entitlements, it created a job training corps (called VISTA), agricultural loan programs, incentive loans to hire the hard-core unemployed, and educational benefits, plus later programs such as Head Start and Upward Bound. While some of this amounted to sleight-of-hand transfers of existing programs to a new agency, a substantial portion of the OEO represented an innovative, broad-scale attack on poverty.

By mid-1964, Johnson had clearly established legitimate claims to the office of president. His renomination was assured. The only question was a running mate. The Democratic convention, meeting in Atlantic City, New Jersey, in August, chose liberal senator Hubert Humphrey of Minnesota. Campaign strategy centered on defending Johnson's legislative record and turning the conservative Republican opponent, Barry Goldwater of Arizona, into an issue.

Goldwater attacked the Johnson administration on domestic and foreign policy. Goldwater's grass-roots campaign in the Republican party represented a temporary triumph over political professionals. He aroused considerable enthusiasm among voters who opposed Johnson's use of the federal government to redress social and economic inequalities. Much of his support was concentrated in the rapidly growing Sunbelt areas of the South and Southwest, where opposition to integration was strongest and where economic growth made social programs seem less necessary.

In some ways, the Goldwater movement was premature. His campaign was troubled by public distrust of some of his right-wing supporters. And he did not completely capitalize on growing hostility to civil rights demonstrations and liberal legislation. Governor George Wallace of Alabama had demonstrated the significance of this backlash vote in primary elections in Wisconsin, Maryland, and Indiana. But Goldwater could not build a movement strong enough to block the Johnson landslide.

One relatively unimportant campaign issue was the war in Vietnam. During his year in office, Johnson proceeded cautiously, without calling attention to the implications of his actions, but he moved the United States toward far greater involvement in the war. Early in 1964, he made several important decisions. He approved plans for covert harassment of North Vietnam, and he agreed to bombing missions against the North in the event of provocation. He also appointed General William Westmoreland to head military operations. These moves rested on two assumptions: first, that North Vietnam was responsible for and could control the insurgent Viet Cong in the South; second, that American intervention in the form of air strikes and ground troops could be decisive. Johnson and his advisers did not believe that American actions would increase the fighting in the South or cause an uncontrollable infiltration of troops and arms from the North.

The pretext for full-scale intervention came in late July 1964. On July 30, South Vietnamese P.T. boats attacked bases in the Gulf of Tonkin inside North Vietnamese waters. Simultaneously, the *Maddox,* an American destroyer, steamed into the area to disrupt North Vietnamese communication facilities. On August 2, possibly seeing the two separate missions as a combined maneuver against them, North Vietnam sent out several P.T. boats to attack the destroyer. The *Maddox* fired, sinking one of the attackers, then radioed the news to Washington. Johnson ordered another ship into the bay. On August 3, both destroyers reported another attack—although somewhat later, the commander of the *Maddox* radioed that he was not sure. Nonetheless, the president ordered American planes to retaliate.

Johnson then sought congressional support and justification for his action. He quickly received it. Senator William Fulbright guided a resolution through his Foreign Relations Committee and then through the Senate in less than a week. Fulbright's reason was perhaps related to his fear that Barry Goldwater might use the Vietnam issue in the forthcoming election. Neither he nor anyone else in the Senate had been told all the facts about the Gulf of Tonkin skirmish, and later critics would question whether or not an attack had actually occurred.

In his first years in office, Johnson prided himself on the consensus he had achieved in domestic and foreign affairs. In dealing with Vietnam he appeared to be a moderate. And in some respects he was. But he locked himself in by three assumptions that gradually convinced him to commit more men and more resources to the Indochina war. The first of these beliefs was the "domino theory," propounded by Eisenhower

## AMERICANS AT WAR

## The War in Vietnam

The war for Vietnam began in 1945, at the end of Japanese occupation, and terminated in 1975, when North Vietnamese and Viet Cong soldiers marched into Saigon, thus putting an end to the last American-supported government. This thirty-year struggle by communist-led forces, sought to eliminate first French and then American influence in Vietnam. Essentially a civil war, it was complicated by French colonialism, by international agreements, by encouragement and aid from outside nations, and by a massive effort of the United States to thwart the success of the communists.

When the French reconquered most of their former colony of Vietnam after World War II, communist forces inspired by Ho Chi Minh began an uprising that eventually defeated the French in 1954 at the battle of Dien Bien Phu. From 1950, the United States supplied the French but refused direct intervention. During the Eisenhower administration, the president and his advisers sympathized with the French and hoped to prevent the further spread of communist influence in Asia. But Eisenhower also understood the extreme risks of involvement in another Asian war after the unpopular conflict in Korea.

Exhausted and defeated after Dien Bien Phu, the French agreed to a peace conference in Geneva, Switzerland, in July 1954. The Geneva Accords provided for French withdrawal and temporarily divided Vietnam into two administrative areas: the north, occupied by the communist Viet Minh, and the south organized by pro-French Vietnamese. Reunification elections were mandated to decide the permanent fate of the nation. The United States sent observers to the Geneva confer-

ence but did not sign the accords. In fact, the Central Intelligence Agency worked secretly to undermine the agreements, to disrupt the economy of the north and to install a pro-

THE WAR IN VIETNAM

American ruler in the south. This last goal was accomplished when Ngo Dinh Diem became prime minister of the south. Diem asked for and received advice and aid from the United States. And he refused to participate in reunification. Partly to counter this, Diem's opponents, aided by the north, turned to insurgency.

From this time onward, American financial and military support poured in as five American presidents, from Eisenhower to Ford, attempted to salvage American interests in the area. For the United States, however, intervention had no really distinct beginning. War was never officially declared, although the Gulf of Tonkin Resolution passed by Congress in early August 1964 authorized the president to protect American forces and interests in the area. American participation grew in small increments, sometimes openly and sometimes secretly. By 1965, there were 181,000 American troops in South Vietnam; by 1968, there were 536,000.

Like the Korean War, the war in Vietnam was fought within serious constraints. The ultimate suppliers of war materiel—the United States, the U.S.S.R., and China—were not attacked, and supply lines into Vietnam remained open on both sides for most of the war. The victory the United States sought was the permanent establishment of a Western-oriented nation in South Vietnam. But the means to achieve this were, from the beginning, controversial.

The nature of warfare in Vietnam was determined by the jungle terrain and by the sympathy of many South Vietnamese for the rebels. In the absence of fronts or battle lines, the Viet Cong (South Vietnamese rebels) and North Vietnamese troops could choose the time and place of engagement. After a battle, they could slip into dense jungles or hide among supporters in the peasantry. Their weapons were sometimes crude—they used booby traps and captured arms—but they also possessed more sophisticated Russian and Chinese equipment. The United States, adapting to jungle warfare, relied most heavily on helicopters, which gave great flexibility to troop movements. After 1964, American

### A VIETNAMESE CASUALTY

Both sides in the Vietnam War inflicted heavy casualties on innocent civilians. Photographs such as this one, featured in American newspapers and on nightly television newscasts, convinced many Americans that the fight could never be won without a savagery and brutality that they would not support. (©P. J. Griffiths/Magnum)

**AN AMERICAN SOLDIER IN VIETNAM**

The American army in Vietnam faced an enemy that melted into the South Vietnamese population. The Vietcong used ambushes, ingenious mines and booby traps to counteract the vastly superior firepower of U.S. combat troops. (*©Donald McCullin/Magnum*)

tactics focused on preventing supplies from reaching rebels in the South. Intensive bombing and defoliation with herbicides disrupted supplies, but eventually intensive bombing of North Vietnam was undertaken to cut supplies off at the source.

Given the ambiguous American goals in this enormously costly conflict, presidents Johnson and Nixon found that they faced a deeply divided public opinion. The devastation caused by bombing and combat operations persuaded a great many Vietnamese to support the rebels. Thus in the struggle for "hearts and minds," the American government found itself in a difficult situation. By 1969, American troops were being phased out of combat; and three years later, no ground troops remained. A final truce ended the war in early 1973. The United States continued restricted support for the South Vietnamese government. Nonetheless, the last American-supported government fell on April 30, 1975, when a massive assault by the North Vietnamese and Viet Cong destroyed the South Vietnamese army.

originally. This notion assumed that if South Vietnam fell to the communist-supported insurgents, other Southeast Asian nations would topple into the communist camp. The second assumption was that gradual escalation, covert action, and misinformation could hide the war from the American people and thus preserve consensus. (The war would be over before anyone realized its extent or cost.) Finally, Johnson wanted to save face. He believed that the United States could not afford to withdraw or back down without inviting a barrage of accusation that he had sold out to the communists. Having lived through one period of McCarthyism, he was determined to prevent another.

Believing the optimistic appraisals of his military advisers and the "hawks" in his administration, he gradually committed American troops

and prestige to the jungle war. He cut himself off from the "doves" (war opponents) in Congress. Planning strategy and defending his decisions against mounting public criticism became his preoccupation. By pursuing this policy, he convinced many Americans that the Democratic party had fallen to the control of a narrow group of professional politicians.

The Vietnam War was only one factor that undercut support for the liberal consensus on which Johnson depended. There were growing numbers of critics of the federal activism of the Kennedy and Johnson administrations. Opponents of integration and conservatives in general rejected the notion that government should intervene in the economic and social order to guarantee a fair distribution of opportunity and rewards. From the opposite point of view,

ROBERT F. KENNEDY

In 1964, "Bobby" Kennedy ran a successful campaign for election as a U.S. senator from New York: here, he is overwhelmed by upstate admirers. During the presidential primaries of 1968, Kennedy attracted equally enthusiastic crowds and growing support. Acceptable to some Democratic party bosses as well as much of the antiwar movement, he was, perhaps, the only candidate who might have held the party together. His assassination in June 1968 prevented this. (©Cornell Capa/Magnum)

students, the civil rights movement, the poor, and then the growing women's movement criticized the federal government for delaying social reforms.

## THE NEW RIGHT

One of the largest groups of disaffected Americans joined the "new right." Born in the troubled 1950s, this movement captured the Republican party temporarily in 1964 and exercised a strong influence on the direction of the party thereafter. It originated in dissatisfaction with the Eisenhower administration and, in particular, with the Warren Court decisions that liberalized American society. Besides *Brown* v. *Board of Education,* the Warren Court in *Watkins* v. *United States* (1957)

upheld the rights of witnesses testifying before a congressional committee. In effect, this decision made it harder for future McCarthy-like hearings. Another decision, *Reynolds* v. *Sims* (1964), ruled that state legislative districts had to be apportioned evenly according to population. This decision deprived rural (and generally conservative) areas of much of the political power they had exercised in state government. A later case, *Miranda* v. *State of Arizona* (1966), ruled that a person apprehended for a crime must be informed of his or her rights—including the right to remain silent—before any statement relating to the crime could become legal evidence.

These Court decisions, together with many others—on civil rights, on definitions of obscenity, on protection of free speech—greatly strengthened minority civil rights. They opened the federal courts to a wide variety of lawsuits brought by groups claiming discrimination. The Warren Court thus took the lead in expanding the rights of citizens and the power of the federal government to intervene in the lives of every American. Because of this activism, the Court also became the target of extensive and angry criticism.

The John Birch Society, founded in 1958 by candy manufacturer Robert Welch, became the most strident center of criticism of the Warren Court. Welch had been deeply disappointed by Eisenhower's refusal to undo New Deal reforms. He concluded, in fact, that the Republican party had been infiltrated by communist agents. Welch discovered support for his views across America and particularly in southern California and the nation's Eastern suburban areas. In 1960, the Birch society launched an "Impeach Earl Warren" campaign. By 1964, Birch members controlled a significant portion of the Republican party—enough to ensure the nomination of Goldwater.

A growing number of right-wing intellectuals were among those who attacked government-mandated egalitarianism. One of the most important among them was William F. Buckley, whose *National Review,* founded in 1955, became a center for opposition to the liberal postwar consensus. Other conservative forces, which were at first less clearly focused or politically motivated, centered around Protestant revivalism. The early leader of this movement was the Reverend Billy Graham. Beginning in the early 1950s, Graham led successful revival crusades in cities across the nation. Although the political message of his sermons and books was sometimes muted, he preached salvation by individual redemption, not by government regulation. He appealed to elements in society who were disturbed—or left behind—by rapid social change. Praising "rugged individualism," he criticized social legislation and labor unions while remaining silent on questions like integration. This stand captivated a strong element of white Southerners, who were most affected by the turbulence of civil rights.

In fact, the gains of civil rights caused con-

sternation among many white Americans, and not just those of the South. Repeatedly, Gallup polls in the 1950s and 1960s demonstrated America's divided conscience on this issue. Gradually, most Americans, even in the South, accepted the goal of integration. But most at the same time feared the means used to accomplish it, such as marches and demonstrations.

Some of the opposition to integration rallied to Governor George Wallace of Alabama. Defeated in several local showdowns with federal officials over Alabama's segregation policies, Wallace became a symbol of resistance to federal

WALLACE SUPPORTERS, LANSING, MICHIGAN

Confusion in the Democratic party and the moderate line taken by Republican candidate Richard Nixon in 1968 bolstered third-party presidential hopeful George Wallace of Alabama. Wallace gained support from disgruntled conservatives frustrated with the limited war policy in Vietnam, demonstrations, and racial integration. *(©Kubota/Magnum)*

erosion of local power. In 1964, he found significant support as a presidential candidate inside the Democratic party, although not enough to win the nomination. In 1968, he ran for president on the ticket of the American Independent party and won about 13 percent of the popular vote, coming close to forcing the election into the House of Representatives. He campaigned on a platform calling for "law and order"—the suppression of urban rioting and protest marches against the war in Vietnam.

## SPLINTERING OF THE LEFT

The most important element to break away from the liberal consensus was the civil rights movement. In some respects, this break was only partial. Organizations such as the NAACP and the Urban League continued to work closely with the Democratic party and the federal government. Black voters repeatedly demonstrated their allegiance to Democratic candidates. Congress and the courts still played a major role in enforcing and extending the rights of minorities. But what Martin Luther King, Jr., had feared might happen did occur after the summer of 1963 and the passage of the 1964 Civil Rights Act. Despite the progress in legal rights, the plight of many black Americans remained little changed. Integration proceeded slowly; job opportunities especially remained scarce. In order to gain support, the civil rights movement had aroused the expectations of every black American. Inevitably these expectations were frustrated.

Lack of visible progress toward either racial equality or improved living standards became apparent in Northern cities during the mid-1960s. Fed by rapid population increases from the rural South during and after World War II, the black population in Northeastern cities more than doubled between 1950 and 1970 while the white population actually fell in the same areas. Consequently, urban tax bases eroded, and city social services were overburdened. At the same time, discrimination in hiring, poor schools, and in-

adequate training kept much of the black population unemployed or underemployed. The network of federal social services could not fill every gap. Inflamed by incautious police enforcement and violent incidents, urban ghettos exploded into rioting in the summers of 1964–1967 and particularly 1968.

Increasing violence precipitated a split in the unwieldy civil rights movement that Martin Luther King, Jr., had tried to guide. The black community had never been entirely unified. Enormous regional and class gulfs split the black population. Generational differences divided leadership. Gradually, a gulf widened between proponents of alliances with white liberals and the federal government and advocates of all-black organizations. The charismatic Black Muslim leader Malcolm X, for example, preached a separatism that appealed to many urban blacks. Although Malcolm X was assassinated in 1965, his position continued to attract the more radical elements of the Northern ghettos.

The first major urban riot occurred in the summer of 1964 in Harlem. Then violence exploded in the Watts section of Los Angeles the following summer. Other cities were struck in 1965, 1966, 1967, and 1968. Most of these disturbances followed the same pattern. An incident in the ghetto would bring police action. Unable to control the situation, police would call for reinforcements. Then ghetto residents would pour out of tenement buildings, attacking and looting stores, and setting fires. As the conflagration spread, snipers sometimes appeared. Police, and finally, the National Guard, would isolate a riot area, proclaim a curfew, and arrest thousands of residents. Frequently the police and guard put down riots with excessive force. During 1967, a year in which seventy cities were besieged by riots, more than eighty people died—most of them black—and thousands were arrested.

King still clung to nonviolence in the midst of this disintegration. But groups like SNCC were less cautious about condoning violence. In 1966, Stokely Carmichael, the leader of SNCC, advocated self-defense for blacks. He also popularized the phrase "black power," which implied cutting ties with white liberals and pushing for gains with exclusively black organizations.

After 1967, relations between black civil rights leaders and the administration deteriorated sharply. In the spring, Martin Luther King, Jr., broke with the president over the war in Vietnam. For the civil rights leader, this was an anguished moment. In 1965, King had briefly criticized the war; but Johnson had applied enormous pressure, and King had reversed himself. Now, however, he believed that the war could not be ignored. Its incessant funding demands had skinned the flesh from poverty programs. College deferments (primarily exercised by young white men) and the draft placed a disproportionate percentage of black soldiers on the Asian front lines. Despite the company of white radicals and black power advocates that an antiwar stance placed him in, King sharply attacked the war. The United States, he declared, was "the greatest purveyor of violence in the world today." As Carl T. Rowan, a black journalist wrote: "By urging Negroes not to respond to the draft or to fight in Vietnam, he has taken a tack that many Americans of all races consider utterly irresponsible."

The black civil rights movement endured one further, and perhaps fatal, loss in the spring of 1968. King was planning a "poor people's campaign" and demonstration in Washington to rekindle the smoldering movement. He also participated in a strike of black garbage workers in Memphis, Tennessee. The strike was a bitter one, called after two workers were accidentally killed on the job. The strikers demanded better wages and working conditions. King worked hard to prevent violence. On the evening of April 4, as he prepared to leave his Memphis motel for dinner, King stepped out on the balcony for a moment to speak to his driver below. A rifle cracked and King fell, mortally wounded from a bullet that struck him in the neck.

The news of King's death blew through the ghettos of American cities like a ravaging wind. Riots erupted in over 100 cities. Buildings burned, businesses were looted. The National Guard and police once more moved in with force.

**AFTERMATH OF GHETTO RIOTS**
National Guardsmen and police restored order to America's urban black ghettos after repeated summer riots throughout the mid-1960s. In many cases, burned-out and looted stores and businesses never reopened. This scene was photographed in Washington, D.C., following riots triggered by the assassination of Martin Luther King, Jr., in April 1968. (©*Burt Glinn/Magnum*)

Mayor Daley of Chicago, which suffered one of the worst riots, spoke of a need to "shoot to maim or cripple" looters if riots broke out again. When the soldiers and police finally withdrew, the civil rights movement, and much of the sympathy it had engendered, had been gutted.

## STUDENT RADICALS

King and other black civil rights leaders had, by their example, inspired the country's student radicals. Young white Americans were also among the most enthusiastic supporters of President John

Kennedy. His New Frontier appealed to a generation that rejected the secure and smug middle-class world they associated with their parents and the suburbs where they lived. Kennedy's inaugural address in early 1961 struck a responsive chord. The new president dedicated his administration to reviving America's traditional mission in the world: the protection and extension of political freedom. To the "tempered," "disciplined," and "proud" new generation of Americans he addressed, he promised an endeavor whose glow would be a beacon for the world. He asked of others only what he required of himself: "not what America will do for you," but "what together we can do for the freedom of man." But these were words of warning as well as promise, for implicit in their fervent rhetoric of sacrifice lay the seeds of the confrontational policies that led to intervention in Cuba and escalation in Vietnam.

Such lofty goals as Kennedy articulated were inevitably compromised in the real and hard world of politics. Like civil rights advocates, with whom they shared much in common, young white Americans had rising expectations for their society. They desired not only civil rights for blacks but a much greater voice for themselves in the direction of society. Their goals consisted of a patchwork of radical reforms—of politics, of culture, of universities and schools, and of social and sexual relationships. These aims were eventually focused in two related movements: the "new left" and the "counterculture." At first, student radicals found themselves in alliance with the Kennedy and Johnson administrations. Pleased by some of the reform legislation and inspired by the stirring rhetoric, the new left and the counterculture nonetheless gradually moved away from the political center of American society. By 1968, they were in open confrontation with it.

The new left and the counterculture originated in the 1950s. The more politically minded students were profoundly dissatisfied with the politics of the Eisenhower era. The slow pace of integration, the tense stand-off between the United States and the Soviet Union, Mc-Carthyism, and widespread poverty and social discrimination inspired a group of university students in 1962 to found a new sort of political organization, the Students for a Democratic Society (SDS). Unlike the "old left," which they dismissed as ineffectual and conservative, these young student radicals wanted to break with the prevailing liberal consensus—or at least to stretch it far beyond its current dimensions. With other young radicals, Tom Hayden, a student at the University of Michigan, wrote the "Port Huron Statement"—a document that proposed a new political system of "participatory democracy" and called for an end to racial discrimination and the cold war.

By the early 1960s, SDS was only part of a larger political stirring on campuses across the country. Much of this movement took its inspiration from and some of it participated in the civil rights marches and demonstrations. Northern white students joined in picketing national corporations such as Woolworths that practiced discrimination in their Southern branches. Or they joined in freedom marches and voter registration drives in the South. Other students became politically active around opposition to the investigations of the House Un-American Activities Committee (HUAC). By 1964, the radical movement had organized on several large university campuses: Michigan, the University of Chicago, Wisconsin, and, particularly, Berkeley.

Berkeley became the center of national attention during the fall of 1964. The centerpiece of the prestigious California system of higher education, Berkeley enjoyed a reputation for liberal regulations and a distinguished faculty. But as an institution it was also large, impersonal, and bureaucratic. In 1964, the administration altered rules governing campus areas set aside for student political meetings and recruitment drives. Students reacted quickly and angrily. They organized a Free Speech movement and held large demonstrations and sit-ins. Eventually they took over administration buildings. Most of these tactics were borrowed from the civil rights movement.

Frightened by the rising anger and organization on campus, and pressured by state officials, the university called in the police. Now the students declared a general strike and shut down most of the campus. Eventually, the new restrictions were lifted. But the student movement remained strong. Indeed, Berkeley set an example for students across the country, who in turn began to protest unwanted rules and restrictions on their own campuses.

Whatever coherence the radical student movement attained depended in part on a growing network of counterculture. The counterculture was not necessarily political in orientation, but it was opposed to many of the practices of adult culture. It traced its origins to the 1950s and rock-'n'-roll music, which at first was almost entirely a teen-age phenomenon.

By the 1960s, this youth culture had spread and deepened. The anti-Establishment character of the youth rebellion became more and more explicit. The youth culture acquired advocates like writers Allen Ginsberg, Jack Kerouac, and Paul Goodman—whose book *Growing Up Absurd,* published in 1960, explored the anguish of the younger generation. Also by the 1960s, the counterculture had absorbed more sophisticated versions of rock-'n'-roll in the music of the Beatles and the protest songs of Bob Dylan. Most important, many young people had begun to experiment with drugs: marijuana, hashish, and LSD.

The young people who experimented with drugs and new sexual relationships were seeking a congenial and hospitable environment. Their life styles represented a sharp contrast to the daily grind of work shifts and overtime. So some of them "dropped out" or sought comradeship in communal living on farms or in rural areas. By the late 1960s, this emphasis on a return to nature and a rejection of modern industrial life, materialism, and artificiality had become a strong ele-

### THE BEATLES, 1965

The Beatles, four young men from Liverpool, England, became international heroes to 1960s youth. Wherever they went, the Beatles attracted huge crowds of adoring fans. Pictured here (left to right) are George Harrison, Paul McCartney, Ringo Starr and his wife Maureen, and Cynthia and John Lennon. The band broke up in 1970, and Lennon was killed in New York City, where he had taken up residence, in December 1980. *(UPI)*

**THE COUNTERCULTURE**

During the 1960s, two symbols represented the counter-culture: a "V" sign, meaning peace in Vietnam, and the word "love." Both signified the desire of many young Americans to revise the nature of sexual, social, and political relationships. (©*Burt Glinn/Magnum*)

# JOHNSON'S SECOND ADMINISTRATION

After his electoral triumph of 1964—now president in his own right—Johnson believed he had created a durable political consensus for further domestic reforms and for broader intervention in the Vietnam War. He was aware of opposition from the political right and left, but he was also sure of his mastery of government. Consequently in 1965 and 1966, he placed before Congress an astonishing program of reform legislation. And Congress passed and funded Medicare insurance for the elderly and Medicaid to provide free medical services for those unable to afford them. An important Voting Rights Act of August 1965 eliminated literacy tests and other obstacles to participation in elections by minority voters. In the same month, Johnson fulfilled Kennedy's promise to establish the Department of Housing and Urban Development (HUD). Other legislation poured out of the hopper: a Clean Air Act, highway beautification, federal funding of urban transit. Each act testified to the president's legislative skill.

Nonetheless, many of these "Great Society" programs lacked coordination or adequate funding. Legislation sometimes promised much more than it could deliver. Johnson himself seemed more interested in passing laws than in their administration. Most ominous however, was the war in Vietnam, which by 1965 and 1966 had begun to divert funds away from social programs into the bottomless pit of an Asian land war.

Although the Gulf of Tonkin Resolution gave Johnson a mandate to protect American lives and interests in Vietnam, its implications were not clear until early 1965. Then, on February 6, Viet Cong rebels attacked an American base at Pleiku. In response, the president ordered sustained bombing of the north. He also authorized search-and-destroy sorties by American troops and, by the end of the year, had approved the dispatch of nearly 180,000 American personnel to Vietnam. A stepped-up strategic enclave policy was also initiated. During the summer of 1965, the presi-

ment—not just in the counterculture but in the rest of American society as well.

By the mid-1960s, many young people had come to reject the liberal consensus of Kennedy and Johnson. They did so largely because of the war in Vietnam. Not only did war starve social programs that many young radicals supported; the war weighed heavily upon their own lives because of the draft. Many of them received deferments while in college or graduate school. But this special status, which exempted them from duty in the jungles of Asia, only increased their uneasiness with their privileged positions in society.

Increasingly, the war split America. It cut off students, the civil rights movement, and intellectuals from the established consensus. And it divided those who believed the war could not be won from those who believed it must be won at all costs. Justification for the war, however, rested on the basic assumptions of postwar American foreign policy. Thus failure either to win the battle in Asia or to convince the American public to support it wholeheartedly frayed the fabric of faith in policies that had been unchallenged for twenty years.

## PERCENT OF BLACK VOTING AGE POPULATION REGISTERED IN ELEVEN SOUTHERN STATES, 1960–1980

|      | *Total*                | *Ala.* | *Ark.* | *Fla.* | *Ga.* | *La.* | *Miss.* | *N.C.* | *S.C.* | *Ten.* | *Tx.* | *Va.* |
|------|------------------------|--------|--------|--------|-------|-------|---------|--------|--------|--------|-------|-------|
| 1960 | 29.1% (White— 61.1%)   | 13.7   | 38.0   | 39.4   | 29.3  | 31.1  | 5.2     | 39.1   | 13.7   | 59.1   | 35.5  | 23.1  |
| 1975 | 58.3% (White— 60.8%)   | 55.8   | 92.2   | 53.1   | 69.5  | 58.8  | 60.7    | 49.2   | 44.0   | 64.2   | 61.9  | 49.8  |
| 1980 | 57.7% (White— 79.4%)   | 57.5   | 59.9   | 61.4   | 51.9  | 61.3  | 64.1    | 55.3   | 55.8   | 66.7   | 54.8  | 54.1  |

Source: U.S. Department of Commerce, Bureau of the Census, *Statistical Abstract of the United States, 1981* (Washington, D.C.: Government Printing Office, 1981), p. 495.

dent added to the bombing by approving regular B-52 saturation raids on enemy strongholds in the south and increased strategic raids on the North.

By the beginning of 1966, a seemingly unchanging pattern had been established in which several interlocking factors relentlessly escalated the war. American bombing and added troop strength (which mounted to 486,000 in 1967 and 536,000 in 1968) destabilized South Vietnamese society and increased Northern infiltration. And Northern infiltration further destabilized the south and led to even greater U.S. intervention.

Johnson did not present the issues or the costs of the war to the American public in a forthright manner. He underestimated costs in 1966 and declined to ask for increased war taxes until early 1968. (Eventually the war cost the United States about $100 billion, with defense spending rising 16 percent in 1966, 15 percent in 1967, and 3 percent in 1968.) He responded to his critics with scorn, sarcasm, and charges of unpatriotic behavior. Nonetheless, he tried to give the impression of flexibility. On several occasions—December 1966, February and December 1967, and March 1968—he ordered a halt to the bombing and suggested negotiations. But neither North Vietnam nor the Viet Cong would agree to his terms, which were intended to guarantee the independence of South Vietnam.

Because the war remained unresolved and promises of an early victory proved false, Johnson faced mounting opposition. The burgeoning

student radical movement, intellectuals, civil rights groups, Republicans angry that the war dragged on without victory, and many others chided the president. A Gallup poll revealed profound public division and confusion about the war. American goals seemed unclear. In part because of his inability to articulate clear and believable aims, the president's popularity plummeted. His carefully constructed consensus, built around fulfilling the idealism of the Kennedy years, disintegrated.

Meanwhile, continuing summer outbreaks of riot in American cities took their toll on Johnson's civil rights achievements. Not only split over the war in Vietnam, the United States was quickly becoming more seriously divided than ever over racial questions. Johnson attempted to prevent this polarization and to preserve the ties of the civil rights movement with his administration. In 1967, he appointed a National Advisory Commission on Civil Disorders, headed by Governor Otto Kerner of Illinois. The report, when issued in 1968, warned of the degeneration of American society into two warring racial cultures. The commission also blamed "white racism" for the urban riots. But a Gallup poll found that only a third of Americans accepted this conclusion.

Following the disorders of 1967, Johnson also secured passage of a new civil rights act in early 1968 that barred discrimination in most American housing. But while he recognized the need for quick action to correct social injustice, Johnson opposed riot and confrontation as a means of

# Helen Gurley Brown

(Cosmopolitan/The Hearst Corporation)

I think marriage is insurance for the *worst* years of your life. During your best years you don't need a husband. You do need a man of course every step of the way, and they are often cheaper emotionally and a lot more fun by the dozen.

These words, appearing in the opening pages of Helen Gurley Brown's *Sex and the Single Girl* (1962), announced the death of America's faith in the marriage ideology of the 1950s and declared the sexual liberation of single women. Brown's aggressive and unrelenting defense of sex for the unmarried girl won her book a prominent place on the best-seller list of 1962. It also earned her the status of a celebrity. Answering letters of appreciation and requests for advice, she marketed her responses as a column, beginning in 1964, called "Woman Alone," distributed to fifty magazines and newspapers. In March 1965, she assumed editorship of *Cosmopolitan,* a women's periodical with a long history and a rapidly declining readership. By 1969, she had rebuilt its circulation to over a million copies monthly, sold almost solely from newsstands and grocery stores, making it one of the most successful commercial periodicals. In 1967, she launched a television interview show, *Outrageous Opinions.*

Helen Gurley was born in Arkansas in 1922, neither rich, beautiful, nor cosmopolitan. She suffered an impoverished childhood and, after World War II, attended business school in Los Angeles. Between the ages of eighteen and twenty-five, she held eighteen different secretarial jobs, until she found a position in an advertising firm in 1948. Picking up the trade as she went along, she became first a copy editor and then an advertising executive. In 1959 she married David Brown, a director and story editor at 20th Century Fox Studios. After reading some of her old love letters to a former boyfriend, her husband suggested that she write an advice book for single women. The result was her best seller and a new career.

Although *Sex and the Single Girl* declared sexual freedom for women, it did so in a curious fashion. In one sense, Brown only articulated major changes occurring in American culture: the open and explicit discussion of sex; the increasing use of birth-control measures such as the intrauterine device or "the pill"; and the growing respectability of soft-core pornographic magazines such as *Playboy.* But Brown's advice was strongly tempered with traditional attitudes. If marriage was out, dependency on men was not. In fact, the single girl as Brown described her lives for nothing else so much as multiple sexual encounters. Everything about her—job, diet, friends, apartment—is designed to attract men. Men are still the aggressors; women always temptresses. By comparison, it might be argued, the narrowest suburban housewife, confined by babies, house and garden, husband, and PTA, has a rich and busy life next to the ever-aging single girl trying to market her attractions.

Brown's celebration of casual sexual encounters deeply upset traditional moralists, who upheld the sanctity of marriage. She helped make explicit the changing mores of American society. She assured women that extramarital sexual behavior was acceptable and desirable. She could not, however, provide any answers to women who wanted fulfillment in ways other than a "man-loved kind of life."

attaining such goals. After the riots of 1967, he declared: "Violence must be stopped, quickly, finally, and permanently."

The president faced still other political problems because of a backlash against his social programs. After midterm Democratic congressional losses in 1966, he faced a more independent-minded and stronger opposition. Funds for some of his projects, such as the War on Poverty, dwindled. Yet Johnson continued to advocate reform, if only to hold the sympathy of his liberal constituency.

A disastrous turn of events in Vietnam during early 1968 effectively ended Johnson's presidency. Beginning in January and extending for more than a month, the Viet Cong challenged American and South Vietnamese forces everywhere: in defended hamlets, in the countryside, in the cities, even in front of the American embassy in Saigon. This Tet offensive (so named because it coincided with the Tet lunar new year) marked a turning point in the war. Although the Viet Cong eventually lost most of their gains, the gruesome battle convinced many Americans that the war could not be won.

This growing doubt registered in Johnson's disappointing showing in the New Hampshire Democratic primary. Young people by the hundreds flocked to the state to organize support for Senator Eugene McCarthy, who had declared his opposition to the war. Their efforts led to a near-defeat of the president. Johnson realized that even if he won renomination, his candidacy would rip apart the Democratic party. Thus on March 31, he surprised the nation by announcing his withdrawal from the race.

Yet Johnson's withdrawal could not stop the escalation of either the war or the dissension at home. Nor did it prevent the president from intervening in the convention to ensure that his policies would be defended by the party platform and by the candidate it chose. The expectations

AN ANTIWAR DEMONSTRATION IN CHICAGO, 1968
Peace, anger, frustration, and defiance were the conflicting motives of demonstrators who marched in American cities in the late 1960s and early 1970s to protest the Vietnam War. (©Roger Malloch/Magnum)

that he had helped to arouse had now soured. His administration, as versatile and innovative as any in the twentieth century, was about to be condemned on the overriding issue of the war. Civil rights, economic progress, the peace of American society—all seemed to hang in the balance of a struggle thousands of miles away. That struggle and the war came home in the summer of 1968. The stage was set for its re-enactment as Yippie theater in the streets of Chicago.

# SUGGESTED READINGS, CHAPTERS 43–44

## SOCIAL UPHEAVALS

Even if the promise of the Kennedy-Johnson years remained unfulfilled, the 1960s was nonetheless a decade of fascinating social changes. One of the most important documents of that change and an influential book in its own right is Betty Friedan, *The Feminine Mystique* (1963). Another such influential work is Michael Harrington, *The Other America: Poverty in the United States* (1963). This work by a leading American socialist helped inspire the antipoverty programs of the 1960s. Explanations for such reforms have abounded. One of the most challenging interpretations is by William G. McLoughlin, in *Revivals, Awakenings, and Reform* (1978), which places the 1960s in the context of other periods of intense moral reform in American history. Charles A. Reich, in *The Greening of America* (1970), argues that Americans developed a wholly new consciousness of themselves, their environment, and their society. Kirkpatrick Sale's *SDS* (1973) is an indispensable guide to the largest student radical group of the decade. At the other end of the political spectrum, George H. Nash, in *The Conservative Intellectual Movement in America Since 1945* (1976), explores the decade's growing conservative challenge to American liberalism.

## KENNEDY AND JOHNSON

During the 1960s, American presidents inspired both admiration and profound disillusionment. Consequently the evaluation of Kennedy and Johnson has been marked by controversy. In the first of several incisive books on American elections, Theodore White in *The Making of the President, 1960* (1961) provides a very readable account of the issues and personalities in the election that brought John Kennedy to the White House. Several memoirs by Kennedy aides have offered insights into Kennedy's style of governing. Among the best is Pierre Salinger, *With Kennedy* (1966). A much more critical account, which stresses the failures of the administration, is Henry Fairlie, *The Kennedy Promise: The Politics of Expectation* (1973). Lyndon Johnson's presidency was, if anything, more controversial. Doris Kearns's *Lyndon Johnson and the American Dream* (1976) is a loving portrait of an unlovely man. Jim F. Heath, *Decade of Disillusionment: The Kennedy-Johnson Years* (1975) is a readable critical history of the 1960s.

## THE WAR IN VIETNAM

Of all the issues that divided Americans during the 1960s, the Vietnam War was probably the most important. George C. Herring, *America's Longest War: The United States and Vietnam, 1950–1975* (1979) is a thorough history of the struggle. David Halberstam's brilliant *The Best and the Brightest* (1972) recounts the ultimate failure of the generation of promising political advisers who counseled involvement in Vietnam. Godfrey Hodgson, *American in Our Time* (1976), is a delightful general history of the era in which Vietnam became the single most important issue.

# 45 ▪ Three Mile Island: An Accident Waiting to Happen

Several miles down the muddy Susquehanna River from Harrisburg, Pennsylvania, the Three Mile Island nuclear generating plant quietly pulsed electricity into the grids of the Metropolitan Edison Company. In the damp, predawn hours of March 28, 1979, a skeleton maintenance crew was operating Unit 2 of the installation. Unit 1 was still "cold" and undergoing its annual shutdown for inspection and refueling.

Unit 2 was a new reactor designed by Babcock and Wilcox Corporation of Lynchburg, Virginia. It was part of a family of reactor systems that used pressurized water to cool and convey heat from the atomic core to steam turbines. The generation of electricity in this plant derived from the interaction of two closed systems. The primary system, containing the nuclear reactor, consisted of a circuit of pipes that pumped pressurized water over the atomic core, picking up heat, and then carrying it through the heat exchanger. The secondary system led from the heat exchanger to turbines that generated electricity. The heat exchanger was partly filled with water. As superheated water in pipes from the reactor flowed through it, the water turned to steam, rushed out of the exchanger, and turned the turbine generators. Then the steam lost its heat, condensed back into water, and flowed back into the exchanger (see p. 922).

Neither system was readily visible from the exterior, so control depended entirely on the accuracy of gauges and alarms. Furthermore, the danger always existed that the reactor system would lose pressure or water or both, causing the atomic pile to uncover and heat uncontrollably.

Unit 2 had been completed for almost a year, but frequent problems—faulty valves and other parts, and quirks in the operation—had kept it shut

**THREE MILE ISLAND**

This photograph shows the nuclear power plant, with its large cooling towers, on Three Mile Island in the Susquehanna River, during the partial meltdown. None of the effects of the accident are visible here; most of them were confined by the plant's safety systems. *(UPI)*

down for most of the year. On this morning, however, it was operating at almost 100 percent capacity.

Quiet, almost serene-looking in its stark modern exterior, the Three Mile Island reactor system was, in fact, seething with energy and motion. Miles of pipes throbbed with the rapid motion of pressurized water and steam. In the control room, away from the reactor and the turbine, operators had to monitor scores of electrical commands registered by lights in the panels. These were attached to alarms. The plant's computer system recorded the various changes in the operation of the systems.

Shortly before 4:00 A.M., two technicians were working to clear the polishers (filters) of the feedwater pipes in the turbine system. This was a normal procedure, something regularly done while the plant was in operation. Unable to unclog the pipe, the engineers decided to blow the residues out with air—like expelling a pea from a pea shooter. Forcing air through the pipe and into the system, however, caused a sudden shutdown of all the water intakes. "All of a sudden," Frederick Scheimann, the Unit 2 foreman said, "I started hearing loud, thunderous noises, like a couple of freight trains."

Three Mile Island: An Accident Waiting to Happen    921

What Scheimann heard in the next half minute was the automatic working of the plant's first-line emergency equipment slamming into place. Starved of fresh, cooled water, the turbine system heated too rapidly and the turbines shut off automatically. Pressurized, superheated water from the reactor continued to flow through the heat transfer area, but because little heat was being extracted, this system also overheated rapidly. As temperatures rose in the reactor, pressure also built. Then a special emergency relief valve on the pressurizer opened. Thus far only six seconds had elapsed.

The reactor continued to function because of a delay mechanism built into its shutdown procedures. Then, as pressure and heat built, the reactor system "tripped." Damping rods fell into the core, shutting off most of the nuclear reaction. Heat and pressure began to fall in the reactor system. About ten seconds later, auxiliary pumps in the turbine system began to operate. The incident should have been over.

Except for two mechanical problems. In the reactor system, the emergency relief valve did not spring shut as it should have when pressure fell. Superheated steam continued to spurt out of the valve, further lowering pressure in the system. In the turbine system nothing happened. The three emergency pumps churned furiously but no water flowed through the pipes. During a previous maintenance operation, the emergency pump valves had been shut—and left shut. In effect, phase one of the accident had already passed before anyone had had time to react. The first set of safety devices failed. Now the second line of defense went into operation.

Although the accident had begun in the turbine system, the emergency shifted to the reactor unit. As pressure fell there, two auxiliary pumps kicked on, pushing hundreds of gallons of water into the core. This was sufficient to keep the core covered and cool until the open emergency relief valve was discovered.

In the control room, lights on the horseshoe panel began flashing and several of the plant's alarms sounded. The overnight operators, Craig Faust and Edward Frederick, and supervisor William Zewe, knew the company procedures handbook well. They paid special attention to the warning: "Never take the plant solid." What that meant, simply, was not to let the reactor system get too much water in it. If it did, then any shock to the system might break it open. Protection against this sort of accident was maintained by keeping air in the pressurizer chamber below the emergency relief valve. Without this pillow of air to absorb changes in pressure, the reactor system would be in danger.

From the information available in the control room, this is precisely what appeared to happening. The water level in the pressurizer moved up, indicating that the whole system was becoming superflooded. Thus the operators shut down the flow of emergency water into the reactor. At eight minutes into the incident, Faust discovered that the valves of the turbine system were closed. He turned them on and water began to flow back into that system. Once again the plant seemed to stabilize. The operators had followed instructions exactly.

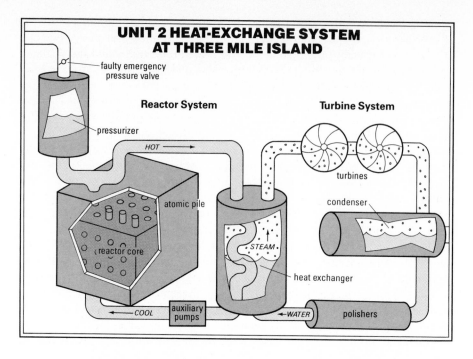

## UNIT 2 HEAT-EXCHANGE SYSTEM AT THREE MILE ISLAND

But they had gravely misinterpreted the problem. Instead of being awash with coolant, the core system was still rapidly leaking through the broken relief valve. Water had risen in the pressure tank, but it had been forced there by steam now forming over the reactor and throughout the system. As pressure inside the system fell, the water began to boil, bubbling steam to the top of the reactor and then into the pipes that ran in and out of the core, blocking them and preventing cooling water from flowing through. The water level in the core began to drop dangerously. If the atomic pile uncovered, it would start to melt.

In the control room, the crew began to realize that a serious malfunction had occurred. Lights flashed and new alarms sounded. The computer reported problems throughout the plant, but in helter-skelter fashion. It was hours before it finally recorded the malfunction in the broken pressurizer valve. The third and last system of defense was about to be called into operation.

This system, unlike the first two, was designed to contain a nuclear accident. Should radioactivity escape from the plant it could seriously endanger the lives of millions of people in its wake. However, the Three Mile Island containment building, which held the reactor system, was designed to prevent such an occurrence. This twenty-story high, 2-foot thick concrete-and-steel enclosure was designed to withstand the force of a jet airliner crashing into it at full speed. More important, it could withstand large increases in the pressure of gases that might build up inside. The only possible leakage from the containment was through the sump pump system that took water off the floor of the building and into a storage tank in the unshielded auxiliary building. But the sump pumps were protected by a cutoff that stopped them if radioactivity was detected in the water.

At about twenty minutes into the accident, operators called Gary Miller, the station emergency director, who arrived at Unit 2 about an hour later. Operating crews believed that they had the plant under control. They knew that overflow water was gushing onto the floor of the containment building and then moving through the sump pump system into tanks in the auxiliary building. But they believed this was turbine water. As Frederick said, "We decided it was a nonradioactive leak, therefore it must be the steam system and not the reactor coolant system. The symptoms are identical except for the radiation alarm." That alarm had malfunctioned, however, and did not sound until 6:50. By that time, hundreds of gallons of radioactive waste had poured into the auxiliary building, some of it spilling out and venting small amounts of radioactive gas into the building and out into the atmosphere.

In the control room, operators followed accident procedures precisely, but they were puzzled by new alarms and flashing lights. Since they could not see inside the reactor system, they did not realize that their emergency actions had actually intensified the accident. The atomic core in shutdown position was still creating considerable decay heat. This, in turn, was increasing the steam trapped at the top of the reactor core and pushing more steam into the intake and outflow pipes. Steam bubbles shot through the system and the regular cooling pumps began to shudder and vibrate. At about 5:20, one set of pumps had to be shut off. At 5:41, a second pair shut down automatically. This further diminished the flow of water over the reactor. With the pressure emergency valve still trapped open, the system continued to leak. The nuclear core was about to be uncovered and no one knew it.

As the core water level fell, it exposed the nuclear fuel, causing three serious reactions. Radioactive discharges from the system increased rapidly, contaminating the coolant water and, eventually, the containment building. The very high temperatures, together with the continuing chain reaction, caused some of the oxygen in the water to combine with metals in the core, giving off highly flammable hydrogen gas as a by-product. Most dangerous, the exposed fuel heated rapidly, melting the tubes that held it, and increasing the reaction. The 100 tons of uranium fuel, arranged in stacked pellets, began to melt together, touching off a larger chain reaction. The plant now clearly risked a melt-down, in which fuel would fall into a searing radioactive heap at the bottom of the reactor. The intense heat—over 5,000°F.—would melt through the 12-inch steel encasement of the reactor, and uranium would tumble onto the floor of the containment building. Then, it might melt through the cement base, cracking the building open and allowing the deadly release of gases and radioactive sludge.

However, neither the officials from Metropolitan Edison nor the plant operators, worried about this risk because they did not realize that the core was uncovered. Their only measurements of water in the system were indirect—and these indicated, falsely, that the reactor was brimming with water. Shortly after 6:00 A.M., Brian Mehler, the Metropolitan Edison shift supervisor arrived. At 6:22, after checking through other systems, he recognized that the emergency relief valve above the pressurizer had jammed open. He immediately ordered it shut. The leak in the reactor finally stopped, but no one started the emergency pumps. The core remained uncovered.

Starved of coolant, the reactor smoldered and crumbled. The damping rods overheated, swelled, and ruptured. Tubes containing the uranium pellets melted. Over the next sixteen hours or so, about one-third of the core fell into a superheated, poisonous mass. Hundreds of gallons of radioactive water flowed into the auxiliary building and gases escaped into the air.

Finally, at 6:50, radiation alarms in the auxiliary building sounded. Miller, the emergency director, declared a "site emergency" and began notifying authorities of a "slight problem at Three Mile Island." He also called the Pennsylvania Emergency Management Agency, the Bureau of Radiation Protection, and the regional headquarters of the U.S. Nuclear Regulatory Commission (NRC). Shortly thereafter, he declared a general emergency. The public was about to receive its first news of a nuclear accident that experts at the plant had yet to understand.

For the next several days, misleading statements, misinformation, confusion, and rumor plagued public understanding of what had happened. This is not surprising. Confusion had always surrounded the atomic power industry and issues of regulation and safety. In part, this came from the extraordinary complexity of the technology. The public understood very little of how this complicated plant worked and yet they had to make decisions that deeply affected their lives on the basis of what they expected to happen. There could be no more dramatic proof of the distance between modern science and the population at large. The accident also revealed an astounding inability to communicate: a panicky press, and government agencies and private corporations that distorted or misinterpreted what had happened. In the rush to protect groups that had an important stake in atomic energy, truthfulness and genuine accountability were lost.

In large industrial accidents, it is sometimes possible to discover "paper trails"—that is, memos, letters, and reports that warn of weaknesses in a system that eventually fails. In the case of Three Mile Island, there were several of these trails, but none led to any action. Each warning about the reactor system was sidetracked by bureaucracy, special interests, and communications breakdowns. Ignorance, ineptitude, and fear of upsetting the precarious nuclear industry combined to block warnings of impending problems.

One reason for the breakdown of Unit 2 lay in the design of the reactor–heat transfer system, its installation, and its operation. All of these areas concerned the manufacturer and designer of the reactor, Babcock and Wilcox. Metropolitan Edison, the generating company, operated the equipment according to B & W instructions. Modifications in procedures continually flowed from B & W headquarters as the company monitored the operations at the generating plants it designed.

Just such a monitoring process led Joe Kelly, a B & W engineer, to ask the company in November 1977 to change its instructions for dealing with a depressurization incident (such as occurred at Three Mile Island). The company worried most about too much coolant entering the reactor system and so instructed operators to shut down emergency pumps if the system suddenly lost pressure. But Kelly argued that instructions should be changed to read that emergency pumps should never be turned off except during a normal shutdown. If operators had received this advice, the Three Mile Island accident would have ended without danger.

Kelly reached his conclusions after investigating an incident at the Davis-Bessie generating plant near Toledo, Ohio. Using a B & W system, the Davis-Bessie plant was operating at about 9 percent capacity in September 1977 when a loss-of-coolant accident occurred. With safety and measurement equipment giving confused signals, the plant operators responded according to B & W instructions and shut off the emergency cooling system. Had the reactor been operating at full capacity, Kelly reasoned, these actions might have caused major fuel damage and a dangerous melt-down.

In November 1977, Kelly collected his suggestions and submitted them in a memo to B & W executives concerned with safety procedures and customer relations. He enlisted others in the emergency–safety management service division. New guidelines were drawn up, but the department failed to send them out to B & W equipment operators. Kelly, however, did not realize this.

The company also had warnings from another source. In September 1977, Carlyle Michelson, a Tennessee Valley Authority engineer and consultant for the Nuclear Regulatory Commission, submitted a report on B & W equipment. He concluded that in a loss-of-coolant accident, the pressurizer gauge would mislead operators as to the amount of water in the system. Michelson submitted his report to the NRC. Nothing happened. So several months later, he shook the bureaucratic tree again to stimulate action. No decisions were taken. Babcock and Wilcox also received a copy of the report, but the company merely filed it away. Michelson sent two letters to B & W headquarters; the second arrived in February 1979, but the company did not respond—or warn its customers.

The Nuclear Regulatory Commission was aware of these warnings about B & W equipment. The Michelson report had been pushed into the agency paper flow in 1977. More important, however, the NRC had done its own investigation of the Davis-Bessie incident, and their investigator agreed with Kelly and Michelson.

James S. Cresswell, an NRC reactor inspector, worried about the Davis-Bessie incident. After studying the problem there, he concluded that all B & W systems were susceptible to such incidents, and he tried to spur the NRC into action. He talked to a number of NRC officials, who generally rejected his conclusions. Finally, on January 8, 1979, he issued a formal memorandum on Babcock and Wilcox plants, in effect, leapfrogging the immediate bureaucracy and making his findings public. But the company continued to reassure the NRC that their systems were safely insulated against accidents and that their instructions were appropriate.

Frustrated in his efforts, Cresswell went to the top of the agency in the spring of 1979 and finally got a meeting with two NRC commissioners. Both were impressed with his evidence, and one of them sent a request to the agency to act on the information. The commissioner's request arrived at the agency on March 29, one day after the Three Mile Island accident began.

The company and the NRC acted slowly on these warnings for several reasons. For one thing, NRC "nugget" files (records of operating problems) showed hundreds of incidents in the operation of nuclear plants. It was not immediately clear that this particular problem with B & W equipment was any more dangerous than scores of others. Also, changes in equipment and operating procedures were expensive. Caught in a serious price squeeze, the nuclear industry was trying to save itself, and the NRC wanted to help.

Actually, the history of regulating nuclear electrical generation was an ambiguous one. The industry began in 1953 with the announcement of President Eisenhower's Atoms for Peace program. Atomic power plant construction began a year later, and the first generating unit was completed in 1958. From the beginning, the federal government subsidized the industry by allocating funds for research and development. The Atomic Energy Commission acted both as advocate for the industry and as regulator—a contradictory mission. In addition, Congress passed the Price-Anderson Act of 1957, which limited to $560 million the total liability of a nuclear generating plant in the case of accident. In effect, the government declared that victims of a serious accident would have to pay for most damages themselves.

Protected, encouraged, and screened by the government, the nuclear industry boomed during the 1960s. Low costs for uranium fuel (below $7 a ton in 1970), rapid rises in demand for electrical power (about 7 percent a year), and increasing unreliability of oil and gas supplies, plus pollution and accident problems associated with coal burning and mining, made nuclear energy seem to be a perfect replacement. Over seventy plants had been constructed by 1979, and they produced about 13 percent of the nation's electrical energy.

Nonetheless, by the mid-1970s, the industry was facing hard times. Uranium ore prices had shot up. Construction costs in plants had risen astronomically, due in part to stricter regulation—some directives were as thick as a telephone book. General inflation had also pushed construction costs upward, so that nuclear-generated electricity cost about ten times as much in 1979 as it had in 1970. Cost overruns in plants like Three Mile Island were huge. The original expense was projected to be about $130 million, but Unit 2 cost $700 million when completed.

The 1970s also raised problems because of a sudden drop in the growth of energy requirements. The huge increase in oil prices after 1973–1974 did not result in a switch to nuclear alternatives. Instead, sluggish economic growth and conservation cut demands for electricity. Optimistic predictions about a fifty percent nuclear future proved to be very wide of the mark. As *Business Week* commented in December 1978: "One by one, the lights are going out for the U.S. nuclear power industry. Reactor orders have plummeted from a high of 41 in 1973 to zero this year."

The federal government in 1974 had tried to reorganize the industry through the creation of better regulation. By creating the Nuclear Regulatory Agency that year, Congress recognized the contradiction between advocacy and regulation. It abolished the AEC and substituted the NRC. Nonetheless, many of the AEC employees, most of them nuclear enthusiasts, transferred to the new agency.

The NRC proved to be reluctant to tighten regulations at a time when the industry was beginning to nose-dive. Expensive safety retrofitting of reactors was not ordered. The NRC hesitated to issue instructions that would make operations more expensive. And it had to contend with opponents of nuclear power plants. With the industry in crisis and with growing public clamor to shut down plants, the NRC was reluctant to interfere with the operation of new plants such as Three Mile Island.

Another paper trail to the accident in Pennsylvania existed in consumer opposition to nuclear energy. Headed by consumer advocate Ralph Nader, antinuclear forces significantly slowed the licensing process of plants, at hearings and through lawsuits. Nader's objections rested on several grounds. He believed evidence that any increase in radiation was a health and genetic danger to plant workers and nearby residents. Since all nuclear plants emitted some radiation, he concluded that this constituted technological victimization. Nader also worried about possible theft of radioactive fuels, sabotage, unresolved waste disposal problems, and the credibility of the government and the nuclear industry.

In his book *The Menace of Atomic Energy,* published in 1977, Nader cited AEC tests of 1970 and 1971 that showed emergency malfunctioning in a loss-of-coolant accident. These tests, he concluded, demonstrated that water

**RALPH NADER**

Beginning with his exposé of unsafe automobiles in the 1960s, consumer advocate Ralph Nader and his "Raiders" investigated other potentially hazardous industries. Nuclear-powered electrical energy plants were among their chief targets. *UPI)*

pumped into the system at low pressure would turn to steam and block the intake and outlet pipes to the reactor. The core would then become exposed and melt. In such an event, the containment floor would also fail, and the "China syndrome" would occur—the molten mass of uranium fuel would burn through the building, into the ground, and downward toward the earth's core, polluting groundwater as it went.

Nader's use of the term "China syndrome" to describe a melt-down accident was nothing more than the adoption of industry slang—a kind of joke, that the molten mass would pass through the earth and come to rest in China on the opposite side of the globe. But the seriousness of such an accident was no joke. A secret AEC report, pried out of the agency in 1973, predicted that in the worst possible accident, 45,000 people would die, 100,000 would sustain injury, and an area that "might be equal to that of the state of Pennsylvania" would be devastated.

This same reference to Pennsylvania occurred in the film *The China Syndrome,* produced by Mike Douglas and released in March 1979, two weeks before the accident at Three Mile Island. This was no coincidence—only another paper trail.

In 1976, Mike Gray, a documentary film maker approached producer Mike Douglas with a completed film script about a near accident at a nuclear generating plant. Gray had studied AEC reports and investigated minor incidents at plants near Detroit and Chicago. The results of his study went into the script. Douglas liked the idea and approached actress Jane Fonda about joining the venture. She agreed but changed the script, writing in a character for herself to play—a television news commentator trying to find out about and then report honestly on a dangerous incident at a nuclear plant. Douglas hired nuclear engineers to provide expertise on plant operations. The film also incorporated testimony from hearings on nuclear plants.

Melodramatic though it was, the film accurately portrayed the sequence of events in a near melt-down accident. And the drama confronted the larger issue of credibility. The action begins when Kimberly Wells, a commentator for *California Close-up* on the evening news, accidentally films a serious incident at the Ventura power plant while doing a feature story. After showing the film to a nuclear engineer, she becomes convinced that she has witnessed a near accident. The engineer explains:

LOWELL: If that's true, then we came very close to the China Syndrome.
KIMBERLY: The what?
LOWELL: If the core is exposed for whatever reason the fuel heats beyond coreheat tolerance in a matter of minutes. Nothing can stop it. And it melts right down through the bottom of the plant, theoretically to China, but, of course, as soon as it hits ground water it blasts into the atmosphere and sends out clouds of radioactivity. The number of people killed would depend on which way the wind is blowing [and] render an area the size of Pennsylvania permanently uninhabitable.

A plant engineer named Godell (played by actor Jack Lemmon) recognizes that the welds supporting cooling pumps are faulty, and he tries to prevent the plant from going back into operation. Holding the control room at gunpoint he demands a live interview on television. Kimberly, eager to get the story, rushes to the plant with her crew. But when Godell tries to explain, he fails completely:

GODELL: I mean, that happened, but that's not why I'm here. It's—I'm not making any sense.

KIMBERLY: No, it's all right.

GODELL: It's so complicated, but there . . . there's something else. There's this—see, it's so complicated . . . yet so simple . . . simple . . . it's terribly complex . . . and it's very difficult.

Action piles on action: Godell is shot by a special police squad; the plant shuts down safely; and Kimberly files her story. As Godell realized, nuclear technology is too complicated to explain to the public, which must depend upon the credibility of government and industry. When that fails, only a feature reporter's chance persistence saves California from disaster.

Predictably, the nuclear industry attacked the film. In a public letter dated nine days before the opening of the film and two weeks before Three Mile Island, Southern California Edison charged that the movie had "no scientific credibility and is in fact ridiculous." But if anything, the film underplayed the danger.

One final trail led to the accident. This was the short but troubled history of Unit 2 operations. After a long and expensive construction period, the second reactor at Three Mile Island "went critical" (began operation) on March 28, 1978. At ceremonies in September, Metropolitan Edison representatives, the lieutenant governor of Pennsylvania, and U.S. Deputy Secretary of Energy John F. O'Leary dedicated the new facility. O'Leary addressed the assembly and called for keeping "the nuclear option open." He urged even more: "Our goal is to achieve a balance of 50 percent coal and 50 percent nuclear." The facility, he concluded, was "a sort of a miracle in many ways."

Residents of the area generally accepted this view. The plant pumped thousands of dollars in construction jobs into the region and employment for the "nukes," as permanent employees called themselves. But there was scattered opposition, centered primarily in a small group, the Three Mile Island Alert, and a small underground tabloid, the *Harrisburg*.

The utility company replied to all adverse publicity with soothing words about safety, stressing the nuclear industry's exemplary record. They cited the industry motto: "Defense in depth—backup systems to back up backup systems." They noted that half of the investment in Unit 2 was for safety devices. As a Metropolitan Edison flier, called "Your Personal Radiation Inventory," said: If the worst conceivable accident "were to occur at the Three Mile Island nuclear station, because of safeguards, a man could remain at a spot less than a half-mile from the reactor for 24 hours a day for an entire year and be exposed to only 2 mrems of radiation." (A millirem (mrem) is one-thousandth of a rem. Exposure to 600 rems is generally a fatal dose.)

This was a negligible amount compared to the 100 mrems that all Americans received each year from natural causes.

Although utility officials exuded public confidence, Unit 2 proved unreliable and accident-prone. The emergency relief valve stuck open more than once, and operators installed an indirect gauge to determine its position—but even this gauge sometimes malfunctioned. And the valve leaked slightly. Other problems flared up in the complicated cooling and heat transfer systems. Employees complained that the alarm system was too extensive and hence meaningless in an emergency. Nonetheless, Metropolitan Edison put the plant on line on December 30, 1978. They did so for two reasons. The company wanted to take advantage of tax breaks for 1978. And they were seeking a rate increase to help cover operating expenses. This was granted in March 1979. However, the flawed system remained out of operation for much of the time.

Plant operators, the utility company, and the NRC did not suspect the gravity of the Three Mile Island accident in its early stages. Communications between the plant and the NRC in Bethesda, Maryland, near Washington, were confused and difficult. When the utility did begin to realize the problem of a partial melt-down, it refused to admit so publicly. At first, the NRC accepted Metropolitan Edison assurances. As a result, the credibility of information flowing over the media from the plant and from the NRC degenerated. The local population was restrained by meaningless assurances and then panicked by rumors.

At 7:30 Wednesday morning, once the general emergency had been declared, the most immediate problem was whether or not to evacuate the nearby public. This decision depended on accurate information. With the coolant system out of control—it remained so for about twelve more hours—the risk of total melt-down and radiation discharge increased. Plant operators, utility experts, B&W scientists, and the NRC only gradually realized the extent of the damage. But they could not advise state officials about evacuation until they knew what was happening on site.

At the plant, emergency director Gary Miller tried to establish control of the reactor and also coordinate public communications. But he recalled, "I was constantly pulled to the phone by senior persons in the state government, the NRC, and my own management. . . . The phone, the pressure, the fact that the plant was in a state that I had never been schooled in combined to make it almost intolerable."

Those in charge of evacuation had even less information. The Pennsylvania Emergency Management Agency (PEMA), headed by Lieutenant Governor William Scranton, was charged with directing emergency procedures. Evacuation plans existed, but they had not been made public for fear of arousing anxiety. PEMA, located in a radiation-proof building in Harrisburg, prepared to act, but it had to have facts. And the man who would instruct it to begin, Governor Richard Thornburgh, had received contradictory advice from Metropolitan Edison and the NRC.

The public first heard of the accident at about 8:00 A.M. A local broadcaster

**THREE MILE ISLAND REACTOR**

This photograph pictures the top portion of nuclear reactor Unit 1 at Three Mile Island. Had a complete meltdown of Unit 2 occurred, the blistering hot, radioactive pile would have fallen through the reactor floor (not visible here). *(UPI)*

discovered that local civil defense authorities had ordered fire equipment on alert. He called Metropolitan Edison, and the company reported a "minor problem" at Three Mile Island. Later in the morning, the company released its first public statement:

> The nuclear reactor at Three Mile Island Unit 2 was shut down as prescribed when a malfunction related to a feedwater pump occurred about four A.M. Wednesday. The entire unit was systematically shut down and will be out of service for about a week while equipment is checked and repairs made.

Metropolitan Edison continued to maintain for several days—against all evidence—that less than 1 percent of the fuel in the reactor core had been damaged. By underestimating the problem, the company quickly lost credibility with government officials and the public. While company experts worked to correct what they knew was an increasingly dangerous situation, they continued to reassure the public that no danger existed. By Wednesday afternoon, Lieutenant Governor Scranton publicly criticized the company for misrepresenting the extent of the accident. The company had "given you and us conflicting information."

Communications between the plant and the NRC offices were difficult to establish. Although NRC inspectors arrived at Three Mile Island at 10:00 in the morning, phone lines to headquarters did not function well. Accurate information about the accident remained sparse in Washington. President Carter had been notified at 9:00, but he let the NRC monitor the problem.

At about 11:30 A.M., plant operators tried to reestablish the blocked flow of coolant into the reactor by depressuring the system, bleeding more steam out through the pressurizer. Their strategy failed. Indeed, it may have uncovered the core even further. Then at 1:50 P.M., the computer recorded an unnoticed pressure spike (a sudden rise in pressure in the containment building). Almost simultaneously, containment spray turned on and emergency liquid shot into the building to neutralize radioactive iodine. Operators shut off the spray. They did not realize, until later, that a bubble of escaped hydrogen, produced in the core, had exploded. This event, when recognized, became the source of fear that hydrogen might explode inside the reactor, creating the worst devastation imaginable and a total melt-down.

Finally, in late afternoon, plant operators attempted to repressurize the system. Gradually they succeeded. Steam began to dissipate, and by 7:50 that evening, coolant water again began to flow through the system. The core was re-covered. It was now time to assess the damage.

To do this, a sample of core coolant water had to be taken and analyzed for radioactive discharges that would indicate fuel damage. Results of this test became available at 6:00 P.M. the next day. At last, officials understood the seriousness of an accident they could not see or measure directly. On Wednesday evening, however, the most immediate problem was how to eliminate the radioactive water and gas trapped in the containment and the auxiliary building. Whether they wanted to or not, company officials decided they had to discharge some of this into the air and into the Susquehanna River.

On Thursday morning, plant officials decided to dump mildly radioactive water into the river. If they did not, it would spill out anyway because storage tanks were completely filled. At about 2:45 P.M., technicians started to empty this pollutant into the Susquehanna. State officials strenuously objected, and at 6:00 P.M., the NRC ordered a halt to the dumping. But by midnight, all parties had agreed to resume the discharge. All day, conflicting stories reached the news media about releases of gas and water. Joseph Hendry, chairman of the NRC, briefed Congress, reporting that there might be some minor cracks in "perhaps about one per cent" of the fuel rods, but he assured Washington that there was no serious risk.

Reporters and television crews began to flood the Harrisburg area. But unlike other sorts of accidents, this one attracted no spectators. The possibility of a deadly release of radiation kept bystanders at home. All of the media attention did little to improve the flow of information or restore credibility. The technological and scientific aspects of the accident were difficult to understand, and scientists themselves disagreed sharply about the accident. News flowing to the governor remained contradictory. But by 11:00 P.M., he knew how serious the incident was: core samples confirmed a partial melt-down.

Friday was the most confused day yet. Communications among civil authorities concerning evacuation became scrambled. The public believed less and less of what it heard. Serious amounts of radioactive gas still had to be vented. And technicians realized that a large hydrogen bubble was building in the reactor. It seemed only a matter of time before a fatal explosion.

The population around Harrisburg was obviously jittery. A quick telephone survey revealed that most area residents feared another nuclear accident even if this one ended uneventfully. Other residents confided their deep-seated fears about radiation to reporters. Paul Holowka, a dog breeder living near the reactor claimed: "Last year I lost twelve dogs. They died of cancer. That never used to happen."

By the end of the day, the area was in turmoil. Phone circuits were jammed, schools were closed, and lines had formed in front of gasoline stations. Toll booth operators on the Pennsylvania Turnpike noted a sudden spurt of heavy traffic, with most cars filled with families. A general exodus that eventually reached almost 140,000 people had begun. One of those fleeing said frankly: "The main reason we're leaving is I don't trust the information they are giving us. No one really knows what happened Wednesday morning."

Even Governor Thornburgh admitted as much. "I am very skeptical of any one set of facts," he told a sweltering news conference in the capitol building (the air conditioning had been shut off to prevent circulation of radiation). At 12:30 P.M., Thornburgh ordered a partial evacuation. Radio broadcasts throughout the morning had warned of such an eventuality. After NRC officials received news that vented radioactivity had reached 1,200 mrems per hour, they phoned the state and suggested a general evacuation. Then they rescinded the suggestion. But Thornburgh advised all pregnant women and preschool children within 5 miles of the plant to leave. Other residents were asked to stay indoors.

Thornburgh, the NRC, and President Carter (more involved now in watching the crisis) grew increasingly worried about the hydrogen bubble. Operators now realized that the earlier pressure spike represented a small hydrogen explosion. If, as many scientists warned was possible, the bubble continued to grow and if oxygen in the core reached sufficient levels, then the reactor and the entire containment might explode. Metropolitan Edison officials declared that there was little danger of this—but no one listened. Instead, newspapers and television blared the news. Areas close to the Three Mile Island plant, such as the King River Haven mobile home park, became ghost towns.

Imagination of a hydrogen explosion translated the accident into an occasion for venting people's worst fears. Some residents recalled stories of the terrible, fiery crash of the German dirigible, the *Hindenburg* in New Jersey in 1937. A child told reporters of a dream she had had: "It was a big ball, and you know the way things glow? It glowed just like that. And then there was a witch and the big ball killed everybody. And all the cats and dogs and rabbits were all dead." To some residents, the hydrogen bubble represented the beginning of the end of the world—the first stage in a chain reaction leading to the Last Judgment. Yet there were some local residents who knew

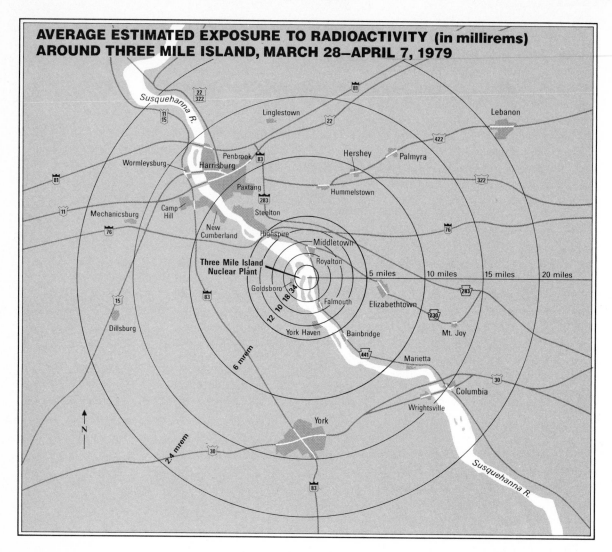

**AVERAGE ESTIMATED EXPOSURE TO RADIOACTIVITY (in millirems) AROUND THREE MILE ISLAND, MARCH 28–APRIL 7, 1979**

almost nothing about the accident or the danger. These were the Amish, the "plain people," who lived on nearby farms, not using automobiles, tractors, modern plumbing—or electricity.

After the confusion over evacuation, and because of scrambled stories coming from the facility, President Carter designated Harold Denton as chief and sole spokesman on the accident site. His first task was to restore the public's faith in the information it was receiving. Denton arrived at Three Mile Island about 2:30 Friday afternoon and quickly took charge. He also stepped into what seemed like the most critical moment of the accident.

During the next day, Denton worked to keep control of news coming from the plant. He warned Governor Thornburgh of a possible general evacuation of the area. For the next harrowing hours, he oversaw attempts to determine the danger of a hydrogen explosion. In Washington, Health, Education, and Welfare Secretary Joseph Califano advised Carter to order a general evacuation. But the president insisted that Denton make such decisions. Nonetheless, the federal government took precautions to order massive amounts of potassium iodide shipped to the area. This drug, if taken before exposure to severe nuclear radiation (radioactive iodine), saturates the thyroid gland to prevent any absorption of dangerous iodine.

By late Saturday evening, Denton and experts working on the accident realized that the danger had passed. The bubble had begun to shrink. The site would be safe enough for President Carter to visit next day. Quite clearly a publicity gesture, the visit would signal that the crisis had passed. Denton informed the media: the president would visit the plant the next afternoon.

On Sunday, the president flew to Harrisburg and then went to the plant for an inspection. Mrs. Carter stopped to visit local residents. Shortly after the visit, scientists at Three Mile Island recognized that they had miscalculated the quantities of hydrogen and oxygen in the reactor. Late that night they confirmed that the bubble was disappearing. By midday on Monday, April 2, it had all but disappeared. The most dangerous phase of the accident had ended.

The Three Mile Island accident ended when operators recovered control over the reactor at 7:50 P.M. on April 4, but the radioactive pollution it released will probably outlast civilization. The reactor came, perhaps, within half an hour of complete melt-down. Although eventually contained, the event had serious and lasting effects on the utility company, the industry, the federal and state regulatory agencies, and the local population—and on the credibility of government and the scientific establishment.

Gradually, the Three Mile Island plant was cleaned up. During the operation to extract the radioactive poisons and permanently remove the nuclear core, the core remained covered by cooling liquids. Worker safety, locating a dump site for wastes, and constant monitoring of the plant presented difficult problems. Over the four years of decontaminating the site, about 1,000 workers were employed and close to a billion dollars had to be spent. If the costs of Metropolitan Edison's purchase of replacement electricity are added in, the total price is about $3 billion—over three times the initial cost of Unit 2 and almost twenty-five times the original estimated cost of the unit.

In the years following the accident, local residents continued to worry about periodic radioactive releases into the air and into the Susquehanna. In March 1980, for example, a citizen living three miles from the plant told the NRC:

> Met Ed's alleged concern for my safety insults me. . . . I have been blitzed by their PR campaigns and their charts and their fancy numbers and their smiling assurances that the levels of radiation to be vented are within Federal safety limits. But who knows if the Federal safety limits are safe?

Bruce Smith, chairman of the board of supervisors in Newberry Township near the site declared: "I am so angry about Three Mile that I have become one of the leaders in the movement to close TMI forever as a nuclear plant."

Plant workers received far higher doses of radiation during the accident than most area residents. Many of them absorbed the maximum safe yearly amount in a few moments. Measured in millirems, a level of 500,000 causes immediate death in 50 percent of a population; 100,000 mrems causes radiation sickness in most. Standard yearly maximums for plant employees had been set at 8,000 mrems. As Joe Hipple, a health physicist told the press during the accident: "I was the hottest I've been in a long time. I hit the frisker [the radiation counter] and it went boing! I probably got half my year's exposure in a day, probably in four minutes."

This exposure to high radiation caused a shortage of technicians. To fill the gap and attract new employees, Metropolitan Edison ran a want ad in the *New York Times:* "Immediate ground floor opportunities for dedicated scientists and engineering personnel who want to be in the forefront of emerging technologies."

Public opinion in the United States and the rest of the world reacted strongly to the accident. Antinuclear sentiment mounted in the United States,

**NO-NUKES RALLY, 1979**

Following the accident at Three Mile Island, sentiment against nuclear power plants mounted. At this rally in Washington on May 6, 1979, Tom Hayden (former leader of SDS and coordinator of the Chicago demonstrations of 1968) and Jane Fonda, his wife and star of *The China Syndrome*, addressed the crowd. *(UPI)*

as evidenced by a large rally in Washington on May 6, 1979. Local opposition to bringing new plants on line, or to planning for the future expansion of facilities, stiffened. In Europe, antinuclear opinion emerged as a strong force in countries like Germany. During the accident, 35,000 Germans marched, chanting, "We all live in Pennsylvania." Added to hugely mounting costs, delays, and new regulations, this growing skepticism hurt an already crippled industry.

The accident and the ensuing communications failure at Three Mile Island also undercut the faith of many Americans in their political, scientific, and economic institutions. Several congressional investigations faulted the NRC for its lack of leadership and candor. A separate presidential report criticized information provided to the public by the NRC and Metropolitan Edison. Exaggeration, ignorance, and rumor had dominated reporting of the event, at least until Harold Denton took control of communications. When the accident was at its most dangerous stage, the public received the advice that nothing was wrong. After the crisis had passed, the media and even state safety officials exaggerated the danger and incited a mass exodus.

Revelation of the existence of paper trails leading to the accident fueled public suspicion that the government and the nuclear industry had conspired to conceal atomic power plant dangers. Regulators did not regulate sufficiently, and companies cut corners to sustain a sick industry. Publication in 1979 of a report on a nuclear disaster in the Soviet Union added to the controversy. A Russian emigré scientist described an accident that had occurred in 1957 or 1958 in the Ural Mountains at a nuclear dump site. He maintained that it had caused devastation of thousands of square miles and killed hundreds of people—and that U.S. government officials had known about the accident for two decades. They had not reported it to the public for security reasons and, he speculated, to protect America's nuclear industry from public criticism.

The accident at Three Mile Island was, in the final analysis, an accident that did not really happen. The worst predictions did not come true. The third line of defense in the containment building held. The core did not melt down completely, and the China syndrome was avoided. And yet the accident had a profound effect. It spread a further cloud of doubt over American society at a time when many Americans were asking agonizing questions about social, economic, and political institutions that also did not seem to work well.

# A Crisis
# of
# Credibility

The accident at Three Mile Island and its aftershocks of disbelief and doubt epitomized the growing problem of accountability in American society during the 1970s. As the economy, technology, government bureaucracy, and social problems became more complex, Americans wanted to know who was responsible. Often, it was impossible to find a straightforward answer to this question. In the case of Three Mile Island, the war in Vietnam, Watergate, and other major events of the decade, it was difficult to find a person, an agency, or an institution that would take responsibility. Increasingly, companies, government bureaucrats, and officials of all sorts, masked their activities behind public relations, the object of which was to convince and persuade the public, but not necessarily to inform it.

## AMERICAN SOCIETY AT A CROSSROAD

Ironically, this reliance on credibility and persuasiveness came at a time when private and public institutions were growing ever larger and more complex. The world of computers, nuclear plants, and space travel could not be translated into simple explanations. The technology of nuclear power plants performed remarkable tasks—in silence, out of sight, and beyond the comprehension of most Americans. There were no familiar spinning gears, whirling belts, or clanging machines in such new industries. They performed marvels of production, but they also sometimes released deadly—and invisible—pollutants. Their operation in the public interest demanded knowledge, skill, and honesty. The public had no other choice but to trust its experts.

Trust was also crucial for the success of government. During the 1970s, the federal government took up difficult—perhaps impossible—tasks. Special interest groups increasingly demanded that government redress grievances and balance old inequalities in social relations. Rising expectations about what government could do to solve problems transformed complex social, economic, and even personal and family issues, into political issues. This was not all. The federal government also had to confront new and contradictory economic problems such as rising inflation, low productivity, and energy shortages.

In this complicated and difficult world, institutions and bureaucracies often used public relations and the mass media to maintain their credibility. Indeed, "credibility" became a widely used political word in this decade. It meant confidence in the honesty and reliability of a government official, a company spokesman, a labor union representative, a consumer advocate. But it did not necessarily mean truthfulness. Inevitably during the 1970s, times of crisis were also credibility crises. The accident at Three Mile Island was a credibility crisis because the public began to doubt official statements and reports, to distrust experts, and to question the intentions of elected representatives. More than ever, Americans wanted government to solve problems—and more than ever, they feared it could not.

The 1970s were years of limitation and readjustment. Many of the institutions whose stability a generation of Americans had taken for granted suddenly appeared weak and ineffectual. The period from 1945 to about 1968 had been exceptional in American history because of its sustained economic growth and dramatic social progress. But Americans had come to accept such successes as normal. Prior to World War II, the nation had experienced prolonged depressions as well as booms, bitter social struggles, and political crises. The 1970s served to remind Americans that economic progress is erratic. But this was not a welcome lesson to a nation that had come to expect uninterrupted progress.

Economic problems in the 1970s were complex and interrelated. The delayed impact of expenditures for the war in Vietnam pushed inflation higher. Small rises in productivity rates after 1966 indicated that many American industries were falling behind Japanese and West European competitors in adopting modern technology. Profligate use of cheap energy made energy shortages and steep price hikes painful to absorb. In time, the energy crisis fueled inflation and slowed economic growth. And the shrinking margin of competitiveness of American goods destabilized the dollar and turned the international balance of payments against the United States. Large budget deficits, high interest rates, and inaction often compounded these problems. The economy did grow during this period, and real wages for most workers did increase—but not at the pace set in the 1960s.

Social change, too, tested the resilience and credibility of American institutions. Political demonstrations and violence occurred sporadically in the early 1970s. And crime rates rose relentlessly: Between 1968 and 1978, aggravated assaults increased by about 60 percent. Larceny and theft rates increased at about the same rate. Heavily concentrated in cities, these crimes were well publicized and visible. There seemed to be a direct link between the size and congestion of a city and its crime rate.

Other indicators suggested a transformation in the family—once the most stable of institutions and now split by divorce and altered by changing relationships between men and women in American society. After a low point in the mid-1950s, divorce rates almost tripled by the end of the 1970s. The size of American families shrank as the postwar baby boom ended. This in turn affected the age structure of the population. America was growing older, and this older population was becoming increasingly active politically.

Perhaps most important in terms of life styles was the change in women's roles. Masked by the domestic ideology of the late 1940s and 1950s, women's lives in fact changed rapidly after World War II. Most significant was the increased participation of women in the work force. In 1947 only about 27 percent of workers in the labor force were women. In 1981, women constituted about 43 percent of the labor force. Put another way, in 1947 about 30 percent of women worked. In 1981 almost 50 percent worked. Together with increasing recognition of their past treatment as second-class citizens, this new economic power convinced many women to challenge the customs of family and society that had restricted their roles. Women demanded equality, respect, and an end to formal and informal restrictions on opportunities and careers. Many of their endeavors were highly visible: more women elected to public office, a large increase of interest in women's sports, and perhaps equally important, the rediscovery of a hidden history of past achievements.

However, a change of this magnitude could not occur without challenges. Increasingly during the 1970s, disputes over women's roles focused on the proposed Equal Rights Amendment to the Constitution. Little more, in fact, than a ratification of the rights to equal treatment that many women already enjoyed and that most Americans supported, the ERA came to symbolize those

## MARRIAGE AND DIVORCE RATES IN THE UNITED STATES

| Year | Total Divorces | Divorce Rate per 1,000 | Marriage Rate per 1,000 |
|------|----------------|------------------------|-------------------------|
| 1965 | 479,000 | 2.5 | 9.3 |
| 1970 | 708,000 | 3.5 | 10.6 |
| 1975 | 1,036,000 | 4.9 | 10.1 |
| 1980 | 1,182,000 | 5.3 | 10.9 |

Source: U.S. Department of Commerce, Bureau of the Census, *Statistical Abstract of the United States, 1981* (Washington, D.C.: Government Printing Office, 1981), pp. 57 and 81.

**REPRESENTATIVE SHIRLEY CHISHOLM**
During the 1960s and 1970s, an increasing number of blacks and women were elected to local, state, and federal office. Shirley Chisholm of New York City was a pioneer, serving in the House of Representatives from 1969 to 1982. (©Lee Goff/Magnum)

changes in modern society that more conservative Americans opposed. In this dispute, both sides viewed the government as the ultimate arbitrator. Although the amendment failed in 1982, public opinion supporting it did not diminish.

Much of the same sort of struggle prevailed in questions of race relations. Increasing ethnic and racial self-confidence in the late 1960s gave rise to strong pressure groups, but it also fed resentment and controversy over the gains of minorities through legislation and court mandate. Many Americans came to believe that the federal government operated in favor of special interest groups—whether racial minorities, the poor, and women, or the oil companies and the nuclear industry. This kind of thinking fed a general tendency toward less political participation that began in the mid-1960s. Percentages of eligible voters who cast ballots—despite the increased ease of doing so—declined. Political scandals, corruption, and favoritism disillusioned and alienated

voters, convincing many that their votes did not count.

The general transformation of political and social change into stalemate was partly generated by a new individualist ethic. This new morality of unlimited self-expression has caused the 1970s to be aptly characterized as the decade of the "me generation." The term refers to a decline of belief in community, of working together to solve problems, and an emphasis on the private individual. In some cases, this celebration of the self led to an increasing frankness about sexuality and life styles that would have been unthinkable ten years earlier. Movements of personal liberation included such groups as the handicapped, gay men and women, and children's rights advocates. Whether or not this development benefited society, however, became an increasingly disputed question.

Above all else, the war in Vietnam was the catalyst in creating the tone of political and institutional crisis in the 1970s. President Johnson's decision not to seek reelection in 1968—and Richard Nixon's defeat of Hubert Humphrey for the presidency—reflected public opposition to continuing the war. But paradoxically, Americans did not wish to lose in Vietnam. Thus it took five more painful years before the United States finally extricated itself from the war.

## NIXON AND SOUTHEAST ASIA

The career of Richard M. Nixon was marked by recurrent controversy, triumph, and defeat—or as he put it, "crises." Born into a Quaker family in 1913 in Yorba Linda, California, Nixon earned a law degree at Duke University. He set up a law practice in Whittier, California, shortly before the beginning of World War II. During the war, he served as a naval supply officer in the Pacific. After the conflict ended, he returned home to California and began his rapid rise in national politics—from representative, to senator, to vice president. From the first, his campaigns, if not actually dishonest, were marred by political

# Norman Lear

(UPI)

At 9:30 P.M. on January 12, 1971, CBS television inaugurated a new series by warning its viewers that the contents of the program might seem offensive or inappropriate to some viewers. What followed was the first showing of Norman Lear's *All in the Family,* in which the leading character, Archie Bunker, vented his petty prejudices against "Hebes," "Spics," "Greasers," and "Coons." This offensive language decorated equally offensive opinions. Archie Bunker represented bigotry. His wife, Edith, however, was naive and good-hearted; and his son-in-law, Mike ("Meathead"), was a liberal. The sparks that flew between family members illuminated serious tensions in American society, but the program was always light-hearted and satiric. Archie Bunker lost each week's battle, although he was never at a loss for expressing a new prejudice in the next episode. Audiences did not flinch from this tough satire; they loved it. By May, Lear's series had become the most popular show on television, and CBS moved it to prime time.

Lear's fertile imagination quickly concocted other shows. One spin-off was *Maude,* which first aired in September 1972. In this production, the heroine was a liberal counterpart of Archie Bunker, and as stubborn and rigid in her opinions as he was in his. Other shows inaugurated by Lear included *Good Times,* the story of a black family living in a housing project, and *Mary Hartman, Mary Hartman,* a satire of afternoon soap operas. In each of these programs, Lear's touch was obvious. The worlds he created and satirized were those of stereotypes—in politics, popular culture, and American society.

In some respects, Lear wrote his own past into his best productions. Archie Bunker was based on his father, an ineffectual entrepreneur who often shouted at his mother, "Stifle yourself!" and, at Norman, "You're the laziest white kid I ever saw." Lear fought his way into show business as a comedy writer. During the late 1950s, he became a regular television script writer, and during the 1960s, he dabbled in film writing and production. After working out the story idea and writing sample scripts for *All in the Family,* he tried to sell the program to ABC-TV. The company praised the idea but rejected it as too controversial. So Lear turned to CBS, which accepted the proposal.

CBS, however, did not always support Lear. In-house program censors sometimes tried—unsuccessfully—to cut potentially offensive material. In late spring of 1975, CBS, ABC, and NBC created a "family hour" to run from 7 to 9 P.M. (6 to 8 in the Midwest). This special time segment, it was agreed, would limit violence and present programming suitable for everyone in the family. *All in the Family* was not considered by CBS to be suitable for this time period, so the company rescheduled the program for a later hour. Lear was furious and brought suit against the network. In late November 1976, a federal judge decided in Lear's favor, and the "family hour" agreement was rescinded. Lear won this battle, but he ultimately lost the war for American audiences. By the late 1970s, several of his newer productions had disappeared. Lear's social sitcoms gave way to sexcoms like *Charlie's Angels.* By 1980, Lear had, by and large, abandoned his innovative role in American television.

smears and innuendos about the patriotism of his opponents. He served in Congress and achieved prominence for his pursuit of Alger Hiss while a member of the House Un-American Activities Committee. By 1952 he represented the best compromise candidate for the vice presidency.

During his eight-year tenure in Eisenhower's shadow, Nixon worked hard to build his leadership of the Republican party. In 1960, he was an easy winner of the presidential nomination and only a narrow loser in the election. Back after defeat in a race for governor of California, Nixon won the Republican nomination in 1968, again by occupying the center of his party. In the campaign, he benefited from growing dismay over the war and the social strife that it was causing at home. He promised to resolve the Vietnam conflict but refused to say how.

Nixon's attitude toward government was a curious blend of admiration, suspicion, and hostility. He enjoyed the power and pomp of office. But because of longstanding enmities with the press and the Democratic party, he saw himself as an outsider—a representative of those who distrusted government. This sort of division showed up in his political appointments. Most members of his cabinet were men with Washington connections, or they were well-known in Republican circles—like Henry Kissinger, his special assistant for national security. But Nixon's personal staff was made up of men who distrusted the Washington political establishment. The White House inner circle was ruled by H. R. (Bob) Haldeman, the chief of staff, and John Dean, the president's legal counsel.

Promising an open government, Nixon in fact shut many of his most important decisions away from public scrutiny. He and Henry Kissinger were both convinced that the United States had to maintain credibility in opposing the Soviet Union and still end American participation in the Vietnam War. To achieve this contradictory end, the president decided to withdraw American forces from combat and yet deny victory to the Viet Cong and North Vietnam through air

power. This tactic was named "Vietnamization." Over the next two years, he withdrew almost 500,000 American troops until only 50,000 remained in late 1972. At the same time, he stepped up air raids and approved the invasion of Cambodia and Laos to cut off enemy supply lines.

In bombing Cambodia, early in his administration, Nixon altered the rules of the war. The president had ordered an attack on a nation that was officially neutral. He wanted to keep the intervention a secret, especially from the American public. When news of the raids leaked to the *New York Times,* Nixon and Kissinger were furious. The White House ordered wiretaps on the telephones of five newsmen and several employees of the National Security Agency to find out who had told the press. In effect, Nixon's crisis of credibility had begun.

The president's anger at the press and television did not prevent him from using the media to try to defuse protests against his Vietnamization policy. During the summer of 1969, he attacked demonstrators in speeches and news conferences. But his efforts proved ineffective. On October 15, thousands of Americans demonstrated against the war in several cities. An even larger coalition, supported now by important congressmen and newspapers, began to solidify around the peace issue.

Nixon and his aides concluded that if the American public believed the criticisms of the administration appearing in the media, then it was time to attack the integrity and objectivity of the media. Thus the president approved Vice President Spiro Agnew's accusing the press and the major television networks of biased reporting. The President also approved Agnew's bitter denunciation of student protesters as an "effete corps of impudent snobs who characterized themselves as intellectuals." Both tactics, the administration hoped, would split the nation and polarize opinion. If antiwar opinion could be isolated, it might also be quieted. As Agnew put it, "it is time for a positive polarization."

Nixon's policy of diverting war casualties to

the Vietnamese and deflecting criticism at home had achieved some success by early 1970. On April 4 a large group of prowar demonstrators congregated in Washington. The overthrow of neutral Prince Sihanouk of Cambodia and his replacement by the pro-American Lon Nol, made it possible to take more drastic action to cut off supplies reaching the Viet Cong through that country. In late April, Nixon authorized an invasion of Cambodia. But he miscalculated the domestic effects of this action. The antiwar movement suddenly sprang to life with demonstrations and strikes on college campuses throughout the nation. Police and the National Guard were called out to restore order in a number of places. At Kent State University in Ohio, National Guard troops opened fire on a crowd of students on May 4, killing four of them. Shortly afterward, at Jackson State University in Mississippi two black protesters were shot and killed. In his angry comments on such incidents, the president appeared to blame the demonstrators.

With pressure mounting for an end to the war, Nixon tried to enlist the country's "silent majority" to turn back war opponents. His chance came during the fall congressional elections, but the results were inconclusive. The Republicans gained two Senate seats, but lost nine places in the House and eleven governorships. Rather than isolating war critics, the president had begun to isolate himself.

In early 1971, Nixon showed a more conciliatory mood, but this dissolved in the wake of further serious opposition to the war. A South Vietnamese invasion of Laos with American air support brought little vocal opposition. But two events riveted national attention on war critics. The first was a large, disruptive demonstration in Washington on May 2 and 3 by the "Mayday Tribe," which resulted in 10,000 arrests. Much more serious was publication of the "Pentagon Papers," beginning June 13 in the *New York Times*. This history of U.S. involvement in Vietnam, culled from secret government files by Daniel Ellsberg, a former Kissinger aide, showed the extent of covert American involvement in Southeast Asia and exposed the intrigue and deception of three administrations.

President Nixon tried to stop publication of these damning government documents, but the Supreme Court ruled in favor of the public's right to know. No documents implicated the Nixon administration, but the history of America's secret and growing involvement in Southeast Asia undercut the reputations of three previous presidents. Nixon did not dispute the truthfulness of the history. His charge was that its publication would undermine the credibility of government.

As the war in Vietnam continued its bloody course, Nixon and Kissinger pursued another, different goal in foreign policy. Both leaders were convinced that the United States must recognize the rising power of other nations. Europe, Japan, the Soviet Union, and China all represented separate poles of power. With Europe pursuing a more independent course, the president believed the time was ripe to upgrade relations with China. He also wished to reach a limited arms control agreement with the Soviet Union.

The president initiated his policy secretly, in part because he did not wish to stir criticism from the right wing of his own party, which vigorously opposed détente with the Chinese communists and the Russians. Nonetheless, signs of a thaw with the Chinese were unmistakable. In April 1971, a U.S. table tennis team traveled to mainland China for a series of matches. In July the president announced that he would visit China, as a result of negotiations carried out by Henry Kissinger. Inevitably these moves seriously compromised support for America's staunch ally nationalist China, which still occupied Taiwan. On October 12, Nixon announced a similar trip to the Soviet Union. Both of these initiatives represented major changes in American policy because they softened U.S. opposition toward an accommodation with the two major communist powers. After the president's dramatic, week-long visit to China in February 1972, the United States began to normalize relations

with that nation. Warmer relations with the Chinese, in turn, convinced the Soviet Union to seek closer ties with the United States.

The results of bargaining with the Russians bore fruit in the spring and summer of 1972. When Nixon returned from the Soviet Union in late May he had cemented two major agreements. The first was a Strategic Arms Limitation Treaty (SALT I), signed with Soviet leader Leonid Brezhnev on May 26 and limiting U.S. and Soviet deployment of antiballistic missile systems. The second was a large Russian purchase of American grain, announced in July.

But the president failed to persuade either China or the U.S.S.R. to abandon North Vietnam. Indeed, the Vietnam crisis worsened. The South Vietnamese government made no real advance in winning the support of its population. Militarily, the situation remained bleak. With diminished numbers of American troops in the country, U.S. power relied more on air strikes. And time obviously favored the insurgents. Do-

mestic support for the war continued to crumble. In a symbolic act in 1971, the Senate rescinded the Gulf of Tonkin resolution. During the spring and summer and into the fall of 1972, the United States and North Vietnam conducted peace negotiations in Paris. Partly to influence the 1972 presidential elections, Kissinger announced during the fall that a peace treaty was imminent. But negotiations faltered, and the president ordered new, saturation bombing of the North. Finally, in January 1973, a treaty was signed. American prisoners of war were to be released, and the South Vietnamese regime was to remain in power. But North Vietnam was allowed to keep troops in the South. In effect, the United States had abandoned the South for which it had fought so long.

Although it ratified a military reverse of major proportions, the treaty was in one sense a positive accomplishment. Nixon had ended the war and yet had avoided the right-wing backlash that two presidents before him had deeply feared. Added to the rapprochement with the Chinese and the Russians, ending the war represented a significant turning point in American foreign relations.

# NIXON'S CREDIBILITY AT HOME

In domestic policy, President Nixon faced two obstacles: a Congress dominated by the Democratic party and a government bureaucracy unresponsive and unsympathetic to his policies. These stumbling blocks constituted a major impediment to the credibility of his administration. The president focused on four issues, but each of them proved highly resistant to change: He attempted to strengthen legal weapons against crime and political violence. He sought a major overhaul of social welfare policy. He attempted to cope with a serious bout of economic stagnation, inflation, and energy shortages. And he tried to reorganize the executive branch.

Elected partly because he had promised decisive action against social disorder, Nixon secured a tough new criminal justice law in the District of Columbia. His attorney general, John Mitchell, sought to isolate student and radical groups by infiltrating their ranks and prosecuting them under an antiriot law passed in 1968. Since many administration members as well as voters believed that civil rights was a major source of social unrest, he also tried to slow federal desegregation actions. Attorney General Mitchell testified against extending the Voting Rights Act, due to expire in August 1970. But Congress renewed the act anyway.

Striking at another institution that had loosened social restraints, Nixon tried to transform the Supreme Court. Early in his administration, the president had to fill two Court openings, one of them the chief justice position. Nixon first nominated two undistinguished, conservative Southern appeals court judges. The Senate rejected both on the grounds of incompetence and because of their extreme views on race relations. Stung by these defeats, Nixon found two acceptable justices, Warren Burger (chief justice) and Harry Blackmun. With two more appointments during his second term, Nixon hoped to affect the complexion of Court, but it still continued to deliver integration decisions; and in 1973, in a landmark decision, it declared constitutional a woman's right to have an abortion.

The issue of welfare payments to nonworking mothers and children was part of the larger question of providing social services and income maintenance to the poor and elderly. Some Americans believed that the poor should suffer the consequences of their fate, and that the federal government should provide only minimal assistance. The president did not share this harsh view, but he did oppose the tangle of agencies and programs left over from the Great Society. His first plan to correct this confusion was the Family Assistance Plan—a plan to provide a guaranteed income of $1,600 for a family of four (plus $820 in food stamps). Twice passed by the House, the act failed in the Senate, and Nixon abandoned it in 1971.

Taking a different tack, the administration did succeed in shifting some federal social programs to the states in the 1972 State and Local Fiscal Assistance Act. This law created "revenue sharing" for the states. In effect it provided block grants to state authorities, with general standards set for expenditures of money but wide discretion left to local administration.

Some of the president's difficulties in passing new social legislation lay in the sluggish economy. As the leader of a political party that ritualistically proclaimed its faith in the private sector, Nixon used federal fiscal and monetary instruments to fight economic problems. At one point he even declared himself a follower of Keynesian economics, "I am now a Keynesian," he told a group of journalists. But his administration lacked an overall, consistent policy.

Shortly after entering the White House, Nixon had promised to nudge the lethargic economy with increased federal expenditures. But by mid-1971, fighting inflation took top priority. In the summer, the president acted on several fronts. Calling this Phase I of his economic program, he

# ECONOMICS AND HISTORY

## The Inflation Game: Winners and Losers

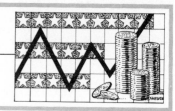

Each year during the 1970s and 1980s, Chrysler, General Motors, Ford, and American Motors announced price increases for many of their automobiles and trucks. As a reason, they blamed rising labor costs, increased prices for raw materials, the cost of government safety regulations, and growing transportation expenses. Added into the general price index, these rising prices for automobiles accounted for a substantial part of annual increases in consumer prices. Rising prices—or general inflation—in turn, has become a widespread and tenacious problem for most advanced market economies in the world, including the United States.

Inflation results from scarcity: a shortage of capital available for investment, which makes interest rates rise; a tight labor market, resulting in higher wages; a scarcity of raw materials and energy, which forces up the costs of manufacturing; and a short supply of manufactured products, which causes their prices to mount. The principle is easy to understand. Shortages force buyers to pay higher prices. If spread over the whole economy, such shortages can cause a general inflation.

However, increased demand need not in itself spur inflation. Inflation will not occur if production rises along with purchasing power. Wages may also rise, provided they keep pace with productivity. In other words, if the costs of production per unit fall because of worker efficiency, then wages may be increased without raising costs. If, however, wages increase and productivity does not, then the cost per unit must increase, with a resulting rise in costs and prices.

The effects of inflation are partly psychological and partly real. For example, if general prices rise by 6 percent per year and wages and salaries go up by about 6.5 percent per year, and individual will increase his or her real earnings by only about 0.5 percent. Over a long period of time, it may seem as if wages and income are diminishing. Furthermore, with a graduated income tax system, as wages rise, taxable income creeps upward from lower to higher tax brackets, and thus taxes mount. Also, in times of very high inflation, people may lose confidence in their currency and in their government. In such circumstances, fears of a "shrinking dollar" may enter the political marketplace, to the detriment of reasonable discussion.

During periods of inflation there are, of course, real losers. Those who exist on fixed incomes and private pensions are one example. Their incomes may not rise as fast as prices. On the other hand, persons on government pensions and social security generally gain, for their benefits are tied (or indexed) to the general inflation rate. In the inflationary years of the late 1970s and early 1980s, two groups lost ground: landlords and stockholders. Neither the value of rents nor the earnings on stocks kept pace with rising prices. Other groups, such as salaried employees and union members generally received increases at least as large as the inflation rate.

If there are losers at times of inflation, there must also be gainers. Money paid for the higher prices goes to those who possess items in short supply—in particular, persons who have tended to be speculators in such items—for example, food, land (real estate), gold, oil, and so on. High interest rates during inflation times also benefit those who have capital to lend at high rates.

## INFLATION: ANNUAL PERCENTAGE INCREASE IN CONSUMER PRICES, 1970–1981

| Year | Rate |
|------|------|
| 1970 | 5.9% |
| 1971 | 4.3 |
| 1972 | 3.3 |
| 1973 | 6.2 |
| 1974 | 11.0 |
| 1975 | 9.1 |
| 1976 | 5.8 |
| 1977 | 6.5 |
| 1978 | 7.7 |
| 1979 | 11.3 |
| 1980 | 13.5 |
| 1981 | 9.8 |

## INFLATION: AVERAGE FIVE-YEARLY PRICE CHANGES, 1960–1980

| | |
|------|------|
| 1960–1965 | 1.3% |
| 1965–1970 | 4.2 |
| 1970–1975 | 6.7 |
| 1975–1980 | 8.9 |

Source: U.S. Department of Commerce, Census Bureau, *Statistical Abstract of the United States, 1981* (Washington, D.C.: U.S. Government Printing Office, 1981), p. 459.

Although it may not be absolutely necessary for economic health, low inflation has been the goal of most recent governments in the United States. The aim is easily stated, but no path toward it is without peril. In recent years, three methods have been tried, all of them having serious drawbacks.

1. *Wage and price controls.* In 1971, as a result of mounting inflation, the Nixon administration established a wage and price freeze. With some adjustments, the policy, while in force, maintained relatively constant prices and wages. But this was only a temporary measure. And prices tended to creep upward while wages did not, which increased political pressure to lift the controls. When controls were eliminated in 1973, prices rose sharply.

2. *Intentional recession.* A recession to "cool" the economy and lower prices may be engineered by the federal government through fiscal means (by shrinking expenditures or raising taxes or both) or by monetary policy (by making the cost of borrowing so high as to discourage investment and expansion). In either case, the result may be higher unemployment and, eventually, lessened demand for goods and services. Prices then begin to fall. This policy was employed to a greater or lesser extent by President Nixon in 1969, by President Ford in 1976, by President Carter in 1980, and by President Reagan in 1981–1982. Its effects have been mixed. Generally inflation has declined, but the decline was substantial only during the last recession, which was also the most severe. Unfortunately, recessions also create undesirable side effects—including unemployment, which most severely affects groups that are already relatively disadvantaged: women, blacks, Hispanics, young workers, and the unskilled.

3. *Massive price shocks.* Price shocks—dramatic cuts in the prices of certain goods or services—may be administered by the federal government acting to begin a sustained downward spiral of prices in one sector with the hopes of setting off ripple effects elsewhere in the economy. During the Carter administration, price shock was implemented by means of airline deregulation. To have a marked overall effect, however, this policy must be applied fairly broadly, risking instability and even increased bankruptcies.

If there is any constant to the problem of inflation, it is complexity. Each solution has its drawbacks. On the other hand, unchecked inflation is equally risky. But as in any economic development, so too with inflation: there are winners and losers.

froze wages and prices for ninety days, slapped a 10 percent surcharge on imports, and devalued the American dollar.

A second phase began in the summer of 1973, when the president reimposed a price freeze for sixty days. When these controls were relaxed, prices soared again. One reason for this sudden, uncontrollable inflation was the steep increase in imported oil prices. By 1973, the United States was importing about one-third of its total crude oil. More than half that total came from OPEC— the Organization of Petroleum Exporting Countries. These nations, among them Saudi Arabia, Kuwait, Libya, Iran, Iraq, Nigeria, and Venezuela, had jointly raised oil prices about 400 percent above 1970 prices. In addition, during the winter of 1973–1974, Arab members of OPEC embargoed all shipments of oil to the United States and other Western nations that supported Israel during the 1973 Yom Kippur War against Egypt and Syria. Spot shortages appeared in the United States, with long lines of automobiles snaking around filling stations.

Unable to develop a consistent and effective economic program, Nixon also discovered enormous inertia in government itself. Of all the problems he faced, none frustrated the president as much as his lack of control over the federal bureaucracy. Twice, Nixon and his advisers tried to reorganize the executive branch. But both efforts, in 1970 and in 1973, failed. In particular, his attempts to subordinate Cabinet heads to the White House staff met spirited opposition.

Finding himself stalemated in several directions, and feeling besieged by the press and Congress, the president tried to undercut the institutions that blocked him. In doing so, he created a submerged, secret branch of government that depended on intrigue and conspiracy. The first such instance was the phone taps used after the bombing of Cambodia. He took a more serious step in the fall of 1970. Tom Huston, a White House aide, prepared a program of domestic spying to be implemented by the president's staff. J. Edgar Hoover, head of the FBI, refused to agree, in part because it would undercut his own agency. When this proposal failed, the administration created the White House investigation unit known as "the plumbers," whose job it was to plug information leaks.

Losses in the election of 1970 and continued criticism of his Vietnam policy convinced the president to act. After publication of the Pentagon Papers, the White House approved plans to break into Daniel Ellsberg's psychiatrist's office to search for material that might incriminate him. The operation was financed with money received in a secret donation from the milk industry, given in return for administration support of higher milk price supports.

In 1972, the administration plunged deeper into illegal activities. Many of these originated in the Committee for the Re-election of the President (CREEP). CREEP hoped to shape the election of 1972 to Nixon's advantage. It willfully misinformed the public and broke the law. Using secret contributions solicited from corporate donors, the group employed "dirty tricks" that injected false issues into Democratic party primaries. CREEP also broke into Democratic party headquarters in May 1972 to install wiretaps and to photograph documents. When the group returned in mid-June to obtain more material, a night watchman alerted the Washington, D.C., police. They arrived quickly at the Watergate complex that housed the headquarters and arrested several of the burglars. A few were Cuban refugees, but two were ex-employees of CREEP.

The Democratic party denounced the break-in, but administration spokesmen dismissed it as a "third-rate burglary attempt." As an election issue, Watergate died. The Democratic candidate, George McGovern, tried to galvanize his party around opposition to the Vietnam War and promises of social reform. But his own credibility was compromised when he supported Senator Thomas Eagleton of Missouri for vice president and then dropped him after information about the senator's history of mental illness surfaced. Much of his early support fell away, and traditional sources of Democratic power in urban political machines and in the labor movement refused to work for him. Nixon's campaign stressed his accomplishments: dramatic changes in foreign policy and a revived economy. He won every state but Massachusetts and the District of Columbia. But the Democrats retained their majority in Congress.

In his second inaugural address, the president spoke words that came to have a bitter irony for his next years:

> From this day forward let each of us make a solemn commitment in his own heart: to bear his responsibility, to do his part, to live his ideals.

At the beginning of 1973, Nixon moved to assert firmer control of the executive branch and to dismantle the Great Society. Even though he impounded funds (refused to spend appropriated money), he made little headway. Instead, he found himself increasingly mired in explanations of the Watergate break-in and other campaign irregularities.

The Watergate scandal hinged on the question of credibility. For Nixon and all his advisers, the problem of truthfulness was rarely an issue. Rather, the Watergate defendants tried again and again to create credible explanations for their behavior, willfully mixing truth with invention and misinformation. As they retreated, more and more of the real story emerged. The administration's problems began when Judge John Sirica, presiding over the trial of the burglars in early 1973, pressed the defendants. One of them, James McCord, implicated high administration figures in the planning of election espionage. He accused John Mitchell and White House staff members Jeb Magruder and John Dean. *Washington Post* reporters picked up loose ends of evidence that emerged in the trial and began weaving together the story of a painstaking plot to cover up ties between the Watergate burglars and the White House.

When John Dean testified during June hear-ings before the Presidential Campaign Committee, set up in the Senate, he used this forum to escape what he believed was a White House decision to make him a scapegoat for Watergate. He even implicated the president in the cover-up. With this new evidence, the investigation intensified. A grand jury began to weigh evidence against a mounting list of accused conspirators. Other material surfaced through efforts of a special prosecutor, Archibald Cox, appointed to oversee the investigation in the attorney general's office. Surrounded, and with his own defenses crumbling, the president worked publicly to investigate what he privately tried to hide. As he instructed John Mitchell:

> I want you all to stonewall it, let them plead the Fifth Amendment, cover-up or anything else, if it'll save it—save the plan.

One by one the president's close advisers resigned. In October 1973, Vice President Agnew left office, pleading no contest to charges of income tax fraud after a grand jury discovered that he had accepted bribes and payoffs while governor of Maryland. The most startling discovery, however, came when a White House aide told of hundreds of tapes of recorded conversations between Nixon and his advisers made secretly over the previous two years. These could establish the president's guilt or innocence.

Nixon's refusal to submit any of the tapes to Cox, the grand jury, or the Senate committee further damaged his credibility. He tried every means to keep the material secret, invoking "executive privilege," and fighting with law suits and delays. He even fired prosecutor Cox. But Cox's replacement, Leon Jaworski, persisted in demanding the evidence. Finally, in April 1974, Nixon released edited versions of the tapes. Even in abridged form, the documents revealed that the president was deeply involved in the Watergate cover-up. They also uncovered the private Nixon—a man who was as ruthless and vulgar in private as he was cautious and well spoken in

## WATERGATE ROSTER

| | Position | Role in Watergate | Sentence | Amount of Sentence Served |
|---|---|---|---|---|
| **Richard M. Nixon** | President of the United States | Unindicted coconspirator | Pardoned | |
| **Dwight L. Chapin** | Presidential appointments secretary | Convicted of lying to a grand jury | Sentenced to serve 10 to 30 months | Served 8 months |
| **Charles W. Colson** | Special Counsel to the president | Pleaded guilty to obstruction of justice | Sentenced to serve 1 to 3 years; fined $5,000 | Served 7 months |
| **John W. Dean III** | Counsel to the president | Pleaded guilty to conspiracy | Sentenced to serve 1 to 4 years | Served 4 months |
| **John D. Ehrlichman** | Domestic Council chief | Convicted of conspiracy to obstruct justice, conspiracy, and perjury | Sentenced to serve concurrent terms of 20 months to 8 years | Served 18 months |
| **H. R. Haldeman** | Chief of the White House staff | Convicted of conspiracy and perjury | Sentenced to serve 30 months to 8 years | Served 18 months |
| **E. Howard Hunt** | White House aide | Pleaded guilty to conspiracy, burglary, and wiretapping | Sentenced to serve 30 months to 8 years; fined $10,000 | Served 33 months |
| **Herbert W. Kalmbach** | Personal attorney to the president | Pleaded guilty to violation of Federal Corrupt Practices Act and promising federal employment as a reward for political activity | Sentenced to serve 6 to 18 months; fined $10,000 | Served 6 months |
| **Richard G. Kleindienst** | Attorney General of the United States | Pleaded guilty to refusal to answer pertinent questions before a Senate committee | Sentenced to serve 30 days; fined $100 | Sentence suspended |
| **Egil Krogh, Jr.** | White House aide | Pleaded guilty to conspiracy | Sentenced to serve 2 to 6 years (all but 6 months suspended) | Served 4½ months |
| **Frederick C. LaRue** | Assistant to John Mitchell | Pleaded guilty to conspiracy | Sentenced to serve 1 to 3 years (all but 6 months suspended) | Served 5½ months |
| **G. Gordon Liddy** | White House aide | Convicted of conspiracy, burglary, and wiretapping | Sentenced to serve 6 years and 8 months to 20 years; fined $40,000 | Served 52 months |
| **Jeb S. Magruder** | White House aide | Pleaded guilty to conspiracy, wiretapping, and fraud | Sentenced to serve 10 months to 4 years | Served 7 months |

## WATERGATE ROSTER *(continued)*

| | *Position* | *Role in Watergate* | *Sentence* | *Amount of Sentence Served* |
|---|---|---|---|---|
| **John N. Mitchell** | Attorney General of the United States | Convicted of conspiracy and perjury | Sentenced to serve 30 months to 8 years | Served 19 months |
| **Donald H. Segretti** | "Dirty tricks" specialist | Pleaded guilty to campaign violations and conspiracy | Sentenced to serve 6 months | Served 4½ months |
| **Maurice H. Stans** | Finance Director of Committee for the Re-Election of the President | Pleaded guilty to misdemeanor violations of the Federal Elections Campaign Act | Fined $5,000 | |
| **Bernard L. Barker** | Watergate burglar | Pleaded guilty to conspiracy, burglary, wiretapping, and unlawful possession of intercepting devices | Sentenced to serve 18 months to 6 years | Served 12 months |
| **Virgilio R. Gonzalez** | Watergate burglar | Pleaded guilty to conspiracy, burglary, wiretapping, and unlawful possession of intercepting devices | Sentenced to serve 1 to 4 years | Served 15 months |
| **James W. McCord, Jr.** | Watergate burglar | Convicted of conspiracy, burglary, wiretapping, and unlawful possession of intercepting devices | Sentenced to serve 1 to 5 years | Served 4 months |
| **Eugenio R. Martinez** | Watergate burglar | Pleaded guilty to conspiracy, burglary, wiretapping and unlawful possession of intercepting devices | Sentenced to serve 1 to 4 years | Served 15 months |
| **Frank A. Sturgis** | Watergate burglar | Pleaded guilty to conspiracy, burglary, wiretapping, and unlawful possession of intercepting devices | Sentenced to serve 1 to 4 years | Served 13 months |

**"NIXON RESIGNS"**

President Nixon's desperate attempt to remain in office, despite the Watergate scandal that swirled about him, was adversely affected by revelations regarding wrongdoing in his administration printed in the *Washington Post*. (*©Alex Webb/Magnum*)

public. The House Judiciary Committee began hearings on impeachment.

As Nixon was forced to release more tapes, impressions of his guilt became firmer. Two new groups of tapes released over the summer disclosed the president's direct participation in the cover-up of the Watergate burglary. On August 8, after his administration had almost ceased to govern—and facing probable impeachment—the president resigned. But he would admit no wrongdoing, only "bad judgment." As Nixon boarded a plane for California, Gerald Ford, Vice President Agnew's replacement, became president.

The turmoil of Watergate and the dramatic exposures of corruption in government convinced many Americans that all politicians were either inept or immoral. True, the system had worked to replace a government that had sub-

verted some of the most important institutions of democracy. But the process was so wrenching that it undercut faith in government itself. New revelations in the media about kickbacks and other scandals, and stories of CIA and FBI illegal activities, added to the growing credibility gap.

## CONSUMERS LOSE FAITH

The reputations of private institutions were also tarnished in the early 1970s. The consumer movement carried on a spirited attack on private corporations for their shoddy and dangerous practices. Consumerism had had an active history in the early decades of the twentieth century, but it was reborn in the mid-1960s. Critics such as Ralph Nader and Barry Commoner wrote exposés of dangerous flaws in automobile design, adulteration of foods, pollution, and, especially, nuclear hazards. They helped to stimulate a wave of consumer protection legislation, such as the Consumer Product Safety Act and the Hazardous Substances Act. These laws aided the removal of dangerous products from the market.

Nader's efforts coincided with an important social movement of the early 1970s—a movement that grew out of the counterculture. Many Americans began to lead what they believed was a less artificial life, stressing vegetarian diet, natural childbirth, communal and rural living, a more natural sexuality, less differentiated sex roles, and the use of solar energy. Many of the thousands of participants in this movement rejected competitive, urban living. They were wary of the great technological feats of the era, such as the U.S. moon landing in July 1969 and the generation of nuclear power. They viewed industrial and scientific progress with deep suspicion.

Perhaps most symbolic of this new mood was a change in automobile design. To increase fuel efficiency and compete with Japanese and European imports, American auto makers shortened and lightened their cars. They lopped off the titanic fins, chrome strips, and long hoods and trunks that had added weight, horsepower, and

**MOON LANDING**

Neil A. Armstrong took this photograph of fellow astronaut Edwin E. Aldrin during the American landing on the surface of the moon, July 20, 1969. This historic event was spurred on by competition between the United States and the Soviet Union for achievements in outer space. Many Americans, influenced by the values of the counterculture, were dubious about this triumph because they mistrusted technological advances. *(UPI)*

expense. The dream of owning a shiny new car did not end, of course; but it did take a more practical bent.

# GERALD FORD AND THE FAILURE OF LEADERSHIP

Gerald Ford, the new president-by-appointment, had the difficult task of restoring belief in American institutions in a moment of deep crisis. A well-liked congressman from Michigan, Ford had almost no national reputation and little experience with the difficult administrative tasks of his new office. He faced a leadership crisis that was intensified by a serious recession, continuing energy shortages, and the final, bleak days of the war in Vietnam. Of his inherited administration, he kept Henry Kissinger; but he replaced most of the White House staff. To fill the vacant vice presidency, he appointed Nelson Rockefeller, who was governor of New York. The choice proved politically damaging. Rockefeller was without a following in the Republican party—disliked by the large and growing right wing and without much vocal support from moderates.

Soon after taking office, Ford made his most controversial move. He granted a general pardon to ex-President Nixon. As he said, "My conscience tells me that only I, as President, have the constitutional power to firmly shut and seal this book." But his act sealed only the lips of Richard Nixon, who did not reveal or admit the extent of his involvement in Watergate. Many Americans believed that Ford had struck a deal with the beleaguered president—although there was no evidence to support this suspicion.

Despite the damage of the pardon, Ford benefited from his reputation for honesty and openness. His wife, Betty, strengthened this impression of candor by speaking openly of a breast cancer operation she underwent in late 1974 and by supporting her own political causes, such as the Equal Rights Amendment. But Gerald Ford also had a reputation as a bumbler and a man not up to the intellectual rigors of the presidency. This impression of ineptness continued for the next two years, fed by the merciless satire of such popular television programs as *Saturday Night Live*.

The new president inherited the final debacle of Vietnam. Now prevented by law from committing any American forces to this Asian conflict, Ford could do nothing when the North Vietnamese army routed the forces of the South and drove toward Saigon in the spring of 1975. An emergency airlift rescued remaining Americans

THE BICENTENNIAL

Celebrations of the two hundredth anniversary of the Declaration of Independence took place all across the United States during 1976. Here, President Gerald Ford greets a Springfield, Illinois, drummer band dressed for the occasion in Revolutionary Era garb. *(UPI)*

and thousands of South Vietnamese officials linked to the United States. The longest war in American history ended in scenes of hasty and confused retreat.

However, there were few domestic recriminations. And America's reputation for decisive action was partly restored when Ford ordered the rescue of an American merchant ship, the *Mayaguez,* seized by the Cambodians in May. Ford ordered ships, planes, and men into action. Although the expedition was costly in terms of lives lost, the 39-man crew was recaptured. Congress and much of the press applauded the president's attempt to restore credibility, although they realized the action might have been unnecessary.

On the domestic front, Ford had few successes. His antirecession plans failed to pass Congress. Infighting and indecision in the administration convinced the public that weak leadership persisted. On questions of energy, conservation, and the environment, Ford relinquished leadership to Congress. Increasingly, he vetoed measures, only to see them passed again over his objections.

By early 1976, Ford announced that he would seek election to a full term as president. He possessed the significant advantage of incumbency, but he had few concrete accomplishments. His party split into two factions, with the most vocal and highly organized portion supporting former governor of California Ronald Reagan. Reagan challenged Ford in primaries across the country, attacking his foreign policy, détente with the Russians, and the continued influence of Henry Kissinger. He filled his speeches with old-fashioned homilies and invited nostalgia for a vaguely remembered American past. This strategy almost succeeded. In a closely divided convention, Ford had to accept a "morality in foreign policy" plank that, in effect, criticized his own foreign policy. Nonetheless Ford narrowly won the nomination.

The Democratic party in 1976 was, if anything, more deeply divided than the Republicans. The multiple leadership of the party and the new rules for delegate selection made it difficult for any one candidate to emerge. The most obvious choice was Senator Edward Kennedy of Massachusetts. But Kennedy's chances remained seriously compromised by an accident on Chappaquiddick Island on July 18, 1969. A woman companion riding in his car had been killed, and Kennedy could never satisfactorily explain the circumstances of the accident. Other candidates lacked national support. As a result, the most persistent candidate, James (Jimmy) Carter, former governor of Georgia, won the nomination.

Carter won a narrow victory in November after a campaign highlighted by televised debates. Carter's margin was provided by an exaggerated turn-out of two traditional Democratic constituencies: the South (proud of its native son) and black voters. But beneath the surface, this coalition was shaky. Blacks and white workers could be split apart, as George Wallace's campaigns over several years had proven. Labor unions, once the backbone of the Democratic party, had declined in membership during the 1970s. They had also lost power in the party as a result of the new rules that gave proportional representation to women and minorities.

The South was solid for Carter, but the region had become increasingly diverse and Republican. While the Voting Rights Act had enfranchised large numbers of black voters, industrialization, large population increases, and traditional conservatism had brought a strong resurgence of Republicanism. Other, traditionally strong Republican areas also gained strength during the 1970s, particularly the Southwest and the West. The census of 1980 confirmed a massive trend in population flow after World War II, out of the North and East to the South and West. For the first time, the population center of the nation crossed the Mississippi River.

The election of 1976 demonstrated another long-term trend in American voting patterns, away from voter participation. Registration was easier, and whole new populations were enfranchised, but the percentage of persons voting continued to decline. So did party identification. The effect of this nonparticipation was to increase the power of special-interest groups and small, well-organized segments of the population. Furthermore, the mass media exercised an increased power in the campaign, with advertising and pollsters largely determining the issues and an-

swers for candidates. But apparently, as Americans learned more of the intimate details of politics, they were less keen to participate.

The only substantial exception to this trend appeared among America's growing elderly population. During the 1970s, the average life expectancy increased more than two and a half years, continuing a tendency to longevity that added millions to the number of retirees. Among older Americans, issues of cuts in social security or medical benefit programs were a matter of life or death. So not only did the elderly vote in large numbers, they also organized pressure groups such as the Gray Panthers.

Jimmy Carter appealed to many disaffected voters. His campaign criticized the Washington establishment and the lingering problems of Watergate. He promised never to deceive the American public. And he stressed traditional values and honesty in government. His strenuous and persistent campaigning paid off.

Born into a Georgia farm family, Carter attended the U.S. Naval Academy and, after World War II, worked in the new nuclear submarine fleet. Retiring from the navy, he returned to Plains, Georgia, and started a successful peanut warehouse and distributing business. He entered Georgia state politics in 1962, and won the governorship in 1970. Widely known as a representative of the "new South"—that is, a South that accepted integration—Carter in 1976 also had strong ties to the old South, with its tradition of evangelical Protestantism. The tone of his campaign stressed the personal virtues he could bring to the office: truthfulness, family values, decency, and principle. He promised nuclear disarmament, open and competent government, and a restoration of faith in America.

# JIMMY CARTER AND THE CREDIBILITY CRISIS

The new president appointed several Washington professionals to his cabinet, including Cyrus Vance as secretary of state and Joseph Califano as

ENERGY SOURCE BY TYPE
(in quadrillions of BTU's)

|  | 1960 | 1970 | 1980 |
|---|---|---|---|
| Refined petroleum | 19.9 | 29.5 | 34.3 |
| Natural gas | 12.4 | 21.8 | 20.4 |
| Coal | 10.1 | 12.7 | 15.7 |
| Nuclear | — | .2 | 2.7 |
| Hydroelectric | 1.7 | 2.7 | 3.1 |
| Other | — | — | .1 |
| Total | 44.1 | 66.9 | 76.3 |

Source: U.S. Department of Commerce, Bureau of the Census, *Statistical Abstract of the United States, 1981* (Washington, D.C.: Government Printing Office, 1981), p. 578.

IMPORTED ENERGY BY TYPE
(in quadrillions of BTU's)

|  | 1960 | 1970 | 1980 |
|---|---|---|---|
| Crude oil | 2.2 | 2.8 | 11.1 |
| Refined petroleum | 1.8 | 4.7 | 3.4 |
| Natural gas | .2 | .9 | 1.0 |
| Percentage of supply imported | 9.2% | 12.1% | 19.8% |

Source: U.S. Department of Commerce, Bureau of the Census, *Statistical Abstract of the United States, 1981* (Washington, D.C.: Government Printing Office, 1981), p. 578.

secretary of health, education, and welfare. He appointed Patricia Harris, a black woman, as secretary of housing and urban development. And large numbers of lower-level administrative appointments went to women and blacks. Nonetheless, Carter's White House staff was headed by Hamilton Jordan, with other Georgians occupying leading roles—among them Bert Lance as head of the Office of Management and Budget and Andrew Young as U.S. ambassador to the United Nations. For national security adviser, Carter called on Columbia professor Zbigniew Brzezinski.

Almost from the beginning, Carter's inexperience in national politics and his indecisiveness (perhaps reflecting the conflicts in his electoral majority) hurt his relations with the Democratic-controlled Congress. Energy took priority with the new president. Personally rejecting the extravagant style sometimes associated with the presidency, Carter urged all Americans to conserve energy and live simpler lives. His major energy legislation, introduced in April 1977, was designed to ease American dependence on OPEC oil and induce domestic conservation. Sections of the proposed program encouraged a return to coal use and mandated energy savings in automobile design.

By August 1977 the energy bill had sailed through the House, practically intact. But it stalled in the Senate, primarily over the issue of deregulating natural gas. Although a new Department of Energy began operating in October 1977, Carter's principal energy legislation did not pass until a year later. In five linked acts, Congress approved measures to encourage home energy conservation, to enforce the use of coal in electrical generating, to encourage auto efficiency, and to increase natural gas prices. Several key questions remained unanswered, however, such as the timing and extent of oil price deregulation and the fate of the nuclear industry.

Carter called the energy crisis the "moral equivalent of war." For his presidency, at least, this slogan proved to be apt. The president recognized that because of recurrent gasoline shortages, many Americans did not trust the oil companies. Were they withholding gasoline from the market in order to raise prices, as many suspected? The president declared that this might be the case. Yet he did not act. A long, bitter coal strike over the winter of 1977–1978, in which the president did not intervene quickly, also added to the impression of his inability to show leadership on the issue of energy.

Energy policy reached an impasse in the spring of 1979. Political turmoil in Iran in late 1978 and 1979 cut that country's oil production to almost nothing. Although Iran supplied only about 5 percent of U.S. needs, the cutoff was significant. Rapid price hikes and serious shortages resulted by spring. Particularly in California and in Washington, D.C., long lines formed around filling stations. Americans believed the oil shortage to have been deliberately engineered, but there was little conclusive evidence, and the government failed to confirm or deny this speculation. Carter's response was a limited decontrol of oil prices and a windfall oil profits tax passed in 1980.

The Three Mile Island catastrophe in early spring 1979 compounded Carter's energy worries. Although, after the incident, he spoke enthusiastically about preserving the U.S. commitment to nuclear power, the nuclear industry did not recover. Alternative energy sources—such as gasohol, solar, wind, and geothermal—did not prove as promising as originally hoped. The conservation that did occur in this period came from increased auto efficiency and a lower use of energy dictated by rapidly rising costs.

Carter's energy problems were matched by difficulties elsewhere. Fueled by expensive oil, large budget deficits, administered prices (prices not determined by the market), and high wage demands, inflation shot upward in 1978, to 7.7 percent. The stock market registered its lack of confidence in the president's economic program by declining sharply in the spring. The economy was hit by stagflation—the double bind of inflation and slow growth.

Carter's leadership in these circumstances faltered. His difficulties with Congress, bickering among his staff, and revelations of improper campaign and banking practices by Bert Lance, which led to his resignation in late 1977, compounded the president's problems. Growing national frustration with government and with mounting taxes became apparent in California, where voters approved Proposition 13, cutting property taxes by more than 50 percent. Carter's reaction to this mood of disenchantment was to reorganize his cabinet and try to work more closely with Congress. Yet part of his response was quixotic—musing in public about a "national malaise" that he should have recognized as partly attributable to his own lack of leadership.

Foreign relations questions provided the president with several accomplishments—and his final undoing. The weakness of the dollar, huge energy price increases, and controversial problems forced the president to make unpopular choices. His foreign policy of emphasis on "human rights," while commendable, was very difficult to pursue. It proved disruptive to American

SADAT, CARTER, AND BEGIN

This portrait, taken at the beginning of the ceremony marking the signing of the Camp David accords, symbolized the achievement of President Jimmy Carter (center) in negotiating a peace treaty between President Anwar Sadat of Egypt (left) and Israeli Prime Minister Menachem Begin in March 1979. (UPI)

alliances to insist that friendly nations respect an internal climate of political freedom in order to receive American aid. But on the question of disarmament, Carter negotiated a new agreement with the Russians—SALT II, limiting weapons systems—on June 18, 1979. The Senate, however, refused to ratify it. Passage of the Panama Canal Treaties, although bitterly opposed in Congress, returned the Canal Zone and eventual control of the American-built canal to the government of Panama. And the United States also established formal ties with the Chinese People's Republic in 1979.

The president's most lasting achievement was a negotiated settlement between Egypt and Israel in March 1979. Intense negotiations between President Anwar Sadat of Egypt and Prime Minister Menachem Begin of Israel, urged on by Carter, took place in late 1978 at Camp David, Maryland, the presidential vacation retreat. For eleven days, Begin, and Sadat, and Carter debated the outstanding issues between Israel and Egypt. When the conference finally ended, Egypt and Israel, after years of hatred and intermittent war, were at peace. The Camp David agreement cemented the gradual peacemaking process that

had begun in the aftermath of the Yom Kippur War of 1973. It increased hopes for a final settlement of the explosive antagonism in the Middle East between Israel and its neighbors.

Relations with the Soviet Union, despite SALT, cooled. Expansion of Soviet power and influence in Africa, especially in Angola and Ethiopia, and—even more—the Russian invasion and occupation of its neighbor Afghanistan, brought American-Soviet relations to a low point. Many Americans also believed that the Russians were near to achieving military superiority over the United States. Pressure built for increased defense expenditures, and Carter responded in 1979 with a larger defense budget and plans to install the complex MX missile system and to develop a neutron bomb.

Frustration over foreign policy intensified in November 1979, after angry Iranians stormed the U.S. embassy in Teheran and took the American staff as hostages and held them until January 1981. Early in that year, the Ayatollah Khomeini had returned from exile to lead a Muslim fundamentalist revolution against the American-supported shah of Iran. The hostage crisis was precipitated when the deposed shah, then in exile,

**AMERICAN HOSTAGES IN IRAN**

In early November 1979, Iranian militants seized the American embassy in Teheran and took its occupants hostage. Photographs such as this one infuriated the American public and increased their frustration with Jimmy Carter's foreign policy. *(UPI)*

was granted entry into the United States to receive cancer treatment. The student captors, with the support of the Iranian revolutionary government, demanded the return of the shah to Iran. President Carter refused this demand and froze Iranian assets. Then he cut off imports of Iranian oil into the United States. But there was little else he could do to force the Iranians to release the hostages—short of war. An ill-planned and ill-executed rescue mission in April 1980 only increased the public's sense of the president's impotence. Nightly news broadcasts, which amounted to some of the most persistent coverage of any event in American history, cut away Carter's support and credibility.

By the spring of 1980, the president's popularity had sunk. Senator Kennedy challenged Carter in presidential primaries. After months of acrimonious and inconclusive campaigning, Carter won the nomination. But the damage of this skirmish was enormous. The president was unable to create a workable electoral coalition around the programs he supported, such as the ERA, or around his accomplishments in foreign policy.

Indeed, many of these accomplishments were turned against him by Ronald Reagan, who captured the Republican nomination. Reagan, a former movie star, a favorite of the Republican party right wing, and a longtime presidential aspirant, ran a remarkably well-focused and well-financed campaign. He capitalized on the antagonism to Carter and to government in general. Among a minority of voters, he inspired fervent support with his promises of a huge tax cut, a balanced budget, sharp increases in defense spending, and a much reduced federal commitment to social legislation. To a number of other voters, he simply represented the possibility of change—and of leadership. Despite the third-party candidacy of Republican moderate John Anderson of Illinois, Reagan won a decisive victory in November 1980. More significant, the Republicans gained control of the Senate and achieved an effective majority in the House—with the help of conservative Southern Democrats.

**PRESIDENT RONALD REAGAN**

Ronald Reagan's successful campaign for the presidency and his initial successes in office depended in part on his ability to evoke patriotic feelings in the American public. Many of his speeches self-consciously appealed to such symbols as the American flag. *(UPI)*

## RONALD REAGAN: RECESSION AND RECOVERY

For the next year, the new Republican president enjoyed what his predecessors had sorely lacked: an almost complete absence of criticism from Congress or the media. Beyond the traditional "honeymoon" period for a new leader, these months signified, perhaps more than anything, that Americans wanted to believe in leadership and in the presidency again. They wanted to trust the institutions that had been so sorely tested and found wanting in the difficult days of the 1970s.

In part, this absence of criticism was a response to Reagan's personal warmth and his ability to project good intentions. Enormously secure in his traditional beliefs about family, social order, capitalism, and patriotism, Reagan projected confidence and competence. Unlike Carter, he did not agonize over the details of governing; he calmly presided over his administration. He made no pretense to extensive knowledge of complicated budgetary matters or foreign policy. Consequently, his advisers kept him relatively isolated from free exchanges with the press corps. Also unlike Carter, Reagan exercised leadership by refusing to compromise on first principles. Although this made the early days of his administration highly ideological, it brought him success, particularly when linked to the major efforts of the Republican party and its business allies to pass his legislative program.

That program proved, however, to have contradictory effects. Reagan, reflecting on the previous thirty years, called them deeply troubled and economically perilous. He vowed to revise the priorities of government. His plan included a massive 30 percent tax cut for individuals, an action justified by "supply-side" economics, which theorized that a return of tax dollars to the public would initiate more investment, higher growth rates—and, in the end, higher tax revenues. Added to this were transfers of federal

funds out of social and welfare programs and into defense. To stimulate investment and production, he promised business incentive tax cuts and revision of federal regulations in the fields of environmental safety. To fight inflation, he signaled his support for Federal Reserve Board attempts to keep interest rates high and the money supply low.

In the first few dramatic months of his presidency, which included an assassination attempt, all of these plans were put into place. A three-year 25 percent tax cut (5 percent the first year, and 10 percent in the second and third years) passed Congress in early August 1981, after feeble and uncoordinated criticisms from Democrats. The federal budgets for 1982 and 1983 slashed social programs and raised real defense expenditures (after inflation) by 12.7 percent in 1982 and about 13 percent in 1983.

The effects of this program were, however, unanticipated. The tax cut plus rising costs of entitlement programs for health and retirement, along with huge defense appropriations, pushed the federal budget deficit to new records (over $110 billion for 1982). This high deficit, which forced the government to borrow vast amounts of money, kept interest rates high. With these two enormously powerful forces (deficits and high interest rates) pushing against each other, economic activity began to diminish and unemployment rose rapidly. A recession that began in the summer of 1981 spread across 1982, until unemployment reached almost 11 percent in December—the highest since the 1930s. Over 12 million workers were without jobs.

Those who bore the brunt of this downturn were the poor, the undereducated, the unemployed, minorities, and other groups that under previous administrations had been sustained by a safety net of social programs. Certain areas of the nation—especially Michigan, Wisconsin, Ohio, Illinois, and Minnesota—were struck with depressionlike conditions, as steel and auto plants shut down and construction sagged. Several banks failed. Farm income dropped precipitously. The world economy, in general, suffered a rapid

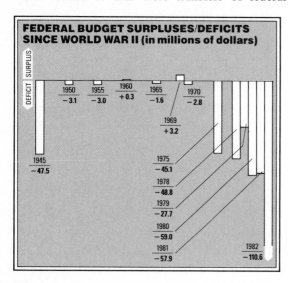

**FEDERAL BUDGET SURPLUSES/DEFICITS SINCE WORLD WAR II (in millions of dollars)**

DEFICIT    SURPLUS

| 1950 | 1955 | 1960 | 1965 | 1970 |
| −3.1 | −3.0 | +0.3 | −1.6 | −2.8 |

1969
+3.2

1945
−47.5

1975
−45.1

1978
−48.8

1979
−27.7

1980
−59.0

1981
−57.9

1982
−110.6

**THE FACES OF UNEMPLOYMENT**

On October 26, 1982, 2,000 applicants jammed the offices of the New York Association of Builders and Carpenters to apply for 400 job openings. High unemployment accounted for serious Republican losses in the House of Representatives and governorships in the national elections held a month later. *(A. Tannenbaum/Sygma)*

decline. Under these circumstances, inflation rates began to fall in the United States and elsewhere. But the price in productivity more than offset the benefits of lowered inflation.

Reagan's defense program also had some unexpected results. Administration talk of the possibility of fighting a controlled nuclear war, or even surviving nuclear attack, made many Europeans extremely anxious. As the United States prepared to station short-range missiles aimed at Russia in Europe, this anxiety blossomed into a strong antinuclear movement in Germany, England, Italy, and the Netherlands. Europeans recognized that they were merely contested terrain between two superpowers and would suffer the worst consequences if war broke out. Tension with Europeans increased when the Reagan administration unsuccessfully attempted to block sales of turbines and construction materials by French, German, British, and Italian firms to

Russia for construction of a natural-gas pipeline to Western Europe.

In other areas, Reagan had more success. When, in April 1982, Argentina invaded the British-controlled Falkland Islands near its shores, the United States faced a dilemma. Which ally should it support? Ostensibly neutral at first, the Reagan administration eventually sided with the British, who retook the islands by force. This position did not, however, permanently injure American relations with the rest of South America and it bolstered the alliance with Britain. The Middle East also provided Reagan with a moderate success. Israel invaded neighboring Lebanon in June 1982 to eliminate Palestine Liberation Organization (PLO) forces operating against Israel from refugee camps. After decisively defeating the PLO and their Syrian allies, Israel agreed to U.S. suggestions for negotiations and the establishment of an independent Lebanon. But here tensions remained high and crisis threatened to recur.

The results of the congressional elections of 1982, which were a referendum on the Reagan administration's economic policies, suggested both anger and indecision. Democrats won seven new governorships (bringing their total to 34) and pushed up their majority in the House of Representatives by 26 seats, for a total of 267 to 166. But they failed to gain in the Senate. Later, in the spring of 1983, the economy began an accelerating recovery. Prices remained stable, yet production, consumer spending, and investment increased. Unemployment declined perceptibly. But the built-in dilemma of the Reagan economic plan stood unresolved. Huge budget deficits remained for a future accounting.

This moment demanded decisions. Should the president abandon his ideological purity, his commitment to increased defense expenditures, tax cuts and deregulation for business, and cuts in social programs for the poor? Should he relinquish his support for constitutional amendments to reinstate prayer in public schools, to outlaw abortion, and to legislate a balanced federal budget? Should he compromise a foreign policy that threatened to mire the United States in a civil war in El Salvador and a rebellion against the leftist government of Nicaragua? Should he move toward the center of his own party, not only to embrace it more fully but to compromise with the opposition Democrats? That he had such a luxury of choice is testimony to the support he could generate whatever his decision. For even in their displeasure with politics and with the economy, many Americans still wanted to believe in their president.

## SUGGESTED READINGS, CHAPTERS 45–46

### THREE MILE ISLAND, ECONOMICS, AND ENERGY

Some of the specific economic and energy problems that contributed to the political instability of the United States during the 1970s are explained in Lester C. Thurow, *The Zero-Sum Society: Distribution and the Possibilities for Economic Change* (1981). Tad Szulc, *The Energy Crisis,* rev. ed. (1978), is a useful explanation of the oil shortages of the mid-1970s. The beginning of the consumer movement, which cast doubt on the quality of American production, is Ralph Nader's exposure of the auto industry, *Unsafe at Any Speed* (1965). An excellent and thorough description of the bureaucratic tangles that aggravated the crisis at Three Mile Island is Daniel Ford, *Three Mile Island* (1982).

### THE 1970s

The 1970s were a complex period in which economic issues, problems of political leadership, and foreign relations assumed critical importance. An excellent account of the interrelationship of these problems is Richard Kirkendall, *A Global Power: America Since the Age of Roosevelt,* 2nd ed. (1980). Richard J. Barnet, in his essay *The Lean Years: Politics in the Age of Scarcity* (1980), examines the impact of diminished productivity and scarcity of resources on the politics of the 1970s. Jonathan Schell's very readable *The Time of Illusion* (1976) stresses the impact of the Vietnam War on American society.

### THREE PRESIDENTS

As in the previous decade, there was a rapid turnover of presidents and administrations during the 1970s. Nonetheless, the central figure of the decade was Richard M. Nixon. An excellent place to begin further reading about Nixon is his own *Memoirs of Richard Nixon* (1978). Fawn Brodie, in her recent and controversial *Richard Nixon: The Shaping of His Character* (1981), suggests psychological explanations for the president's complex and sometimes quixotic behavior. Patrick J. Buchanan, in *The New Majority: President Nixon at Mid-Passage* (1973), outlines the basis of a new conservative electoral majority inspired by Nixon. Of several books on Watergate, the most intriguing remains the account by the two *Washington Post* reporters who uncovered much of the story: Carl Bernstein and Bob Woodward, *All the President's Men* (1974). On the interim presidency of Gerald Ford, John Osborne, *White House Watch: The Ford Years* (1977), is one of the best works. Henry Kissinger, secretary of state under Nixon and Ford, offers interesting insights in *Years of Upheaval* (1982). Jimmy Carter's *Keeping Faith* (1982) is a readable, if self-justifying, appraisal of his one-term presidency.

# The Declaration of Independence

In Congress, July 4, 1776. *The unanimous Declaration of the thirteen United States of America.*

When in the Course of human events, it becomes necessary for one people to dissolve the political bands which have connected them with another, and to assume among the powers of the earth, the separate and equal station to which the Laws of Nature and of Nature's God entitle them, a decent respect to the opinions of mankind requires that they should declare the causes which impel them to the separation.—

We hold these truths to be self-evident, that all men are created equal, that they are endowed by their Creator with certain unalienable Rights, that among these are Life, Liberty and the pursuit of Happiness.—

That to secure these rights, Governments are instituted among Men, deriving their just powers from the consent of the governed,—

That whenever any Form of Government becomes destructive of these ends, it is the Right of the People to alter or to abolish it, and to institute new Government, laying its foundation on such principles and organizing its powers in such form, as to them shall seem most likely to effect their Safety and Happiness. Prudence, indeed, will dictate that Governments long established should not be changed for light and transient causes; and accordingly all experience hath shown, that mankind are more disposed to suffer, while evils are sufferable, than to right themselves by abolishing the forms to which they are accustomed. But when a long train of abuses and usurpations, pursuing invariably the same Object evinces a design to reduce them under absolute Despotism, it is their right, it is their duty, to throw off such Government, and to provide new Guards for their future security.—

Such has been the patient sufferance of these Colonies; and such is now the necessity which constrains them to alter their former Systems of Government. The history of the present King of Great Britain is a history of repeated injuries and usurpations, all having in direct object the establishment of an absolute Tyranny over these States. To prove this, let Facts be submitted to a candid world.—

He has refused his Assent to laws, the most wholesome and necessary for the public good.—

He has forbidden his Governors to pass Laws of immediate and pressing importance, unless suspended in their operation till his Assent should be obtained; and when so suspended, he has utterly neglected to attend to them.—

He has refused to pass other Laws for the accommodation of large districts of people, unless those people would relinquish the right of Representation in the Legislature, a right inestimable to them and formidable to tyrants only.—

He has called together legislative bodies at places unusual, uncomfortable, and distant from the depository of their public Records, for the sole purpose of fatiguing them into compliance with his measures.—

He has dissolved Representative Houses repeatedly, for opposing with manly firmness his invasions on the rights of the people.—

He has refused for a long time, after such dissolutions, to cause others to be elected;

whereby the Legislative powers, incapable of Annihilation, have returned to the People at large for their exercise; the State remaining in the mean time exposed to all the dangers of invasion from without, and convulsions within.—

He has endeavoured to prevent the population of these States; for that purpose obstructing the Laws for Naturalization of Foreigners; refusing to pass others to encourage their migrations hither, and raising the conditions of new Appropriations of Lands.—

He has obstructed the Administration of Justice, by refusing his Assent to Laws for establishing Judiciary powers.—

He has made Judges dependent on his Will alone, for the tenure of their offices, and the amount and payment of their salaries.—

He has erected a multitude of New Offices, and sent hither swarms of Officers to harrass our people, and eat out their substance.—

He has kept among us in times of peace, Standing Armies without the Consent of our legislatures.—

He has affected to render the Military independent of and superior to the Civil power.—

He has combined with others to subject us to a jurisdiction foreign to our constitution, and unacknowledged by our laws; giving his Assent to their Acts of pretended Legislation:—

For quartering large bodies of armed troops among us:—

For protecting them, by a mock Trial, from punishment for any Murders which they should commit on the Inhabitants of these States:—

For cutting off our Trade with all parts of the world:—

For imposing Taxes on us without our Consent:—

For depriving us in many cases, of the benefits of Trial by Jury:—

For transporting us beyond Seas to be tried for pretended offences:—

For abolishing the free System of English Laws in a neighbouring Province, establishing therein an Arbitrary government, and enlarging its Boundaries so as to render it at once an example and fit instrument for introducing the same absolute rule in these Colonies:—

For taking away our Charters, abolishing our most valuable Laws, and altering fundamentally the Forms of our Government:—

For suspending our own Legislatures, and declaring themselves invested with power to legislate for us in all cases whatsoever.—

He has abdicated Government here, by declaring us out of his Protection and waging War against us.—

He has plundered our seas, ravaged our Coasts, burnt our towns, and destroyed the lives of our people.—

He is at this time transporting large Armies of foreign Mercenaries to compleat the works of death, desolation and tyranny, already begun with circumstances of Cruelty & perfidy scarcely paralleled in the most barbarous ages, and totally unworthy the Head of a civilized nation.—

He has constrained our fellow Citizens taken Captive on the high Seas to bear arms against their Country, to become the executioners of their friends and Brethren, or to fall themselves by their Hands.—

He has excited domestic insurrections amongst us, and has endeavoured to bring on the inhabitants of our frontiers, the merciless Indian Savages, whose known rule of warfare, is an undistinguished destruction of all ages, sexes and conditions.

In every stage of these Oppressions We have Petitioned for Redress in the most humble terms: Our repeated Petitions have been answered only by repeated injury. A

Prince, whose character is thus marked by every act which may define a Tyrant, is unfit to be the ruler of a free people.

Nor have We been wanting in attentions to our British brethren. We have warned them from time to time of attempts by their legislature to extend an unwarrantable jurisdiction over us. We have reminded them of the circumstances of our emigration and settlement here. We have appealed to their native justice and magnanimity, and we have conjured them by the ties of our common kindred to disavow these usurpations, which, would inevitably interrupt our connections and correspondence. They too have been deaf to the voice of justice and of consanguinity. We must, therefore, acquiesce in the necessity, which denounces our Separation, and hold them, as we hold the rest of mankind, Enemies in War, in Peace Friends.—

We, therefore, the Representatives of the united States of America, in General Congress, Assembled, appealing to the Supreme Judge of the world for the rectitude of our intentions, do, in the Name, and by Authority of the good People of these Colonies, solemnly publish and declare, That these United Colonies are, and of Right ought to be, Free and Independent States; that they are absolved from all Allegiance to the British Crown, and that all political connection between them and the State of Great Britain, is and ought to be totally dissolved; and that as Free and Independent States they have full Power to levy War, conclude Peace, contract Alliances, establish Commerce, and to do all other Acts and Things which Independent States may of right do.—

And for the support of this Declaration, with a firm reliance on the protection of divine Providence, we mutually pledge to each other our Lives, our Fortunes and our sacred Honor.

### John Hancock
#### (MASSACHUSETTS)

**New Hampshire**
Josiah Bartlett
William Whipple
Matthew Thornton

**Massachusetts**
Samuel Adams
John Adams
Robert Treat Paine
Elbridge Gerry

**Delaware**
Caesar Rodney
George Read
Thomas McKean

**New York**
William Floyd
Philip Livingston
Francis Lewis
Lewis Morris

**New Jersey**
Richard Stockton
John Witherspoon
Francis Hopkinson
John Hart
Abraham Clark

**North Carolina**
William Hooper
Joseph Hewes
John Penn

**Maryland**
Samuel Chase
William Paca
Thomas Stone
Charles Carroll
   of Carrollton

**South Carolina**
Edward Rutledge
Thomas Heywood, Jr.
Thomas Lynch, Jr.
Arthur Middleton

**Rhode Island**
Stephen Hopkins
William Ellery

**Connecticut**
Roger Sherman
Samuel Huntington
William Williams
Oliver Wolcott

**Pennsylvania**
Robert Morris
Benjamin Rush
Benjamin Franklin
John Morton
George Clymer
James Smith
George Taylor
James Wilson
George Ross

**Virginia**
George Wythe
Richard Henry Lee
Thomas Jefferson
Benjamin Harrison
Thomas Nelson, Jr.
Francis Lightfoot Lee
Carter Braxton

**Georgia**
Button Gwinnett
Lyman Hall
George Walton

# The Constitution of the United States of America

The preamble establishes the principle of government by the people, and lists the six basic purposes of the Constitution.

W e the People of the United States, in Order to form a more perfect Union, establish Justice, insure domestic Tranquility, provide for the common defence, promote the general Welfare, and secure the Blessings of Liberty to ourselves and our Posterity, do ordain and establish this Constitution for the United States of America.

## ARTICLE I • LEGISLATIVE DEPARTMENT

**Section 1.**  All legislative Powers herein granted shall be vested in a Congress of the United States, which shall consist of a Senate and House of Representatives.

Representatives serve two-year terms. They are chosen in each state by those electors (that is, voters) who are qualified to vote for members of the lower house of their own state legislature.

**Section 2.**  The House of Representatives shall be composed of Members chosen every second Year by the People of the several States, and the Electors in each State shall have the Qualifications requisite for Electors of the most numerous Branch of the State Legislature.

No Person shall be a Representative who shall not have attained to the Age of twenty-five Years, and have been seven Years a Citizen of the United States, and who shall not, when elected, be an Inhabitant of that State in which he shall be chosen.

The number of representatives allotted to a state is determined by the size of its population. The 14th Amendment has made obsolete the reference to "all other persons"—that is, slaves.

A census must be taken every ten years to determine the number of representatives to which each state is entitled. There is now one representative for about every 470,000 persons.

Representatives and direct Taxes shall be apportioned among the several States which may be included within this Union, according to their respective Numbers, which shall be determined by adding to the whole Number of free Persons, including those bound to Service for a Term of Years, and excluding Indians not taxed, three-fifths of all other Persons. The actual Enumeration shall be made within three Years after the first Meeting of the Congress of the United States, and within every subsequent Term of ten Years, in such Manner as they shall by Law direct. The Number of Representatives shall not exceed one for every thirty Thousand, but each State shall have at Least one Representative; and until such enumeration shall be made, the State of New Hampshire shall be entitled to chuse three, Massachusetts eight, Rhode Island and Providence Plantations one, Connecticut five, New York six, New Jersey four, Pennsylvania eight, Delaware one, Maryland six, Virginia ten, North Carolina five, South Carolina five, and Georgia three.

"Executive authority" refers to the governor of a state.

The Speaker, chosen by and from the majority party, presides over the House. Impeachment is the act of bringing formal charges against an official. (See also Section 3.)

When vacancies happen in the Representation from any State, the Executive Authority thereof shall issue Writs of Election to fill such Vacancies.

The House of Representatives shall chuse their Speaker and other Officers; and shall have the sole Power of Impeachment.

*Source:* House Document #529. U.S. Government Printing Office, 1967.
[*Note:* The Constitution and the amendments are reprinted here in their original form. Portions that have been amended or superseded are underlined.] The words printed in the margins explain some of the more difficult passages.

**Section 3.**   The Senate of the United States shall be composed of two Senators from each State, chosen by the Legislature thereof, for six Years; and each Senator shall have one Vote.

Immediately after they shall be assembled in Consequence of the first Election, they shall be divided as equally as may be into three Classes. The Seats of the Senators of the first Class shall be vacated at the Expiration of the second Year, of the second Class at the Expiration of the fourth Year, and of the third Class at the Expiration of the sixth Year, so that one third may be chosen every second Year; and if Vacancies happen by Resignation, or otherwise, during the Recess of the Legislature of any State, the Executive thereof may make temporary Appointments until the next Meeting of the Legislature, which shall then fill such Vacancies.

No Person shall be a Senator who shall not have attained to the Age of thirty Years, and been nine Years a Citizen of the United States, and who shall not, when elected, be an Inhabitant of that State for which he shall be chosen.

The Vice President of the United States shall be President of the Senate, but shall have no Vote, unless they be equally divided.

The Senate shall chuse their other Officers, and also a President pro tempore, in the absence of the Vice President, or when he shall exercise the Office of President of the United States.

The Senate shall have the sole Power to try all Impeachments. When sitting for that Purpose, they shall be on Oath or Affirmation. When the President of the United States is tried, the Chief Justice shall preside: And no Person shall be convicted without the Concurrence of two thirds of the Members present.

Judgment in Cases of Impeachment shall not extend further than to removal from Office, and disqualification to hold and enjoy any Office of Honor, Trust or Profit under the United States: but the Party convicted shall nevertheless be liable and subject to Indictment, Trial, Judgment and Punishment, according to Law.

**Section 4.**   The Times, Places and Manner of holding Elections for Senators and Representatives, shall be prescribed in each State by the Legislature thereof; but the Congress may at any time by Law make or alter such Regulations, except as to the Place of chusing Senators.

The Congress shall assemble at least once in every Year, and such Meeting shall be on the first Monday in December, unless they shall by Law appoint a different Day.

**Section 5.**   Each House shall be the Judge of the Elections, Returns and Qualifications of its own Members, and a Majority of each shall constitute a Quorum to do Business; but a smaller number may adjourn from day to day, and may be authorized to compel the Attendance of absent Members, in such Manner, and under such Penalties as each House may provide.

Each House may determine the Rules of its Proceedings, punish its Members for disorderly Behavior, and, with the Concurrence of two thirds, expel a Member.

Each House shall keep a Journal of its Proceedings, and from time to time publish the same, excepting such Parts as may in their Judgment require Secrecy; and the Yeas and Nays of the Members of either House on any question shall, at the Desire of one fifth of those Present, be entered on the Journal.

Neither House, during the Session of Congress, shall, without the Consent of the other, adjourn for more than three days, nor to any other Place than that in which the two Houses shall be sitting.

---

The 17th Amendment changed this method to direct election.

The 17th Amendment also provides that a state governor shall appoint a successor to fill a vacant Senate seat until a direct election is held.

The Vice President may cast a vote in the Senate only in order to break a tie.

The president *pro tempore* of the Senate is a temporary officer; the Latin words mean "for the time being."

No President has every been successfully impeached. In 1868 the Senate fell one vote short of the two-thirds majority needed to convict Andrew Johnson. Twelve other officials—ten federal judges, one senator, and one Secretary of War—have been impeached; four of the judges were convicted.

Elections for Congress are held on the first Tuesday after the first Monday in November in even-numbered years.

The 20th Amendment designates January 3 as the opening of the congressional session.

Each house of Congress decides whether a member has been elected properly and is qualified to be seated. (A quorum is the minimum number of persons required to be present in order to conduct business.) The House once refused admittance to an elected representative who had been guilty of a crime. The Senate did likewise in the case of a candidate whose election campaign lent itself to "fraud and corruption."

Congressmen have the power to fix their own salaries. Under the principle of *congressional immunity,* they cannot be sued or arrested for anything they say in a congressional debate. This provision enables them to speak freely.

This clause reinforces the principle of separation of powers by stating that, during his term of office, a member of Congress may not be appointed to a position in another branch of government. Nor may he resign and accept a position created during his term.

The House initiates tax bills but the Senate may propose changes in them.

By returning a bill unsigned to the house in which it originated, the President exercises a *veto.* A two-thirds majority in both houses can override the veto. If the President receives a bill within the last ten days of a session and does not sign it, the measure dies by *pocket veto.* Merely by keeping the bill in his pocket, so to speak, the President effects a veto.

The same process of approval or disapproval by the President is applied to resolutions and other matters passed by both houses (except adjournment).

These are the *delegated,* or *enumerated,* powers of Congress.

*Duties* are taxes on imported goods; *excises* are taxes on goods manufactured, sold, or consumed within the country. *Imposts* is a general term including both duties and excise taxes.

*Naturalization* is the process by which an alien becomes a citizen.

Government *securities* include savings bonds and other notes.

Authors' and inventors' rights are protected by copyright and patent laws.

**Section 6.**   The Senators and Representatives shall receive a Compensation for their Services, to be ascertained by Law, and paid out of the Treasury of the United States. They shall in all Cases, except Treason, Felony and Breach of the Peace, be privileged from Arrest during their Attendance at the Session of their respective Houses, and in going to and returning from the same; and for any Speech or Debate in either House, they shall not be questioned in any other Place.

No Senator or Representative shall, during the Time for which he was elected, be appointed to any civil Office under the Authority of the United States, which shall have been created, or the Emoluments whereof shall have been encreased during such time; and no Person holding any Office under the United States, shall be a Member of either House during his Continuance in Office.

**Section 7.**   All Bills for raising Revenue shall originate in the House of Representatives; but the Senate may propose or concur with Amendments as on other Bills.

Every Bill which shall have passed the House of Representatives and the Senate, shall, before it become a Law, be presented to the President of the United States; If he approve he shall sign it, but if not he shall return it, with his Objections to that House in which it shall have originated, who shall enter the Objections at large on their Journal, and proceed to reconsider it. If after such Reconsideration two thirds of that House shall agree to pass the Bill, it shall be sent, together with the Objections, to the other House, by which it shall likewise be reconsidered, and if approved by two thirds of that House, it shall become a Law. But in all such Cases the Votes of both Houses shall be determined by Yeas and Nays, and the Names of the Persons voting for and against the Bill shall be entered on the Journal of each House respectively. If any Bill shall not be returned by the President within ten Days (Sundays excepted) after it shall have been presented to him, the Same shall be a Law, in like Manner as if he had signed it, unless the Congress by their Adjournment prevent its Return, in which Case it shall not be a Law.

Every Order, Resolution, or Vote to which the Concurrence of the Senate and House of Representatives may be necessary (except on a question of Adjournment) shall be presented to the President of the United States; and before the Same shall take Effect, shall be approved by him, or being disapproved by him, shall be repassed by two thirds of the Senate and House of Representatives, according to the Rules and Limitations prescribed in the Case of a Bill.

**Section 8.**   The Congress shall have Power to lay and collect Taxes, Duties, Imposts and Excises, to pay the Debts and provide for the common Defence and general Welfare of the United States; but all Duties, Imposts and Excises shall be uniform throughout the United States;

To borrow money on the credit of the United States;

To regulate Commerce with foreign Nations, and among the several States, and with the Indian Tribes;

To establish an uniform Rule of Naturalization, and uniform Laws on the subject of Bankruptcies throughout the United States;

To coin Money, regulate the Value thereof, and of foreign Coin, and fix the Standard of Weights and Measures;

To provide for the Punishment of counterfeiting the Securities and current Coin of the United States;

To establish Post Offices and post Roads;

To promote the Progress of Science and useful Arts, by securing for limited Times to Authors and Inventors the exclusive Right to their respective Writings and Discoveries;

To constitute Tribunals inferior to the superior Court;

To define and punish Piracies and Felonies committed on the high Seas, and Offenses against the Law of Nations;

To declare War, grant Letters of Marque and Reprisal, and make Rules concerning Captures on Land and Water;

To raise and support Armies, but no Appropriation of Money to that Use shall be for a longer Term than two Years;

To provide and maintain a Navy;

To make Rules for the Government and Regulation of the land and naval Forces;

To provide for calling forth the Militia to execute the Laws of the Union, suppress Insurrections and repel Invasions;

To provide for organizing, arming, and disciplining the Militia, and for governing such Part of them as may be employed in the Service of the United States, reserving to the States respectively, the Appointment of the Officers, and the Authority of training the Militia according to the discipline prescribed by Congress;

To exercise the exclusive Legislation in all Cases whatsoever, over such District (not exceeding ten Miles square) as may, by Cession of particular States, and the acceptance of Congress, become the Seat of the Government of the United States, and to exercise like Authority over all Places purchased by the Consent of the Legislature of the State in which the Same shall be, for the Erection of Forts, Magazines, Arsenals, dock-Yards, and other needful Buildings;—And

To make all Laws which shall be necessary and proper for carrying into Execution the foregoing Powers, and all other Powers vested by this Constitution in the Government of the United States, or in any Department or Officer thereof.

**Section 9.** The Migration or Importation of such Persons as any of the States now existing shall think proper to admit, shall not be prohibited by the Congress prior to the Year one thousand eight hundred and eight, but a tax or duty may be imposed on such Importation, not exceeding ten dollars for each Person.

The privilege of the Writ of Habeas Corpus shall not be suspended unless when in Cases of Rebellion or Invasion the public Safety may require it.

No Bill of Attainder or ex post facto Law shall be passed.

No capitation, or other direct, Tax shall be laid, unless in Proportion to the Census or Enumeration herein before directed to be taken.

No Tax or Duty shall be laid on Articles exported from any State.

No Preference shall be given by any Regulation of Commerce or Revenue to the Ports of one State over those of another; nor shall Vessels bound to, or from, one State, be obliged to enter, clear, or pay Duties in another.

No Money shall be drawn from the Treasury, but in Consequence of Appropriations made by Law; and a regular Statement and Account of the Receipts and Expenditures of all public Money shall be published from time to time.

No Title of Nobility shall be granted by the United States: And no Person holding any Office of Profit or Trust under them, shall, without the Consent of the Congress, accept of any present, Emolument, Office, or Title, of any kind whatever, from any King, Prince, or foreign State.

**Section 10.** No State shall enter into any Treaty, Alliance, or Confederation; grant Letters of Marque and Reprisal; coin Money; emit Bills of Credit; make any Thing but gold and silver Coin a Tender in Payment of Debts; pass any Bill of Attainder, ex post facto Law, or Law impairing the Obligation of Contracts, or grant any Title of Nobility.

No State shall, without the Consent of the Congress, lay any Imposts or Duties on Imports or Exports, except what may be absolutely necessary for executing its

---

*Sidebar notes:*

Congress may establish lower federal courts.

Only Congress may declare war. *Letters of marque and reprisal* grant merchant ships permission to attack enemy vessels.

*Militia* refers to national guard units, which may become part of the United States Army during an emergency. Congress aids the states in maintaining their national guard units.

This clause gives Congress the power to govern what became the District of Columbia, as well as other federal sites.

Known as the *elastic clause*, this provision enables Congress to exercise many powers not specifically granted to it by the Constitution.

This clause concerns the slave trade, which Congress did ban in 1808.

The *writ of habeas corpus* permits a prisoner to appear before a judge to inquire into the legality of his or her detention.

A *bill of attainder* is an act of legislation that declares a person guilty of a crime and punishes him or her without a trial. An *ex post facto* law punishes a person for an act that was legal when performed but later declared illegal.

The object of Clause 4 was to bar direct (per person) taxation of slaves for the purpose of abolishing slavery. The 16th Amendment modified this provision by giving Congress the power to tax personal income.

States are hereby forbidden to exercise certain powers. Some of these powers belong to Congress alone; others are considered undemocratic.

inspection Laws: and the net Produce of all Duties and Imposts, laid by any State on Imports or Exports, shall be for the Use of the Treasury of the United States; and all such Laws shall be subject to the Revision and Controul of the Congress.

No State shall, without the Consent of Congress, lay any duty of Tonnage, keep Troops, or Ships of War in time of Peace, enter into any Agreement or Compact with another State, or with a foreign Power, or engage in War, unless actually invaded, or in such imminent Danger as will not admit of delay.

## ARTICLE II • EXECUTIVE DEPARTMENT

**Section 1.**    The executive Power shall be vested in a President of the United States of America. He shall hold his Office during the Term of four Years, and, together with the Vice President, chosen for the same Term, be elected, as follows.

**States cannot, without congressional authority, tax goods that enter or leave, except for a small inspection fee.**

Each State shall appoint, in such Manner as the Legislature thereof may direct, a Number of Electors, equal to the whole Number of Senators and Representatives to which the State may be entitled in the Congress: but no Senator or Representative, or Person holding an office of Trust or Profit under the United States, shall be appointed an Elector.

**Federal officials are ineligible to serve as presidential electors.**

The Electors shall meet in their respective States, and vote by Ballot for two persons, of whom one at least shall not be an Inhabitant of the same State with themselves. And they shall make a List of all the Persons voted for, and of the Number of Votes for each; which List they shall sign and certify, and transmit sealed to the Seat of the Government of the United States, directed to the President of the Senate. The President of the Senate shall, in the Presence of the Senate and House of Representatives, open all the Certificates, and the Votes shall then be counted. The Person having the greatest Number of Votes shall be the President, if such Number be a Majority of the whole Number of Electors appointed; and if there be more than one who have such Majority, and have an equal Number of Votes, then the House of Representatives shall immediately chuse by Ballot one of them for President; and if no Person have a Majority, then from the five highest on the List the said House shall in like Manner chuse the President. But in chusing the President, the Votes shall be taken by States, the Representation from each State having one Vote; a quorum for this Purpose shall consist of a Member or Members from two thirds of the States, and a Majority of all the States shall be necessary to a Choice. In every Case, after the Choice of the President, the Person having the greatest Number of Votes of the Electors shall be the Vice President. But if there should remain two or more who have equal Votes, the Senate shall chuse from them by Ballot the Vice President.

**The 12th Amendment superseded this clause. The weakness of the original constitutional provision became apparent in the election of 1800, when Thomas Jefferson and Aaron Burr received the same number of electoral votes. The 12th Amendment avoids this possibility by requiring electors to cast separate ballots for President and Vice President.**

The Congress may determine the Time of chusing the Electors, and the Day on which they shall give their Votes; which Day shall be the same throughout the United States.

No person except a natural born Citizen, or a Citizen of the United States, at the time of the Adoption of this Constitution, shall be eligible to the Office of President; neither shall any Person be eligible to that Office who shall not have attained to the Age of Thirty-five Years, and been fourteen Years a Resident within the United States.

**A naturalized citizen may not become President.**

In Case of the Removal of the President from Office, or of his Death, Resignation, or Inability to discharge the Powers and Duties of the said Office, the same shall devolve on the Vice-President, and the Congress may by Law provide for the Case of Removal, Death, Resignation or Inability, both of the President and the Vice President, declaring what Officer shall then act as President, and such Officer shall act accordingly, until the Disability be removed, or a President shall be elected.

**The Vice President is next in line for the presidency. A federal law passed in 1947 determined the order of presidential succession as follows: (1) Speaker of the House; (2) president pro tempore of the Senate; and (3) Cabinet officers in the order in which their departments were created. (So far, death has been the only circumstance under which a presidential term has been cut short.) This clause has been amplified by the 25th Amendment.**

The President shall, at stated Times, receive for his Services, a Compensation, which shall neither be encreased nor diminished during the Period for which he shall have been elected, and he shall not receive within that Period any other Emolument from the United States, or any of them.

Before he enter on the Execution of his Office, he shall take the following Oath or Affirmation:—"I do solemnly swear (or affirm) that I will faithfully execute the Office of the President of the United States, and will to the best of my Ability, preserve, protect and defend the Constitution of the United States."

**Section 2.**    The President shall be Commander in Chief of the Army and Navy of the United States, and of the Militia of the several States, when called into the actual Service of the United States; he may require the Opinion in writing, of the principal Officer in each of the executive Departments, upon any subject relating to the Duties of their respective Offices, and he shall have Power to Grant Reprieves and Pardons for Offenses against the United States, except in Cases of Impeachment.

He shall have Power, by and with the Advice and Consent of the Senate, to make Treaties, provided two thirds of the Senators present concur; and he shall nominate, and by and with the Advice and Consent of the Senate, shall appoint Ambassadors, other public Ministers and Consuls, Judges of the supreme Court, and all other Officers of the United States, whose Appointments are not herein otherwise provided for, and which shall be established by Law: but the Congress may by Law vest the Appointment of such inferior Officers, as they think proper, in the President alone, in the Courts of Law, or in the Heads of Departments.

The President shall have Power to fill up all Vacancies that may happen during the Recess of the Senate, by granting Commissions which shall expire at the End of their next Session.

**Section 3.**    He shall from time to time give to the Congress Information of the State of the Union, and recommend to their Consideration such Measures as he shall judge necessary and expedient; he may, on extraordinary Occasions, convene both Houses, or either of them, and in Case of Disagreement between them, with Respect to the Time of Adjournment, he may adjourn them to such Time as he shall think proper; he shall receive Ambassadors and other public Ministers; he shall take Care that the Laws be faithfully executed, and shall Commission all the Officers of the United States.

**Section 4.**    The President, Vice President and all civil Officers of the United States, shall be removed from Office on Impeachment for, and Conviction of, Treason, Bribery, or other high Crimes and Misdemeanors.

## ARTICLE III • JUDICIAL DEPARTMENT

**Section 1.**    The judicial Power of the United States, shall be vested in one supreme Court, and in such inferior Courts as the Congress may from time to time ordain and establish. The Judges, both of the supreme and inferior Courts, shall hold their Offices during good Behaviour, and shall, at stated Times, receive for their Services, a Compensation, which shall not be diminished during their Continuance in Office.

**Section 2.**    The judicial Power shall extend to all Cases, in Law and Equity, arising under this Constitution, the Laws of the United States, and Treaties made, or which shall be made, under their Authority;—to all Cases affecting Ambassadors,

---

This clause suggests written communication between the President and "the principal officer in each of the executive departments." As it developed, these officials comprise the Cabinet—whose members are chosen, and may be replaced, by the President.

Senate approval is required for treaties and presidential appointments.

Without the consent of the Senate, the President may appoint officials only on a temporary basis.

The President delivers a "State of the Union" message at the opening of each session of Congress. Woodrow Wilson was the first President since John Adams to read his messages in person. Franklin D. Roosevelt and his successors followed Wilson's example.

Federal judges hold office for life and may not have their salaries lowered while in office. These provisions are intended to keep the federal bench independent of political pressure.

This clause describes the types of cases that may be heard in federal courts.

other public Ministers and Consuls;—to all Cases of admiralty and maritime Jurisdiction;—to Controversies to which the United States shall be a Party;—to Controversies between two or more States;—between a State and Citizens of another State;—between Citizens of different states;—between Citizens of the same State claiming Lands under Grants of different States, and between a State, or the Citizens thereof, and foreign States, Citizens or Subjects.

In all Cases affecting Ambassadors, other public Ministers and Consuls, and those in which a State shall be Party, the supreme Court shall have original Jurisdiction. In all the other Cases before mentioned, the supreme Court shall have appellate Jurisdiction, both as to Law and Fact, with such Exceptions, and under such Regulations as the Congress shall make.

The trial of all Crimes, except in Cases of Impeachment, shall be by Jury; and such Trial shall be held in the State where the said Crimes shall have been committed; but when not committed within any State, the Trial shall be at such Place or Places as the Congress may by Law have directed.

**Section 3.**   Treason against the United States, shall consist only in levying War against them, or in adhering to their Enemies, giving them Aid and Comfort. No Person shall be convicted of Treason unless on the Testimony of two Witnesses to the same overt Act, or on Confession in open Court.

The Congress shall have Power to declare the Punishment of Treason, but no Attainder of Treason shall work Corruption of Blood, or Forfeiture except during the Life of the Person attainted.

## ARTICLE IV • RELATIONS AMONG THE STATES

**Section 1.**   Full Faith and Credit shall be given in each State to the public Acts, Records, and judicial Proceedings of every other State. And the Congress may by general Laws prescribe the Manner in which such Acts, Records and Proceedings shall be proved, and the Effect thereof.

**Section 2.**   The Citizens of each State shall be entitled to all Privileges and Immunities of Citizens in the several States.

A Person charged in any State with Treason, Felony, or other Crime, who shall flee from Justice, and be found in another State, shall on demand of the executive Authority of the State from which he fled, be delivered up, to be removed to the State having Jurisdiction of the Crime.

No Person held in Service or Labour in one State, under the laws thereof, escaping into another, shall, in Consequence of any Law or Regulation therein, be discharged from such Service or Labour, but shall be delivered up on Claim of the Party to whom such Service or Labour may be due.

**Section 3.**   New States may be admitted by the Congress into this Union; but no new State shall be formed or erected within the Jurisdiction of any other State; nor any State be formed by the Junction of two or more States, or parts of States, without the Consent of the Legislatures of the States concerned as well as of the Congress.

The Congress shall have Power to dispose of and make all needful Rules and Regulations respecting the Territory or other Property belonging to the United States; and nothing in this Constitution shall be so construed as to Prejudice any Claims of the United States, or of any particular State.

---

The 11th Amendment prevents a citizen from suing a state in a federal court.

The Supreme Court handles certain cases directly. It may also review cases handled by lower courts, but Congress in some cases may withhold the right to appeal to the highest court, or limit appeal by setting various conditions.

The 6th Amendment strengthens this clause on trial procedure.

Treason is rigorously defined. A person can be convicted only if two witnesses testify to the same obvious act, or if he confesses in court.

Punishment for treason extends only to the person convicted, not to his or her descendants. ("Corruption of blood" means that the heirs of a convicted person are deprived of certain rights.)

States must honor each other's laws, court decisions, and records (for example, birth, marriage, and death certificates).

Each state must respect the rights of citizens of other states.

The process of returning a person accused of a crime to the governmental authority (in this case a state) from which he or she has fled is called *extradition.*

The 13th Amendment, which abolished slavery, makes this clause obsolete.

A new state may not be created by dividing or joining existing states unless approved by the legislatures of the states affected and by Congress. An exception to the provision forbidding the division of a state occurred during the Civil War. In 1863 West Virginia was formed out of the western region of Virginia.

**Section 4.**  The United States shall guarantee to every State in this Union a Republican Form of Government, and shall protect each of them against Invasion; and on Application of the Legislature, or of the Executive (when the Legislature cannot be convened) against domestic Violence.

A *republican* form of government is one in which citizens choose representatives to govern them. The federal government must protect a state against invasion and, if state authorities request it, against violence within a state.

## ARTICLE V • AMENDING THE CONSTITUTION

The Congress, whenever two thirds of both Houses shall deem it necessary, shall propose Amendments to this Constitution, or, on the Application of the Legislatures of two thirds of the several States, shall call a Convention for proposing Amendments, which, in either Case, shall be valid to all Intents and Purposes, as part of this Constitution, when ratified by the Legislatures of three fourths of the several States, or by Conventions in three fourths thereof, as the one or the other Mode of Ratification may be proposed by the Congress: Provided that no Amendment which may be made prior to the Year One thousand eight hundred and eight shall in any Manner affect the first and fourth Clauses in the Ninth Section of the first Article; and that no State, without its Consent, shall be deprived of its equal Suffrage in the Senate.

An amendment to the Constitution can be proposed (a) by Congress, with a two-thirds vote of both houses, or (b) by a convention called by Congress when two-thirds of the state legislatures request it. An amendment is ratified (a) by three-fourths of the state legislatures, or (b) by conventions in three-fourths of the states. The twofold procedure of proposal and ratification reflects the seriousness with which the framers of the Constitution regarded amendments. Over 6,900 amendments have been proposed; only 26 have been ratified.

## ARTICLE VI • GENERAL PROVISIONS

All Debts contracted and Engagements entered into, before the Adoption of this Constitution, shall be as valid against the United States under this Constitution, as under the Confederation.

This Constitution, and the Laws of the United States which shall be made in Pursuance thereof; and all Treaties made, or which shall be made, under the Authority of the United States, shall be the supreme Law of the Land; and the Judges in every State shall be bound thereby, any Thing in the Constitution or Laws of any State to the Contrary notwithstanding.

The *supremacy clause* means that if a federal and a state law conflict, the federal law prevails.

The Senators and Representatives before mentioned, and the Members of the several State Legislatures, and all executive and judicial Officers, both of the United States and of the several States, shall be bound by Oath or Affirmation, to support this Constitution; but no religious Test shall ever be required as a Qualification to any Office or public Trust under the United States.

Religion may not be a condition for holding public office.

## ARTICLE VII • RATIFICATION

The Ratification of the Conventions of nine States shall be sufficient for the Establishment of this Constitution between the States so ratifying the Same.

DONE in Convention by the Unanimous Consent of the States present the Seventeenth Day of September in the Year of our Lord one thousand seven hundred and eighty-seven and of the Independence of the United States of America the Twelfth. In Witness whereof We have hereunto subscribed our Names.

The Constitution would become the law of the land upon the approval of nine states.

*G⁰ WASHINGTON*
Presid^t and deputy from
**VIRGINIA**

Attest: *William Jackson,* Secretary

**Delaware**
Geo: Read
Gunning Bedford, jun
John Dickinson
Richard Bassett
Jaco:Broom

**Maryland**
James McHenry
Dan: of St Thos Jenifer
Danl Carroll

**Virginia**
John Blair
James Madison Jr.

**North Carolina**
Wm Blount
Richd Dobbs Spaight
Hu Williamson

**South Carolina**
J. Rutledge
Charles Cotesworth
    Pinckney
Charles Pinckney
Pierce Butler

**Georgia**
William Few
Abr Baldwin

**New Hampshire**
John Langdon
Nicholas Gilman

**Massachusetts**
Nathaniel Gorham
Rufus King

**Connecticut**
Wm Saml Johnson
Roger Sherman

**New York**
Alexander Hamilton

**New Jersey**
Wil: Livingston
David Brearley
Wm Paterson
Jona: Dayton

**Pennsylvania**
B Franklin
Thomas Mifflin
Robt. Morris
Geo. Clymer
Thos. FitzSimons
Jared Ingersoll
James Wilson
Gouv Morris

# Amendments

[*The date following each amendment number is the year of ratification.*]

## AMENDMENT I • (1791)

*Establishes freedom of religion, speech, and the press; gives citizens the rights of assembly and petition.*

Congress shall make no law respecting an establishment of religion, or prohibiting the free exercise thereof: or abridging the freedom of speech, or of the press; or the right of the people peaceably to assemble, and to petition the Government for a redress of grievances.

## AMENDMENT II • (1791)

*States have the right to maintain a militia.*

A well regulated Militia, being necessary to the security of a free State, the right of the people to keep and bear Arms, shall not be infringed.

## AMENDMENT III • (1791)

*Limits the army's right to quarter soldiers in private homes.*

No Soldier shall, in time of peace, be quartered in any house, without the consent of the Owner, nor in time of war, but in a manner to be prescribed by law.

## AMENDMENT IV • (1791)

*Search warrants are required as a guarantee of a citizen's right to privacy.*

The right of the people to be secure in their persons, houses, papers, and effects, against unreasonable searches and seizures, shall not be violated, and no Warrants shall issue, but upon probable cause, supported by Oath or affirmation, and particularly describing the place to be searched, and the persons or things to be seized.

## AMENDMENT V • (1791)

No person shall be held to answer for a capital, or otherwise infamous crime, unless on a presentment or indictment of a Grand Jury, except in cases arising in the land or naval forces, or in the Militia, when in actual service in time of War or public danger; nor shall any person be subject for the same offence to be twice put in jeopardy of life or limb; nor shall be compelled in any criminal case to be a witness against himself, nor be deprived of life, liberty, or property, without due process of law; nor shall private property be taken for public use, without just compensation.

To be prosecuted for a serious crime, a person must first be accused *(indicted)* by a grand jury. No one can be tried twice for the same crime *(double jeopardy)*. Nor can a person be forced into self-incrimination by testifying against himself or herself.

## AMENDMENT VI • (1791)

In all criminal prosecutions, the accused shall enjoy the right to a speedy and public trial, by an impartial jury of the State and district wherein the crime shall have been committed, which district shall have been previously ascertained by law, and to be informed of the nature and cause of the accusation; to be confronted with the witnesses against him; to have compulsory process for obtaining witnesses in his favor, and to have the Assistance of Counsel for his defense.

Guarantees a defendant's right to be tried without delay and to face witnesses testifying for the other side.

## AMENDMENT VII • (1791)

In suits at common law, where the value in controversy shall exceed twenty dollars, the right of trial by jury shall be preserved, and no fact tried by a jury, shall be otherwise reexamined in any Court of the United States, than according to rules of the common law.

A jury trial is guaranteed in federal civil suits involving more than twenty dollars.

## AMENDMENT VIII • (1791)

Excessive bail shall not be required, nor excessive fines imposed, nor cruel and unusual punishments inflicted.

## AMENDMENT IX • (1791)

The enumeration in the Constitution, of certain rights, shall not be construed to deny or disparage others retained by the people.

The listing of specific rights in the Constitution does not mean that others are not protected.

## AMENDMENT X • (1791)

The powers not delegated to the United States by the Constitution, nor prohibited by it to the States, are reserved to the States respectively, or to the people.

Limits the federal government to its specific powers. Powers not prohibited the states by the Constitution may be exercised by them.

## AMENDMENT XI • (1798)

The Judicial power of the United States shall not be construed to extend to any suit in law or equity, commenced or prosecuted against one of the United States by Citizens of another State, or by Citizens or Subjects of any Foreign State.

A state cannot be sued by a citizen of another state in a federal court. Such a case can be tried only in the courts of the state being sued.

## AMENDMENT XII • (1804)

Revises the process by which the President and Vice President were elected (see Article II, Section 1, Clause 3). The major change requires electors to cast separate ballots for President and Vice President. If none of the presidential candidates obtains a majority vote, the House of Representatives—with each state having one vote—chooses a President from the three candidates having the highest number of votes. If no vice presidential candidate wins a majority, the Senate chooses from the two candidates having the highest number of votes. The portion printed in color was superseded by Section 3 of the 20th Amendment.

The Electors shall meet in their respective states and vote by ballot for President and Vice-President, one of whom, at least, shall not be an inhabitant of the same state with themselves; they shall name in their ballots the person voted for as President, and in distinct ballots the person voted for as Vice-President, and they shall make distinct lists of all persons voted for as President, and of all persons voted for as Vice-President, and of the number of votes for each, which lists they shall sign and certify, and transmit sealed to the seat of the government of the United States, directed to the President of the Senate;—The President of the Senate shall, in presence of the Senate and House of Representatives, open all the certificates and the votes shall then be counted;—The person having the greatest number of votes for President, shall be the President, if such number be a majority of the whole number of Electors appointed; and if no person have such majority, then from the persons having the highest numbers not exceeding three on the list of those voted for as President, the House of Representatives shall choose immediately, by ballot, the President. But in choosing the President, the votes shall be taken by states, the representation from each state having one vote; a quorum for this purpose shall consist of a member or members from two-thirds of the states, and a majority of all the states shall be necessary to a choice. And if the House of Representatives shall not choose a President whenever the right of choice shall devolve upon them, before the fourth day of March next following, then the Vice-President shall act as President, as in the case of the death or other constitutional disability of the President.—The person having the greatest number of votes as Vice-President, shall be the Vice-President, if such number be a majority of the whole number of Electors appointed, and if no person have a majority, then from the two highest numbers on the list, the Senate shall choose the Vice-President; a quorum for the purpose shall consist of two-thirds of the whole number of Senators, and a majority of the whole number shall be necessary to a choice. But no person consitutionally ineligible to the office of President shall be eligible to that of Vice-President of the United States.

## AMENDMENT XIII • (1865)

Abolishes slavery.

**Section 1.**    Neither slavery nor involuntary servitude, except as a punishment for crime whereof the party shall have been duly convicted, shall exist within the United States, or any place subject to their jurisdiction.

**Section 2.**    Congress shall have power to enforce this article by appropriate legislation.

## AMENDMENT XIV • (1868)

This section confers full civil rights on former slaves. Supreme Court decisions have interpreted the language of Section 1 to mean that the states, as well as the federal government, are bound by the Bill of Rights.

**Section 1.**    All persons born or naturalized in the United States, and subject to the jurisdiction thereof, are citizens of the United States and of the State wherein they reside. No state shall make or enforce any law which shall abridge the privileges or immunities of citizens of the United States; nor shall any State deprive any person of life, liberty, or property, without due process of law; nor deny any person within its jurisdiction the equal protection of the laws.

**Section 2.**    Representatives shall be apportioned among the several States according to their respective numbers, counting the whole number of persons in each State, excluding Indians not taxed. But when the right to vote at any election for the choice of electors for President and Vice-President of the United States, Representatives in Congress, the Executive and Judicial officers of a State, or the members of the Legislature thereof, is denied to any of the male inhabitants of such State, being twenty-one years of age, and citizens of the United States, or in any way abridged, except for participation in rebellion, or other crime, the basis of representation therein shall be reduced in the proportion which the number of such male citizens shall bear to the whole number of male citizens twenty-one years of age in such State.

A penalty of a reduction in congressional representation shall be applied to any state that refuses to give all adult male citizens the right to vote in federal elections. This section has never been applied. The portion printed in color was superseded by Section 1 of the 26th Amendment. (This section has also been amplified by the 19th Amendment.)

**Section 3.**    No person shall be a Senator or Representative in Congress, or elector of President and Vice-President, or hold any office, civil or military, under the United States, or under any State, who, having previously taken an oath, as a member of Congress, or as an officer of the United States, or as a member of any State legislature, or as an executive or judicial officer of any State, to support the Constitution of the United States, shall have engaged in insurrection or rebellion against the same, or given aid or comfort to the enemies thereof. But Congress may by a vote of two-thirds of each House, remove such disability.

Any former federal or state official who served the Confederacy during the Civil War could not become a federal official again unless Congress voted otherwise.

**Section 4.**    The validity of the public debt of the United States, authorized by law, including debts incurred for payment of pensions and bounties for services in suppressing insurrection or rebellion, shall not be questioned. But neither the United States nor any State shall assume or pay any debt or obligation incurred in aid of insurrection or rebellion against the United States, or any claim for the loss or emancipation of any slave; but all such debts, obligations and claims shall be held illegal and void.

Makes legal the federal Civil War debt, but at the same time voids all Confederate debts incurred in the war.

**Section 5.**    The Congress shall have power to enforce, by appropriate legislation, the provisions of this article.

## AMENDMENT XV • (1870)

**Section 1.**    The right of citizens of the United States to vote shall not be denied or abridged by the United States or by any State on account of race, color, or previous condition of servitude.

Gives blacks the right to vote.

**Section 2.**    The Congress shall have power to enforce this article by appropriate legislation.

## AMENDMENT XVI • (1913)

The Congress shall have power to lay and collect taxes on incomes, from whatever source derived, without apportionment among the several States, and without regard to any census or enumeration.

Allows Congress to levy taxes on incomes.

## AMENDMENT XVII • (1913)

The Senate of the United States shall be composed of two Senators from each State, elected by the people thereof, for six years; and each Senator shall have one vote. The electors in each State shall have the qualifications requisite for electors of the most numerous branch of the State legislature.

When vacancies happen in the representation of any State in the Senate, the Executive authority of such State shall issue writs of election to fill such vacancies:

Provides for election of senators by the people of a state, rather than the state legislature.

*Provided,* That the legislature of any State may empower the executive thereof to make temporary appointments until the people fill the vacancies by election as the legislature may direct.

This amendment shall not be so construed as to affect the election or term of any Senator chosen before it becomes valid as part of the Constitution.

## AMENDMENT XVIII • (1919)

Legalizes *prohibition*—that is, forbidding the making, selling, or transporting of intoxicating beverages. Superseded by the 21st Amendment.

**Section 1.**    After one year from the ratification of this article, the manufacture, sale, or transportation of intoxicating liquors within, the importation thereof into, or the exportation thereof from the United States and all territory subject to the jurisdiction thereof for beverage purposes is hereby prohibited.

**Section 2.**    The Congress and the several States shall have concurrent power to enforce this article by appropriate legislation.

**Section 3.**    This article shall be inoperative unless it shall have been ratified as an amendment to the Constitution by the legislatures of the several States, as provided in the Constitution, within seven years from the date of the submission hereof to the States by the Congress.

## AMENDMENT XIX • (1920)

Gives women the right to vote.

The right of citizens of the United States to vote shall not be denied or abridged by the United States or by any State on account of sex.

Congress shall have power to enforce this article by appropriate legislation.

## AMENDMENT XX • (1933)

The "lame duck" amendment allows the President to take office on January 20, and members of Congress on January 3. The purpose of the amendment is to reduce the term in office of defeated incumbents—known as "lame ducks."

**Section 1.**    The terms of the President and Vice-President shall end at noon on the 20th day of January, and the terms of Senators and Representatives at noon on the 3d day of January, of the years in which such terms would have ended if this article had not been ratified; and the terms of their successors shall then begin.

**Section 2.**    The Congress shall assemble at least once in every year, and such meeting shall begin at noon on the 3d day of January, unless they shall by law appoint a different day.

**Section 3.**    If, at the time fixed for the beginning of the term of the President, the President elect shall have died, the Vice-President elect shall become President. If a President shall not have been chosen before the time fixed for the beginning of his term, or if the President elect shall have failed to qualify, then the Vice-President elect shall act as President until a President shall have qualified; and the Congress may by law provide for the case wherein neither a President elect nor a Vice-President elect shall have qualified, declaring who shall then act as President, or the manner in which one who is to act shall be selected, and such person shall act accordingly until a President or Vice-President shall have qualified.

**Section 4.**    The Congress may by law provide for the case of the death of any of the persons from whom the House of Representatives may choose a President whenever the right of choice shall have devolved upon them, and for the case of the death of any of the persons from whom the Senate may choose a Vice-President whenever the right of choice shall have devolved upon them.

**Section 5.**   Sections 1 and 2 shall take effect on the 15th day of October following the ratification of this article.

**Section 6.**   This article shall be inoperative unless it shall have been ratified as an amendment to the Constitution by the legislatures of three-fourths of the several States within seven years from the date of its submission.

## AMENDMENT XXI • (1933)

**Section 1.**   The eighteenth article of amendment to the Constitution of the United States is hereby repealed.

Repeals the 18th Amendment.

**Section 2.**   The transportation or importation into any State, Territory, or possession of the United States for delivery or use therein of intoxicating liquors, in violation of the laws thereof, is hereby prohibited.

States may pass prohibition laws.

**Section 3.**   This article shall be inoperative unless it shall have been ratified as an amendment to the Constitution by conventions in the several States, as provided in the Constitution, within seven years from the date of the submission hereof to the States by the Congress.

## AMENDMENT XXII • (1951)

**Section 1.**   No person shall be elected to the office of the President more than twice, and no person who has held the office of President, or acted as President, for more than two years of a term to which some other person was elected President shall be elected to the office of the President more than once. But this Article shall not apply to any person holding the office of President when this Article was proposed by the Congress, and shall not prevent any person who may be holding the office of President, or acting as President, during the term within which this Article becomes operative from holding the office of President or acting as President during the remainder of such term.

Limits a President to only two full terms plus two years of a previous President's term.

**Section 2.**   This article shall be inoperative unless it shall have been ratified as an amendment to the Constitution by the legislatures of three-fourths of the several States within seven years from the date of its submission to the States by the Congress.

## AMENDMENT XXIII • (1961)

**Section 1.**   The District constituting the seat of Government of the United States shall appoint in such manner as the Congress may direct:

By giving the District of Columbia three electoral votes, Congress enabled its residents to vote for President and Vice President.

A number of electors of President and Vice-President equal to the whole number of Senators and Representatives in Congress to which the District would be entitled if it were a State, but in no event more than the least populous State; they shall be in addition to those appointed by the States, but they shall be considered, for the purposes of the election of President and Vice-President, to be electors appointed by a State; and they shall meet in the District and perform such duties as provided by the twelfth article of amendment.

**Section 2.**   The Congress shall have power to enforce this article by appropriate legislation.

# AMENDMENT XXIV • (1964)

Forbids the use of a poll tax as a requirement for voting in federal elections.

**Section 1.**    The right of citizens of the United States to vote in any primary or other election for President or Vice-President, for electors for President or Vice-President, or for Senator or Representative in Congress, shall not be denied or abridged by the United States or any State by reason of failure to pay any poll tax or other tax.

**Section 2.**    The Congress shall have power to enforce this article by appropriate legislation.

# AMENDMENT XXV • (1967)

Outlines the procedure to be followed in case of presidential disability.

**Section 1.**    In case of the removal of the President from office or of his death or resignation, the Vice-President shall become President.

**Section 2.**    Whenever there is a vacancy in the office of the Vice-President, the President shall nominate a Vice-President who shall take office upon confirmation by a majority vote of both Houses of Congress.

**Section 3.**    Whenever the President transmits to the President pro tempore of the Senate and the Speaker of the House of Representatives his written declaration that he is unable to discharge the powers and duties of his office, and until he transmits to them a written declaration to the contrary, such powers and duties shall be discharged by the Vice-President as Acting President.

**Section 4.**    Whenever the Vice-President and a majority of either the principal officers of the executive departments or of such other body as Congress may by law provide, transmit to the President pro tempore of the Senate and the Speaker of the House of Representatives their written declaration that the President is unable to discharge the powers and duties of his office, the Vice-President shall immediately assume the powers and duties of the office as Acting President.

Thereafter, when the President transmits to the President pro tempore of the Senate and the Speaker of the House of Representatives his written declaration that no inability exists, he shall resume the powers and duties of his office unless the Vice-President and a majority of either the principal officers of the executive department or of such other body as Congress may by law provide, transmit within four days to the President pro tempore of the Senate and the Speaker of the House of Representatives their written declaration that the President is unable to discharge the powers and duties of his office. Thereupon Congress shall decide the issue, assembling within forty-eight hours for that purpose if not in session. If the Congress, within twenty-one days after receipt of the latter written declaration, or, if Congress is not in session, within twenty-one days after Congress is required to assemble, determines by two-thirds vote of both Houses that the President is unable to discharge the powers and duties of his office, the Vice-President shall continue to discharge the same as Acting President; otherwise, the President shall resume the powers and duties of his office.

# AMENDMENT XXVI • (1971)

Lowers the voting age to eighteen.

**Section 1.**    The right of citizens of the United States, who are eighteen years of age or older, to vote shall not be denied or abridged by the United States or any state on account of age.

**Section 2.**    The Congress shall have the power to enforce this article by appropriate legislation.

# Index

# About the Authors

R. JACKSON WILSON is a Professor of History at Smith College, where he also teaches American studies and philosophy. His special field of interest is cultural history, and he is currently at work on a study of nineteenth-century American writers. His books include *In Quest of Community: Social Philosophy in the United States* and *Darwinism and the American Intellectual*. He has taught at an unusually wide range of institutions, including the University of Wisconsin, the University of Arizona, Columbia University, Yale University, Hartford College for Women, the University of Massachusetts, Amherst College, Teacher's College (Columbia), and the Flinders University, South Australia.

JAMES GILBERT received his B.A. from Carleton College and his M.A. and Ph. D. from the University of Wisconsin. He has taught at Teachers College, Columbia University, the Centre for Social History at Warwick University, Coventry, England, and at the University of Maryland. In 1978, he was chosen distinguished Scholar-Teacher at Maryland. In 1968, he published *Writers and Partisans*. His other books include *Designing the Industrial State* (1972), *Work Without Salvation* (1978), and *Another Chance: Postwar America, 1945–1968* (1981). In 1977, his "Wars of the Worlds" was named the best article of the year by the Popular Culture Association. He has been a Fellow of the Woodrow Wilson Foundation and the National Endowment for the Humantites.

STEPHEN NISSENBAUM is a Professor of History at the University of Massachusetts, Amherst, where he teaches intellectual and social history and directs his department's graduate program. His previous books include *Salem Possessed: The Social Origins of Witchcraft* (with Paul Boyer) and *Sex, Diet, and Debility in Jacksonian America*. He is now writing a book about Nathaniel Hawthorne and the social history of literature in the Jacksonian period. He has held fellowships from the National Endowment for the Humanities, Harvard University, and the American Antiquarian Society. He has taught at Hampshire College, Mount Holyoke College, and Smith College.

DONALD M. SCOTT teaches American history at Brown University and is an Associate Dean of the College. He is a graduate of Harvard College and received his Ph.D. from the University of Wisconsin. He is the author of *From Office to Profession: The New England Ministry, 1750–1850* and is co-author of *America's Families: A Documentary History*. He has been a Fellow at the Davis Center for Historical Studies, Princeton University, and a National Endowment for the Humanities Fellow at the American Antiquarian Society. He is currently at work on a book on the formation of public culture in nineteenth-century America.

CARVILLE EARLE is Associate Professor of Geography at the University of Maryland— Baltimore County, where he has taught since completing his Ph.D. at the University of Chicago in 1973. He is a former Charles Warren Center Fellow at Harvard University and the author of *The Evolution of a Tidewater Settlement System*, along with various scholarly articles on the historical geography of the United States.

RONALD HOFFMAN is Associate Professor of History at the University of Maryland. He received his Ph.D. from the University of Wisconsin in 1969. He is currently editing the papers of Charles Carroll of Carrollton and is directing a series of annual symposia on the Revolutionary and Confederation eras for the United States Capitol Historical Society. Professor Hoffman is the author of *A Spirit of Dissention: Economics, Politics, and the Revolution in Maryland* (1973) and has co-edited several volumes of essays including *Sovereign States in an Age of Uncertainty* (1981), with Peter J. Albert, and *Slavery and Freedom in the Age of the American Revolution* (1983), with Ira Berlin. He has also contributed articles and essays to a number of academic journals and collections including *The American Historical Review, Perspectives in American History,* and *The American Revolution: Explorations in the History of American Radicalism,* edited by Alfred F. Young.

# A Note on the Type

The text of this book has been set via computer-driven cathode-ray tube in a typeface named Bembo. The roman is a copy of a letter cut for the celebrated Venetian printer Aldus Manutius by Francesco Griffo and first used in Cardinal Bembo's *De Aetna* of 1495—hence the name of the revival. Griffo's type is now generally recognized, thanks to the researches of Mr. Stanley Morison, to be the first of the old face group of types. The companion italic is an adaptation of the chancery script type designed by the Roman calligrapher and printer Lodovico degli Arrighi, called Vincentino, and used by him during the 1520s.

Composed by
Ruttle, Shaw & Wetherill, Inc.
Philadelphia, Pennsylvania

Printed and bound by
Von Hoffmann Press, Inc.
St. Louis, Missouri

Inserts printed by
Universal Printing Co., Inc.
St. Louis, Missouri